CHILTON'S
CAMA
1967 to
1981

Covers all Camaro models

Managing Editor KERRY A. FREEMAN, S.A.E.
Senior Editor RICHARD J. RIVELE, S.A.E.
Editor DEAN F. MORGANTINI, S.A.E.

President WILLIAM A. BARBOUR
Executive Vice President JAMES A. MIADES
Vice President and General Manager JOHN P. KUSHNERICK

CHILTON BOOK COMPANY
Radnor, Pennsylvania
19089

SAFETY NOTICE

Proper service and repair procedures are vital to the safe, reliable operation of all motor vehicles, as well as the personal safety of those performing repairs. This book outlines procedures for servicing and repairing vehicles using safe, effective methods. The procedures contain many NOTES, CAUTIONS and WARNINGS which should be followed along with standard safety procedures to eliminate the possibility of personal injury or improper service which could damage the vehicle or compromise its safety.

It is important to note that repair procedures and techniques, tools and parts for servicing motor vehicles, as well as the skill and experience of the individual performing the work vary widely. It is not possible to anticipate all of the conceivable ways or conditions under which vehicles may be serviced, or to provide cautions as to all of the possible hazards that may result. Standard and accepted safety precautions and equipment should be used when handling toxic of flammable fluids, and safety goggles or other protection should be used during cutting, grinding, chiseling, prying, or any other process that can cause material removal or projectiles.

Some procedures require the use of tools specially designed for a specific purpose. Before substituting another tool or procedure, you must be completely satisfied that neither your personal safety, nor the performance of the vehicle will be endangered.

Although the information in this guide is based on industry sources and is as complete as possible at the time of publication, the possibility exists that the manufacturer made later changes which could not be included here. While striving for total accuracy, Chilton Book Company cannot assume responsibility for any errors, changes, or omissions that may occur in the compilation of this data.

PART NUMBERS

Part numbers listed in this reference are not recommendations by Chilton for any product by brand name. There are references that can be used with interchange manuals and aftermarket supplier catalogs to locate each brand supplier's discrete part number.

ACKNOWLEDGMENTS

The Chilton Book Company expresses its appreciation to the Chevrolet Motor Division, General Motors Corporation for their generous assistance.

Information has been selected from Chevrolet shop manuals, owners manuals, service bulletins and technical training manuals.

Copyright © 1981 by Chilton Book Company
All Rights Reserved
Published in Radnor, Pa. by Chilton Book Company
and simultaneously in Ontario, Canada
by Nelson Canada, Limited

Manufactured in the United States of America
234567890   098765432

Chilton's Repair & Tune-Up Guide: Camaro 1967–81
ISBN 0-819-7045-8 pbk.
Library of Congress Catalog Card No. 81-68125

CONTENTS

1 General Information and Maintenance
- 1 How to Use this Book
- 2 Tools and Equipment
- 15 Routine Maintenance and Lubrication

2 Tune-Up
- 46 Tune-Up Procedures
- 47 Tune-Up Specifications

3 Engine and Engine Rebuilding
- 85 Engine Electrical System
- 99 Engine Service and Specifications
- 142 Engine Rebuilding

4 Emission Controls and Fuel System
- 164 Emission Control System and Service
- 189 Fuel System Service

5 Chassis Electrical
- 226 Accessory Service
- 232 Instrument Panel Service
- 235 Lights, Fuses and Flashers

6 Clutch and Transmission
- 239 Manual Transmission
- 244 Clutch
- 248 Automatic Transmission

7 Drive Train
- 258 Driveshaft and U-Joints
- 261 Rear Axle

8 Suspension and Steering
- 264 Front Suspension
- 271 Rear Suspension
- 274 Steering

9 Brakes
- 286 Front Brakes
- 294 Rear Brakes
- 297 Brake Specifications

10 Body
- 303 Repairing Scratches and Small Dents
- 307 Repairing Rust
- 313 Body Care

11 Troubleshooting
- 318 Problem Diagnosis

350 Appendix
354 Index

220 Chilton's Fuel Economy and Tune-Up Tips

Quick Reference Specifications For Your Vehicle

Fill in this chart with the most commonly used specifications for your vehicle. Specifications can be found in Chapters 1 through 3 or on the tune-up decal under the hood of the vehicle.

Tune-Up

Firing Order_____

Spark Plugs:

    Type_____

    Gap (in.)_____

Point Gap (in.)_____

Dwell Angle (°)_____

Ignition Timing (°)_____

    Vacuum (Connected/Disconnected)_____

Valve Clearance (in.)

    Intake_____ Exhaust_____

Capacities

Engine Oil (qts)

    With Filter Change_____

    Without Filter Change_____

Cooling System (qts)_____

Manual Transmission (pts)_____

    Type_____

Automatic Transmission (pts)_____

    Type_____

Front Differential (pts)_____

    Type_____

Rear Differential (pts)_____

    Type_____

Transfer Case (pts)_____

    Type_____

FREQUENTLY REPLACED PARTS
Use these spaces to record the part numbers of frequently replaced parts.

PCV VALVE   **OIL FILTER**   **AIR FILTER**

Manufacturer_____   **Manufacturer**_____   **Manufacturer**_____

Part No._____   **Part No.**_____   **Part No.**_____

General Information and Maintenance

HOW TO USE THIS BOOK

Chilton's Repair and Tune-Up Guide for the Camaro is intended to teach you more about the inner workings of your automobile and save you money on its upkeep. Chapters One and Two will probably be the most frequently used in the book. The first chapter contains all the information that may be required at a moment's notice. Aside from giving the location of various serial numbers and the proper towing instructions, it also contains all the information on basic day-to-day maintenance that you will need to ensure good performance and long component life. Chapter Two contains the necessary tune-up procedures to assist you not only in keeping the engine running properly and at peak performance levels, but also in restoring some of the more delicate components to operating condition in the event of a failure. Chapters Three through Eleven cover repairs (rather than maintenance) for various portions of your car, with each chapter covering either one separate system or two related systems. The appendix then lists general information which may be useful in rebuilding the engine or performing some other operation on any car.

When using the Table of Contents, refer to the bold listings for the subject of the chapter and the smaller listings (or the index) for information on a particular component.

In general, there are three things a proficient mechanic has which must be allowed for when a non-professional does work on his/her car. These are:

1. A sound knowledge of the construction of the parts he is working with; their order of assembly, etc.
2. A knowledge of potentially hazardous situations; particularly how to prevent them.
3. Manual dexterity.

This book provides step-by-step instructions and illustrations whenever possible. Use them carefully and wisely—don't just jump headlong into disassembly. When there is doubt about being able to readily reassemble something, make a careful drawing of the component before taking it apart. Assembly always looks simple when everything is still assembled.

"CAUTIONS," "WARNINGS" and "NOTES" will be provided where appropriate to help prevent you from injuring yourself or damaging your car. Consequently, you should always read through the entire procedure before beginning the work so as to familiarize yourself with any special problems which may occur during the given procedure. Since no number of warnings could cover every possible situation, you should

2 GENERAL INFORMATION AND MAINTENANCE

work slowly and try to envision what is going to happen in each operation ahead of time.

When it comes to tightening things, there is generally a slim area between too loose to properly seal or resist vibration and so tight as to risk damage or warping. When dealing with major engine parts, or with any aluminum component, it pays to buy a torque wrench and go by the recommended figures.

When reference is made in this book to the "right side" or the "left side" of the car, it should be understood that the positions are always to be viewed from the front seat. This means that the left side of the car is the driver's side and the right side is the passenger's side. This will hold true throughout the book, regardless of how you might be looking at the car at the time.

We have attempted to eliminate the use of special tools whenever possible, substituting more readily available hand tools. However, in some cases, the special tools are necessary. These tools can usually be purchased from your local Chevrolet dealer or from an automotive parts store.

Always be conscious of the need for safety in your work. Never get under a car unless it is firmly supported by jack stands or ramps. Never smoke near, or allow flame to get near the battery or the fuel system. Keep your clothing, hands and hair clear of the fan and pulleys when working near the engine if it is running. Most importantly, try to be patient, even in the midst of an argument with a stubborn bolt; reaching for the largest hammer in the garage is usually a cause for later regret and more extensive repair. As you gain confidence and experience, working on your car will become a source of pride and satisfaction.

TOOLS AND EQUIPMENT

It would be impossible to catalog each and every tool that you may need to perform all the operations included in this book. It would also not be wise for the amateur to rush out and buy an expensive set of tools on the theory that he may need one of them at some time. The best approach is to proceed slowly, gathering together a good quality set of those tools that are used most frequently. Don't be misled by the low cost of bargain tools. It is far better to spend a little more for quality, name brand tools. Forged wrenches, 10 or 12 point sockets and fine-tooth ratchets are by far preferable to their less expensive counterparts. As any good mechanic can tell you, there are few worse experiences than trying to work on a car or truck with bad tools. Your monetary savings will be far outweighed by frustration and mangled knuckles.

Begin accumulating those tools that are used most frequently; those associated with routine maintenance and tune-up. In addition to the normal assortment of screwdrivers and pliers, you should have the following tools for routine maintenance jobs:

1. SAE wrenches, sockets and combination open end/box end wrenches.
2. Jackstands—for support;
3. Oil filter wrench;
4. Oil filler spout or funnel;
5. Grease gun—for chassis lubrication;
6. Hydrometer—for checking the battery;
7. A low flat pan for draining oil;
8. Lots of rags for wiping up the inevitable mess.

In addition to these items there are several others which are not absolutely necessary, but handy ot have around. These include a transmission funnel and filler tube, a drop light on a long cord, and adjustable wrench and a pair of slip joint pliers.

A more advanced set of tools, suitable for tune-up work, can be drawn up easily. While the tools are slightly more sophisticated, they need not be outrageously expensive. The key to these purchases is to make them with an eye towards adaptability and wide range. A basic list of tune-up tools could include:

1. Tachometer/dwell meter;
2. Spark plug gauge and gapping tool;
3. Feeler gauges for valve and point adjustment;
4. Timing light.

A tachometer/dwell meter will ensure accurate tune-up work on cars without electronic ignition. The choice of a timing light should be made carefully. A light which works on the DC current supplied by the car battery is the best choice; it should have a xenon tube for brightness. Since some later models have an electronic ignition system, the timing light should have an inductive pickup which clamps around the No. 1 spark plug cable (the timing light illustrated has one of these pickups).

In addition to these basic tools, there are several other tools and gauges which, though not particularly necessary for basic tune-up

GENERAL INFORMATION AND MAINTENANCE

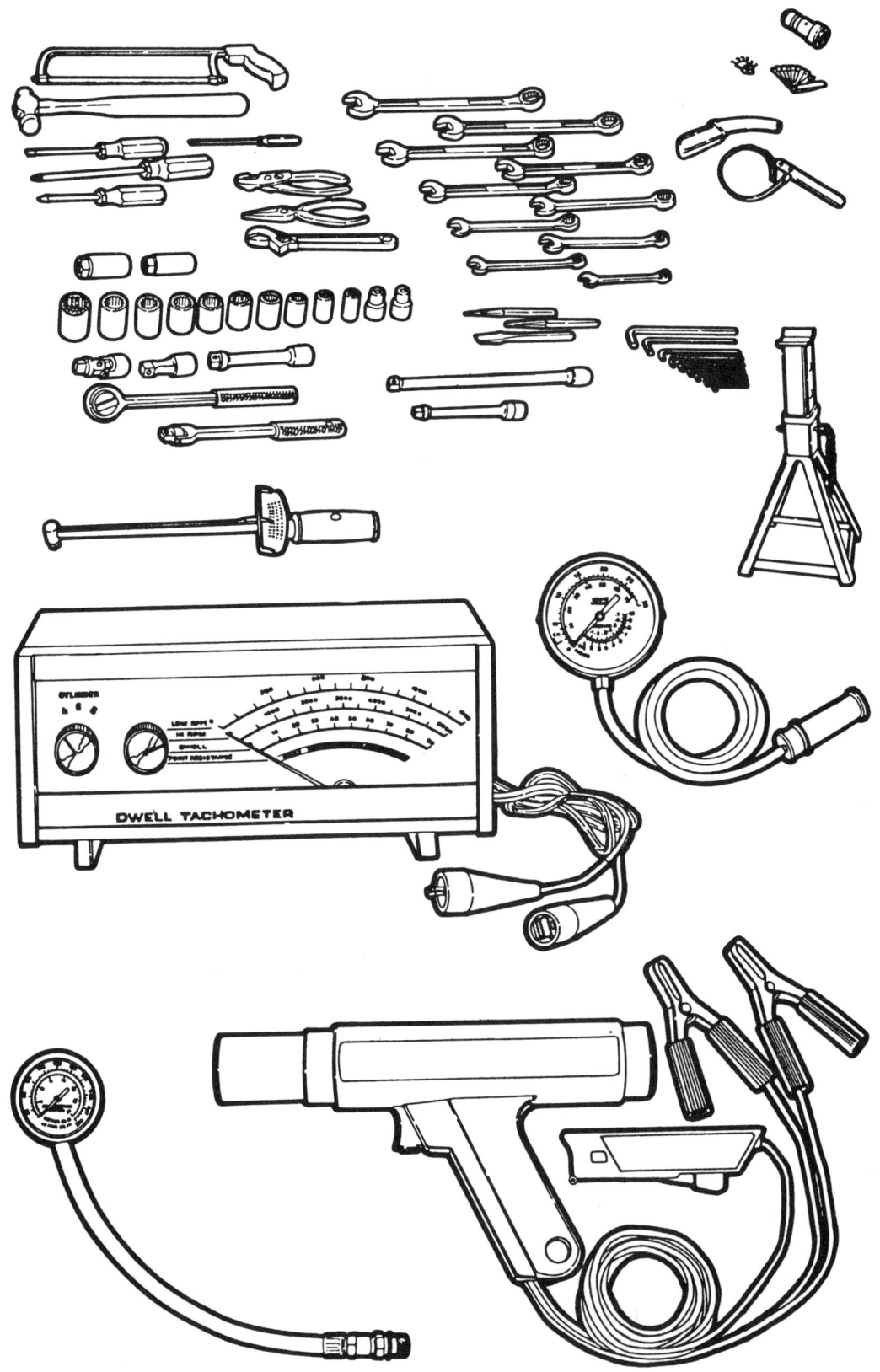

You need only a basic assortment of hand tools for most maintenance and repair jobs

4 GENERAL INFORMATION AND MAINTENANCE

work, you may find to be quite useful. These include:

1. A compression gauge. The screw-in type is slower to use but eliminates the possibility of a faulty reading due to escaping pressure;
2. A manifold vacuum gauge;
3. A test light;
4. A combination volt/ohmmeter;
5. An induction meter, used to determine whether or not there is current flowing through a wire. An extremely helpful tool for electrical troubleshooting.

Finally, you will find a torque wrench necessary for all but the most basic of work. The beam-type models are perfectly adequate. The newer click-type (breakaway) torque wrenches are more accurate, but are also much more expensive and must be periodically recalibrated.

Special Tools

Most of the jobs covered in this guide can be accomplished with commonly available hand tools. However, in some cases special tools are required. Your Chevrolet dealer can probably supply the necessary tools or they can be ordered from:

Service Tool Division
Kent-Moore Corporation
1501 South Jackson St.
Jackson, MI. 49203

HISTORY

In 1967, Chevrolet entered the "pony car" market with an all-new car, the Camaro. Available in two body styles, a convertible and a two-door sports coupe, the Camaro could be ordered with one of five engines. Choices ranged from the economical 230 cubic inch (cu in.) six-cylinder to the new 350 cu in., 295 horsepower (hp) eight. The 350 engine was new in 1967. The 350 is actually a 327 that has been enlarged by increasing the stroke from 3.25 inches (in.) to 3.48 in. Installed in the SS 350 (a sporty, performance model), the engine produced a respectable 0–60 miles per hour (mph) time of 7.8 seconds. Later in that model year Chevrolet released a limited number of high-performance Camaros. The Z28, as it was called, came equipped with one standard engine, the 302 cu in. V8 rated very conservatively at 290 hp. Dual exhausts, four-barrel carburetor, four-speed transmission, solid valve lifters and high-compression pistons and heads were just a few of the standard equipment heavy-duty components. The 1967 Z28, easily recognized by its contrasting color racing stripes and throaty roar, has become a highly desirable car among Camaro enthusiasts. The 1968 Camaro changed little in appearance while the 302 Z28 increased in popularity and production. The 1969 model showed minor styling changes and offered as standard V8 engines the 307 and the 350. Due to a complete restyling, the 1970 Camaro didn't appear in the showrooms until February of that year. The convertible was killed by lagging public demand and high insurance rates.

As the muscle car field diminished, it was felt that the Camaro would either have to change radically or vanish altogether from the field. It did neither; instead gradually losing the fire-breathing, street racer image and V8s larger than 350 cu in. to become a sporty grand touring car. While the engines gradually lessened in size and performance, the rest of the Camaro has been upgraded to form a responsive handling car.

MODEL IDENTIFICATION

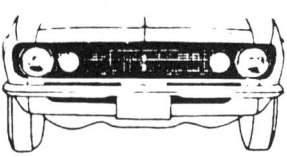

1967 Camaro

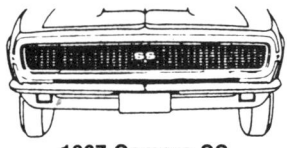

1967 Camaro SS

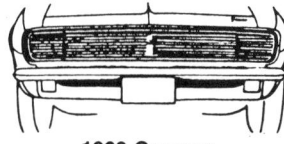

1968 Camaro

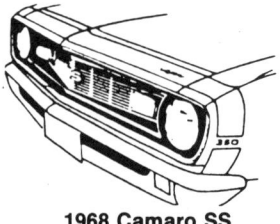

1968 Camaro SS

GENERAL INFORMATION AND MAINTENANCE

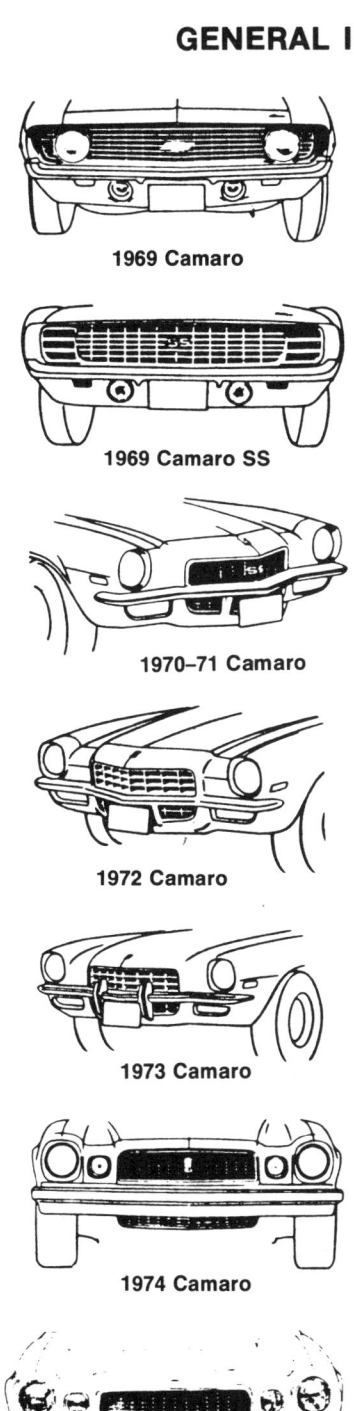

1969 Camaro

1969 Camaro SS

1970-71 Camaro

1972 Camaro

1973 Camaro

1974 Camaro

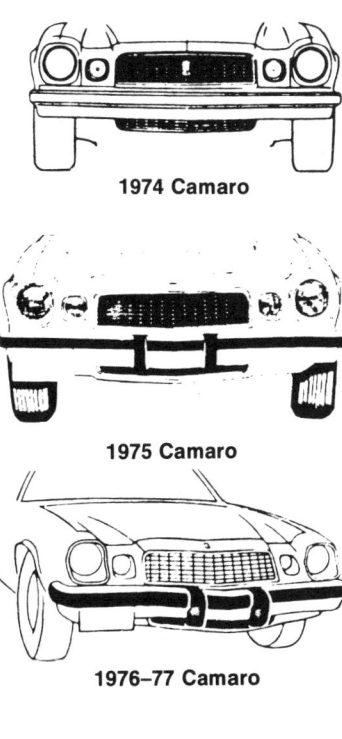

1975 Camaro

1976-77 Camaro

1978-79 Camaro

1980-81 Camaro

SERVICING YOUR CAR SAFELY

It is virtually impossible to anticipate all of the hazards involved with automotive maintenance and service, but care and common sense will prevent most accidents.

The rules of safety for mechanics range from "don't smoke around gasoline," to "use the proper tool for the job." The trick to avoiding injuries is to develop safe work habits and take every possible precaution.

Dos

• Do keep a fire extinguisher and first aid kit within easy reach.
• Do wear safety glasses or goggles when cutting, drilling, grinding or prying, even if you have 20-20 vision. If you wear glasses for the sake of vision, they should be made of hardened glass that can serve also as safety glasses, or wear safety goggles over your regular glasses.
• Do shield your eyes whenever you work around the battery. Batteries contain sulphuric acid. In case of contact with the eyes or skin, flush the area with water or a mixture of water and baking soda and get medical attention immediately.
• Do use safety stands for any undercar service. Jacks are for raising vehicles; safety stands are for making sure the vehicle stays raised until you want to come down. Whenever the car is raised, block the wheels remaining on the ground and set the parking brake.
• Do use adequate ventilation when working with any chemicals or hazardous materials. Like carbon monoxide, the asbestos dust resulting from brake lining wear can be poisonous in sufficient quantities.

6 GENERAL INFORMATION AND MAINTENANCE

Always support the car securely with jackstands; never use cinder blocks, tire changing jacks or the like

• Do disconnect the negative battery cable when working on the electrical system. The secondary ignition system can contain up to 40,000 volts.

• Do follow manufacturer's directions whenever working with potentially hazardous materials. Both brake fluid and antifreeze are poisonous if taken internally.

• Do properly maintain your tools. Loose hammerheads, mushroomed punches and chisels, frayed or poorly grounded electrical cords, excessively worn screwdrivers, spread wrenches (open end), cracked sockets, slipping ratchets, or faulty droplight sockets can cause accidents.

• Do use the proper size and type of tool for the job being done.

• Do when possible, pull on a wrench handle rather than push on it, and adjust your stance to prevent a fall.

• Do be sure that adjustable wrenches are tightly closed on the nut or bolt and pulled so that the face is on the side of the fixed jaw.

• Do select a wrench or socket that fits the nut or bolt. The wrench or socket should sit straight, not cocked.

• Do strike squarely with a hammer; avoid glancing blows.

• Do set the parking brake and block the drive wheels if the work requires the engine running.

Don'ts

• Don't run an engine in a garage or anywhere else without proper ventilation—EVER! Carbon monoxide is poisonous; it takes a long time to leave the human body and you can build up a deadly supply of it in your system by simply breathing in a little every day. You may not realize you are slowly poisoning yourself. Always use power vents, windows, fans or open the garage doors.

• Don't work around moving parts while wearing a necktie or other loose clothing. Short sleeves are much safer than long, loose sleeves; hard-toed shoes with neoprene soles protect your toes and give a better grip on slippery surfaces. Jewelry such as watches, fancy belt buckles, beads or body adornment of any kind is not safe working around a car. Long hair should be hidden under a hat or cap.

• Don't use pockets for toolboxes. A fall or bump can drive a screwdriver deep into your body. Even a wiping cloth hanging from the back pocket can wrap around a spinning shaft or fan.

• Don't smoke when working around gasoline, cleaning solvent or other flammable material.

• Don't smoke when working around the battery. When the battery is being charged, it gives off explosive hydrogen gas.

• Don't use gasoline to wash your hands; there are excellent soaps available. Gasoline may contain lead, and lead can enter the body through a cut, accumulating in the body until you are very ill. Gasoline also removes all the natural oils from the skin so that bone dry hands will suck up oil and grease.

• Don't service the air conditioning system unless you are equipped with the necessary tools and training. The refrigerant, R-12, is extremely cold when compressed, and when released into the air will instantly freeze any surface it contacts, including your eyes. Although the refrigerant is normally non-toxic, R-12 becomes a deadly poisonous gas in the presence of an open flame. One good whiff of the vapors from burning refrigerant can be fatal.

SERIAL NUMBER IDENTIFICATION

Vehicle Serial Number

1967

The vehicle serial number is stamped on a plate attached to the left front door hinge pillar.

1968–81

The vehicle identification number (VIN) is stamped on a plate located on the top left-

GENERAL INFORMATION AND MAINTENANCE

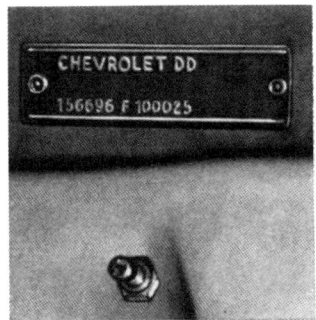

Vehicle serial number location on 1967 cars (© Chevrolet Motor Division)

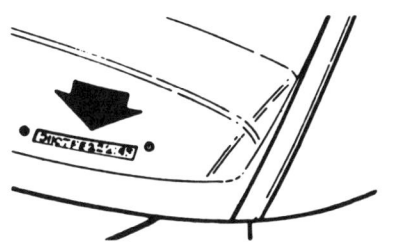

Vehicle serial number location on 1968 and later cars

VIN Chart 1968–71

Mfr Identity ①	Body Style ②	Model Year ③	Assy Plant ④	Unit No. ⑤
1	5645	8	F	100025

① Manufacturer's identity number assigned to all Chevrolet built vehicles
② Model identification
③ Last number of model year (1968)
④ F-Flint
⑤ Unit numbering will start at 100,001 at all plants

hand side (driver's side) of the instrument panel so that it can be seen by looking through the windshield.

Engine Serial Number

The engine serial number for six and eight-cylinder cars shows the manufacturing plant signified by a letter (F for Flint, T for Tonawanda, etc.), the month of manufacture, the day of manufacture, and the transmission and

VIN Chart 1972–80

Mfr Identity ①	Series Code Letter ②	Body Style ③	Engine Model ④	Model Year ⑤	Assembly Plant ⑥	Unit Number ⑦
1	Q	87	F	2	F	000001

① Manufacturer's identity number assigned to all Chevrolet built vehicles
② Series Code
③ Body Style
④ Engine code
⑤ Last number of model year (1972)
⑥ F-Flint
⑦ Unit numbering will start at 000001 or 100,001 depending on the model

VIN Chart 1981

Nation of Origin ①	Mfr ②	Mke ③	Resr Sys ④	Ser Code ⑤	Body Type ⑥	Eng Type ⑦	Chk Dig ⑧	Mod Yr ⑨	Assy Plant ⑩	Un Num ⑪
1	G	1	A	P	37	A	6	B	R	000001

① Nation of origin; 1-U.S.A. 2-Canada
② Manufacturer; G-General Motors
③ Make and type; 1-Chevrolet
④ Restraint system; A-Non-passive B-Passive/belts C-Passive/airbag
⑤ Carline/Series; P-Sport coupe S-Berlinetta
⑥ Body type
⑦ Engine type and make; see Engine Identification Chart for explanation
⑧ Check digit
⑨ Model year; B(81) - M(91)
⑩ Assembly plant
⑪ Unit numbering will start at 000001 or 100001, depending on the model

GENERAL INFORMATION AND MAINTENANCE

Engine Identification Chart 1967–75

The fifth digit in the VIN designates the installed engine in 1972 and later General Motors cars. However, there is one problem. Unlike other car makers, GM occasionally uses the same letter or number to identify different engines (as long as they are made by different divisions). For instance, the letter S was used in 1976 to identify the 454 CID V8 used in Chevrolets. S was also used to identify the 455 CID V8 used in Pontiacs. Because of this, it is necessary to be sure of the make and model year of the car before a firm identification is made according to the 5th digit letter code.

No. Cyls	Displacement (cu in.)	Type	1967	1968	1969	1970	1971	1972	1973	1974	1975
6	230	3 or 4 Spd	LA	BA	AM						
6	230	3 or 4 Spd AC	LB	BD							
6	230	HDC AC		BB							
6	230	HDC		BC							
6	230	3 or 4 Spd w/ex EM	LC								
6	230	3 or 4 Spd AC w/ex EM	LD								
6	230	PG, Torque Dr	LE								
6	230	PG, AC	LF	BF	AN						
6	230	PG, w/ex EM	LG	BH	AQ						
6	230	PG, AC, w/ex EM	LH								
6	230	Hyd 350			AO						
6	230	AC			AP						
6	230	Hyd 350, AC			AR						
6	230	PG, w/ex EM	LG								
6	250	3 or 4 Spd	LN	CM	BE	COG, OCL		CBG			
6	250	3 or 4 Spd		CN		CRF, CRG					
6	250	3 or 4 Spd AC	LO								
6	250	M.T., w/ex EM	LP					CAM	CCB	CCW	
6	250	M.T., w/NB2						CBA	CCP		
6	250	PG, w/NB2						CJD			
6	250	M.T. w/ex EM	LQ								
6	250	AC			BF						
6	250	PG, Torque Dr	FM	CQ	BB			CBJ			
6	250	PG, AC	FR	CR	BC						
6	250	PG, w/ex EM	GP		CDL						
6	250	PG, AC, w/ex EM	GQ		BD						
6	250	Hyd 350			BH						
6	250	Hyd 350, AC						CAA	CCA	CCX	CJL, CJT
6	250	M.T. (all 1975)							CCC	CCR	CJU

GENERAL INFORMATION AND MAINTENANCE

Cyl	CID		MD	MD	DZ*	CAB
6	250	PG				
6	250	(all 1976)				
8	302	Z28				
8	307	M.T.			DA	CKG CHB
8	307	PG			DC	CKH
8	307	Hyd 350			DD	CTK CHH
8	307	M.T. w/NB2				CAY CHJ
8	307	PG w/NB2				CAZ
8	307	Hyd 350 w/NB2				CMZ CHK
8	307	4 Spd			DE	CCA
8	307	M.T.				CCA
8	307	PG			CND	
8	327	3 or 4 Spd (210)	MA	MA		
8	327	3 or 4 Spd w/ex EM	MB	ME		
8	327	PG, (210 HP)	ME			
8	327	PG, w/ex EM (210)	MF			
8	327	3 or 4 Spd (275 HP)	MK			
8	327	3 or 4 Spd w/ex EM	ML			
8	327	PG (275 HP)	MM			
8	327	PG, w/ex EM	MN			
8	350	3 or 4 Spd	MS	MS	HA, HQ	CNJ(300)
8	350	3 or 4 Spd w/ex EM	MT	MU	HE, HR	CNK(300)
8	350	PG	MU			
8	350	PG, w/ex EM	MV			
8	350	Hyd 350			HB, HS	CRE(300)
8	350	M.T., w/ex EM				
8	350	Hyd 350 w/ex EM				
8	350	M.T. ('74 and later—2-bbl)				
8	350	Hyd 350				CKA(L65)
8	350	M.T. w/NB2				CTL(L65)
8	350	Hyd 350, w/NB2				CRG(L65)
8	350					CRD(L65)
8	350					CKK(L48) CKH
8	350					CKD(L48) CLL
8	350					CMH(L65) CKX CMC
8	350					CMB(L65) CKD
8	350	M.T., w/NB2				CDG(L48) CLM CKD
8	350	Hyd 350, w/NB2				CKY CKH
8	350	M.T., Z28				CDD(L48) CKA
8	350	Hyd 400, Z28				CKS(Z28) CLJ CLJ
8	350	2-bbl			HC	CNI(250) CKT(Z28)
8	350	350 2-bbl			HD	CNN(250) CMA

Engine Identification Chart (cont.)

No. Cyls	Displacement (cu in.)	Type	1967	1968	1969	1970	1971	1972	1973	1974	1975
8	350	PG, 2-bbl			HF	CNM(250)					
8	350	370 HP (new Z28)				NA					
8	350	PG				CNK(300)	CBG(245)				
8	350	Hyd 400				CTC(320)	CCR(330)		CLK	CLK	
8	350	M.T. ('74 and later, 4-bbl)				CTB(320)	CGK(270)		CKB	CKB	
8	350	Hyd 350				CRE(300)	CJG(270)		CKW		
							CGL(270)		CKU	CKU	
							CJD(270)				
8	350	M.T. ('75 all models)					CGP(330)				CMU, CMB CRX, CHW CML
8	396	M.T. & PG	MW	MW							
8	396	M.T. & PG w/ex EM	MX								
8	396	Hyd 400	MY	MY	JG	CJI(350)					
8	396	Hyd w/ex EM	MZ								
8	396	SHP	MQ	MQ	JH						
8	396	HP, Hyd 400	EQ	MR	JI						
8	396	HP, w/ex EM	EY								
8	396	SHP, w/ex EM	MR								

GENERAL INFORMATION AND MAINTENANCE

8	396	SHP, ALUM HEADS			MT	JF		
8	396	HP		EI	MX	JB		
8	396	PG				JJ, KE		
8	396	M.T., ALUM HEADS				JL		CJL(375)
8	396	SHP, Hyd 400				JM		
8	396	Hyd 400 ALUM HEADS				JU		CJF(350)
8	396	M.T.				KA, KC		CJH(375)
8	396	M.T., SHP						
8	402	Hyd 400 (Mk. IV)						CTW(350)
								CKN(325)
								CTY(375)
8	402	M.T. (Mk. IV)						CTX(350)
								CKO(375)
8	402	Hyd 400 (Mk. IV)					CLD(350)	CLB
8	402	M.T. (Mk. IV)					CLC(350)	CLA
8	402	Hyd w/ex EM						CTB
8	402	M.T. w/ex EM						CTA

AC—air conditioned
HDC—heavy-duty clutch
HP—high-performance
SHP—special high-performance
M.T.—manual transmission
PG—Powerglide transmission
w/ex EM—with exhaust emission (AIR)

4-bbl—four-barrel carburetor
2-bbl—two-barrel carburetor
Hyd—Hydramatic transmission (350 or 400)
*—CNA = late production
w/NB2—Calif emission equipment
NA—not applicable

GENERAL INFORMATION AND MAINTENANCE

Engine Identification Chart 1976–81

1976				1977				1978			
Code	Engine	Carb	Engine Manuf.	Code	Engine	Carb	Engine Manuf.	Code	Engine	Carb	Engine Manuf.
D	6-250	1V	Chev	D	6-250	1V	Chev	D	6-250	1V	Chev
L	V8-350	2V	Chev	U	V8-305	2V	Chev	U	V8-305	2V	Chev
M	V8-350	2V	Chev	L	V8-350	4V	Chev	L	V8-350	4V	Chev
Q	V8-305	2V	Chev	H	V8-305	4V	Chev	4	V8-350	4V	Chev
V	V8-350	2V	Chev								
X	V8-350	4V	Chev								

1979				1980–81			
Code	Engine	Carb	Engine Manuf.	Code	Engine	Carb	Engine Manuf.
D	6-250	1V	Chev	K	V6-229	2V	Chev
G	V8-305	2V	Chev	A	V6-231	2V	Buick
L	V8-350	4V	Chev	J	V8-267	2V	Chev
				H	V8-305	4V	Chev
				L	V8-350	4V	Chev

engine type represented by a two or three-letter code. A typical engine serial number would be F1005FA. The F represents the manufacturing plant (Flint), the 10 signifies the month of manufacture (October), 05 signifies the day of manufacture, and FA signifies the engine and transmission type. Beginning with 1968 models, a VIN is stamped on the cylinder block next to the engine serial number. The VIN (up to 1971) is the same as the vehicle serial number stamped on the instrument panel except that it does not include the four numbers representing body style.

In 1972, the VIN changed somewhat. A typical VIN for a 1972 Camaro might be: IQ87F2F000001 identifying this particular car as the first (000001) 1972 Camaro to roll off the Flint assembly line. It includes the manufacturer's identity number (number 1 representing Chevrolet products), a series code letter (Q representing Camaro), a two-digit body style number (87 representing 2 Dr. Sport Coupe), an engine code letter (letters listed below), a one-digit model year number (2 representing 1972), an assembly plant letter (F signifying Flint), and a unit number signifying order of production. According to the VIN, this car had a 307 cu in. engine with two-barrel carburetor represented by the engine code letter "F."

This basic format is utilized through the 1981 model year, although specific letter/number designations may change from year to year.

INLINE 6 CYLINDER ENGINES (1967–81)

On six-cylinder engines, the serial number is found on a pad at the front right-hand side of the cylinder block, just to the rear of the distributor.

Engine serial number location—six cylinder (© Chevrolet Motor Division)

V8 AND V6 ENGINES (1967–81)

On the 229 V6 and all V8 engines, the serial number is found on a pad at the front right-hand side of the cylinder block, just below the cylinder head. On the 231 V6, the number is stamped on a pad at the left rear of the cylinder block, where the engine meets the transmission.

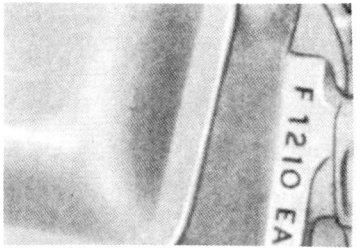

Engine serial number location-eight cylinder (© Chevrolet Motor Division)

GENERAL INFORMATION AND MAINTENANCE

Transmission Serial Number

A transmission serial number is stamped on each transmission. Beginning with 1968 models, a VIN is stamped on each cylinder block and on every transmission, in addition to the serial number. The VIN is the same as the vehicle serial number stamped on the instrument panel except that it does not include the four numbers representing body style. The location of the transmission serial number on each transmission is as follows:

Serial number location-Turbo Hydra-Matic (© Chevrolet Motor Division)

Serial number location-Saginaw 3 and 4 speed (© Chevrolet Motor Division)

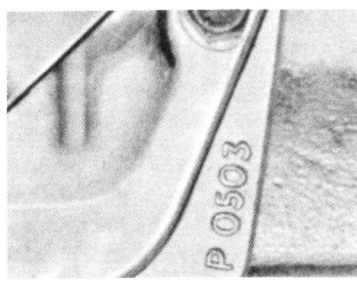

Serial number location-Muncie 4 speed (© Chevrolet Motor Division)

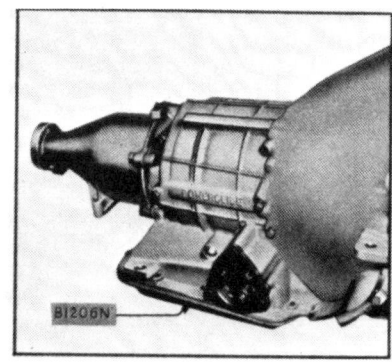

Serial number location on the 1967-68 Powerglide

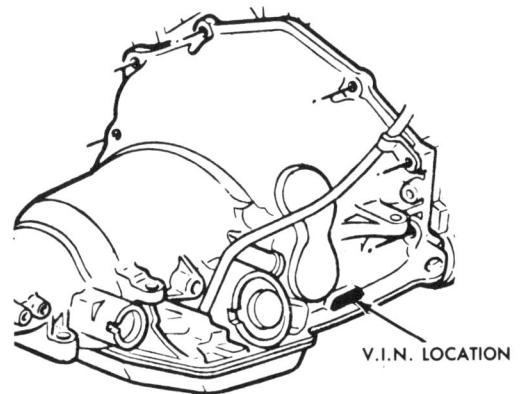

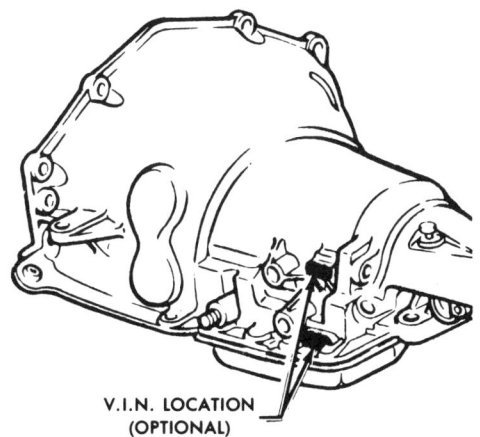

Serial number location on the 1979-81 Turbo Hydra-matic 350

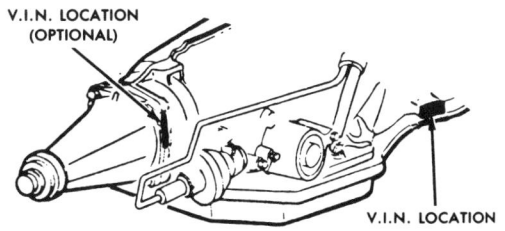

Serial number location on the 1981 Turbo Hydramatic 250 and the 1979-81 200

GENERAL INFORMATION AND MAINTENANCE

Transmission Identification Chart

Type	Serial Number Location
AUTOMATIC	
Powerglide 1967–68	Right rear vertical surface of the transmission oil pan
1969–72 (Turbo)	Upper left flange of the torque converter opening
1973 (Turbo)	Lower right side of the torque converter housing
Hydra-Matic 1967–68 (Turbo)	Light blue plate on the right side of the transmission case
Hydra-Matic 400 1969–72 (Turbo)	Upper left flange of the torque converter opening
1973 (Turbo)	Left side of the transmission case, to the rear of the manual control lever
1974–77 (Turbo)	Blue tag on the right side of the transmission case
Hydra-Matic 350 1969–72 (Turbo)	Upper left flange of the torque converter opening
1973 (Turbo)	Left side of the transmission case, to the rear of the manual control lever
1974–78 (Turbo)	Right rear vertical surface of the transmission oil pan
1979–81 (Turbo)	Lower right side of the transmission case (also located at the left rear side occasionally)
Hydra-Matic 250 1974–77 (Turbo)	Right rear vertical surface of the transmission oil pan
1981 (Turbo)	Lower right side at the front of the transmission case (also located at the right rear side occasionally)
Hydra-Matic 200 1978	Tag on the right side of the transmission extension
1979–81	Lower right side at the front of the transmission case (also located at the right rear side occasionally)
MANUAL	
Borg-Warner 1967–68 (3 speed)	Right rear corner of the extension housing
Saginaw 1967–68 (3 & 4 speed)	Lower left side of the transmission case, next to the rear of the cover
1969–76 (3 & 4 speed)	Lower right side of the transmission case, next to the rear of the cover
Muncie 1967–68 (4 speed)	Left side of the transmission case at the lower rear of the cover flange
1969–76 (4 speed)	Right side of the transmission case at the lower rear of the cover flange
1969–76 (3 speed)	Directly above the filler plug
76MM 1977–78 (3 speed-Saginaw)	Left side of the transmission case, below the side cover
1979–81 (3 speed-Saginaw)	Upper right side of the transmission case, near the rear
1977–78 (4 speed-Saginaw)	Left side of the transmission case, below the side cover
1979–81 (4 speed-Saginaw)	Upper right side of the transmission case, near the rear
83MM 1977–78 (4 speed-Warner)	Left side of the transmission case, at the rear of the side cover
1979–81 (4 speed-Warner)	Upper right side of the transmission case, near the rear

GENERAL INFORMATION AND MAINTENANCE

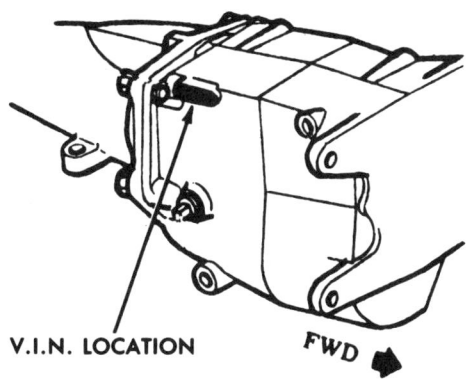

Manual transmission serial number location—1979-81

Unscrew the wing nut and remove the cover

ROUTINE MAINTENANCE

Air Cleaner

The air cleaner has a dual purpose. It not only filters the air going to the carburetor, but also acts as a flame arrester if the engine should backfire through the carburetor. If an engine maintenance procedure requires the temporary removal of the air cleaner, remove it; otherwise, never run the engine without it. Operating a car without its air cleaner results in some throaty sounds from the carburetor giving the impression of increased power but will only cause trouble. Unfiltered air to the carburetor will eventually result in a dirty, inefficient carburetor and engine. A dirty carburetor increases the chances of carburetor backfire and, without the protection of an air cleaner, fire becomes a probable danger. The air cleaner assembly consists of the air cleaner itself, which is the large metal container that fits over the carburetor, the element (paper or polyurethane) contained within, and the flame arrester located in the base of the air cleaner. If your Camaro is equipped with the paper element, it should be inspected at its first 12,000 miles, rechecked every 6,000 miles thereafter, and replaced after 24,000 miles. 1975 and later Camaro air cleaners should be replaced at 30,000 mile intervals if the paper type, and 15,000 miles if the oil wetted type. Inspections and replacements should be more frequent if the car is operated in a dirty, dusty environment. When inspecting the element, look for dust leaks, holes or an overly dirty appearance. If the element is excessively dirty, it may cause a reduction in clean air intake. If air has trouble getting through a dirty element, the carburetor fuel mixture

Remove and discard the old filter

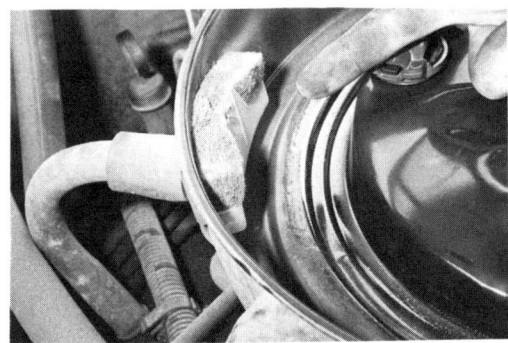

Check the small crankcase breather

will become richer (more gas, less air), the idle will be rougher, and the exhaust smoke will be noticeably black. To check the effectiveness of your paper element, remove the air cleaner assembly and, if the idle increases, then the element is restricting airflow and should be replaced. If a polyurethane element is installed, replace it every 12,000 miles. If you choose to clean it, do so with kerosene or another suitable solvent. Squeeze out all of the solvent, soak in en-

16 GENERAL INFORMATION AND MAINTENANCE

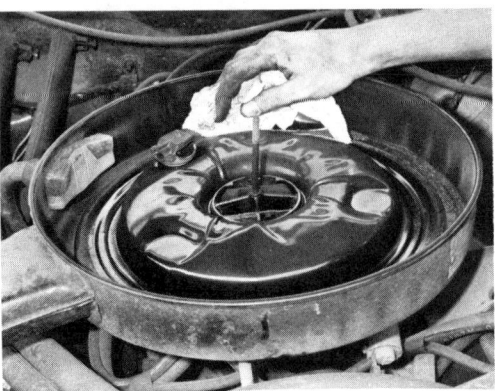

Using a clean rag or paper towel, wipe out the inside of the air cleaner

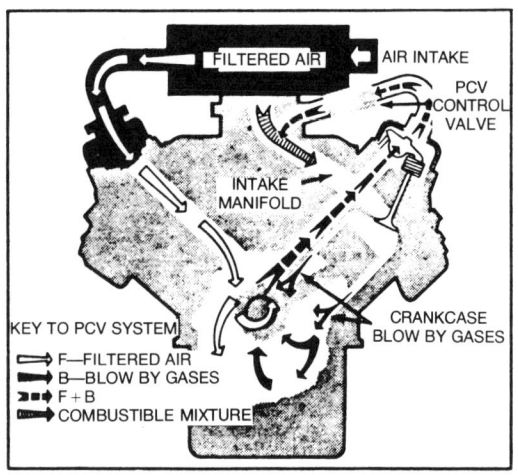

PCV system schematic; V8 engine (others similar)

gine oil, and then squeeze out the oil using a clean, dry cloth to remove the excess. The flame arrester, located at the base of the carburetor, should be cleaned in solvent (kerosene) once every 12,000 miles.

Positive Crankcase Ventilation Valve (PCV)

The crankcase ventilation system (PCV) must be operating properly in order to allow evaporation of fuel vapors and water from the crankcase. This system should be checked at every oil change and serviced after one year or 12,000 miles. The PCV valve is replaced after 2 years or 24,000 miles. For 1975 and later cars, the service interval has been upgraded to one year or 15,000 miles, with PCV valve replacement scheduled for two years or 30,000 miles. Normal service entails cleaning the passages of the system hoses with solvent, inspecting them for cracks and breaks, and replacing them as necessary. The PCV valve contains a check valve and, when working properly, this valve will make a rattling sound when the outside case is tapped. If it fails to rattle, then it is probably stuck in a closed position and needs to be replaced.

The PCV system is designed to prevent the emission of gases from the crankcase. It does this by connecting a crankcase outlet (valve cover, oil filler tube, back of engine) to the intake manifold with a hose. The crankcase gases travel through the hose to the intake manifold where they are returned to the combustion chamber to be burned. If maintained properly, this system reduces condensation in the crankcase and the resultant formation of harmful acids and oil dilution. A clogged PCV valve will often cause a slow or rough idle due to a richer fuel mixture. A car equipped with a PCV system has air going through a hose to the intake manifold from an outlet at the valve cover, oil filler tube, or rear of the engine. To compensate for this extra air going to the manifold, carburetor specifications require a richer (more gas) mixture at the carburetor. If the PCV valve or hose is clogged, this air doesn't go to the intake manifold and the fuel mixture is too rich. A rough, slow idle results. The valve should be checked before making any carburetor adjustments. Disconnect the valve from the engine or merely clamp the hose shut. If the engine speed decreases less than 50 rpm, the valve is clogged and should be replaced. If the engine speed decreases much more than 50 rpm, then the valve is good. The PCV valve is an inexpensive item and it is suggested that it be replaced. If the new valve doesn't noticeably improve engine idle, the problem might be a restriction in the PCV hose. For further details on PCV valve operation see Chapter 4.

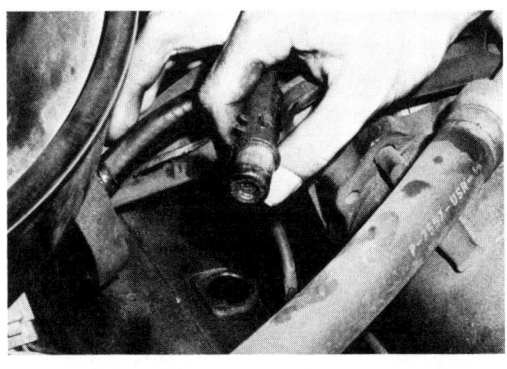

Pulling out the PCV valve from the rocker cover

GENERAL INFORMATION AND MAINTENANCE

Evaporative Emissions Control System

This system, standard since 1970, eliminates the release of unburned fuel vapors into the atmosphere. The only periodic maintenance required is an occasional check of the connecting lines of the system for kinks or other damage and deterioration. Lines should only be replaced with quality fuel line or special hose marked "evap." On 1970 and 1971 vehicles, every 12,000 miles or 12 months, the filter in the bottom of the carbon canister which is located in the engine compartment should be removed and replaced. On 1972–1976 vehicles, this service interval is 24,000 miles or 24 months. For 1977–1981 vehicles, the mileage interval has been increased to 30,000 miles, while the time interval remains the same. For further details on the Evaporative Emission Control System please refer to Chapter 4.

FILTER REPLACEMENT

1. Tag and disconnect all hoses connected to the charcoal canister.
2. Loosen the retaining clamps and then lift out the canister.
3. Grasp the filter in the bottom of the canister with your fingers and pull it out. Replace it with a new one.
4. Installation of the remaining components is in the reverse order of removal.

Battery

SPECIFIC GRAVITY (EXCEPT "MAINTENANCE FREE" BATTERIES)

At least once a year, check the specific gravity of the battery. It should be between 1.20 and 1.26 at room temperature.

The specific gravity can be checked with the use of an hydrometer, an inexpensive instrument available from many sources, including auto parts stores. The hydrometer has a squeeze bulb at one end and a nozzle at the other. Battery electrolyte is sucked into the hydrometer until the float is lifted from its seat. The specific gravity is then read by noting the position of the float. Generally, if after charging, the specific gravity between any two cells varies more than 50 points (.050), the battery is bad and should be replaced.

It is not possible to check the specific gravity in this manner on sealed ("maintenance free") batteries. Instead, the indicator built into the top of the case must be relied on to display any signs of battery deterioration. If the indicator is dark, the battery can be assumed to be OK. If the indicator is light, the specific gravity is low, and the battery should be charged or replaced.

CABLES AND CLAMPS

Once a year, the battery terminals and the cable clamps should be cleaned. Loosen the clamps and remove the cables, negative ca-

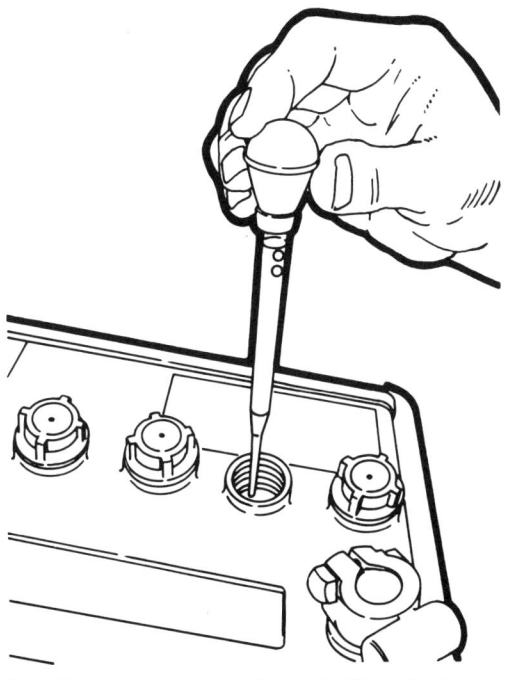

Specific gravity can be checked with an hydrometer

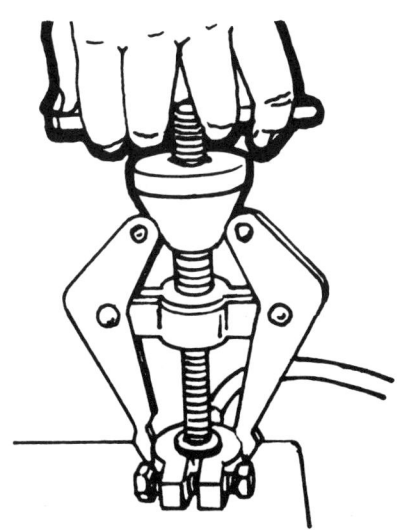

Pullers make clamp removal easier

18 GENERAL INFORMATION AND MAINTENANCE

Clean the posts with a wire brush, or a terminal cleaner made for the purpose (shown)

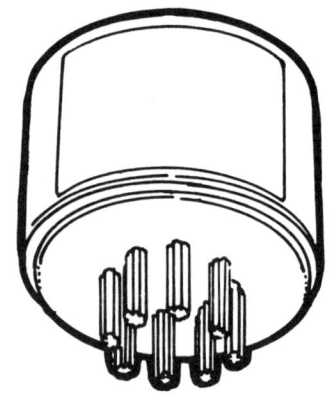

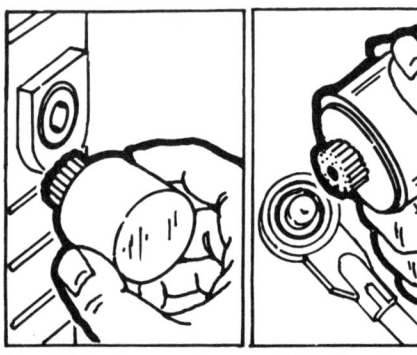

Special tools are also available for cleaning the posts and clamps on side terminal batteries

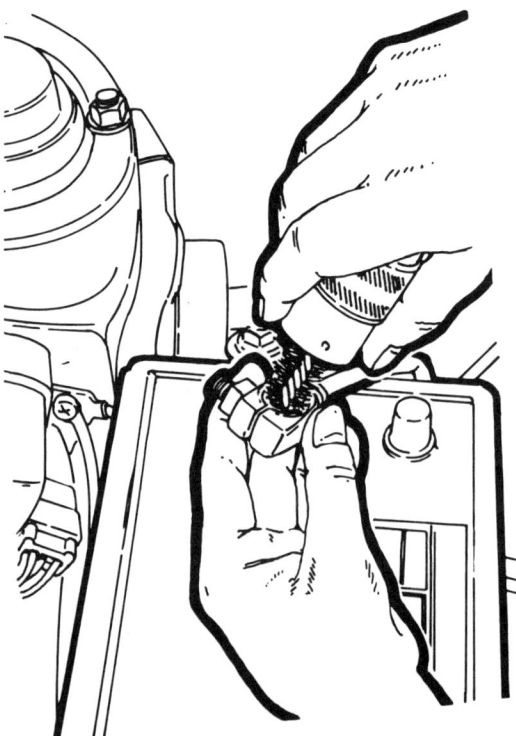

Clean the inside of the clamps with a wire brush, or the special tool

ble first. On batteries with posts on top, the use of a puller specially made for the purpose is recommended. These are inexpensive, and available in auto parts stores. Side terminal battery cables are secured with a bolt.

Clean the cable clamps and the battery terminal with a wire brush, until all corrosion, grease, etc. is removed and the metal is shiny. It is especially important to clean the inside of the clamp thoroughly, since a small deposit of foreign material or oxidation there will prevent a sound electrical connection and inhibit either starting or charging. Special tools are available for cleaning these parts, one type for conventional batteries and another type for side terminal batteries.

Before installing the cables, loosen the battery hold-down clamp or strap, remove the battery and check the battery tray. Clear it of any debris, and check it for soundness. Rust should be wire brushed away, and the metal given a coat of anti-rust paint. Replace the battery and tighten the hold-down clamp or strap securely, but be careful not to overtighten, which will crack the battery case.

After the clamps and terminals are clean, reinstall the cables, negative cable last; do not hammer on the clamps to install. Tighten

GENERAL INFORMATION AND MAINTENANCE

the clamps securely, but do not distort them. Give the clamps and terminals a thin external coat of grease after installation, to retard corrosion.

Check the cables at the same time that the terminals are cleaned. If the cable insulation is cracked or broken, or if the ends are frayed, the cable should be replaced with a new cable of the same length and gauge.

NOTE: *Keep flame or sparks away from the battery; it gives off explosive hydrogen gas. Battery electrolyte contains sulphuric acid. If you should splash any on your skin or in your eyes, flush the affected area with plenty of clear water; if it lands in your eyes, get medical help immediately.*

REPLACEMENT

When it becomes necessary to replace the battery, select a battery with a rating equal to or greater than the battery originally installed. Deterioration, embrittlement and just plain aging of the battery cables, starter motor, and associated wires makes the battery's job harder in successive years. The slow increase in electrical resistance over time makes it prudent to install a new battery with a greater capacity than the old. Details on battery removal and installation are covered in Chapter 3.

Manifold Heat Control Valve (Heat Riser) 1967–74

This valve is located in the exhaust manifold under the carburetor on in-line engines, and in either the right or left side exhaust manifold on V engines. It can be identified by looking for an external thermostatic spring and weight, and hinge pins that run through the walls of the manifold. Check the valve for free operation every 6,000 miles and, if it binds or is frozen, free it up with a solvent.

Early Fuel Evaporation (EFE) System 1975 and Later

This is a more effective form of heat riser which is vacuum actuated. It is used on Camaros built in 1975 and later. It heats incoming mixture during the engine warm-up process, utilizing a ribbed heat exchanger of thin metal that is located in the intake manifold. This pre-heating allows the choke to open more rapidly, thus reducing emissions. Problems in this system might be indicated by poor engine operation during warm-up.

This valve should be checked initially at 6 months/7500 miles, and, thereafter, at 18 month/22,500 mile intervals.

To check, move the valve through its full stroke by hand, making sure that the linkage does not bind and is properly connected. If the valve sticks, free it with a solvent. Also check that all vacuum hoses are properly connected and free of cracks or breaks. Replace hoses or broken or bent linkage parts as necessary.

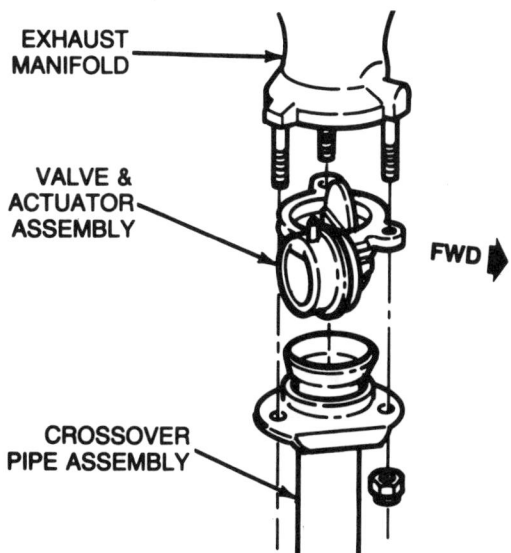

EFE valve

Typical heater riser valve (six cylinder shown) (© Chevrolet Motor Div.)

Belts

TENSION CHECKING AND ADJUSTMENT

Check the drive belts every 7,500 miles or six months for evidence of wear such as cracking, fraying, and incorrect tension. Determine belt tension at a point halfway be-

20 GENERAL INFORMATION AND MAINTENANCE

HOW TO SPOT WORN V-BELTS

V-Belts are vital to efficient engine operation—they drive the fan, water pump and other accessories. They require little maintenance (occasional tightening) but they will not last forever. Slipping or failure of the V-belt will lead to overheating. If your V-belt looks like any of these, it should be replaced.

This belt has deep cracks, which cause it to flex. Too much flexing leads to heat build-up and premature failure. These cracks can be caused by using the belt on a pulley that is too small. Notched belts are available for small diameter pulleys.

Cracking or weathering

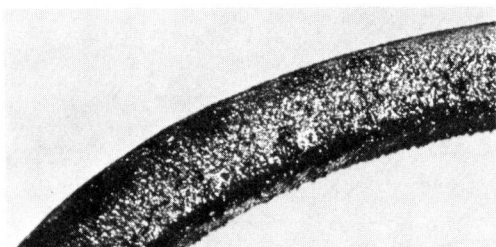

Oil and grease on a belt can cause the belt's rubber compounds to soften and separate from the reinforcing cords that hold the belt together. The belt will first slip, then finally fail altogether.

Softening (grease and oil)

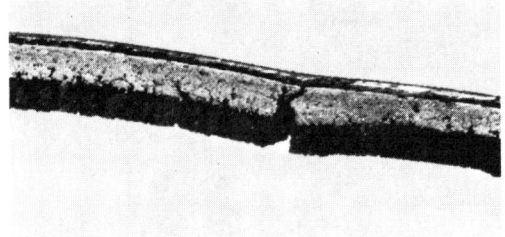

Glazing is caused by a belt that is slipping. A slipping belt can cause a run-down battery, erratic power steering, overheating or poor accessory performance. The more the belt slips, the more glazing will be built up on the surface of the belt. The more the belt is glazed, the more it will slip. If the glazing is light, tighten the belt.

Glazing

The cover of this belt is worn off and is peeling away. The reinforcing cords will begin to wear and the belt will shortly break. When the belt cover wears in spots or has a rough jagged appearance, check the pulley grooves for roughness.

Worn cover

This belt is on the verge of breaking and leaving you stranded. The layers of the belt are separating and the reinforcing cords are exposed. It's just a matter of time before it breaks completely.

Separation

GENERAL INFORMATION AND MAINTENANCE

tween the pulleys by pressing on the belt with moderate thumb pressure. If the distance between the pulleys (measured at the center of the pulley) is 13–16 in., the belt should deflect ½ in. at the halfway point or ¼ in. if the distance is 7–10 in. If the deflection is found to be too much or too little, loosen the mounting bolts and make the adjustments.

Before you attempt to adjust any of your engine's belts, you should take an old rag soaked in solvent and clean the mounting bolts of any road grime which has accumulated there. On some of the harder-to-reach bolts, an application of penetrating oil will make them easier to loosen. When you're adjusting belts, especially on late model V8's with air conditioning and power steering, it

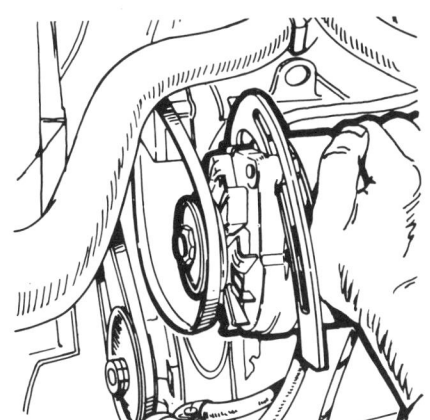

Push the component toward the engine and slip off the belt

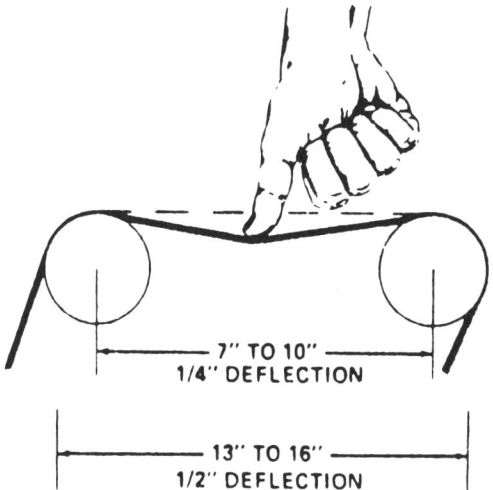

A gauge is recommended, but you can check belt tension with thumb pressure (© Chevrolet Motor Div.)

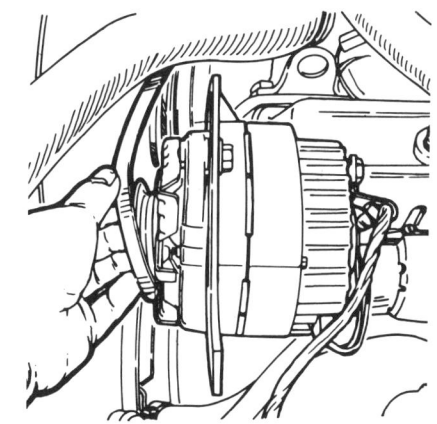

Slip the new belt over the pulley

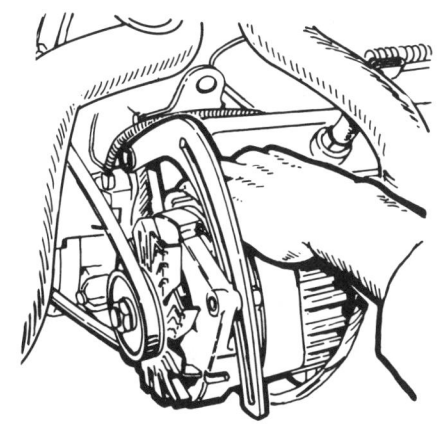

Pull outward on the component and tighten the mounting bolts

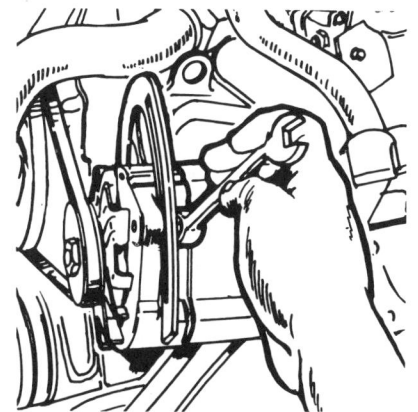

To adjust belt tension or to replace belts, first loosen the component's mounting and adjusting bolts slightly

would be especially helpful to have a variety of socket extensions and universals to get to those hard-to-reach bolts.

NOTE: *When adjusting the air pump belt, if you are using a pry bar, make sure that*

22 GENERAL INFORMATION AND MAINTENANCE

HOW TO SPOT BAD HOSES

Both the upper and lower radiator hoses are called upon to perform difficult jobs in an inhospitable environment. They are subject to nearly 18 psi at under hood temperatures often over 280°F., and must circulate nearly 7500 gallons of coolant an hour—3 good reasons to have good hoses.

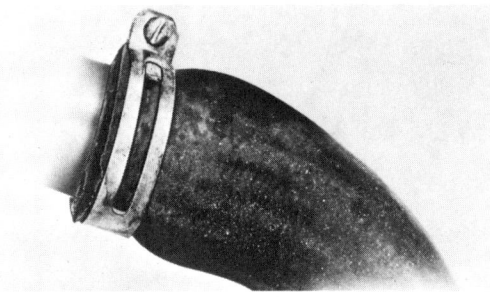

Swollen hose

A good test for any hose is to feel it for soft or spongy spots. Frequently these will appear as swollen areas of the hose. The most likely cause is oil soaking. This hose could burst at any time, when hot or under pressure.

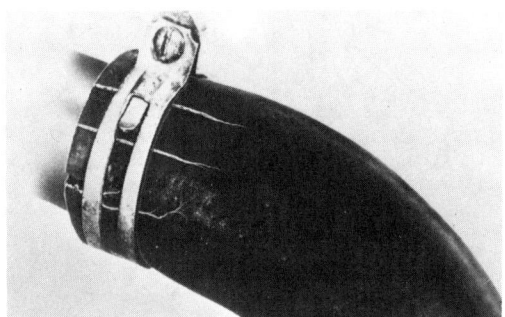

Cracked hose

Cracked hoses can usually be seen but feel the hoses to be sure they have not hardened; a prime cause of cracking. This hose has cracked down to the reinforcing cords and could split at any of the cracks.

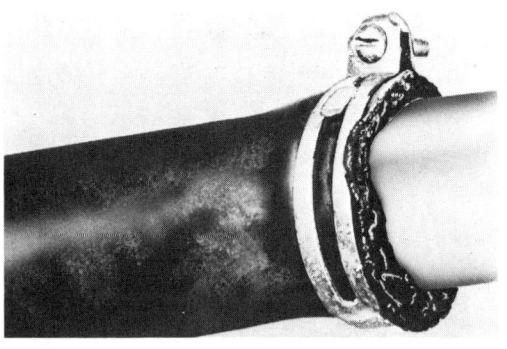

Frayed hose end (due to weak clamp)

Weakened clamps frequently are the cause of hose and cooling system failure. The connection between the pipe and hose has deteriorated enough to allow coolant to escape when the engine is hot.

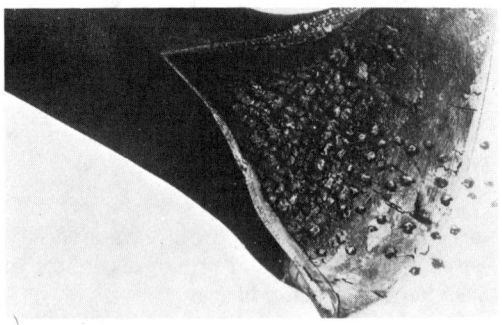

Debris in cooling system

Debris, rust and scale in the cooling system can cause the inside of a hose to weaken. This can usually be felt on the outside of the hose as soft or thinner areas.

GENERAL INFORMATION AND MAINTENANCE

you pry against the cast iron end cover and not against the aluminum housing. Excessive force on the housing itself will damage it.

Hoses

Upper and lower radiator hoses and all heater hoses should be checked for deterioration, leaks and loose hose clamps every 15,000 miles. To remove the hoses:
1. Drain the radiator as detailed later in this chapter.
2. Loosen the hose clamps at each end of the hose to be removed.
3. Working the hose back and forth, slide it off its connection and then install a new hose if necessary.
4. Position the hose clamps at least ¼ in. from the end of the hose and tighten them.
NOTE: *Always make sure that the hose clamps are beyond the bead and placed in the center of the clamping surface before tightening them.*

Cooling System

Dealing with the cooling system can be a dangerous matter unless the proper precautions are observed. It is best to check the coolant level in the radiator when the engine is cold. On early models this is accomplished by carefully removing the radiator cap and checking that the coolant is within 2 in. of the bottom of the filler neck. On later models, the cooling system has, as one of its components, a coolant recovery tank. If the coolant level is at or near the "FULL COLD" line (engine cold) or the "FULL HOT" line (engine hot), the level is satisfactory. Always be

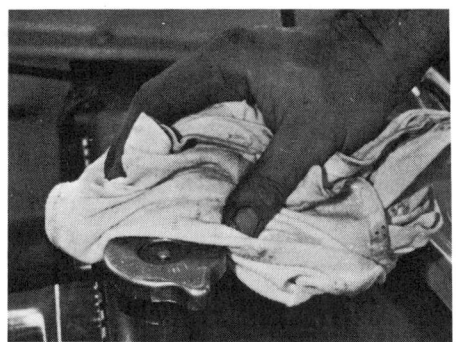

If the engine is hot, cover the radiator cap with a rag

Some radiator caps have pressure release levers

certain that the filler caps on both the radiator and the recovery tank are closed tightly.

In the event that the coolant level must be checked when the engine is hot on engines without a coolant recovery tank, place a thick rag over the radiator cap and slowly turn the cap counterclockwise until it reaches the first detent. Allow all hot steam to escape. This will allow the pressure in the system to drop gradually, preventing an explosion of hot coolant. When the hissing noise stops, remove the cap the rest of the way.

If the coolant level is found to be low, add a 50/50 mixture of ethylene glycol-based antifreeze and clean water. On older models, coolant must be added through the radiator filler neck. On newer models with the recovery tank, coolant may be added either through the filler neck on the radiator or directly into the recovery tank.

CAUTION: *Never add coolant to a hot engine unless it is running. If it is not running you run the risk of cracking the engine block.*

If the coolant level is chronically low or rusty, refer to Chapter 11 for diagnosis of the problem.

On models without a coolant recovery tank, the coolant level should be about 2 in. below the filler neck (engine cold)

24 GENERAL INFORMATION AND MAINTENANCE

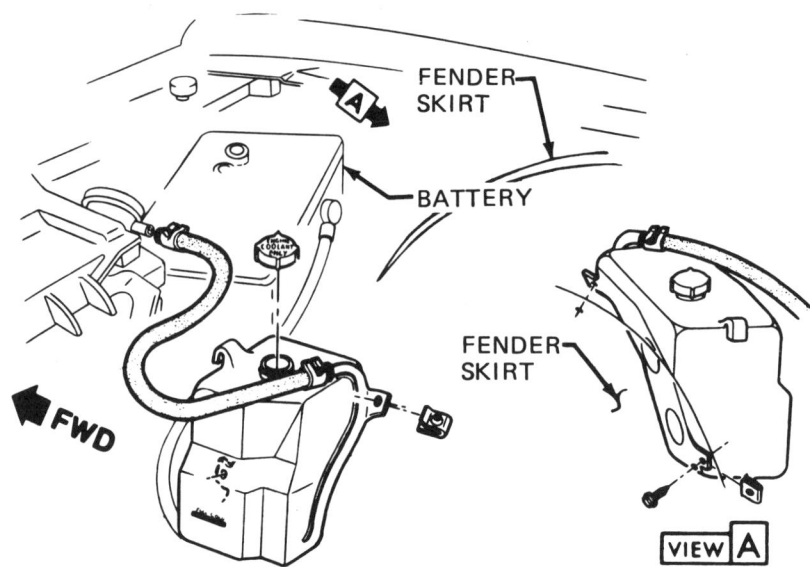

The coolant recovery tank is attached to the right fender skirt

The radiator hoses and clamps and the radiator cap should be checked at the same time as the coolant level. The radiator cap gasket should be checked for any obvious tears, cracks or swelling, or any signs of incorrect seating in the radiator filler neck.

Air Conditioning

Regular maintenance for the air conditioning system includes periodic checks of the drive belt tension. In addition, the system should be operated for at least five minutes every month. This ensures an adequate supply of lubricant to the bearings and also helps to prevent the seals and hoses from drying out. To do this comfortably in the winter months, turn the air conditioning on, the temperature control lever to the WARM or HI position and turn the blower fan to its highest setting. This will engage the compressor, circulating lubricating oils within the system, but prevent the discharge of cold air. The system should also be checked for proper refrigerant charge using the procedure given below.

SYSTEM CHECKS

CAUTION: *Do not attempt to charge or discharge the refrigerant system unless you are thoroughly familiar with its operation and the hazards involved. The compressed refrigerant used in the air conditioning system expands and evaporates (boils) into the atmosphere at a temperature of −21.7°F (−29.8°C) or less. This will freeze any surface that it comes in contact with, including your eyes. In addition, the refrigerant decomposes into a poisonous gas in the presence of flame.*

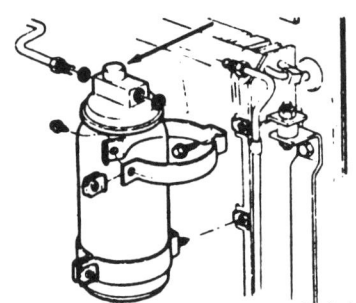

Air conditioner sight glass (arrow)

1967–77 Camaros with factory installed air conditioners have a sight glass for checking the refrigerant charge. The sight glass is on top of the VIR (valves-in-receiver) which is located in the front of the engine compartment, usually on the left side of the radiator.

1978 and later models utilize a different system which does not include a sight glass.

NOTE: *If your car is equipped with an aftermarket air conditioner, the following system checks may not apply. Contact the manufacturer of the unit for instructions on system checks.*

1967–77

This test works best if the outside air temperature is warm (above 70°F).

1. Place the automatic transmission in

GENERAL INFORMATION AND MAINTENANCE

Park or the manual in Neutral. Set the parking brake.

2. With the help of a friend, run the engine at a fast idle (about 1500 rpm).

3. Set the controls for maximum cold with the blower on high.

4. Look at the sight glass on top of the VIR. If a steady stream of bubbles is present in the sight glass, the system is low on charge. Very likely there is a leak in the system.

5. If no bubbles are present, the system is either fully charged or completely empty. Feel the high and low pressure lines at the compressor, if no appreciable temperature difference is felt, the system is empty or nearly so.

6. If one hose is warm (high pressure) and the other is cold (low pressure), the system may be OK. However, you are probably making these tests because there is something wrong with the air conditioner, so proceed to the next step.

7. Either disconnect the compressor clutch wire or have a friend in the car turn the fan control on and off to operate the compressor clutch. Watch the sight glass.

8. If bubbles appear when the clutch is disengaged and disappear when it is engaged, the system is properly charged.

9. If the refrigerant takes more than 45 seconds to bubble when the clutch is disengaged, the system is more than likely overcharged. This condition will usually result in poor cooling at low speeds.

NOTE: *If it is determined that the system has a leak, it should be repaired as soon as possible. Leaks may allow moisture to enter the system, causing an expensive rust problem.*

1978 and Later

The air conditioning system on these cars has no sight glass.

1. Run the engine until it reaches normal operating temperature.

2. Open the hood and all doors.

3. Turn the air conditioning on, move the temperature selector to the first detent to the right of COLD (outside air) and then turn the blower on HI.

4. Idle the engine at 1000 rpm.

5. Feel the temperature of the evaporator inlet and the accumulator outlet with the compressor clutch engaged.

6. Both lines should be cold. If the inlet pipe is colder than the outlet pipe, the sys-

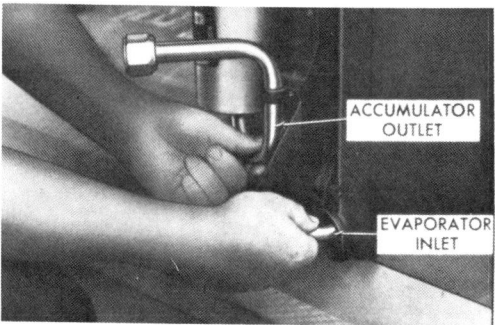

Checking the evaporator inlet and the accumulator outlet line temperatures—1978 and later

tem is low on charge. Do not attempt to charge the system yourself.

Windshield Wipers

For maximum effectiveness and longest element life, the windshield and wiper blades should be kept clean. Dirt, tree sap, road tar and so on will cause streaking, smearing and blade deterioration if left on the glass. It is advisable to wash the windshield carefully with a commercial glass cleaner at least once a month. Wipe off the rubber blades with the wet rag afterwards. Do not attempt to move the wipers back and forth by hand; damage to the motor and drive mechanism will result.

If the blades are found to be cracked, broken or torn, they should be replaced immediately. Replacement intervals will vary with usage, although ozone deterioration usually limits blade life to about one year. If the wiper pattern is smeared or streaked, or if the blade chatters across the glass, the blades should be replaced. It is easiest and most sensible to replace them in pairs.

There are basically three different types of wiper blade refills, which differ in their method of replacement. One type has two release buttons, approximately one-third of the way up from the ends of the blade frame. Pushing the buttons down releases a lock and allows the rubber blade to be removed from the frame. The new blade slides back into the frame and locks in place.

The second type of refill has two metal tabs which are unlocked by squeezing them together. The rubber blade can then be withdrawn from the frame jaws. A new one is installed by inserting it into the front frame jaws and sliding it rearward to engage the remaining frame jaws. There are usually four jaws; be certain when installing that the refill

GENERAL INFORMATION AND MAINTENANCE

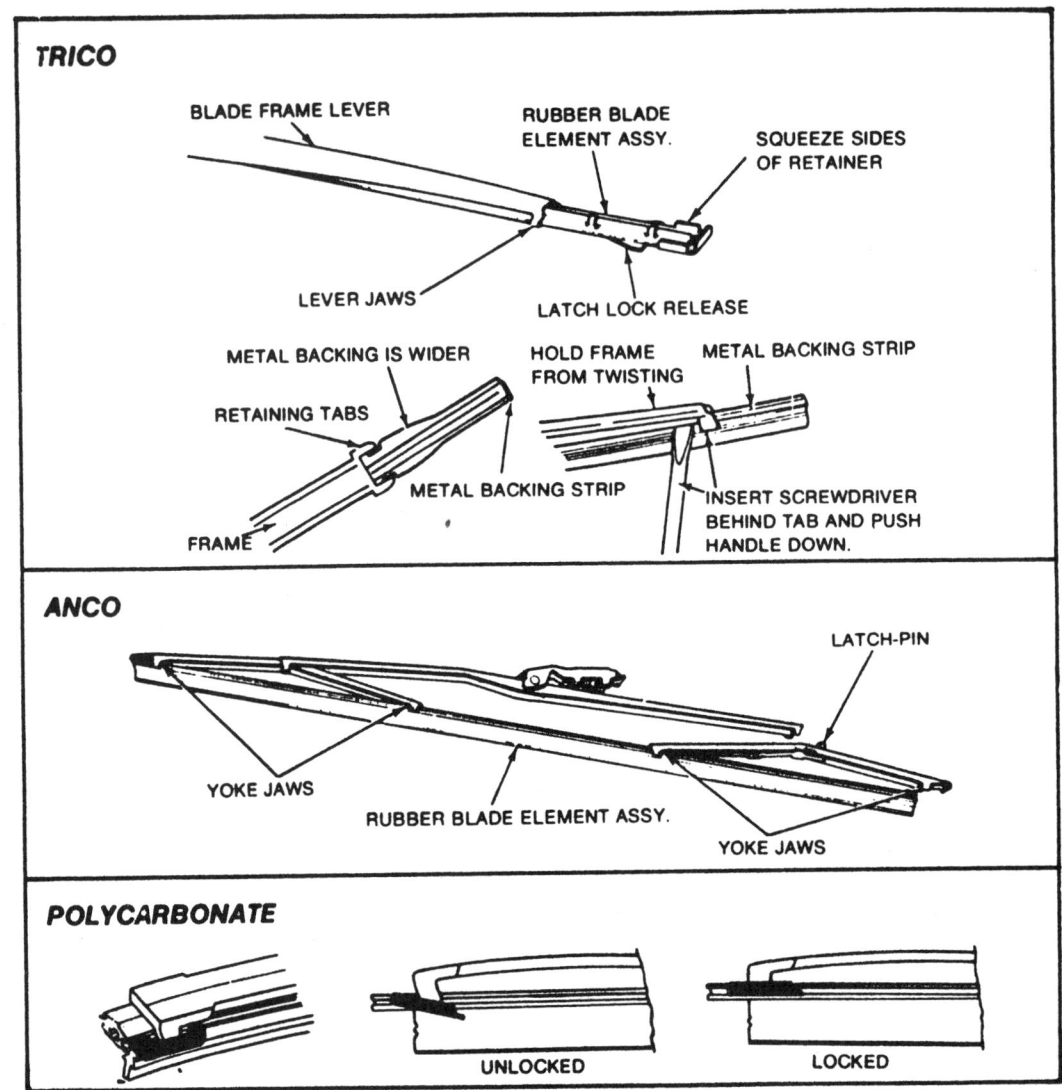

The three types of wiper blade retention

is engaged in all of them. At the end of its travel, the tabs will lock into place on the front jaws of the wiper blade frame.

The third type is a refill made from polycarbonate. The refill has a simple locking device at one end which flexes downward out of the groove into which the jaws of the holder fit, allowing easy release. By sliding the new refill through all the jaws and pushing through the slight resistance when it reaches the end of its travel, the refill will lock into position.

Regardless of the type of refill used, make sure that all of the frame jaws are engaged as the refill is pushed into place and locked. The metal blade holder and frame will scratch the glass if allowed to touch it.

Fluid Level Checks
ENGINE OIL

Every time you stop for fuel, check the engine oil as follows:

1. Make sure the car is parked on level ground.
2. When checking the oil level it is best for the engine to be at normal operating temperature, although checking the oil immediately after stopping will lead to a false reading. Wait a few minutes after turning off the engine to allow the oil to drain back into the crankcase.
3. Open the hood and locate the dipstick which will be on either the right or left side depending upon your particular engine. Pull

GENERAL INFORMATION AND MAINTENANCE

The oil level is checked with the dipstick

The oil level should be between the 'ADD' and 'FULL' marks on the dipstick

the dipstick from its tube, wipe it clean and then reinsert it.

4. Pull the dipstick out again and, holding it horizontally, read the oil level. The oil should be between the "FULL" and "ADD" marks on the dipstick. If the oil is below the "ADD" mark, add oil of the proper viscosity through the capped opening in the top of the cylinder head cover. See the "Oil and Fuel Recommendations" chart in this chapter for the proper viscosity and rating of oil to use.

5. Replace the dipstick and check the oil level again after adding any oil. Be careful not to overfill the crankcase. Approximately one quart of oil will raise the level from the "ADD" mark to the "FULL" mark. Excess oil will generally be consumed at an accelerated rate.

TRANSMISSION

Manual

The oil in the manual transmission should be checked at least every 6,000 miles for 1967–74 models or every 7,500 miles for all 1975 and later models.

1. With the car parked on a level surface, remove the filler plug from the side of the transmission housing.

2. If the lubricant begins to trickle out of the hole, there is enough and you need not go any further. Otherwise, carefully insert your finger (watch out for sharp threads) and check to see if the oil is up to the edge of the hole.

3. If not, add oil through the hole until the level is at the edge of the hole. Most gear lubricants come in a plastic squeeze bottle with a nozzle; making additions simple. You can also use a common kitchen baster. Use only standard GL-5 hypoid-type gear oil—SAE 80W or SAE 80W/90.

4. Replace the filler plug, run the engine and check for leaks.

Automatic

Check the automatic transmission fluid level at least every 6,000 miles (7,500 miles for 1975 and later models). The dipstick can be found in the rear of the engine compartment. The fluid level should be checked only when the transmission is hot (normal operating temperature). The transmission is considered hot after about 20 miles of highway driving.

1. Park the car on a level surface with the engine idling. Shift the transmission into Neutral and set the parking brake.

2. Remove the dipstick, wipe it clean and then reinsert it firmly. Be sure that it has been pushed all the way in. Remove the dipstick again and check the fluid level while holding it horizontally. With the engine running, the fluid level should be between the second notch and the "FULL HOT" line. If the fluid must be checked when it is cool, the level should be between the first and second notches.

3. If the fluid level is below the second notch (engine hot) or the first notch (engine cold), add DEXRON® (1967–75) or DEXRON® II (1976 and later) automatic

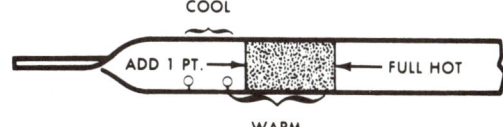

Automatic transmission dipstick marks; the proper level is within the shaded area

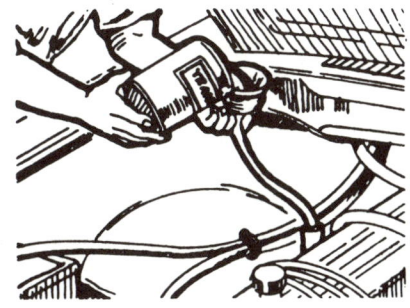

Add automatic transmission fluid through the dipstick tube

28 GENERAL INFORMATION AND MAINTENANCE

transmission fluid through the dipstick tube. This is easily done with the aid of a funnel. Check the level often as you are filling the transmission. Be extremely careful not to overfill it. Overfilling will cause slippage, seal damage and overheating. Approximately one pint of ATF will raise the fluid level from one notch/line to the other.

NOTE: *Always use DEXRON® or DEXRON® II AFT. The use of AFT Type F or any other fluid will cause severe damage to the transmission.*

The fluid on the dipstick should always be a bright red color. If it is discolored (brown or black), or smells burnt, serious transmission troubles, probably due to overheating, should be suspected. The transmission should be inspected by a qualified technician to locate the cause of the burnt fluid.

BRAKE MASTER CYLINDER

The brake master cylinder is located under the hood, in the left rear section of the engine compartment. It is divided into two sections (reservoirs) and the fluid must be kept within ¼ in. of the top edge of both reservoirs. The level should be checked at least every 6,000 miles (7,500 miles for 1975 and later models).

NOTE: *Any sudden decrease in the level of fluid indicates a possible leak in the system and should be checked out immediately.*

To check the fluid level, simply pry off the retaining bar and then lift off the top cover of the master cylinder. When making additions of brake fluid, use only fresh, uncontaminated brake fluid which meets or exceeds DOT 3 standards. Be careful not to spill any brake fluid on painted surfaces, as it eats

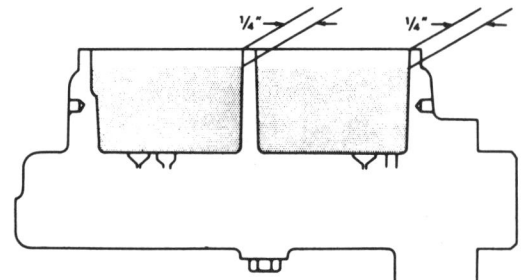

The fluid level in the master cylinder reservoir should be within ¼ in. of the top edge

paint. Do not allow the brake fluid container or the master cylinder reservoir to remain open any longer than necessary; brake fluid absorbs moisture from the air, reducing its effectiveness and causing corrosion in the lines.

RADIATOR COOLANT

It's a good idea to check the coolant level every time that you stop for fuel. If the engine is hot, let it cool for a few minutes and then check the level following the procedure given earlier in this chapter.

Check the freezing protection rating at least once a year, preferably just before the winter sets in. This can be done with an antifreeze tester (most service stations will have one on hand and will probably check it for you, if not, they are available at an auto parts store). Maintain a protection rating of at least $-20°F$ $(-29°C)$ to prevent engine damage as a result of freezing and to assure the proper engine operating temperature.

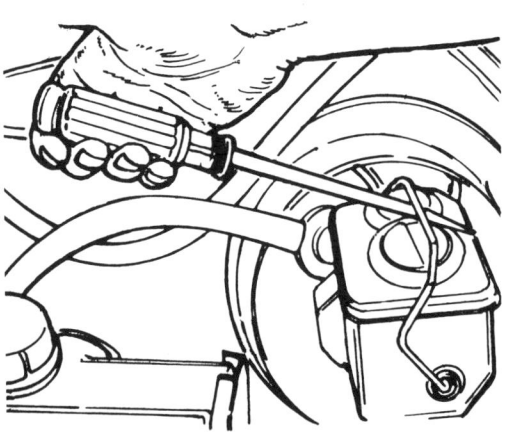

Pry the retaining bail from the master cylinder reservoir cap to check the fluid level

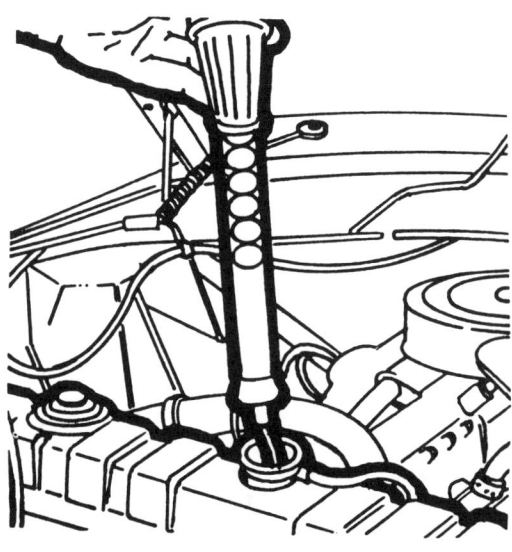

Coolant protection can be checked with a simple, float-type tester

GENERAL INFORMATION AND MAINTENANCE

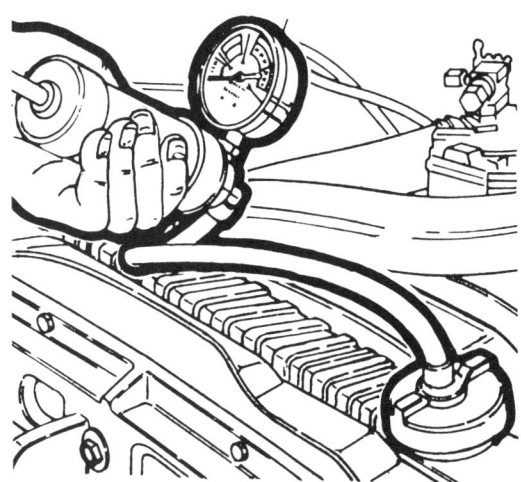

The system should be pressure tested at least once a year

POWER STEERING RESERVOIR

Power steering fluid level should be checked at least once every 6,000 miles (7,500 miles for 1975 and later models). To prevent possible overfilling, check the fluid level only when the fluid has warmed to operating temperatures and the wheels are turned straight ahead. If the level is low, fill the pump reservoir with DEXRON® Automatic Transmission Fluid required by the transmission on 1976 and earlier cars. 1977–81 cars require GM power steering fluid, until the fluid level measures "full" on the reservoir dipstick. Low fluid level usually produces a moaning sound as the wheels are turned (especially when standing still or parking) and increases steering wheel effort.

REAR AXLE

The oil in the differential should be checked at least every 6,000 miles (7,500 miles for 1975 and later models).

1. With the car on a level surface, remove the filler plug from the front side of the differential.
2. If the oil begins to trickle out of the hole, there is enough. Otherwise, carefully insert your finger (watch out for sharp threads) into the hole and check that the oil is up to the bottom edge of the filler hole.
3. If not, add oil through the hole until the level is at the edge of the hole. Most gear oils come in a plastic squeeze bottle with a nozzle; making additions is simple. You can also use a common kitchen baster. Use only standard GL-5 hypoid-type gear oil—SAE 80W or SAE 80W/90.

NOTE: *On all models equipped with the positraction/limited slip rear axle, GM recommends that you use only the special lubricant which is available at your local Chevrolet parts department.*

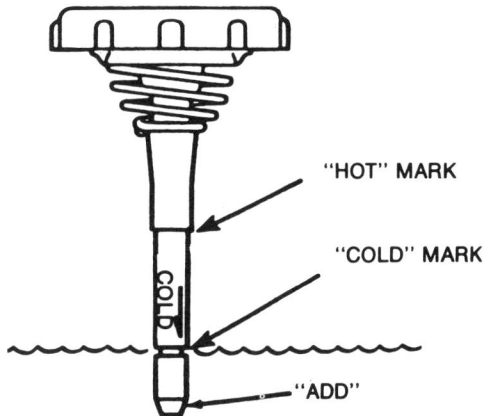

Use the dipstick to check the power steering fluid

BATTERY

Check the battery fluid level (except in Maintenance Free batteries) at least once a month, more often in hot weather or during extended periods of travel. The electrolyte

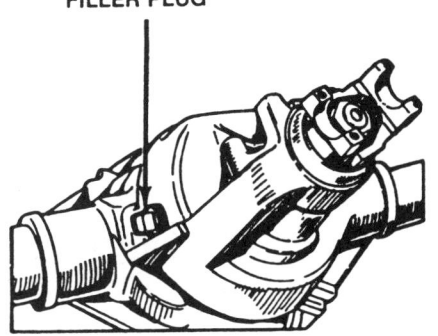

Remove the filler plug to check the lubricant level in the rear axle

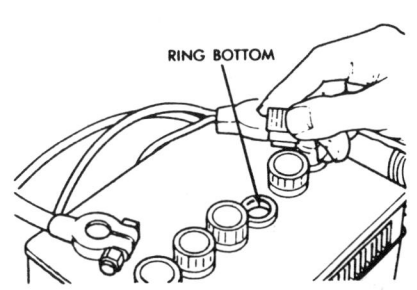

Fill each battery cell to the bottom of the split ring with distilled water

GENERAL INFORMATION AND MAINTENANCE

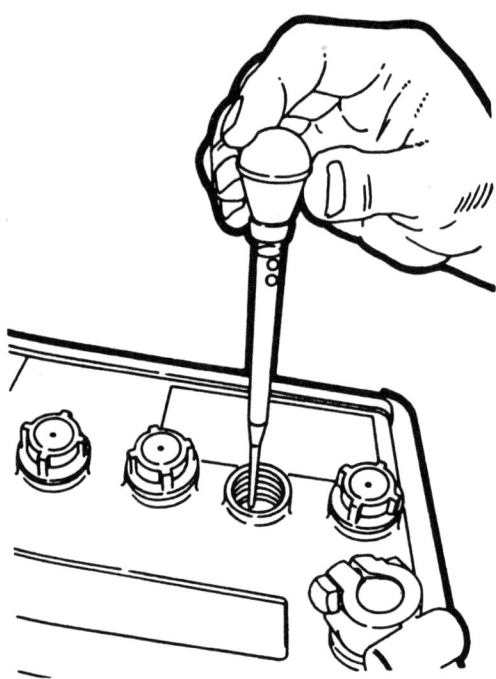

The specific gravity of the battery can be checked with a simple float-type hydrometer

level should be up to the bottom of the split ring in each cell. All batteries are equipped with an "eye" in the cap of one cell. If the "eye" glows or has an amber color to it, this means that the level is low and only distilled water should be added. Do not add anything else to the battery. If the "eye" has a dark appearance the battery electrolyte level is high enough. It is also wise to check each cell individually.

At least once a year, check the specific gravity of the battery. It should be between 1.20–1.26. Clean and tighten the clamps and apply a thin coat of petroleum jelly to the terminals. This will help to retard corrosion. The terminals can be cleaned with a stiff wire brush or with an inexpensive terminal cleaner designed for this purpose.

Battery State of Charge at Room Temperature

Specific Gravity Reading	Charged Condition
1.260–1.280	Fully Charged
1.230–1.250	¾ Charged
1.200–1.220	½ Charged
1.170–1.190	¼ Charged
1.140–1.160	Almost no Charge
1.110–1.130	No Charge

If water is added during freezing weather, the car should be driven several miles to allow the electrolyte and water to mix. Otherwise the battery could freeze.

If the battery becomes corroded, a solution of baking soda and water will neutralize the corrosion. This should be washed off after making sure that the caps are securely in place. Rinse the solution off with cold water.

Some batteries were equipped with a felt terminal washer. This should be saturated with engine oil approximately every 6,000 miles. This will also help to retard corrosion.

If a "fast" charger is used while the battery is in the car, disconnect the battery before connecting the charger.

NOTE: *Keep flame or sparks away from the battery; it gives off explosive hydrogen gas.*

Testing the Maintenance-Free Battery

All later model cars are equipped with maintenance-free batteries, which do not require normal attention as far as fluid level checks are concerned. However, the terminals require periodic cleaning, which should be performed at least once a year.

The sealed-top battery cannot be checked for charge in the normal manner, since there is no provision for access to the electrolyte. To check the condition of the battery:

1. If the indicator eye on top of the battery is dark, the battery has enough fluid. If the eye is light, the electrolyte fluid is too low and the battery must be replaced.
2. If a green dot appears in the middle of the eye, the battery is sufficiently charged. Proceed to Step 4. If no green dot is visible, charge the battery as in Step 3.
3. Charge the battery at this rate:

Charging Rate Amps	Time
75	40 min
50	1 hr
25	2 hr
10	5 hr

CAUTION: *Do not charge the battery for more than 50 amp/hours. If the green dot appears, or if electrolyte squirts out of the vent hole, stop the charge and proceed to Step 4.*

It may be necessary to tip the battery from side to side to get the green dot to appear after charging.

GENERAL INFORMATION AND MAINTENANCE

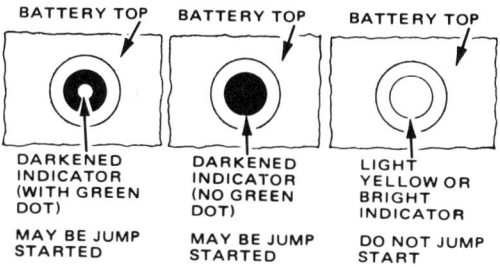

Maintenance-free batteries contain their own built in hydrometer

4. Connect a battery load tester and a voltmeter across the battery terminals (the battery cables should be disconnected from the battery). Apply a 300 amp load to the battery for 15 seconds to remove the surface charge. Remove the load.

5. Wait 15 seconds to allow the battery to recover. Apply the appropriate test load, as specified in the following chart:

Battery	Test Load
Y85-4	130 amps
R85-5	170 amps
R87-5	210 amps
R89-5	230 amps

Apply the load for 15 seconds while reading the voltage. Disconnect the load.

6. Check the results against the following chart. If the battery voltage is at or above the specified voltage for the temperature listed, the battery is good. If the voltage falls below what's listed, the battery should be replaced.

Temperature (°F)	Minimum Voltage
70 or above	9.6
60	9.5
50	9.4
40	9.3
30	9.1
20	8.9
10	8.7
0	8.5

Tires

Tires should be checked weekly for proper air pressure. A chart, located either in the glove compartment or on the driver's or passenger's door, gives the recommended inflation pressures. Maximum fuel economy and

Tread wear indicators will appear when the tire is worn out

tire life will result if the pressure is maintained at the highest figure given on the chart. Pressures should be checked before driving since pressure can increase as much as six pounds per square inch (psi) due to heat buildup. It is a good idea to have your own accurate pressure gauge, because not all gauges on service station air pumps can be trusted. When checking pressures, do not neglect the spare tire. Note that some spare tires require pressures considerably higher than those used in the other tires.

While you are about the task of checking air pressure, inspect the tire treads for cuts, bruises and other damage. Check the air valves to be sure that they are tight. Replace any missing valve caps.

Check the tires for uneven wear that might indicate the need for front end alignment or tire rotation. Tires should be replaced when a tread wear indicator appears as a solid band across the tread.

When buying new tires, give some thought to the following points, especially if

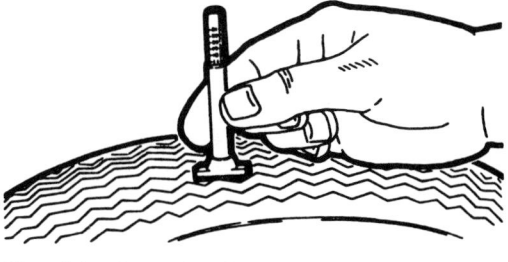

Tread depth can be checked with an inexpensive gauge

32 GENERAL INFORMATION AND MAINTENANCE

A penny works as well as anything for checking tire tread depth; when you can see the top of Lincoln's head, it's time for a new tire

you are considering a switch to larger tires or a different profile series:

1. All four tires must be of the same construction type. This rule cannot be violated. Radial, bias, and bias-belted tires must not be mixed.
2. The wheels should be the correct width for the tire. Tire dealers have charts of tire and rim compatibility. A mismatch will cause sloppy handling and rapid tire wear. The tread width should match the rim width (inside bead to inside bead) within an inch. For radial tires, the rim width should be 80% or less of the tire (not tread) width.
3. The height (mounted diameter) of the new tires can change speedometer accuracy, engine speed at a given road speed, fuel mileage, acceleration, and ground clearance. Tire manufacturers furnish full measurement specifications.
4. The spare tire should be usable, at least for short distance and low speed operation, with the new tires.
5. There shouldn't be any body interference when loaded, on bumps, or in turns.

TIRE ROTATION

Tire rotation is recommended every 6000 miles or so, to obtain maximum tire wear. The pattern you use depends on whether or not your car has a usable spare. Radial tires should not be cross-switched (from one side of the car to the other); they last longer if their direction of rotation is not changed. Snow tires sometimes have directional arrows molded into the side of the carcass; the arrow shows the direction of rotation. They will wear very rapidly if the rotation is reversed. Studded tires will lose their studs if their rotational direction is reversed.

NOTE: *Mark the wheel position or direction of rotation on radial tires or studded snow tires before removing them.*

STORAGE

Store the tires at the proper inflation pressure if they are mounted on wheels. Keep them in a cool dry place, laid on their sides. If the tires are stored in the gargage or basement, do not let them stand on a concrete floor; set them on strips of wood.

Fuel Filter

The carburetor inlet fuel filter should be replaced every 12,000 miles (15,000 miles for

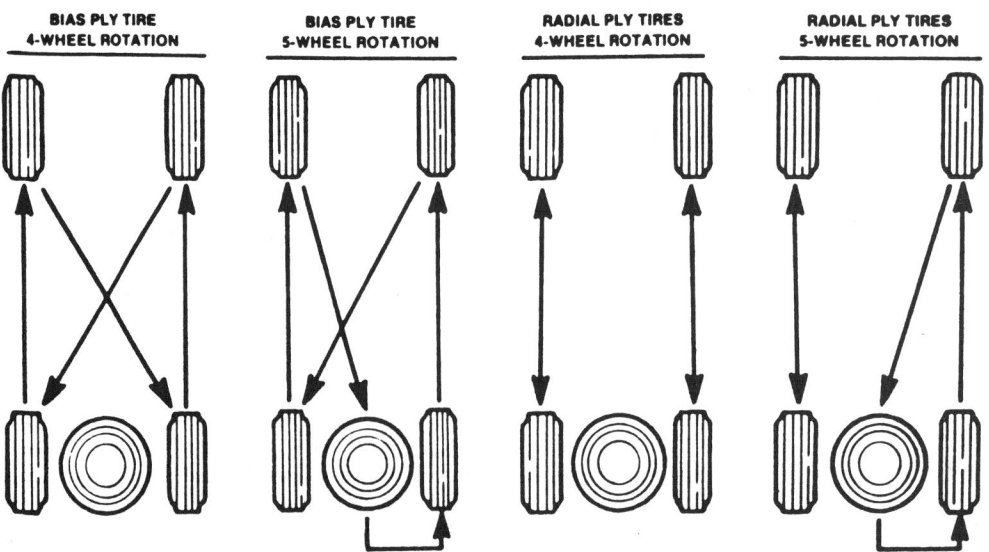

Tire rotation diagrams; note that radials should not be cross-switched

GENERAL INFORMATION AND MAINTENANCE

Capacities

| Year | Engine No. Cyl Displacement (cu in.) | Engine Crankcase Add 1 qt for New Filter | Transmission Pts to Refill After Draining | | | Drive Axle (pts) | Gasoline Tank (gals) | Cooling System (qts) | |
| | | | Manual | | | | | | |
			3-Speed	4-Speed	Automatic ●			With Heater	With A/C
1967	6—230	4	3①	3③	6	3.5	18	14	14
	6—250	4	3①	3①	6	3.5	18	14	14
	8—327	4	3①	3①	6	3.5	18	15	18
	8—350	4	3①	3①	6	3.5	18	17	17
	8—396	4	3①	3①	6	3.5	18	23	23
1968	6—230	4	3	3	6	3.5	18	12	12
	6—250	4	3	3	6	3.5	18	12	12
	8—302	4	3	3	6	3.5	18	16	—
	8—327	4	3	3	6	3.5	18	16	16
	8—350	4	3	3	6	3.5	18	16	16
	8—396	4	3	3	6⑥	3.5	18	23	23
1969	6—230	4	3①	—	6⑦	3.5②	18	13	13
	6—250	4	3①	—	6⑦	3.5②	18	13	13
	8—302	4	3①	3	6⑦	3.5②	18	17	—
	8—307	4	3①	3	6⑦	3.5②	18	17	18
	8—327	4	3①	3	6	3.5②	18	16	16
	8—350	4	3①	3	6⑦	3.5②	18	16	17
	8—396	4	3①	3	8	3.5②	18	23	24
1970	6—250	4	3	—	6⑦	3.75③	19	12	13
	8—307	4	3	—	6⑦	3.75③	19	15	16
	8—350	4	3	3	6.5④⑦	3.75③	19	16	16
	8—396	4	3	3	8	3.75③	19	23	24
1971	6—250	4	3	—	8	3.75	17	12	—

Capacities (cont.)

| Year | Engine No. Cyl Displacement (cu in.) | Engine Crankcase Add 1 qt for New Filter | Transmission Pts to Refill After Draining | | | Drive Axle (pts) | Gasoline Tank (gals) | Cooling System (qts) | |
| | | | Manual | | | | | | |
			3-Speed	4-Speed	Automatic ●			With Heater	With A/C
1971	8—307	4	3	—	6⑦	3.75	17	15	16
	8—350	4	3	3	6.5⑦	3.75	17	16	16
	8—402⑧	4	3	3	8	3.75	17	23	23
1972	6—250	4	3	—	6⑦	4.25	18	12	—
	8—307	4	3	—	6⑦	4.25	18	15	16
	8—350	4	3	3	6.5⑤⑦	4.25	18	16	16
	8—402⑧	4	—	3	8	4.25	18	24	24
1973	6—250	4	3	—	6	4.25	18	12	—
	8—307	4	3	—	5	4.25	18	15	16
	8—350	4	3	3	6⑨	4.25	18	16	16
1974	6—250	4	3	—	8	4.25	21	14	—
	8—350	4	3	—	8⑩	4.25	21	18	19
1975	6—250	4	3	—	8	4.25	21	14	15
	8—350	4	3	3	8⑩	4.25	21	18	19
1976	6—250	4	3	—	8	4.25	21	14.6	14.7
	8—305	4	3	3	8	4.25	21	17.2	17.9
	8—350	4	3	3	8	4.25	21	17.3	18.0
1977	6—250	4	3	—	8	4.25	21	15	16
	V8—305	4	—	3	8	4.25	21	17.5	18.5
	V8—350	4	—	3	8	4.25	21	17.5	18.5
1978	6—250	4	3	—	6	4.25⑪	21	15	16
	V8—305	4	—	3	6	4.25⑪	21	17.5	18.5
	V8—350	4	—	3	6	4.25⑪	21	17.5	18.5

GENERAL INFORMATION AND MAINTENANCE

Capacities (cont.)

Year	Engine No. Cyl Displacement (cu in.)	Engine Crankcase Add 1 qt for New Filter	Transmission Pts to Refill After Draining			Drive Axle (pts)	Gasoline Tank (gals)	Cooling System (qts)	
			Manual					With Heater	With A/C
			3-Speed	4-Speed	Automatic ●				
1979	6-250	4	3	—	7	4.25⑪	21	15	16
	V8-305	4	—	3.4	7	4.25⑪	21	17.5	18.5
	V8-350	4	—	3.4	7	4.25⑪	21	17.5	18.5
1980-81	V6-229	4⑫	3	—	7⑬	4.25⑭	21	14.5	15.5
	V6-231	4⑫	—	—	7⑬	4.25⑭	21	12	13
	V8-267	4	—	—	7⑬	4.25⑭	21	15	16
	V8-305	4	—	3.4	7⑬	4.25⑭	21	15	16
	V8-350	4	—	—	7⑬	4.25⑭	21	16	17

● Specifications do not include torque converter
① 3.5 pts with heavy duty transmission
② 4 pts with 8.875 in. ring gear
③ 4.25 pts with 8.875 in. ring gear
④ 8 pts with 360 hp engine
⑤ 8 pts with Z-28 350
⑥ 8 pts with Turbo Hydramatic 400
⑦ 5 pts with Turbo Hydramatic 350
⑧ 402 is actually 396 V8 with a slight overbore
⑨ 8 pts with the Z-28
⑩ 9 pts with the Z-28
⑪ W/7.5 in. ring gear—3.5 pts.
⑫ Figure is the same with or without filter change
⑬ W/350c—6 pts.
⑭ W/7.5 in. ring gear—3.5 pts.; W/8.75 in. ring gear—5.4 pts.

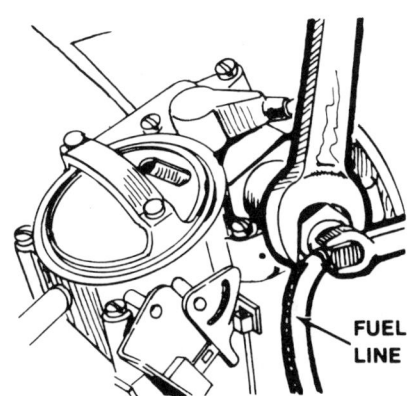

The fuel filter is located behind the large fuel line inlet nut on the carburetor

1975 and later models) or more often if necessary. Two types of fuel filters are used in the carburetor body, a bronze type and a paper element type. Either one may be encountered at any given time. However, the replacement filter should be of the same type as the one removed. Inline fuel filters may be used on some engines which should be changed at the same time as the filter in the carburetor body. Filter replacement should be attempted only when the engine is cold. Additionally, it is a good idea to place some absorbent rags under the fuel fittings to catch the gasoline which will spill out when the lines are loosened. To replace the filter found in the carburetor body:

36 GENERAL INFORMATION AND MAINTENANCE

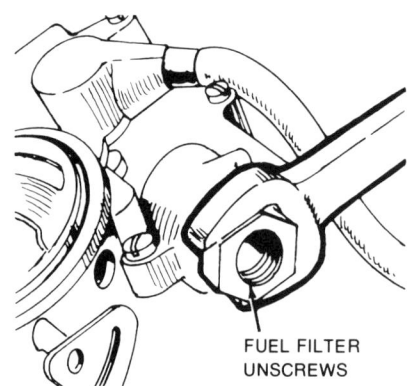

Remove the retaining nut and the filter will pop out under spring pressure

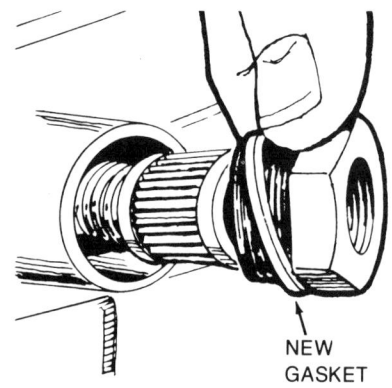

Install the new filter and spring. Certain early models use a bronze filter element, but most are made of paper

1. Disconnect the fuel line connection at the intake fuel filter nut. Plug the opening to prevent loss of fuel.
2. Remove the intake fuel filter nut from the carburetor with a 1 in. box wrench or socket.
3. Remove the filter element and spring.
4. Check the element for restrictions by blowing on the cone end. Air should pass freely.
5. Clean or replace the element, as necessary.
6. Install the element spring, then the filter elements in the carburetor. Bronze filters should have the small section of the cone facing out.
7. Install a new gasket on the intake fuel nut. Install the nut in the carburetor body and tighten securely.
8. Install the fuel line and tighten the connector.

Some models may have an inline filter. This is a can-shaped device located in the fuel line between the pump and the carburetor. It may be made of either plastic or metal. To replace the filter:

1. Place some absorbent rags under the filter; remember, it will be full of gasoline when removed.
2. Use a pair of pliers to expand the clamp on one end of the filter, then slide the clamp down past the point to which the filter pipe extends in the rubber hose. Do the same with the other clamp.
3. Gently twist and pull the hoses free of the filter pipes. Remove and discard the old filter.
4. Install the new filter into the hoses, slide the clamps back into place, and check for leaks with the engine idling.

LUBRICATION

Oil and Fuel Recommendations

OIL

The SAE (Society of Automotive Engineers) grade number indicates the viscosity of the engine oil and thus its ability to lubricate at a given temperature. The lower the SAE grade number, the lighter the oil; the lower the viscosity, the easier it is to crank the engine in cold weather.

Oil viscosities should be chosen from those oils recommended for the lowest anticipated temperatures during the oil change interval.

Multi-viscosity oils (10W-30, 20W-50 etc.) offer the important advantage of being adaptable to temperature extremes. They allow easy starting at low temperatures, yet they give good protection at high speeds and engine temperatures. This is a decided advantage in changeable climates or in long distance touring.

The API (American Petroleum Institute) designation indicates the classification of engine oil used under certain given operating conditions. Only oils designated for use "Service SE" should be used. Oils of the SE type perform a variety of functions inside the engine in addition to the basic function as a lubricant. Through a balanced system of metallic detergents and polymeric dispersants, the oil prevents the formation of high and low temperature deposits and also keeps sludge and particles of dirt in suspension. Acids, particularly sulfuric acid, as well as other by-products of combustion, are neutralized. Both the SAE grade number and the API

GENERAL INFORMATION AND MAINTENANCE

designation can be found on top of the oil can.

For recommended oil viscosities, refer to the chart.

NOTE: *As of late 1980, the API has come out with a new designation of motor oil, SF. Oils designated for use "Service SF" are equally acceptable in your Camaro.*

CAUTION: *Non-detergent or straight mineral oils should not be used in your car.*

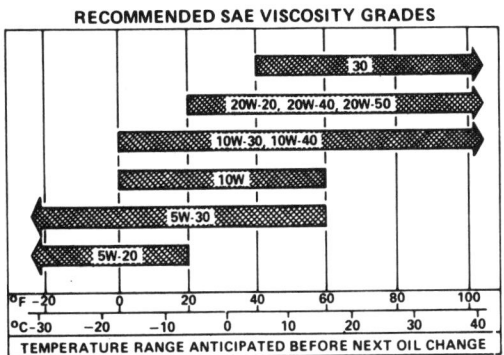

Oil viscosity chart

FUEL

All 1967–74 Camaros are designed to run on either regular or premium grade fuel depending upon the particular engine's compression ratio. All engines having a compression ratio of 9.0:1 or less can run efficiently on regular gasoline, while any engines with a higher ratio must use premium fuel. All 1975 and later models have been designed to run on unleaded fuel. The use of a leaded fuel in a car requiring unleaded fuel will plug the catalytic converter and render it inoperative. It will also increase exhaust backpressure to the point where engine output will be severely reduced. In all cases, the minimum octane rating of the unleaded fuel being used must be at least 91 RON (87 CLC). All unleaded fuels sold in the U.S. are required to meet this minimum rating.

The use of a fuel too low in octane (a measurement of anti-knock quality) will result in spark knock. Since many factors such as altitude, terrain, air temperature and humidity affect operating efficiency, knocking may result even though the recommended fuel is being used. If persistant knocking occurs, it may be necessary to switch to a higher grade of fuel. Continuous or heavy knocking may result in engine damage.

NOTE: *Your engine's fuel requirement can change with time, mainly due to carbon buildup, which will in turn change the compression ratio. If your engine pings, knocks, or runs on, switch to a higher grade of fuel. Sometimes just changing brands will cure the problem. If it becomes necessary to retard the timing from the specifications, don't change it more than a few degrees. Retarded timing will reduce power output and fuel mileage, in addition to increasing the engine temperature.*

OPERATION IN FOREIGN COUNTRIES

If you plan to drive your car outside the United States or Canada, there is a possibility that fuels will be too low in anti-knock quality and could produce engine damage. Send to Chevrolet Owner Relations Department the Vehicle Identification Number, compression ratio of your engine and the countries in which you plan to operate and they will send you details of adjustments or modifications that can be made to your engine. It is also wise to consult with local authorities upon arrival in a foreign country to determine the best fuels available.

Fluid Changes

ENGINE OIL AND FILTER

The oil should be changed every four months or 6,000 miles on all 1967–74 Camaros. On 1975–78 models, the interval is six months or 7,500 miles. 1979 and later models increased the time interval to 12 months while keeping the mileage (7,500) the same. Make sure that you change the oil based on whichever interval comes first.

The oil drain plug is located on the bottom of the oil pan (bottom of the engine, underneath the car). The oil filter is located on the right side of the inline six cylinder engine and on the left side of all other engines.

The mileage figures given are the Chevrolet recommended intervals assuming normal driving and conditions. If your car is used under dusty, polluted or off-road conditions, change the oil and filter more often than specified. The same goes for cars driven in stop-and-go traffic or only for short distances at a time. Always drain the engine oil after the engine has been running long enough to bring it up to normal operating temperature. Hot oil will flow easier and more contaminants will be removed along with the oil than

GENERAL INFORMATION AND MAINTENANCE

if it were drained cold. To change the oil and filter:

1. Run the engine until it reaches normal operating temperature.
2. Jack up the front of the car and support it on safety stands.
3. Slide a drain pan of at least 6 quarts capacity under the oil pan.
4. Loosen the drain plug. Turn the plug out by hand. By keeping an inward pressure on the plug as you unscrew it, oil won't escape past the threads and you can remove it without being burned by hot oil.
5. Allow the oil to drain completely and then install the drain plug. Don't overtighten the plug, or you'll be buying a new pan or a trick replacement plug for stripped threads.
6. Using a strap wrench, remove the oil filter. Keep in mind that it's holding about one quart of dirty, hot oil.
7. Empty the old filter into the drain pan and dispose of the filter.
8. Using a clean rag, wipe off the filter adapter on the engine block. Be sure that the rag doesn't leave any lint which could clog an oil passage.
9. Coat the rubber gasket on the filter with fresh oil. Spin it onto the engine *by hand;* when the gasket touches the adapter surface give it another ½–¾ turn. No more, or you'll squash the gasket and it will leak.
10. Refill the engine with the correct amount of fresh oil. See the "Capacities" chart.
11. Check the oil level on the dipstick. It is normal for the level to be a bit above the

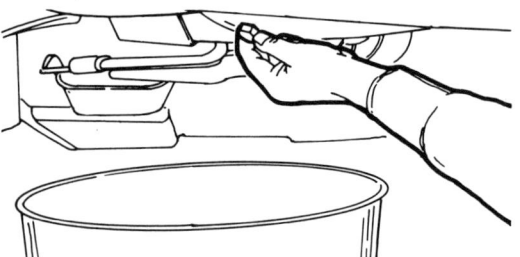

By keeping an inward pressure on the plug as you unscrew it, oil won't escape past the threads

Recommended Lubricants

Item	Lubricant
Engine Oil	API "SE" or "SF"
Manual Transmission	SAE 80W GL-5 or SAE 80W/90 GL-5
Automatic Transmission	DEXRON® or DEXRON® 11 ATF
Rear Axle–Standard	SAE 80W GL-5 or SAE 80W/90 GL-5
Positraction/Limited Slip	GM Part #1052271 or 1052272
Power Steering Reservoir	DEXRON® ATF—1967–76 Power Steering Fluid—1977 and later
Brake Fluid	DOT 3
Antifreeze	Ethylene Glycol
Front Wheel Bearings	GM Wheel Bearing Grease
Clutch Linkage	Engine Oil
Hood and Door Hinges	Engine Oil
Chassis Lubrication	NLGI #1 or NLGI #2
Lock Cylinders	WD-40 or Powdered Graphite

GENERAL INFORMATION AND MAINTENANCE

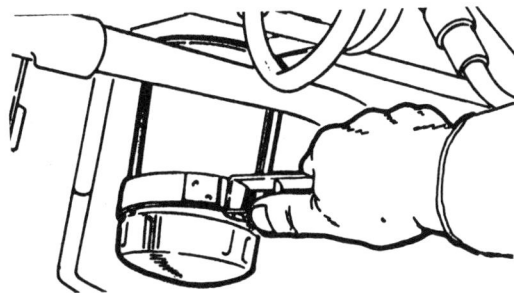
Remove the oil filter with a strap wrench

Coat the new oil filter gasket with clean oil

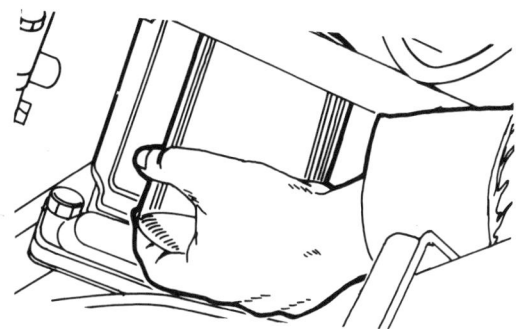
Install the new oil filter by hand

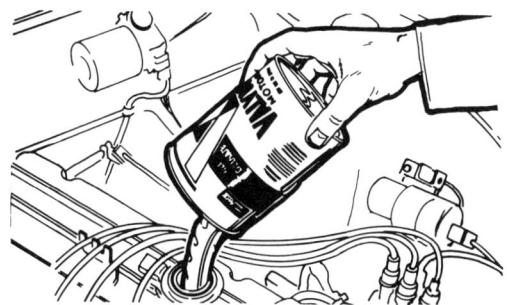
Add oil through the capped opening in the cylinder head cover

full mark. Start the engine and allow it to idle for a few minutes.

CAUTION: *Do not run the engine above idle speed until it has built up oil pressure, indicated when the oil light goes out.*

12. Shut off the engine, allow the oil to drain for a minute, and check the oil level. Check around the filter and drain plug for any leaks, and correct as necessary.

MANUAL TRANSMISSION

There is no recommended interval for the manual transmission but it is always a good idea to change the fluid if you have purchased the car used or if it has been driven in water high enough to reach the axles.

1. The oil must be hot before it is drained. Drive the car until the engine reaches normal operating temperature.
2. Remove the filler plug to provide a vent.
3. Place a large container underneath the transmission and then remove the drain plug.
4. Allow the oil to drain completely. Clean off the drain plug and replace it; tighten it until it is just snug.
5. Fill the transmission with the proper lubricant as detailed earlier in this chapter. Refer to the "Capacities" chart for the correct amount of lubricant.
6. When the oil level is up to the edge of the filler hole, replace the filler plug. Drive the car for a few minutes, stop, and check for any leaks.

AUTOMATIC TRANSMISSION

The procedures for automatic transmission fluid drain and refill, filter change and band adjustment are all detailed in Chapter 6.

REAR AXLE

There is no recommended change interval for the rear axle but it is always a good idea to change the fluid if you have purchased the car used or if it has been driven in water high enough to reach the axle.

1. Park the car on a level surface and set the parking brake.
2. Remove the filler plug.
3. Place a large container underneath the rear axle.
4. Unscrew the retaining bolts and remove the rear cover. This will allow the lubricant to drain out into the container.
5. Install the rear cover using a new gasket and sealant. Tighten the retaining bolts in a crosswise pattern.
6. Refill with the proper grade and quantity of lubricant as detailed earlier in this chapter. Replace the filler plug, run the car and then check for any leaks.

40   GENERAL INFORMATION AND MAINTENANCE

RADIATOR COOLANT

The cooling system should be drained, thoroughly flushed and then refilled at least every 30,000 miles. This should be done with the engine cold.

1. Remove the radiator cap and the expansion tank cap (if so equipped).
2. With the caps removed, run the engine until the upper radiator hose is hot. This means that the thermostat is open and the coolant is flowing through the system.
3. Turn off the engine, place a large container underneath the radiator and open the drain valve at the bottom of the radiator.

NOTE: *Drainage may be speeded by removing the drain plugs on the sides of the cylinder block.*

4. Close the drain valve and add water until the system is filled.
5. Repeat Steps 3 and 4 several times until the drained liquid is nearly colorless.
6. Tighten the drain valve and then fill the radiator with a 50/50 mixture of ethylene glycol and water.
7. With the radiator cap still removed, run the engine until the upper radiator hose is hot. Add coolant if necessary, replace the caps and check for any leaks.

Chassis Greasing

Chassis greasing can be performed with a pressurized grease gun or it can be performed at home by using a hand-operated grease gun. Wipe the grease fittings clean before greasing in order to prevent the possibility of forcing any dirt into the component.

Body Lubrication
TRANSAXLE SHIFT LINKAGE

Lubricate the manual transaxle shift linkage contact points with the EP grease used for chassis greasing, which should meet G.M. specification 6031M. The automatic transaxle linkage should be lubricated with clean engine oil.

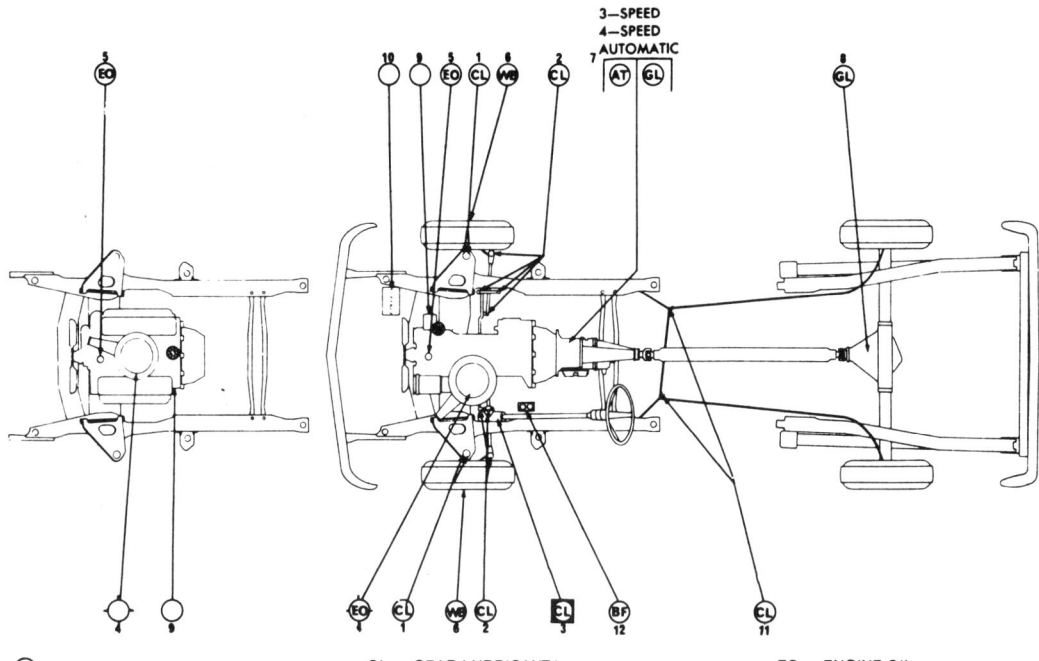

○ LUBRICATE EVERY 6000 MILES
◇ LUBRICATE EVERY 12000 MILES
□ LUBRICATE EVERY 36000 MILES

GL — GEAR LUBRICANT*
WB — WHEEL BEARING LUBRICANT
    (WHENEVER BRAKES ARE SERVICED)
CL — CHASSIS LUBRICANT

EO — ENGINE OIL
AT — AUTOMATIC TRANSMISSION
    FLUID (TYPE A)
BF — BRAKE FLUID

*Refill positraction rear axle with special lubricant only.

1. Front suspension
2. Steering linkage
3. Steering gear
4. Air cleaner
5. Crankcase breather cap
6. Front wheel bearings
7. Transmission
8. Rear axle
9. Oil filter
10. Battery
11. Parking brake
12. Brake master cylinder

Lubrication diagram—1967

GENERAL INFORMATION AND MAINTENANCE

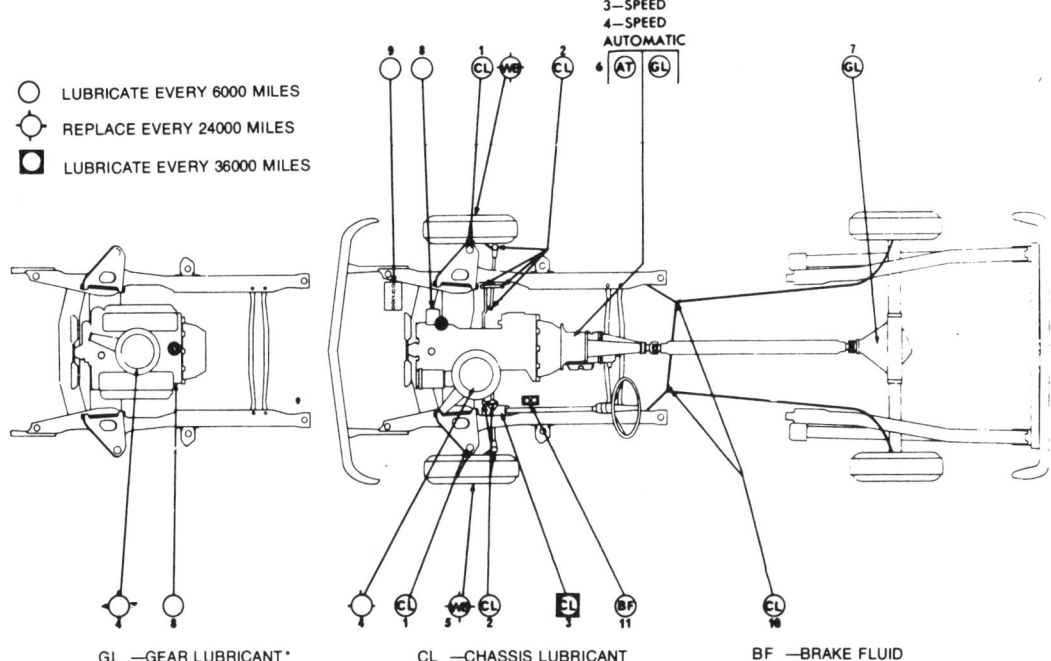

1. Front suspension
2. Steering linkage
3. Steering gear
4. Air cleaner
5. Front wheel bearings
6. Transmission
7. Rear axle
8. Oil filter
9. Battery
10. Parking brake
11. Brake master cylinder

Lubrication diagram—1968–69

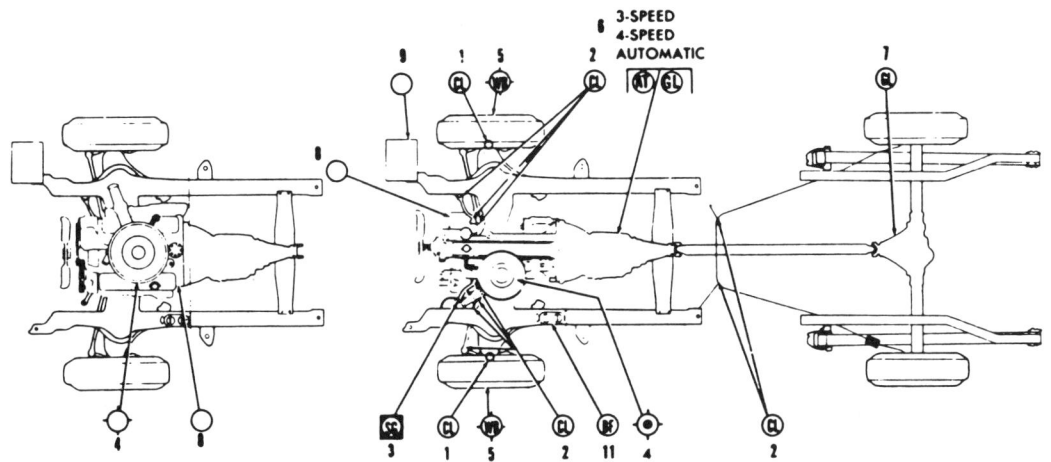

1. Front suspension
2. Steering linkage
3. Steering gear
4. Air cleaner
5. Front wheel bearings
6. Transmission
7. Rear axle
8. Oil filter
9. Battery
10. Parking brake
11. Brake master cylinder

Lubrication diagram—1970–76

42 GENERAL INFORMATION AND MAINTENANCE

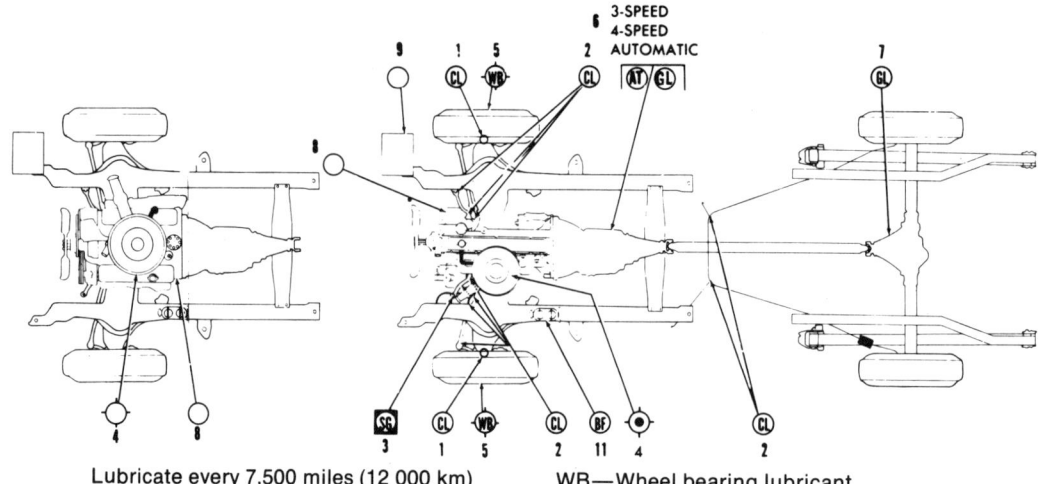

Lubricate every 7,500 miles (12 000 km)
Replace every 15,000 miles (24 000 km)
Replace every 30,000 miles (48 000 km)
Check for grease leakage
    every 30,000 miles (48 000 km)
GL—Gear lubricant*

WB—Wheel bearing lubricant
CL—Chassis lubricant
AT—DEXRON-II® Automatic
    transmission fluid or equivalent
BF—Brake fluid
SG—Steering gear lubricant

*Refill positraction rear axle with special lubricant only.

1. Front suspension
2. Steering linkage
3. Steering gear
4. Air cleaner
5. Front wheel bearings
6. Transmission
7. Rear axle
8. Oil filter
9. Battery
10. Parking brake
11. Brake master cylinder

Lubrication diagram—1977 and later

HOOD LATCH AND HINGES

Clean the latch surfaces and apply clean engine oil to the latch pilot bolts and the spring anchor. Use the engine oil to lubricate the hood hinges as well. Use a chassis grease to lubricate all the pivot points in the latch release mechanism.

DOOR HINGES

The gas tank filler door, car door, and rear hatch or trunk lid hinges should be wiped clean and lubricated with clean engine oil. Silicone spray also works well on these parts, but must be applied more often. Use engine oil to lubricate the trunk or hatch lock mechanism and the lock bolt and striker. The door lock cylinders can be lubricated easily with a shot of silicone spray or one of the many dry penetrating lubricants commercially available.

PARKING BRAKE LINKAGE

Use chassis grease on the parking brake cable where it contacts the guides, links, levers, and pulleys. The grease should be a water-resistant one for durability under the car.

ACCELERATOR LINKAGE

Lubricate the carburetor stud, carburetor lever, and the accelerator pedal lever at the support inside the car with clean engine oil.

Wheel Bearings

Once every 12 months or 12,000 miles, clean and repack wheel bearings with a wheel bearing grease. Use only enough grease to completely coat the rollers. Remove any excess grease from the exposed surface of the hub and seal.

It is important that wheel bearings be properly adjusted after installation. Improperly adjusted wheel bearings can cause steering instability, front-end shimmy and wander, and increased tire wear. For complete lubrication and adjustment procedures, see the "Wheel Bearing" section in Chapter 9.

PUSHING AND TOWING

Push Starting

This is the last recommended method of starting a car and should be used only in an

GENERAL INFORMATION AND MAINTENANCE 43

JUMP STARTING A DEAD BATTERY

The chemical reaction in a battery produces explosive hydrogen gas. This is the safe way to jump start a dead battery, reducing the chances of an accidental spark that could cause an explosion.

Jump Starting Precautions

1. Be sure both batteries are of the same voltage.
2. Be sure both batteries are of the same polarity (have the same grounded terminal).
3. Be sure the vehicles are not touching.
4. Be sure the vent cap holes are not obstructed.
5. Do not smoke or allow sparks around the battery.
6. In cold weather, check for frozen electrolyte in the battery.
7. Do not allow electrolyte on your skin or clothing.
8. Be sure the electrolyte is not frozen.

Jump Starting Procedure

1. Determine voltages of the two batteries; they must be the same.
2. Bring the starting vehicle close (they must not touch) so that the batteries can be reached easily.
3. Turn off all accessories and both engines. Put both cars in Neutral or Park and set the handbrake.
4. Cover the cell caps with a rag—do not cover terminals.
5. If the terminals on the run-down battery are heavily corroded, clean them.
6. Identify the positive and negative posts on both batteries and connect the cables in the order shown.
7. Start the engine of the starting vehicle and run it at fast idle. Try to start the car with the dead battery. Crank it for no more than 10 seconds at a time and let it cool off for 20 seconds in between tries.
8. If it doesn't start in 3 tries, there is something else wrong.
9. Disconnect the cables in the reverse order.
10. Replace the cell covers and dispose of the rags.

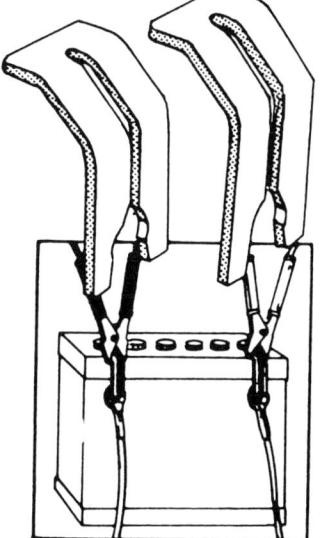

Side terminal batteries occasionally pose a problem when connecting jumper cables. There frequently isn't enough room to clamp the cables without touching sheet metal. Side terminal adaptors are available to alleviate this problem and should be removed after use.

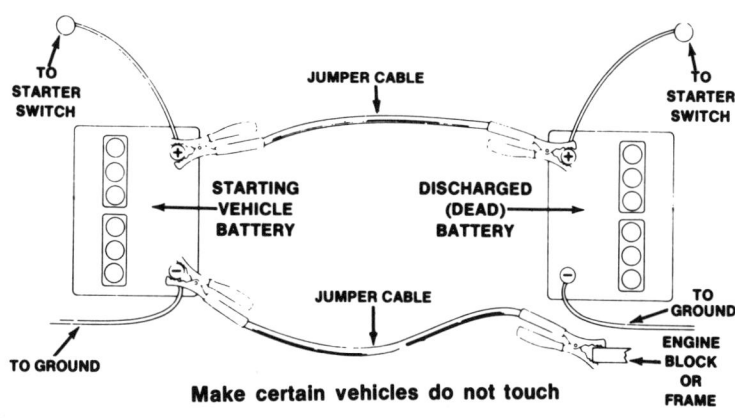

Make certain vehicles do not touch

This hook-up for negative ground cars only

44 GENERAL INFORMATION AND MAINTENANCE

extreme case. Chances of body damage are high, so be sure that the pushcar's bumper does not override your bumper. If your Chevrolet has an automatic transmission it cannot be push started. In an emergency, you can start a manual transmission car by pushing. With the bumpers evenly matched, get in your car, switch on the ignition, and place the gearshift in Second or Third gear—do not engage the clutch. Start off slowly. When the speed of the car reaches about 15–20 mph, release the clutch.

Towing

The car can be towed safely (with the transmission in Neutral) from the front at speeds of 35 mph or less. The car must either be towed with the rear wheels off the ground or the driveshaft disconnected if: towing speeds are to be over 35 mph, or towing distance is over 50 miles, or transmission or rear axle problems exist.

When towing the car on its front wheels, the steering wheel must be secured in a straight-ahead position and the steering column unlocked. Tire-to-ground clearance should not exceed 6 in. during towing.

Jacking

The standard jack utilizes slots in the bumper to raise the car. The jack supplied with the car should never be used for any service operation other than tire changing. Never get under the car while it is supported by only a jack. Always block the wheels when changing tires.

The service operations in this book often require that one end or the other, or both, of the car be raised and safely supported. The ideal method, of course, would be a hydraulic hoist. Since this is beyond both the resource and requirement of the do-it-yourselfer, a small hydraulic, screw or scissors jack will suffice for the procedures in this guide. Two sturdy jackstands should be acquired if you intend to work under the car at any time. An alternate method of raising the car would be drive-on ramps. These are available commercially or can be fabricated from heavy boards or steel. Be sure to block

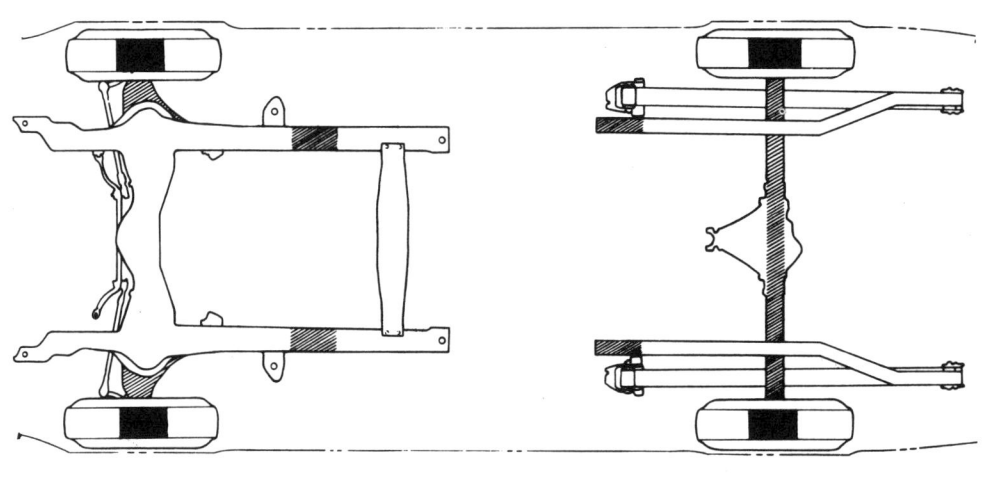

■ DRIVE ON HOIST   ▨ FLOOR JACK OR HOIST LIFT

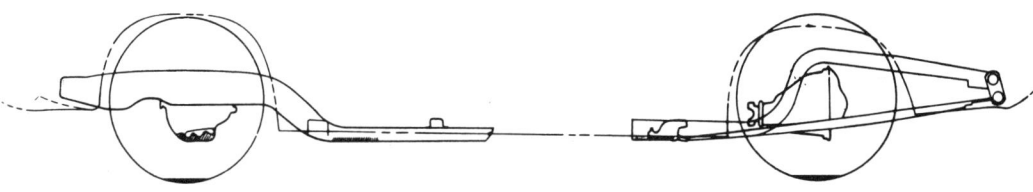

Vehicle hoisting and jacking points

GENERAL INFORMATION AND MAINTENANCE 45

the wheels when using ramps. Never use concrete blocks to support the car. They may break if the load is not evenly distributed.

Regardless of the method of jacking or hoisting the car, there are only certain areas of the undercarriage and suspension you can safely use to support it. See the illustration below, and make sure that only the shaded areas are used. In addition, be especially careful on vehicles built after 1974 that you do not damage the catalytic converter. Remember that various cross braces and supports on a lift can sometimes contact low-hanging parts of the car.

Tune-Up

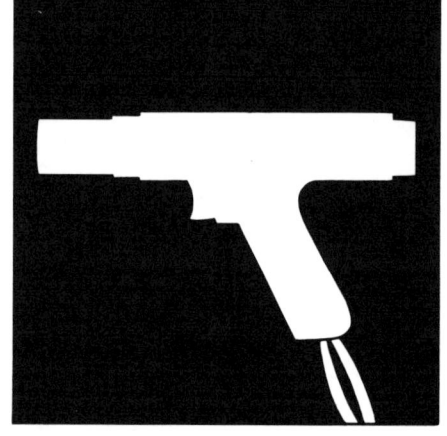

TUNE-UP PROCEDURES

In order to extract the full measure of performance and economy from your engine it is essential that it is properly tuned at regular intervals. A regular tune-up will keep your Camaro's engine running smoothly and will prevent the annoying breakdowns and poor performance associated with an untuned engine.

NOTE: *All Camaros used a conventional breaker point ignition system through 1974. In 1975, Chevrolet switched to a fully electronic ignition system known as HEI.*

A complete tune-up should be performed at least every 15,000 miles (12,000 miles for early models) or twelve months, whichever comes first.

NOTE: *1981 models have increased their interval to 30,000 miles.*

This interval should be halved if the car is operated under severe conditions such as trailer towing, prolonged idling, start-and-stop driving, or if starting or running problems are noticed. It is assumed that the routine maintenance described in Chapter 1 has been kept up, as this will have a decided effect on the results of a tune-up. All of the applicable steps of a tune-up should be followed in order, as the result is a cumulative one.

If the specifications on the underhood tune-up sticker in the engine compartment of your car disagree with the "Tune-Up Specifications" chart in this chapter, the figures on the sticker must be used. The sticker often reflects changes made during the production run.

Spark Plugs

A typical spark plug consists of a metal shell surrounding a ceramic insulator. A metal electrode extends downward through the center of the insulator and protrudes a small distance. Located at the end of the plug and attached to the side of the outer metal shell is the side electrode. This side electrode bends in at 90° so its tip is even with, and parallel to, the tip of the center electrode. This distance between these two electrodes (measured in thousandths of an inch) is called spark plug gap. The spark plug in no way produces a spark but merely provides a gap across which the current can arc. The coil produces 20,000–25,000 V (the HEI transistorized ignition produces considerably more voltage than the standard type, approximately 50,000 volts), which travels to the distributor where it is distributed through the spark plug wires to the plugs. The current passes along the center electrode and jumps

Tune-Up Specifications

When analyzing compression test results, look for uniformity among cylinders rather than specific pressures.

Year	Engine No. Cyl Displacement (cu in.)	hp	Spark Plugs Type	Spark Plugs Gap (in.)	Distributor Point Dwell (deg)	Distributor Point Gap (in.)	Ignition Timing ▲ (deg) ● Man Trans	Ignition Timing ▲ (deg) ● Auto Trans	Intake Valve Opens ■ (deg) ●	Fuel Pump Pressure (psi)	Idle Speed ● (rpm) ▲ Man Trans	Idle Speed ● (rpm) ▲ Auto Trans
1967	6—230	140	46N	0.035	31–34	0.019	4B	4B	62	3½–4½	500②	500②
	6—230①	140	46N	0.035	31–34	0.019	4B	4B	62	3½–4½	700	500
	6—250	155	46N	0.035	31–34	0.019	4B	4B	62	3½–4½	500②	500②
	6—250①	155	46N	0.035	31–34	0.019	4B	4B	62	3½–4½	700	500
	8—302	290	43	0.035	28–32	0.019	4B	—	NA	5¼–6½	900	—
	8—327	210	44	0.035	28–32	0.019	2B	2B	36	5¼–6½	500②	600②
	8—327①	210	44	0.035	28–32	0.019	2B	2B	36	5¼–6½	700	600
	8—327	275	44	0.035	28–32	0.019	8B	8B	38	5¼–6½	500②	500②
	8—327①	275	44	0.035	28–32	0.019	6B	6B	38	5¼–6½	700	600
	8—350	295	44	0.035	28–32	0.019	4B	4B	38	5¼–6½	500②	500②
	8—350①	295	44	0.035	28–32	0.019	4B	4B	38	5¼–6½	700②	500②
	8—396	325	43N	0.035	28–32	0.019	4B	4B	40	5–8½	700	600
	8—396	375	43N	0.035	28–32	0.019	4B	—	NA	5–8½	700	—

Tune-Up Specifications (cont.)

When analyzing compression test results, look for uniformity among cylinders rather than specific pressures.

Year	Engine No. Cyl Displacement (cu in.)	hp	Spark Plugs Type	Gap (in.)	Distributor Point Dwell (deg)	Point Gap (in.)	Ignition Timing ▲ (deg) ● Man Trans	Ignition Timing ▲ (deg) ● Auto Trans	Intake Valve Opens ■ (deg) ●	Fuel Pump Pressure (psi)	Idle Speed ● (rpm) ▲ Man Trans	Idle Speed ● (rpm) ▲ Auto Trans
1968	6—230	140	46N	0.035	31–34	0.019	TDC	4B	16	3½–4½	700	600②/400
	6—250	155	46N	0.035	31–34	0.019	TDC	4B	16	3½–4½	700	600②/400
	8—302	290	43	0.035	28–32	0.019	4B	—	NA	5¼–6½	900	—
	8—327	210	44	0.035	28–32	0.019	2A	2B	28	5–6½	700	600
	8—327	275	44	0.035	28–32	0.019	TDC	4B	28	5–6½	700②	600
	8—350	295	44	0.035	28–32	0.019	TDC	4B	28	5–6½	700	600
	8—396	325	43N	0.035	28–32	0.019	4B	4B	40	7–8½	700	600
	8—396	350	43N	0.035	28–32	0.019	TDC	4B	40	7–8½	700	600
	8—396	375	43N	0.035	28–32	0.019	4B	—	NA	7–8½	750	—
1969	6—230	140	R-46N	0.035	31–34	0.019	TDC	4B	16	4–5	700	500/400③
	6—250	155	R-46N	0.035	31–34	0.019	TDC	4B	16	4–5	700	500/400③
	8—302	290	R-43	0.035	28–32	0.019	4B	—	NA	5–6½	900	—
	8—307	200	R-45S	0.035	28–32	0.019	2B	2B	28	5–7½	700	600
	8—327	210	R-45S	0.035	28–32	0.019	2A	2B	28	5–6½	700	600

TUNE-UP

	Engine	HP	Spark Plug	Gap								
	8—350	255	R-44	0.035	28–32	0.019	TDC	4B	28	5–6½	700	600
	8—350	300	R-44	0.035	28–32	0.019	TDC	4B	28	5–6½	700	600
	8—396	325	R-44N	0.035	28–32	0.019	4B	4B	28	5–8½	800	600
	8—396	350	R-43N	0.035	28–32	0.019	TDC	4B	56	5–8½	800	600
	8—396	375	R-43N	0.035	28–32	0.019	4B	4B	NA	5–8½	750	750/500
1970	6—250	155	R-46T	0.035	29–31	0.019	TDC	4B	16	3½–4½	750	650/400 ③
	8—307	200	R-43	0.035	31–34	0.019	2B	8B	28	5–6½	700	600/450 ③
	8—350	250	R-44	0.035	29–31	0.019	TDC	4B	28	7–8½	750	600/450 ③
	8—350	300	R-44	0.035	29–31	0.019	TDC	4B	28	7–8½	700	600
	8—350	360	R-43	0.035	29–31	0.019	8B	8B	42½	7–8½	800	750/500 ③
	8—396	350	R-44T	0.035	29–31	0.019	TDC	4B	56	5–8½	700	600
	8—396	375	R-43T	0.035	29–31	0.019	4B	4B	NA	5–8½	750	700
1971	6—250	145	R-46TS	0.035	31–34	0.019	4B	4B	16	3½–4½	550	550 ②
	8—307	200	R-45TS	0.035	29–31	0.019	4B	8B	28	5–6½	600	550 ②
	8—350	245	R-45TS	0.035	29–31	0.019	2B	6B	28	7–8½	600	550 ②
	8—350	270	R-44TS	0.035	29–31	0.019	4B	8B	28	7–8½	600	550 ②
	8—350	330	R-43TS	0.035	29–31	0.019	8B	12B	42⅔	7–8½	700	700
	8—402	300	R-44TS	0.035	28–30	0.019	8B	8B	28	7–8½	600	600

Tune-Up Specifications (cont.)

When analyzing compression test results, look for uniformity among cylinders rather than specific pressures.

Year	Engine No. Cyl Displacement (cu in.)	hp	Spark Plugs Type	Spark Plugs Gap (in.)	Distributor Point Dwell (deg)	Distributor Point Gap (in.)	Ignition Timing ▲ (deg) ● Man Trans	Ignition Timing ▲ (deg) ● Auto Trans	Intake Valve Opens (deg) ■	Fuel Pump Pressure (psi)	Idle Speed ● (rpm) ▲ Man Trans	Idle Speed ● (rpm) ▲ Auto Trans
1972	6—250	110	R-46T	0.035	31–34	0.019	4B	4B	16	3½–4½	700	600
	8—307	130	R-44T	0.035	29–31	0.019	4B	8B	28	5–6½	900	600
	8—350	165	R-44T	0.035	29–31	0.019	6B	6B	28(44)	7–8½	900	600
	8—350	200	R-44T	0.035	29–31	0.019	4B	8B	28(44)	7–8½	800	600
	8—350	255	R-44T	0.035	29–31	0.019	8B	12B	42⅔	7–8½	900	700
	8—402	240	R-44TS	0.035	28–30	0.019	8B	8B	28	7–8½	800	600
1973	6—250	100	R-46T	0.035	31–34	0.019	6B	6B	16	3½–4½	700/450③	600/450
	8—307	115	R-44T	0.035	29–31	0.019	4B	4B	28	5–6½	900/450③	600/450
	8—350	145	R-44T	0.035	29–31	0.019	8B	8B	28	7½–8½	900/450③	600/450
	8—350	175	R-44T	0.035	29–31	0.019	8B	12B	28	7½–8½	900/450③	600/450
	8—350	245	R-44T	0.035	29–31	0.019	8B	12B	52	7½–8½	900/450③	700/450
1974	6—250	100	R-46T	0.035	31–34	0.019	6B	6B	16	4–5	800/450③	600/450

TUNE-UP

Year	Engine	HP	Spark Plug	Gap	Point Gap	Dwell	Timing (Man)	Timing (Auto)	Valve	Fuel Pump	Idle (Man)	Idle (Auto)
	8—350	145	R-44T	0.035	29–31	0.019	4B	8B	28	7½–9	900/450③	600/450
	8—350	160	R-44T	0.035	29–31	0.019	4B	8B	44	7½–9	900/450③	600/450
	8—350	185	R-44T	0.035	29–31	0.019	4B	8B	28	7½–9	900/450③	600/450
	8—350	245	R-44T	0.035	29–31	0.019	8B	8B	52	7½–9	900/450③	700/450
1975	6—250	105	R-46TX	0.060	Electronic		10B	10B	16	4–5	800/425③	550/425③④ (600/425)
	8—350	145	R-44TX	0.060	Electronic		6B	6B	28	7½–9	800	600
	8—350	155	R-44TX	0.060	Electronic		6B	8B(6B)	28	7½–9	800	600
1976	6—250	105	R-46TS	0.035	Electronic		6B	6B	16	3½–4½	850	550② (600)
	8—305	140	R-45TS	0.045	Electronic		6B	8B(TDC)	28	7–8½	800	600
	8—350	165	R-45TS	0.045	Electronic		8B(6B)	8B(6B)	28	7–8½	800	600
1977	6—250	105	R-46TS	0.035	Electronic		6B	8B(6B)⑤	16	4–5	⑥	550(600)
	8—305	140	R-45TS	0.045	Electronic		8B	8B(6B)	28	7½–9	600	500
	8—350	165	R-45TS	0.045	Electronic		8B	8B	28	7½–9	700	500
1978	6—250	105	R-46TS	0.035	Electronic		6B	10B⑦(6B)	16	4½–6	800	550(600)
	8—305	140	R-45TS	0.045	Electronic		4B	4B(6B)	28	7½–9	600	500

TUNE-UP

Tune-Up Specifications (cont.)

When analyzing compression test results, look for uniformity among cylinders rather than specific pressures.

Year	Engine No. Cyl Displacement (cu in.)	hp	Spark Plugs Type	Gap (in.)	Distributor Point Dwell (deg)	Distributor Point Gap (in.)	Ignition Timing (deg) ▲ ● Man Trans	Ignition Timing (deg) ▲ ● Auto Trans	Intake Valve Opens ■ (deg) ●	Fuel Pump Pressure (psi)	Idle Speed (rpm) ▲ ● Man Trans	Idle Speed (rpm) ▲ ● Auto Trans
	8—350	165	R-45TS	0.045	Electronic		6B	6B(8B)	28	7½–9	700	500⑧
1979	6—250	115	R-46TS	0.035	Electronic		12B	8B(6B)	16	4½–6	800	675(600)
	8—305	130	R-45TS	0.045	Electronic		4B	4B	28	7½–9	600	500(600)
	8—350	165	R-45TS	0.045	Electronic		6B	6B(8B)	28	7½–9	700	500⑧
	6—229	115	R-T5TS ⑨	0.045	Electronic		8B	12B	42	4½–6	700	600
	6—231	110	R-45TSX	0.060	Electronic		—	15B	16	4¼–5¾	—	600
1980	8—267	120	R-45TS	0.045	Electronic		—*	4B	28	7½–9	—	500
	8—305	155 ⑩	R-45TS	0.045	Electronic		4B	4B	28	7½–9	700	500(550)
	8—350	190	R-45TS	0.045	Electronic		6B	6B	28	7½–9	700	500

TUNE-UP

Year	Engine No. Cyl-Disp.	HP	Spark Plugs Type	Gap (in.)	Distributor	Ign. Timing (deg) Man Trans	Ign. Timing (deg) Auto Trans	Valves Intake Opens (deg)	Fuel Pump Pressure	Idle Speed (rpm) Man Trans	Idle Speed (rpm) Auto Trans
1981	6—229	110	R-45TS	0.045	Electronic	6B	6B	42	4½–6	700⑪	600⑪
	6—231	110	R-45TS8	0.080	Electronic	—	15B	16	4¼–5¾	—	500⑪
	8—267	115	R-45TS	0.045	Electronic	—	6B	44	7½–9	—	500⑪
	8—305	150⑩	R-45TS	0.045	Electronic	6B	6B	44	7½–9	700	500
	8—350	175	R-45TS	0.045	Electronic	—	6B	38	7½–9	—	500⑪

▲ See text for procedure
● Figures in parentheses indicate California
■ All figures Before Top Dead Center
① Equipped with Air Injection Reaction System
② A/C on
③ Lower figure is with idle solenoid disconnected
④ W/O intake manifold integral with head—600/450
⑤ Except engine code #CCC which is 8B; High altitude engine—10B
⑥ 750 with A/C; 800 without A/C
⑦ 8B with A/C
⑧ High altitude engine—600
⑨ With A/T— R-45TS
⑩ Z/28—165
⑪ Equipped with Idle Speed Control
TDC Top Dead Center
A After TDC
B Before TDC
— Not applicable
NA Not available

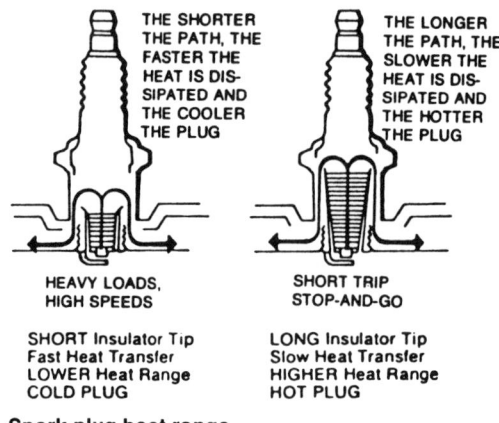

Spark plug heat range

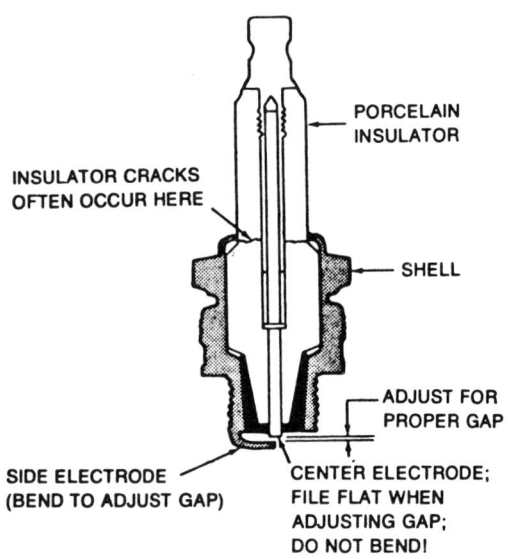

Cross section of a spark plug

amount of heat that the plug absorbs is determined by the length of the lower insulator. The longer the insulator (it extends farther into the engine), the hotter the plug will operate; the shorter it is, the cooler it will operate. A plug that has a short path for heat transfer and remains too cool will quickly accumulate deposits of oil and carbon since it is not hot enough to burn them off. This leads to plug fouling and consequently to misfiring. A plug that has a long path for heat transfer will have no deposits but, due to the excessive heat, the electrodes will burn away quickly and, in some instances, pre-ignition may result. Pre-ignition takes place when plug tips get so hot that they glow sufficiently to ignite the fuel/air mixture before the spark does. This early ignition will usually cause a pinging (sounding much like castanets) during low speeds and heavy loads. In severe cases, the heat may become enough to start the fuel/air mixture burning throughout the combustion chamber rather than just to the front of the plug as in normal operation. At this time, the piston is rising in the cylinder making its compression stroke. The burning mass is compressed and an explosion results producing tremendous pressure. Something has to give, and it does—pistons are often damaged. Obviously, this detonation (explosion) is a destructive condition that can be avoided by installing a spark plug designed and specified for your particular engine.

A set of spark plugs usually requires replacement after 10,000 to 12,000 miles depending on the type of driving (this interval has been increased to 22,500 miles for all 1975–79 models and 30,000 miles for all 1980–81 models). The electrode on a new spark plug has a sharp edge but, with use, this edge becomes rounded by erosion causing the plug gap to increase. In normal operation, plug gap increases about 0.001 in. in every 1,000–2,000 miles. As the gap increases, the plug's voltage requirement also increases. It requires a greater voltage to jump the wider gap and about two to three times as much voltage to fire a plug at high speeds and acceleration than at idle.

The higher voltage produced by the HEI ignition coil is one of the primary reasons for the prolonged replacement interval for spark plugs in 1975 and later cars. A consistently hotter spark prevents the fouling of plugs for much longer than could normally be expected; this spark is also able to jump across a larger gap more efficiently than a spark

the gap to the side electrode and, in so doing, ignites the air/fuel mixture in the combustion chamber. All plugs used in Camaros since 1969 have a resistor built into the center electrode to reduce interference to any nearby radio and television receivers. The resistor also cuts down on erosion of plug electrodes caused by excessively long sparking. Resistor spark plug wiring is original equipment on all Camaros.

Spark plug life and efficiency depend upon the condition of the engine and the temperatures to which the plug is exposed. Combustion chamber temperatures are affected by many factors such as compression ratio of the engine, fuel/air mixtures, exhaust emission equipment, and the type of driving you do. Spark plugs are designed and classified by number according to the heat range at which they will operate most efficiently. The

from a conventional system. However, even plugs used with the HEI system wear after time in the engine.

Worn plugs become obvious during acceleration. Voltage requirement is greatest during acceleration and a plug with an enlarged gap may require more voltage than the coil is able to produce. As a result, the engine misses and sputters until acceleration is reduced. Reducing acceleration reduces the plug's voltage requirement and the engine runs smoother. Slow, city driving is hard on plugs. The long periods of idle experienced in traffic creates an overly rich gas mixture. The engine isn't running fast enough to completely burn the gas and, consequently, the plugs are fouled with gas deposits and engine idle becomes rough. In many cases, driving under right conditions can effectively clean these fouled plugs.

NOTE: *There are several reasons why a spark plug will foul and you can usually learn which is at fault by just looking at the plug. A few of the most common reasons for plug fouling, and a description of the fouled plug's appearance, can be found in the color insert in this book.*

Accelerate your car to the speed where the engine begins to miss and then slow down to the point where the engine smooths out. Run at this speed for a few minutes and then accelerate again to the point of engine miss. With each repetition this engine miss should occur at increasingly higher speeds and then disappear altogether. Do not attempt to shortcut this procedure by hard acceleration. This approach will compound problems by fusing deposits into a hard permanent glaze. Dirty, fouled plugs may be cleaned by sandblasting. Many shops have a spark plug sandblaster. After sandblasting, the electrode should be filed to a sharp, square shape and then gapped to specifications. Gapping a plug too close will produce a rough idle while gapping it too wide will increase its voltage requirement and cause missing at high speeds and during acceleration.

The type of driving you do may require a change in spark plug heat range. If the majority of your driving is done in the city and rarely at high speeds, plug fouling may necessitate changing to a plug with a heat range number one higher than that specified by the car manufacturer. For example, a 1970 Camaro with a 350 cu in. (300 hp) engine requires an R44 plug. Frequent city driving may foul these plugs making engine operation rough. An R45 is the next hottest plug in the AC heat range (the higher the AC number, the hotter the plug) and its insulator is longer than the R44 so that it can absorb and retain more heat than the shorter R44. This hotter R45 burns off deposits even at low city speeds but would be too hot for prolonged turnpike driving. Using this plug at high speeds would create dangerous pre-ignition. On the other hand, if the aforementioned Camaro were used almost exclusively for long distance high speed driving, the specified R44 might be too hot resulting in rapid electrode wear and dangerous pre-ignition. In this case, it might be wise to change to a colder R43. If the car is used for abnormal driving (as in the examples above), or the engine has been modified for higher performance, then a change to a plug of a different heat range may be necessary. For a modified car it is always wise to go to a colder plug as a protection against pre-ignition. It will require more frequent plug cleaning, but destructive detonation during acceleration will be avoided.

REMOVAL

When you're removing spark plugs, you should work on one at a time. Don't start by removing the plug wires all at once because unless you number them, they're going to get mixed up. On some models though, it will be more convenient for you to remove all the wires before you start to work on the plugs. If this is necessary, take a minute before you begin and number the wires with tape before you take them off. The time you spend here will pay off later on.

1. Twist the spark plug boot and remove the boot from the plug. You may also use a plug wire removal tool designed especially for this purpose. *Do not pull on the wire itself.* When the wire has been removed, take a wire brush and clean the area around the plug. Make sure that all the grime is removed so that none will enter the cylinder after the plug has been removed.

2. Remove the plug using the proper size socket, extensions, and universals as necessary. For all engines through 1969, and all V8s through 1971, use a 13/16 in. spark plug socket. Six-cylinder engines from 1970 and V8s from 1972 are equipped with tapered seat plugs which require a 5/8 in. socket.

3. If removing the plug is difficult, drip some penetrating oil on the plug threads, allow it to work, then remove the plug. Also,

56 TUNE-UP

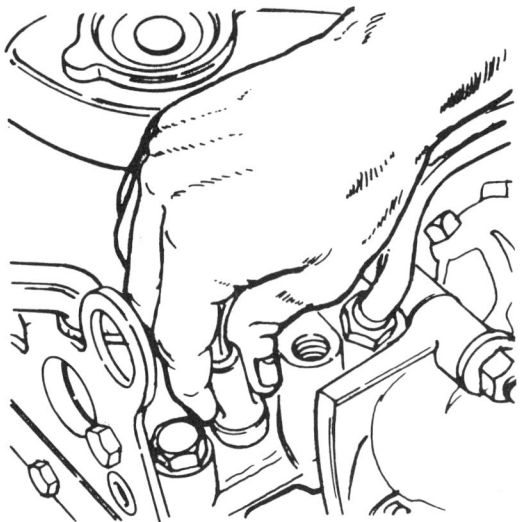

Twist and pull on the rubber boot to remove the spark plug wires; never pull on the wire itself

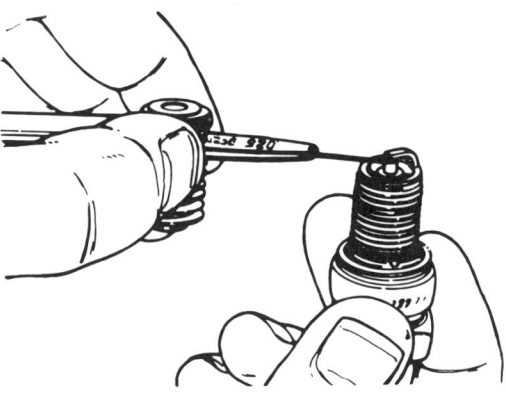

Always use a wire gauge to check the electrode gap

be sure that the socket is straight on the plug, especially on those hard to reach plugs.

INSPECTION

Check the plugs for deposits and wear. If they are not going to be replaced, clean the plugs thoroughly. Remember that any kind of deposit will decrease the efficiency of the plug. Plugs can be cleaned on a spark plug cleaning machine, which can sometimes be found in service stations, or you can do an acceptable job of cleaning with a stiff brush. If the plugs are cleaned, the electrodes must be filed flat. Use an ignition points file, not an emery board or the like, which will leave deposits. The electrodes must be filed perfectly flat with sharp edges; rounded edges reduce the spark plug voltage by as much as 50%.

Check spark plug gap before installation. The ground electrode (the L-shaped one connected to the body of the plug) must be parallel to the center electrode and the specified size wire gauge (see "Tune-Up Specifications") should pass through the gap with a slight drag. Always check the gap on new plugs, too; they are not always set correctly at the factory. Do not use a flat feeler gauge when measuring the gap, because the reading will be inaccurate. Wire gapping tools usually have a bending tool attached. Use that to adjust the side electrode until the proper distance is obtained. *Absolutely never bend the center electrode.* Also, be careful not to bend the side electrode too far or too often; it may weaken and break off within the engine, requiring removal of the cylinder head to retrieve it.

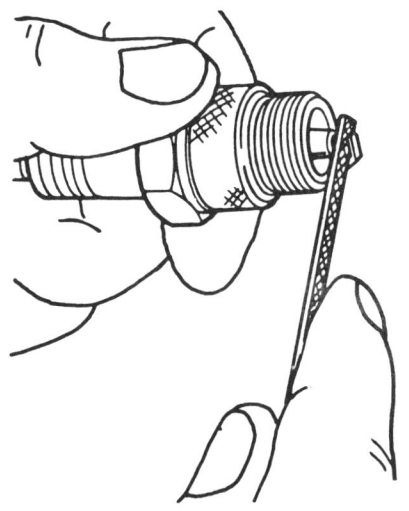

Plugs that are in good condition can be filed and re-used

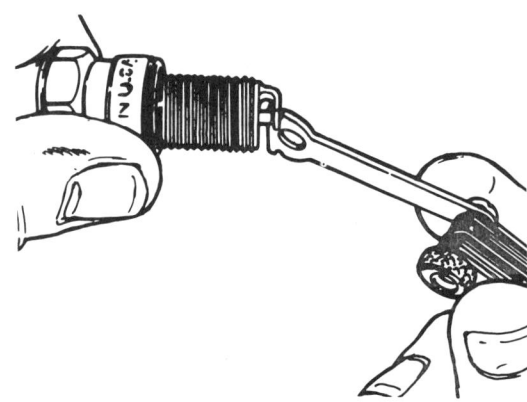

Adjust the electrode gap by bending the side electrode

TUNE-UP 57

INSTALLATION

1. Lubricate the threads of the spark plugs with a drop of oil. Install the plugs and tighten them hand-tight. Take care not to cross-thread them.
2. Tighten the spark plugs with the socket. Do not apply the same amount of force you would use for a bolt; just snug them in. If a torque wrench is available, tighten to 11–15 ft. lbs.
3. Install the wires on their respective plugs. Make sure the wires are firmly connected. You will be able to feel them click into place.

CHECKING AND REPLACING SPARK PLUG WIRES

Every 15,000 miles, inspect the spark plug wires for burns, cuts, or breaks in the insulation. Check the boots and the nipples on the distributor cap. Replace any damaged wiring.

Every 45,000 miles or so, the resistance of the wires should be checked with an ohmmeter. Wires with excessive resistance will cause misfiring, and may make the engine difficult to start in damp weather. Generally, the useful life of the cables is 45,000–60,000 miles.

To check resistance, remove the distributor cap, leaving the wires in place. Connect one lead of an ohmmeter to an electrode within the cap; connect the other lead to the corresponding spark plug terminal (remove it from the spark plug for this test). Replace anh wire which shows a resistance over 30,000 ohms. A chart in Chapter 11 gives resistance values as a function of length. Generally speaking, however, resistance should not be over 25,000 ohms, and 30,000 ohms must be considered the outer limit of acceptability.

It should be remembered that resistance is also a function of length; the longer the wire, the greater the resistance. Thus, if the wires on your car are longer than the factory originals, resistance will be higher, quite possibly outside these limits.

When installing new wires, replace them one at a time to avoid mixups. Start by replacing the longest one first. Install the boot firmly over the spark plug. Route the wire over the same path as the original. Insert the nipple firmly onto the tower on the distributor cap, then install the cap cover and latches to secure the wires.

Breaker Points and Condenser

The points function as a circuit breaker for the primary circuit of the ignition system. The ignition coil must boost the 12 volts of electrical pressure supplied by the battery to as much as 25,000 volts in order to fire the plugs. To do this, the coil depends on the points and the condenser to make a clean break in the primary circuit.

The coil has both primary and secondary circuits. When the ignition is turned on, the battery supplies voltage through the coil and onto the points. The points are connected to ground, completing the primary circuit. As the current passes through the coil, a magnetic field is created in the iron center core of the coil. When the cam in the distributor turns, the points open, breaking the primary circuit. The magnetic field in the primary circuit of the coil then collapses and cuts through the secondary circuit windings around the iron core. Because of the physical principle called "electromagnetic induction," the battery voltage is increased to a level sufficient to fire the spark plugs.

When the points open, the electrical charge in the primary circuit tries to jump the gap created between the two open contacts of the points. If this electrical charge were not transferred elsewhere, the metal contacts of the points would start to change rapidly.

The function of the condenser is to absorb excessive voltage from the points when they open and thus prevent the points from becoming pitted or burned.

If you have ever wondered why it is necessary to tune-up your engine occasionally, consider the fact that the ignition system must complete the above cycle each time a spark plug fires. On a four-cylinder, four-cycle engine, two of the four plugs must fire once for every engine revolution. If the idle speed of your engine is 800 revolutions per minute (800 rpm), the breaker points open and close two times for each revolution. For every minute your engine idles, your points open and close 1,600 times ($2 \times 800 = 1,600$). And that is just at idle. What about at 60 mph?

There are two ways to check breaker point gap: with a feeler gauge or with a dwell meter. Either way you set the points, you are adjusting the amount of time (in degrees of distributor rotation) that the points will remain open. If you adjust the points with a

58 TUNE-UP

feeler gauge, you are setting the maximum amount the points will open when the rubbing block on the points is on a high point of the distributor cam. When you adjust the points with a dwell meter, you are measuring the number of degrees (of distributor cam rotation) that the points will remain closed before they start to open as a high point of the distributor cam approaches the rubbing block of the points.

If you still do not understand how the points function, take a friend, go outside, and remove the distributor cap from your engine. Have your friend operate the starter (make sure that the transmission is not in gear) as you look at the exposed parts of the distributor.

There are two rules that should always be followed when adjusing or replacing points. *The points and condenser are a matched set; never replace one without replacing the other. If you change the point gap or dwell of the engine, you also change the ignition timing. Therefore, if you adjust the points, you must also adjust the timing.*

REMOVAL AND INSTALLATION
Through 1974

The usual procedure is to replace the condenser each time the point set is replaced. Although this is not always necessary, it is easy to do at this time and the cost is negligible. Every time you adjust or replace the breaker points, the ignition timing must be checked and, if necessary, adjusted. No special equipment other than a feeler gauge is required for point replacement or adjustment, but a dwell meter is strongly advised. A magnetic screwdriver is handy to prevent the small points and condenser screws from falling down into the distributor.

Point sets using the push-in type wiring terminal should be used on those distributors equipped with an R.F.I. (Radio Frequency Interference) shield (1970–74). Points using a lockscrew-type terminal may short out due to contact between the shield and the screw.

1. Push down on the spring-loaded V8 distributor cap retaining screws and give them a half-turn to release. Unscrew the captive six-cylinder cap retaining screws. Remove the cap. You might have to unclip or detach some or all of the plug wires to remove the cap. If so, number the wires and the cap before removal.

2. Clean the cap inside and out with a

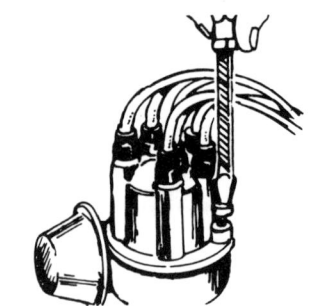

The six cylinder distributor cap is retained by two captive screws

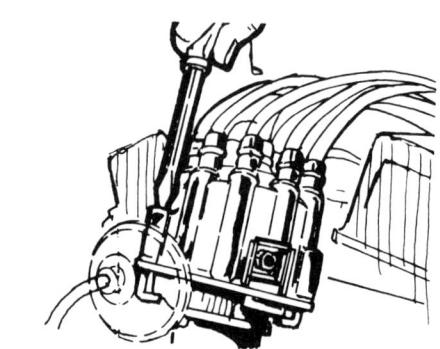

The eight cylinder distributor cap has spring latches

clean rag. Check for cracks and carbon paths. A carbon path shows up as a dark line, usually from one of the cap sockets or inside terminals to a ground. Check the condition of the carbon button inside the center of the cap and the inside terminals. Replace the cap as necessary. Carbon paths cannot usually be successfully scraped off. It is better to replace the cap.

3. Pull the six-cylinder rotor up and off the shaft. Remove the two screws and lift the round V8 rotor off. There is less danger of losing the screws if you just back them out all the way and lift them off with the rotor. Clean off the metal outer tip if it is burned or corroded. Don't file it. Replace the rotor as necessary or if one came with your tune-up kit.

4. Remove the radio frequency interference shield if your distributor has one. Watch out for those little screws! The factory says that the points don't need to be replaced if they are only slightly rough or pitted. However, sad experience shows that it is more economical and reliable in the long run to replace the point set while the distributor is open, than to have to do this at a later (and possibly more inconvenient) time.

5. Pull off the two wire terminals from

TUNE-UP 59

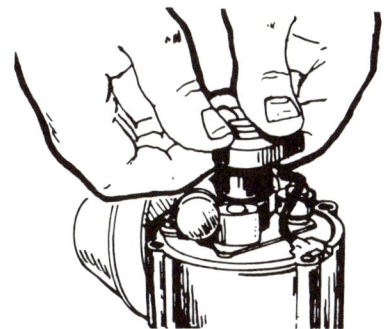
Pull the six cylinder rotor straight up to remove it

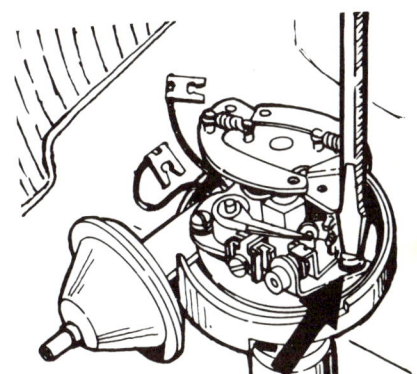
The points are retained by screws; use a magnetic screwdriver to avoid losing them

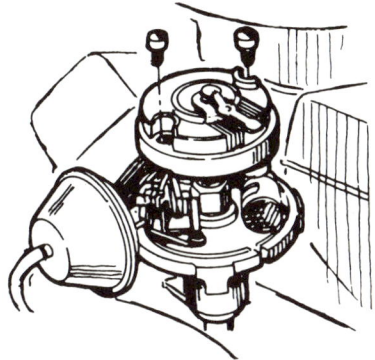
The eight cylinder rotor is held on by two screws

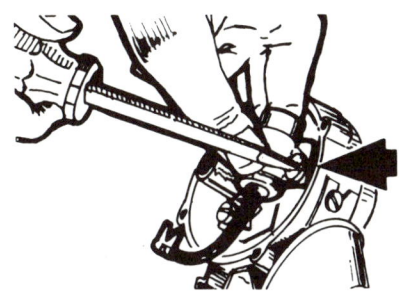
The condenser is held in place by a screw and a clamp

the point assembly. One wire comes from the condenser and the other comes from within the distributor. The terminals are usually held in place by spring tension only. There might be a clamp screw securing the terminals on some older versions. There is also available a one-piece point/condenser assembly for V8s. The radio frequency interference shield isn't needed with this set. Loosen the point set hold-down screw(s). Be very careful not to drop any of these little screws inside the distributor. If this happens, the distributor will probably have to be removed to get at the screw. If the hold-down screw is lost elsewhere, it must be replaced with one that is no longer than the original to avoid interference with the distributor workings. Remove the point set, even if it is to be reused.

6. If the points are to be reused, clean them with a few strokes of a special point file. This is done with the points removed to prevent tiny metal filings getting into the distributor. Don't use sandpaper or emery cloth; they will cause rapid point burning.

7. Loosen the condenser hold-down screw and slide the condenser out of the clamp. This will save you a struggle with the clamp, condenser, and the tiny screw when you install the new one. If you have the type of clamp that is permanently fastened to the condenser, remove the screw and the condenser. Don't lose the screw.

8. Attend to the distributor cam lubricator. If you have the round kind, turn it around on its shaft at the first tune-up and replace it at the second. If you have the long kind, switch ends at the first tune-up and replace it at the second.

NOTE: *Don't oil or grease the lubricator. The foam is impregnated with a special lubricant.*

If you didn't get any lubricator at all, or if it looks like someone took it off, don't worry. You don't really need it. Just rub a matchhead size dab of grease on the cam lobes.

9. Install the new condenser. If you left the clamp in place, just slide the new condenser into the clamp.

10. Replace the point set and tighten the screws on a V8. Leave the screw slightly loose on a six. Replace the two wire terminals, making sure that the wires don't interfere with anything. Some V8 distributors have a ground wire that must go under one of the screws.

11. Check that the contacts meet squarely. If they don't, bend the tab supporting the fixed contact.

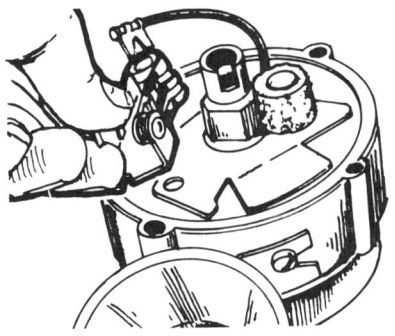

Install the point set on the breaker plate and then attach the wires

NOTE: *If you are installing preset points on a V8, go ahead to Step 16. If they are preset, it will say so on the package. It would be a good idea to make a quick check on point gap, anyway. Sometimes those preset points aren't.*

12. Turn the engine until a high point on the cam that opens the points contacts the rubbing block on the point arm. You can turn the engine by hand if you can get a wrench on the crankshaft pulley nut, or you can grasp the fan belt and turn the engine with the spark plugs removed.

CAUTION: *If you try turning the engine by hand, be very careful not to get your fingers pinched in the pulleys.*

On a stick-shift you can push it forward in High gear. Another alternative is to bump the starter switch or use a remote starter switch.

13. On a six, there is a screwdriver slot near the contacts. Insert a screwdriver and lever the points open or closed until they appear to be at about the gap specified in the "Tune-Up Specifications." On a V8, simply insert a ⅛ in. allen wrench into the adjustment screw and turn. The wrench sometimes comes with a tune-up kit.

14. Insert the correct size feeler gauge

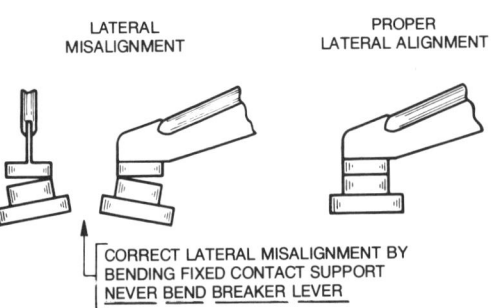

Check the points for proper alignment after installation

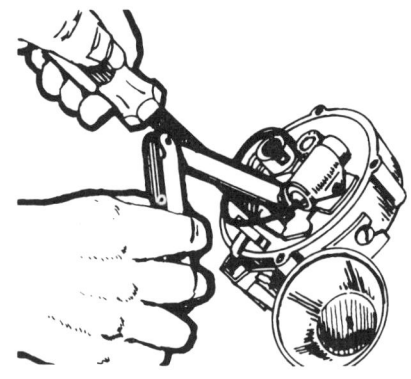

Use a screwdriver to lever the points closer together or farther apart on the six cylinder models

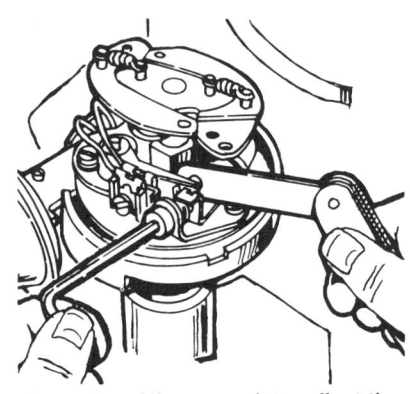

You will need an Allen wrench to adjust the point gap on the V8 engine

and adjust the gap until you can push the gauge in and out between the contacts with a slight drag, but without disturbing the point arm. This operation takes a bit of experience to obtain the correct feel. Check by trying the gauges 0.001–0.002 larger and smaller than the setting size. The larger one should disturb the point arm, while the smaller one should not drag at all. Tighten the six-cylinder point set hold-down screw. Recheck the gap, because it often changes when the screw is tightened.

15. After all the point adjustments are complete, pull a white index card through (between) the contacts to remove any traces of oil. Oil will cause rapid contact burning

NOTE: *You can adjust six-cylinder dwell at this point, if you wish. Refer to Step 18.*

16. Replace the radio frequency interference shield, if any. You don't need it if you are installing the one-piece point/condenser set. Push the rotor firmly down into place. It will only go on one way. Tighten the V8 rotor screws. If the rotor is not installed properly, it will probably break when the starter is operated.

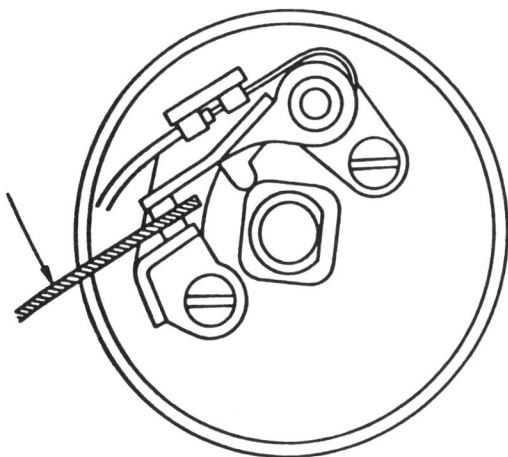

The arrow indicates the feeler gauge used to check the point gap

17. Replace the distributor cap.
18. If a dwell meter is available, check the dwell. The dwell meter hookup is shown in the "Troubleshooting" chapter.

NOTE: *This hookup may not apply to electronic, capacitive discharge, or other special ignition systems. Some dwell meters won't work at all with such systems.*

1975 and Later

These engines use the breakerless HEI (High Energy Ignition) system. Since there is no mechanical contact, there is no wear or need for periodic service. There is an item in the distributor that resembles a condenser; it is a radio interference suppression capacitor which requires no service.

Dwell Angle

Dwell angle is the amount of time (measured in degrees of distributor cam rotation) that the contact points remain closed. Initial point gap determines dwell angle. If the points are set too wide they open gradually and dwell angle (the time they remain closed) is small. This wide gap causes excessive arcing at the points and, because of this, point burning. This small dwell doesn't give the coil sufficient time to build up maximum energy and so coil output decreases. If the points are set too close, the dwell is increased but the points may bounce at higher speeds and the idle becomes rough and starting is made harder. The wider the point opening, the smaller the dwell and the smaller the gap, the larger the dwell. Adjusting the dwell by making the initial point gap setting with a feeler gauge is sufficient to get the car started but a finer adjustment should be made. A dwell meter is needed to check the adjustment.

Connect the red lead (positive) wire of the meter to the distributor primary wire connection on the positive (+) side of the coil, and the black ground (negative) wire of the meter to a good ground on the engine. The dwell angle may be checked either with the engine cranking or running, although the reading will be more accurate if the engine is running. With the engine cranking, the reading will fluctuate between zero degrees dwell and the maximum figure for that angle. While cranking, the maximum figure is the correct one.

Dwell angle is permanently set electronically on HEI distributors, requiring no adjustment or checking.

ADJUSTMENT
1967-74

Dwell can be checked with the engine running or cranking. Decrease dwell by increasing the point gap; increase by decreasing the gap. Dwell angle is simply the number of degrees of distributor shaft rotation during which the points stay closed. Theoretically, if the point gap is correct, the dwell should also be correct or nearly so. Adjustment with a dwell meter produces more exact, consistent results since it is a dynamic adjustment. If dwell varies more than 3 degrees from idle speed to 1,750 engine rpm, the distributor is worn.

1. To adjust dwell on a six, trial and error point adjustments are required. On a V8,

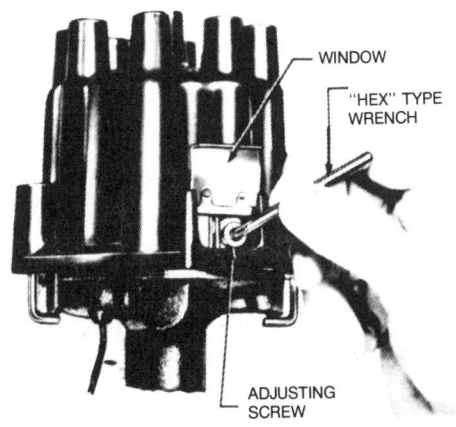

To set the dwell on a V8, lift the window and then turn the adjusting screw

62 TUNE-UP

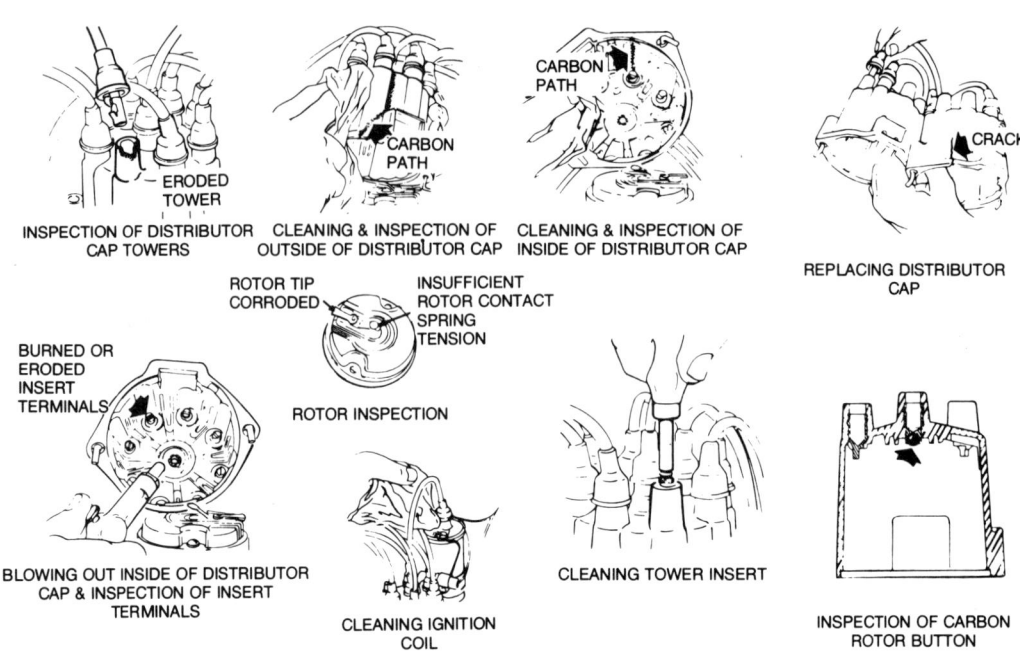

Inspection points for the distributor, rotor, cap and coil

simply open the metal window on the distributor and insert a ⅛ in. allen wrench. Turn until the meter shows the correct reading. Be sure to snap the window closed.

2. An approximate dwell adjustment can be made without a meter on a V8. Turn the adjusting screw clockwise until the engine begins to misfire, then turn it out ½ turn.

3. If the engine won't start, check:
   a. That all the spark plug wires are in place.
   b. That the rotor has been installed.
   c. That the two (or three) wires inside the distributor are connected.
   d. That the points open and close when the engine turns.
   e. That the gap is correct and the hold-down screw (on a six) is tight.

4. After the first 200 miles or so on a new set of points, the point gap often closes up due to initial rubbing block wear. For best performance, recheck the dwell (or gap) at this time. This quick initial wear is the reason the factory recommends 0.003 in. more gap on new points.

5. Since changing the gap affects the ignition timing, the timing should be checked and adjusted as necessary after each point replacement or adjustment.

1975 and Later

The Dwell angle on these models is preset at the factory and not adjustable.

High Energy Ignition (HEI) System

The General Motors HEI system is a pulse-triggered, transistor-controlled, inductive discharge ignition system. Except on inline six-cylinder models through 1977, the entire HEI system is contained within the distributor cap. Inline six-cylinder engines through 1977 have an external coil. Otherwise, the systems are the same.

The distributor, in addition to housing the mechanical and vacuum advance mechanisms, contains the ignition coil (except on some inline six engines), the electronic control module, and the magnetic triggering device. The magnetic pick-up assembly contains a permanent magnet, a pole piece with internal "teeth," and a pick-up coil (not to be confused with the ignition coil).

For 1981, an HEI distributor with Electronic Spark Timing is used (for more information on EST, refer to Chapter 4). This system uses a one piece distributor with the ignition coil mounted in the distributor cap, similar to 1980.

All spark timing changes in the 1981 distributors are done electronically by the Electronic Control Module (ECM) which moniters information from various engine sensors, computes the desired spark timing and then signals the distributor to change the timing

TUNE-UP

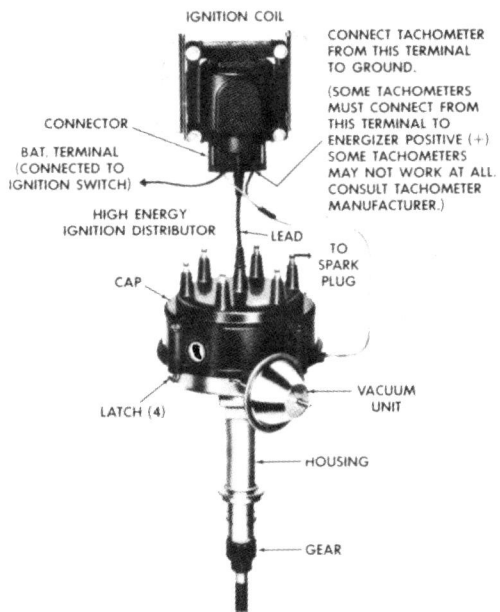

Early six cylinder engines with the HEI distributor had an external coil

accordingly. No vacuum or mechanical advance systems are used whatsoever.

In the HEI system, as in other electronic ignition systems, the breaker points have been replaced with an electronic switch—a transistor—which is located *within* the control module. This switching transistor performs the same function the points did in a conventional ignition system; it simply turns coil primary current on and off at the correct time. Essentially then, electronic and conventional ignition systems operate on the same principle.

The module which houses the switching transistor is controlled (turned on and off) by a magnetically generated impulse induced in the pick-up coil. When the teeth of the rotating timer align with the teeth of the pole piece, the induced voltage in the pick-up coil signals the electronic module to open the coil primary circuit. The primary current then decreases, and a high voltage is induced in the ignition coil secondary windings which is then directed through the rotor and high voltage leads (spark plug wires) to fire the spark plugs.

In essence then, the pick-up coil module system simply replaces the conventional breaker points and condenser. The condenser found within the distributor is for radio suppression purposes only and has nothing to do with the ignition process. The module automatically controls the dwell period, increasing it with increasing engine speed. Since dwell is automatically controlled, it cannot be adjusted. The module itself is non-adjustable and non-repairable and must be replaced if found defective.

HEI SYSTEM PRECAUTIONS

Before going on to troubleshooting, it might be a good idea to take note of the following precautions:

Timing Light Use

Inductive pick-up timing lights are the best kind to use with HEI. Timing lights which connect between the spark plug and the spark plug wire occasionally (not always) give false readings.

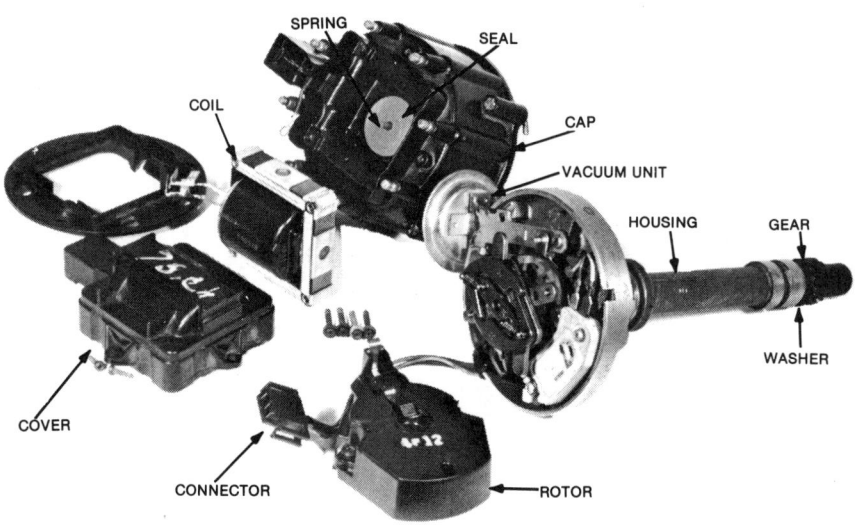

V8 HEI distributor components—1975-80 (1978-80 6-cyl. similar)

64 TUNE-UP

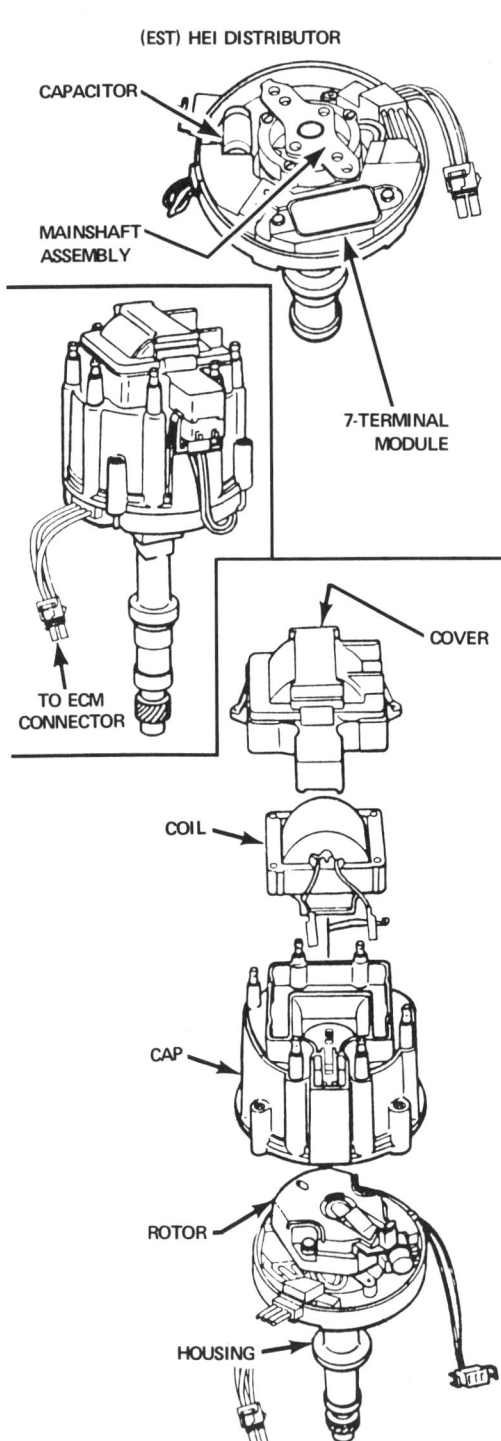

HEI EST distributor components—1981 (note absence of vacuum advance unit)

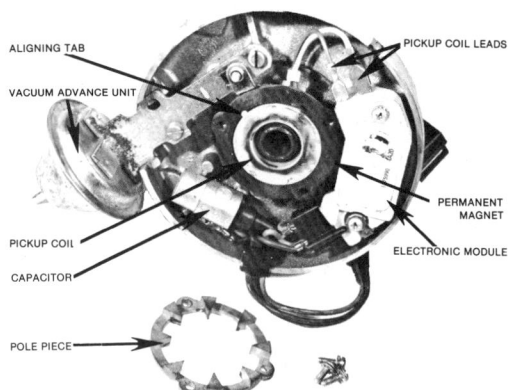

All HEI circuitry is contained within the distributor body (1980 shown)

get the correct wires, since conventional wires won't carry the voltage. Also, handle them carefully to avoid cracking or splitting them and *never* pierce them.

Tachometer Use

Not all tachometers will operate or indicate correctly when used on a HEI system. While some tachometers may give a reading, this does not necessarily mean the reading is correct. In addition, some tachometers hook up differently from others. If you can't figure out whether or not your tachometer will work on your car, check with the tachometer manufacturer. Dwell readings, of course, have no significance at all.

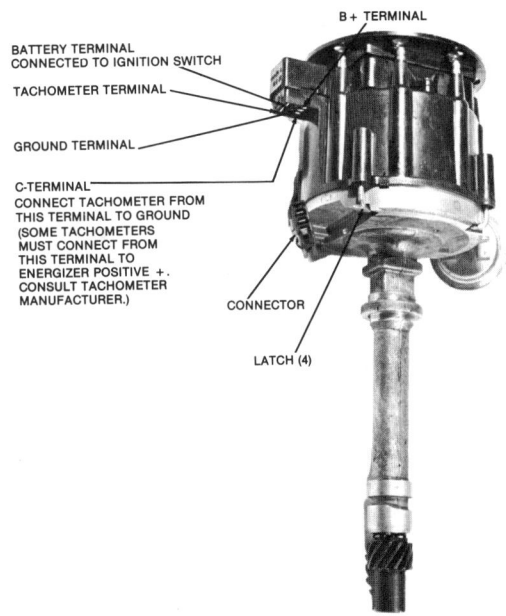

Typical HEI distributor connections

Spark Plug Wires

The plug wires used with HEI systems are of a different construction than conventional wires. When replacing them, make sure you

TUNE-UP 65

HEI System Testers

Instruments designed specifically for testing HEI systems are available from several tool manufacturers. Some of these will even test the module itself. However, the tests given in the following section will require only an ohmmeter and a voltmeter.

TROUBLESHOOTING THE HEI SYSTEM

The symptoms of a defective component within the HEI system are exactly the same as those you would encounter in a conventional system. Some of these symptoms are:
- Hard or no Starting
- Rough Idle
- Poor Fuel Economy
- Engine misses under load or while accelerating

If you suspect a problem in your ignition system, there are certain preliminary checks which you should carry out before you begin to check the electronic portions of the system. First, it is extremely important to make sure the vehicle battery is in a good state of charge. A defective or poorly charged battery will cause the various components of the ignition system to read incorrectly when they are being tested. Second, make sure all wiring connections are clean and tight, not only at the battery, but also at the distributor cap, ignition coil, and at the electronic control module.

Since the only change between electronic and conventional ignition systems is in the distributor component area, it is imperative to check the secondary ignition circuit first. If the secondary circuit checks out properly, then the engine condition is probably not the fault of the ignition system. To check the secondary ignition system, perform a simple spark test. Remove one of the plug wires and insert some sort of extension in the plug socket. An old spark plug with the ground electrode removed makes a good extension. Hold the wire and extension about ¼ in. away from the block and crank the engine. If a normal spark occurs, then the problem is most likely *not* in the ignition system. Check for fuel system problems, or fouled spark plugs.

If, however, there is no spark or a weak spark, then further ignition system testing will have to be done. Troubleshooting techniques fall into two categories, depending on the nature of the problem. The categories are (1) Engine cranks, but won't start or (2) Engine runs, but runs rough or cuts out. To begin with, let's consider the first case.

Engine Fails to Start

If the engine won't start, perform a spark test as described earlier. This will narrow the problem area down considerably. If no spark occurs, check for the presence of normal battery voltage at the battery (BAT) terminal in the distributor cap. The ignition switch must be in the "on" position for this test. Either a voltmeter or a test light may be used for this test. Connect the test light wire to ground and the probe end to the BAT terminal at the distributor. If the light comes on, you have voltage to the distributor. If the light fails to come on, this indicates an open circuit in the ignition primary wiring leading to the distributor. In this case, you will have to check wiring continuity back to the ignition switch using a test light. If there is battery voltage at the BAT terminal, but no spark at the plugs, then the problem lies within the distributor assembly. Go on to the distributor components test section.

Engine Runs, But Runs Rough or Cuts Out

1. Make sure the plug wires are in good shape first. There should be no obvious cracks or breaks. You can check the plug wires with an ohmmeter, but *do not* pierce the wires with a probe. Check the chart for the correct plug wire resistance.

HEI Plug Wire Resistance Chart

Wire Length	Minimum	Maximum
0–15 inches	3000 ohms	10,000 ohms
15–25 inches	4000 ohms	15,000 ohms
25–35 inches	6000 ohms	20,000 ohms
Over 35 inches		25,000 ohms

2. If the plug wires are OK, remove the cap assembly and check for moisture, cracks, chips, or carbon tracks, or any other high voltage leaks or failures. Replace the cap if any defects are found. Make sure the timer wheel rotates when the engine is cranked. If everything is all right so far, go on to the distributor components test section following.

66 TUNE-UP

DISTRIBUTOR COMPONENTS TESTING

If the trouble has been narrowed down to the units within the distributor, the following tests can help pinpoint the defective component. An ohmmeter with both high and low ranges should be used. These tests are made with the cap assembly removed and the battery wire disconnected. If a tachometer is connected to the TACH terminal, disconnect it before making these tests.

1. Connect an ohmmeter between the TACH and BAT terminals in the distributor cap. The primary coil resistance should be less than one ohm.

2. To check the coil secondary resistance, connect an ohmmeter between the rotor button and the BAT terminal. Note the reading. Connect the ohmmeter between the rotor button and the TACH terminal. Note the reading. The resistance in both cases should be between 6,000 and 30,000 ohms. Be sure to test between the rotor button and both the BAT and TACH terminals.

3. Replace the coil *only* if the readings in Step 1 and Step 2 are infinite.

NOTE: *These resistance checks will not disclose shorted coil windings. This condition can only be detected with scope analysis or a suitably designed coil tester. If*

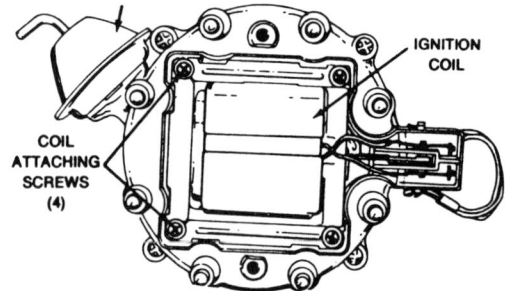

The coil on all but the 1975–77 six cylinder engine is accessible by removing the four attaching screws

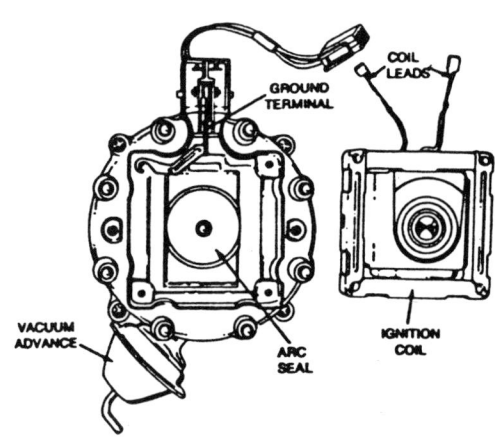

Check the condition of the arc seal under the coil

these instruments are unavailable, replace the coil with a known good coil as a final coil test.

4. To test the pick-up coil, first disconnect the white and green module leads. Set the ohmmeter on the high scale and connect it between a ground and either the white or green lead. Any resistance measurement *less* than infinity requires replacement of the pick-up coil.

5. Pick-up coil continuity is tested by connecting the ohmmeter (on low range) between the white and green leads. Normal resistance is between 650 and 850 ohms, or 500 and 1500 ohms on 1977 and later models. Move the vacuum advance arm while performing this test. This will detect any break in coil continuity. Such a condition can cause intermittent misfiring. Replace the pick-up coil if the reading is outside the specified limits.

6. If no defects have been found at this time, and you still have a problem, then the

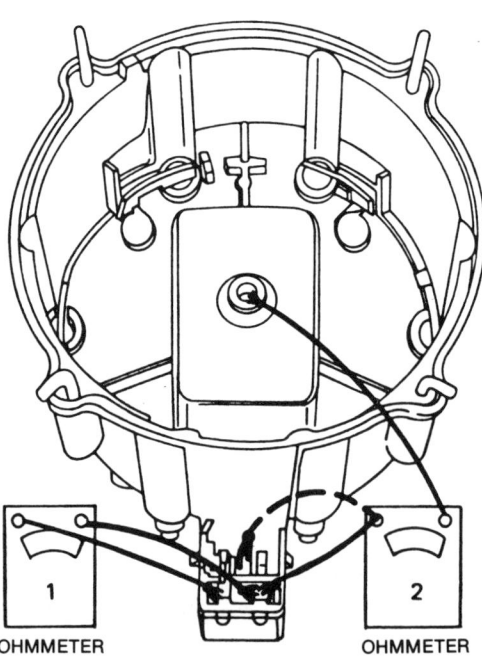

Ohmmeter 1 shows the primary coil resistance connection. Ohmmeter 2 shows the secondary resistance connection. (1980 shown, most models similar).

TUNE-UP 67

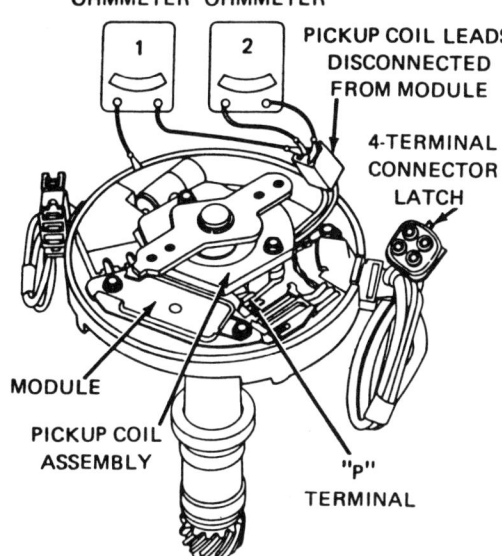

Ohmmeter 1 shows the connections for testing the pickup coil. Ohmmeter 2 shows the connections for testing the pickup coil continuity (1980 shown, most models similar)

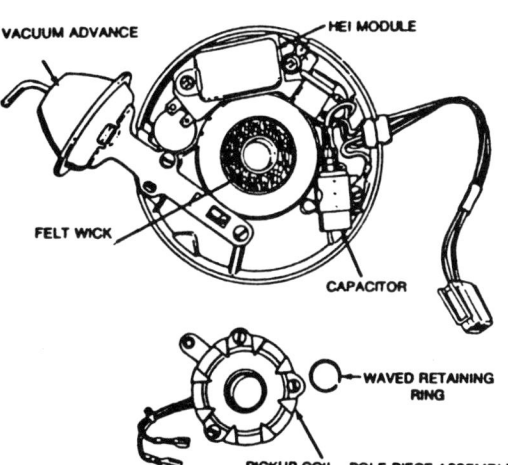

Pickup coil removal (1981 models have no vacuum advance unit)

module will have to be checked. If you do not have access to a module tester, the only possible alternative is a substitution test. If the module fails the substitution test, replace it.

HEI SYSTEM MAINTENANCE

Except for periodic checks of the spark plug wires, and an occasional check of the distributor cap for cracks (see Steps 1 and 2 under

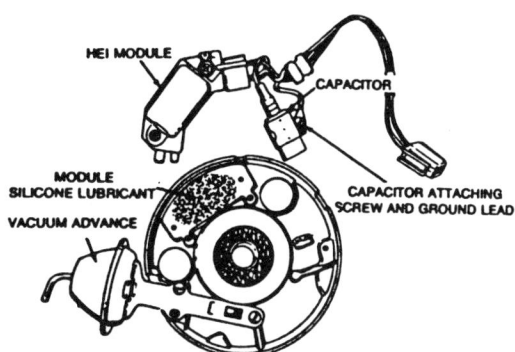

Module replacement, be sure to coat the mating surfaces with silicone lubricant

"Engine Runs, But Runs Rough or Cuts Out" for details), no maintenance is required on the HEI System. No periodic lubrication is necessary; engine oil lubricates the lower bushing, and an oil-filled reservoir lubricates the upper bushing.

COMPONENT REPLACEMENT

Integral Ignition Coil

1. Disconnect the feed and module wire terminal connectors from the distributor cap.
2. Remove the ignition set retainer.
3. Remove the 4 coil cover-to-distributor cap screws and the coil cover.
4. Remove the 4 coil-to-distributor cap screws.
5. Using a blunt drift, press the coil wire spade terminals up out of distributor cap.
6. Lift the coil up out of the distributor cap.
7. Remove and clean the coil spring, rubber seal washer and coil cavity of the distributor cap.
8. Coat the rubber seal with a dielectric lubricant furnished in the replacement ignition coil package.
9. Reverse the above procedures to install.

Distributor Cap

1. Remove the feed and module wire terminal connectors from the distributor cap.
2. Remove the retainer and spark plug wires from the cap.
3. Depress and release the 4 distributor cap-to-housing retainers and lift off the cap assembly.
4. Remove the 4 coil cover screws and cover.

TUNE-UP

5. Using a finger or a blunt drift, push the spade terminals up out of the distributor cap.

6. Remove all 4 coil screws and lift the coil, coil spring and rubber seal washer out of the cap coil cavity.

7. Using a new distributor cap, reverse the above procedures to assemble being sure to clean and lubricate the rubber seal washer with dielectric lubricant.

Rotor

1. Disconnect the feed and module wire connectors from the distributor.

2. Depress and release the 4 distributor cap-to-housing retainers and lift off the cap assembly.

3. Remove the two rotor attaching screws and rotor.

4. Reverse the above procedure to install.

Vacuum Advance (1975–80)

1. Remove the distributor cap and rotor as previously described.

2. Disconnect the vacuum hose from the vacuum advance unit.

3. Remove the two vacuum advance retaining screws, pull the advance unit outward, rotate and disengage the operating rod from its tang.

4. Reverse the above procedure to install.

Module

1. Remove the distributor cap and rotor as previously described.

2. Disconnect the harness connector and pick-up coil spade connectors from the module. Be careful not to damage the wires when removing the connector.

3. Remove the two screws and module from the distributor housing.

4. Coat the bottom of the new module with dielectric lubricant supplied with the new module. Reverse the above procedure to install.

HEI SYSTEM TACHOMETER HOOKUP

There is a terminal marked TACH on the distributor cap. Connect one tachometer lead to this terminal and the other lead to a ground. On some tachometers, the leads must be connected to the TACH terminal and to the battery positive terminal.

CAUTION: *Never ground the TACH terminal; serious module and ignition coil damage will result. If there is any doubt as to the correct tachometer hookup, check with the tachometer manufacturer.*

1975–77 models with a six cylinder engine utilize an HEI distributor with an external coil. For these particular vehicles, connect one tachometer lead to the TACH terminal on the ignition coil and connect the other one to a suitable ground.

Ignition Timing

Ignition timing is the measurement, in degrees of crankshaft rotation, of the point at which the spark plugs fire in each of the cylinders. It is measured in degrees before or after Top Dead Center (TDC) of the compression stroke.

Because it takes a fraction of a second for the spark plug to ignite the mixture in the cylinder, the spark plug must fire a little before the piston reaches TDC. Otherwise, the mixture will not be completely ignited as the piston passes TDC and the full power of the explosion will not be used by the engine.

The timing measurement is given in degrees of crankshaft rotation before the piston reaches TDC (BTDC). If the setting for the ignition timing is 5° BTDC, the spark plug must fire 5° before each piston reaches TDC. This only holds true, however, when the engine is at idle speed.

As the engine speed increases, the pistons go faster. The spark plugs have to ignite the fuel even sooner if it is to be completely ignited when the piston reaches TDC. To do this, the distributor has two means to advance the timing of the spark as the engine speed increases. This is accomplished by centrifugal weights within the distributor, and a vacuum diaphragm mounted on the side of the distributor.

If the ignition is set too far advanced (BTDC), the ignition and expansion of the fuel in the cylinder will occur too soon and tend to force the piston down while it is still traveling up. This causes engine ping. If the ignition spark is set too far retarded, after TDC (ATDC), the piston will have already passed TDC and started on its way down when the fuel is ignited. This will cause the piston to be forced down for only a portion of its travel. This will result in poor engine performance and lack of power.

Timing marks consist of a notch on the rim of the crankshaft pulley and a scale of degrees attached to the front of the engine. The notch corresponds to the position of the piston in the number 1 cylinder. A stroboscopic (dynamic) timing light is used, which is hooked into the circuit of the No. 1 cylinder spark plug. Every time the spark plug fires, the timing light flashes. By aiming the timing light at the timing marks, the exact position of the piston within the cylinder can be read, since the stroboscopic flash makes the mark on the pulley appear to be standing still. Proper timing is indicated when the notch is aligned with the correct number on the scale.

There are three basic types of timing lights available. The first is a simple neon bulb with two wire connections (one for the spark plug and one for the plug wire, connecting the light in series). This type of light is quite dim, and must be held closely to the marks to be seen, but it is quite inexpensive. The second type of light operates from the car's battery. Two alligator clips connect to the battery terminals, while a third wire connects to the spark plug with an adapter. This type of light is more expensive, but the xenon bulb provides a nice bright flash which can even be seen in sunlight. The third type replaces the battery source with 110 volt house current. Some timing lights have other functions built into them, such as dwell meters, tachometers, or remote starting switches. These are convenient, in that they reduce the tangle of wires under the hood, but may duplicate the functions of tools you already have.

If your Camaro has electronic ignition, you should use a timing light with an inductive pickup. This pickup simply clamps onto the No. 1 spark plug wire, eliminating the adapter. It is not susceptible to crossfiring or false triggering, which may occur with a conventional light, due to the greater voltages produced by electronic ignition.

Typical ignition timing marks

CHECKING AND ADJUSTMENT

1. Warm the engine to normal operating temperature. Shut off the engine and connect the timing light to the No. 1 spark plug (left front on V8, front on a six). Do not, under any circumstances, pierce a wire to hook up a light.

2. Clean off the timing marks and mark the pulley or damper notch and the timing scale with white chalk or paint. The timing notch on the damper or pulley can be elusive. Bump the engine around with the starter or turn the crankshaft with a wrench on the front pulley bolt to get it to an accessible position.

3. Disconnect and plug the vacuum advance hose at the distributor, to prevent any distributor advance. The vacuum line is the rubber hose connected to the metal cone-shaped canister on the side of the distributor. A short screw, pencil, or a golf tee can be used to plug the hose.

NOTE: *1981 models with Electronic Spark Timing have no vacuum advance, therefore you may skip the previous step.*

4. Start the engine and adjust the idle speed to that specified in the "Tune-Up Specifications" chart. Some cars require that the timing be set with the transmission in Neutral. You can disconnect the idle solenoid, if any, to get the speed down. Otherwise, adjust the idle speed screw. This is to prevent any centrifugal advance of timing in the distributor.

The tachometer hookup for cars through 1974 is the same as that shown for the dwell meter in the "Tune-Up" section. On 1975–77 HEI systems, the tachometer connects to the TACH terminal on the distributor for V8s, or on the coil for sixes, and to a ground. For 1978 and later models, all tachometer connections are to the TACH terminal. Some tachometers must connect to the TACH terminal and to the positive battery terminal. Some tachometers won't work at all with HEI. Consult the tachometer manufacturer if the instructions supplied with the unit do not give the proper connection.

CAUTION: *Never ground the HEI TACH terminal; serious system damage will result, including module burnout.*

5. Aim the timing light at the timing marks. Be careful not to touch the fan, which may appear to be standing still. Keep your clothes and hair, and the light's wires clear of the fan, belts, and pulleys. If the pulley or

70 TUNE-UP

damper notch isn't aligned with the proper timing mark (see the "Tune-Up Specifications" chart), the timing will have to be adjusted.

NOTE: *TDC or Top Dead Center corresponds to 0 degrees; B, or BTDC, or Before Top Dead Center, may be shown as BEFORE; A, or ATDC, or After Top Dead Center, may be shown as AFTER.*

6. Loosen the distributor base clamp locknut. You can buy special wrenches which make this task a lot easier on V8s. Turn the distributor slowly to adjust the timing, holding it by the body and not the cap. Turn the distributor in the direction of rotor rotation (found in the "Firing Order" illustration in Chapter 3) to retard, and against the direction to advance.

7. Tighten the locknut. Check the timing, in case the distributor moved as you tightened it.

8. Replace the distributor vacuum hose, if removed. Correct the idle speed.

9. Shut off the engine and disconnect the light.

Valve Lash

MECHANICAL LIFTERS

Relatively few engines ever used in Camaros utilize mechanical valve lifters. Those that do are listed in the following chart.

Mechanical Valve Lifter Clearance

Year	Engine		Intake (Hot) In.	Exhaust (Hot) In.
1967–1969	V8—302	290 hp	0.030	0.030
1970	V8—350	360 hp	0.024	0.030
1971	V8—350	330 hp	0.024	0.030
1972	V8—350	255 hp	0.024	0.030

Engine Running

1. Run the engine to reach normal operating temperature.
2. Remove the valve covers and gaskets by tapping the end of the cover rearward. Do not attempt to pry the cover off.
3. To avoid being splashed with hot oil, use oil deflector clips. Place one over each oil hole in the rocker arm.

Oil deflector clips will prevent splatter when adjusting the valves with the engine running

4. Measure between the rocker arm and the valve stem with a flat feeler gauge, then adjust the rocker arm stud nut until clearance agrees with the specifications in the chart.

5. After adjusting all the valves, stop the engine, clean the gasket surfaces, and install the valve covers with new gaskets.

Engine Not Running

These are initial adjustments usually required after assembling an engine or doing a valve job. They should be followed up by an adjustment with the engine running as described above.

1. Set the engine to the no. 1 firing position.

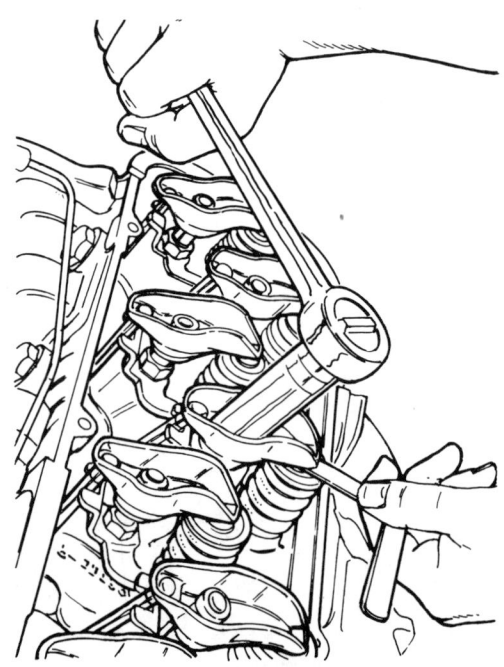

Adjusting the mechanical valve lifters

TUNE-UP 71

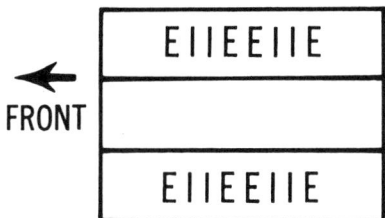

Valve arrangement—302, 350 V8

2. Adjust the clearance between the valve stems and the rocker arms with a feeler gauge. Check the Chart for the proper clearance. Adjust the following valves in the No. 1 firing position: Intake No. 2, 7, Exhaust No. 4, 8.

3. Turn the crankshaft one-half revolution clockwise. Adjust the following valves: Intake No. 1, 8, Exhaust No. 3, 6.

4. Turn the crankshaft one-half revolution clockwise to No. 6 firing position. Adjust the following valves in the No. 6 firing position: Intake No. 3, 4, Exhaust No. 5, 7.

5. Turn the crankshaft one-half revolution clockwise. Adjust the following valves: Intake No. 5, 6, Exhaust No. 1, 2.

6. Run the engine until the normal operating temperature is reached. Reset all clearances, using the procedure listed above under "Engine Running."

HYDRAULIC LIFTERS

All Camaros, with the exception of those few already discussed, use a hydraulic tappet system with adjustable rocker mounting nuts to obtain zero lash. No periodic adjustment is necessary.

Carburetor

Idle mixture and speed adjustments are critical aspects of exhaust emission control. It is important that all tune-up instructions be carefully followed to ensure satisfactory engine performance and minimum exhaust pollution. The different combinations of emission systems application on the different engine models have resulted in a great variety of tune-up specifications. See the "Tune-Up Specifications" at the beginning of this section. Beginning in 1968, all models have a decal conspicuously placed in the engine compartment giving tune-up specifications.

When adjusting a carburetor with two idle mixture screws, adjust them alternately and evenly, unless otherwise stated.

IDLE SPEED AND MIXTURE ADJUSTMENT

See Chapter 4 for illustrations and adjustment specifications of Carter and Rochester carburetors. In the following adjustment procedures the term "lean roll" means turning the mixture adjusting screws in (clockwise) from otpimum setting to obtain an obvious drop in engine speed (usually 20 rpm).

1967 Without Air

Adjust with air cleaner removed.

1. Remove the air cleaner.
2. Connect a tachometer and vacuum gauge to the engine, set the parking brake, and place the transmission in Neutral.
3. Turn in the idle mixture screws until they *gently* seat, then back out 1½ turns.
4. Start the engine and allow it to come to the normal operating temperature. Make sure the choke is fully open, then adjust the idle speed screw to obtain the specified idle speed (automatic in Drive, manual in Neutral).
5. Adjust the idle mixture screw(s) to obtain the highest steady vacuum at the specified idle speed, except for the Rochester BV. For this carburetor, adjust the idle mixture screw out ¼ turn from lean "drop-off," the point where a 20–30 rpm drop is achieved by leaning the mixture.

NOTE: *On carburetors having a hot idle compensator valve (A/C models,) hold the brass valve down with a pencil while making the mixture adjustment.*

6. Repeat Steps four and five if necessary.
7. Turn off the engine, remove the gauges, and install the air cleaner.

1967 With Air

Adjust with the air cleaner removed.

NOTE: *During this adjustment, air conditioning should be turned off on 327 and 350 cu in. engines.*

1. Remove the air cleaner.
2. Connect a tachometer and a vacuum gauge to the engine, set the parking brake, and place the transmission in Neutral.
3. Turn in the idle mixture screw(s) until they *gently* seat, then back them out three turns.
4. Start the engine and allow it to reach normal operating temperature. Make sure the choke is fully open, then adjust the idle speed screw(s) to obtain the specified idle speed (automatic in Drive, manual in Neutral).

72 TUNE-UP

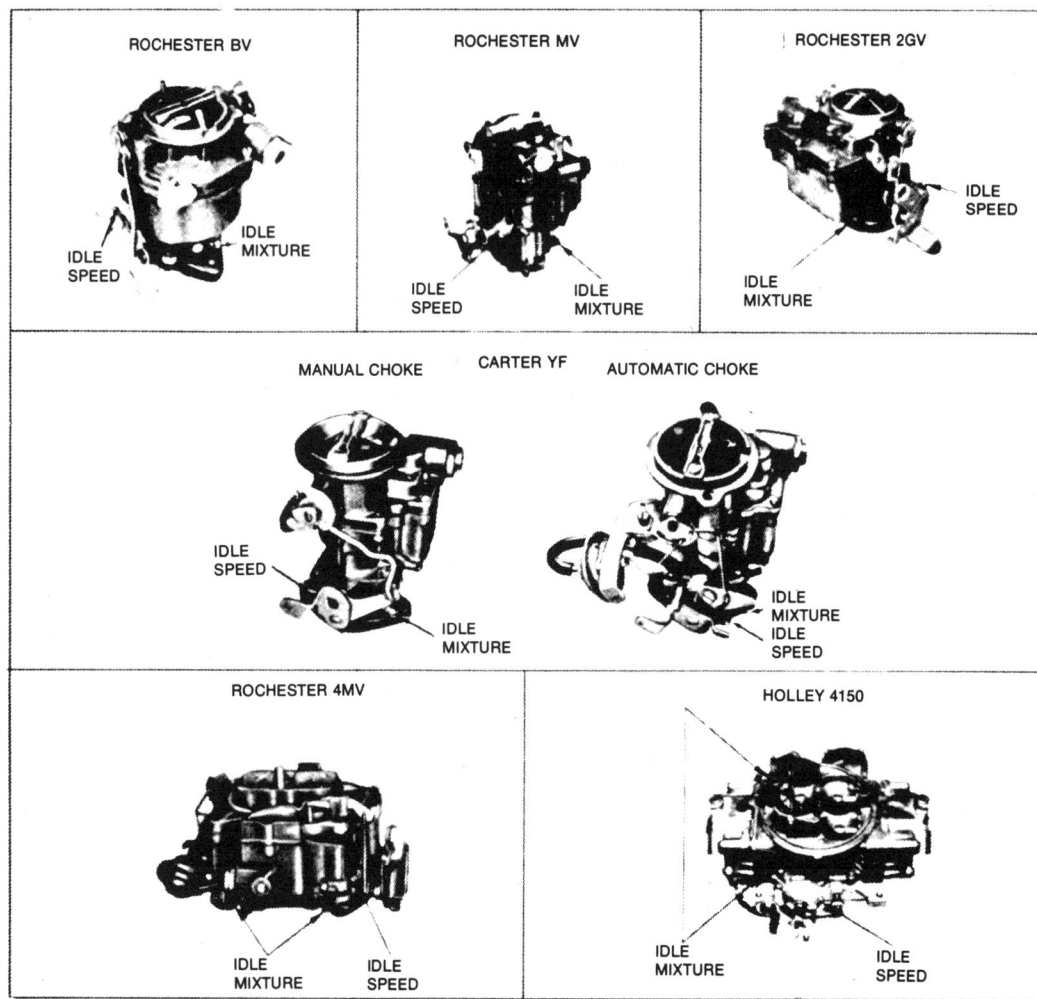

Idle speed and mixture screw location—1967-70

5. Turn the idle mixture screw(s) clockwise (in) to the point where a 20-30 rmp drop in speed is achieved—this is the lean "drop off" point. Back out the screws ¼ turn from this point.

6. Repeat Steps four and five if necessary.

7. Turn off the engine, remove the gauges, and install the air cleaner.

1968-69

Adjust with the air cleaner installed.

NOTE: *Turn off the air conditioner (if applicable) unless your car is a 1968 model with the 6 cylinder engine and automatic transmission. These cars should have the air conditioner turned on when setting the idle.*

1. Turn in the idle mixture screw(s) until they seat gently, then back them out three turns.

2. Start the engine and allow it to reach operating temperature. Make sure the choke is fully open and the preheater valve is open, then adjust the idle speed scew to obtain the specified idle speed (automatic in Drive, manual in Neutral).

3. Adjust the idle mixture screw(s) to obtain the highest steady idle speed, then readjust the idle speed screw to obtain the specified speed. On cars with an idle stop solenoid adjust as follows:

a. Adjust the idle speed to 500 rpm (6) or 600 rpm (1968 V8) by turning the hex on the solenoid plunger. Refer to the tune-up decal in the engine compartment for 1969 idle speeds.

b. Disconnect the wire at the solenoid. This allows the throttle lever to seat against the idle screw.

c. Adjust the idle screw to obtain 400

rpm (1968), then reconnect the wire. On 1969 models, adjust the idle to that specified on the tune-up decal in the engine compartment.

4. Adjust one mixture screw to obtain a 20 rpm drop in idle speed, and back out the screw ¼ turn from this point.

5. Repeat Steps three and four for the second mixture screw (if so equipped).

6. Readjust the idle speed to obtain the specified idle speed.

1970—Initial Adjustments

Adjust with the air cleaner installed.

1. Disconnect the fuel tank line from the vapor canister (EEC).

2. Connect a tachometer to the engine, start the engine and allow it to reach operating temperature. Make sure the choke and preheater valves are fully open.

3. Turn off the air conditioner and set the parking brake. Disconnect and plug the distributor vacuum line.

4. Make the following adjustments:

6-250

1. Turn in the mixture screw until it *gently* seats, then back out the screw four turns.

2. Adjust the solenoid screw to obtain 830 rpm for manual transmissions (in Neutral) or 630 rpm for automatic transmissions (in Drive).

3. Adjust the mixture screw to obtain 750 rpm for manual transmissions (in Neutral) or 600 rpm for automatic transmissions (in Drive).

4. Disconnect the solenoid wire and set the idle speed to 400 rpm, then reconnect it.

5. Reconnect the distributor vacuum line.

V8-307

1. Turn in the mixture screws until they seat *gently,* then back them out four turns.

2. Adjust the carburetor idle speed screw to obtain 800 rpm for manual transmissions (in Neutral), or adjust the solenoid screw to obtain 630 rpm for automatic transmissions (in Drive).

3. Adjust both mixture screws equally inward to obtain 700 rpm for manual transmissions, 600 rpm for automatic transmissions (in Drive).

4. On cars with automatic transmissions, disconnect the solenoid wire, set the carburetor idle screw to obtain 450 rpm and reconnect the solenoid.

5. Reconnect the distributor vacuum line.

V8-350 (250 HP)

1. Turn in the mixture screws until they *gently* seat, then back them out four turns.

2. Adjust the solenoid screw to obtain 830 rpm for manual transmissions (in Neutral), or 630 rpm for automatic transmissions (in Drive).

3. Adjust both mixture screws equally inward to obtain 750 rpm for manual transmissions or 600 rpm for automatics (in Drive).

4. Disconnect the solenoid wire, set the carburetor idle screw to obtain 450 rpm, and reconnect the solenoid.

5. Reconnect the distributor vacuum line.

V8-350 (300 HP)

1. Turn in both mixture screws until they *gently* seat, then back them out four turns.

2. Adjust the carburetor idle screw to obtain 775 rpm for manual transmissions, 630 rpm for automatics (in Drive).

3. Adjust the mixture screws equally to obtain 700 rpm for manual transmissions, 600 rpm for automatics (in Drive).

4. Reconnect the distributor vacuum line.

V8-350 (360 HP Z28)

1. Set the mixture screws to obtain maximum idle rpm and adjust the idle speed screw to obtain 750 rpm in Neutral.

V8-396 (350 HP)

1. Turn in both mixture screws until they *gently* seat, then back them out four turns.

2. Adjust the carburetor idle screw to obtain 700 rpm for manual transmissions or 630 rpm for automatics (in Drive).

3. For cars with automatic transmissions: adjust the mixture screws equally to obtain 600 rpm with the transmission in Drive.

4. For cars with manual transmissions: turn in *one* mixture screw until the speed drops to 400 rpm, then adjust the carburetor idle screw to obtain 700 rpm. Turn in the *other* mixture screw until the speed drops 400 rpm, then regain 700 rpm by adjusting the carburetor idle screw.

5. Reconnect the distributor vacuum line.

1971–72—Initial Adjustments

Adjust with air cleaner installed. The following initial idle adjustments are part of the normal engine tune-up. There is a tune-up

74 TUNE-UP

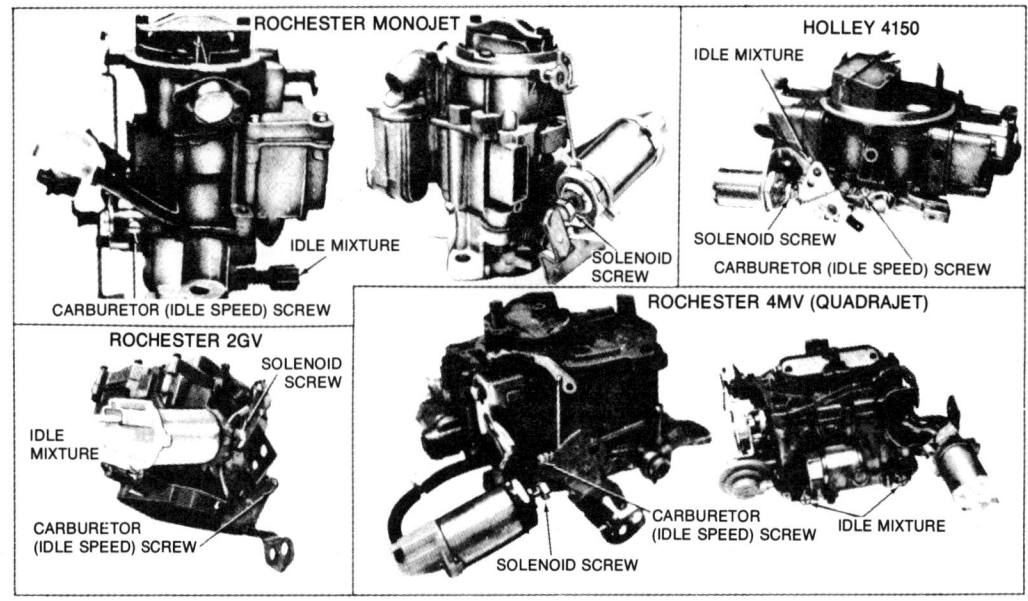

Idle speed and mixture screw location—1971

decal placed conspicuously in the engine compartment outlining the specific procedure and settings for each engine application. Follow all of the instructions when adjusting the idle. These tuning procedures are necessary to obtain the delicate balance of variables for the maintenance of both reliable engine performance and efficient exhaust emission control.

NOTE: *All engines have limiter caps on the mixture adjusting screws. The idle mixture is preset and the limiter caps installed at the factory in order to meet emission control standards. Do not remove these limiter caps unless all other possible causes of poor idle condition have been thoroughly checked out. The solenoid used on 1971 carburetors is different from the one used on earlier models. The Combination Emission Control System (C.E.C.) solenoid valve regulates distributor vacuum as a function of transmission gear position.*

CAUTION: *The C.E.C. solenoid is adjusted only after: 1) replacement of the solenoid, 2) major carburetor overhaul, or 3) after the throttle body is removed or replaced.*

All initial adjustments described below are made:

1. With the engine warmed up and running.
2. With the choke fully open.
3. With the fuel tank line disconnected from the Evaporative Emission canister on all models.
4. With the vacuum hose disconnected at the distributor and plugged.

Be sure to reconnect the distributor vacuum hose and to connect the fuel tank-to-evaporative emission canister line or install the gas cap when idle adjustments are complete.

6-250

1. Adjust the carburetor idle speed screw to obtain 550 rpm (700 rpm for 1972) for manual transmissions (in Neutral) or 500 rpm (600 rpm for 1972) for automatics (in Drive). *Do not adjust the solenoid screw.* Using the solenoid screw to set idle or incorrectly adjusting it may result in a decrease in engine braking.
2. Reconnect the vapor line and distributor vacuum advance line.

V8-307 and 350 (2-BBL)

1. On 1971 models, adjust the carburetor idle speed screw to obtain 600 rpm for manual transmission (in Neutral) with the air conditioning turned off, or 550 rpm for automatic transmissions (in Drive) with the air conditioning turned on. *Do not adjust the solenoid screw.* On 1972 models, turn the air conditioning off and adjust the idle stop solenoid screw to obtain 900 rpm for manual transmissions (in Neutral) or 600 rpm for automatics

(in Drive). Place the transmission in Park or Neutral and adjust the fast idle cam screw to get 1,850 rpm on 307 engines and 2,200 rpm on 350 engines.

2. Reconnect the vapor line and distributor vacuum advance line.

V8-350 (4-BBL EXCEPT Z28)

1. On 1971 models, adjust the carburetor idle speed screw to obtain 600 rpm for manual transmissions (in Neutral) with the air conditioning turned off, or 550 rpm for automatics (in Drive) with the air conditioning turned on. *Do not adjust the solenoid screw.* On 1972 models, turn the air conditioning off and adjust the idle stop solenoid screw to get 800 rpm for manual transmissions (in Neutral) or 600 rpm for automatic transmissions (in Drive).

2. For both 1971 and 1972 models, place the fast idle cam follower on the second step of the fast idle cam, turn the air conditioning off and adjust the fast idle to 1,350 rpm for manual transmissions (in Neutral) or 1,500 rpm for automatics (in Park).

3. Reconnect the vapor line and the distributor vacuum advance line on all models.

V8-350 (Z28)

1. On 1971 models, perform Steps 1–3. Adjust the mixture screws to obtain the maximum speed (rpm at idle), then adjust the carburetor idle speed screw to obtain 700

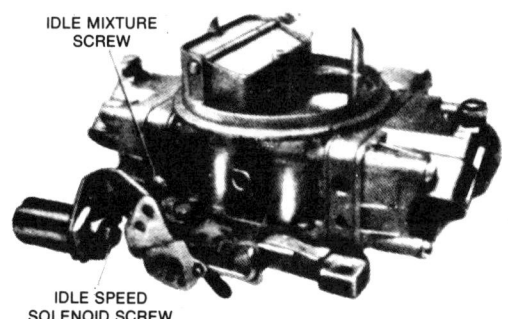

Idle speed and mixture screw location—1972 Holley 4150

rpm (manual in Neutral and automatic in Drive).

2. Turn in one mixture screw to obtain a 20 rpm drop in speed, then back out ¼ turn.

3. Repeat step b for the other mixture screw, then reset the idle to 700 rpm. *Do not adjust the solenoid screw.*

4. On 1972 models, turn the air conditioning off and adjust the idle stop solenoid screw to obtain 900 rpm (in Neutral) for manual transmission and 700 rpm (in Drive) for automatic. Proceed with step e.

5. Reconnect the vapor line and the distributor vacuum line.

V8-396 (CALLED 402 IN 1972)

1. On 1971 models, turn off the air conditioner and adjust the carburetor idle speed screw to obtain 600 rpm with manual trans-

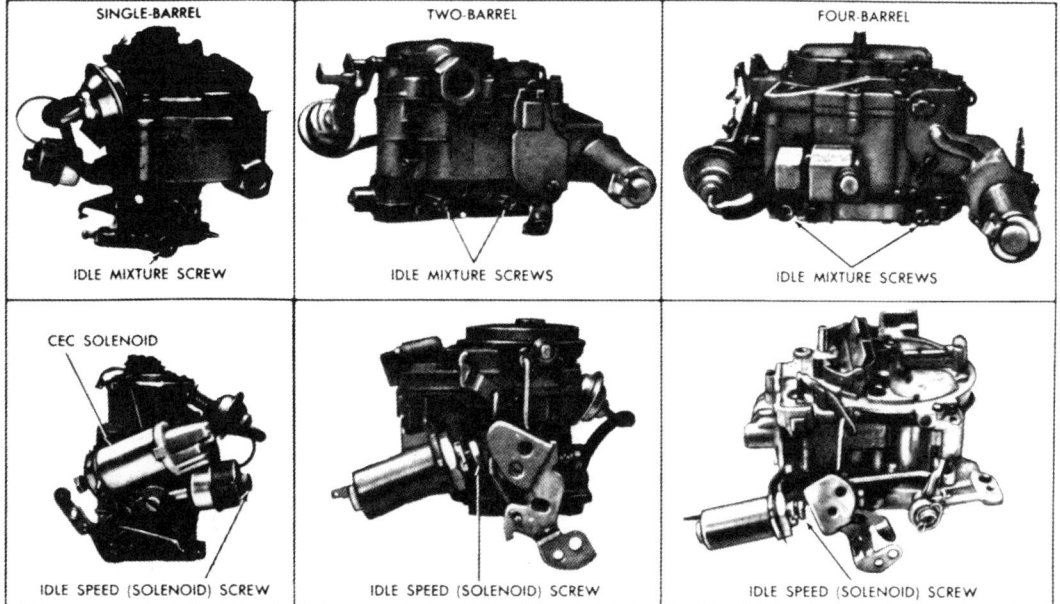

Idle speed and mixture screw location—1972–75

missions in Neutral and automatics in Drive. *Do not adjust the solenoid screw.* On 1972 cars, turn off the air conditioning and adjust the idle stop solenoid screw to 800 rpm (in Neutral) for manual transmissions and 600 rpm (in Drive) for automatics.

2. On both 1971 and 1972 cars, place the fast idle cam follower on the second step of the fast idle cam, turn off the air conditioner and adjust the fast idle to 1,350 rpm for manual transmissions (in Neutral) or 1,500 rpm for automatics (in Park).

3. Reconnect the vapor line and the distributor vacuum line on 1971 and 1972 cars.

1973—Initial Adjustments

All models are equipped with idle limiter caps and idle solenoids. Disconnect the fuel tank line from the evaporative canister. The engine must be running at operating temperature, choke off, parking brake on, and rear wheels blocked. Disconnect the distributor vacuum hose and plug it. After adjustment, reconnect the vacuum and evaporative hoses.

6-250

Adjust the idle stop solenoid for 700 rpm on manual transmission models or 600 rpm on automatics (in Drive). On manual models, make no attempt to adjust the CEC solenoid (the larger of the two carburetor solenoids) or a decrease in engine braking could result.

V8-307 & 350 (2-BBL)

1. With the air conditioning Off, adjust the idle stop solenoid screw for a speed of 900 rpm on manual models; 600 rpm for automatics in Drive.

2. Disconnect the idle stop solenoid electrical connector and adjust the idle speed screw (screw resting on lower step of the cam) for 450 rpm on all 307 cu in. engines, 400 rpm on 350 engines with automatic transmissions, or 500 rpm on 350 cu in. engine with manual transmissions.

V8-350 (4-BBL)

1. Adjust the idle stop solenoid screw for 900 rpm on manual, 600 rpm on automatic (in Drive).

2. Connect the distributor vacuum hose and position the fast idle cam follower on the top step of the fast idle cam (turn air conditioning off) and adjust the fast idle to 1300 rpm on manual transmission 350 engines; 1600 rpm for all automatics in Park.

V8-350 (Z-28)

1. With the air conditioning off, adjust the idle stop solenoid screw to 900 rpm for the manual transmission; 700 rpm with the automatic transmission in Drive.

2. Connect the distributor vacuum hose and place fast idle cam follower on the top step of the fast idle cam. Adjust the fast idle to 1300 rpm for manual transmission; and 1600 rpm for automatic transmissions (in Park).

1974

The same preliminary adjustments as for 1973 apply.

6-250

1. Using the hex nut on the end of the solenoid body, turn the entire solenoid to get 850 rpm for the manual transmission; 600 rpm for automatic transmissions in Drive.

V8-350 (2-BBL)

1. Turn the air conditioning off. Adjust the idle stop solenoid screw for 900 rpm on manual; 600 rpm on automatic (in Drive).

2. De-energize the solenoid and adjust the carburetor idle cam screw (on low step of cam) for 400 rpm on automatic models (in Drive); 500 rpm on 350 engines with manual transmission.

V8-350 (4-BBL)

1. Turn the air conditioning off. Adjust the idle stop solenoid screw for 900 rpm on manual transmission models; 600 rpm on automatic (in Drive).

2. Connect the distributor vacuum hose. Position the fast idle cam follower on the top step of the fast idle cam and adjust the fast idle speed to 1300 rpm on manual; 1600 on automatic (in Park).

V8-350 (Z-28)

1. With the air conditioning off, adjust the idle stop solenoid screw for 900 rpm with the manual transmission; 700 with the automatic transmission in Drive.

2. Reconnect the distributor vacuum advance hose and place the fast idle cam follower on the top step of the fast idle cam. With the air conditioning off, adjust the fast idle to 1300 rpm for manual transmissions; 1600 rpm for all automatics in Park.

1975-76

6-250 (1-BBL)

1. Idle speed is adjusted with the engine at normal operating temperature, air cleaner on, choke open, and air conditioning off (air conditioning on—1976 automatic transmission models). Hook up a tachometer to the engine.
2. Block the rear wheels and apply the parking brake.
3. Disconnect the fuel tank hose from the evaporative canister.
4. Disconnect and plug the distributor vacuum advance hose.
5. Start the engine and check the ignition timing. Adjust if necessary. Reconnect the vacuum hose. To adjust the idle speed, turn the solenoid in or out to obtain the higher of the two specifications listed on the decal. With the automatic transmission in Drive or the manual transmission in Neutral, disconnect the solenoid electrical connector and turn the 1/8 in. allen screw in the end of the solenoid body to the lower idle speed.
6. Place the shift lever in Drive on cars with automatic transmissions and have an assistant apply the brakes. On cars with manual transmissions, put it into Neutral.
7. Cut the tab off the mixture limiter cap, but don't remove the cap. Turn the screw counterclockwise until the highest idle speed is reached.
8. Set the idle speed to the higher of the two listed idle speeds by turning the solenoid in or out.
9. Check the tachometer and turn the mixture screw clockwise until the idle speed is at the lower of the two listed idle speeds.
10. Shut off the engine, remove the tachometer, and reconnect the carbon canister hose.

V8-350; 1975 (2-BBL)
V8-305; 1976 (2-BBL)

1. Idle speed is adjusted with the engine at normal operating temperature, air cleaner on, choke open, and air conditioning off. Hook up a tachometer to the engine.
2. Block the rear wheels and apply the parking brake.
3. Disconnect the fuel tank hose from the evaporative canister.
4. Disconnect and plug the distributor vacuum advance hose.
5. Start the engine and check the ignition timing. Adjust if necessary. Reconnect the vacuum hose.

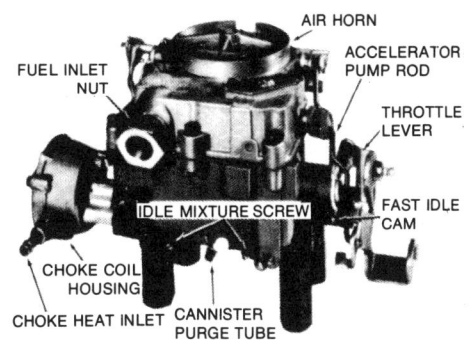

Idle mixture screw location—1976-77 2GC

6. Adjust the idle speed screw to the specified rpm. If the figures given in the "Tune-Up Specifications" chart differ from those on the tune-up decal, those on the decal take precedence. Automatic transmissions should be in Drive, manual transmissions should be in Neutral.

CAUTION: *Make doubly sure that the rear wheels are blocked and the parking brake applied.*

Adjust the idle speed to the higher of the two figures on the tune-up decal. Back out the two mixture screws equally until the highest idle is reached. Reset the speed if necessary to the higher one on the tune-up decal. Next, turn the screws in equally until the lower of the two figures on the decal is obtained.

7. Shut off engine, reconnect hose to evaporative canister, and remove blocks from wheels.

V8-350 (4-BBL)

1975 four-barrel carburetors are equipped with idle stop solenoids. There are two idle speeds, one with the solenoid energized and second with the solenoid de-energized. Both are set with the solenoid. The slower speed (solenoid de-energized) is necessary to prevent dieseling by allowing the throttle plates to close further than at a normal idle speed.

1. Idle speed is set with the engine at normal operating temperature, air cleaner on, choke open, and air conditioning off. Hook up a tachometer to the engine.
2. Block the rear wheels and apply the parking brake.
3. Disconnect the fuel tank hose from the evaporative canister.
4. Disconnect and plug the distributor vacuum advance hose.
5. Start the engine and check the ignition timing. Adjust if necessary. Reconnect the vacuum hose.

TUNE-UP

6. Disconnect the electrical connector at the idle solenoid.

7. Set the transmission in Drive. Adjust the low idle speed screw for the lower of the two figures given for idle speed.

CAUTION: *Make sure that the drive wheels are blocked and the parking brake is applied.*

8. Reconnect the idle solenoid and open the throttle slightly to extend the solenoid plunger.

9. Turn the solenoid plunger screw in or out to obtain the higher of the two idle speed figures (this is normal curb-idle).

To adjust the mixture, break off the limiter caps. Make sure that the idle is at the higher of the two speeds listed on the decal. Turn the mixture screws out equally to obtain the highest idle. Reset the idle speed with the plunger screw if necessary. Turn the mixture screws in until the lower of the two figures on the decal is obtained.

10. Shut off engine, remove blocks from drive wheels, and reconnect hose to evaporative canister.

For 1976, the idle solenoid has been dropped. To adjust the idle, follow the preceding Steps 1–5. Skip Steps 6, 7, and 8, then follow Steps 9 and 10, adjusting the idle speed screw.

1977

1. First satisfy all the following requirements:

   A. Set parking brake and block drive wheels.

   B. Bring the engine to operating temperature.

   C. Remove the air cleaner for access, but make sure all hoses stay connected.

   D. Consult the Emission Control Information label under the hood, and disconnect and plug hoses as required by the instructions there.

   E. Connect an accurate tach to the engine.

2. Set ignition timing as described above.

3. Remove the cap(s) from the idle mixture screw(s). Remove caps carefully, to prevent bending these screws.

4. Turn in the screw(s) till they seat *very lightly*, then back screw(s) out just far enough to permit the engine to run.

5. Put automatic transmission in Drive.

6. Back out screw(s) 1/8 turn at a time, going alternately from screw to screw after each 1/8 turn where there are two screws, until the highest possible idle speed is achieved. Then, set the idle speed as follows: 250 CID engine with manual transmission—950; with automatic—575; with automatic in California—640; with automatic used in high altitude area—650; 305 V8 with manual transmission—650; with automatic—550; standard 350 V8, manual transmission—800; standard 350 V8 with automatic—550; 350 V8, manual transmission, used in Z-28—900; 350 V8 automatic used in Z-28—750; 350 V8 used at high altitudes—650.

7. After setting the idle speed, repeat the mixture adjustment to ensure that mixture is at the point where highest idle speed is obtained. Then, if idle speed has increased, repeat idle speed adjustment of Step 6.

8. Now, turn screw(s) in, going evenly in 1/8 turn increments where there are two, until the following idle speeds are obtained: 250 CID engine with manual transmission—750; with automatic—550; with automatic in California—600; with automatic used in high altitude areas—600; 305 V8 with manual transmission—600; with automatic—500; standard 350 V8, manual transmission—700; standard 350 V8 with automatic—500; 350 V8 with manual transmission used in Z-28—800; 350 V8 with automatic used in Z-28—700; 350 V8 used at high altitudes—600.

9. Reset idle speed to the value shown on the engine compartment sticker, if that differs from the final setting in the step above.

10. Check and adjust fast idle as described on the engine compartment sticker. See Chapter 4.

11. Reconnect any vacuum hoses that were disconnected for the procedure, and install the air cleaner.

12. If idle speed has changed, reset ac-

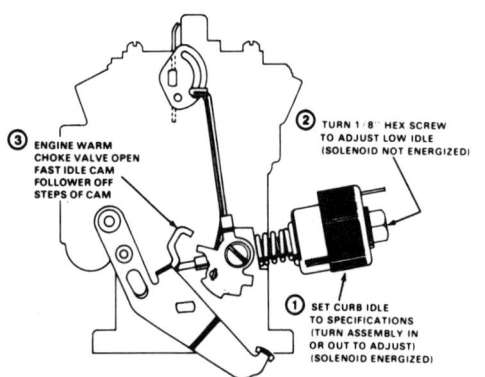

Idle speed adjustment screw location—1976–79 1 BBL

TUNE-UP

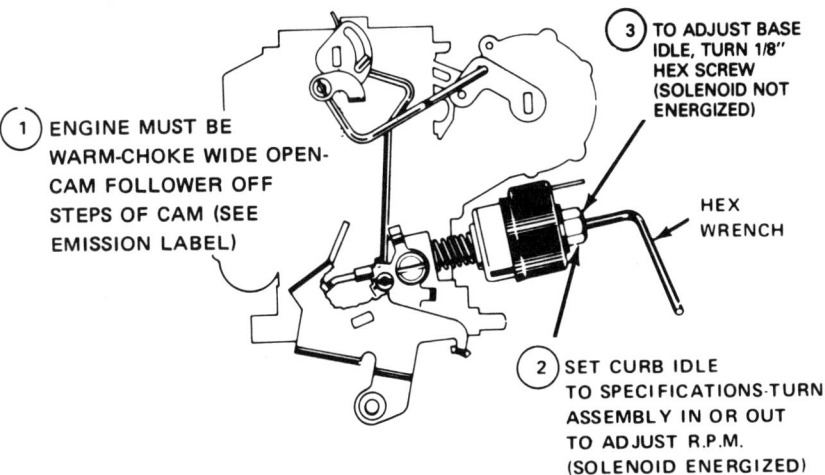

Idle speed adjustment for the six cylinder engine—1976-78

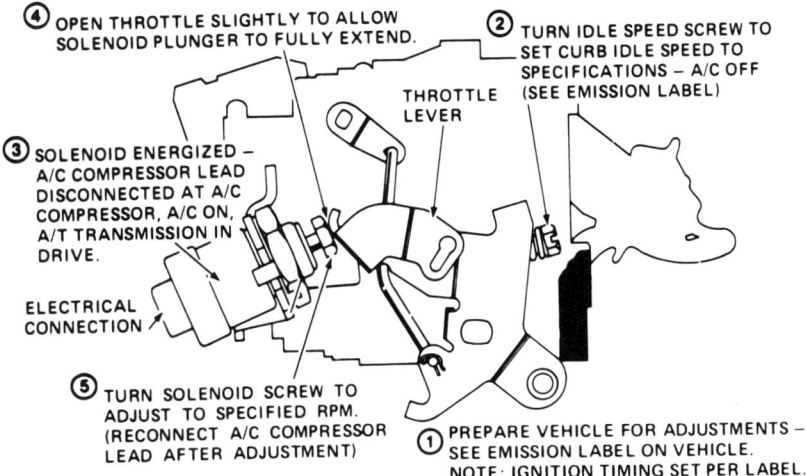

Idle speed adjustment for the the V8, 4 BBL with solenoid—1977

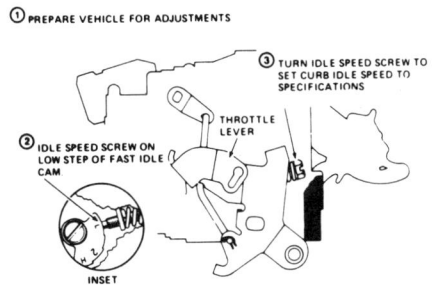

Idle speed adjustment for the V8, 4 BBL without solenoid—1977

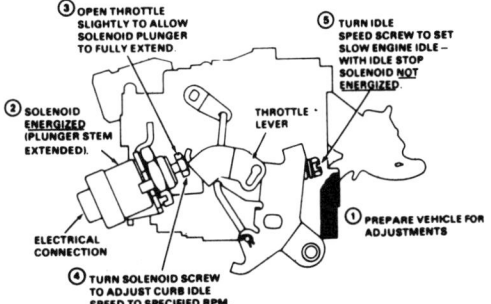

Idle speed adjustment for the 2 BBL with solenoid—1978-79

cording to the engine compartment sticker. Disconnect tach.

1978-81

1978 and later models have sealed idle mixture screws; in most cases these are concealed under staked-in plugs. Idle mixture is adjustable only during carburetor overhaul, and requires the addition of propane as an artificial mixture enrichener.

TUNE-UP

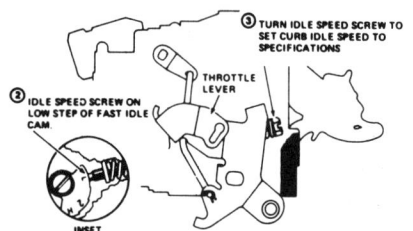

Idle speed adjustment for the 2 BBL without solenoid—1978-79

See the emission control label in the engine compartment for procedures and specifications not supplied here. Prepare the car for adjustment (engine warm, choke open, fast idle screw off the fast idle cam) as per the label instructions.

1 BBL

1. Run the engine to normal operating temperature.
2. Make sure that the choke is fully opened.
3. Turn the A/C Off and disconnect the vacuum line at the vapor canister. Plug the line.
4. Set the parking brake, block the drive wheels and place the transmission in Drive (AT) or Neutral (MT). Connect a tachometer to the engine according to the manufacturer's instructions.
5. Turn the solenoid assembly to achieve the solenoid-on speed.
6. Disconnect the solenoid wire and turn the 1/8 inch hex screw in the solenoid end, to achieve the solenoid-off speed.

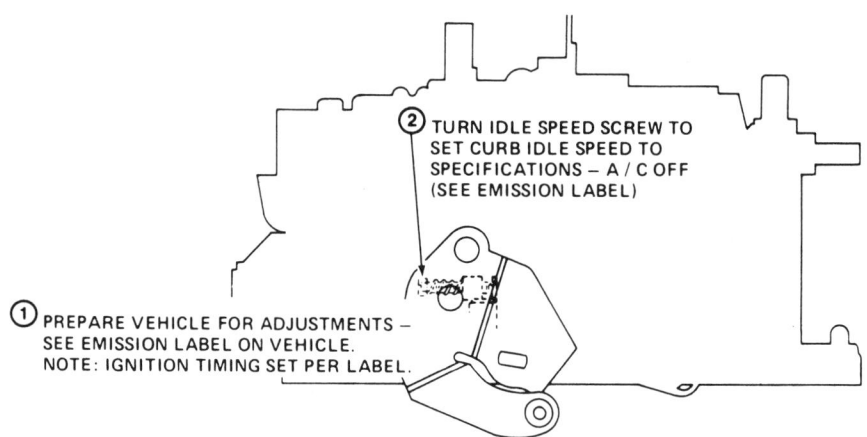

1979-81 4 BBL adjustment without solenoid

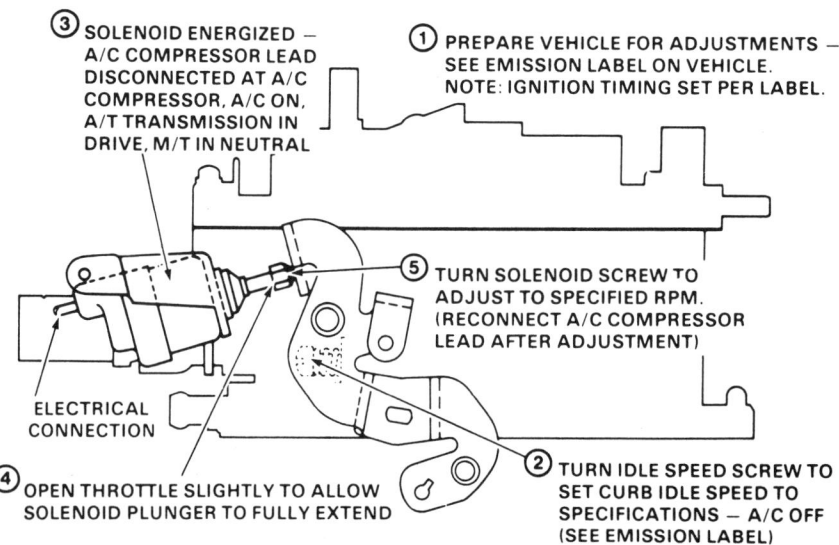

1979-81 4 BBL adjustment with solenoid

TUNE-UP 81

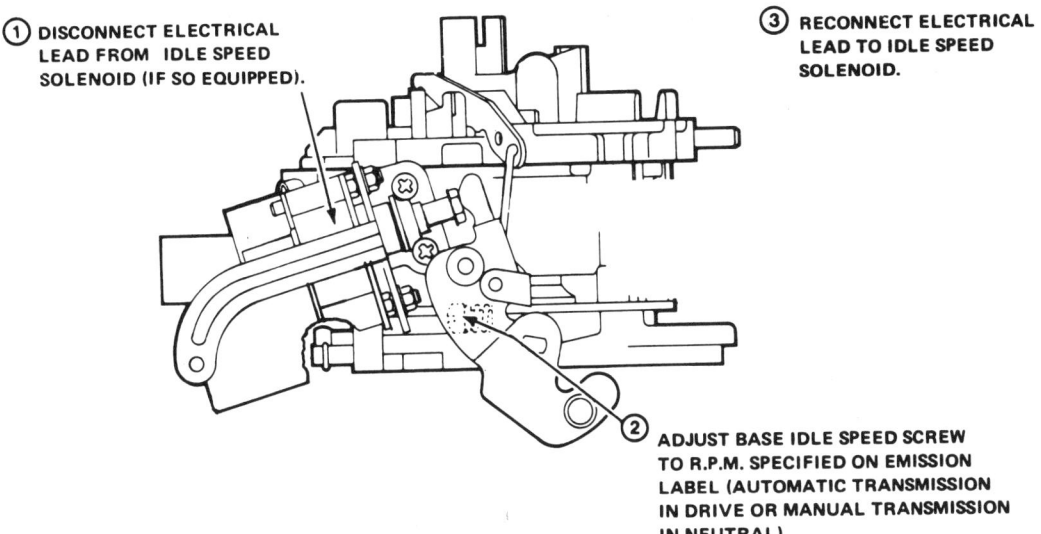

Idle speed adjustment with solenoid—1980 2 BBL

7. Remove the tachometer, connect the canister vacuum line and shut off the engine.

2 BBL and 4 BBL (ALL BUT V8-350)

1. Run the engine to normal operating temperature.
2. Make sure that the choke is fully opened, turn the A/C Off, set the parking brake, block the drive wheels and connect a tachometer to the engine according to the manufacturer's instructions.
3. Disconnect and plug the vacuum hoses at the EGR valve and the vapor canister.
4. Place the transmission in Park (AT) or Neutral (MT).
5. Disconnect and plug the vacuum advance hose at the distributor. Check and adjust the timing.
6. Connect the distributor vacuum line.
7. Manual transmission cars without A/C and without solenoid: place the idle speed screw on the low step of the fast idle cam and turn the screw to achieve the specified idle speed.

Cars with A/C: set the idle speed screw to the specified rpm. Disconnect the compressor clutch wire and turn the A/C On. Open the throttle momentarily to extend the solenoid plunger. Turn the solenoid screw to obtain the specified rpm.

A/C IDLE SPEED ADJUSTMENT (ON VEHICLE)

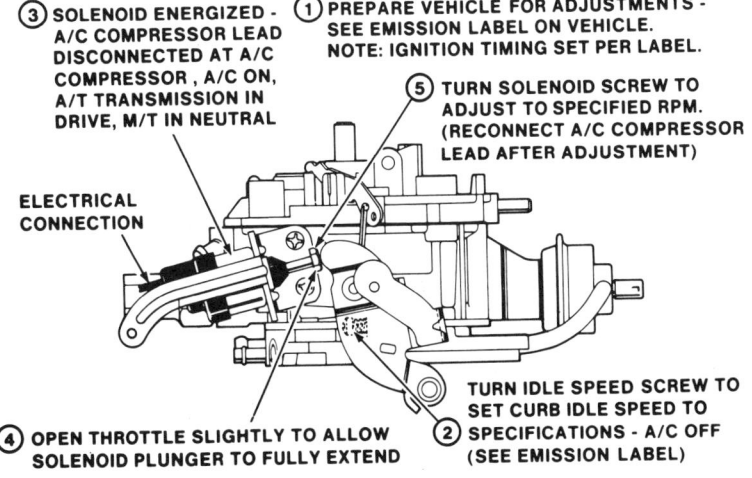

Idle speed adjustment without solenoid—1980 2 BBL

Automatic transmission cars without A/C; manual transmission cars without A/C, solenoid-equipped carburetor: mementarily open the throttle to extend the solenoid plunger. Turn the solenoid screw to obtain the specified rpm. Disconnect the solenoid wire and turn the idle speed screw to obtain the slow engine idle speed.

V8-350

1. Run the engine to normal operating temperature.
2. Set the parking brake and block the drive wheels.
3. Connect a tachometer to the engine according to the manufacturer's instructions.
4. Disconnect and plug the purge hose at the vapor canister. Disconnect and plug the EGR vacuum hose at the EGR valve.
5. Turn the A/C Off.
6. Place the transmission in Park (AT) or Neutral (MT).
7. Disconnect and plug the vacuum advance line at the distributor. Check and adjust the timing.
8. Connect the vacuum advance line. Place the automatic transmission in Drive.
9. Manual transmission cars without A/C: adjust the idle stop screw to obtain the specified rpm. Cars with A/C: with the A/C off, adjust the idle stop screw to obtain the specified rpm. Disconnect the compressor clutch wire and turn the A/C on. Open the throttle slightly to allow the solenoid plunger to extend. Turn the solenoid screw to obtain the solenoid rpm listed on the underhood emission sticker.
10. Connect all hoses and remove the tachometer.

Engine and Engine Rebuilding

UNDERSTANDING THE ENGINE ELECTRICAL SYSTEM

The engine electrical system can be broken down into three separate and distinct systems—(1) the starting system; (2) the charging system; (3) the ignition system.

Battery and Starting System

The battery is the first link in the chain of mechanisms which work together to provide cranking of the automobile engine. In most modern cars, the battery is a lead-acid electrochemical device consisting of six two-volt (2 V) subsections connected in series so the unit is capable of producing approximately 12 V of electrical pressure. Each subsection, or cell, consists of a series of positive and negative plates held a short distance apart in a solution of sulfuric acid and water. The two types of plates are of dissimilar metals. This causes a chemical reaction to be set up, and it is this reaction which produces current flow from the battery when its positive and negative terminals are connected to an electrical appliance such as a lamp or motor. The continued transfer of electrons would eventually convert the sulfuric acid in the electrolyte to water, and make the two plates identical in chemical composition. As electrical energy is removed from the battery, its voltage output tends to drop. Thus, measuring battery voltage and battery electrolyte composition are two ways of checking the ability of the unit to supply power. During the starting of the engine, electrical energy is removed from the battery. However, if the charging circuit is in good condition and the operating conditions are normal, the power removed from the battery will be replaced by the generator (or alternator) which will force electrons back through the battery, reversing the normal flow, and restoring the battery to its original chemical state.

The battery and starting motor are linked by very heavy electrical cables designed to minimize resistance to the flow of current. Generally, the major power supply cable that leaves the battery goes directly to the starter, while other electrical system needs are supplied by a smaller cable. During the starter operation, power flows from the battery to the starter and is grounded through the car's frame and the battery's negative ground strap.

The starting motor is a specially designed, direct current electric motor capable of producing a very great amount of power for its size. One thing that allows the motor to produce a great deal of power is its tremendous rotating speed. It drives the engine through a tiny pinion gear (attached to the starter's armature), which drives the very large flywheel ring gear at a greatly reduces speed. Another factor allowing it to produce so much power is that only intermittent operation is required of it. Thus, little allowance for air circulation is required, and the windings can be built into a very small space.

The starter solenoid is a magnetic device which employs the small current supplied by the starting switch circuit of the ignition switch. This magnetic action moves a plunger which mechanically engages the starter and electrically closes the heavy switch which connects it to the battery. The starting switch circuit consists of the starting switch contained within the ignition switch, a transmission neutral safety switch or clutch pedal switch, and the wiring necessary to connect these with the starter solenoid or relay.

A pinion, which is a small gear, is mounted to a one-way drive clutch. This clutch is splined to the starter armature shaft. When the ignition switch is moved to the "start" position, the solenoid plunger slides the pinion toward the flywheel ring gear via a collar and spring. If the teeth on the pinion and flywheel match properly, the pinion will engage the flywheel immediately. If the gear teeth butt one another, the spring will be compressed and will force the gears to mesh as soon as the starter turns far enough to allow them to do so. As the solenoid plunger reaches the end of its travel, it closes the contacts that connect the battery and starter and then the engine is cranked.

As soon as the engine starts, the flywheel ring gear begins turning fast enough to drive the pinion at an extremely high rate of speed. At this point, the one-way clutch begins allowing the pinion to spin faster than the starter shaft so that the starter will not operate at excessive speed. When the ignition switch is released from the starter position, the solenoid is de-energized, and a spring contained within the solenoid assembly pulls the gear out of mesh and interrupts the current flow to the starter.

Some starters employ a separate relay, mounted away from the starter, to switch the motor and solenoid current on and off. The relay thus replaces the solenoid electrical switch, but does not eliminate the need for a solenoid mounted on the starter used to mechanically engage the starter drive gears. The relay is used to reduce the amount of current the starting switch must carry.

The Charging System

The automobile charging system provides electrical power for operation of the vehicle's ignition and starting systems and all the electrical accessories. The battery serves as an electrical surge or storage tank, storing (in chemical form) the energy originally produced by the engine-driven generator. The system also provides a means of regulating generator output to protect the battery from being overcharged and to avoid excessive voltage to the accessories.

The storage battery is a chemical device incorporating parallel lead plates in a tank containing a sulfuric acid-water solution. Adjacent plates are slightly dissimilar, and the chemical reaction of the two dissimilar plates produces electrical energy when the battery is connected to a load such as the starter motor. The chemical reaction is reversible, so that when the generator is producing a voltage (electrical pressure) greater than that produced by the battery, electricity is forced into the battery, and the battery is returned to its fully charged state.

The vehicle's generator is driven mechanically, through V belts, by the engine crankshaft. It consists of two coils of fine wire, one stationary (the "stator"), and one movable (the "rotor"). The rotor may also be known as the "armature," and consists of fine wire wrapped around an iron core which is mounted on a shaft. The electricity which flows through the two coils of wire (provided initially by the battery in some cases) creates an intense magnetic field around both rotor and stator, and the interaction between the two fields creates voltage, allowing the generator to power the accessories and charge the battery.

There are two types of generators; the earlier is the direct current (DC) type. The current produced by the DC generator is generated in the armature and carried off the spinning armature by stationary brushes contacting the commutator. The commutator is a series of smoooth metal contact plates on the end of the armature. The commutator plates, which are separated from one another by a very short gap, are connected to the armature circuits so that current will flow in one direction only in the wires carrying the generator output. The generator stator consists of two stationary coils of wire which draw some of the output current of the generator to form a powerful magnetic field and

ENGINE AND ENGINE REBUILDING 85

create the interaction of fields which generates the voltage. The generator field is wired in series with the regulator.

Newer automobiles use alternating current generators or "alternators" because they are more efficient, can be rotated at higher speeds, and have fewer brush problems. In an alternator, the field rotates while all the current produced passes only through the stator windings. The brushes bear against continuous slip rings rather than a commutator. This causes the current produced to periodically reverse the direction of its flow. Diodes (electrical one-way switches) block the flow of current from traveling in the wrong direction. A series of diodes is wired together to permit the alternating flow of the stator to be converted to a pulsating, but unidirectional flow at the alternator output. The alternator's field is wired in series with the voltage regulator.

The regulator consists of several circuits. Each circuit had a core, or magnetic coil of wire, which operates a switch. Each switch is connected to ground through one or more resistors. The coil of wire responds directly to system voltage. When the voltage reaches the required level, the magnetic field created by the winding of wire closes the switch and inserts a resistance into the generator field circuit, thus reducing the output. The contacts of the switch cycle open and close many times each second to precisely control voltage.

While alternators are self-limiting as far as maximum current is concerned, DC generators employ a current regulating circuit which responds directly to the total amount of current flowing through the generator circuit rather than to the output voltage. The current regulator is similar to the voltage regulator except that all system current must flow through the energizing coil on its way to the various accessories.

SAFETY PRECAUTIONS

Observing these precautions will ensure safe handling of the electrical system components, and will avoid damage to the vehicle's electrical system:

A. Be *absolutely* sure of the polarity of a booster battery before making connections. Connect the cables positive to positive, and negative to negative. Connect positive cables first and then make the last connection to a ground on the body of the booster vehicle so that arcing cannot ignite hydrogen gas that may have accumulated near the battery. Even momentary connection of a booster battery with the polarity reserved will damage alternator diodes.

B. Disconnect both vehicle battery cables before attempting to charge a battery.

C. Never ground the alternator or generator output or battery terminal. Be cautious when using metal tools around a battery to avoid creating a short circuit between the terminals.

D. Never ground the field circuit between the alternator and regulator.

E. Never run an alternator or generator without load unless the field circuit is disconnected.

F. Never attempt to polarize an alternator.

G. Keep the regulator cover in place when taking voltage and current limiter readings.

H. Use insulated tools when adjusting the regulator.

I. Whenever DC generator-to-regulator wires have been disconnected, the generator *must* be repolarized. To do this with an externally grounded, light duty generator, momentarily place a jumper wire between the battery terminal and the generator terminal of the regulator. With an internally grounded heavy duty unit, disconnect the wire to the regulator field terminal and touch the regulator battery terminal with it.

ENGINE ELECTRICAL

High Energy Ignition (HEI) Distributor

The Delco-Remy High Energy Ignition (HEI) System is a breakerless, pulse triggered, transistor controlled, inductive discharge ignition system available as an option in 1974 and standard in 1975.

There are only nine external electrical connections; the ignition switch feed wire, and the eight spark plug leads. On eight cylinder models through 1977, and all 1978 and later models, the ignition coil is located with the distributor cap, connecting directly to the rotor.

The magnetic pick-up assembly located inside the distributor contains a permanent magnet, a pole piece with internal teeth, and a pick-up coil. When the teeth of the rotating

ENGINE AND ENGINE REBUILDING

timer core and pole piece align, an induced voltage in the pick-up coil signals the electronic module to open the coil primary circuit. As the primary current decreases, a high voltage is induced in the secondary windings of the ignition coil, directing a spark through the rotor and high voltage leads to fire the spark plugs. The dwell period is automatically controlled by the electronic module and is increased with increasing engine rpm. The HEI System features a longer spark duration which is instrumental in firing lean and EGR diluted fuel/air mixtures. The condenser (capacitor) located within the HEI distributor is provided for noise (static) suppression purposes only and is not a regularly replaced ignition system component.

As already noted in Chapter 2, 1981 Camaros continue to use the HEI distributor although it now incorporates an Electronic Spark Timing System (for more information on EST, please refer to Chapter 4). With the new EST system, all spark timing changes are performed electronically by the Electronic Control Module (ECM) which moniters information from various engine sensors, computes the desired spark timing and then signals the distributor to change the timing accordingly. Because all timing changes are controlled electronically, no vacuum or mechanical advance systems are used whatsoever.

Distributor

REMOVAL AND INSTALLATION

Points-Type Ignition 1967-74

1. Remove the distributor cap and position it out of the way.
2. Disconnect the primary coil wire and the vacuum advance hose.
3. Scribe a mark on the distributor body and the engine block showing their relationship. Mark the distributor housing to show the direction in which the rotor is pointing. Note the positioning of the vacuum advance unit.
4. Remove the hold-down bolt and clamp and remove the distributor.

To install the distributor with the engine undisturbed:

5. Reinsert the distributor into its opening, aligning the previously made marks on the housing and the engine block.
6. The rotor may have to be turned either way a slight amount to align the rotor-to-housing marks.
7. Install the retaining clamp and bolt. Install the distributor cap, primary wire or electrical connector, and the vacuum hose.
8. Start the engine and check the ignition timing.

To install the distributor with the engine disturbed:

9. Turn the engine to bring No. 1 piston to the top of its compression stroke. This may be determined by inserting a rag into the No. 1 spark plug hole and slowly turning the engine over. When the timing mark on the crankshaft pulley aligns with the 0 on the timing scale and the rag is blown out by compression, No. 1 piston is at top-dead-center (TDC).

NOTE: On Mark IV (big block) V8 engines there is a punch mark on the distributor drive gear which indicates the rotor position. Thus, the distributor may be installed with the cap in place. Align the punch mark 2° clockwise from the No. 1 cap terminal, then rotate the distributor body 1/8 turn counterclockwise and push the distributor down into the block.

10. Install the distributor to the engine block so that the vacuum advance unit points in the correct direction.
11. Turn the rotor so that it will point to No. 1 terminal in the cap.
12. Install the distributor into the engine block. It may be necessary to turn the rotor a little in either direction in order to engage the gears.
13. Tap the starter a few times to ensure that the oil pump shaft is mated to the distriburor shaft.
14. Bring the engine to No. 1 TDC again and check to see that the rotor is indeed pointing toward the No. 1 terminal of the cap.
15. After correct positioning is assured, turn the distributor housing so that the points are just opening. Tighten the retaining clamp.
16. Install the cap and primary wire. Check the ignition timing. Install the vacuum hose.

HEI Distributor 1975-81

1. Disconnect the ground cable from the battery.
2. Tag and disconnect the feed and module terminal connectors from the distributor cap.

ENGINE AND ENGINE REBUILDING 87

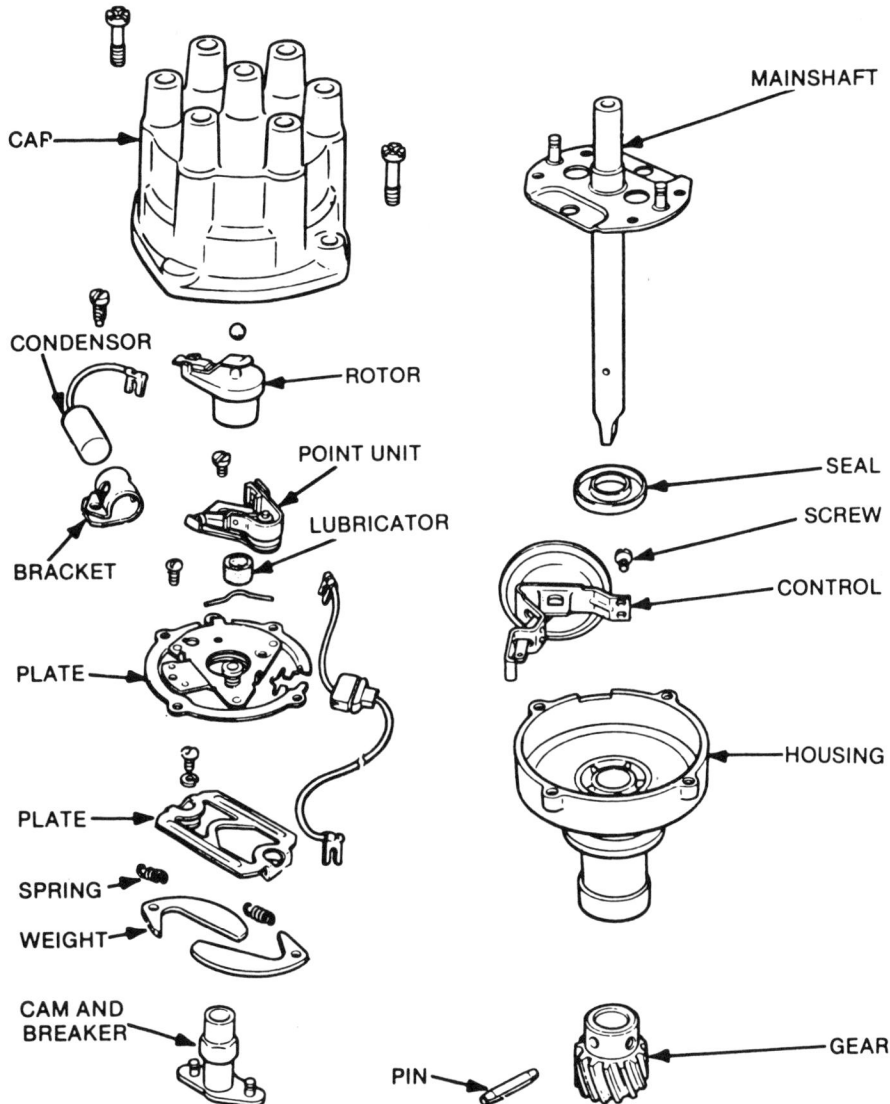

Exploded view of the six cylinder points-type distributor

3. Disconnect the hose at the vacuum advance (1975–80 only).

4. Depress and release the 4 distributor cap-to-housing retainers and lift off the cap assembly.

5. Using crayon or chalk, make locating marks on the rotor and module and on the distributor housing and engine for installation purposes.

6. Loosen and remove the distributor clamp bolt and clamp, and lift distributor out of the engine. Noting the relative position of the rotor and module alignment marks, make a second mark on the rotor to align it with the one mark on the module.

7. With a new O-ring on the distributor housing and the second mark on the rotor aligned with the mark on the module, install the distributor, taking care to align the mark on the housing with the one on the engine. It may be necessary to lift the distributor and turn the rotor slightly to align the gears and the oil pump driveshaft.

8. With the respective marks aligned, install the clamp and bolt finger-tight.

9. Install and secure the distributor cap.

10. Connect the feed and module connectors to the distributor cap.

11. Connect a timing light to the engine and plug the vacuum hose.

12. Connect the ground cable to the battery.

88 ENGINE AND ENGINE REBUILDING

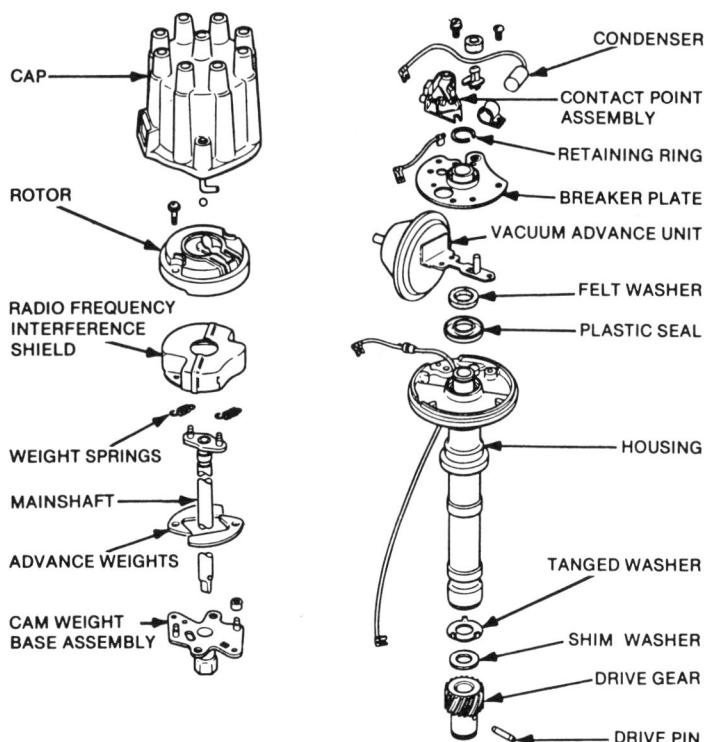

Exploded view of the V8 points-type distributor

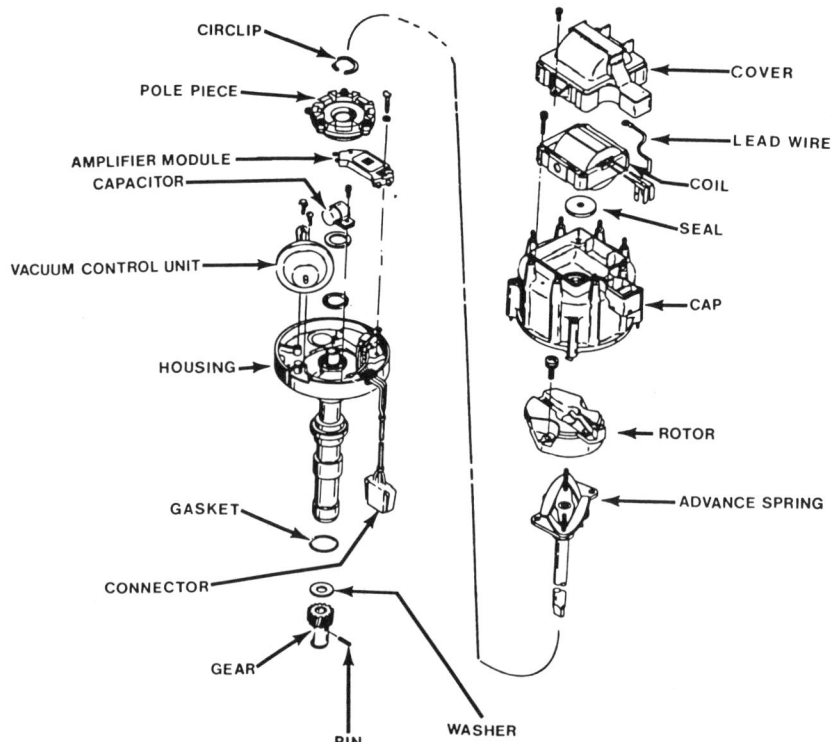

Exploded view of the HEI distributor (1981 models have no vacuum advance unit)

ENGINE AND ENGINE REBUILDING 89

13. Start the engine and set the timing.
14. Turn the engine off and tighten the distributor clamp bolt. Disconnect the timing light and unplug and connect the hose to the vacuum advance.

Firing Order

To avoid confusion, replace spark plug wires one at a time.

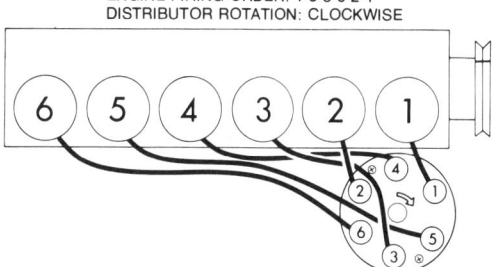

1967–79 six cylinder firing order

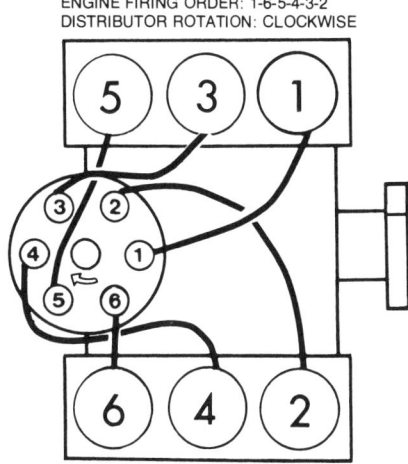

1980–81 229 V6 firing order

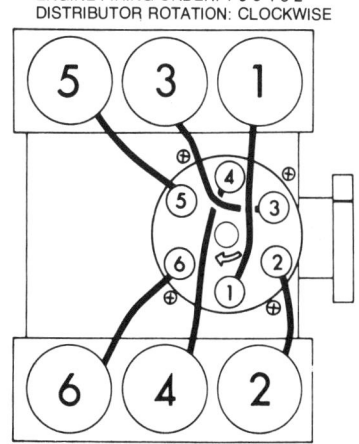

1980–81 231 V6 firing order

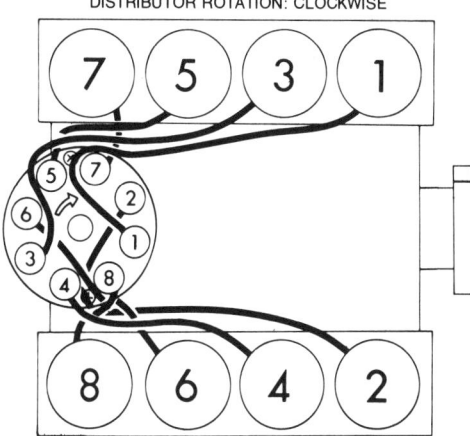

1967–74 V8 firing order

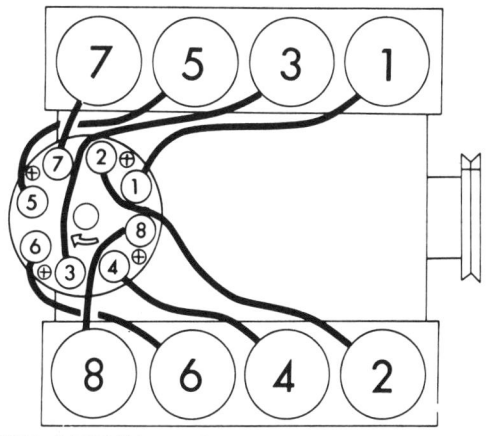

1975–81 V8 firing order

Alternator

The alternating current generator (alternator) supplies a continuous output of electrical energy at all engine speeds. The alternator generates electrical energy and recharges the battery by supplying it with electrical current. This unit consists of four main assemblies: two end frame assemblies, a rotor assembly, and a stator assembly. The rotor assembly is supported in the drive end frame by a ball bearing and at the other end by a roller bearing. These bearings are lubricated during assembly and require no maintenance. There are six diodes in the end frame assembly. These diodes are electrical check valves that also change the alternating current developed within the stator windings to a direct (DC) current at the output (BAT) terminal. Three of these diodes are negative and are mounted flush with the end frame while

90 ENGINE AND ENGINE REBUILDING

the other three are positive and are mounted into a strip called a heat sink. The positive diodes are easily identified as the ones within small cavities or depressions.

ALTERNATOR PRECAUTIONS

To prevent serious damage to the alternator and the rest of the charging system, the following precautions must be observed:

1. When installing a battery, make sure that the positive cable is connected to the positive terminal and the negative to the negative.

2. When jump-starting the car with another battery, make sure that like terminals are connected. This also applies when using a battery charger.

3. Never operate the alternator with the

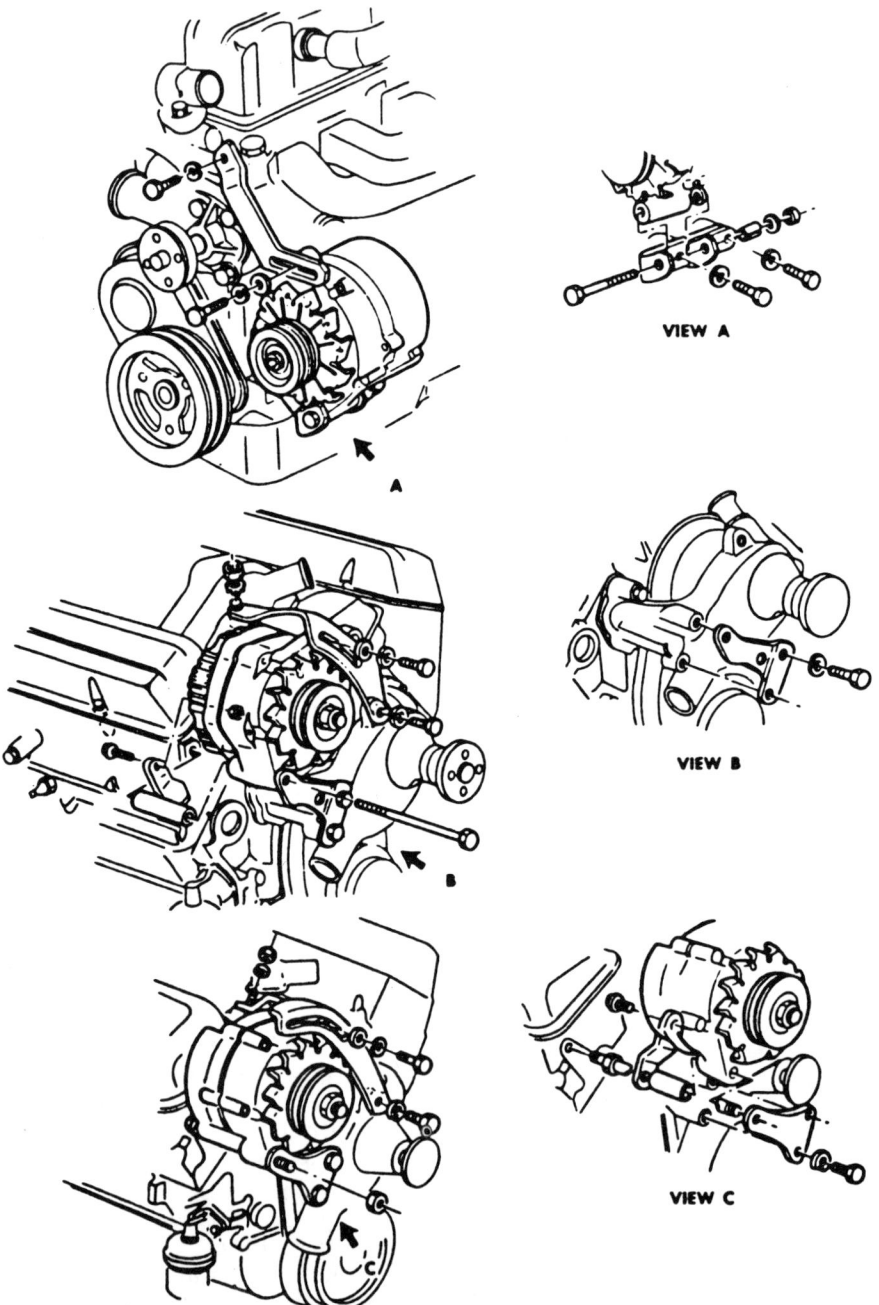

Typical alternator mounting—inline six cylinder (top), V6 and small-block V8 (center) and big-block V8 (bottom)

ENGINE AND ENGINE REBUILDING

battery disconnected or otherwise on an uncontrolled open circuit. Double-check to see that all connections are tight.

4. Do not short across or ground any alternator or regulator terminals.

5. Do not try to polarize the alternator.

6. Do not apply full battery voltage to the field (brown) connector.

7. Always disconnect the battery ground cable before disconnecting the alternator lead.

REMOVAL

1. Disconnect the battery ground cable to prevent diode damage.
2. Tag and disconnect the alternator wiring.
3. Remove the alternator brace bolt. If the car is equipped with power steering, loosen the pump brace and mount nuts. Detach the drive belt(s).
4. Support the alternator and remove the mount bolt(s). Remove the unit from the vehicle.

INSTALLATION AND BELT ADJUSTMENT

To install, reverse the above removal procedure. Alternator belt tension is quite critical. A belt that is too tight may cause alternator bearing failure; one that is too loose will cause a gradual battery discharge. For details on correct belt adjustment, see "Drive Belts" in Chapter one.

Regulator

The voltage regulator combines with the battery and alternator to comprise the charging system. Just as the name implies, the voltage regulator regulates the alternator voltage output to a safe amount. A properly working regulator prevents excessive voltage from burning out wiring, bulbs, or contact points,

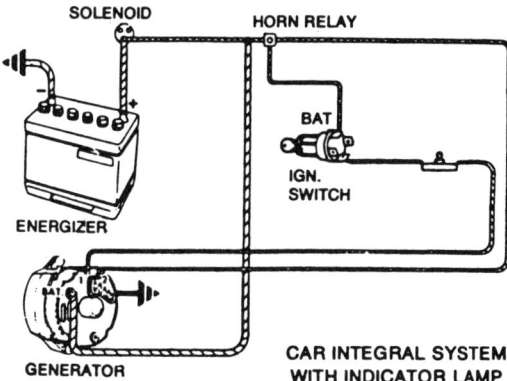

Integral voltage regulator charging system schematic

and prevents overcharging of the battery. Mechanical adjustments (air gap, point opening) must be followed by electrical adjustments and not vice versa.

Since 1973 all GM cars have been equipped with alternators which have built-in solid state voltage regulators. The regulator is in the end frame (inside) of the alternator and requires no adjustment. The following adjustments apply only to pre-1973 units.

NOTE: *Some 1973 Camaros were built using a 1972 type alternator with an external voltage regulator. Cars with serial numbers after N146488 (V8) and N154788 (six-cylinder) are affected. On these cars, check the voltage regulator as you would on a 1972 or earlier model.*

REMOVAL AND INSTALLATION

1. Disconnect the battery ground cable.
2. Disconnect the wiring harness from the regulator.
3. Remove the mounting screws and remove the regulator.
4. Make sure that the regulator base basket is in place before installation.
5. Clean the attaching area for proper grounding.
6. Install the regulator. Do not overtighten the mounting screws, as this will cancel the cushioning effect of the rubber grommets.

ADJUSTMENT—1967-72

Field Relay Adjustments (Mechanical Adjustment)

As explained earlier, mechanical adjustments must be made first and then followed by electrical adjustments.

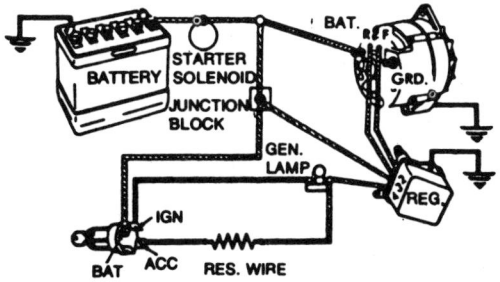

Non-integral voltage regulator charging system schematic

92 ENGINE AND ENGINE REBUILDING

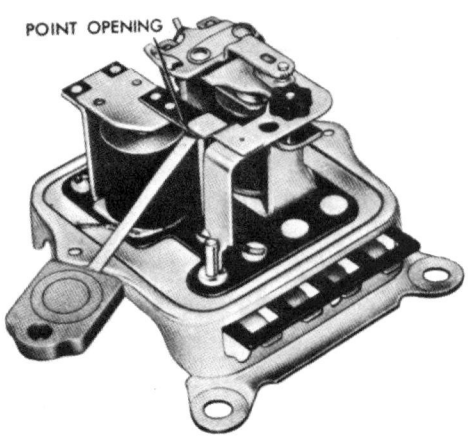

Checking the field relay point opening

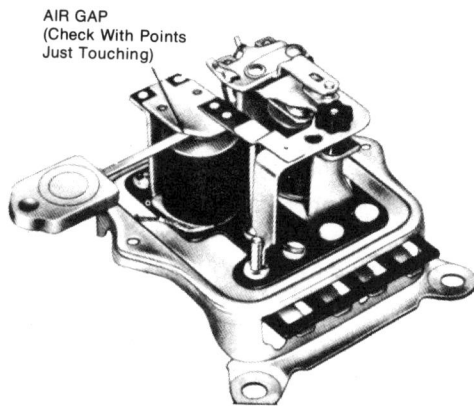

Checking the air gap on the field relay

Point Opening

Using a feeler gauge, check the point opening as illustrated. To change the opening, carefully bend the armature stop. The point opening for all Camaro regulators should be 0.014 in.

Air Gap

Check the air gap with the points just touching. The gap should be 0.067 in. If the point opening setting is correct, then the relay will operate OK even if the air gap is off. To adjust air gap, bend the flat contact spring.

Voltage Adjustment (Electrical Adjustment)

1. Connect a ¼ ohm 25 watt fixed resistor (a knife blade switch using a ¼ ohm resistor) into the charging circuit (as illustrated) at the battery positive terminal. One end of the resistor connects to the battery positive terminal while the other connects to the voltmeter.

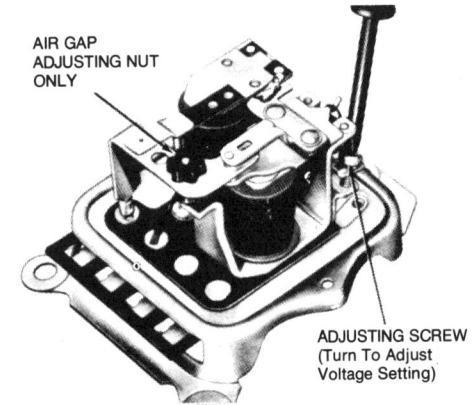

Voltage setting adjustment

2. Operate the engine at 1,500 rpm or more for at least 15 minutes. Disconnect and reconnect the regulator connector and read the voltage on the voltmeter. If the regulator is functioning properly, the reading should be 13.5–15.2V. If the reading is not within this range, keep the engine running at 1,500 rpm and do the following:

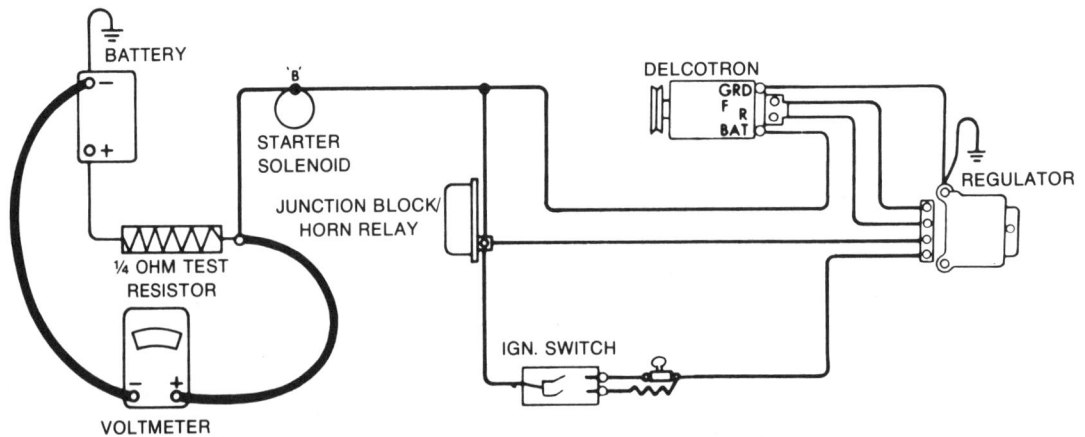

Schematic for testing the regulator voltage setting

ENGINE AND ENGINE REBUILDING

Alternator and Regulator Specifications

	Alternator			Regulator					
				Field Relay			Regulator		
Year	Part No. or Manufacturer	Field Current @ 12 V	Output (amps)	Air Gap (in.)	Point Gap (in.)	Volts to Close	Air Gap (in.)	Point Gap (in.)	Volts @ 75°
1967	1100693	2.2–2.6	37	0.015	0.030	2.3–3.7	0.067	0.014	13.5–14.4
	1100695	2.2–2.6	32	0.015	0.030	2.3–3.7	0.067	0.014	13.5–14.4
	1100794	2.2–2.6	37	0.015	0.030	2.3–3.7	0.067	0.014	13.5–14.4
1968	1100813	2.2–2.6	37	0.015	0.030	2.3–3.7	0.067	0.014	13.5–14.4
	1100693	2.2–2.6	37	0.015	0.030	2.3–3.7	0.067	0.014	13.5–14.4
1969	1100834	2.2–2.6	37	0.015	0.030	2.3–3.7	0.067	0.014	13.5–14.4
	1100836	2.2–2.6	37	0.015	0.030	2.3–3.7	0.067	0.014	13.5–14.4
1970	1100834	2.2–2.6	37	0.015	0.030	2.3–3.7	0.067	0.014	13.5–14.4
	1100837	2.2–2.6	37	0.015	0.030	2.3–3.7	0.067	0.014	13.5–14.4
1971	1100838	2.2–2.6	37	0.015	0.030	2.3–3.7	0.067	0.014	13.5–14.4
	1100839	2.2–2.6	37	0.015	0.030	2.3–3.7	0.067	0.014	13.5–14.4
1972	1100566	2.2–2.6	35	0.015	0.030	1.5–3.2	0.067	0.014	13.8–14.8
	1100917	2.8–3.2	59	0.030	0.030	1.5–3.2	0.067	0.014	13.8–14.8
	1100843	2.8–3.2	58	Integrated with alternator					13.8–14.8
1973	1100497	2.8–3.2	36	Integrated with alternator					13.8–14.8
	1100934	2.8–3.2	37	Integrated with alternator					13.8–14.8
	1102354	4–4.5	63	Integrated with alternator					13.8–14.8
	1100573	4–4.5	42	Integrated with alternator					13.8–14.8
	1100597	4–4.5	61	Integrated with alternator					13.8–14.8
1974	1100934	4–4.5	37	Integrated with alternator					13.8–14.8
	1102347	4–4.5	61	Integrated with alternator					13.8–14.8
	1100497	4–4.5	37	Integrated with alternator					13.8–14.8
	1100573	4–4.5	42	Integrated with alternator					13.8–14.8

ENGINE AND ENGINE REBUILDING

Alternator and Regulator Specifications (cont.)

Year	Alternator Part No. or Manufacturer	Alternator Field Current @ 12 V	Alternator Output (amps)	Regulator — Field Relay Air Gap (in.)	Regulator — Field Relay Point Gap (in.)	Regulator — Field Relay Volts to Close	Regulator — Regulator Air Gap (in.)	Regulator — Regulator Point Gap (in.)	Regulator — Regulator Volts @ 75°
	1100597	4–4.5	61	Integrated with alternator					13.8–14.8
	1100560	4–4.5	55	Integrated with alternator					13.8–14.8
1975	1100497	4–4.5	37	Integrated with alternator					13.8–14.8
	1102397	4–4.5	37	Integrated with alternator					13.8–14.8
	1102483	4–4.5	37	Integrated with alternator					13.8–14.8
	1100597	4–4.5	61	Integrated with alternator					13.8–14.8
	1102347	4–4.5	61	Integrated with alternator					13.8–14.8
1976	1102941	4–4.5	37	Integrated with alternator					13.8–14.8
	1102394	4–4.5	37	Integrated with alternator					13.8–14.8
1977	1102491	4–4.5	37	Integrated with alternator					13.8–14.8
	1102480	4–4.5	61	Integrated with alternator					13.8–14.8
	1102486	4–4.5	61	Integrated with alternator					13.8–14.8
	1102394	4–4.5	37	Integrated with alternator					13.8–14.8
1978	1102491	4–4.5	37	Integrated with alternator					13.8–14.8
	1102480	4–4.5	61	Integrated with alternator					13.8–14.8
	1102481	4–4.5	61	Integrated with alternator					13.8–14.8
	1102394	4–4.5	37	Integrated with alternator					13.8–14.8
1979	1102491	4–4.5	37	Integrated with alternator					13.8–14.8
	1102394	4–4.5	37	Integrated with alternator					13.8–14.8
	1102480	4–4.5	61	Integrated with alternator					13.8–14.8
	1102486	4–4.5	61	Integrated with alternator					13.8–14.8
1980–81	1103161	4–4.5	37	Integrated with alternator					13.8–14.8
	1103118	4–4.5	37	Integrated with alternator					13.8–14.8

ENGINE AND ENGINE REBUILDING

Alternator and Regulator Specifications (cont.)

Year	Alternator Part No. or Manufacturer	Alternator Field Current @ 12 V	Alternator Output (amps)	Field Relay Air Gap (in.)	Field Relay Point Gap (in.)	Field Relay Volts to Close	Regulator Air Gap (in.)	Regulator Point Gap (in.)	Regulator Volts @ 75°
1980–81	1103043	4–4.5	42		Integrated with alternator				13.8–14.8
	1103162	4–45	37		Integrated with alternator				13.8–14.8
	1103092	4–4.5	55		Integrated with alternator				13.8–14.8
	1103088	4–4.5	55		Integrated with alternator				13.8–14.8
	1103085	4–4.5	55		Integrated with alternator				13.8–14.8
	1103044	4–4.5	63		Integrated with alternator				13.8–14.8
	1103091	4–4.5	63		Integrated with alternator				13.8–14.8
	1103169	4–4.5	63		Integrated with alternator				13.8–14.8
	1101044	4–4.5	70		Integrated with alternator				13.8–14.8
	1101071	4–4.5	70		Integrated with alternator				13.8–14.8

a. Disconnect the terminal connector (four terminal connector) and remove the regulator cover. Reconnect the connector and adjust the voltage to 14.2–14.6 by turning the adjusting screw.

CAUTION: *When removing the regulator cover ALWAYS disconnect the connector first to prevent regulator damage by short circuits.*

b. Disconnect the connector, install the cover, and reconnect the connector.

c. Increase the regulator temperature by running the engine at 1,500 rpm for 10 more minutes.

d. Disconnect and reconnect the connector and read the voltmeter. A reading of 13.5–15.2 indicates a good regulator.

Starter

REMOVAL AND INSTALLATION

1. Disconnect the battery cable.
2. Raise the car to a convenient working height.
3. Disconnect all wiring from the starter solenoid. Replace each nut as the connector is removed, as thread sizes differ from connector to connector. Note or tag the wiring positions for installation.
4. Remove the front bracket from the starter and the two mounting bolts. On engines with a solenoid heat shield, remove the front bracket upper bolt and detach the bracket from the starter.

Chilton Time Saver

Starter removal on certain models may necessitate the removal of the frame support. This support runs from the corner of the frame to the front crossmember. To remove:
1. Loosen the mounting bolt that attaches the support to the corner of the frame.
2. Loosen and remove the mounting bolt that attaches the support to the front crossmember and then swing the support out of the way.
3. Installation is in the reverse order of removal.

5. Remove the front bracket bolt or nut. Lower the starter front end first, and then remove the unit from the car.
6. Reverse the removal procedures to install the starter. Torque the two mounting bolts to 25–35 ft. lbs.

96 ENGINE AND ENGINE REBUILDING

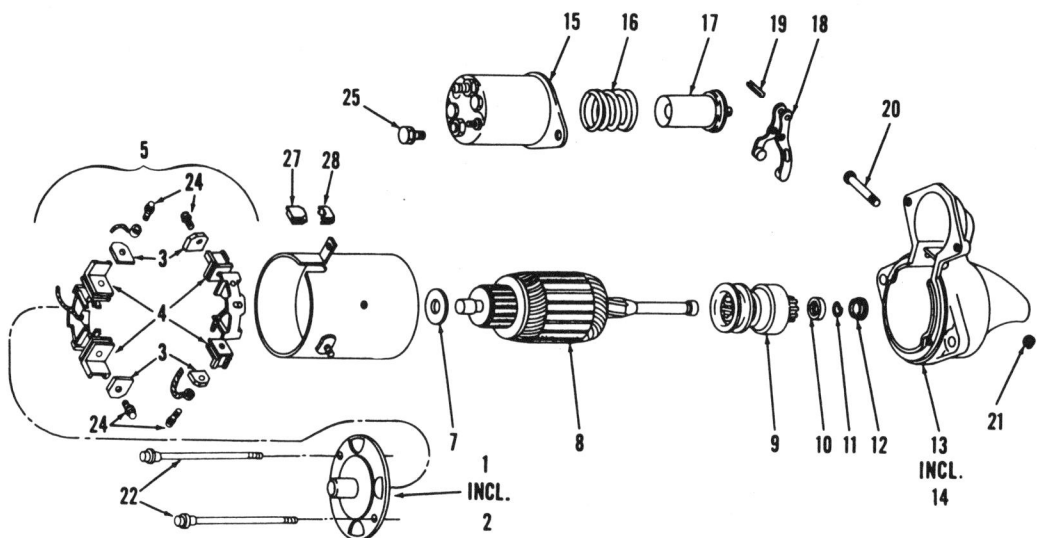

1. Frame—commutator end
2. Brush and holder pkg.
3. Brush
4. Brush holder
5. Housing—drive end
6. Frame and field asm.
7. Solenoid switch
8. Armature
9. Drive asm.
10. Plunger
11. Shift lever
12. Plunger return springer
13. Shift lever shaft
14. Lock washer
15. Screw—brush attaching
16. Screw—field lead to switch
17. Screw—switch attaching
18. Washer—brake
19. Thru bolt
20. Bushing—commutator end
21. Bushing—drive end
22. Pinion stop collar
23. Thrust collar
24. Grommet
25. Grommet
26. Plunger pin
27. Pinion stop retainer ring
28. Lever shaft retaining ring

Exploded view of the starter

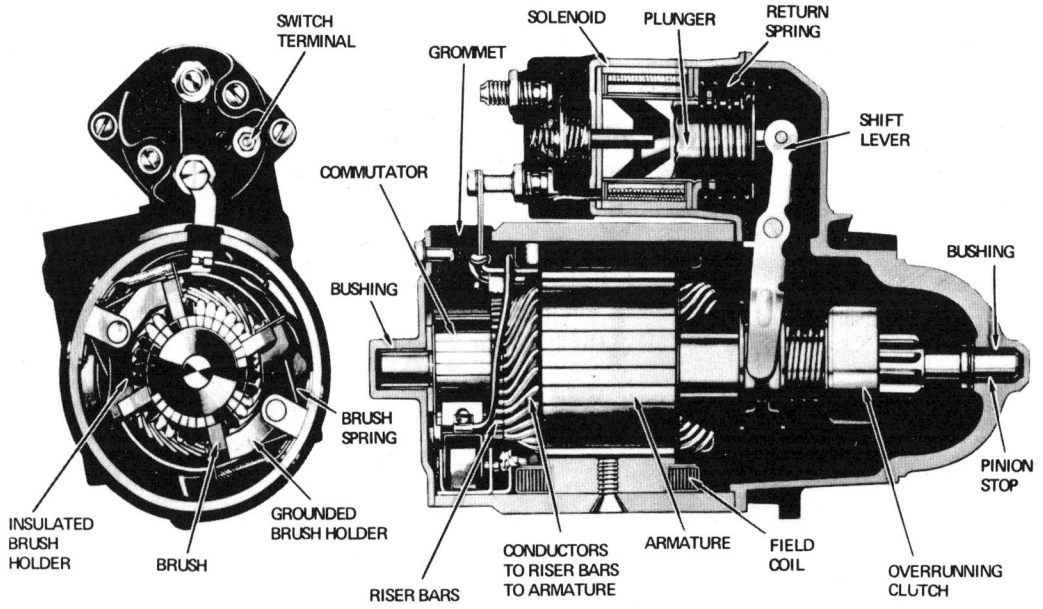

Cross section of a typical starter

ENGINE AND ENGINE REBUILDING

STARTER OVERHAUL
Drive Replacement

1. Disconnect the field coil straps from the solenoid.
2. Remove the through bolts, and separate commutator end frame, field frame assembly, drive housing, and armature assembly from each other.
3. Slide the two piece thrust collar off the end of the armature shaft.
4. Slide a suitably sized metal cylinder, such as a standard half-inch pipe coupling, or an old pinion, onto the shaft so that the end of the coupling or pinion butts up against the edge of the pinion retainer.

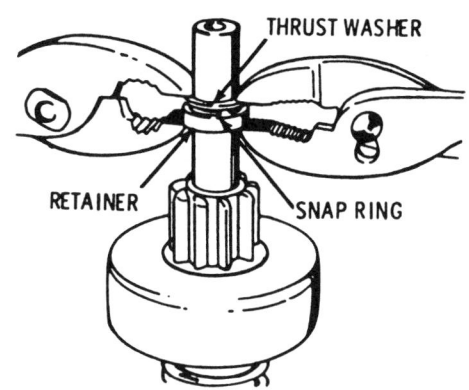

Snap-ring installation

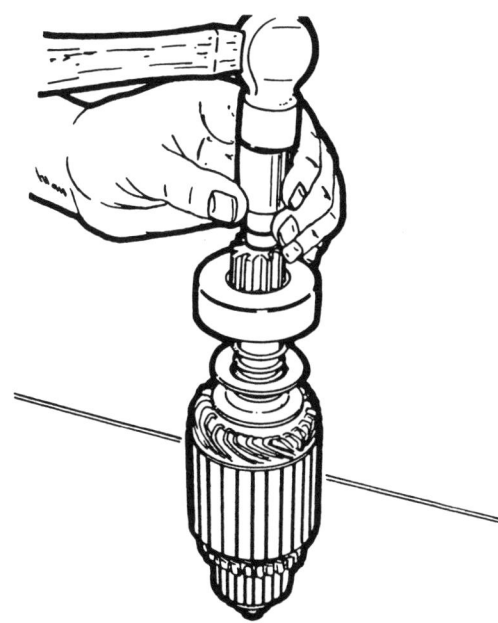

Use a piece of pipe to drive the retainer toward the snap-ring

5. Support the lower end of the armature securely on a soft surface, such as a wooden block, and tap the end of the coupling or pinion, driving the retainer towards the armature end of the snap ring.
6. Remove the snap ring from the groove in the armature shaft with a pair of pliers. Then, slide the retainer and starter drive from the shaft.
7. To reassemble, lubricate the drive end of the armature shaft with silicone lubricant, and then slide the starter drive onto the shaft *with the pinion facing outward*. Slide the retainer onto the shaft *with the cupped surface facing outward*.
8. Again support the armature on a soft surface, with the pinion at the upper end. Center the snap ring on the top of shaft (use a new snap ring if the original was damaged during removal). Gently place a block of wood flat on top of the snap ring so as not to move it from a centered position. Tap the wooden block with a hammer in order to force the snap ring around the shaft. Then, slide the ring down into the snap ring groove.
9. Lay the armature down flat on the surface you're working on. Slide the retainer close up on to the shaft and position it and the thrust collar next to the snap ring. Using two pairs of pliers on opposite sides of the shaft, squeeze the thrust collar and the retainer together until the snap ring is forced into the retainer.
10. Lube the drive housing bushing with a silicone lubricant. Then, install the armature and the clutch assembly into the drive housing, engaging the solenoid shift lever with the clutch, and positioning the front of the armature shaft into the bushing.
11. Apply a sealing compound approved for this application onto the drive housing; then position the field frame around the armature shaft and against the drive housing. *Work slowly and carefully to prevent damaging the starter brushers.*
12. Lubricate the bushing in the commutator end frame with a silicone lubricant, place the leather brake washer onto the armature shaft, and then slide the commutator end frame over the shaft and into position against the field frame. Line up the bolt holes, and then install and tighten the thru-bolts.
13. Reconnect the field coil straps to the "motor" terminal of the solenoid.

NOTE: *If replacement of the starter drive fails to cure improper engagement of starter pinion to flywheel, there are probably defective parts in the solenoid and/or*

ENGINE AND ENGINE REBUILDING

Battery and Starter Specifications

Year	Engine No. Cyl Displacement (cu in.)	Battery Ampere Hour Capacity	Volts	Terminal Grounded	Lock Test Amps	Lock Test Volts	Lock Test Torque (ft. lbs.)	No-Load Test Amps	No-Load Test Volts	No-Load Test RPM	Brush Spring Tension (oz)
1967	6	44	12	Neg	Not Recommended			49–76	10.6	7,800	35
	8—302, 327, 350, 396	61	12	Neg	Not Recommended			65–100	10.6	4,200 ①	35
1968–69	6, 8—307	45	12	Neg	Not Recommended			—	10.6	—	35
	8—302, 327, 350, 396	61	12	Neg	Not Recommended			—	9	—	35
1970–71	6, 8—307	45	12	Neg	Not Recommended			50–80	9	5,500–10,500	35
	8—350	61	12	Neg	Not Recommended			55–80	9	3,500–6,000	35
	8—402(396)	61	12	Neg	Not Recommended			65–95	9	7,500–10,000	35
1972	6	45	12	Neg	Not Recommended			50–80	9	5,500–10,500	35
	8—307	61	12	Neg	Not Recommended			50–80	9	5,500–10,500	35
	8—350, 402	61	12	Neg	Not Recommended			65–95	9	7,500–10,500	35
1973	6—250	45	12	Neg	Not Recommended			50–80	9	5,500–10,500	35
	8—307	61	12	Neg	Not Recommended			50–80	9	5,500–10,500	35
	8—350	76	12	Neg	Not Recommended			65–95	9	7,500–10,500	35
1974	6—250	2300 ②	12	Neg	Not Recommended			50–80	9	5,500–10,500	35
	8—350	2900 ②	12	Neg	Not Recommended			65–95	9	7,500–10,500	35
1975–76	6—250	2500 ②	12	Neg	Not Recommended			50–80	9	5,500–10,500	35
	8—305, 350	3200 ②	12	Neg	Not Recommended			65–95	9	7,500–10,000	35
1977–79	6—250	275 ③	12	Neg	Not Recommended			50–80	9	5,500–10,500	35
	8—305	350 ③	12	Neg	Not Recommended			50–80	9	5,500–10,500	35
	8—350	350 ③	12	Neg	Not Recommended			65–95	9	7,500–10,500	35
1980–81	6—229	350 ③	12	Neg	Not Recommended			50–80	10.6	7,500–11,400	35

Battery and Starter Specifications (cont.)

Year	Engine No. Cyl Displacement (cu in.)	Battery			Starter						Brush Spring Tension (oz)
		Ampere Hour Capacity	Volts	Terminal Grounded	Lock Test			No-Load Test			
					Amps	Volts	Torque (ft. lbs.)	Amps	Volts	RPM	
	6—231	350③	12	Neg	Not Recommended			50–80	10.6	7,500–11,400	35
	8—267	350③	12	Neg	Not Recommended			50–80	10.6	7,500–11,400	35
	8—305	350③	12	Neg	Not Recommended			50–8;	10.6	7,500–11,400	35
	8—350	350③	12	Neg	Not Recommended			65–95	10.6	7,500–10,500	35

① 6—230 and 8—327—9,750
② Cranking power in watts @ 0°F is for 1974–76
③ Cranking power in amps @ 0°F is given for 1977–81

shift lever. The best procedure would probably be to take the assembly to a shop where a pinion clearance check can be made by energizing the solenoid on a test bench. If the pinion clearance is incorrect, disassemble the solenoid and shift lever, inspect, and replace worn parts.

Brush Replacement

1. Disassemble the starter by following Steps 1 and 2 of the "Drive Replacement" procedure above.
2. Replace the brushes one at a time to avoid having to mark wiring. For each brush: remove the brush holding screw; remove the old brush and position the new brush in the same direction (large end toward center of field frame; position wire connector on top of brush, line up holes, and reinstall screw. Make sure screw is snug enough to ensure good contact.
3. Reassemble starter according to Steps 10–13 above.

Solenoid Replacement

1. Remove the screw and washer from the motor connector strap terminal.
2. Remove the two solenoid retaining screws.
3. Twist the solenoid housing clockwise to remove the flange key from the keyway in the housing. Then remove the housing.
4. To re-install the unit, place the return spring on the plunger and place the solenoid body on the drive housing. Turn counterclockwise to engage the flange key. Place the two retaining screws in position and install the screw and washer which secures the strap terminal. Install the unit on the starter.

ENGINE MECHANICAL

Design

All Chevrolet engines, whether inline sixes (L6), V6 or V8, are water-cooled, overhead valve powerplants. All engines use cast iron cylinder blocks and heads.

The crankshaft in the 230 and 250 cu. in. inline six cylinder engines is supported in seven main bearings, with the thrust being taken by the No. 7 bearing. The camshaft is low in the block and driven by the crankshaft gear; no timing chain is used. Relatively long pushrods actuate the valves through ball-jointed rocker arms.

The small-block family of engines, which includes the 283, 305, 307, 327, 350, and 400 cu in. blocks, have all sprung from the basic design of the 1955, 265 cu in. engine. It was this engine that introduced the ball-joint, rocker arm design which is now used by many car makers. This line of engines features a great deal of interchangeability, and later parts may be utilized on earlier engines for increased reliability and/or performance. In 1968, rod and main bearings were increased in size on the small-block family. The 283 was also dropped in that year and replaced by the 307, which is in effect a 327 crankshaft in a 283 block. The 327 and 350 engines share the same cylinder block, with the difference in displacement being pro-

General Engine Specifications

Year	Engine No. Cyl Displacement (cu in.)	Carburetor Type	Horsepower @ rpm ■	Torque @ rpm (ft. lbs.) ■	Bore and Stroke (in.)	Compression Ratio	Oil Pressure @ 1000 rpm
1967	6—230	1 bbl	140 @ 4400	220 @ 1600	3.875 x 3.250	8.5:1	38
	6—250	1 bbl	155 @ 4200	235 @ 1600	3.875 x 3.530	8.5:1	38①
	8—302	4 bbl	290 @ 5800	290 @ 4200	4.000 x 3.000	11.0:1	45
	8—327	2 bbl	210 @ 4600	320 @ 2400	4.001 x 3.250	8.75:1	38①
	8—327	4 bbl	275 @ 4800	355 @ 3200	4.001 x 3.250	10.0:1	38①
	8—350	4 bbl	295 @ 4800	380 @ 3200	4.000 x 3.480	10.25:1	38①
	8—396	4 bbl	325 @ 4800	410 @ 3200	4.094 x 3.760	10.25:1	57
	8—396	4 bbl	350 @ 5200	415 @ 3400	4.094 x 3.760	10.25:1	57
1968	6—230	1 bbl	140 @ 4400	220 @ 1600	3.875 x 3.250	8.5:1	58
	6—250	1 bbl	155 @ 4200	235 @ 1600	3.875 x 3.530	8.5:1	58
	8—302	4 bbl	290 @ 5800	290 @ 4200	4.000 x 3.000	11.0:1	45
	8—327	2 bbl	210 @ 4600	320 @ 2400	4.001 x 3.250	8.75:1	58
	8—327	4 bbl	275 @ 4800	355 @ 3200	4.001 x 3.250	10.0:1	58
	8—350	4 bbl	295 @ 4800	380 @ 3200	4.000 x 3.480	10.25:1	58
	8—396	4 bbl	325 @ 4800	410 @ 3200	4.094 x 3.760	10.25:1	62
	8—396	4 bbl	350 @ 5200	415 @ 3400	4.094 x 3.760	10.25:1	62
	8—396	4 bbl	375 @ 5600	415 @ 3600	4.094 x 3.760	11.0:1	62
1969	6—230	1 bbl	140 @ 4400	220 @ 1600	3.875 x 3.250	8.5:1	58
	6—250	1 bbl	155 @ 4200	235 @ 1600	3.875 x 3.530	8.5:1	58
	8—302	4 bbl	290 @ 5800	290 @ 4200	4.000 x 3.000	11.0:1	45
	8—307	2 bbl	200 @ 4600	300 @ 2400	3.875 x 3.250	9.0:1	58
	8—327	2 bbl	210 @ 4600	320 @ 2400	4.001 x 3.250	9.0:1	58
	8—350	2 bbl	255 @ 4800	345 @ 2800	4.000 x 3.480	9.0:1	62
	8—350	4 bbl	300 @ 4800	380 @ 3200	4.000 x 3.480	10.25:1	62

ENGINE AND ENGINE REBUILDING

General Engine Specifications (cont.)

Year	Engine No. Cyl Displacement (cu in.)	Carburetor Type	Horsepower @ rpm ■	Torque @ rpm (ft. lbs.) ■	Bore and Stroke (in.)	Compression Ratio	Oil Pressure @ 1000 rpm
	8—396	4 bbl	325 @ 4800	410 @ 3200	4.094 x 3.760	10.25:1	62
	8—396	4 bbl	350 @ 5200	415 @ 3400	4.094 x 3.760	10.25:1	62
	8—396	4 bbl	375 @ 5600	415 @ 3600	4.094 x 3.760	11.0:1	62
1970	6—250	1 bbl	155 @ 4200	235 @ 1600	3.875 x 3.530	8.5:1	40
	8—307	2 bbl	200 @ 4600	300 @ 2400	3.875 x 3.250	9.0:1	40
	8—350	2 bbl	250 @ 4800	345 @ 2800	4.000 x 3.480	9.0:1	40
	8—350	4 bbl	300 @ 4800	380 @ 3200	4.000 x 3.480	10.25:1	40
	8—350	4 bbl	360 @ 6000	380 @ 4000	4.000 x 3.480	11.0:1	40
	8—396	4 bbl	350 @ 5200	415 @ 3400	4.126 x 3.760	10.25:1	40
	8—396	4 bbl	375 @ 5600	415 @ 3600	4.126 x 3.760	11.0:1	62
1971	6—250	1 bbl	145 @ 4200	230 @ 1600	3.875 x 3.530	8.5:1	40
	8—307	2 bbl	200 @ 4600	300 @ 2400	3.875 x 3.250	8.5:1	40
	8—350	2 bbl	245 @ 4800	350 @ 2800	4.000 x 3.480	8.5:1	40
	8—350	4 bbl	270 @ 4800	360 @ 3200	4.000 x 3.480	8.5:1	40
	8—350	4 bbl	330 @ 5000	275 @ 5600	4.000 x 3.480	9.0:1	40
	8—402	4 bbl	300 @ 4800	400 @ 3200	4.126 x 3.760	8.5:1	40
1972	6—250	1 bbl	110 @ 3800	185 @ 1600	3.875 x 3.530	8.5:1	40
	8—307	2 bbl	130 @ 4000	230 @ 2400	3.875 x 3.250	8.5:1	40
	8—350	2 bbl	165 @ 4000	280 @ 2400	4.000 x 3.480	8.5:1	40
	8—350	4 bbl	200 @ 4400	300 @ 2800	4.000 x 3.480	8.5:1	40
	8—350	4 bbl	255 @ 5600	280 @ 4000	4.000 x 3.480	9.0:1	40
	8—402	4 bbl	240 @ 4400	345 @ 3200	4.126 x 3.760	8.5:1	40
1973	6—250	1 bbl	100 @ 3800	175 @ 1600	3.875 x 3.530	8.25:1	40
	8—307	2 bbl	115 @ 4000	205 @ 2000	3.875 x 3.250	8.5:1	40

General Engine Specifications (cont.)

Year	Engine No. Cyl Displacement (cu in.)	Carburetor Type	Horsepower @ rpm ■	Torque @ rpm (ft. lbs.) ■	Bore and Stroke (in.)	Compression Ratio	Oil Pressure @ 1000 rpm
	8—350	2 bbl	145 @ 4000	255 @ 2400	4.000 x 3.480	8.5:1	40
	8—350	4 bbl	175 @ 4400	270 @ 2400	4.000 x 3.480	8.5:1	40
	8—350	4 bbl	245 @ 5200	280 @ 4000	4.000 x 3.480	9.0:1	40
1974	6—250	1 bbl	100 @ 3600	175 @ 1800	3.875 x 3.530	8.25:1	40
	8—350②	2 bbl	145 @ 3600	250 @ 2200	4.000 x 3.480	8.5:1	40
	8—350③	4 bbl	160 @ 3800	245 @ 2400	4.000 x 3.480	8.5:1	40
	8—350	4 bbl	185 @ 4000	270 @ 2600	4.000 x 3.480	8.5:1	40
	8—350/Z28	4 bbl	245 @ 5200	280 @ 4000	4.000 x 3.480	9.0:1	40
1975	6—250	1 bbl	105 @ 3800	185 @ 1200	3.875 x 3.530	8.25:1	40
	8—350②	2 bbl	145 @ 3800	250 @ 2200	4.000 x 3.480	8.5:1	40
	8—350	4 bbl	155 @ 3800	245 @ 2400	4.000 x 3.480	8.5:1	40
1976	6—250	1 bbl	105 @ 3800	185 @ 1200	3.875 x 3.530	8.25:1	40
	8—305	2 bbl	140 @ 3800	245 @ 2000	3.736 x 3.480	8.5:1	40
	8—350	4 bbl	165 @ 3800	260 @ 2400	4.000 x 3.480	8.5:1	40
1977	6—250	1 bbl	105 @ 3800	185 @ 1200	3.875 x 3.530	8.25:1	40
	8—305	2 bbl	140 @ 3800	245 @ 2000	3.736 x 3.480	8.5:1	40
	8—350	4 bbl	165 @ 3800	260 @ 2400	4.000 x 3.480	8.5:1	40
1978	6—250	1 bbl	105 @ 3800	185 @ 1200	3.875 x 3.530	8.1:1	40
	8—305	2 bbl	140 @ 3800	245 @ 2000	3.736 x 3.480	8.0:1	40
	8—350	4 bbl	165 @ 3800	260 @ 2400	4.000 x 3.480	8.0:1	40
1979	6—250	1 bbl	115 @ 3800	190 @ 1300	3.875 x 3.530	8.0:1④	40
	8—305	2 bbl	130 @ 3200	230 @ 2000	3.736 x 3.480	8.4:1	45
	8—350	4 bbl	165 @ 3800	260 @ 2400	4.000 x 3.480	8.2:1	45
1980	6—229	2 bbl	115 @ 4000	175 @ 2000	3.736 x 3.480	8.6:1	45

ENGINE AND ENGINE REBUILDING

General Engine Specifications (cont.)

Year	Engine No. Cyl Displacement (cu in.)	Carburetor Type	Horsepower @ rpm ■	Torque @ rpm (ft. lbs.) ■	Bore and Stroke (in.)	Compression Ratio	Oil Pressure @ 1000 rpm
	6—231	2 bbl	110 @ 3800	190 @ 1600	3.800 x 3.400	8.0:1	45
	8—267	2 bbl	120 @ 3600	215 @ 2000	3.500 x 3.480	8.3:1	45
	8—305	4 bbl	155 @ 4000	240 @ 1600	3.736 x 3.480	8.6:1	45
	8—305 CALIF.	4 bbl	155 @ 4000	230 @ 2400	3.736 x 3.480	8.6:1	45
	8—305/Z28	4 bbl	165 @ 4000	245 @ 2400	3.736 x 3.480	8.6:1	45
	8—350	4 bbl	190 @ 4200	280 @ 2400	4.000 x 3.480	8.2:1	45
1981	6—229	2 bbl	110 @ 4200	170 @ 2000	3.736 x 3.480	8.6:1	45
	6—231	2 bbl	110 @ 3800	190 @ 1600	3.800 x 3.400	8.0:1	45
	8—267	2 bbl	115 @ 4000	200 @ 2400	3.500 x 3.480	8.3:1	45
	8—305	4 bbl	150 @ 3800	240 @ 2400	3.736 x 3.480	8.6:1	45
	8—305/Z28	4 bbl	165 @ 4000	245 @ 2400	3.736 x 3.480	8.6:1	45
	8—350	4 bbl	175 @ 4000	275 @ 2400	4.000 x 3.480	8.2:1	45

■ Starting 1972, horsepower and torque are SAE net figures. They are measured at the rear of the transmission with all accessories installed and operating. Since the figures vary when a given engine is installed in different models, some are representative rather than exact.
① Oil pressure at 1500 rpm
② Not available—Calif.
③ Calif. only
④ Calif.
N/A Not available

Valve Specifications

Year	Engine No. Cyl Displacement (cu in.)	Seat Angle (deg)	Face Angle (deg)	Spring Test Pressure (lbs @ in.)	Spring Installed Height (in.)	Stem to Guide Clearance (in.)		Stem Diameter (in.)	
						Intake	Exhaust	Intake	Exhaust
1967	6—230	46③	45	60 @ 1.66	1²¹/₃₂	0.0010–0.0037	0.0015–0.0052	0.3414	0.3414
	6—250	46③	45	60 @ 1.66	1²¹/₃₂	0.0010–0.0047	0.0015–0.0052	0.3414	0.3414
	8—302	46③	45	80 @ 1.70	1⁵/₃₂	0.0010–0.0037	0.0010–0.0047	0.3414	0.3414
	8—327	46③	45	80 @ 1.70	1⁵/₃₂	0.0010–0.0037	0.0010–0.0047	0.3414	0.3414
	8—350	46③	45	80 @ 1.70	1⁵/₃₂	0.0010–0.0037	0.0010–0.0047	0.3414	0.3414

ENGINE AND ENGINE REBUILDING

Valve Specifications (cont.)

Year	Engine No. Cyl Displacement (cu in.)	Seat Angle (deg)	Face Angle (deg)	Spring Test Pressure (lbs @ in.)	Spring Installed Height (in.)	Stem to Guide Clearance (in.) Intake	Stem to Guide Clearance (in.) Exhaust	Stem Diameter (in.) Intake	Stem Diameter (in.) Exhaust
	8—396①	46③	45	90 @ 1.88	1⁷/₈	0.0010–0.0035	0.0012–0.0047	0.3717	0.3717
	8—396②	46③	45	100 @ 1.88	1⁷/₈	0.0010–0.0035	0.0012–0.0047	0.3717	0.3717
1968	6—230	46③	45	59 @ 1.86	1²¹/₃₂	0.0010–0.0037	0.0015–0.0052	0.3414	0.3414
	6—250	46③	45	59 @ 1.86	1²¹/₃₂	0.0010–0.0037	0.0015–0.0052	0.3414	0.3414
	8—302	46③	45	80 @ 1.70	1⁵/₃₂	0.0010–0.0037	0.0010–0.0047	0.3414	0.3414
	8—327	46③	45	80 @ 1.70	1⁵/₃₂	0.0010–0.0037	0.0010–0.0047	0.3414	0.3414
	8—350	46③	45	80 @ 1.70	1⁵/₃₂	0.0010–0.0037	0.0010–0.0047	0.3414	0.3414
	8—396	46③	45	90 @ 1.88	1⁷/₈	0.0010–0.0035	0.0012–0.0047	0.3719	0.3717
1969	6—230	46③	45	59 @ 1.66	1²¹/₃₂	0.0010–0.0037	0.0015–0.0052	0.3414	0.3414
	6—250	46③	45	59 @ 1.66	1²¹/₃₂	0.0010–0.0037	0.0015–0.0052	0.3414	0.3414
	8—302	46③	45	80 @ 1.70	1⁵/₃₂	0.0010–0.0037	0.0010–0.0047	0.3414	0.3414
	8—307	46③	45	80 @ 1.70	1⁵/₃₂	0.0010–0.0037	0.0010–0.0047	0.3414	0.3414
	8—327	46③	45	80 @ 1.70	1⁵/₃₂	0.0010–0.0037	0.0010–0.0047	0.3414	0.3414
	8—350	46③	45	80 @ 1.70	1⁵/₃₂	0.0010–0.0037	0.0010–0.0047	0.3414	0.3414
	8—396①	46③	45	90 @ 1.88	1⁷/₈	0.0010–0.0035	0.0012–2.0047	0.3719	0.3719
	8—396④	46③	45	100 @ 1.88	1⁷/₈	0.0010–0.0035	0.0012–0.0047	0.3719	0.3719
1970	6—250	46③	45	186 @ 1.27	1²¹/₃₂	0.0010–0.0027	0.0015–0.0032	0.3414	0.3414
	8—307	46③	45	200 @ 1.25	1²³/₃₂	0.0010–0.0027	0.0012–0.0029	0.3414	0.3414
	8—350	46③	45	200 @ 1.25	1²³/₃₂	0.0010–0.0027	0.0012–0.0029	0.3414	0.3414
	8—396	46③	45	⑤	1⁷/₈	0.0010–0.0027	0.0012–0.0027	0.3719	0.3717
1971	6—250	46	45	186 @ 1.27	1²¹/₃₂	0.0010–0.0027	0.0015–0.0032	0.3414	0.3414
	8—307	46	45	200 @ 1.25	1²³/₃₂	0.0010–0.0027	0.0012–0.0027	0.3414	0.3414
	8—350	46	45	200 @ 1.25	1²³/₃₂	0.0010–0.0027	0.0012–0.0027	0.3414	0.3414
	8—402	46	45	240 @ 1.38	1⁷/₈	0.0010–0.0027	0.0012–0.0029	0.3719	0.3717

Valve Specifications (cont.)

Year	Engine No. Cyl Displacement (cu in.)	Seat Angle (deg)	Face Angle (deg)	Spring Test Pressure (lbs @ in.)	Spring Installed Height (in.)	Stem to Guide Clearance (in.) Intake	Stem to Guide Clearance (in.) Exhaust	Stem Diameter (in.) Intake	Stem Diameter (in.) Exhaust
1972	6—250	46	45	186 @ 1.27	1 21/32	0.0010–0.0027	0.0015–0.0032	0.3414	0.3414
	8—307	46	45	200 @ 1.25	1 23/32	0.0010–0.0027	0.0010–0.0027	0.3414	0.3414
	8—350	46	45	200 @ 1.25	1 23/32	0.0010–0.0027	0.0010–0.0027	0.3414	0.3414
	8—402	46	45	240 @ 1.38	1 7/8	0.0010–0.0027	0.0012–0.0029	0.3719	0.3717
1973	6—250	46	45	186 @ 1.27	1 21/32	0.0010–0.0027	0.0015–0.0032	0.3414	0.3414
	8—307	46	45	189 @ 1.20	1 5/8 ⑥	0.0010–0.0027	0.0012–0.0027	0.3414	0.3414
	8—350	46	45	200 @ 1.25	1 23/32 ⑥	0.0010–0.0027	0.0012–0.0027	0.3414	0.3414
1974	6—250	46	45	186 @ 1.27	1 21/32	0.0010–0.0027	0.0015–0.0032	0.3414	0.3414
	8—350	46	45	200 @ 1.25	1 23/32 ⑥	0.0010–0.0027	0.0010–0.0027	0.3414	0.3414
1975	6—250	46	45	186 @ 1.27	1 21/32	0.0010–0.0027	0.0015–0.0032	0.3414	0.3414
	8—350	46	45	200 @ 1.25	1 23/32 ⑥	0.0010–0.0027	0.0012–0.0029	0.3414	0.3414
1976	6—250	46	45	175 @ 1.26	1 21/32	0.0010–0.0027	0.0015–0.0032	0.3414	0.3414
	8—305	46	45	200 @ 1.25	1 23/32 ⑥	0.0010–0.0027	0.0010–0.0027	0.3414	0.3414
	8—350	46	45	200 @ 1.25	1 23/32 ⑥	0.0010–0.0027	0.0010–0.0027	0.3414	0.3414
1977	6—250	46	45	175 @ 1.26	1 21/32	0.0010–0.0027	0.0015–0.0032	0.3414	0.3414
	8—305	46	45	200 @ 1.25	1 23/32 ⑦	0.0010–0.0027	0.0010–0.0027	0.3414	0.3414
	8—350	46	45	200 @ 1.25	1 23/32 ⑦	0.0010–0.0027	0.0010–0.0027	0.3414	0.3414
1978	6—250	46	45	175 @ 1.26	1 23/32	0.0010–0.0027	0.0015–0.0032	0.3414	0.3414
	8—305	46	45	200 @ 1.25	1 23/32	0.0010–0.0027	0.0010–0.0027	0.3414	0.3414
	8—350	46	45	200 @ 1.25	1 23/32	0.0010–0.0027	0.0010–0.0027	0.3414	0.3414
1979	6—250	46	45	175 @ 1.26	1 21/32	0.0010–0.0027	0.0015–0.0032	0.3414	0.3414
	8—305	46	45	200 @ 1.25	1 23/32	0.0010–0.0027	0.0010–0.0027	0.3414	0.3414
	8—350	46	45	200 @ 1.25	1 23/32	0.0010–0.0027	0.0010–0.0027	0.3414	0.3414
1980–81	6—229	46	45	200 @ 1.25	1 23/32	0.0010–0.0027	0.0010–0.0027	0.3414	0.3414

ENGINE AND ENGINE REBUILDING

Valve Specifications (cont.)

Year	Engine No. Cyl Displacement (cu in.)	Seat Angle (deg)	Face Angle (deg)	Spring Test Pressure (lbs @ in.)	Spring Installed Height (in.)	Stem to Guide Clearance (in.)		Stem Diameter (in.)	
						Intake	Exhaust	Intake	Exhaust
	6—231	45	45	168 @ 1.33	NA	0.0015–0.0032	0.0015–0.0032	0.3407	0.3409
	8—267	46	45	200 @ 1.25	1 23/32	0.0010–0.0027	0.0010–0.0027	0.3414	0.3414
	8—305	46	45	200 @ 1.25	1 23/32	0.0010–0.0027	0.0010–0.0027	0.3414	0.3414
	8—350	46	45	200 @ 1.25	1 23/32	0.0010–0.0027	0.0010–0.0027	0.3414	0.3414

① 325 hp
② 360 hp and 375 hp
③ 45° on aluminum heads
④ Inner spring—30 @ 1.78
⑤ 310 hp—315 @ 1.38
  350 hp and 375 hp—240 @ 1.38
⑥ 1 39/64 for exhaust
⑦ 1 19/32 for exhaust
NA Not available at time of publication

vided by a longer stroke crankshaft. The 305 and 350 cu in. engines remain as the most common V8s.

The 396 and 402 cu in. engines are known as the Mark IV engines or big-blocks. These engines feature unusual cylinder heads, in that the intake and exhaust valves are canted at the angle at which their respective port enters the cylinder. The 396 cu in. engine was used from 1967–72. The big-block cylinder heads use ball-joint rockers similar to those on the small block engines.

Engine Removal and Installation

The factory recommended procedure for engine removal is to remove the engine/transmission as a unit and then separate them outside of the car. In the process of removing the engine you will come across a number of steps which call for the removal of a separate component or system, i.e. "Disconnect the exhaust system" or "Remove the radiator." In all of these instances, a detailed removal procedure can be found elsewhere in the chapter, or in some cases, in another chapter which deals with the specific component in question.

1. Remove the hood. Scribe lines around the hinges so that the hood can be installed in its original location.
2. Remove the air cleaner.
3. Disconnect the battery cables at the battery.
4. Remove the radiator and shroud.
5. Remove the fan blade and pulley.
6. Disconnect and label wires at:
    a. C.E.C. solenoid.
    b. Coil.
    c. Temperature switch.
    d. Alternator.
    e. Starter solenoid.
    f. Oil pressure sending unit.
7. Disconnect:
    a. Accelerator linkage at the pedal.
    b. Oil pressure gauge line, if so equipped.
    c. Exhaust pipes at the manifold flanges.
    d. Engine cooler lines, if so equipped.
    e. Vacuum line to the power brake unit, if so equipped.
    f. Fuel line (front tank) at the fuel pump.
    g. Hoses at the carbon canister.
8. If the car has air conditioning, unbolt the compressor, leaving the hoses attached. Set the compressor out of the way. Do not disconnect any air conditioning refrigerant lines unless you are familiar with discharge procedures. Escaping refrigerant can freeze any surface it contacts, including your skin and eyes.
9. Remove the power steering pump,

Crankshaft and Connecting Rod Specifications
(All measurements are given in in.)

Year	Engine No. Cyl Displacement (cu in.)	Crankshaft				Connecting Rod		
		Main Brg Journal Dia	Main Brg Oil Clearance	Shaft End-Play	Thrust on No.	Journal Diameter	Oil Clearance	Side Clearance
1967	6—230	2.2983–2.2993	0.0003–0.0029	0.002–0.006	7	1.999–2.000	0.0007–0.0027	0.009–0.013
	6—250	2.2983–2.2993	0.0003–0.0029	0.002–0.006	7	1.999–2.000	0.0007–0.0027	0.009–0.013
	8—302 (Z28)	⑤	0.0008–0.003	0.003–0.011	5	1.999–2.000	0.0007–0.0028	0.009–0.013
	8—327	⑤	⑦	0.003–0.011	5	1.999–2.000	0.0007–0.0028	0.009–0.013
	8—350	2.24493–2.4493 ⑥	0.0008–0.002 ⑧	0.003–0.011	5	2.099–2.100	0.0007–0.0028	0.009–0.013
	8—396	③	④	0.006–0.010	5	2.199–2.200	0.0007–0.0028	0.015–0.021
1968	6—230	2.2983–2.2993	0.0003–0.0029	0.002–0.006	7	1.999–2.000	0.0007–0.0027	0.009–0.013
	6—250	2.2983–2.2993	0.0003–0.0029	0.002–0.006	7	1.999–2.000	0.0007–0.0027	0.009–0.013
	8—302 (Z28)	2.4479–2.4488	0.0008–0.003	0.003–0.011	5	2.099–2.100	0.0007–0.0028	0.009–0.013
	8—327	2.4484–2.4493 ⑥	0.0008–0.002 ⑧	0.003–0.011	5	2.099–2.100	0.0007–0.0028	0.009–0.013
	8—350	2.4484–2.4493 ⑥	0.0008–0.002 ⑧	0.003–0.011	5	2.099–2.100	0.0007–0.0028	0.009–0.013
	8—396	⑨	⑪	0.006–0.010	5	2.199–2.200	0.0009–0.0025	0.015–0.021
	8—396 (375 H.P.)	⑩	0.0013–0.0025 ⑫	0.006–0.010	5	2.1985–2.1995	0.0014–0.0030	0.019–0.025

Crankshaft and Connecting Rod Specifications (cont.)
(All measurements are given in in.)

Year	Engine No. Cyl Displacement (cu in.)	Crankshaft Main Brg Journal Dia	Crankshaft Main Brg Oil Clearance	Crankshaft Shaft End-Play	Thrust on No.	Connecting Rod Journal Diameter	Connecting Rod Oil Clearance	Connecting Rod Side Clearance
1969	6—230	2.2983–2.2993	0.0003–0.0029	0.002–0.006	7	1.999–2.000	0.0007–0.0027	0.009–0.013
	6—250	2.2983–2.2993	0.0003–0.0029	0.002–0.006	7	1.999–2.000	0.0007–0.0027	0.009–0.013
	8—302 (Z28)	2.4479–2.4488	0.0008–0.003	0.003–0.011	5	2.099–2.100	0.0007–0.0028	0.009–0.013
	8—307	2.4479–2.4488	0.0008–0.002 ⑧	0.003–0.011	5	2.099–2.100	0.0007–0.0027	0.009–0.013
	8—327	2.4479–2.4488	0.0008–0.002 ⑧	0.003–0.011	5	2.099–2.100	0.0007–0.0028	0.009–0.013
	8—350	2.4479–2.4488	0.0008–0.002 ⑧	0.003–0.011	5	2.099–2.100	0.0007–0.028	0.009–0.013
	8—396	⑨	⑪	0.006–0.010	5	2.199–2.200	0.0009–0.0025	0.015–0.021
	8—396 (375 H.P.)	⑩	0.0013–0.0025 ⑫	0.006–0.010	5	2.1985–2.1995	0.0014–0.0030	0.019–0.025
1970	6—250	2.2983–2.2993	0.0003–0.0029	0.002–0.006	7	1.999–2.000	0.0007–0.0027	0.009–0.013
	8—307, 350	2.4484–2.4493 ⑥	0.0003–0.0015 ⑬	0.002–0.006	5	2.099–2.100	0.0007–0.0028	0.008–0.014
	8—350 (Z28)	2.4484–2.4493 ⑥	0.0013–0.0025 ⑭	0.002–0.006	5	2.099–2.100	0.0013–0.0035	0.008–0.014
	8—396	2.7487–2.7496 ⑮	0.0007–0.0019 ⑯	0.006–0.010	5	2.199–2.200	0.0009–0.0025	0.013–0.023
1971	6—250	2.2983–2.2993	0.0003–0.0029	0.002–0.006	7	1.999–2.000	0.0007–0.0027	0.009–0.014
	8—307, 350	2.4484–2.4493 ⑳	0.0008–0.0020 ㉑	0.002–0.006	5	2.099–2.100	0.0013–0.0035	0.008–0.014

Year	Engine							
	8—350 (Z28)	2.4484-2.4493 ⑳	0.0013-0.0025 ⑭	0.002-0.006	5	2.099-2.100	0.0013-0.0035	0.008-0.014
	8—402	2.7487-2.7496 ⑮	0.0007-0.0019 ⑯	0.006-0.010	5	2.199-2.200	0.0009-0.0025	0.013-0.023
1972	6—250	2.2983-2.2993	0.0003-0.0029	0.002-0.006	7	1.999-2.000	0.0007-0.0027	0.009-0.014
	8—307, 350	2.4484-2.4493 ⑳	0.0008-0.0020 ㉑	0.002-0.006	5	2.099-2.100	0.0013-0.0035	0.008-0.014
	8—350 (Z28)	2.4484-2.4493 ⑳	0.0013-0.0025 ⑭	0.002-0.006	5	2.099-2.100	0.0013-0.0035	0.008-0.014
	8—402	2.7487-2.7496 ⑮	0.0007-0.0019 ⑯	0.006-0.010	5	2.199-2.200	0.0009-0.0025	0.013-0.023
1973	6—250	2.2983-2.2993	0.0003-0.0029	0.002-0.006	7	1.999-2.000	0.0007-0.0027	0.007-0.016
	8—305, 707, 350	㉒	㉓	0.002-0.006	5	2.099-2.100	0.0013-0.0035	0.008-0.014
1974	6—250	2.2983-2.2993	0.0003-0.0029	0.002-0.006	7	1.999-2.000	0.0007-0.0027	0.007-0.016
	8—350	㉒	㉓	0.002-0.006	5	2.099-2.100	0.0013-0.0035	0.008-0.014
1975	6—250	2.2983-2.2993	0.0003-0.0029	0.002-0.006	7	1.999-2.000	0.0007-0.0027	0.007-0.016
	8—305, 350	㉒	㉓	0.002-0.006	5	2.099-2.100	0.0013-0.0035	0.008-0.014
1976	6—250	2.2983-2.2993	0.0003-0.0029	0.002-0.006	7	1.999-2.000	0.0007-0.0027	0.007-0.016
	8—305, 350	㉒	㉓	0.003-0.006	5	2.099-2.100	0.0013-0.0035	0.008-0.014
1977	6—250	2.2983-2.2993	0.0003-0.0029	0.002-0.006	7	1.9928-2.000	0.0007-0.0027	0.007-0.016
	8—305, 350	㉒	㉕	0.002-0.006	5	2.099-2.100	0.0013-0.0035	0.008-0.014
1978	6—250	2.2979-2.2994	0.0010-0.0024 ㉔	0.002-0.006	7	1.9928-2.000	0.0010-0.0026	0.006-0.017

Crankshaft and Connecting Rod Specifications (cont.)
(All measurements are given in in.)

Year	Engine No. Cyl Displacement (cu in.)	Crankshaft				Connecting Rod		
		Main Brg Journal Dia	Main Brg Oil Clearance	Shaft End-Play	Thrust on No.	Journal Diameter	Oil Clearance	Side Clearance
	8—305, 350	㉒	㉕	0.002–0.006	5	2.0986–2.0998	0.0013–0.0035	0.008–0.014
1979	6—250	2.2979–2.2994	0.0010–0.0024 ㉔	0.002–0.006	7	1.999–2.000	0.0010–0.0026	0.006–0.017
	8—305, 350	㉒	㉕	0.002–0.006	5	2.0986–2.0998	0.0013–0.0035	0.006–0.014
1980–81	6—229	㉒	㉕	0.002–0.006	4	2.0986–2.0998	0.0013–0.0035	0.006–0.014
	6—231	2.4995	0.0004–0.0015	0.004–0.008	2	2.2495–2.2487	0.0005–0.0026	0.006–0.027
	8—267	㉒	㉕	0.002–0.006	5	2.0986–2.0998	0.0013–0.0035	0.006–0.014
	8—305	㉒	㉕	0.002–0.006	5	2.0986–2.0998	0.0013–0.0035	0.006–0.014
	8—350	㉒	㉕	0.002–0.006	5	2.0986–2.0998	0.0013–0.0035	0.006–0.014

① Not used
② Not used
③ Nos. 1-2—2.7487-2.7497
   Nos. 3-4—2.7482-2.7492
   No. 5—2.7478-2.7488
④ Nos. 1-2—0.0004-0.002
   Nos. 3-4—0.0009-0.0025
   No. 5—0.0013-0.0029
⑤ No. 1—2.2984-2.2993
   Nos. 2-4—2.2983-2.2993
   No. 5—2.2978-2.2988
⑥ Nos. 2.4478-2.4488
⑦ No. 1—0.0008-0.002
   Nos. 2-4—0.0018-0.002
   No. 5—0.0010-0.0036
⑧ No. 5—0.0018-0.0034
⑨ Nos. 1-2—2.7484-2.7493
   Nos. 3-4—2.7481-2.7490
   No. 5—2.7478-2.7488
⑩ No. 1—2.7484-2.7493
   Nos. 2-4—2.7481-2.7490
   No. 5—2.7478-2.7488
⑪ Nos. 1-2—0.0010-0.0022
   Nos. 3-4—0.0013-0.0025
   No. 5—0.0015-0.0031
⑫ No. 5—0.0015-0.0031
⑬ Nos. 2-4—0.0006-0.0018
   No. 5—0.0008-0.0023
⑭ w/Man trans—No. 5—0.0023-0.0033

w/Auto trans—No. 1—0.0019-0.0031
   Nos. 2-4—0.0013-0.0025
   No. 5—0.0023-0.0033
⑮ Nos. 3-4—2.7481-2.7490
   No. 5—2.7473-2.7483
⑯ Nos. 2-4—0.0013-0.0025
   No. 5—0.0019-0.0035
⑰ Not used
⑱ No. 5—2.6479-2.6488
⑲ Not used
⑳ Nos. 2-4—2.4481-2.4490
   No. 5—2.4479-2.4488
㉑ Nos. 2-4—0.0011-0.0023
   No. 5—0.0017-0.0033
㉒ No. 1—2.4484-2.4493
   Nos. 2, 3, 4—2.4481-2.4490
   No. 5—2.4479-2.4488
㉓ 8—307:
   No. 1—0.0008-0.002
   Nos. 2, 3, 4—0.0011-0.0023
   8—305, 350:
   Auto. No. 1—0.0019-0.0031
      Nos. 2, 3, 4—0.0013-0.0025
      No. 5—0.0023-0.0033
   Man. Nos. 1, 2, 3, 4—0.0013-0.0025
      No. 5—0.0023-0.0033
㉔ Applies to brgs. 1-6; 7—0.0015-0.0035
㉕ No. 1—0.0008-0.0020
   Nos. 2, 3, 4—0.0011-0.0023
   No. 5—0.0017-0.0032

Ring Gap
(All measurements are given in in.)

Year	Engine	Top Compression	Bottom Compression	Year	Engine	Oil Control
1967-79	6—230, 250 8—307, 396, 402	0.010-0.020	0.010-0.020	1967-81	All engines except 8—396	0.015-0.055
1967-69	8—302, 327	0.013-0.023①	0.013-0.025①	1967-70	8—396	0.010-0.030
1976-81	8—305	0.010-0.020	0.010-0.025	1980-81	6—231	0.015-0.035
1967-68	8—350	0.010-0.020	0.013-0.023			
1969	8—350	0.013-0.023	0.013-0.025			
1970-72	8—350	0.010-0.020②	0.013-0.025②			
1973-77	8—350	0.010-0.020	0.013-0.025③			
1978-81	8—350	0.010-0.020	0.010-0.025			
1980-81	6—229 8—267	0.010-0.020	0.010-0.025			
1980-81	6—231	0.010-0.020	0.010-0.020			

① 325, 350 hp—Top 0.010-0.020
                2nd 0.013-0.023
② 255, 330, 360 hp—Top 0.010-0.020
                      2nd 0.013-0.023
③ 2bbl—0.010-0.020

leaving the hoses attached to the pump. Set the pump aside, out of the way.
10. Raise the car on a hoist.
11. Drain the crankcase.
12. Remove the driveshaft.
NOTE: *If a plug for the driveshaft opening in the transmission is not available, drain the transmission.*
13. Disconnect:
    a. Shift linkage at the transmission.
    b. Speedometer cable at the transmission.
    c. Transmission cooler lines, if so equipped.
    d. TCS switch at the transmission.
14. On vehicles with manual transmissions, disconnect the clutch linkage at the cross-shaft then remove the cross-shaft at the frame bracket.
15. Lower the vehicle, remove the rocker arm covers and install an engine lifting adapter on the cylinder heads.
16. Raise the engine enough to take the weight off the front mounts, then remove the front mount thru-bolts.
17. Remove the rear mount-to-cross member bolts.
NOTE: *Make sure, on 1977 and later models, that the same number of transmission mount shims are reinstalled. These are used to adjust driveshaft angle.*
18. Raise the engine enough to take the weight off the rear mount, then remove the crossmember.
NOTE: *It is necessary to remove the mount from the transmission before the crossmember can be removed.*
19. Remove the engine/transmission assembly as a unit.
20. To remove the clutch and manual transmission from the engine:
    a. Remove the clutch housing cover plate screws.
    b. Remove the clutch housing-to-engine

ENGINE AND ENGINE REBUILDING

Ring Side Clearance
(All measurements are given in in.)

Year	Engine	Top Compression	Bottom Compression	Year	Engine	Oil Control
1967–72	6—230 8—302, 307, 327	0.0012–0.0027	0.0012–0.0032	1966–76	6—230, 250 8—302, 307, 327, 350	0.0000–0.0050 ③
1967	8—396	0.0012–0.0032	0.0012–0.0032	1967	8—396	0.0012–0.0060
1968–69	8—396	0.0017–0.0032	0.0017–0.0032	1968–72	8—396, 402	0.0005–0.0065
1967	6—250	0.0020–0.0035	0.0020–0.0040	1977	6—250 8—305, 350	0.002–0.007
1968–79	6—250	0.0012–0.0027	0.0012–0.0032	1978	6—250	0.000–0.005
1967–77	8—305, 350	0.0012–0.0032 ②	0.0012–0.0027 ①	1978–81	8—305, 350	0.002–0.007
1970–72	8—402	0.0017–0.0032	0.0017–0.0032	1980–81	6—229 8—267	0.002–0.007
1978–81	8—305, 350	0.0012–0.0032	0.0012–0.0032	1980–81	6—231	0.0035 Max
1980–81	6—229 8—267	0.0012–0.0032	0.0012–0.0032			
1980–81	6—231	0.003–0.005	0.003–0.005			

① 165, 245, 250 hp 350 cu in. engine 0.0012–0.0032
② 1975 350 2 bbl:
Top—0.0012–0.0027
2nd—0.0012–0.0032
1975 350 4 bbl:
Top—0.0012–0.0032
2nd—0.0012–0.0032
③ 0.002–0.007 for 1970–74
350 2 bbl and 1974–76
350 4 bbl, except 1974 Z28

attaching bolts, then, remove the transmission and clutch housing as a unit.
CAUTION: *Do not let the weight of the transmission hang on the spline because the clutch disc may be easily damaged.*
  c. Remove the starter and clutch housing rear cover plate.
  d. Loosen the clutch mounting bolts one turn at a time (to prevent distortion of the clutch cover) until the spring pressure is released. Remove all the bolts, clutch disc and pressure plate assembly.
21. To remove the automatic transmission:
  a. Remove the starter and the converter housing underpan.
  b. Remove the flywheel-to-converter attaching bolts.
  c. Supporting both the engine and transmission, remove the transmission-to-engine mounting bolts.
  d. Slowly guide the engine from the transmission.
To install:
1. Attach the engine to the transmission in the reverse order of removal.
2. Bolt the engine lifting tool to the engine and then lower the engine and the transmission into the chassis as a unit. Guide the engine so as to align the front engine mounts with the mounts on the frame.
3. Install one rear transmission crossmember side bolt, swing the crossmember up under the transmission mount and install the bolt in the opposite side rail.
4. Align and install the rear mount bolts.

Piston Clearance

Year	Engine No. Cyl Displacement (cu in.)	Piston to Bore Clearance (in.)
1967–68	6—230	0.0005–0.0011
	6—250	0.0005–0.0011
	8—302	0.0024–0.0030
	8—327	0.0005–0.0011
	8—350	0.0007–0.0013 ①
	8—396	0.0007–0.0013
	8—396 ⑤	0.0036–0.0047
1969	6—230	0.005–0.0015
	6—250	0.005–0.0015
	8—302	0.0024–0.0030
	8—307	0.0005–0.0011
	8—327	0.0005–0.0011
	8—350	0.0005–0.0011
	8—350 ⑤	0.0026–0.0030
	8—396	0.0010–0.0018
	8—396 ⑤	0.0036–0.0044
1970	6—230	0.0005–0.0015
	8—307	0.0005–0.0011
	8—350	0.0007–0.0013
	8—350 ⑤	0.0036–0.0042
	8—396	0.0018–0.0026
	8—396 ⑤	0.0036–0.0046

Piston Clearance (cont.)

Year	Engine No. Cyl Displacement (cu in.)	Piston to Bore Clearance (in.)
1971–72	6—250	0.0005–0.0015
	8—307	0.0005–0.0011
	8—350	0.0007–0.0013
	8—350 ④	0.0036–0.0042
	8—402	0.0018–0.0026
1973	6—250	0.0005–0.0015
	8—307	0.0005–0.0011
	8—350 ①	0.0007–0.0013
	8—350 ④	0.0036–0.0042
1974–75	6—250	0.0005–0.0015
	8—350 ②	0.0005–0.0011
	8—350 ③	0.0007–0.0013
1976–79	6—250	0.0010–0.0020
	8—305, 350	0.0007–0.0017
1980–81	6—229	0.0007–0.0017
	6—231	0.0008–0.0020
	8—267	0.0007–0.0017
	8—305	0.0007–0.0017
	8—350	0.0007–0.0017

① 1967 8—350—0.0005–0.0011
② 2 bbl carb
③ 4 bbl carb
④ 9:1 compression
⑤ 11:1 compression

ENGINE AND ENGINE REBUILDING

Camshaft Specifications
(All measurements in inches)

Year	Engine	Journal Diameter					Lobe Lift		Camshaft End Play
		1	2	3	4	5	Intake	Exhaust	
1970	6—250	1.8682–1.8692	1.8682–1.8692	1.8682–1.8692	1.8682–1.8692	—	0.2217	0.2217	0.001–0.005
	8—307	1.8682–1.8692	1.8682–1.8692	1.8682–1.8692	1.8682–1.8692	1.8682–1.8692	0.2600	0.2733	NA
	8—350	1.8682–1.8692	1.8682–1.8692	1.8682–1.8692	1.8682–1.8692	1.8682–1.8692	0.2600	0.2733	NA
	8—396 (350 hp)	1.9487–1.9497	1.9487–1.9497	1.9487–1.9497	1.9487–1.9497	1.9487–1.9497	0.2714	0.2824	NA
	8—396 (375 hp)	1.9487–1.9497	1.9487–1.9497	1.9487–1.9497	1.9487–1.9497	1.9487–1.9497	0.3057	0.3057	NA
1971	6—250	1.8682–1.8692	1.8682–1.8692	1.8682–1.8692	1.8682–1.8692	—	0.2217	0.2217	0.001–0.005
	8—307	1.8682–1.8692	1.8682–1.8692	1.8682–1.8692	1.8682–1.8692	1.8682–1.8692	0.2600	0.2733	NA
	8—350 (245 hp)	1.8682–1.8692	1.8682–1.8692	1.8682–1.8692	1.8682–1.8692	1.8682–1.8692	0.2600	0.2733	NA
	8—350 (270 hp)	1.8682–1.8692	1.8682–1.8692	1.8682–1.8692	1.8682–1.8692	1.8682–1.8692	0.2600	0.2733	NA
	8—350 (330 hp)	1.8682–1.8692	1.8682–1.8692	1.8682–1.8692	1.8682–1.8692	1.8682–1.8692	0.3057	0.3234	NA
	8—402	1.9482–1.9492	1.9482–1.9492	1.9482–1.9492	1.9482–1.9492	1.9482–1.9492	0.2343	0.2343	NA
1972	6—250	1.8682–1.8692	1.8682–1.8692	1.8682–1.8692	1.8682–1.8692	—	0.2217①	0.2217①	0.001–0.005
	8—307	1.8682–1.8692	1.8682–1.8692	1.8682–1.8692	1.8682–1.8692	1.8682–1.8692	0.2600①	0.2733①	NA
	8—350 (165 hp)	1.8682–1.8692	1.8682–1.8692	1.8682–1.8692	1.8682–1.8692	1.8682–1.8692	0.2600①	.02733①	NA
	8—350 (200 hp)	1.8682–1.8692	1.8682–1.8692	1.8682–1.8692	1.8682–1.8692	1.8682–1.8692	0.2600①	0.2733①	NA
	8—350 (255 hp)	1.8682–1.8692	1.8682–1.8692	1.8682–1.8692	1.8682–1.8692	1.8682–1.8692	0.3057	0.3234	NA
	8—402	1.9482–1.9492	1.9482–1.9492	1.9482–1.9492	1.9482–1.9492	1.9482–1.9492	0.2343	0.2343	NA
1973	6—250	1.8682–1.8692	1.8682–1.8692	1.8682–1.8692	1.8682–1.8692	—	0.2217①	0.2217①	0.001–0.005

ENGINE AND ENGINE REBUILDING

Camshaft Specifications (cont.)
(All measurements in inches)

Year	Engine	Journal Diameter					Lobe Lift		Camshaft End Play
		1	2	3	4	5	Intake	Exhaust	
1973	8—307	1.8682–1.8692	1.8682–1.8692	1.8682–1.8692	1.8682–1.8692	1.8682–1.8692	0.2600①	0.2733①	NA
	8—350 (145 hp)	1.8682–1.8692	1.8682–1.8692	1.8682–1.8692	1.8682–1.8692	1.8682–1.8692	0.2600①	0.2733①	NA
	8—350 (175 hp)	1.8682–1.8692	1.8682–1.8692	1.8682–1.8692	1.8682–1.8692	1.8682–1.8692	0.2600①	0.2733①	NA
	8—350 (245 hp)	1.8682–1.8692	1.8682–1.8692	1.8682–1.8692	1.8682–1.8692	1.8682–1.8692	0.3057	0.3234	NA
1974	6—250	1.8682–1.8692	1.8682–1.8692	1.8682–1.8692	1.8682–1.8692	—	0.2217	0.2217	0.001–0.005
	8—350	1.8682–1.8692	1.8682–1.8692	1.8682–1.8692	1.8682–1.8692	1.8682–1.8692	0.2600	0.2733	NA
	8—350 (Z28)	1.8682–1.8692	1.8682–1.8692	1.8682–1.8692	1.8682–1.8692	1.8682–1.8692	0.3057	0.3234	NA
1975	6—250	1.8682–1.8692	1.8682–1.8692	1.8682–1.8692	1.8682–1.8692	—	0.2217	0.2217	0.001–0.005
	8—350	1.8682–1.8692	1.8682–1.8692	1.8682–1.8692	1.8682–1.8692	1.8682–1.8692	0.3000	0.3070	NA
1976–79	6—250	1.8677–1.8697	1.8677–1.8697	1.8677–1.8697	1.8677–1.8697	—	0.2217	0.2315	0.003–0.008
	8—305	1.8682–1.8692	1.8682–1.8692	1.8682–1.8692	1.8682–1.8692	1.8682–1.8692	0.2485	0.2733②	0.004–0.012
	8—350	1.8682–1.8692	1.8682–1.8692	1.8682–1.8692	1.8682–1.8692	1.8682–1.8692	0.2600	0.2733	0.004–0.012
1980–81	6—229	1.8682–1.8692	1.8682–1.8692	1.8682–1.8692	1.8682–1.8692	—	0.3570	0.3900	0.004–0.012
	6—231	1.7850–1.7860	1.7850–1.7860	1.7850–1.7860	1.7850–1.7860	1.7850–1.7860	NA	NA	NA
	8—267	1.8682–1.8692	1.8682–1.8692	1.8682–1.8692	1.8682–1.8692	1.8682–1.8692	0.3570	0.3900	0.004–0.012
	8—305	1.8682–1.8692	1.8682–1.8692	1.8682–1.8692	1.8682–1.8692	1.8682–1.8692	0.2484	0.2667	0.004–0.012
	8—350	1.8682–1.8692	1.8682–1.8692	1.8682–1.8692	1.8682–1.8692	1.8682–1.8692	0.2600	0.2733	0.004–0.012

① California camshafts: # 6262810 (6—250)—Inlet 0.2217; Exhaust 0.2315
　　　　　　　　　　　　# 3864896 (6—250)—Inlet 0.2217; Exhaust 0.2315
　　　　　　　　　　　　# 6262944 (small V8)—Inlet 0.2671; Exhaust 0.2733
② 1978–79　0.2267

Torque Specifications
(All readings in ft. lbs.)

Year	Engine No. Cyl Displacement (cu in.)	Cylinder Head Bolts	Rod Bearing Bolts	Main Bearing Bolts	Crankshaft Pulley Bolts	Flywheel to Crankshaft Bolts	Manifold Intake	Manifold Exhaust
1967–79	6—230, 250	95 ⑨	35	65	—	60	30 ⑦	25 ⑥ ⑧
1967	8—327	65	35	80	60 ⑤	60	30	20
1967–76	8—302, 305, 307, 327, 350	65	45	75 ②	60 ⑤	60	30	④
1967–72	8—396, 402	80 ①	50	105 ③	85 ⑤	65	30	30
1978–81	8—305, 350	65	45	70	60	60	30	20 ⑩
1980–81	6—229 8—267	65	45	70	60	60	30	20
1980–81	6—231	80	40	100	175	60	45	25

① Aluminum heads—short bolts—65; long bolts—75
② Engines with 4-bolt mains—outer bolts 65
③ 1967–68 2-bolt mains—95
   1967 4-bolt mains—115
④ Center bolts—27; end bolts—17
⑤ Where applicable
⑥ Exhaust-to-intake
⑦ Manifold-to-head
⑧ 74 and later 250 has intake manifold integral with head—30 center, 20 on four end bolts
⑨ 78–79—L.H. front head bolt—85
⑩ Inside bolts on 350—30

5. Install the engine front mount bolts and then remove the lifting tool from the engine.
6. Installation of the remaining components is in the reverse order of removal.

Cylinder Head

REMOVAL AND INSTALLATION

Six Cylinder 1967–79

1. Drain the cooling system and remove the air cleaner. Disconnect the P.C.V. hose.
2. Disconnect the accelerator pedal rod at the bell crank on the manifold, and the fuel and vacuum lines at the carburetor.
3. Disconnect the exhaust pipe at the manifold flange, then remove the manifold bolts and clamps and remove the manifolds and carburetor as an assembly. There is a ring gasket at the exhaust manifold flange, and a gasket for each of the manifolds at the head. These will have to be replaced. On 1977 and later models with an integral intake manifold, remove the carburetor at the intake manifold, and remove the exhaust manifold.
4. Remove the fuel and vacuum line retaining clip from the water outlet. Then disconnect the wire harness from the heat sending unit and coil, leaving the harness clear of the clips on the rocker arm cover.
5. Disconnect the radiator hose at the water outlet housing and the battery ground strap at the cylinder head.
6. Number the spark plug wires, then remove the wires and spark plugs. Disconnect the coil-to-distributor primary wire lead at the coil and remove the coil (except integral coil HEI).

118 ENGINE AND ENGINE REBUILDING

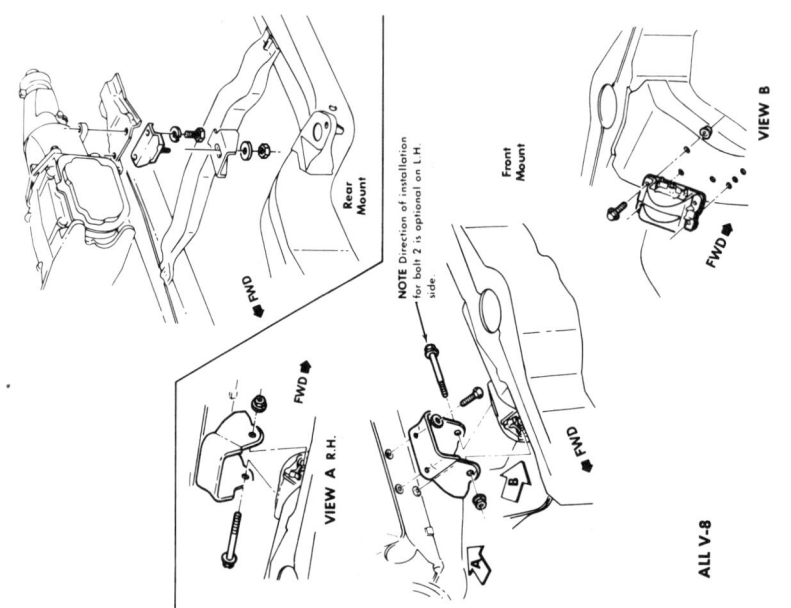

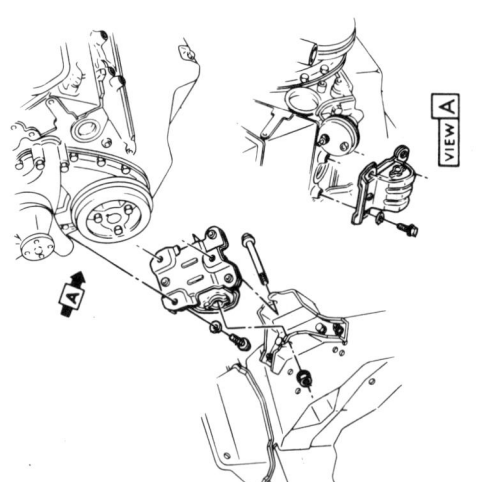

Engine mounts for the 1980 model (most years similar)

ENGINE AND ENGINE REBUILDING

7. Remove the rocker arm cover. Back off the rocker arm nuts, pivot the rocker arms to clear the pushrods and remove the pushrods. Be certain to keep the pushrods in the order in which they came out. They must be returned to their original positions.

NOTE: *1977 and later model sixes do not use a rocker arm cover gasket. RTV sealer is used in its place.*

8. Remove the cylinder head bolts, cylinder head and gasket.

To install:

1. Clean the mating surfaces of the cylinder head and block. Check the cylinder head and block for warpage with a straight-edge and feeler gauge. Warpage must not exceed 0.006 in. over a six inch span. If this limit is exceeded, the head or block should be milled flat.

2. Clean the head bolts and the threads in the cylinder block, since dirt will affect torque readings.

3. Install a new head gasket over the dowel pins. Do not use sealer on combination steel/asbestos gaskets.

4. Guide and lower the cylinder head into place over dowels and gasket.

5. Oil the cylinder head bolts, install and run them down snug.

6. Tighten the cylinder head bolts a little at a time with a torque wrench in the correct sequence. Final torque should be 90 to 95 ft. lbs. except for the left front head bolt, which should be torqued to 85 ft. lbs.

7. Install the valve pushrods down through the cylinder head openings and seat them in their lifter sockets.

8. Install the rocker arms, balls and nuts and then tighten the rocker arm nuts until all pushrod play is taken up.

9. Install the thermostat, thermostat housing and water outlet using new gaskets. Then connect the radiator hose.

10. Install the heat sending switch and torque to 15–20 ft. lbs.

11. Clean the spark plugs or install new ones.

12. Install the coil then connect the heat sending unit and the coil primary wires, and connect the battery ground cable at the cylinder head.

13. Clean the surfaces of the manifold(s) and install a new gasket or gaskets over the manifold studs. Install the manifold(s). Clean and oil the bolts, then install and torque them in sequence to the specified values. Connect the exhaust pipe to the manifold, using a new ring gasket.

14. Install the carburetor if it was removed, and reconnect the carburetor linkage.

15. Connect the P.C.V., fuel and vacuum lines and then secure the lines in the clip at water outlet.

16. Fill the cooling system and check for leaks.

17. Adjust the valve lash.

18. Install the rocker arm cover and position the wiring harness in the clips.

19. Clean and install the air cleaner.

V-6 and V-8 1967–81 (all but 231 V-6)

1. Drain the coolant. Remove the air cleaner.
2. Disconnect:
   a. Battery
   b. Radiator and heater hose from manifold
   c. Throttle linkage
   d. Fuel line
   e. Coil wires
   f. Temperature sending unit
   g. Power brake hose, distributor vacuum hose, and crankcase vent hoses.
3. Remove:
   a. Distributor, marking position
   b. Alternator upper bracket
   c. Coil and its bracket (where so equipped)

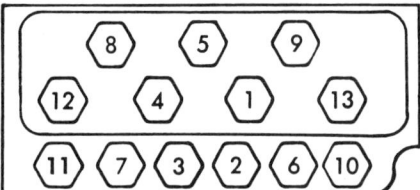

Cylinder head torque sequence—229 V6

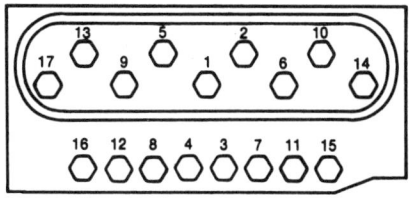

Cylinder head torque sequence—small block V8

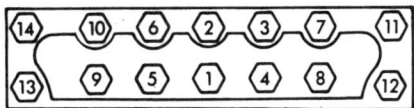

Cylinder head torque sequence—inline six cylinder

4. On 1977 and later engines, remove all of the following with which the engine is equipped:
   a. Air cleaner bracket
   b. Air pump bracket
   c. Accelerator return spring and bracket
   d. Accelerator bellcrank

5. Remove all manifold attaching bolts, and remove the intake manifold.
6. Disconnect the air manifold and tubes, and spark plug wires, remove the air cleaner preheater and spark plug heat shields, loosen and remove the exhaust manifold flange nuts, then lower the exhaust pipe assembly and hang it from the frame with wire.
7. Remove the manifold end bolts, then the center ones and remove the manifold from the engine.
8. Remove rocker cover(s). Loosen rocker nuts and pivot rockers 90° to permit removal of pushrods. Remove pushrods, marking the location of each.
9. Remove the cylinder head bolts, cylinder head, and gasket.

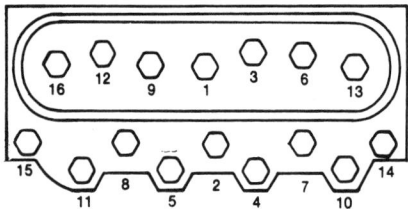

Cylinder head torque sequence—big-block V8

To install:
1. Inspect the gasket surfaces on the head(s). All surface must be clean and free of nicks and burrs. The threads on bolts and inside the boltholes in the block must be clean. Inspect the head for warpage as described in the engine rebuilding section below.
2. Install, reversing the removal procedures, keeping the following important points in mind:
   a. Tighten the head bolts in several stages, going in the pattern specified in the illustration.
   b. Coat new gaskets (both sides) and headbolts with sealer, unless a combination steel-asbestos gasket is used; in that case, put sealer on the head bolts only, and let the gasket dry.
   c. Make sure to relocate pushrods according to their markings. Adjust the valves according to the procedure labeled "Engine Not Running" before running the engine. Then, readjust the valves with the engine hot and running.
   d. Coat *new* rocker cover gaskets with sealer, and tighten cover bolts to specified torque evenly in several stages.

231 V-6 1980–81

NOTE: *On vehicles equipped with AIR, disconnect the rubber hose at the injection tubing check valve. This way the tubing will not have to be removed from the exhaust manifold.*

1. Remove the intake manifold as detailed later in this chapter.
2. When removing the right cylinder head:
   a. Loosen and remove all drive belts.
   b. Tag and disconnect the wires leading from the rear of the alternator.
   c. Remove the air conditioning compressor (if so equipped) and position it out of the way with all the hoses still connected.
   d. Remove the alternator and its mounting bracket.
3. When removing the left cylinder head:
   a. Remove the oil gauge rod.
   b. Remove the power steering pump (if so equipped) and its bracket and then position it out of the way with the hoses still attached.
4. Tag and disconnect the spark plug wires and then remove the spark plug wire clips from the cylinder head cover studs.
5. Remove the exhaust manifold mounting bolts from the head which is being removed, and then pull the manifold away from the head.
6. Use an air hose if available, or a bunch of clean rags and clean the dirt off the head and surrounding areas thoroughly. It is extremely important to avoid getting dirt into the hydraulic valve lifters.
7. Remove the cylinder head cover from the top of the head that you wish to remove.

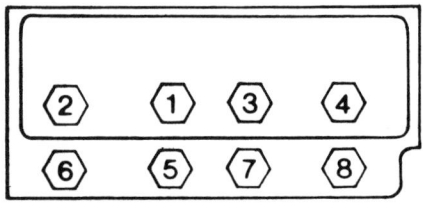

Cylinder head torque sequence—231 V6

ENGINE AND ENGINE REBUILDING 121

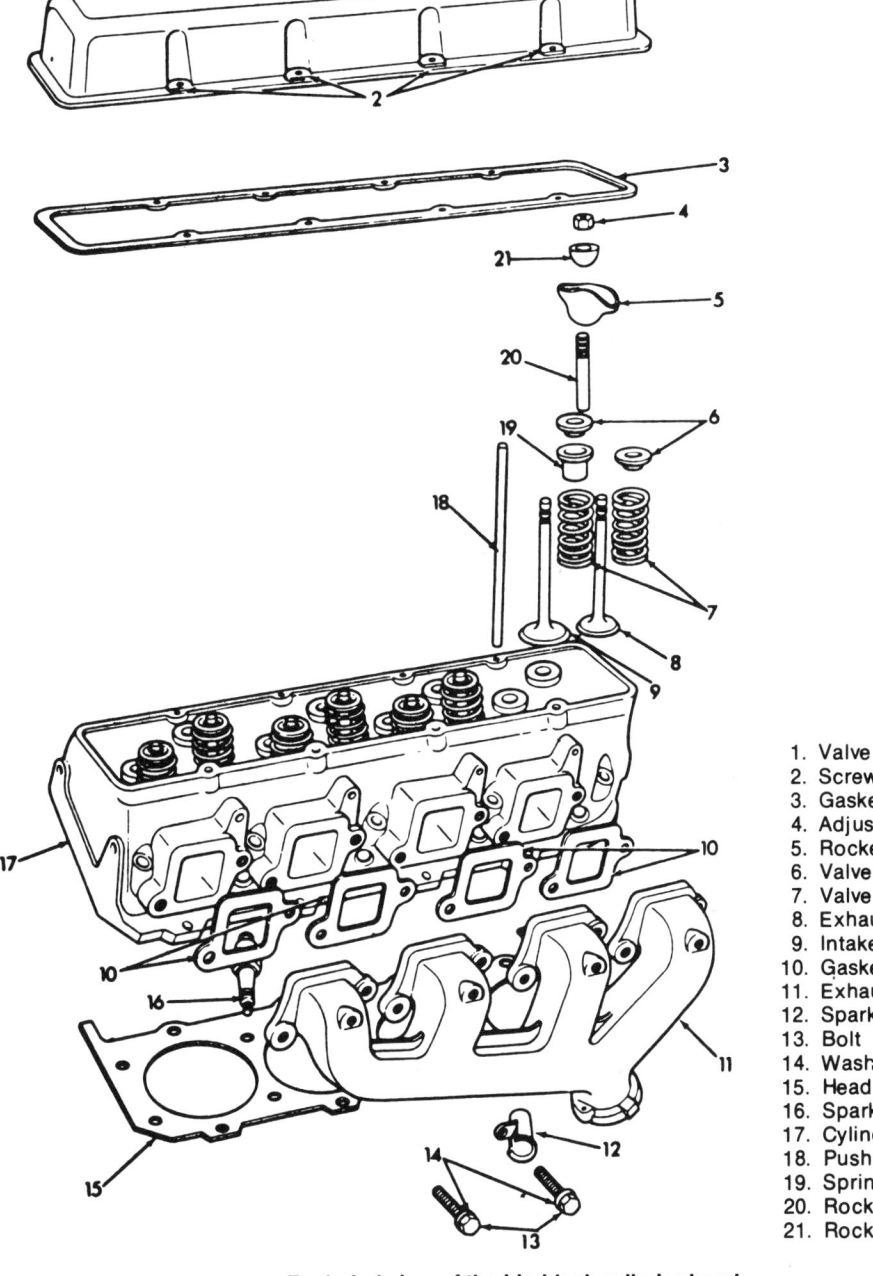

1. Valve cover
2. Screw reinforcements
3. Gasket
4. Adjusting nut
5. Rocker arm
6. Valve spring retainer
7. Valve spring
8. Exhaust valve
9. Intake valve
10. Gasket
11. Exhaust manifold
12. Spark plug shield
13. Bolt
14. Washer
15. Head gasket
16. Spark plug
17. Cylinder head
18. Pushrod
19. Spring shield
20. Rocker arm stud
21. Rocker arm ball

Exploded view of the big-block cylinder head

8. Remove the rocker arm and shaft assembly from the cylinder head and then remove the pushrods.

NOTE: *If the valve lifters are to be serviced, remove them at this time. Otherwise, protect the lifters and the camshaft from dust and dirt by covering the entire area with a clean cloth. Whenever the lifters or the pushrods are removed from the head it is always a good idea to place them in a wooden block with numbered holes to keep them identified as to their position in the engine.*

9. Loosen and remove all the cylinder head bolts and then lift off the head.

To install:

1. Clean the engine block gasket surface thoroughly. Make sure that no foreign mate-

122 ENGINE AND ENGINE REBUILDING

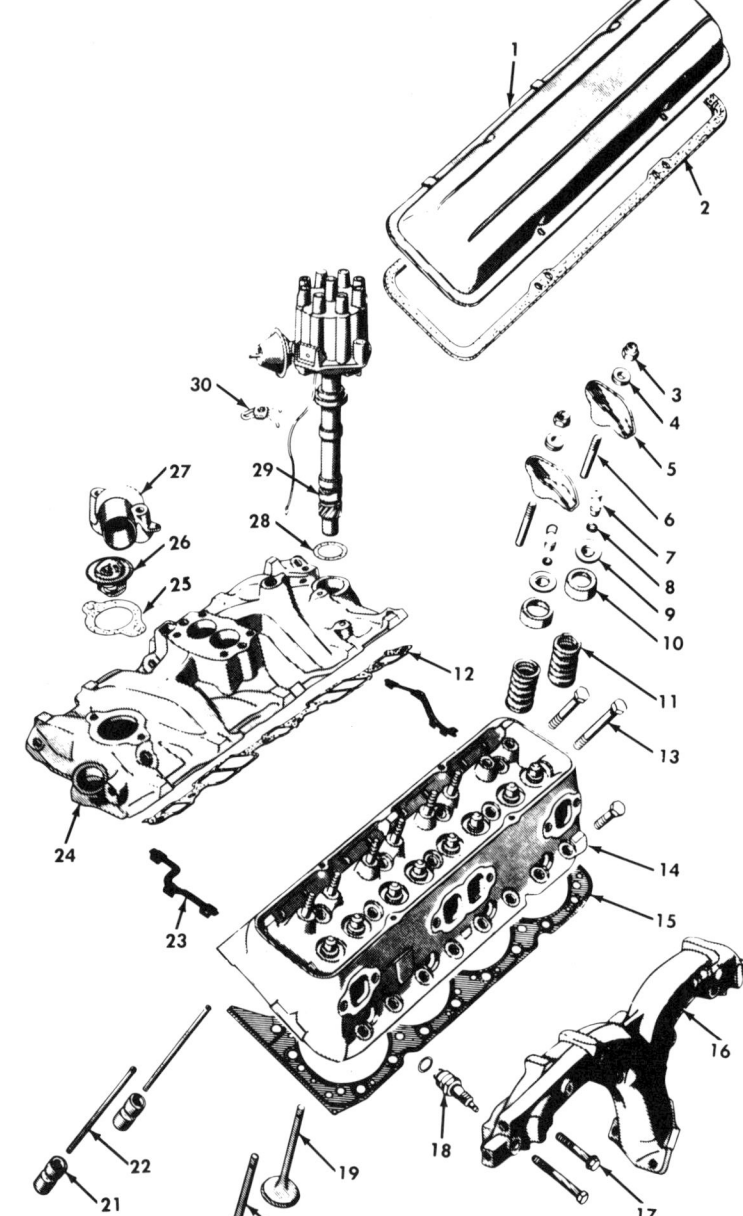

1. Rocker arm cover
2. Gasket
3. Nut
4. Ball
5. Rocker arms
6. Rocker arm studs
7. Valve keeper locks
8. O-ring seals
9. Valve spring cap
10. Shield
11. Spring
12. Gasket
13. Bolts
14. Cylinder head
15. Head gasket
16. Exhaust manifold
17. Bolts
18. Spark plug and gasket
19. Intake valve
20. Exhaust valve
21. Hydraulic lifters
22. Push rods
23. Intake manifold gaskets
24. Intake manifold
25. Gasket
26. Thermostat
27. Thermostat housing
28. Gasket
29. Distributor
30. Clamp

Exploded view of the small-block cylinder head

rial has fallen into the cylinder bores, the bolt holes or into the valve lifter area. It is always a good idea to clean out the bolt holes with an air hose if one is available.

2. Install a new head gasket with the bead facing down toward the cylinder block. The dowels in the block will hold the gasket in place.

3. Clean the gasket surface of the cylinder head and carefully set it into place on the dowels in the cylinder block.

4. Use a heavy body thread sealer on all of the head bolts since the bolt holes go all the way through into the coolant.

5. Install the head bolts. Tighten the bolts a little at a time about three times around in the sequence shown in the illustration. Tighten the bolts to a final torque equal to that given in the "Torque Specifications" chart.

6. Installation of the remaining components is in the reverse order of removal.

ENGINE AND ENGINE REBUILDING

VALVE GUIDES

Valve guides are integral with the cylinder head on all engines. Valve guide bores may be reamed to accommodate oversize valves. If wear permits, valve guides can be knurled to allow the retention of standard valves. Maximum allowable valve stem-to-guide bore clearances are listed under valve specifications.

Rocker Arms

REMOVAL AND INSTALLATION

All Except 231 V6

Rocker arms are removed by removing the adjusting nut. Be sure to adjust the valve lash after replacing the rocker arms. Coat the replacement rocker arm and ball with SAE 90 gear oil before installation.

aftermarket companies produce complete rocker arm stud kits with installation tools. Mark IV and late high performance small-block engines use screw-in studs and pushrod guide plates.

231 V6

1. Remove the rocker arm covers.
2. Remove the rocker arm shaft assembly bolts.
3. Remove the rocker arm shaft assembly.
4. To remove the rocker arms from the shaft, the nylon arm retainers must be removed. They can be removed with a pair of water pump pliers, or they can be broken by hitting them below the head with a chisel.

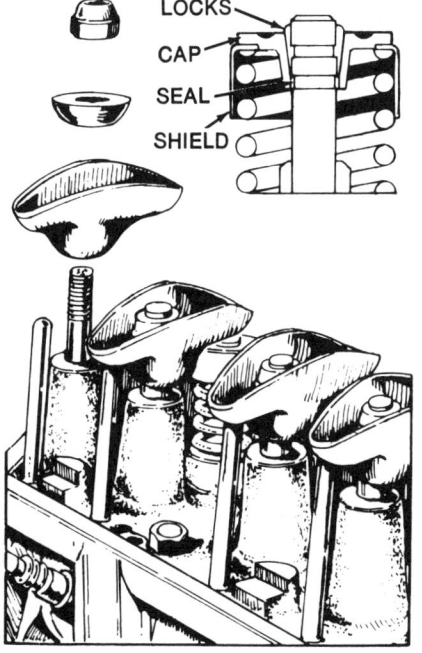

Six cylinder rocker arm components (V8's similar)

NOTE: *When replacing an exhaust rocker, move an old intake rocker to the exhaust rocker arm stud and install the new rocker arm on the intake stud. This will prevent burning of the new rocker arm on the exhaust position.*

Rocker arms studs that have damaged threads or are loose in the cylinder heads may be replaced by reaming the bore and installing oversize studs. Oversizes available are .003 and .013 in. The bore may also be tapped and screw-in studs installed. Several

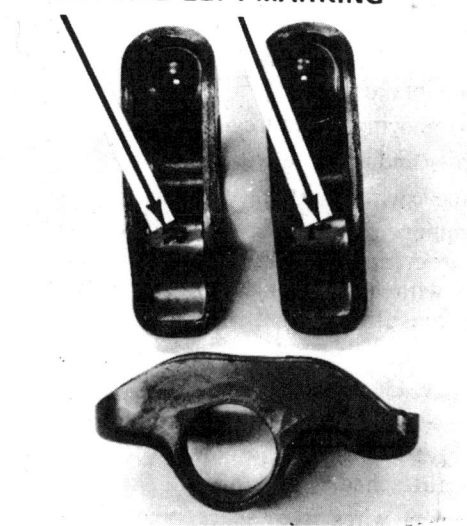

Replacement rocker arm identification—231 V6

Position of rocker arms on shaft—231 V6

ENGINE AND ENGINE REBUILDING

5. Remove the rocker arms from the shaft. Make sure you keep them in order. Also note that the external rib on each arm points *away* from the rocker arm shaft bolt located between each pair of rocker arms.

6. If you are installing new rocker arms, note that replacement rocker arms are marked "R" and "L" for right and left side installation. *Do not* interchange them.

7. Install the rocker arms on the shaft and lubricate them with oil.

8. Center each arm on the ¼ in. hole in the shaft. Install new nylon rocker arm retainers in the holes using a ½ in. drift.

9. Locate the push rods in the rocker arms and insert the shaft bolts. Tighten the bolts a little at a time until they are tight.

10. Install the rocker covers using new gaskets.

OVERHAUL

See the Engine Rebuilding Section.

Valve Lash Adjustment

Most engines described in this book use hydraulic lifters, which require no periodic adjustment. In the event of cylinder head removal or any operation that requires disturbing the rocker arms, the rocker arms will have to be adjusted.

1967–71

Normalize the engine temperature by running it for several minutes. Shut the engine off and remove the valve cover(s). After valve cover removal, torque the cylinder heads to specification. The use of oil stopper clips, readily available on the market, is recommended to prevent oil splatter when adjusting valve lash. Restart the engine. Valve lash is set with the engine warm and idling.

Turn the rocker arm nut counterclockwise until the rocker arm begins to clatter. Reverse the direction and turn the rocker arm down slowly until the clatter just stops. This is the zero lash position. Turn the nut down an additional ¼ turn and wait ten seconds until the engine runs smoothly. Continue with additional ¼ turns, waiting ten seconds each time, until the nut has been turned down one full turn from the zero lash position. This one turn, pre-load adjustment must be performed to allow the lifter to adjust itself and prevents possible interference between the valves and pistons. Noisy lifters should be cleaned or replaced.

1972–81

1. Remove the rocker covers and gaskets.
2. Adjust the valves on inline six cylinder engines as follows:
   a. Mark the distributor housing with a piece of chalk at No. 1 and 6 plug wire positions. Remove the distributor cap with the plug wires attached.
   b. Crank the engine until the distributor rotor points to No. 1 cylinder and No. 1 piston is at TDC (both No. 1 cylinder valves closed). At this point, adjust the following valves:
   - No. 1—Exhaust and Intake
   - No. 2—Intake
   - No. 3—Exhaust
   - No. 4—Intake
   - No. 5—Exhaust
   c. Back out the adjusting nut until lash is felt at the pushrod, then turn the adjust-

Oil splash stopper clips will prevent splatter when adjusting the valves with the engine running

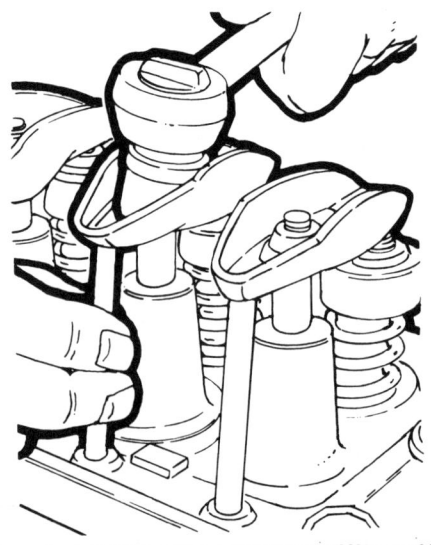

Inline six cylinder valve adjustment (V6's and V8's similar)

ing nut in until all lash is removed. This can be determined by checking pushrod end-play while turning the adjusting nut. When all play has been removed, turn the adjusting nut in 1 full turn.

d. Crank the engine until the distributor rotor points to No. 6 cylinder and No. 6 piston is at TDC (both No. 6 cylinder valves closed). The following valves can be adjusted:
- No. 2—Exhaust
- No. 3—Intake
- No. 4—Exhaust
- No. 5—Intake
- No. 6—Intake and Exhaust

3. Adjust the valves on V8 engines as follows:

a. Crank the engine until the mark on the damper aligns with the TDC or 0° mark on the timing tab and the engine is in No. 1 firing position. This can be determined by placing the fingers on the No. 1 cylinder valves as the marks align. If the valves do not move, it is in No. 1 firing position. If the valves move, it is in No. 6 firing position and the crankshaft should be rotated one more revolution to the No. 1 firing position.

b. The adjustment is made in the same manner as 6 cylinder engines.

c. With the engine in No. 1 firing position, the following valves can be adjusted:
- V8-Exhaust—1,3,4,8
- V8-Intake—1,2,5,7
- V6-Exhaust—1,5,6
- V6-Intake—1,2,3

d. Crank the engine 1 full revolution until the marks are again in alignment. This is No. 6 firing position. The following valves can now be adjusted:
- V8-Exhaust—2,5,6,7
- V8-Intake—3,4,6,8
- V6-Exhaust—2,3,4
- V6-Intake—4,5,6

4. Reinstall the rocker arm covers using new gaskets or sealer.

5. Install the distributor cap and wire assembly.

6. Adjust the carburetor idle speed.

Intake Manifold

REMOVAL AND INSTALLATION

Inline Six Cylinder

NOTE: *1975 and later L6 engines are equipped with an intake manifold which is integral with the cylinder head.*

1. Remove the air cleaner.
2. Disconnect the throttle rods at the bellcrank and remove the throttle return spring.
3. Disconnect the fuel and vacuum lines from the carburetor.
4. Disconnect the crankcase ventilation hose from the valve cover and the evaporation control hose from the carbon canister.
5. Disconnect the exhaust pipe from the manifold and throw away the packing.
6. Remove the manifold assembly and scrape off the gaskets.
7. Check the condition of the manifold. If a manifold is cracked or distorted 0.030 in. or more, it should be replaced to prevent exhaust leakage. To detect distortion, lay a straightedge along the length of the exhaust port faces. If, at any point, a gap of 0.030 in. or more exists between the straightedge and the manifold, distortion of that amount is present.
8. By removing one bolt and two nuts, the manifold can be separated.
9. To install, reverse the removal procedure, using new gaskets. Replace the exhaust pipe packing.

V6 and V8 (Except 231 V6)

1. Remove the air cleaner.
2. Drain the radiator.
3. Disconnect:
   a. Battery cables at the battery.
   b. Upper radiator and heater hoses at the manifold.
   c. Crankcase ventilation hoses as required.

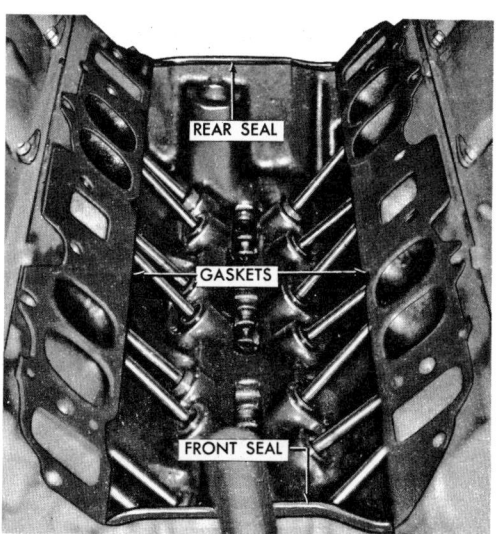

V8 intake manifold and seal location

ENGINE AND ENGINE REBUILDING

 d. Fuel line at the carburetor.
 e. Accelerator linkage.
 f. Vacuum hose at the distributor.
 g. Power brake hose at the carburetor base or manifold, if applicable.
 h. Ignition coil and temperature sending switch wires.
 i. Water pump bypass at the water pump (Mark IV only).

4. Remove the distributor cap and scribe the rotor position relative to the distributor body.

5. Remove the distributor.

6. If applicable, remove the alternator upper bracket. As required, remove the oil filler bracket, air cleaner bracket, air conditioning compressor and bracket, and accelerator bellcrank.

7. Remove the manifold-to-head attaching bolts, then remove the manifold and carburetor as an assembly.

8. If the manifold is to be replaced, transfer the carburetor (and mounting studs), water outlet and thermostat (use a new gasket) heater hose adapter, EGR valve (use new gasket) and, if applicable, TVS switch and the choke coil. 1975–79 engines use a new carburetor heat choke tube which must be transferred to a new manifold.

9. Before installing the manifold, thoroughly clean the gasket and seal surfaces of the cylinder heads and manifold.

10. Install the manifold end seals, folding the tabs if applicable, and the manifold/head gaskets, using a sealing compound around the water passages.

NOTE: *1974–75 350 V8 engines require a new intake manifold side gasket on 4-bbl*

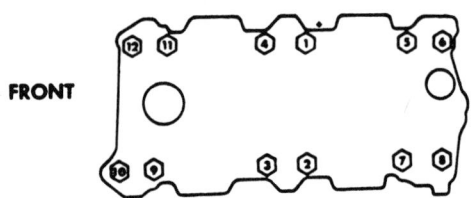

Intake manifold torque sequence—V6 (exc. 231) and small-block V8

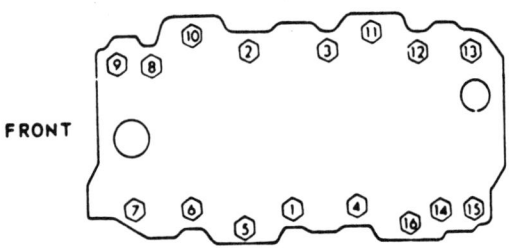

Intake manifold torque sequence—big-block V8

engines. The new gasket has restricted cross-over ports. The 350 2-bbl uses a restricted cross-over gasket on the right-hand side and an open gasket on the left. The 350 4-bbl uses restricted cross-over gaskets on both sides. The correct gaskets are essential.

11. When installing the manifold, care should be taken not to dislocate the end seals. It is helpful to use a pilot in the distributor opening. Tighten the manifold bolts to 30 ft. lbs. in the sequence illustrated.

12. Install the ignition coil.

13. Install the distributor with the rotor in its original location as indicated by the scribe line. If the engine has been disturbed, refer to "Distributor Removal and Installation" at the beginning of this chapter.

14. If applicable, install the alternator upper bracket and adjust the belt tension.

15. Connect all components disconnected in Steps 3 and 6 above.

16. Fill the cooling system, start the engine, check for leaks and adjust the ignition timing and carburetor idle speed and mixture.

231 V6

NOTE: *A special wrench adapter, available from Snap-On and several other tool manufacturers, is necessary to remove the left front intake manifold bolt.*

1. Disconnect the battery and drain the cooling system. Remove the upper radiator hose, and the coolant bypass hose from the manifold.

2. Remove the air cleaner. Disconnect the

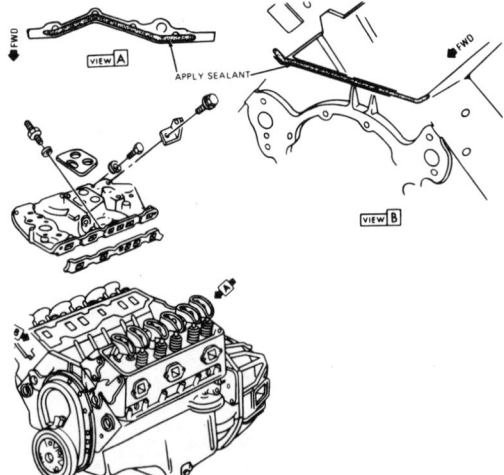

V6 intake manifold and seal location

ENGINE AND ENGINE REBUILDING

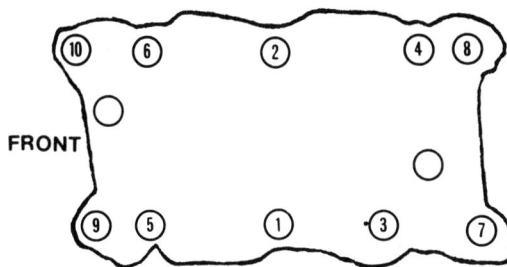

Intake manifold torque sequence—231 V6

Inline six cylinder exhaust manifold torque sequence—1975-79

throttle linkage from the carburetor. Remove the linkage bracket from the manifold. If the car is equipped with an automatic transmission, remove the downshift linkage.

3. Disconnect the fuel line from the carburetor. If equipped with power brakes, disconnect the power brake line from the manifold. Disconnect the choke pipe and all vacuum lines. Disconnect the anti-dieseling solenoid wire.

4. Remove the manifold bolts. It will be necessary to remove the distributor cap and rotor to gain access to the front left manifold bolt. This is the special bolt, known as a torx bolt. Remove the plug wires from the plugs.

5. Remove the manifold.

6. Installation is in the reverse order of removal. Use a new gasket and seals. Coat the ends of the seals with a non-hardening silicone sealer. The pointed end of the seal should be a snug fit against the block and head. When installing the manifold, start with the center bolts (numbers one and two) and slowly tighten them until *snug*. Continue with the rest of the bolts in sequence, tightening them in several stages to the correct torque.

Exhaust Manifold

REMOVAL AND INSTALLATION

Inline Six—1967-74

Exhaust manifold removal for these model years is covered in the "Intake Manifold Removal and Installation" section earlier in this chapter.

Inline Six With Integral Intake Manifold—1975-76

1. Remove the air cleaner.
2. Remove the power steering and air pump brackets.
3. Remove the EFE valve bracket.
4. Disconnect the throttle linkage and return spring.

5. Unbolt the exhaust pipe from the flange.
6. Unbolt and remove the manifold.
7. Reverse the procedure for installation. Tighten the four end bolts to specifications last.

Inline Six With Integral Intake Manifold—1977-79

1. Disconnect negative (−) battery cable and remove air cleaner.
2. Remove the power steering and/or AIR pumps and brackets, where they are present. (You need not disconnect power-steering hoses—just support pump out of the way.)
3. Working from below, with the vehicle safely supported, disconnect the exhaust pipe at the manifold and at the catalytic converter bracket near the transmission mount. If the car uses an exhaust manifold mounted converter, disconnect the pipe at the bottom of the converter, and then remove the converter.
4. Working from above, remove the rear heat shield and accelerator cable bracket.
5. Remove the exhaust manifold bolts, and pull off the manifold.
6. If the manifold is to be replaced, transfer the EFE valve, actuator, and rod assembly to the new part. Otherwise, inspect the manifold as described in Step 7.
7. Clean and then inspect the manifold carefully for cracks, and for free operation of the EFE valve. Repair or replace parts, and free up the EFE valve with solvent, if necessary.
8. Make sure the gasket surface is clean and free of deep scratches. Position a new gasket on the manifold, and then put the manifold in position on the block, and install the bolts hand tight.
9. Torque all bolts *in the proper order* to the specified torque (see illustration).
10. Install the rear heat shield and the accelerator cable bracket.
11. Working from underneath, connect the exhaust pipe at the manifold flange and connect the converter bracket at the trans-

128 ENGINE AND ENGINE REBUILDING

mission mount. If the car has an exhaust manifold converter, first install the converter to the manifold loosely; then attach the exhaust pipe to the converter and align the exhaust system; finally, torque the converter mounting bolts to 15 ft. lbs., in an X pattern, and torquing in several stages.

12. Working from above, install the power steering and A.I.R. pumps as necessary. Then, install the air cleaner and connect the battery ground cable.

V6 and V8

1. If equipped with AIR, remove the air injector manifold assembly. The ¼ in. pipe threads in the manifold are straight threads. Do not use a ¼ in. tapered pipe tap to clean the threads.
2. Disconnect the battery.
3. If applicable, remove the air cleaner pre-heater shroud.
4. Remove the spark plug wire heat shields. On Mark IV, remove spark plugs.
5. On the left exhaust manifold, disconnect and remove the alternator.
6. Disconnect the exhaust pipe from the manifold and hang it from the frame out of the way.
7. Bend the locktabs and remove the end bolts, then the center bolts. Remove the manifold.

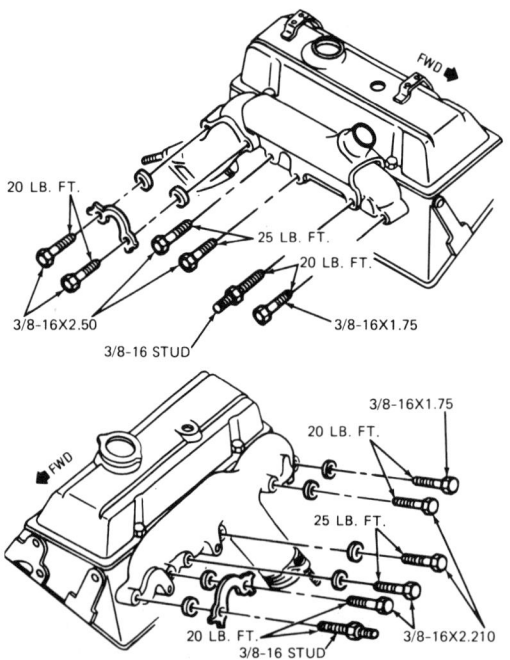

Exhaust manifold installation—V6, V8 (1980 shown, others similar)

NOTE: *A 9/16 in. thin wall 6-point socket, sharpened at the leading edge and tapped onto the head of the bolt, simplifies bending the locktabs.*

NOTE: *When installing a new manifold on the right side on 1978 and later V8s you must transfer the heat stove from the old manifold to the new one.*

8. Installation is the reverse of removal. Clean all mating surfaces and use new gaskets. Torque all bolts to specifications from the inside working out.

Timing Gear Cover

REMOVAL AND INSTALLATION

Inline Six Cylinder

1. Drain the oil and remove the oil pan on models through 1972.
2. Remove the radiator after draining it.
3. Remove the fan, pulley, and belt. Remove any power steering and/or AIR pump drive belts. Remove any braces for the above pumps which will interfere with cover removal and position the pumps out of the way.
4. Remove the crankshaft pulley and damper. Use a puller to remove the damper. Do not attempt to pry or hammer the damper off, or it will be damaged.
5. Remove the retaining bolts, and remove the cover on 1968–72 models.
6. On 1973–79 models, pull the cover forward slightly and cut the oil pan front seal off flush with the block. Remove the cover. On installation, cut the tabs off a new oil pan front seal and install it on the cover.
7. On installation, coat the gasket with sealer and use a ⅛ in. bead of silicone sealer at the oil pan-to-cylinder block joint. Replace the damper before tightening the cover bolts

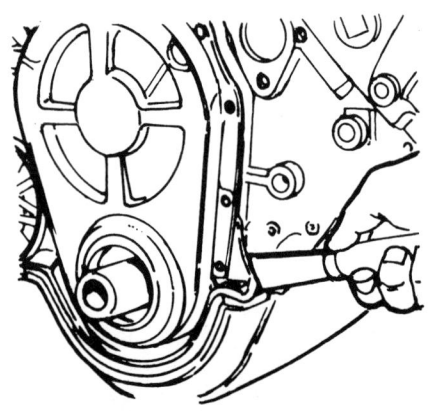

Cut the oil pan seal flush with the front of the cylinder block (V8 shown, others similar)

ENGINE AND ENGINE REBUILDING 129

When the timing gear cover is replaced on most engines, the oil pan front seal must be modified

down, so that the cover seal will align. The damper must be drawn into place. Hammering it will destroy it.

8. Replace the oil pan if it was removed, and fill the crankcase with oil.

V6 and V8

REMOVAL: ALL SMALL BLOCK V6 (EXCEPT 231) V8 AND 1967-72 MARK IV

1. Drain the oil and remove the oil pan. The pan need not be removed on 1974 and later small block engines.
2. Drain and remove the radiator.
3. Remove the fan, pulley, and belt. Remove any power steering and/or AIR pump drive belts. Remove any braces for these pumps which will interfere with cover removal and position the pumps out of the way.
4. Remove the water pump.
5. Remove the crankshaft pulley and damper. Use a puller on the damper. Do not attempt to pry or hammer the damper off.
6. Remove the retaining bolts, and remove the timing cover.

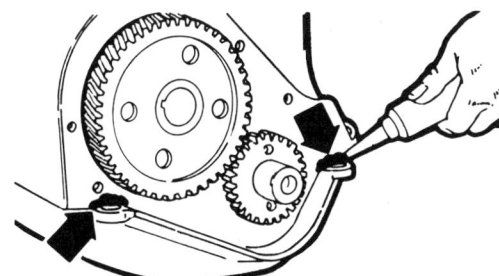

Use sealer at the timing cover-to-oil pan and the oil pan-to-cylinder block joints

INSTALLATION: 1967-74 SMALL BLOCK V8 AND 1967-72 MARK IV

Reverse the preceding steps to install the cover. Use a damper installation tool to pull the damper on. Apply an ⅛ in. bead of silicone rubber sealer to the oil pan and cylinder block joint faces. Lightly coat the bottom of the seal with engine oil.

Refill the engine with oil.

INSTALLATION: 1975-81 SMALL BLOCK V6 (EXC. 231) AND V8

1. Clean the gasket mating surfaces.
2. Remove any oil pan gasket material that may still be adhering to the oil pan-engine block joint face.
3. Apply a ⅛ in. bead of silicone sealant (Part No. 1051435) or the equivalent to the joint formed by the oil pan and cylinder block, as well as to the entire oil pan front lip.
4. Coat the cover gasket with gasket sealer and place it in position on the front cover.
5. Loosely install the front cover on the block. Install the 4 top bolts loosely (about 3 turns). Install two ¼-20 x ½ in. screws in the hole at each side of the front cover and apply a bead of sealant on the bottom of the seal and install it on the cover.
6. Tighten the screws evenly while aligning the dowel pins and holes in the front cover.
7. Remove the ¼-20 x ½ in. screws and install the rest of the cover screws.
8. Further installation is the reverse of removal. Refill the engine with oil.

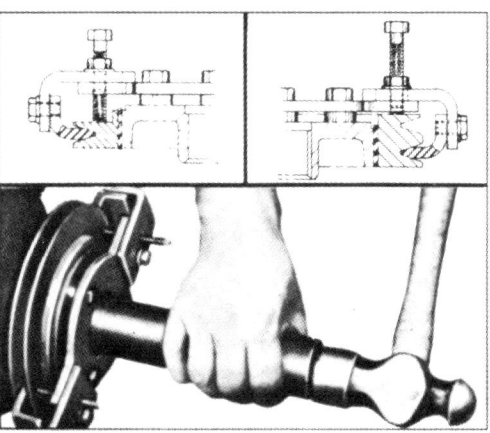

Installing the drive-on torsional damper

231 V6

1. Drain the cooling system. Remove the radiator hoses. Remove the radiator.
2. Remove all the drive belts. Remove the fan and fan pulley. Remove the bypass hose.
3. Remove the crank pulley, the fuel pump and the distributor. Note the position of the distributor rotor before you remove the distributor.
4. Remove the alternator and its bracket.

ENGINE AND ENGINE REBUILDING

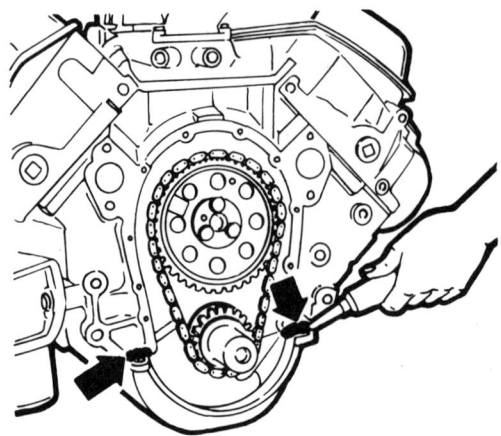

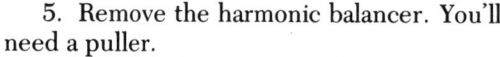

Apply sealer to the front pads at the area shown (V8)

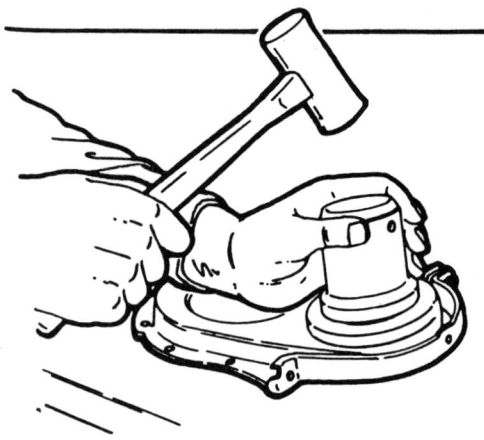

Oil seal installation with the cover removed

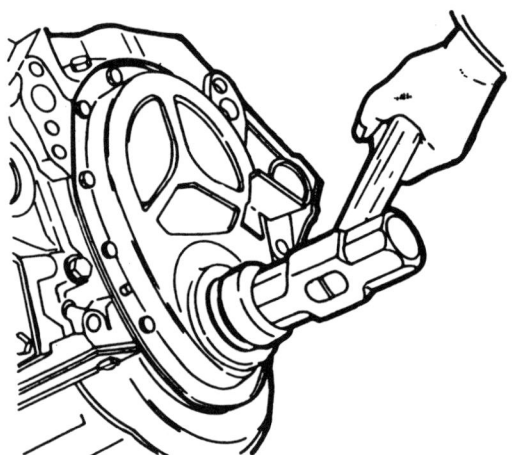

Oil seal installation with the cover installed

5. Remove the harmonic balancer. You'll need a puller.

6. Remove the two bolts which attach the oil pan to the front cover. Remove the bolts which attach the cover to the block.

7. Remove the cover and remove the gasket material.

8. To install, it is first necessary to remove the oil pump cover and pack the space around the oil pump gears completely full of petroleum jelly. *Do not use gear lube.* There must be no air space left inside the pump. Reinstall the pump cover using a new gasket. This step is very important since the oil pump may lose its prime any time the pump, pump cover or timing cover is disturbed. If the pump is not packed, it may not begin to pump oil as soon as the engine is started.

9. Install the cover, using a sealer and new gaskets. Make sure the dowel pins engage the dowel pin holes before starting the bolts. Apply sealer to the bolt threads.

10. Install the harmonic balancer, bolt and washer. It will be necessary to lock the flywheel in some way to torque the balancer bolt to specifications. Most mechanics remove the flywheel cover and lock the flywheel with a bolt-on or hand-held locking device.

11. The rest of the installation is in the reverse order of removal.

TIMING GEAR COVER OIL SEAL REPLACEMENT

All Engines

1. After removing the gear cover, pry the oil seal out of the front of the cover with a small prybar or an oil seal removal tool.

2. Install a new lip seal with the lip (open side of seal) inside and drive or press the seal into place.

3. Lightly coat seal with engine oil before replacing cover on block.

Timing Chain or Gear

REMOVAL AND INSTALLATION

Inline Six Cylinder

The six-cylinder camshaft is gear driven. To remove the camshaft gear, remove the camshaft and press the gear off.

CAUTION: *The thrust plate must be positioned so that the woodruff key in the shaft does not damage it when the shaft is pressed out of the gear. Support the hub of the gear or the gear will be seriously damaged.*

The crankshaft gear may be removed with a gear puller while in place in the block.

ENGINE AND ENGINE REBUILDING 131

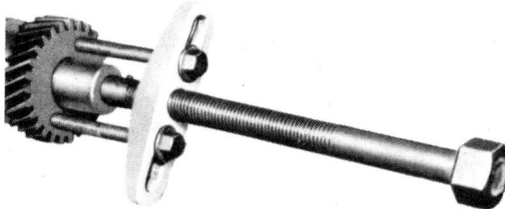

The inline six cylinder crankshaft gear is removed with a gear puller

V6 and V8 (Except 231 V6)

These engines are equipped with a timing chain. To replace the chain, remove the radiator core, water pump harmonic balancer, and the crankcase front cover. This will allow access to the timing chain. Crank the engine until the zero marks punched on both sprockets are closest to one another and in line between the shaft centers. Then, take out the three bolts that hold the camshaft gear to the camshaft. This gear is a light press fit on the camshaft and will come off readily. It is located by a dowel.

The chain comes off with the camshaft gear.

A gear puller will be required to remove the crankshaft gear.

Without disturbing the position of the engine, mount the new crank gear on the shaft, then mount the chain over the camshaft gear. Arrange the camshaft gear in such a way that the timing marks will line up between the shaft centers and the camshaft locating dowel will enter the dowel hole in the cam sprocket.

Place the cam sprocket, with its chain mounted over it, in position on the front of the camshaft and pull up with the three bolts that hold it to the camshaft.

After the gears are in place, turn the en-

V6 and V8 crankshaft sprocket removal

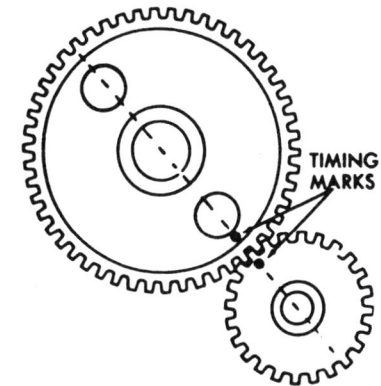

Timing gear alignment—inline six cylinder

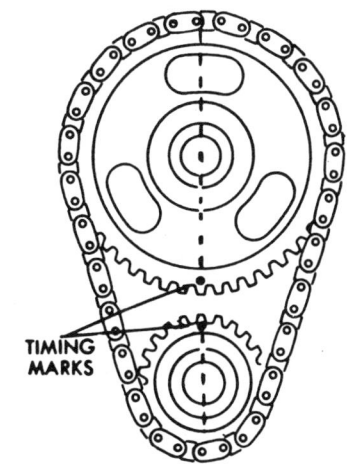

Timing sprocket alignment—1967–78 V8

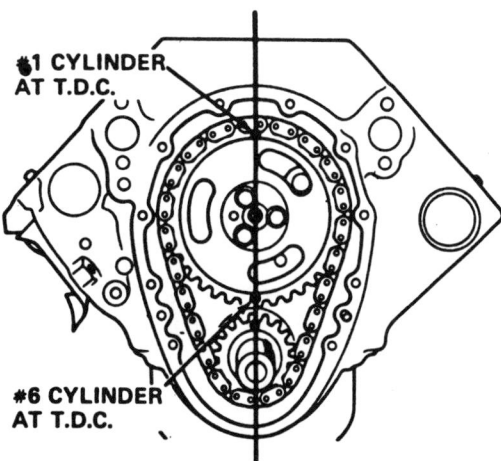

Timing sprocket alignment—1979–81 V6 and V8

gine two full revolutions to make certain that the timing marks are in correct alignment between the shaft centers.

ENGINE AND ENGINE REBUILDING

231 V6

1. Remove the timing chain cover.
2. Before removing anything else, make sure the timing marks on the crankshaft and camshaft sprockets are aligned. This will greatly ease reinstallation of parts.
3. It is not necessary to remove the timing chain tensioners unless they are worn or damaged.
4. Remove the front crankshaft oil slinger.
5. Remove the bolt and the special washer that hold the camshaft distributor drive gear and fuel pump eccentric at the forward end of the camshaft. Remove the eccentric and the gear from the camshaft.
6. Using a gear puller, alternately pull the camshaft sprocket, then the crankshaft sprocket forward until the camshaft sprocket is free.
7. After the camshaft sprocket and chain are removed, finish pulling the crankshaft sprocket off the crankshaft.
8. To install, if the engine has not been disturbed, proceed to Step Eleven.
9. If the engine has been disturbed, turn the crankshaft so that the number one piston is at top dead center.
10. Temporarily install the sprocket key and the camshaft sprocket on the camshaft. Turn the camshaft so that the index mark of the sprocket is pointing downward. Remove the key and the sprocket from the camshaft.
11. Assemble the timing chain and sprockets. Install the keys, sprockets, and chain assembly on the crankshaft and camshaft so that the index marks of both the sprockets are aligned. It will be necessary to hold the chain tensioners out of the way while installing the timing chain and sprocket assembly.
12. Install the front oil slinger on the crankshaft with the concave side toward the front of the engine.
13. Install the fuel pump eccentric with the oil groove forward.
14. Install the distributor drive gear on the camshaft.
15. Install the front cover.

Camshaft

REMOVAL AND INSTALLATION

Inline Six Cylinder

Due to the length of the inline six cylinder camshaft, a large amount of working room will be required in front of the engine to remove the camshaft. There are two ways to go about this task: either remove the engine from the car, or remove the radiator, grille and all supports which are mounted directly in front of the engine. If the second alternative is chosen, you must also disconnect the motor mounts and raise the front of the engine enough to gain the clearance necessary to remove the cam from the engine.

1. In addition to removing the timing gear cover, remove the grille and radiator.
2. Remove the valve cover and gasket, loosen all the valve rocker arm nuts and pivot the arms clear of the pushrods.
3. Remove the distributor and the fuel pump.
4. Remove the coil, the side cover and its gasket. Remove the pushrods and valve lifters.
5. Remove the two camshaft thrust plate retaining screws by working through the holes in the camshaft gear.
6. Remove the camshaft and gear assembly by pulling it out through the front of the block.

NOTE: *If renewing either the camshaft or the camshaft gear, the gear must be pressed off the camshaft. The replacement parts must be assembled in the same manner (under pressure). In placing the gear on the camshaft, press the gear onto the shaft until it bottoms against the gear spacer ring. The end clearance of the thrust plate should be .001 to .005 in.*

7. Install the camshaft assembly in the engine.

Timing chain and gears—231 V6

ENGINE AND ENGINE REBUILDING

NOTE: *Pre-lube the cam lobes with E.O.S. or SAE 90 gear lubricant. Do not dislodge the cam bearings when inserting the camshaft.*

8. Turn the crankshaft and the camshaft to align and bring the timing marks together. Push the camshaft into this aligned position. Install the camshaft thrust plate-to-block screws and torque them to 6–7½ lbs.
9. Runout on either the crankshaft or the camshaft gear should not exceed .003 in.
10. Backlash between the two gears should be between .004 and .006 in.
11. Install the timing gear cover and its gasket.
12. Install the oil pan and gaskets.
13. Install the harmonic balancer.
14. Line up the keyway in the balancer with the key on the crankshaft and the drive balancer onto the shaft until it bottoms against the crankshaft gear.
15. Install the valve lifters and pushrods. Install the side cover with new gasket. Attach the coil wires; install the fuel pump.
16. Install the distributor and set the timing as described under "Distributor Installation" at the beginning of this section.
17. Pivot the rocker arms over the pushrods and then adjust the valves.
18. Add oil to the engine. Install and adjust the fan belt.
19. Install the radiator or shroud.
20. Install the grille assembly.
21. Fill the cooling system, start the engine and check for leaks.
22. Check and adjust the timing.

V6 and V8 (except 231 V6)

1. Remove the intake manifold, valve lifters and timing chain cover, as described in this section.
2. Remove the grille and radiator.
3. Remove the fuel pump and pump pushrod.
4. Remove the camshaft sprocket bolts, the sprocket and the timing chain. A light blow to the lower edge of a tight sprocket should free it (use a plastic mallet).
5. Install two $5/16-18 \times 4$ in. bolts in the cam bolt holes and pull the cam from block.
NOTE: *All camshaft journals are the same diameter and care must be taken while removing the camshaft to avoid damage to the bearings.*
6. To install, reverse removal procedure, aligning the timing marks.

NOTE: *Pre-lube the cam lobes with E.O.S. or SAE 90 gear lubricant. Do not dislodge the cam bearings when installing the camshaft.*

231 V6

1. Drain the engine coolant and remove the radiator and radiator hoses.
2. Remove the water pump and all the drive belts. Remove the alternator.
3. Remove the crankshaft pulley and the vibration damper.
4. Remove the intake manifold. Mark the location of the distributor and remove the distributor.
5. Remove the fuel pump. Remove the timing chain cover and the oil pump.
6. Remove the timing chain and the camshaft sprocket, along with the distributor drive gear and the fuel pump eccentric.
7. Remove the rocker arm covers and the rocker arm assemblies. Mark the pushrods and remove them. Remove the lifters. Mark them so they can be returned to their original position.
8. Carefully remove the camshaft from the engine. Make sure you don't damage the bearings.
9. Installation is in the reverse order of removal. Remember to pack the oil pump with petroleum jelly.

Pistons and Connecting Rods
REMOVAL AND INSTALLATION

1. Drain the crankcase and remove the oil pan. Remove the oil pump as described later in this chapter.
2. Drain the cooling system and remove the cylinder heads.
3. Remove any ridge or deposits from the upper end of the cylinder bores with a ridge reamer. Do this with the piston in the Bottom Dead Center position and a clean rag on top of the piston to collect cuttings.
4. Check the rods and pistons for identification numbers and, if necessary, number them.
5. Remove the connecting rod cap nuts and caps. Push the rods away from the crankshaft and install the caps and nuts loosely to their respective rods.
6. Push the piston and rod assemblies up and out of the cylinders.
7. Before replacing the rings, inspect the cylinder bores. If the cylinder bore is in satisfactory condition, place each ring in its bore

134 ENGINE AND ENGINE REBUILDING

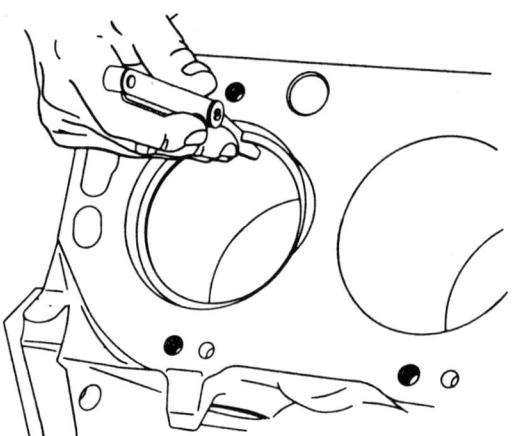

Check the ring end gap with the ring installed in the cylinder

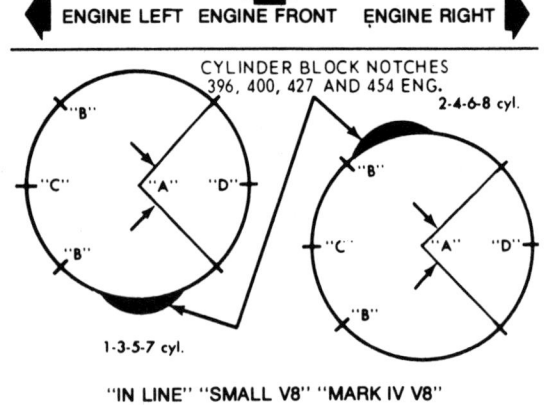

"A" OIL RING SPACER GAP
(Tang in Hole or Slot within Arc)

"B" OIL RING RAIL GAPS

"C" 2ND COMPRESSION RING CAP

"D" TOP COMPRESSION RING GAP

Ring gap location—all engines but 231 V6

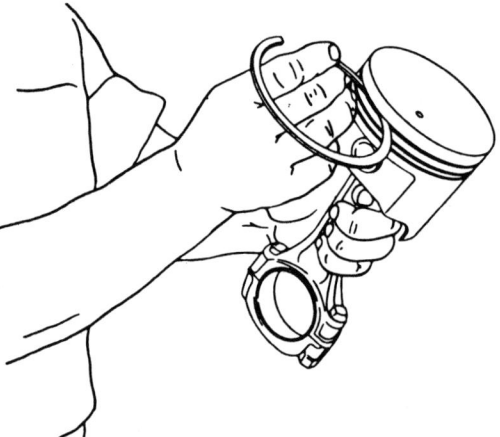

Checking the ring side clearance

in turn and square it in the bore with the head of the piston. Measure the ring endgap. If the gap is greater than the limit, get a new ring. If the gap is less than the limit, file the end of the ring to obtain the correct gap.

8. Check the ring side-clearance by installing the rings on the piston, and inserting a feeler gauge of the correct dimension between the ring and the lower land. The gauge should slide freely around the circumference of the ring without binding. Any wear will form a step on the lower land. Replace any pistons having high steps. Before checking the ring side-clearance be sure the ring grooves are clean and free of carbon, sludge, or grit.

9. Install piston rings with a ring expander. Compression rings have a mark which must face the top of the piston. The top ring is chrome or molybdenum faced. When installing oil rings, do the following: first, install the oil ring in the ring groove and insert the anti-rotation tang into the oil hole; then, holding the ends of the spacer so they butt up against one another, install the lower steel oil ring rail; repeat this procedure to install the upper rail so that the gap will line up with that of the lower rail; flex the oil ring assembly to make sure it is free—if it binds, the ring groove must be dressed at a narrow point, or a distorted ring must be replaced; install the lower compression ring with its gap 120 degrees (one third of a circle) away from oil ring gap; install the top ring with its gap 120 degrees away from that of the second ring. Be sure to install the piston in its original bore. Install the piston and rod assembly with the connecting rod bearing tang slots on the side opposite the camshaft on V8 engines. Inline engine pistons must have the piston notch facing the front of the engine. Install short lengths of rubber tubing over the connecting rod bolts to prevent damage to the rod journals. Lubricate pistons and rod bearings with light engine oil. Install a ring compressor over the rings on the piston. Lower the piston and rod assembly into the bore until the ring compressor contacts the block. Using the wooden handle of a hammer, push the piston into the bore while guiding the rod onto the journal.

ENGINE AND ENGINE REBUILDING

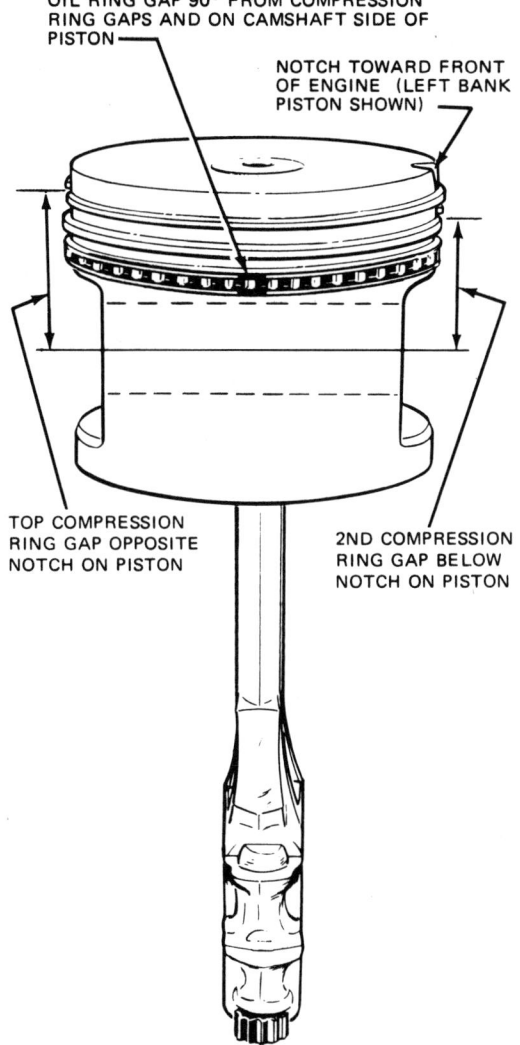

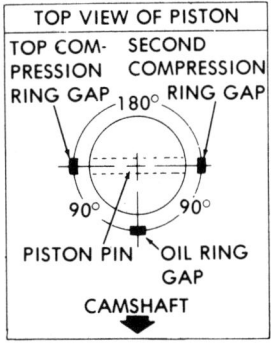

Ring gap location—231 V6

136 ENGINE AND ENGINE REBUILDING

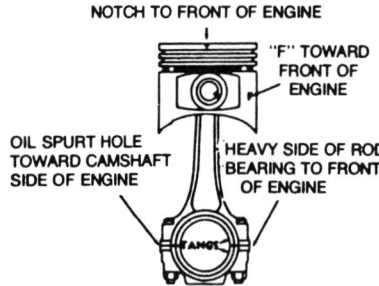

InLine six-cylinder piston-to-rod relationship

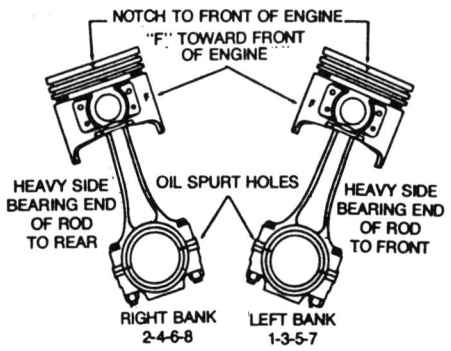

Small block V8 and V6 piston-to-rod relationship

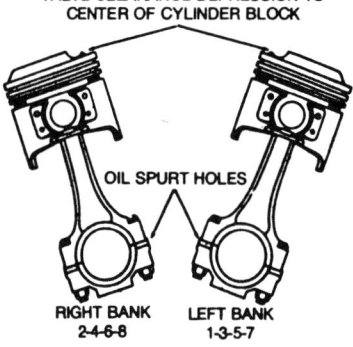

Mark IV V8 piston-to-rod relationship

ENGINE LUBRICATION

Both six-cylinder and V8 engines have pressurized lubrication systems with full-flow oil filters.

Oil Pan

REMOVAL AND INSTALLATION

In Line Six-Cylinder

1. Disconnect the battery ground cable.
2. Remove the upper radiator mounting bolts or side mount bolts. Remove the upper and lower hoses from the water pump.
3. Install a piece of heavy cardboard between the fan and the radiator.
4. Disconnect the fuel suction line from the fuel pump.
5. Raise the car and drain the oil.
6. Remove the starter.
7. Remove the flywheel lower pan or converter lower pan and splash shield.
8. Rotate the crankshaft until the timing mark on the damper is at the six o'clock position.
9. Remove the brake line retaining bolts from the crossmember and move the brake line out of the way.
10. Remove the thru-bolts from the front motor mounts.
11. Remove the oil pan bolts.
12. Slowly raise the engine until the motor mounts can be removed from the frame brackets.
13. Remove the mounts and continue to raise the engine until it has been raised three inches.
14. Remove the oil pan by pulling it down from the engine and then twisting it into the opening left by the removal of the left engine mount.
15. When the pan is clear of the engine, tilt the front up and remove it by pulling it down and to the rear.
16. Install the oil pan gaskets to the engine block.
17. Install the oil pan and torque the side bolts to 6–8 ft. lbs. and the end bolts to 9–12 ft. lbs.
18. Install the motor mounts, and then install the remaining components using a reverse procedure of removal.

1967–68 V8

1. Remove the engine from the chassis.
2. Remove the bellhousing or converter underpan.
3. Remove the starter.
4. Remove the oil pan.
5. Reverse the removal procedure to install the pan.

1969 396, 1969 Manual Transmission, and 1970–72, 396 and 402

1. Disconnect the battery ground cable.
2. Remove the air cleaner, dipstick, distributor cap, radiator shroud and upper mounting panel.
3. On big-block models, place a piece of heavy cardboard between the radiator and the fan.

ENGINE AND ENGINE REBUILDING

4. Disconnect the engine ground straps. Remove the fuel pump on 307 and 350 engines.
5. Disconnect the accelerator control cable.
6. Drain the oil. Remove the filter on 307 and 350 engines.
7. Remove the driveshaft and plug the rear of transmission.
8. Remove the starter.
9. Disconnect the transmission linkage at the transmission or remove the floorshift lever.
10. Disconnect the speedometer cable and the back-up switch connector.
11. On manual transmission vehicles, disconnect the clutch cross-shaft at the frame. On automatic transmission vehicles, disconnect the cooler lines, detent cable, rod or switch wire, and the modulator pipe.
12. Remove the crossmember bolts. Jack up the engine and move the crossmember rearward.
13. Remove the crossover or disconnect the dual exhaust pipes.
14. Remove:
    a. Flywheel housing cover;
    b. Transmission;
    c. Flywheel housing and throwout bearing (manual transmission);
    d. Front engine mount through-bolts.
15. Raise the rear of engine approximately 4 in. Support the engine by hoist.
16. Raise the front of the engine approximately 4 in. and insert 2 in. blocks under the front engine mounts.
17. Rotate the crankshaft until the timing mark on the torsional damper is at the six o'clock position.
18. Unbolt and remove the oil pan.

1969–72 Small Block V8s and All 1973 and Later V8s

1. Disconnect the negative battery cable.
2. As a precaution, remove the distributor cap to keep it from getting broken when the engine is raised.
3. Remove the fan shroud retaining bolts.
4. On earlier models it may be necessary to remove the radiator upper mounting panel.
5. Raise the vehicle on a hoist and drain the engine oil.
6. Disconnect the exhaust pipes or crossover pipes.
7. On automatic transmission equipped vehicles, remove the converter housing underpan and splash shield.
8. Rotate the crankshaft until the timing mark on the torsional dampener is at the six o'clock position.
9. The starter can be swung out of the way by disconnecting the brace at the starter, removing the inboard starter bolt and loosening the outboard starter bolt. On 1970 small V8, remove the fuel pump.
10. Remove the front engine mount through-bolts.
11. Raise the engine and insert blocks, at least three in. thick, under the engine mounts.
12. Remove the oil pan bolts and remove the oil pan.
13. To install, clean all gasket and seal surfaces thoroughly, use new gaskets and seals, and reverse the removal procedure.

NOTE: *If the crankshaft was rotated while the pan was off, place the timing mark at the six o'clock position.*

V6

1. Disconnect the negative battery cable.
2. Remove the upper half of the radiator fan shroud.
3. Raise the front of the car and drain the oil.
4. Unscrew the exhaust pipe cross-over tube mounting nuts at the manifold. Lower the cross-over tube.
5. On models which are equipped with an automatic transmission, remove the torque converter cover.
6. Remove the upper bolt on the starter brace and then remove the inboard starter bolt and swing the starter assembly aside.
7. Loosen and remove the left hand motor mount thru-bolt and then loosen the thru-bolt on the right hand mount.
8. Raise the engine and then reinstall the thru-bolt in the left-hand motor mount. *Do not tighten the bolt.*
9. Unscrew the attaching bolts and remove the oil pan from under the engine.
10. To install, clean all gasket and seal surfaces thoroughly, use new gaskets and seals and reverse the removal procedure.

Rear Main Oil Seal

REPLACEMENT—ALL EXCEPT 231 V6

The rear main bearing seal may be replaced without removing the crankshaft. Seals

138 ENGINE AND ENGINE REBUILDING

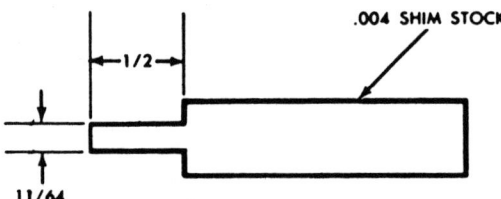

Fabricate an oil seal tool

should only be replaced as a pair. Fabrication of a seal installation tool as shown in the figure will prevent damaging the bead on the cylinder block. The seal lips should face the front of the engine when properly installed.

1. Remove the oil pan and oil pump.
2. Remove the rear main bearing cap, and pry the seal out from the bottom with a small pry bar.
3. Remove the upper seal with a small hammer and a brass pin punch. Tap on one end of the seal until the opposite end can be gripped with pliers.
4. Clean the bearing cap and the crankshaft.
5. Coat the lips and bead of the seal with a light engine oil. Do not get oil on the seal ends.
6. Insert the tip of the installation tool between the crankshaft and the seal seat of the cylinder block. Place the seal between the tip of the tool and the crankshaft, so that the bead contacts the tip of the tool.
7. Be sure that the seal lip is facing the front of the engine, and work the seal around

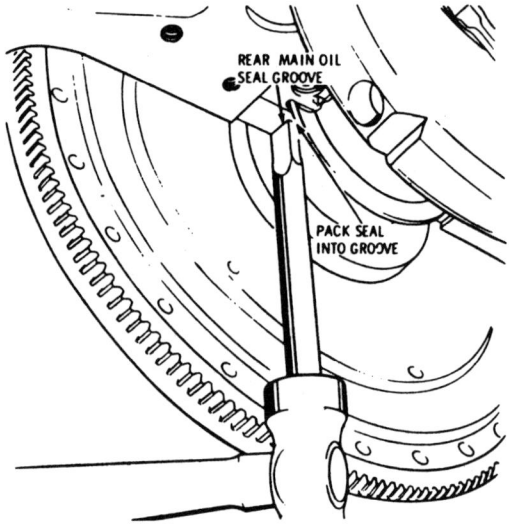

Pack the old seal into the groove

the crankshaft, using the installation tool to protect the seal from the corner of the cylinder block.

NOTE: *Do not remove the tool until the opposite end of the seal is flush with the cylinder block surface.*

8. Remove the installation tool, being careful not to pull the seal out at the same time.
9. Using the same procedure, install the lower seal into the bearing cap. Use your finger and thumb to lever the seal into the cap.
10. Apply sealer to the cylinder block only

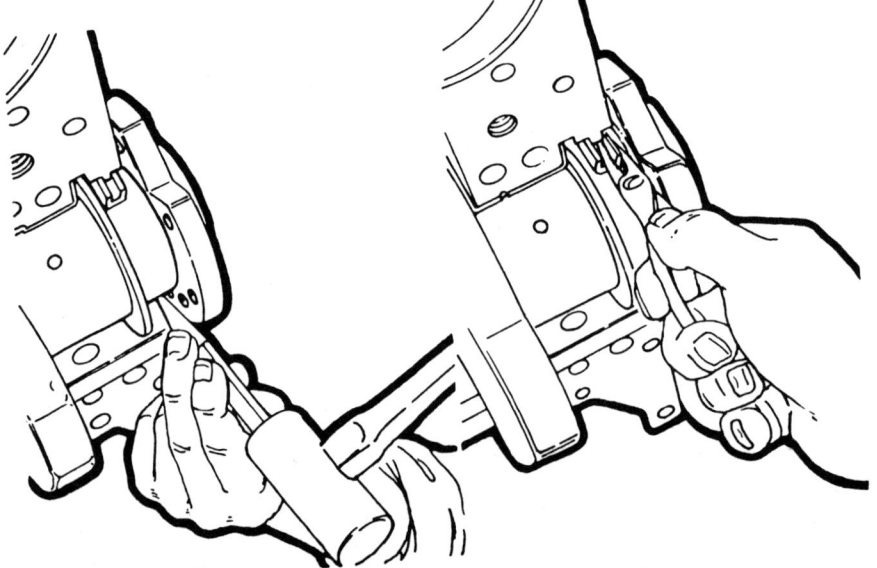

Removing the upper half of the oil seal

ENGINE AND ENGINE REBUILDING

where the cap mates to the surface. Do not apply sealer to the seal ends.

11. Install the rear cap and torque the bolts to specifications. Install the oil pan and pump as previously described.

231 V6

On this engine, the upper half of the rear main bearing oil seal may be repaired, but not replaced, with the crankshaft in place. To completely replace the seal, the crankshaft must be removed. The lower part of the seal may be replaced in the conventional manner when the bearing cap is removed.

1. Remove the oil pan and the rear main bearing cap.
2. Using a blunt-edged tool, drive the upper seal into its groove until it is tightly packed. This is usually ¼–¾ in.
3. Cut pieces of a new seal 1/16 in. longer than required to fill the grooves and install them, packing them into place.
4. Carefully trim any protruding edges of the seal.
5. Remove the old seal from the bearing cap, and install a new seal.
6. Reinstall the cap and the oil pan.

2. Remove the two flange mounting bolts, the pick-up bolt, then remove the pump and screen together.
3. To install, align the oil pump driveshafts to match with the distributor tang and position the flange over the distributor lower bushing. Install the pump mounting bolts.
4. Install the oil pan.

V6 and V8 (Except 231V6)

1. Remove the oil pan as previously described.
2. Remove the pump-to-rear main bearing cap bolts and remove the pump and extension shaft.
3. To install align the slot on the top end of the extension shaft with the drive tang on the lower end of the distributor driveshaft and install the rear main bearing cap bolt.
4. Position the pump screen so that the bottom edge is parallel to the oil pan rails.
5. Install the oil pan.

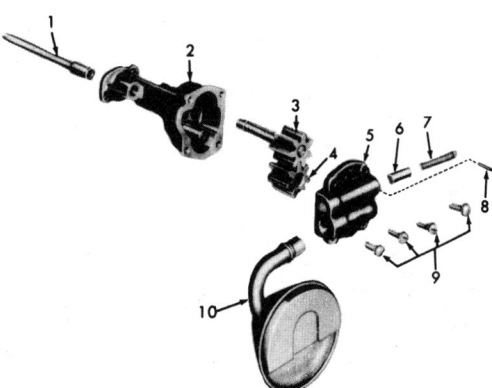

1. Shaft Extension
2. Pump Body
3. Drive Gear and Shaft
4. Idler Gear
5. Pump Cover
6. Pressure Regulator Valve
7. Pressure Regulator Spring
8. Retaining Pin
9. Screws
10. Pickup Screen and Pipe

Exploded view of a small-block V8 oil pump (others similar)

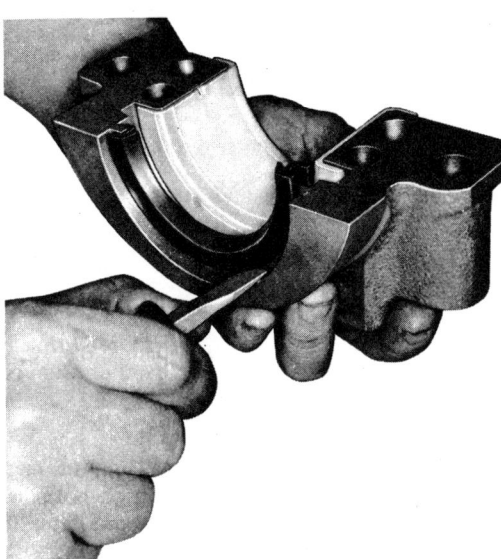

Removing the lower half of the oil seal

Oil Pump

REMOVAL AND INSTALLATION

In Line Six-Cylinder

1. Remove the oil pan as previously described.

231 V6

The oil pump is located in the timing chain cover and is connected by a drilled passage to the oil screen housing and pipe assembly in the oil pan. All oil is discharged from the pump to the oil pump cover assembly, on which the oil filter is mounted.

1. To remove the oil pump cover and gears, first remove the oil filter.
2. Remove the screws which attach the oil

pump cover assembly to the timing chain cover.

3. Remove the cover assembly and slide out the oil pump gears. Clean the gears and inspect them for any obvious defects such as chipping or scoring.

4. Remove the oil pressure relief valve cap, spring and valve. Clean them and inspect them for wear or scoring. Check the relief valve spring to see that it is not worn on its side or collapsed. Replace the spring if it seems questionable.

5. Check the relief valve for a correct fit in its bore. It should be an easy slip fit and no more. If any perceptible shake can be felt, the valve and/or the cover should be replaced.

6. To install, lubricate the pressure relief valve and spring and place them in the cover. Install the cap and the gasket. Torque the cap to 35 ft. lbs.

7. Pack the oil pump gear cavity full of petroleum jelly. Do not use gear lube. Reinstall the oil pump gears so that the petroleum jelly is forced into every cavity of the gear pocket, and between the gear teeth. There must be no air spaces. This step is very important. Unless the pump is packed, it may not begin to pump oil as soon as the engine is started.

8. Install the cover assembly using a new gasket and sealer. Tighten the screws to 10 ft. lbs.

9. Install the oil filter.

ENGINE COOLING

The cooling system consists of a radiator, belt-driven fan, thermostat, and a mechanical water pump. Air conditioned and high-performance engines are equipped with a viscous drive fan. This fan restricts operation at 1500 rpm in cold weather and 3500 rpm during warmer temperatures. This fan requires less horsepower to drive during high rpm operation and reduces under-hood noise. 1977 and later models are equipped with a special pressure relief radiator cap. Be sure any replacement cap used is the same.

Refer to Chapter 1 for the coolant level checking procedure and to the Appendix for "Antifreeze" charts. The coolant should periodically be drained and the system flushed with clean water, at the intervals specified in Chapter 1. Service stations have reverse flushing equipment available; there also permanently-installed do-it-yourself reverse flushing attachments available.

There is a coolant drain cock at the bottom of most radiators. Six-cylinder engines have a coolant drain plug on the left side of the engine block; V8s have one on each side. Some engines don't have any.

The coolant should always be maintained at a minimum of −20°F freezing protection, regardless of the prevailing temperature. This concentration assures rust protection and the highest possible boiling point. It also prevents the heater core from freezing on air-conditioned models.

Two common causes of corrosion are air-suction and exhaust gas leakage. Air may be drawn into the system due to low coolant level in the radiator, a leaky water pump, loose hose connections, a defective radiator pressure cap, or a leaky overflow hose connection to the radiator on the coolant recovery bottle. Exhaust gas may be blown into the cooling system past the cylinder head gasket or through cracks in the cylinder head and block.

Radiator

REMOVAL AND INSTALLATION

1. Drain the cooling system.
2. Disconnect the radiator upper and lower hoses and, if applicable, the transmission coolant lines. Remove the coolant recovery system line, if so equipped.
3. Remove the radiator upper panel if so equipped.
4. If there is a radiator shroud in front of the radiator, the radiator and shroud are removed as an assembly.
5. If there is a fan shroud, remove the shroud attaching screws and let the shroud hang on the fan.
6. Remove the radiator attaching bolts and remove the radiator.
7. Installation is the reverse of the removal procedure.

Water Pump

REMOVAL AND INSTALLATION

NOTE: *Certain steps may not apply to all engines.*

1. Drain the radiator.
2. Loosen the fan pulley bolts.
3. Disconnect the heater hoses, lower radiator hose, and the by-pass hose (if so equipped) at the water pump.

ENGINE AND ENGINE REBUILDING

4. Loosen the alternator swivel bolt (remove the upper brace on V8s) and remove the fan belt.

5. Disconnect the power steering and air conditioning belts and swivel the power steering pump to one side (on Mark IV engines).

6. Remove the fan and pulley.

NOTE: *Viscous drive fans should not be stored horizontally. The silicone fluid can leak out of the fan assembly if it is not kept upright.*

7. Remove the water pump-to-cylinder block bolts and the power steering-to-pump bolts. Remove the water pump. On six-cylinder engines, remove the pump by pulling it straight out of the block.

8. Install the pump on the block with a new gasket.

9. Install the pump pulley and the fan onto the pump.

10. Connect the hoses and refill the cooling system. Install the remaining components, bolts, and belts.

11. Start the engine and check for leaks.

Thermostat

REMOVAL AND INSTALLATION

1. It is not necessary to remove the radiator hose from the thermostat housing.

2. Remove the two retaining bolts from the thermostat housing (located on the front top of the intake manifold on V6s and V8s, and directly in front of the valve cover on in-line sixes), and remove the thermostat.

3. Use a new gasket when replacing the thermostat.

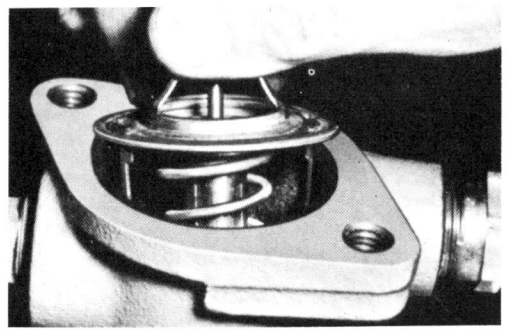

Thermostat removal and installation

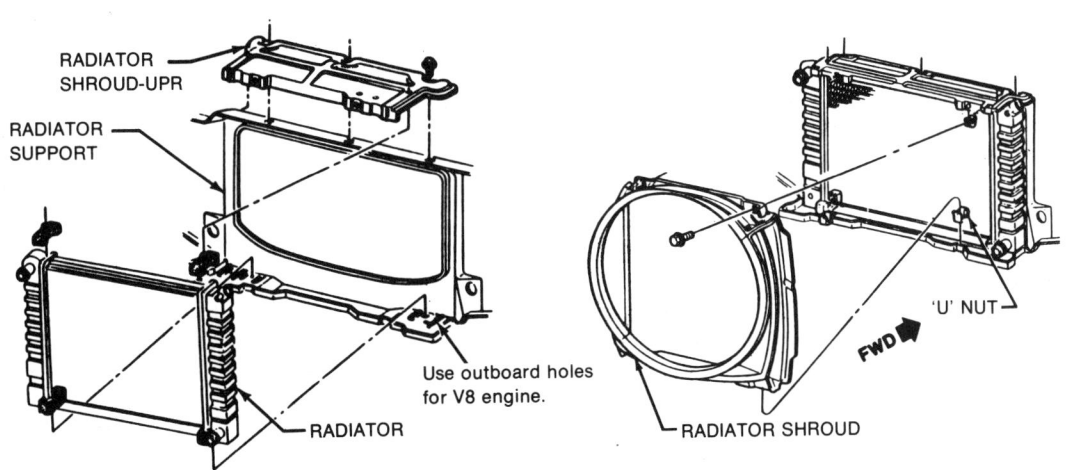

Typical radiator removal

ENGINE REBUILDING

Most procedures involved in rebuilding an engine are fairly standard, regardless of the type of engine involved. This section is a guide accepted rebuilding procedures. Examples of standard rebuilding practices are illustrated and should be used along with specific details concerning your particular engine, found earlier in this chapter.

The procedures given here are those used by any competent rebuilder. Obviously some of the procedures cannot be performed by the do-it-yourself mechanic, but are provided so that you will be familiar with the services that should be offered by rebuilding or machine shops. As an example, in most instances, it is more profitable for the home mechanic to remove the cylinder heads, buy the necessary parts (new valves, seals, keepers, keys, etc.) and deliver these to a machine shop for the necessary work. In this way you will save the money to remove and install the cylinder head and the mark-up on parts.

On the other hand, most of the work involved in rebuilding the lower end is well within the scope of the do-it-yourself mechanic. Only work such as hot-tanking, actually boring the block or Magnafluxing (invisible crack detection) need be sent to a machine shop.

Tools

The tools required for basic engine rebuilding should, with a few exceptions, be those included in a mechanic's tool kit. An accurate torque wrench, and a dial indicator (reading in thousandths) mounted on a universal base should be available. Special tools, where required, are available from the major tool suppliers. The services of a competent automotive machine shop must also be readily available.

Precautions

Aluminum has become increasingly popular for use in engines, due to its low weight and excellent heat transfer characteristics. The following precautions must be observed when handling aluminum (or any other) engine parts:
—Never hot-tank aluminum parts.
—Remove all aluminum parts (identification tags, etc.) from engine parts before hot-tanking (otherwise they will be removed during the process).
—Always coat threads lightly with engine oil or anti-seize compounds before installation, to prevent seizure.
—Never over-torque bolts or spark plugs in aluminum threads. Should stripping occur, threads can be restored using any of a number of thread repair kits available (see next section).

Inspection Techniques

Magnaflux and Zyglo are inspection techniques used to locate material flaws, such as stress cracks. Magnaflux is a magnetic process, applicable only to ferrous materials. The Zyglo process coats the matrial with a fluorescent dye penetrant, and any material may be tested using Zyglo. Specific checks of suspected surface cracks may be made at lower cost and more readily using spot check dye. The dye is sprayed onto the suspected area, wiped off, and the area is then sprayed with a developer. Cracks then will show up brightly.

Overhaul

The section is divided into two parts. The first, Cylinder Head Reconditioning, assumes that the cylinder head is removed from the engine, all manifolds are removed, and the cylinder head is on a workbench. The camshaft should be removed from overhead cam cylinder heads. The second section, Cylinder Block Reconditioning, covers the block, pistons, connecting rods and crankshaft. It is assumed that the engine is mounted on a work stand, and the cylinder head and all accessories are removed.

Procedures are identified as follows:
Unmarked—Basic procedures that must be performed in order to successfully complete the rebuilding process.
Starred (*)—Procedures that should be performed to ensure maximum performance and engine life.
Double starred (**)—Procedures that may be performed to increase engine performance and reliability.

When assembling the engine, any parts that will be in frictional contact must be pre-lubricated, to provide protection on initial start-up. Any product specifically formulated for this purpose may be used. NOTE: *Do not use engine oil.* Where semi-permanent (locked but removable) installation of bolts or nuts is desired, threads should be cleaned and located with Loctite® or a similar product (non-hardening).

ENGINE AND ENGINE REBUILDING 143

Repairing Damaged Threads

Several methods of repairing damaged threads are available. Heli-Coil® (shown here), Keenserts® and Microdot® are among the most widely used. All involve basically the same principle—drilling out stripped threads, tapping the hole and installing a pre-wound insert—making welding, plugging and oversize fasteners unnecessary.

Two types of thread repair inserts are usually supplied—a standard type for most Inch Coarse, Inch Fine, Metric Coarse and Metric Fine thread sizes and a spark plug type to fit most spark plug port sizes. Consult the individual manufacturer's catalog to determine exact applications. Typical thread repair kits will contain a selection of pre-wound threaded inserts, a tap (corresponding to the outside diameter threads of the insert) and an installation tool. Spark plug inserts usually differ because they require a tap equipped with pilot threads and a combined reamer/tap section. Most manufacturers also supply blister-packed thread repair inserts separately in addition to a master kit containing a variety of taps and inserts plus installation tools.

Before effecting a repair to a threaded hole, remove any snapped, broken or damaged bolts or studs. Penetrating oil can be used to free frozen threads; the offending item can be removed with locking pliers or with a screw or stud extractor. After the hole is clear, the thread can be repaired, as follows:

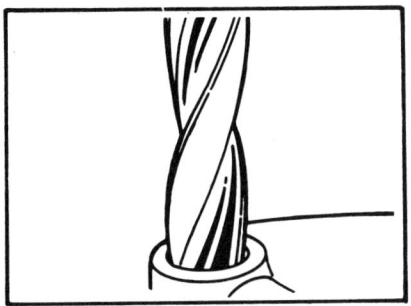

Drill out the damaged threads with specified drill. Drill completely through the hole or to the bottom of a blind hole

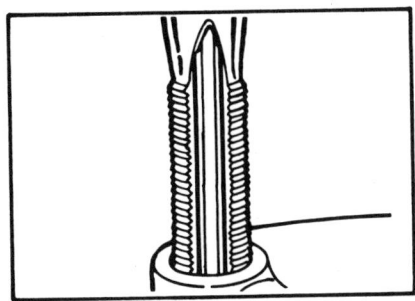

With the tap supplied, tap the hole to receive the thread insert. Keep the tap well oiled and back it out frequently to avoid clogging the threads

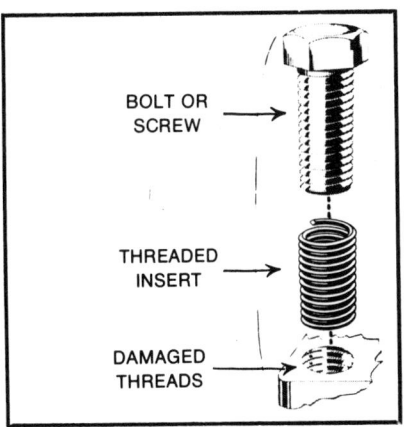

Damaged bolt holes can be repaired with thread repair inserts

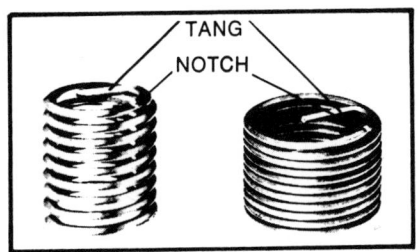

Standard thread repair insert (left) and spark plug thread insert (right)

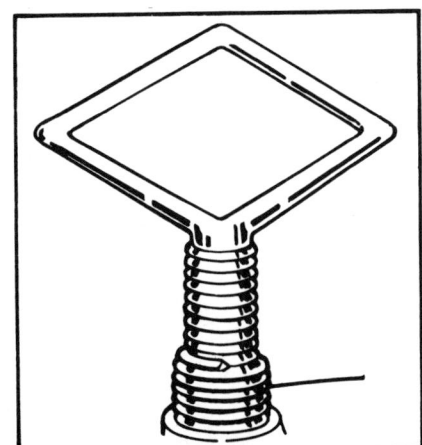

Screw the threaded insert onto the installation tool until the tang engages the slot. Screw the insert into the tapped hole until it is ¼–½ turn below the top surface. After installation break off the tang with a hammer and punch

Standard Torque Specifications and Fastener Markings

The Newton-metre has been designated the world standard for measuring torque and will gradually replace the foot-pound and kilogram-meter. In the absence of specific torques, the following chart can be used as a guide to the maximum safe torque of a particular size/grade of fastener.

- There is no torque difference for fine or coarse threads.
- Torque values are based on clean, dry threads. Reduce the value by 10% if threads are oiled prior to assembly.
- The torque required for aluminum components or fasteners is considerably less.

U. S. BOLTS

SAE Grade Number	1 or 2			5			6 or 7		
Bolt Markings Manufacturer's marks may vary—number of lines always 2 less than the grade number.									
Usage	Frequent			Frequent			Infrequent		
Bolt Size (inches)—(Thread)	Maximum Torque			Maximum Torque			Maximum Torque		
	Ft-Lb	kgm	Nm	Ft-Lb	kgm	Nm	Ft-Lb	kgm	Nm
¼—20	5	0.7	6.8	8	1.1	10.8	10	1.4	13.5
—28	6	0.8	8.1	10	1.4	13.6			
5⁄16—18	11	1.5	14.9	17	2.3	23.0	19	2.6	25.8
—24	13	1.8	17.6	19	2.6	25.7			
3⁄8—16	18	2.5	24.4	31	4.3	42.0	34	4.7	46.0
—24	20	2.75	27.1	35	4.8	47.5			
7⁄16—14	28	3.8	37.0	49	6.8	66.4	55	7.6	74.5
—20	30	4.2	40.7	55	7.6	74.5			
½—13	39	5.4	52.8	75	10.4	101.7	85	11.75	115.2
—20	41	5.7	55.6	85	11.7	115.2			
9⁄16—12	51	7.0	69.2	110	15.2	149.1	120	16.6	162.7
—18	55	7.6	74.5	120	16.6	162.7			
5⁄8—11	83	11.5	112.5	150	20.7	203.3	167	23.0	226.5
—18	95	13.1	128.8	170	23.5	230.5			
¾—10	105	14.5	142.3	270	37.3	366.0	280	38.7	379.6
—16	115	15.9	155.9	295	40.8	400.0			
7⁄8— 9	160	22.1	216.9	395	54.6	535.5	440	60.9	596.5
—14	175	24.2	237.2	435	60.1	589.7			
1— 8	236	32.5	318.6	590	81.6	799.9	660	91.3	894.8
—14	250	34.6	338.9	660	91.3	849.8			

ENGINE AND ENGINE REBUILDING

METRIC BOLTS

NOTE: *Metric bolts are marked with a number indicating the relative strength of the bolt. These numbers have nothing to do with size.*

Description	Torque ft-lbs (Nm)			
Thread size x pitch (mm)	Head mark—4		Head mark—7	
6 x 1.0	2.2–2.9	(3.0–3.9)	3.6–5.8	(4.9–7.8)
8 x 1.25	5.8–8.7	(7.9–12)	9.4–14	(13–19)
10 x 1.25	12–17	(16–23)	20–29	(27–39)
12 x 1.25	21–32	(29–43)	35–53	(47–72)
14 x 1.5	35–52	(48–70)	57–85	(77–110)
16 x 1.5	51–77	(67–100)	90–120	(130–160)
18 x 1.5	74–110	(100–150)	130–170	(180–230)
20 x 1.5	110–140	(150–190)	190–240	(160–320)
22 x 1.5	150–190	(200–260)	250–320	(340–430)
24 x 1.5	190–240	(260–320)	310–410	(420–550)

NOTE: *This engine rebuilding section is a guide to accepted rebuilding procedures. Typical examples of standard rebuilding procedures are illustrated. Use these procedures along with the detailed instructions earlier in this chapter, concerning your particular engine.*

Cylinder Head Reconditioning

Procedure	Method
Remove the cylinder head:	See the engine service procedures earlier in this chapter for details concerning specific engines.
Identify the valves:	Invert the cylinder head, and number the valve faces front to rear, using a permanent felt-tip marker.
Remove the rocker arms:	Remove the rocker arms with shaft(s) or balls and nuts. Wire the sets of rockers, balls and nuts together, and identify according to the corresponding valve.
Remove the valves and springs:	Using an appropriate valve spring compressor (depending on the configuration of the cylinder head), compress the valve springs. Lift out the keepers with needlenose pliers, release the compressor, and remove the valve, spring, and spring retainer. See the engine service procedures earlier in this chapter for details concerning specific engines.
Check the valve stem-to-guide clearance:	Clean the valve stem with lacquer thinner or a similar solvent to remove all gum and varnish. Clean the valve guides using solvent and an expanding wire-type valve guide cleaner. Mount a dial indicator so that the stem is at 90° to the valve stem, as close to the valve guide as possible. Move the valve off its seat, and measure the valve guide-to-stem clearance by rocking the stem back and forth to actuate the dial indicator. Measure the valve stems using a micrometer, and compare to specifications, to determine whether stem or guide wear is responsible for excessive clearance. NOTE: *Consult the Specifications tables earlier in this chapter.*

Check the valve stem-to-guide clearance

146 ENGINE AND ENGINE REBUILDING

Cylinder Head Reconditioning

Procedure	Method
De-carbon the cylinder head and valves: 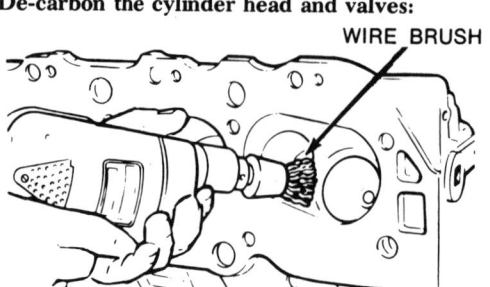 Remove the carbon from the cylinder head with a wire brush and electric drill	Chip carbon away from the valve heads, combustion chambers, and ports, using a chisel made of hardwood. Remove the remaining deposits with a stiff wire brush. NOTE: *Be sure that the deposits are actually removed, rather than burnished.*
Hot-tank the cylinder head (cast iron heads only): CAUTION: *Do not hot-tank aluminum parts.*	Have the cylinder head hot-tanked to remove grease, corrosion, and scale from the water passages. NOTE: *In the case of overhead cam cylinder heads, consult the operator to determine whether the camshaft bearings will be damaged by the caustic solution.*
Degrease the remaining cylinder head parts:	Clean the remaining cylinder head parts in an engine cleaning solvent. Do not remove the protective coating from the springs.
Check the cylinder head for warpage: 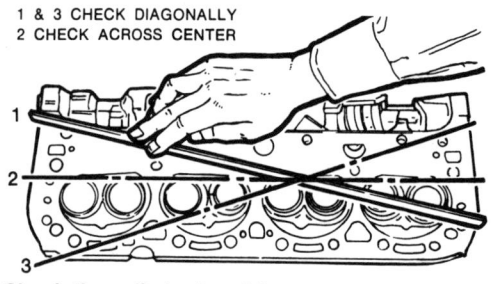 Check the cylinder head for warpage	Place a straight-edge across the gasket surface of the cylinder head. Using feeler gauges, determine the clearance at the center of the straight-edge. If warpage exceeds .003″ in a 6″ span, or .006″ over the total length, the cylinder head must be resurfaced. NOTE: *If warpage exceeds the manufacturer's maximum tolerance for material removal, the cylinder head must be replaced.* When milling the cylinder heads of V-type engines, the intake manifold mounting position is altered, and must be corrected by milling the manifold flange a proportionate amount.
*Knurl the valve guides: 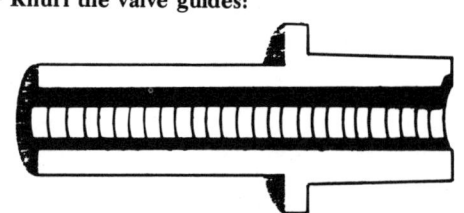 Cut-away view of a knurled valve guide	*Valve guides which are not excessively worn or distorted may, in some cases, be knurled rather than replaced. Knurling is a process in which metal is displaced and raised, thereby reducing clearance. Knurling also provides excellent oil control. The possibility of knurling rather than replacing valve guides should be discussed with a machinist.
Replace the valve guides: NOTE: *Valve guides should only be replaced if damaged or if an oversize valve stem is not available.*	See the engine service procedures earlier in this chapter for details concerning specific engines. Depending on the type of cylinder head, valve guides may be pressed, hammered, or shrunk in. In cases where the guides are shrunk into the head, replacement should be left to an equipped machine shop. In other

ENGINE AND ENGINE REBUILDING

Cylinder Head Reconditioning

Procedure	Method
	cases, the guides are replaced using a stepped drift (see illustration). Determine the height above the boss that the guide must extend, and obtain a stack of washers, their I.D. similar to the guide's O.D., of that height. Place the stack of washers on the guide, and insert the guide into the boss. **NOTE:** *Valve guides are often tapered or beveled for installation.* Using the stepped installation tool (see illustration), press or tap the guides into position. Ream the guides according to the size of the valve stem.

A—VALVE GUIDE I.D. **B**—LARGER THAN THE VALVE GUIDE O.D.

WASHERS

A—VALVE GUIDE I.D. **B**—LARGER THAN THE VALVE GUIDE O.D.

Valve guide installation tool using washers for installation

Replace valve seat inserts:	Replacement of valve seat inserts which are worn beyond resurfacing or broken, if feasible, must be done by a machine shop.
Resurface (grind) the valve face:	Using a valve grinder, resurface the valves according to specifications given earlier in this chapter. **CAUTION:** *Valve face angle is not always identical to valve seat angle.* A minimum margin of 1/32" should remain after grinding the valve. The valve stem top should also be squared and resurfaced, by placing the stem in the V-block of the grinder, and turning it while pressing lightly against the grinding wheel. **NOTE:** *Do not grind sodium filled exhaust valves on a machine. These should be hand lapped.*

FOR DIMENSIONS, REFER TO SPECIFICATIONS

CHECK FOR BENT STEM

DIAMETER

VALVE FACE ANGLE

1/32" MINIMUM

THIS LINE PARALLEL WITH VALVE HEAD

Critical valve dimensions

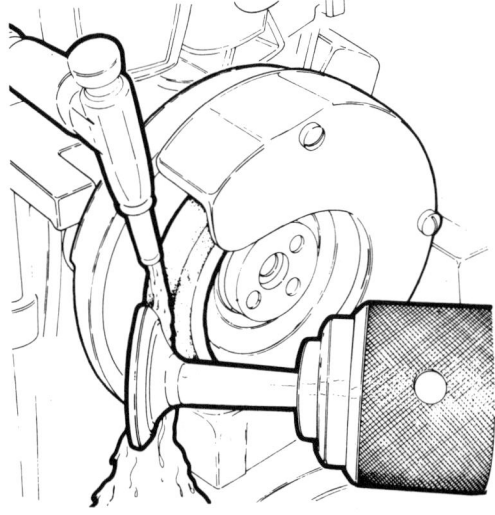

Valve grinding by machine

Cylinder Head Reconditioning

Procedure	Method
Resurface the valve seats using reamers of grinder: 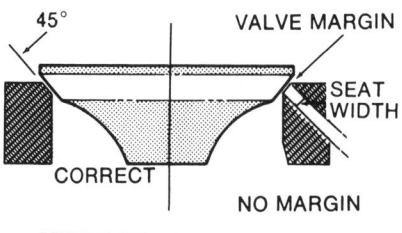 Valve seat width and centering 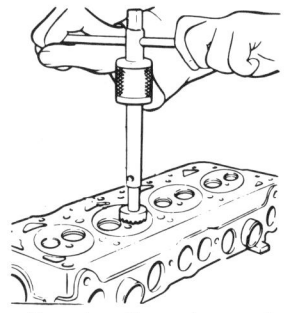 Reaming the valve seat with a hand reamer	Select a reamer of the correct seat angle, slightly larger than the diameter of the valve seat, and assemble it with a pilot of the correct size. Install the pilot into the valve guide, and using steady pressure, turn the reamer clockwise. **CAUTION:** *Do not turn the reamer counterclockwise.* Remove only as much material as necessary to clean the seat. Check the concentricity of the seat (following). If the dye method is not used, coat the valve face with Prussian blue dye, install and rotate it on the valve seat. Using the dye marked area as a centering guide, center and narrow the valve seat to specifications with correction cutters. **NOTE:** *When no specifications are available, minimum seat width for exhaust valves should be 5/64", intake valves 1/16".* After making correction cuts, check the position of the valve seat on the valve face using Prussian blue dye. To resurface the seat with a power grinder, select a pilot of the correct size and coarse stone of the proper angle. Lubricate the pilot and move the stone on and off the valve seat at 2 cycles per second, until all flaws are gone. Finish the seat with a fine stone. If necessary the seat can be corrected or narrowed using correction stones.
Check the valve seat concentricity: 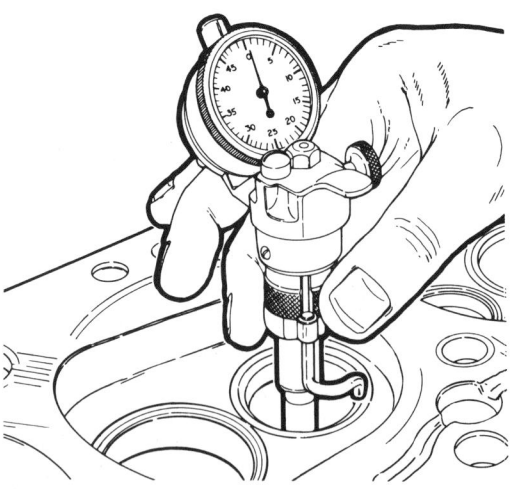 Check the valve seat concentricity with a dial gauge	Coat the valve face with Prussian blue dye, install the valve, and rotate it on the valve seat. If the entire seat becomes coated, and the valve is known to be concentric, the seat is concentric. *Install the dial gauge pilot into the guide, and rest of the arm on the valve seat. Zero the gauge, and rotate the arm around the seat. Run-out should not exceed .002".

ENGINE AND ENGINE REBUILDING

Cylinder Head Reconditioning

Procedure	Method
*Lap the valves: NOTE: *Valve lapping is done to ensure efficient sealing of resurfaced valves and seats.* 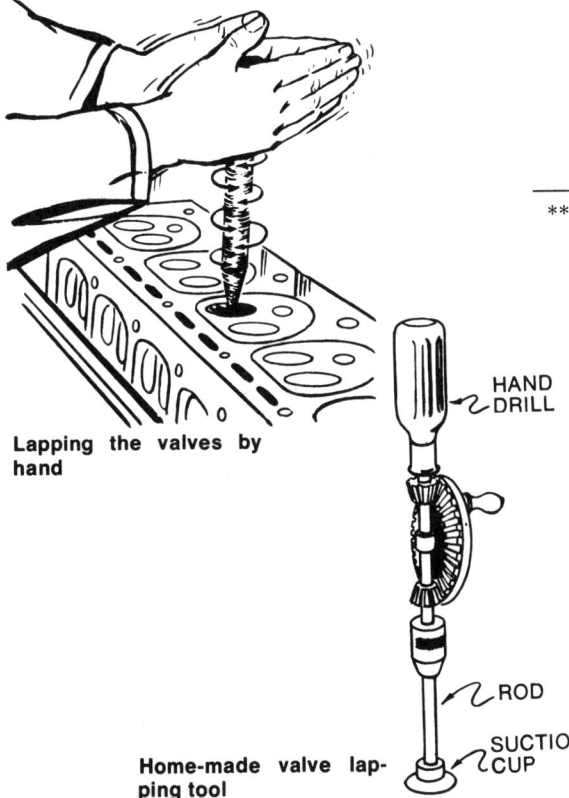 Lapping the valves by hand Home-made valve lapping tool	Invert the cylinder head, lightly lubricate the valve stems, and install the valves in the head as numbered. Coat valve seats with fine grinding compound, and attach the lapping tool suction cup to a valve head. NOTE: *Moisten the suction cup.* Rotate the tool between the palms, changing position and lifting the tool often to prevent grooving. Lap the valve until a smooth, polished seat is evident. Remove the valve and tool, and rinse away all traces of grinding compound. **Fasten a suction cup to a piece of drill rod, and mount the rod in a hand drill. Proceed as above, using the hand drill as a lapping tool. CAUTION: *Due to the higher speeds involved when using the hand drill, care must be exercised to avoid grooving the seat.* Lift the tool and change direction of rotation often.
Check the valve springs: 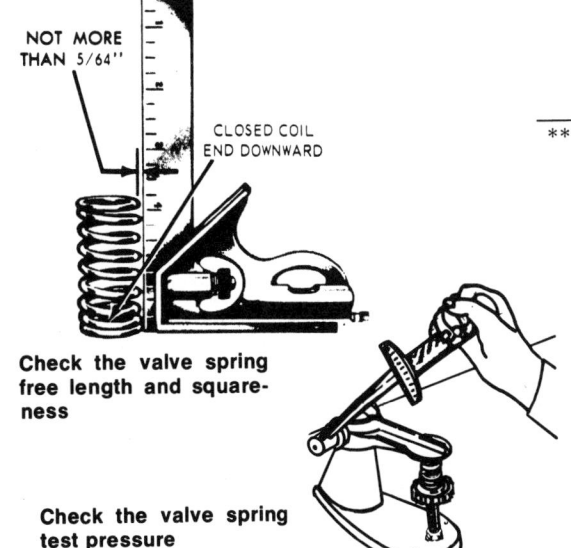 Check the valve spring free length and squareness Check the valve spring test pressure	Place the spring on a flat surface next to a square. Measure the height of the spring, and rotate it against the edge of the square to measure distortion. If spring height varies (by comparison) by more than $1/16''$ or if distortion exceeds $1/16''$, replace the spring. **In addition to evaluating the spring as above, test the spring pressure at the installed and compressed (installed height minus valve lift) height using a valve spring tester. Springs used on small displacement engines (up to 3 liters) should be $\mp$ 1 lb of all other springs in either position. A tolerance of $\mp$ 5 lbs is permissible on larger engines.

ENGINE AND ENGINE REBUILDING

Cylinder Head Reconditioning

Procedure	Method
*Install valve stem seals: 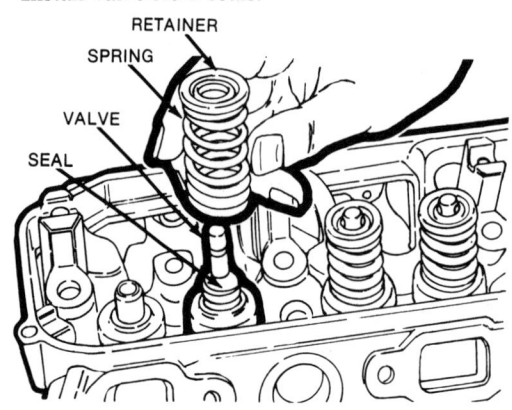 **Install valve stem seals**	*Due to the pressure differential that exists at the ends of the intake valve guides (atmospheric pressure above, manifold vacuum below), oil is drawn through the valve guides into the intake port. This has been alleviated somewhat since the addition of positive crankcase ventilation, which lowers the pressure above the guides. Several types of valve stem seals are available to reduce blow-by. Certain seals simply slip over the stem and guide boss, while others require that the boss be machined. Recently, Teflon guide seals have become popular. Consult a parts supplier or machinist concerning availability and suggested usages. NOTE: *When installing seals, ensure that a small amount of oil is able to pass the seal to lubricate the valve guides; otherwise, excessive wear may result.*
Install the valves:	See the engine service procedures earlier in this chapter for details concerning specific engines. Lubricate the valve stems, and install the valves in the cylinder head as numbered. Lubricate and position the seals (if used) and the valve springs. Install the spring retainers, compress the springs, and insert the keys using needlenose pliers or a tool designed for this purpose. NOTE: *Retain the keys with wheel bearing grease during installation.*
Check valve spring installed height: 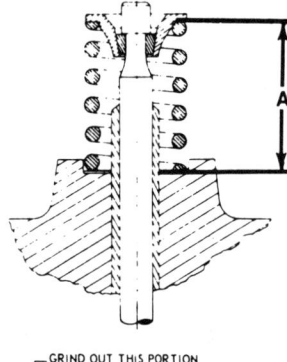 **Valve spring installed height (A)**  **Measure the valve spring installed height (A) with a modified steel rule**	Measure the distance between the spring pad the lower edge of the spring retainer, and compare to specifications. If the installed height is incorrect, add shim washers between the spring pad and the spring. CAUTION: *Use only washers designed for this purpose.*

ENGINE AND ENGINE REBUILDING

Cylinder Head Reconditioning

Procedure	Method
Inspect the rocker arms, balls, studs, and nuts: 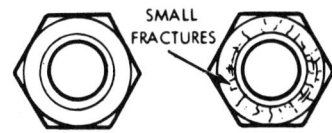 Stress cracks in the rocker nuts	Visually inspect the rocker arms, balls, studs, and nuts for cracks, galling, burning, scoring, or wear. If all parts are intact, liberally lubricate the rocker arms and balls, and install them on the cylinder head. If wear is noted on a rocker arm at the point of valve contact, grind it smooth and square, removing as little material as possible. Replace the rocker arm if excessively worn. If a rocker stud shows signs of wear, it must be replaced (see below). If a rocker nut shows stress cracks, replace it. If an exhaust ball is galled or burned, substitute the intake ball from the same cylinder (if it is intact), and install a new intake ball. NOTE: *Avoid using new rocker balls on exhaust valves.*
Replace rocker studs: 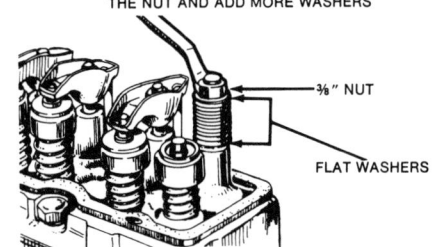 Extracting a pressed-in rocker stud 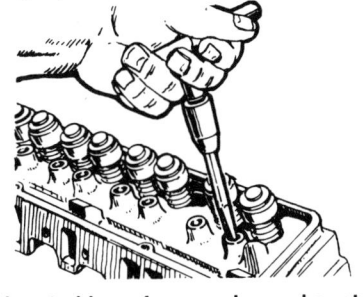 Ream the stud bore for oversize rocker studs	In order to remove a threaded stud, lock two nuts on the stud, and unscrew the stud using the lower nut. Coat the lower threads of the new stud with Loctite, and install. Two alternative methods are available for replacing pressed in studs. Remove the damaged stud using a stack of washers and a nut (see ilustration). In the first, the boss is reamed .005–.006″ oversize, and an oversize stud pressed in. Control the stud extension over the boss using washers, in the same manner as valve guides. Before installing the stud, coat it with white lead and grease. To retain the stud more positively drill a hole through the stud and boss, and install a roll pin. In the second method, the boss is tapped, and a threaded stud installed.
Inspect the rocker shaft(s) and rocker arms: 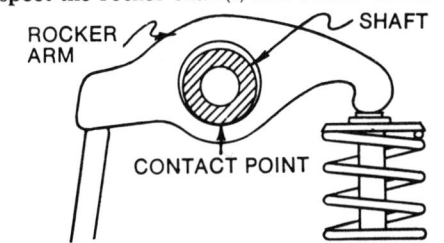 Check the rocker arm-to-rocker shaft contact area	Remove the rocker arms, springs and washers from rocker shaft. NOTE: *Lay out parts in the order as they are removed.* Inspect rocker arms for pitting or wear on the valve contact point, or excessive bushing wear. Bushings need only be replaced if wear is excessive, because the rocker arm normally contacts the shaft at one point only. Grind the valve contact point of rocker arm smooth if necessary, removing as little material as possible. If excessive material must be removed to smooth and square the arm, it should be replaced. Clean out all oil holes and passages in rocker shaft. If shaft is grooved or worn, replace it. Lubricate and assemble the rocker shaft.

152　ENGINE AND ENGINE REBUILDING

Cylinder Head Reconditioning

Procedure	Method
Inspect the pushrods:	Remove the pushrods, and, if hollow, clean out the oil passages using fine wire. Roll each pushrod over a piece of clean glass. If a distinct clicking sound is heard as the pushrod rolls, the rod is bent, and must be replaced.
	*The length of all pushrods must be equal. Measure the length of the pushrods, compare to specifications, and replace as necessary.
*Inspect the valve lifters: CHECK FOR CONCAVE WEAR ON FACE OF TAPPET USING TAPPET FOR STRAIGHT EDGE **Check the lifter face for squareness**	Remove lifters from their bores, and remove gum and varnish, using solvent. Clean walls of lifter bores. Check lifters for concave wear as illustrated. If face is worn concave, replace lifter, and carefully inspect the camshaft. Lightly lubricate lifter and insert it into its bore. If play is excessive, an oversize lifter must be installed (where possible). Consult a machinist concerning feasibility. If play is satisfactory, remove, lubricate, and reinstall the lifter.
*Testing hydraulic lifter leak down:	Submerge lifter in a container of kerosene. Chuck a used pushrod or its equivalent into a drill press. Position container of kerosene so pushrod acts on the lifter plunger. Pump lifter with the drill press, until resistance increases. Pump several more times to bleed any air out of lifter. Apply very firm, constant pressure to the lifter, and observe rate at which fluid bleeds out of lifter. If the fluid bleeds very quickly (less than 15 seconds), lifter is defective. If the time exceeds 60 seconds, lifter is sticking. In either case, recondition or replace lifter. If lifter is operating properly (leak down time 15–60 seconds), lubricate and install it.

Cylinder Block Reconditioning

Procedure	Method
Checking the main bearing clearance: 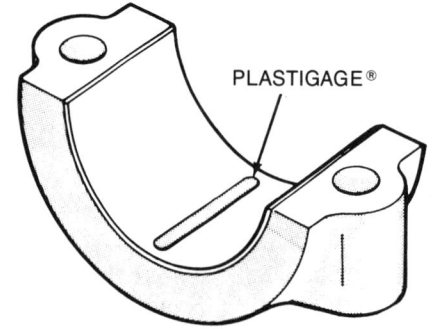 PLASTIGAGE® **Plastigage® installed on the lower bearing shell**	Invert engine, and remove cap from the bearing to be checked. Using a clean, dry rag, thoroughly clean all oil from crankshaft journal and bearing insert. NOTE: *Plastigage® is soluble in oil; therefore, oil on the journal or bearing could result in erroneous readings.* Place a piece of Plastigage along the full length of journal, reinstall cap, and torque to specifications. NOTE: *Specifications are given in the engine specifications earlier in this chapter.* Remove bearing cap, and determine bearing clearance by comparing width of Plastigage to the scale on Plastigage envelope. Journal taper is determined by comparing width of the Plas-

ENGINE AND ENGINE REBUILDING 153

Cylinder Block Reconditioning

Procedure	Method
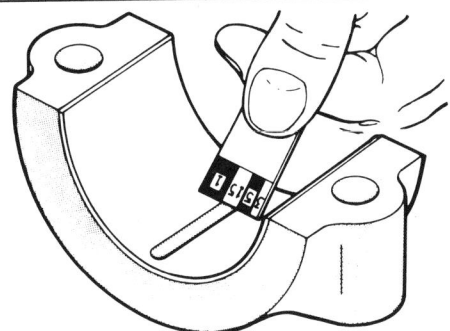 **Measure Plastigage® to determine main bearing clearance**	tigage strip near its ends. Rotate crankshaft 90° and retest, to determine journal eccentricity. **NOTE:** *Do not rotate crankshaft with Plastigage installed.* If bearing insert and journal appear intact, and are within tolerances, no further main bearing service is required. If bearing or journal appear defective, cause of failure should be determined before replacement.
	* Remove crankshaft from block (see below). Measure the main bearing journals at each end twice (90° apart) using a micrometer, to determine diameter, journal taper and eccentricity. If journals are within tolerances, reinstall bearing caps at their specified torque. Using a telescope gauge and micrometer, measure bearing I.D. parallel to piston axis and at 30° on each side of piston axis. Subtract journal O.D. for bearing I.D. to determine oil clearance. If crankshaft journals appear defective, or do not meet tolerances, there is no need to measure bearings; for the crankshaft will require grinding and/or undersize bearings will be required. If bearing appears defective, cause for failure should be determined prior to replacement.
Check the connecting rod bearing clearance:	Connecting rod bearing clearance is checked in the same manner as main bearing clearance, using Plastigage. Before removing the crankshaft, connecting rod side clearance also should be measured and recorded.
	* Checking connecting rod bearing clearance, using a micrometer, is identical to checking main bearing clearance. If no other service is required, the piston and rod assemblies need not be removed.
Remove the crankshaft: 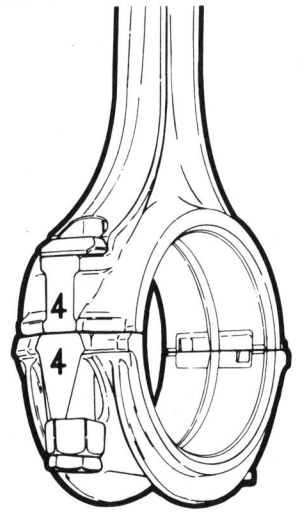 **Match the connecting rod to the cylinder with a number stamp**	Using a punch, mark the corresponding main bearing caps and saddles according to position (i.e., one punch on the front main cap and saddle, two on the second, three on the third, etc.). Using number stamps, identify the corresponding connecting rods and caps, according to cylinder (if no numbers are present). Remove the main and connecting rod caps, and place 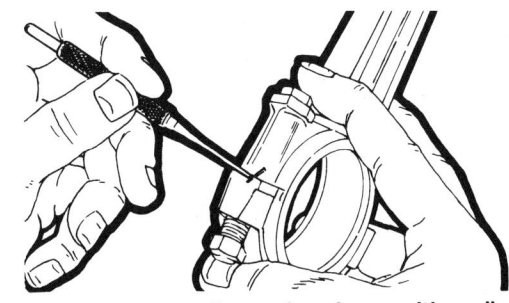 **Match the connecting rod and cap with scribe marks**

ENGINE AND ENGINE REBUILDING

Cylinder Block Reconditioning

Procedure	Method
	sleeves of plastic tubing or vacuum hose over the connecting rod bolts, to protect the journals as the crankshaft is removed. Lift the crankshaft out of the block.
Remove the ridge from the top of the cylinder: Cylinder bore ridge	In order to facilitate removal of the piston and connecting rod, the ridge at the top of the cylinder (unworn area; see illustration) must be removed. Place the piston at the bottom of the bore, and cover it with a rag. Cut the ridge away using a ridge reamer, exercising extreme care to avoid cutting too deeply. Remove the rag, and remove cuttings that remain on the piston. **CAUTION:** *If the ridge is not removed, and new rings are installed, damage to rings will result.*
Remove the piston and connecting rod: Push the piston out with a hammer handle	Invert the engine, and push the pistons and connecting rods out of the cylinders. If necessary, tap the connecting rod boss with a wooden hammer handle, to force the piston out. **CAUTION:** *Do not attempt to force the piston past the cylinder ridge* (see above).
Service the crankshaft:	Ensure that all oil holes and passages in the crankshaft are open and free of sludge. If necessary, have the crankshaft ground to the largest possible undersize.
	** Have the crankshaft Magnafluxed, to locate stress cracks. Consult a machinist concerning additional service procedures, such as surface hardening (e.g., nitriding, Tuftriding) to improve wear characteristics, cross drilling and chamfering the oil holes to improve lubrication, and balancing.
Removing freeze plugs:	Drill a small hole in the middle of the freeze plugs. Thread a large sheet metal screw into the hole and remove the plug with a slide hammer.
Remove the oil gallery plugs:	Threaded plugs should be removed using an appropriate (usually square) wrench. To remove soft, pressed in plugs, drill a hole in the plug, and thread in a sheet metal screw. Pull the plug out by the screw using pliers.

ENGINE AND ENGINE REBUILDING 155

Cylinder Block Reconditioning

Procedure	Method
Hot-tank the block: NOTE: *Do not hot-tank aluminum parts.*	Have the block hot-tanked to remove grease, corrosion, and scale from the water jackets. **NOTE:** *Consult the operator to determine whether the camshaft bearings will be damaged during the hot-tank process.*

Check the block for cracks:	Visually inspect the block for cracks or chips. The most common locations are as follows:
	    Adjacent to freeze plugs.
	    Between the cylinders and water jackets.
	    Adjacent to the main bearing saddles.
	    At the extreme bottom of the cylinders.
	Check only suspected cracks using spot check dye (see introduction). If a crack is located, consult a machinist concerning possible repairs.

	**Magnaflux the block to locate hidden cracks. If cracks are located, consult a machinist about feasibility of repair.
Install the oil gallery plugs and freeze plugs:	Coat freeze plugs with sealer and tap into position using a piece of pipe, slightly smaller than the plug, as a driver. To ensure retention, stake the edges of the plugs. Coat threaded oil gallery plugs with sealer and install. Drive replacement soft plugs into block using a large drift as a driver.
	*Rather than reinstalling lead plugs, drill and tap the holes, and install threaded plugs.
Check the bore diameter and surface: 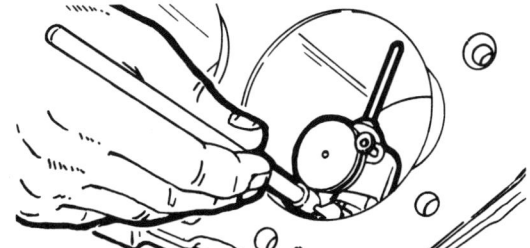 **Measure the cylinder bore with a dial gauge**	Visually inspect the cylinder bores for roughness, scoring, or scuffing. If evident, the cylinder bore must be bored or honed oversize to eliminate imperfections, and the smallest possible oversize piston used. The new pistons should be given to the machinist with the block, so that the cylinders can be bored or honed exactly to the piston size (plus clearance). If no flaws are evident, measure the bore diameter using a telescope gauge and micrometer, or dial gauge, parallel and perpendicular to the engine centerline, at the top (below the ridge) and bottom of the bore. Subtract the bottom measurements from the top to determine taper, and the parallel to

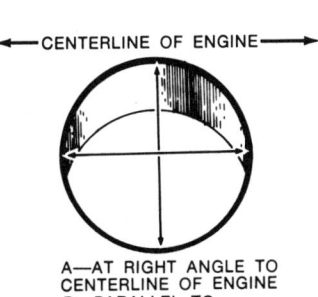

Cylinder bore measuring points
A—AT RIGHT ANGLE TO CENTERLINE OF ENGINE
B—PARALLEL TO CENTERLINE OF ENGINE

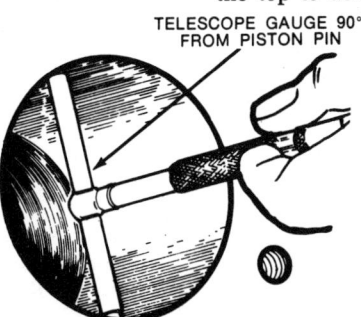

Measure the cylinder bore with a telescope gauge

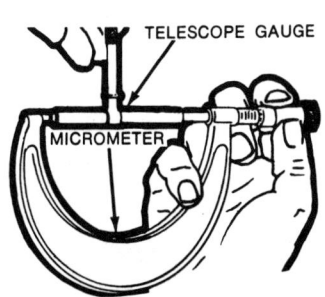

Measure the telescope gauge with a micrometer to determine the cylinder bore

Cylinder Block Reconditioning

Procedure	Method
	the centerline measurements from the perpendicular measurements to determine eccentricity. If the measurements are not within specifications, the cylinder must be bored or honed, and an oversize piston installed. If the measurements are within specifications the cylinder may be used as is, with only finish honing (see below). NOTE: *Prior to submitting the block for boring, perform the following operation(s).*
Check the cylinder block bearing alignment: Check the main bearing saddle alignment	Remove the upper bearing inserts. Place a straightedge in the bearing saddles along the centerline of the crankshaft. If clearance exists between the straightedge and the center saddle, the block must be alignbored.
*Check the deck height:	The deck height is the distance from the crankshaft centerline to the block deck. To measure, invert the engine, and install the crankshaft, retaining it with the center main cap. Measure the distance from the crankshaft journal to the block deck, parallel to the cylinder centerline. Measure the diameter of the end (front and rear) main journals, parallel to the centerline of the cylinders, divide the diameter in half, and subtract it from the previous measurement. The results of the front and rear measurements should be identical. If the difference exceeds .005″, the deck height should be corrected. NOTE: *Block deck height and warpage should be corrected at the same time.*
Check the block deck for warpage:	Using a straightedge and feeler gauges, check the block deck for warpage in the same manner that the cylinder head is checked (see Cylinder Head Reconditioning). If warpage exceeds specifications, have the deck resurfaced. NOTE: *In certain cases a specification for total material removal (cylinder head and block deck) is provided. This specification must not be exceeded.*
Clean and inspect the pistons and connecting rods: 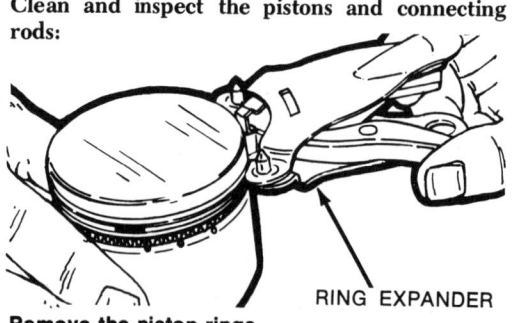 Remove the piston rings	Using a ring expander, remove the rings from the piston. Remove the retaining rings (if so equipped) and remove piston pin. NOTE: *If the piston pin must be pressed out, determine the proper method and use the proper tools; otherwise the piston will distort.* Clean the ring grooves using an appropriate tool, exercising care to avoid cutting too deeply. Thoroughly clean all carbon and varnish from the piston with solvent. CAUTION: *Do not use a wire brush or caustic solvent on pistons.* Inspect the pistons for scuffing, scoring, cracks, pitting, or excessive ring

ENGINE AND ENGINE REBUILDING

Cylinder Block Reconditioning

Procedure	Method
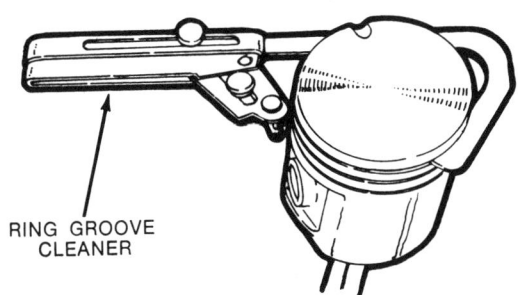 Clean the piston ring grooves	groove wear. If wear is evident, the piston must be replaced. Check the connecting rod length by measuring the rod from the inside of the large end to the inside of the small end using calipers (see illustration). All connecting rods should be equal length. Replace any rod that differs from the others in the engine.
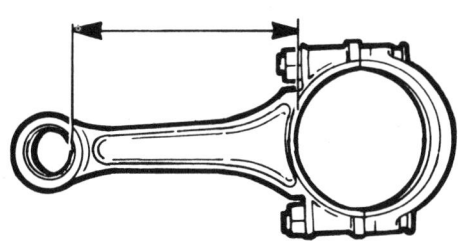 Check the connecting rod length (arrow)	* Have the connecting rod alignment checked in an alignment fixture by a machinist. Replace any twisted or bent rods. * Magnaflux the connecting rods to locate stress cracks. If cracks are found, replace the connecting rod.
Fit the pistons to the cylinders: 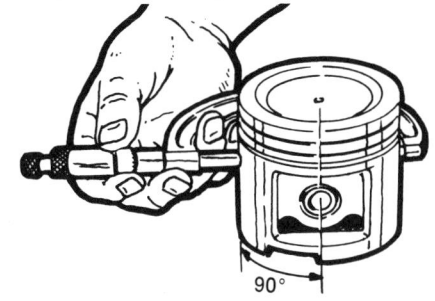 Measure the piston prior to fitting	Using a telescope gauge and micrometer, or a dial gauge, measure the cylinder bore diameter perpendicular to the piston pin, 2½" below the deck. Measure the piston perpendicular to its pin on the skirt. The difference between the two measurements is the piston clearance. If the clearance is within specifications or slightly below (after boring or honing), finish honing is all that is required. If the clearance is excessive, try to obtain a slightly larger piston to bring clearance within specifications. Where this is not possible, obtain the first oversize piston, and hone (or if necessary, bore) the cylinder to size.
Assemble the pistons and connecting rods: 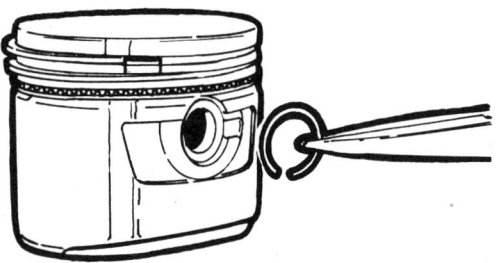 Install the piston pin lock-rings (if used)	Inspect piston pin, connecting rod small end bushing, and piston bore for galling, scoring, or excessive wear. If evident, replace defective part(s). Measure the I.D. of the piston boss and connecting rod small end, and the O.D. of the piston pin. If within specifications, assemble piston pin and rod. **CAUTION:** *If piston pin must be pressed in, determine the proper method and use the proper tools; otherwise the piston will distort.* Install the lock rings; ensure that they seat properly. If the parts are not within specifications, determine the service method for the type of engine. In some cases, piston and pin are serviced as an assembly when either is defective. Others specify reaming the piston and connecting rods for an oversize pin. If the connecting rod bushing is worn, it may in many cases be replaced. Reaming the piston and replacing the rod bushing are machine shop operations.

158　ENGINE AND ENGINE REBUILDING

Cylinder Block Reconditioning

Procedure	Method
Clean and inspect the camshaft: 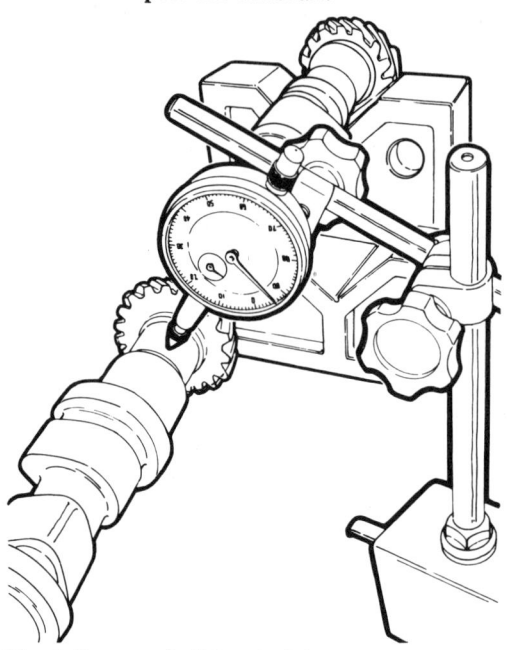 **Check the camshaft for straightness**	Degrease the camshaft, using solvent, and clean out all oil holes. Visually inspect cam lobes and bearing journals for excessive wear. If a lobe is questionable, check all lobes as indicated below. If a journal or lobe is worn, the camshaft must be reground or replaced. NOTE: *If a journal is worn, there is a good chance that the bushings are worn.* If lobes and journals appear intact, place the front and rear journals in V-blocks, and rest a dial indicator on the center journal. Rotate the camshaft to check straightness. If deviation exceeds .001″, replace the camshaft. *Check the camshaft lobes with a micrometer, by measuring the lobes from the nose to base and again at 90° (see illustration). The lift is determined by subtracting the second measurement from the first. If all exhaust lobes and all intake lobes are not identical, the camshaft must be reground or replaced. 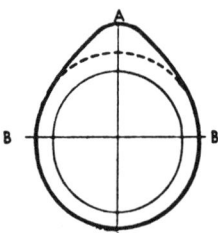 **Camshaft lobe measurement**
Replace the camshaft bearings: 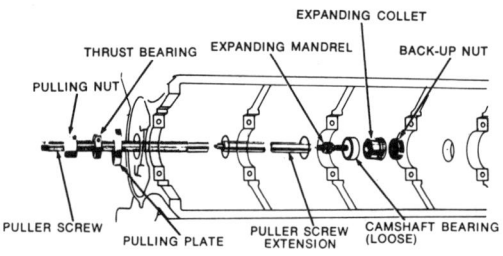 **Camshaft bearing removal and installation tool (OHV engines only)**	If excessive wear is indicated, or if the engine is being completely rebuilt, camshaft bearings should be replaced as follows: Drive the camshaft rear plug from the block. Assemble the removal puller with its shoulder on the bearing to be removed. Gradually tighten the puller nut until bearing is removed. Remove remaining bearings, leaving the front and rear for last. To remove front and rear bearings, reverse position of the tool, so as to pull the bearings in toward the center of the block. Leave the tool in this position, pilot the new front and rear bearings on the installer, and pull them into position. Return the tool to its original position and pull remaining bearings into position. NOTE: *Ensure that oil holes align when installing bearings.* Replace camshaft rear plug, and stake it into position to aid retention.
Finish hone the cylinders:	Chuck a flexible drive hone into a power drill, and insert it into the cylinder. Start the hone, and remove it up and down in the cylinder at a rate which will produce approximately a 60° cross-hatch pattern. NOTE: *Do not extend the hone below the cylinder bore.* After developing the pattern, remove

ENGINE AND ENGINE REBUILDING

Cylinder Block Reconditioning

Procedure	Method
 Cylinder bore after honing	the hone and recheck piston fit. Wash the cylinders with a detergent and water solution to remove abrasive dust, dry, and wipe several times with a rag soaked in engine oil.
Check piston ring end-gap: 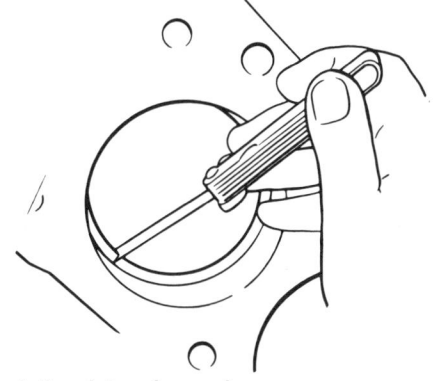 Check the piston ring end gap	Compress the piston rings to be used in a cylinder, one at a time, into that cylinder, and press them approximately 1″ below the deck with an inverted piston. Using feeler gauges, measure the ring end-gap, and compare to specifications. Pull the ring out of the cylinder and file the ends with a fine file to obtain proper clearance. **CAUTION:** *If inadequate ring end-gap is utilized, ring breakage will result.*
Install the piston rings: 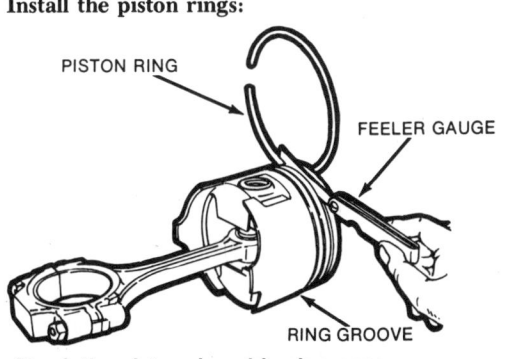 Check the piston ring side clearance	Inspect the ring grooves in the piston for excessive wear or taper. If necessary, recut the groove(s) for use with an overwidth ring or a standard ring and spacer. If the groove is worn uniformly, overwidth rings, or standard rings and spacers may be installed without recutting. Roll the outside of the ring around the groove to check for burrs or deposits. If any are found, remove with a fine file. Hold the ring in the groove, and measure side clearance. If necessary, correct as indicated above. **NOTE:** *Always install any additional spacers above the piston ring.* The ring groove must be deep enough to allow the ring to seat below the lands (see illustration). In many cases, a "go-no-go" depth gauge will be provided with the piston rings. Shallow grooves may be corrected by recutting, while deep grooves require some type of filler or expander

160 ENGINE AND ENGINE REBUILDING

Cylinder Block Reconditioning

Procedure	Method
	behind the piston. Consult the piston ring supplier concerning the suggested method. Install the rings on the piston, lowest ring first, using a ring expander. **NOTE:** *Position the rings as specified by the manufacturer.* Consult the engine service procedures earlier in this chapter for details concerning specific engines.
Install the camshaft:	Liberally lubricate the camshaft lobes and journals, and install the camshaft. **CAUTION:** *Exercise extreme care to avoid damaging the bearings when inserting the camshaft.* Install and tighten the camshaft thrust plate retaining bolts. See the engine service procedures earlier in this chapter for details concerning specific engines.
Check camshaft end-play (OHV engines only): Check the camshaft end-play with a feeler gauge DIAL INDICATOR CAMSHAFT Check the camshaft end-play with a dial indicator	Using feeler gauges, determine whether the clearance between the camshaft boss (or gear) and backing plate is within specifications. Install shims behind the thrust plate, or reposition the camshaft gear and retest endplay. In some cases, adjustment is by replacing the thrust plate. See the engine service procedures earlier in this chapter for details concerning specific engines. *Mount a dial indicator stand so that the stem of the dial indicator rests on the nose of the camshaft, parallel to the camshaft axis. Push the camshaft as far in as possible and zero the gauge. Move the camshaft outward to determine the amount of camshaft endplay. If the endplay is not within tolerance, install shims behind the thrust plate, or reposition the camshaft gear and retest. See the engine service procedures earlier in this chapter for details concerning specific engines.
Install the rear main seal:	See the engine service procedures earlier in this chapter for details concerning specific engines.
Install the crankshaft: INSTALLING BEARING SHELL REMOVING BEARING SHELL **Remove or install the upper bearing insert using a roll-out pin**	Thoroughly clean the main bearing saddles and caps. Place the upper halves of the bearing inserts on the saddles and press into position. **NOTE:** *Ensure that the oil holes align.* Press the corresponding bearing inserts into the main bearing caps. Lubricate the upper main bearings, and lay the crankshaft in position. Place a strip of Plastigage on each of the crankshaft journals, install the main caps, and torque to specifications. Remove the main caps, and compare the Plastigage to the scale on the Plastigage envelope. If clearances are within tolerances, remove the Plastigage, turn the crankshaft 90°, wipe off all oil and retest. If all clearances are correct,

ENGINE AND ENGINE REBUILDING

Cylinder Block Reconditioning

Procedure	Method
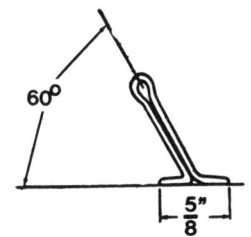 Home-made bearing roll-out pin	remove all Plastigage, thoroughly lubricate the main caps and bearing journals, and install the main caps. If clearances are not within tolerance, the upper bearing inserts may be removed, without removing the crankshaft, using a bearing roll out pin (see illustration). Roll in a bearing that will provide proper clearance, and retest. Torque all main caps, excluding the thrust bearing cap, to specifications. Tighten the thrust bearing cap finger tight. To properly align the thrust bearing, pry the crankshaft the extent of its axial travel several times, the last movement held toward the front of the engine, and torque the thrust bearing cap to specifications. Determine the crankshaft end-play (see below), and bring within tolerance with thrust washers.

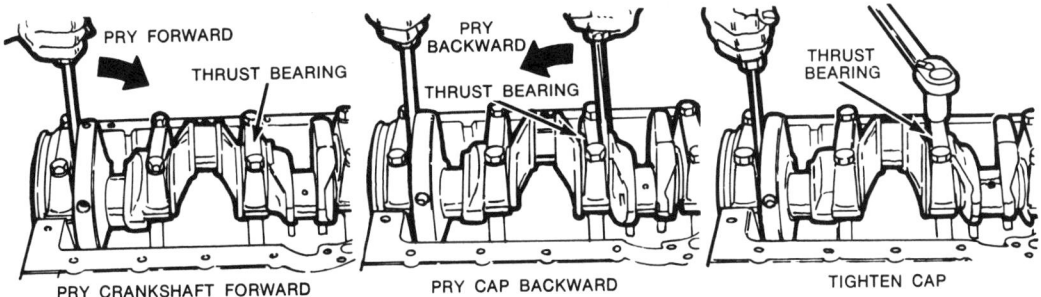

Aligning the thrust bearing

Measure crankshaft end-play:	Mount a dial indicator stand on the front of the block, with the dial indicator stem resting on the nose of the crankshaft, parallel to the crankshaft axis. Pry the crankshaft the extent of its travel rearward, and zero the indicator. Pry the crankshaft forward and record crankshaft end-play. NOTE: *Crankshaft end-play also may be measured at the thrust bearing, using feeler gauges (see illustration).*

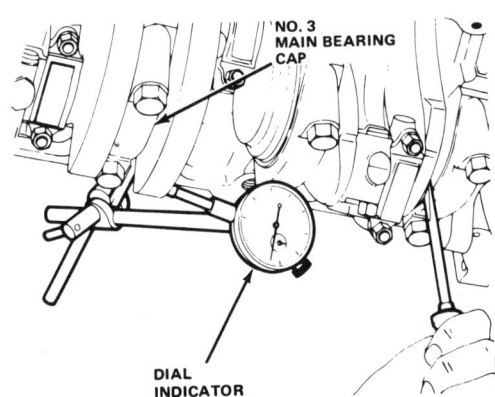

Check the crankshaft end-play with a dial indicator

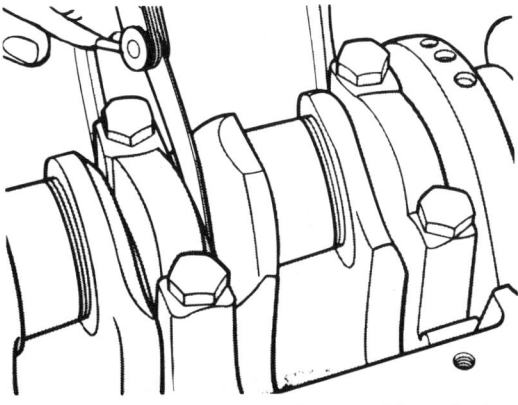

Check the crankshaft end-play with a feeler gauge

ENGINE AND ENGINE REBUILDING

Cylinder Block Reconditioning

Procedure	Method
Install the pistons: 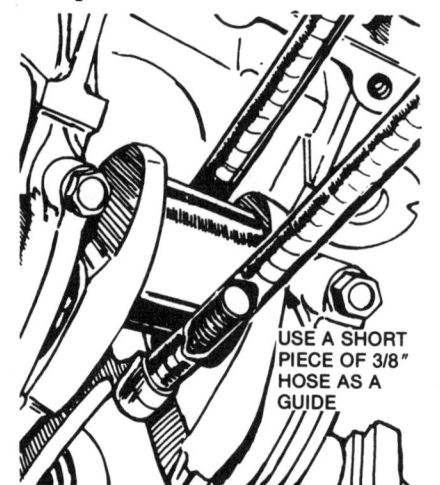 Use lengths of vacuum hose or rubber tubing to protect the crankshaft journals and cylinder walls during piston installation  Install the piston using a ring compressor	Press the upper connecting rod bearing halves into the connecting rods, and the lower halves into the connecting rod caps. Position the piston ring gaps according to specifications (see car section), and lubricate the pistons. Install a ring compresser on a piston, and press two long (8″) pieces of plastic tubing over the rod bolts. Using the tubes as a guide, press the pistons into the bores and onto the crankshaft with a wooden hammer handle. After seating the rod on the crankshaft journal, remove the tubes and install the cap finger tight. Install the remaining pistons in the same manner. Invert the engine and check the bearing clearance at two points (90° apart) on each journal with Plastigage. NOTE: *Do not turn the crankshaft with Plastigage installed.* If clearance is within tolerances, remove *all* Plastigage, thoroughly lubricate the journals, and torque the rod caps to specifications. If clearance is not within specifications, install different thickness bearing inserts and recheck. CAUTION: *Never shim or file the connecting rods or caps.* Always install plastic tube sleeves over the rod bolts when the caps are not installed, to protect the crankshaft journals.
Check connecting rod side clearance: 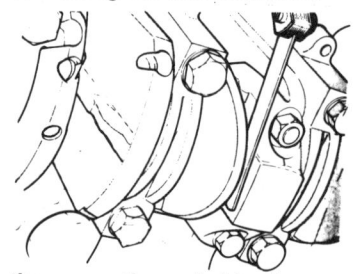 Check the connecting rod side clearance with a feeler gauge	Determine the clearance between the sides of the connecting rods and the crankshaft using feeler gauges. If clearance is below the minimum tolerance, the rod may be machined to provide adequate clearance. If clearance is excessive, substitute an unworn rod, and recheck. If clearance is still outside specifications, the crankshaft must be welded and reground, or replaced.
Inspect the timing chain (or belt):	Visually inspect the timing chain for broken or loose links, and replace the chain if any are found. If the chain will flex sideways, it must be replaced. Install the timing chain as specified. Be sure the timing belt is not stretched, frayed or broken. NOTE: *If the original timing chain is to be reused, install it in its original position.*

ENGINE AND ENGINE REBUILDING

Cylinder Block Reconditioning

Procedure	Method
Check timing gear backlash and runout (OHV engines):  Check the camshaft gear backlash	Mount a dial indicator with its stem resting on a tooth of the camshaft gear (as illustrated). Rotate the gear until all slack is removed, and zero the indicator. Rotate the gear in the opposite direction until slack is removed, and record gear backlash. Mount the indicator with its stem resting on the edge of the camshaft gear, parallel to the axis of the camshaft. Zero the indicator, and turn the camshaft gear one full turn, recording the runout. If either backlash or runout exceed specifications, replace the worn gear(s). 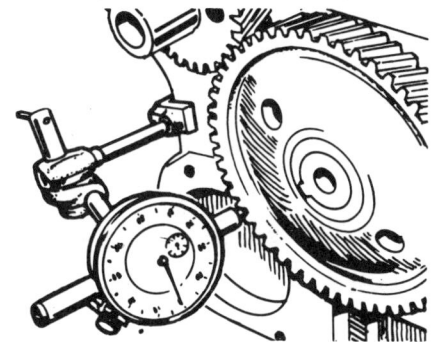 Check the camshaft gear run-out

Completing the Rebuilding Process

Follow the above procedures, complete the rebuilding process as follows:

Fill the oil pump with oil, to prevent cavitating (sucking air) on initial engine start up. Install the oil pump and the pickup tube on the engine. Coat the oil pan gasket as necessary, and install the gasket and the oil pan. Mount the flywheel and the crankshaft vibration damper or pulley on the crankshaft.

NOTE: *Always use new bolts when installing the flywheel.* Inspect the clutch shaft pilot bushing in the crankshaft. If the bushing is excessively worn, remove it with an expanding puller and a slide hammer, and tap a new bushing into place.

Position the engine, cylinder head side up. Lubricate the lifters, and install them into their bores. Install the cylinder head, and torque it as specified. Insert the pushrods and install the rocker shaft(s) or position the rocker arms on the pushrods. Adjust the valves.

Install the intake and exhaust manifolds, the carburetor(s), the distributor and spark plugs. Adjust the point gap and the static ignition timing. Mount all accessories and install the engine in the car. Fill the radiator with coolant, and the crankcase with high quality engine oil.

Break-in Procedure

Start the engine, and allow it to run at low speed for a few minutes, while checking for leaks. Stop the engine, check the oil level, and fill as necessary. Restart the engine, and fill the cooling system to capacity. Check the point dwell angle and adjust the ignition timing and the valves. Run the engine at low to medium speed (800–2500 rpm) for approximately ½ hour, and retorque the cylinder head bolts. Road test the car, and check again for leaks.

Follow the manufacturer's recommended engine break-in procedure and maintenance schedule for new engines.

Emission Controls and Fuel System

EMISSION CONTROLS

There are three sources of automotive pollutants: Crankcase fumes, exhaust gases and gasoline evaporation. The pollutants formed from these substances fall into three categories: unburnt hydrocarbons (HC), carbon monoxide (CO) and oxides of nitrogen (NOx). The equipment that is used to limit these pollutants is commonly called emission control equipment.

Positive Crankcase Ventilation

OPERATION

In 1967, Camaros were available with two types of crankcase ventilation systems: the closed type found on all California cars and some non-California cars, or the open type. The open ventilation system (non-California cars) receives outside air through a vented oil filler cap. This filtered cap permits outside air to enter the valve cover and also allows crankcase vapors to escape from the valve cover into the atmosphere. 1967 California law and later Federal law requires that this filler cap be non-vented to prevent the emission of vapors into the air. To supply this closed system with fresh air, a hose runs from the carburetor air cleaner to an inlet hole in the valve cover. The carburetor end of the hose fits into a cup-shaped flame arrestor and filter in the air cleaner cover. In the event of a carburetor back-fire, this arrestor prevents the spread of fire to the valve cover where it could create an explosion. Included in the system is a PCV (positive crankcase ventilation) valve that fits into an outlet hole in the top of the valve cover. A hose connects this valve to a vacuum outlet at the intake manifold. Contained within the valve housing is a valve (pointed at one end, flat at the other) positioned within a coiled spring. During

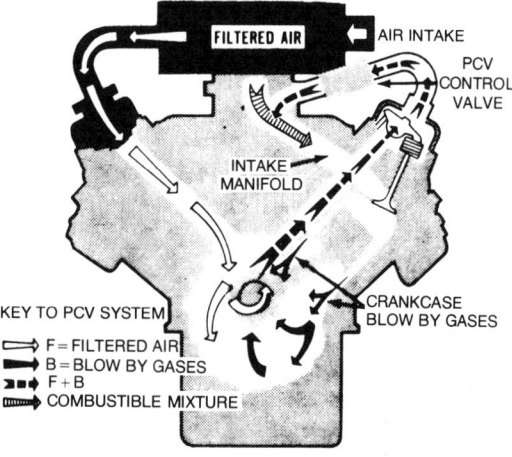

Schematic of PCV system (© Chevrolet Motor Division)

EMISSION CONTROLS AND FUEL SYSTEM

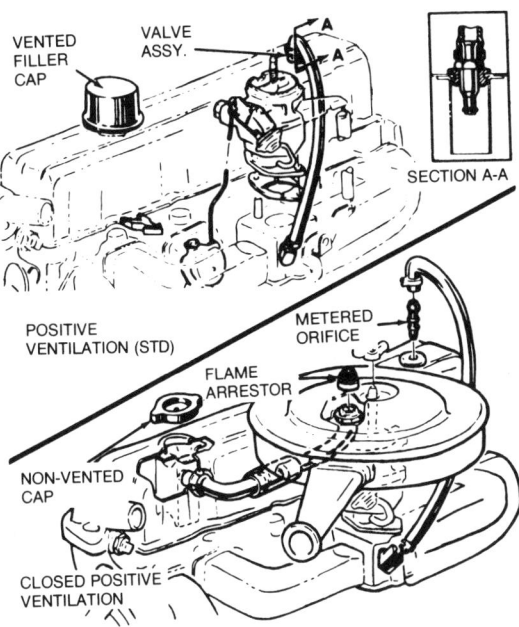

Closed and positive ventilation systems

idle or low speed operation, when manifold vacuum is highest, the valve spring tension is overcome by the high vacuum pull and, as a result, the valve is pulled up to very nearly seal off the manifold end of the valve housing. This restricts the flow of crankcase vapors to the intake manifold at a time when crankcase pressures are lowest and least disruptive to engine performance. At times of acceleration or constant speed, intake manifold vacuum is reduced to a point where it can no longer pull against the valve spring and so, spring force pulls the valve away from the housing outlet allowing crankcase vapors to escape through the hose to the intake manifold. Once inside the manifold, the gases enter the combustion chambers to be reburned. At times of engine backfire (at the carburetor) or when the engine is turned off, manifold vacuum ceases permitting the spring to pull the valve against the inlet (crankcase end) end of the valve housing. This seals off the inlet, thereby stopping the entrance of crankcase gases into the valve and preventing the possibility of a backfire spreading through the hose and valve to ignite these gases. The carburetor used with this system is set to provide a richer gas mixture to compensate for the additional air and gases going to the intake manifold. A valve that is clogged and stuck closed will not allow this extra air to reach the manifold. Consequently, the engine will run roughly and

plugs will foul due to the creation of an overly rich air/fuel mixture. It can be said that the PCV system performs three functions. It reduces air pollution by reburning the crankcase gases rather than releasing them to the atmosphere, and it increases engine life and gas economy. By recirculating crankcase gases, oil contamination that is harmful to engine parts is kept to a minimum. Recirculated gases returned to the intake manifold are combustible and, when combined with the air/fuel mixture from the carburetor, become fuel for operation, slightly increasing gas economy. In 1968, all cars were required to use the closed system and vented filler caps became a thing of the past. For more information on PCV, see Chapter One.

SERVICE

Inspect the PCV system hose and connections at each tune-up and replace any deteriorated hoses. Check the PCV valve at every tune-up and replace it every 24,000 miles on 1967–74 cars, and every 30,000 miles on later cars. See Chapter One for testing procedure.

REMOVAL AND INSTALLATION

The valve is inserted into a rubber grommet in the valve cover at the large end. At the narrow end, it is inserted into a hose and clamped. To remove it, gently pull it out of the valve cover, then open the clamp with a pair of pliers. Hold the clamp open while sliding it an inch or two down the hose (away from the valve), and then remove the valve. If the end of the hose is hard or cracked where it holds the valve, it may be feasible to cut the end off if there is plenty of extra hose. Otherwise, replace the hose. Replace the grommet in the valve cover if it is cracked or hard. Replace the clamp if it is broken or weak. In replacing the valve, make sure it is fully inserted in the hose, that the clamp is moved over the ridge on the valve so that the valve will not slip out of the hose, and that the valve is fully inserted into the grommet in the valve cover.

PCV FILTER REMOVAL AND INSTALLATION

1. Slide the rubber coupling that joins the tube coming from the valve cover to the filter off the filter nipple. Then, remove the top of the air cleaner. Slide the spring clamp off the filter, and remove the filter.

2. Inspect the rubber grommet in the valve cover and the rubber coupling for brit-

EMISSION CONTROLS AND FUEL SYSTEM

tleness or cracking. Replace parts as necessary.

3. Insert the new PCV filter through the hole in the air cleaner with open portion of the filter upward. Make sure the square portion of filter behind the nipple fits into the (square) hole in the air cleaner.

4. Install a new spring clamp onto the nipple. Make sure the clamp goes under the ridge on the filter nipple all the way around. Then, reconnect the rubber coupling and install the air cleaner cover.

Evaporative Emission Control
OPERATION

This system which was introduced to California cars in 1970, and other cars in 1971, reduces the amount of escaping gasoline vapors. Float bowl emissions are controlled by internal carburetor modifications. Redesigned bowl vents, reduced bowl capacity, heat shields, and improved intake manifold-to-carburetor insulation reduce vapor loss into the atmosphere. The venting of fuel tank vapors into the air has been stopped by means of the carbon canister storage method. This method transfers fuel vapors to an activated carbon storage device which absorbs and stores the vapor that is emitted from the engine's induction system while the engine is not running. When the engine is running, the stored vapor is purged from the carbon storage device by the intake air flow and then consumed in the normal combustion process. As the manifold vacuum reaches a certain point, it opens a purge control valve atop the charcoal storage canister. This allows air to be drawn into the canister, thus forcing the existing fuel vapors back into the engine to be burned normally.

In 1981, the purge function on the 231 V6 engine is electronically controlled by a purge solenoid in the line which is itself controlled by the Electronic Control Module (ECM). When the system is in the "Open Loop" mode, the solenoid valve is energized, blocking all vacuum to the purge valve. When the system is in the "Closed Loop" mode, the solenoid is de-energized, thus allowing existing vacuum to operate the purge valve. This releases the trapped fuel vapor and it is forced into the induction system.

Most carbon canisters used on Camaros

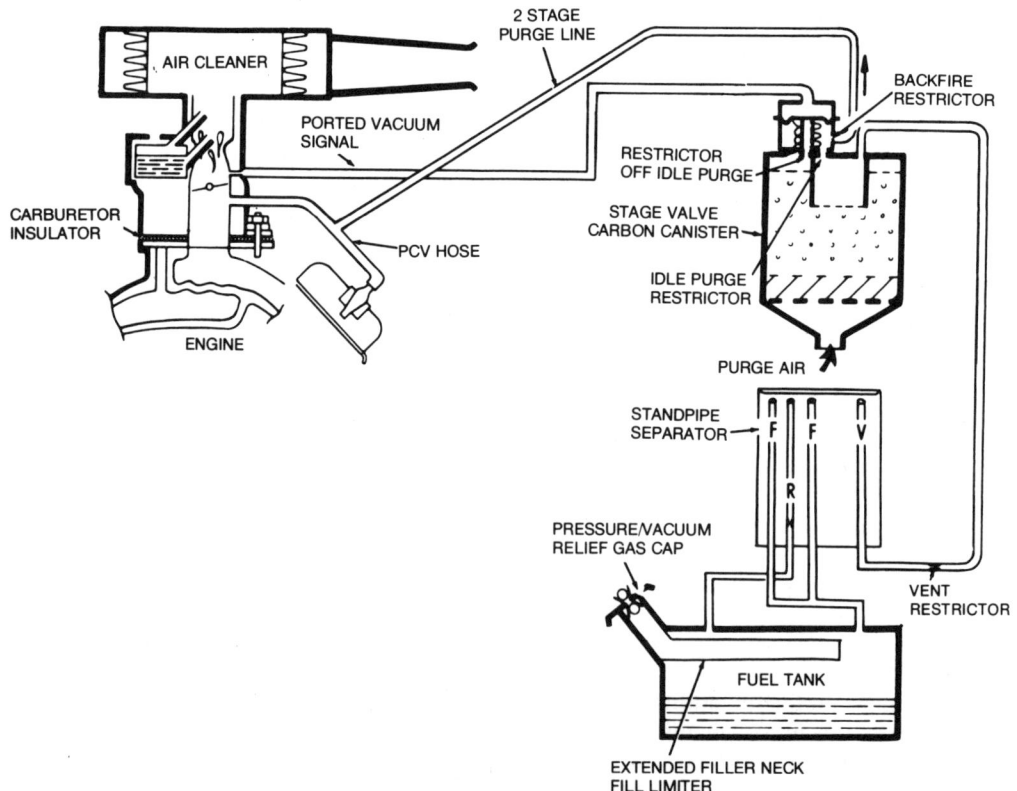

Schematic of the evaporative emission system (open)—1972 (most models similar)

EMISSION CONTROLS AND FUEL SYSTEM

are of the 'Open' design, meaning that air is drawn in through the bottom (filter) of the canister. Some (1981 231 V6) canisters are of the 'Closed' design which means that the incoming air is drawn directly from the air cleaner.

SERVICE

The only service required is the periodic replacement of the canister filter (if so equipped). This procedure is covered in Chapter 1. If the fuel tank cap on your Camaro ever requires replacement, make sure that it is of the same type as the original.

Exhaust Emission Controls

Exhaust emission control systems constitute the largest body of emission control devices installed on your Camaro. Included in this category are: Thermostatic Air Cleaner (THERMAC); Air Injection Reactor System (A.I.R., 1967–80); Air Management System (1981); Anti-Dieseling Solenoid; Transmission Controlled Spark (TCS, 1970–74); Early Fuel Evaporation System (EFE, 1975–81); Exhaust Gas Recirculation (EGR, 1973–81); Controlled Combustion System (CCS); Computer Controlled Catalytic Converter System (C-4); Computer Command Control System (CCC); Mixture Control Solenoid (M/C); Throttle Position Sensor (TPS); Idle Speed Control (ISC); Electronic Spark Timing (EST); Transmission Converter Clutch (TCC); Catalytic Converter and the Oxygen Sensor System. A brief description of each system and any applicable service procedures follows.

Thermostatic Air Cleaner (THERMAC)

All late model engines utilize the THERMAC system (in 1978 it was called TAC, but was the same). This system is designed to warm the air entering the carburetor when underhood temperatures are low, and to maintain a controlled air temperature into the carburetor at all times. By allowing preheated air to enter the carburetor, the amount of time the choke is on is reduced, resulting in better fuel economy and lower emissions. Engine warm-up time is also reduced.

The Thermac system is composed of the air cleaner body, a filter, sensor unit, vacuum diaphragm, damper door, and associated hoses and connections. Heat radiating from the exhaust manifold is trapped by a heat stove and is ducted to the air cleaner to supply heated air to the carburetor. A movable door in the air cleaner case snorkel allows air to be drawn in from the heat stove (cold operation) or from underhood air (warm operation). The door position is controlled by the vacuum motor, which receives intake manifold vacuum as modulated by the temperature sensor.

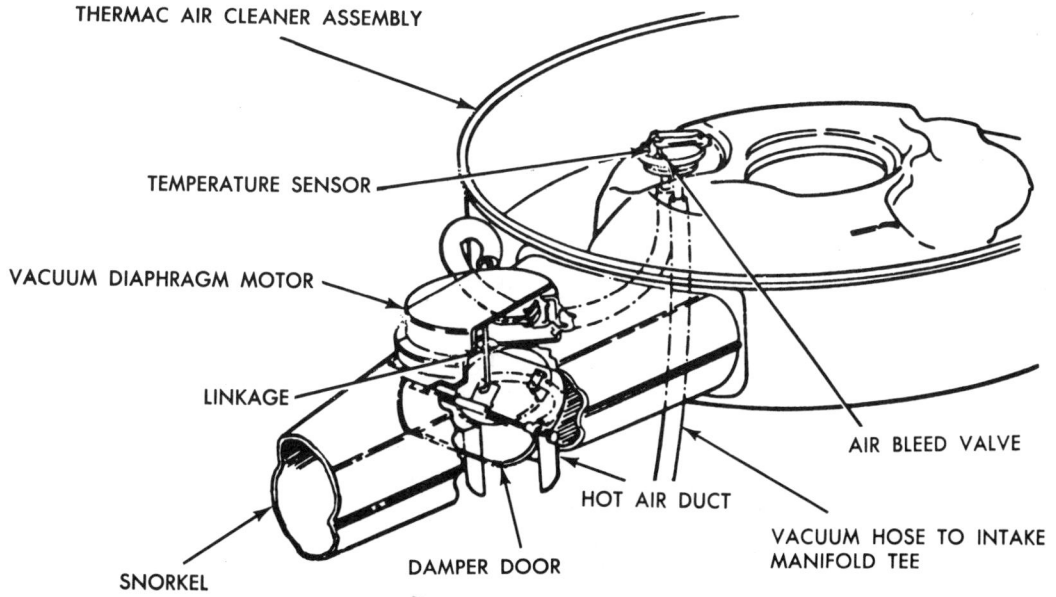

Typical THERMAC air cleaner

EMISSION CONTROLS AND FUEL SYSTEM

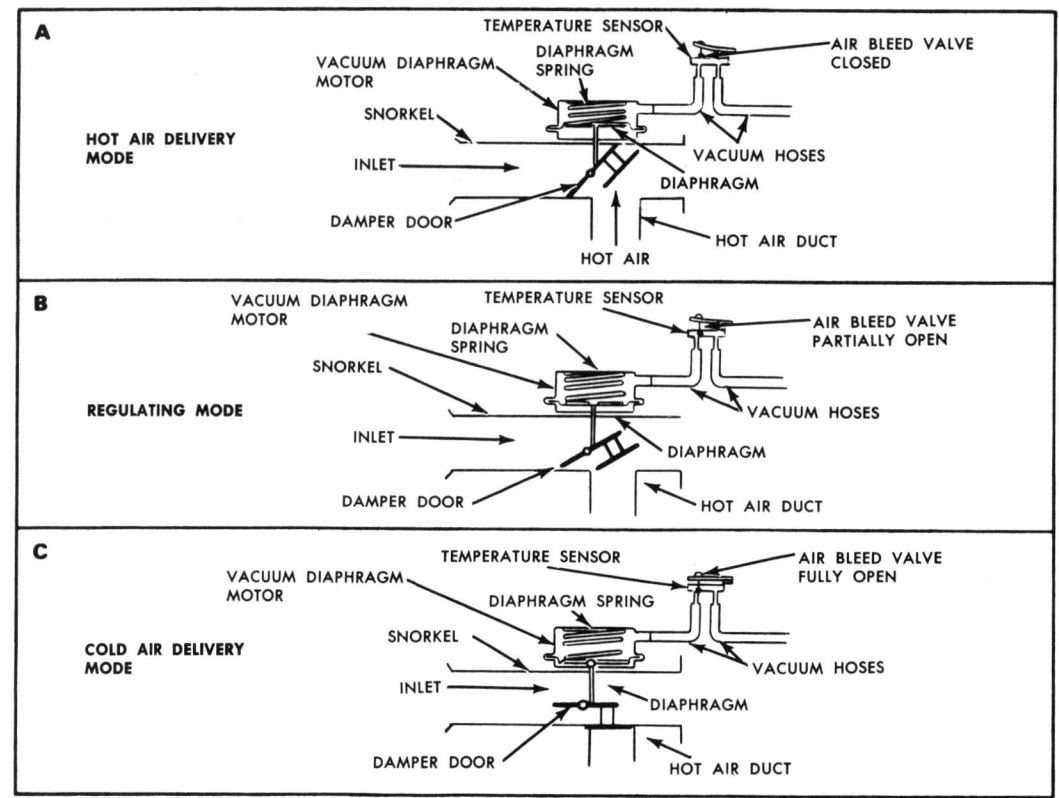

Schematic of the vacuum motor operation

SYSTEM CHECKS

1. Check the vacuum hoses for leaks, kinks, breaks, or improper connections and correct any defects.
2. With the engine off, check the position of the damper door within the snorkel. A mirror can be used to make this job easier. The damper door should be open to admit outside air.
3. Apply at least 7 in. Hg of vacuum to the damper diaphragm unit. The door should close. If it doesn't, check the diaphragm linkage for binding and correct hookup.
4. With vacuum still applied and the door closed, clamp the tube to trap the vacuum. If the door doesn't remain closed, there is a leak in the diaphragm assembly.

Air Injection Reactor System (A.I.R.) — 1967–80

This system was first introduced on California cars in 1967. The AIR system injects compressed air into the exhaust system, near enough to the exhaust valves to continue the burning of the normally unburned segment of the exhaust gases. To do this it employs an air injection pump and a system of hoses, valves, tubes, etc., necessary to carry the compressed air from the pump to the exhaust manifolds. Carburetors and distributors for AIR engines have specific modifications to adapt them to the air injection system; those components should not be interchanged with those intended for use on engines that do not have the system.

A diverter valve is used to prevent backfiring. The valve senses sudden increases in manifold vacuum and ceases the injection of air during fuel-rich periods. During coasting, this valve diverts the entire air flow through the pump muffler and during high engine speeds, expels it through a relief valve. Check valves in the system prevent exhaust gases from entering the pump.

NOTE: *The AIR system on the 231 V6 engine is slightly different, but its purpose remains the same.*

SERVICE

The AIR system's effectiveness depends on correct engine idle speed, ignition timing,

EMISSION CONTROLS AND FUEL SYSTEM 169

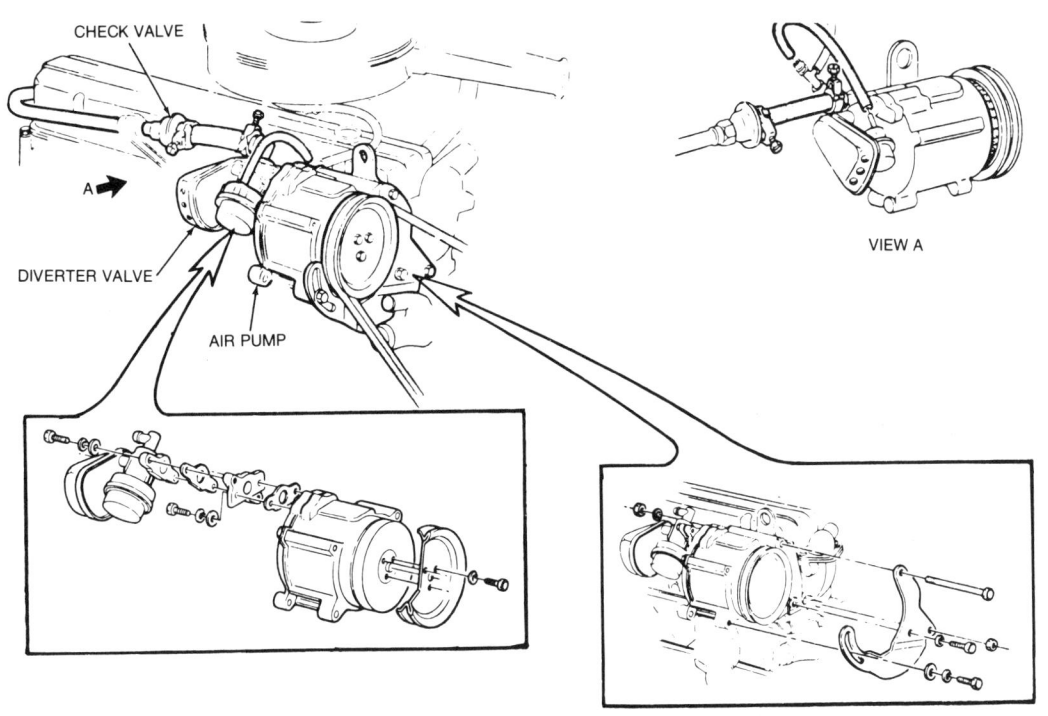

AIR system—inline six cylinder

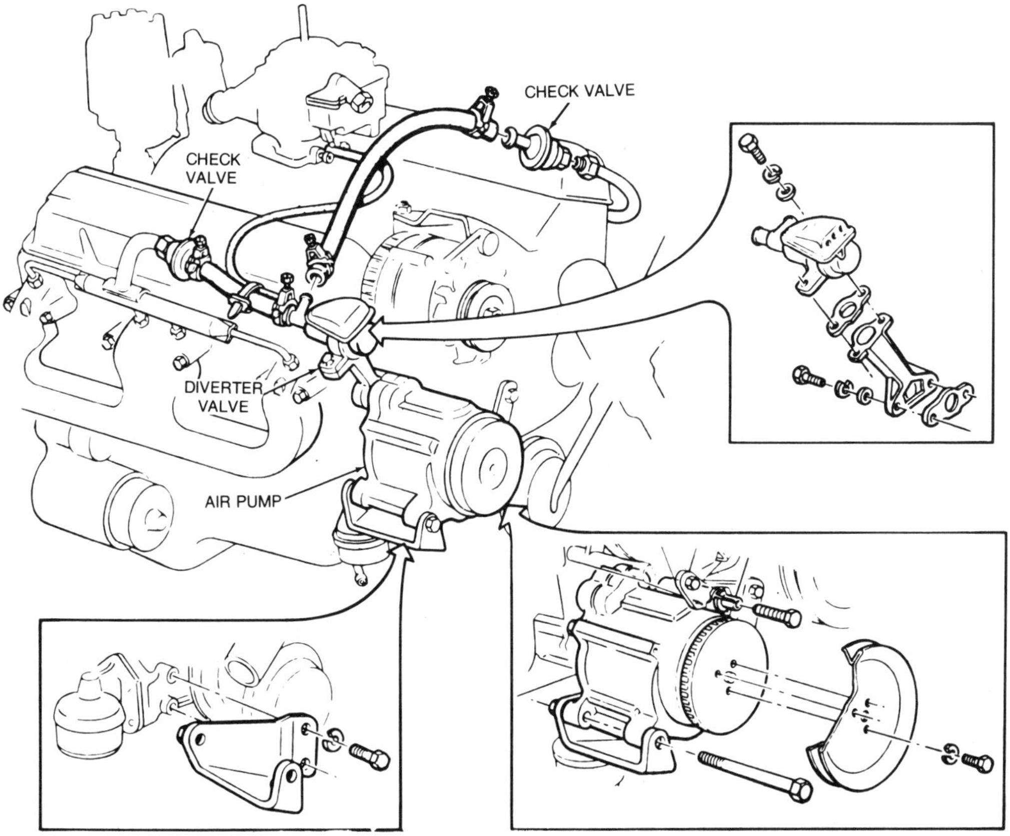

AIR system—V8 (229 V6 similar)

170 EMISSION CONTROLS AND FUEL SYSTEM

and dwell. These settings should be strictly adhered to and checked frequently. All hoses and fittings should be inspected for condition and tightness of connections. Check the drive belt for wear and tension every 12 months or 12,000 miles.

COMPONENT REMOVAL

Air Pump

CAUTION: *Do not pry on the pump housing or clamp the pump in a vise: the housing is soft and may become distorted.*

1. Disconnect the air hoses at the pump.
2. Hold the pump pulley from turning and loosen the pulley bolts.
3. Loosen the pump mounting bolt and adjustment bracket bolt. Remove the drive belt.
4. Remove the mounting bolts, and then remove the pump.
5. Install the pump using a reverse of the removal procedure.

Diverter (Anti-afterburn) Valve

1. Detach the vacuum sensing line from the valve.
2. Remove the other hose(s) from the valve.
3. Unfasten the diverter valve from the elbow or the pump body.

Installation is performed in the reverse order of removal. Always use a new gasket. Tighten the valve securing bolts to 85 in. lbs.

Air Management System—1981

The Air Management System is used to provide additional oxygen to continue the combustion process after the exhaust gases leave the combustion chamber; much the same as the AIR system described earlier in this chapter. Air is injected into either the exhaust port(s), the exhaust manifold(s) or the catylytic converter by an engine driven air pump. The system is in operation at all times and will bypass air only momentarily during deceleration and at high speeds. The bypass function is performed by the Air Management Valve, while the check valve protects the air pump by preventing any backflow of exhaust gases.

The AIR system helps to reduce HC and CO content in the exhaust gases by injecting air into the exhaust ports during cold engine operation. This air injection also helps the catalytic converter to reach the proper temperature quicker during warm-up. When the engine is warm (closed loop), the AIR system injects air into the beds of a three-way converter to lower the HC and CO content in the exhaust.

The Air Management System utilizes the following components:

1. An engine driven air pump
2. Air management valves (Air Control and Air Switching)
3. Air flow and control hoses
4. Check valves

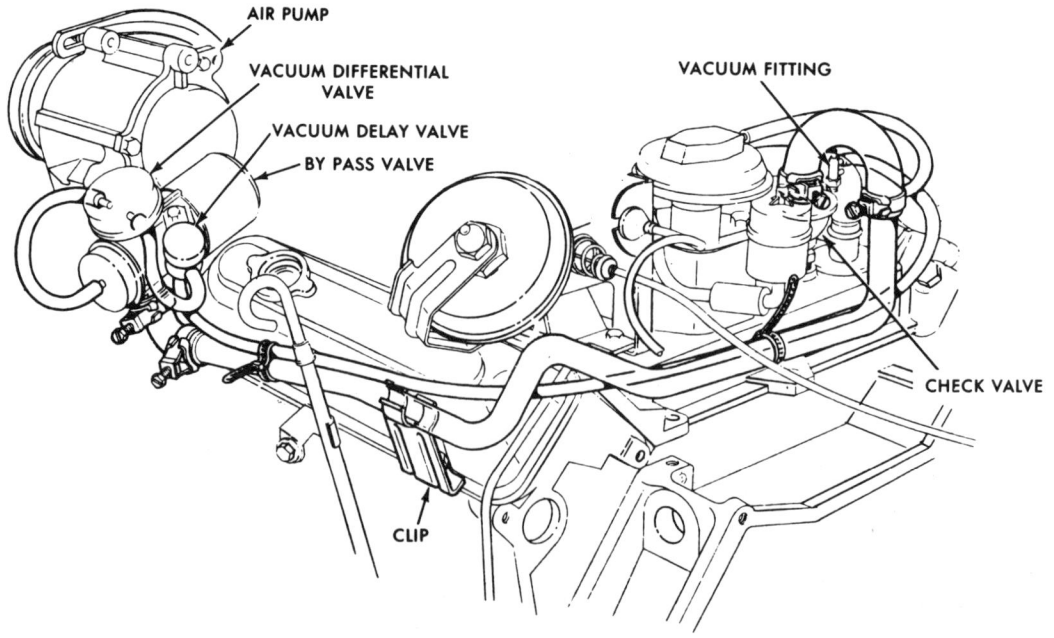

AIR system—231 V6

EMISSION CONTROLS AND FUEL SYSTEM

5. A dual-bed, three-way catalytic converter

The belt driven, vane-type air pump is located at the front of the engine and supplies clean air to the system for pusposes already stated. When the engine is cold, the Electronic Control Module (ECM) energizes an air control solenoid. This allows air to flow to the air switching valve. The air switching valve is then energized to direct air into the exhaust ports.

When the engine is warm, the ECM de-energizes the air switching valve, thus directing the air between the beds of the catalytic converter. This then provides additional oxygen for the oxidizing catalyst in the second bed to decrease HC and CO levels, while at the same time keeping oxygen levels low in the first bed, enabling the reducing catalyst to effectively decrease the levels of NOx.

If the air control valve detects a rapid increase in manifold vacuum (deceleration), certain operating modes (wide open throttle, etc.) or if the ECM self-diagnostic system detects any problems in the system, air is diverted to the air cleaner or directly into the atmosphere.

The primary purpose of the ECM's divert mode is to prevent backfiring. Throttle closure at the beginning of deceleration will temporarily create air/fuel mixtures which are too rich to burn completely. These mixtures will become burnable when they reach the exhaust if they are combined with injection air. The next firing of the engine will ignite the mixture causing an exhaust backfire. Momentary diverting of the injection air from the exhaust prevents this.

The Air Management System check valves and hoses should be checked periodically for any leaks, cracks or deterioration.

REMOVAL AND INSTALLATION
Air Pump

1. Remove the valves and/or adapter at the air pump.
2. Loosen the air pump adjustment bolt and remove the drive belt.
3. Unscrew the three mounting bolts and then remove the pump pulley.
4. Unscrew the pump mounting bolts and then remove the pump.
5. Installation is in the reverse order of removal. Be sure to adjust the drive belt tension after installing it.

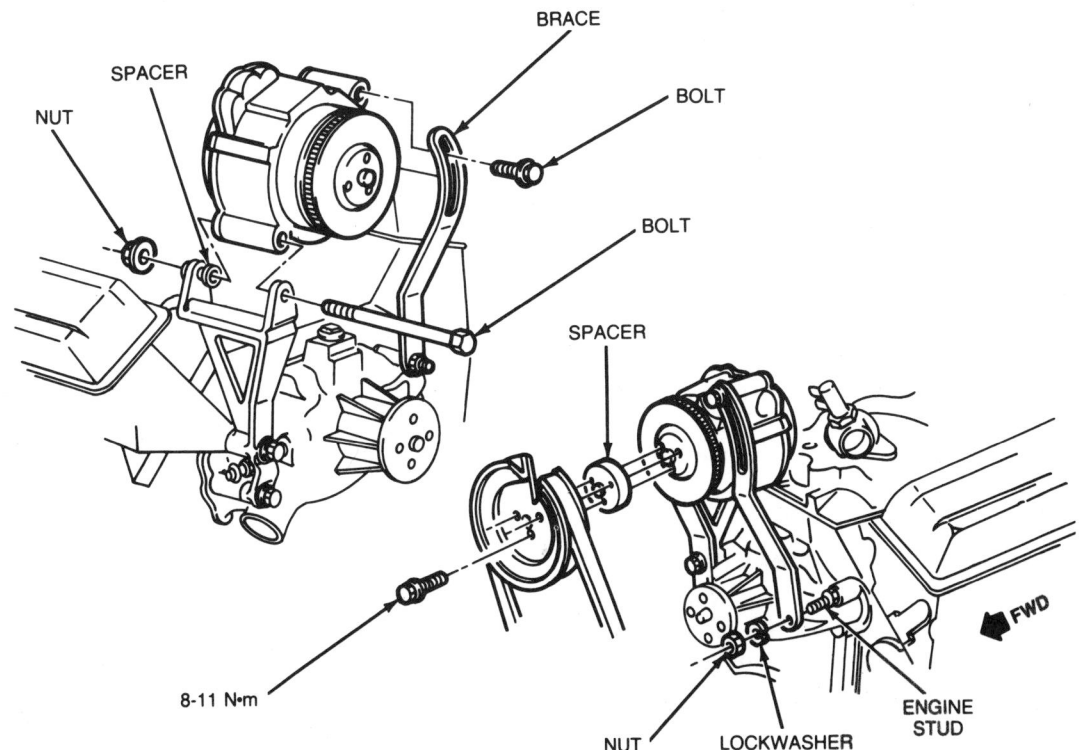

Removing the air pump; 1981 air management system

172 EMISSION CONTROLS AND FUEL SYSTEM

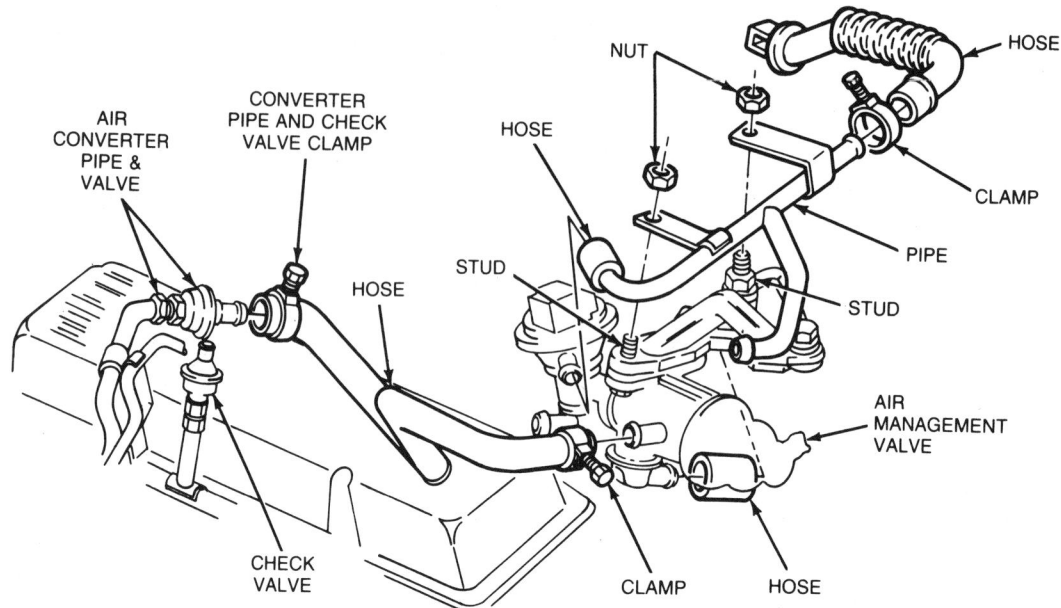

Check valve and hoses—1981 air management system

Check Valve

1. Release the clamp and disconnect the air hoses from the valve.
2. Unscrew the check valve from the air injection pipe.
3. Installation is in the reverse order of removal.

Air Management Valve

1. Disconnect the negative battery cable.
2. Remove the air cleaner.
3. Tag and disconnect the vacuum hose from the valve.
4. Tag and disconnect the air outlet hoses from the valve.
5. Bend back the lock tabs and then remove the bolts holding the elbow to the valve.
6. Tag and disconnect any electrical connections at the valve and then remove the valve from the elbow.
7. Installation is in the reverse order of removal.

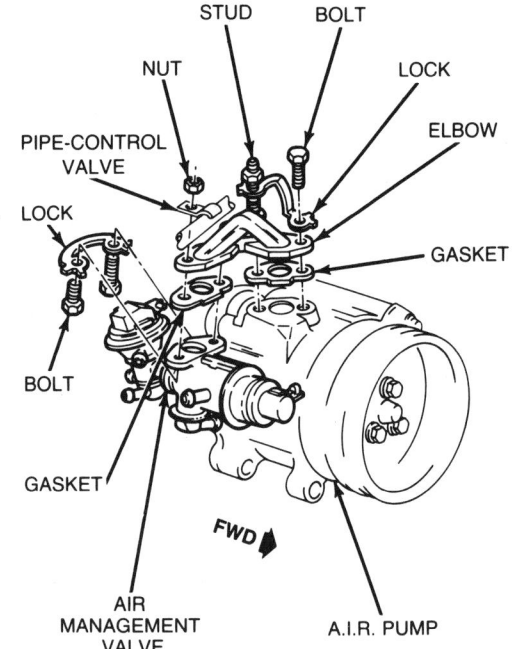

Removing the air management valve

Anti-Dieseling Solenoid

Beginning in 1968 some models may have an idle speed solenoid on the carburetor. All 1972–75 models have idle solenoids. Due to the leaner carburetor settings required for emission control, the engine may have a tendency to "diesel" or "run-on" after the ignition is turned off. The carburetor solenoid, energized when the ignition is on, maintains the normal idle speed. When the ignition is turned off, the solenoid is de-energized and permits the throttle valves to fully close, thus preventing run-on. For adjustment of carburetors with idle solenoids see the section on carburetor adjustments later in this chapter.

EMISSION CONTROLS AND FUEL SYSTEM

Anti-dieseling solenoid

Transmission Controlled Spark (TCS)—1970–74

Introduced in 1970, this system controls exhaust emissions by eliminating vacuum advance in the lower forward gears.

The 1970 system consists of a transmission switch, solenoid vacuum switch, time delay relay, and a thermostatic water temperature switch. The solenoid vacuum switch is energized in the lower gears via the transmission switch and closes off distributor vacuum. The two-way transmission switch is activated by the shifter shaft on manual transmissions, and by oil pressure on automatic transmissions. The switch de-energizes the solenoid in High gear, the plunger extends and uncovers the vacuum port, and the distributor receives full vacuum. The temperature switch overrides the system when engine temperature is below 63° or above 232°. This allows vacuum advance in all gears. A time delay relay opens 15 seconds after the ignition is switched on. Full vacuum advance during this delay eliminates the possibility of stalling.

The 1971 system is similar, except that the vacuum solenoid (now called a Combination Emissions Control or CEC solenoid) serves two functions. One function is to control distributor vacuum; the added function is to act as a deceleration throttle stop in High gear. This cuts down on emissions when the vehicle is coming to a stop in High gear. The CEC solenoid is controlled by a temperature switch, a transmission switch, and a 20 second time delay relay. This system also contains a reversing relay, which energizes the solenoid when the transmission switch, temperature switch or time delay completes the CEC circuit to ground. This system is directly opposite the 1970 system in operation. The 1970 vacuum solenoid was normally open to allow vacuum advance and when energized, closed to block vacuum. The 1971 system is normally closed blocking vacuum advance and when energized, opens to allow vacuum advance. The temperature switch completes the CEC circuit to ground when engine temperature is below 82°. The time delay relay allows vacuum advance (and raised idle speed) for 20 seconds after the ignition key is turned to the "on" position. Models with an automatic transmission and air conditioning also have a solid state timing device which engages the air conditioning compressor for three seconds after the ignition key is turned to the "off" position to prevent the engine from running-on.

The 1972 six-cylinder system is similar to that used in 1971, except that an idle stop solenoid has been added to the system. In the energized position, the solenoid maintains engine speed at a predetermined fast idle. When the solenoid is de-energized by turning off the ignition, the solenoid allows the throttle plates to close beyond the normal idle position; thus cutting off their air supply and preventing engine run-on. The six-cylinder is the only 1972 engine with a C.E.C. valve, which serves the same deceleration function as in 1971. The 1972 time delay relay delays full vacuum 20 seconds after the transmission is shifted into High gear. V8 engines use a vacuum advance solenoid similar to that used in 1970. This relay is normally closed to block vacuum and opens when energized to allow vacuum advance. The solenoid controls distributor vacuum advance and performs no throttle positioning function. The idle stop solenoid used operates in the same manner as the one on six-cylinder engines. All air-conditioned cars have an additional anti-diesel (run-on) solenoid which engages the compressor clutch for three seconds after the ignition is switched off. The 1973 TCS system differs from the 1972 system in three ways. The 23 second upshift delay has been replaced by a 20 second starting relay. This relay closes to complete the TCS circuit and open the TCS solenoid, allowing vacuum advance, for 20 seconds after the key is turned to the "on" position. The operating temperature of the temperature override switch has been raised to 93°, and the switch which was used to engage the A/C compressor when the key was turned "off" has been eliminated. All models are equipped with an electric throttle control solenoid to prevent run-on. The 1973 TCS system is used on all

174 EMISSION CONTROLS AND FUEL SYSTEM

models equipped with a 307 engine and all V8 models equipped with a manual transmission.

The 1974 TCS system is used only on manual transmission models. System components remain unchanged from 1973. The vacuum advance solenoid is located on the coil bracket. The TCS system is not used in 1975 and later cars.

TESTING

If there is a TCS system malfunction, first connect a vacuum gauge in the hose between the solenoid valve and the distributor vacuum unit. Drive the vehicle or raise it on a frame lift and observe the vacuum gauge. If full vacuum is available in all gears, check for the following:
1. Blown fuse.
2. Disconnected wire at solenoid-operated vacuum valve.
3. Disconnected wire at transmission switch.
4. Temperature override switch energized due to low engine temperature.
5. Solenoid failure.

If no vacuum is available in any gear, check the following:
1. Solenoid valve vacuum lines switched.
2. Clogged solenoid vacuum valve.
3. Distributor or manifold vacuum lines leaking or disconnected.
4. Transmission switch or wire grounded.

Test for individual components are as follows:

Idle Stop Solenoid

This unit may be checked simply by observing it while an assistant switches the ignition on and off. It should extend further with the current switched on. The unit is not repairable.

Solenoid Vacuum Valve

Check that proper manifold vacuum is available. Connect the vacuum gauge in the line between the solenoid valve and the distributor. Apply 12 volts to the solenoid. If vacuum is still not available, the valve is defective, either mechanically or electrically. The unit is not repairable. If the valve is satisfactory, check the relay next.

Relay

1. With the engine at normal operating temperature and the ignition on, ground the solenoid vacuum valve terminal with the black lead. The solenoid should energize (no vacuum) if the relay is satisfactory.
2. With the solenoid energized as in Step 1, connect a jumper from the relay terminal with the green/white stripe lead to ground. The solenoid should deenergize (vacuum available) if the relay is satisfactory.
3. If the relay worked properly in Steps 1 and 2, check the temperature switch. The relay unit is not repairable.

Temperature Switch

The vacuum valve solenoid should be de-energized (vacuum available) with the engine cold. If it is not, ground the green/white stripe wire from the switch. If the solenoid now de-energizes, replace the switch. If the switch was satisfactory, check the transmission switch.

Transmission Switch

With the engine at normal operating temperature and the transmission in one of the no-vacuum gears, the vacuum valve solenoid should be energized (no vacuum). If not, remove and ground the switch electrical lead. If the solenoid energizes, replace the switch.

Early Fuel Evaporation System (EFE)—1975–81

1975 and later models are equipped with this system to reduce engine warm-up time, improve driveability, and reduce emissions. On start-up, a vacuum motor acts to close a heat valve in the exhaust manifold which causes exhaust gases to enter the intake manifold heat riser passages. Incoming fuel mixture is then heated and more complete fuel evaporation is provided during warm-up.

The system consists of a Thermal Vacuum

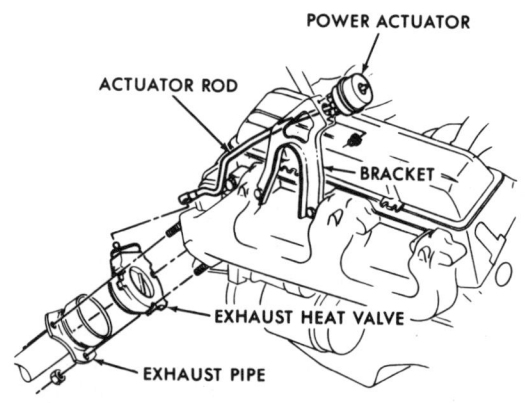

EFE system—V8 models

EMISSION CONTROLS AND FUEL SYSTEM

Switch, and an Exhaust Heat Valve and actuator. The Thermal Vacuum Switch is located on the coolant outlet housing on V8s, and on the block on in-line six cylinder engines. When the engine is cold, the TVS conducts manifold vacuum to the actuator to close the valve. When engine coolant or, on 6 cylinder engines, oil warms up, vacuum is interrupted and the actuator should open the valve.

NOTE: *On 1981 models with the 231 V6 engine, the EFE system is controlled by the ECM.*

CHECKING THE EFE SYSTEM

1. With the engine overnight cold, have someone start the engine while you observe the Exhaust Heat Valve. The valve should snap to the closed position.

2. Watch the valve as the engine warms up. By the time coolant starts circulating through the radiator (V type engines) or oil is hot (in-line engines), the valve should snap open.

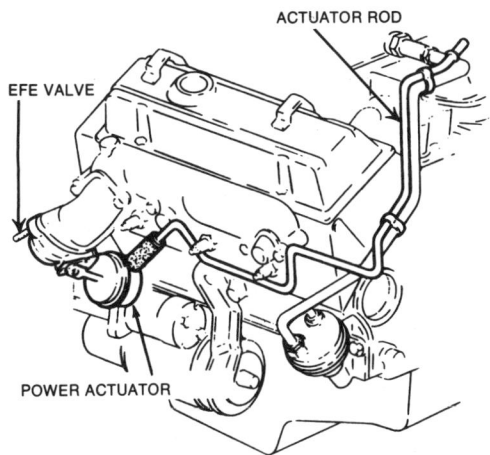

EFE system—229 V6

3. If the valve does not close, immediately disconnect the hose at the actuator, and check for vacuum by placing your finger over the end of the hose, or with a vacuum gauge. If there is vacuum, replace the actuator. If there is no vacuum, immediately disconnect the hose leading to the TVS from the manifold *at the TVS*. If there is vacuum here, but not at the actuator, replace the TVS. If vacuum does not exist at the hose going to the TVS, check that the vacuum hose is free of cracks or breaks and tightly connected at the manifold, and that the manifold port is clear.

4. If the valve does not open when the engine coolant or oil warms up, disconnect the hose at the actuator, and check for vacuum by placing your finger over the end of the hose or using a vacuum gauge. If there is vacuum, replace the TVS. If there is no vacuum, replace the actuator.

TVS REMOVAL AND INSTALLATION

On V8 engines, drain coolant until the level is below the coolant outlet housing. No oil need be drained on 6 cylinder engines. Apply sealer to threads on V8 engines. Use no sealer on 6 cylinder engines. Note that the valve must be installed until just snug (120 in-lb) and then turned by hand just far enough to line up the fittings for hose connection.

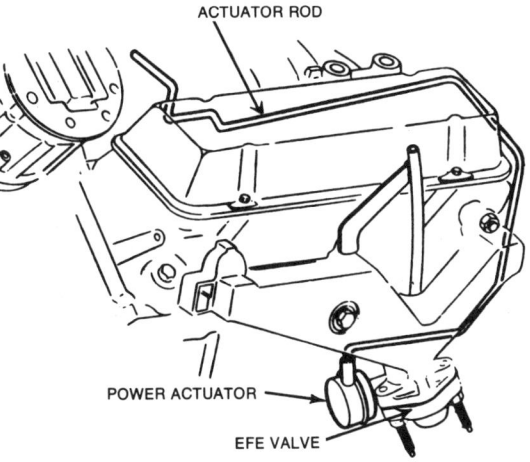

EFE system—231 V6

Exhaust Gas Recirculation (EGR)—1973–81

All 1973–81 engines are equipped with exhaust gas recirculation (EGR). This system consists of a metering valve, a vacuum line to the carburetor, and cast-in exhaust gas passages in the intake manifold. The EGR valve is controlled by carburetor vacuum, and accordingly opens and closes to admit exhaust gases into the fuel/air mixture. The exhaust gases lower the combustion temperature, and reduce the amount of oxides of nitrogen (NO_x) produced. The valve is closed at idle between the two extreme throttle positions.

In most installations, vacuum to the EGR valve is controlled by a thermal vacuum switch (TVS); the switch, which is installed into the engine block, shuts off vacuum to the EGR valve until the engine is hot. This pre-

176 EMISSION CONTROLS AND FUEL SYSTEM

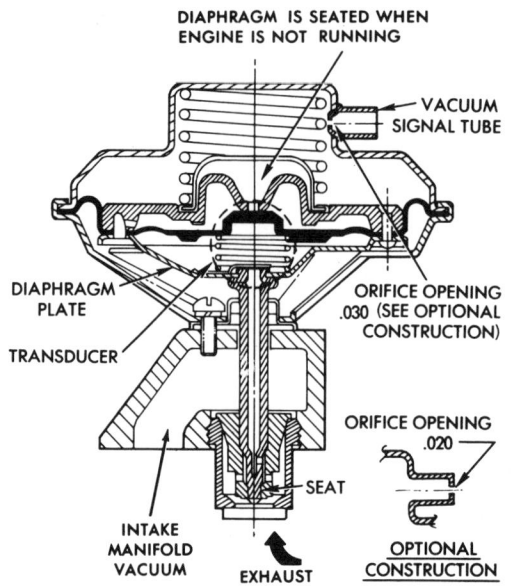

Negative backpressure EGR valve

vents the stalling and lumpy idle which would result if EGR occurred when the engine was cold.

As the car accelerates, the carburetor throttle plate uncovers the vacuum port for the EGR valve. At 3–5 in. Hg, the EGR valve opens and then some of the exhaust gases are allowed to flow into the air/fuel mixture to lower the combustion temperature. At full-throttle the valve closes again.

Some California engines are equipped with a dual diaphragm EGR valve. This valve further limits the exhaust gas opening (compared to the single diaphragm EGR valve) during high intake manifold vacuum periods, such as high-speed cruising, and provides more exhaust gas recirculation during acceleration when manifold vacuum is low. In addition to the hose running to the thermal vacuum switch, a second hose is connected directly to the intake manifold.

For 1977, all California models and cars delivered in areas above 4000 ft are equipped with back pressure EGR valves. This valve is also used on all 1978–81 models. The EGR valve receives exhaust back pressure through its hollow shaft. This exerts a force on the bottom of the control valve diaphragm, opposed by a light spring. Under low exhaust pressure (low engine load and partial throttle), the EGR signal is reduced by an air bleed. Under conditions of high exhaust pressure (high engine load and large throttle opening), the air bleed is closed and the EGR valve responds to an unmodified vacuum signal. At wide open throttle, the EGR flow is reduced in proportion to the amount of vacuum signal available.

1979 and late models have a ported signal vacuum EGR valve. The valve opening is controlled by the amount of vacuum obtained from a ported vacuum source on the carburetor and the amount of backpressure in the exhaust system.

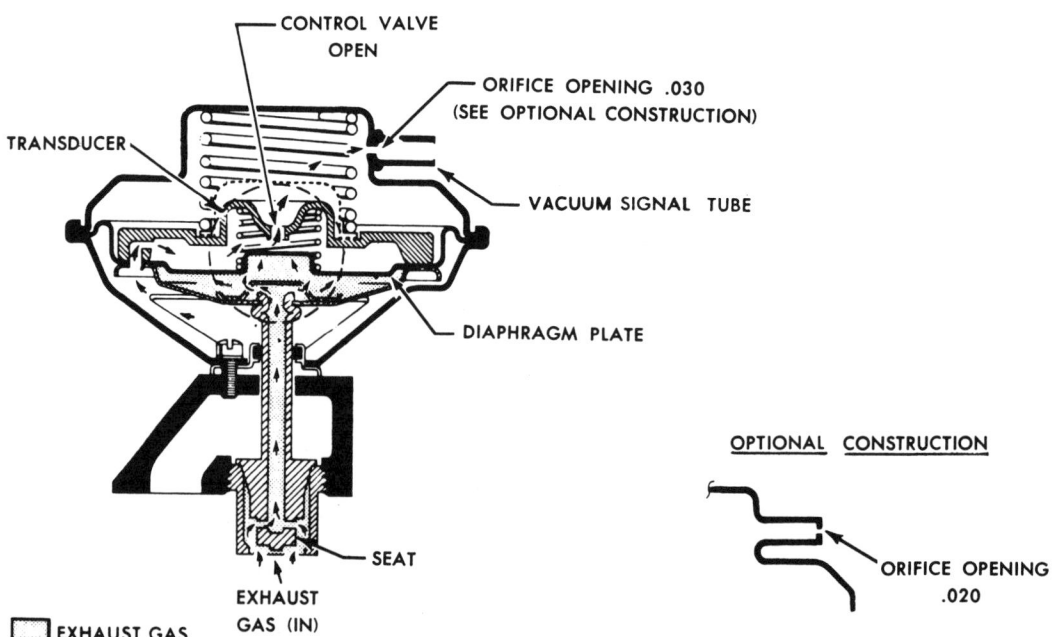

Cross section of a positive backpressure EGR valve

EMISSION CONTROLS AND FUEL SYSTEM

EGR VALVE REMOVAL AND INSTALLATION

1. Detach the vacuum lines from the EGR valve.
2. Unfasten the two bolts or bolt and clamp which attach the valve to the manifold. Withdraw the valve.
3. Installation is the reverse of removal. Always use a new gasket between the valve and the manifold. On dual diaphragm valves, attach the carburetor vacuum line to the tube at the top of valve, manifold vacuum line to tube at center of valve.

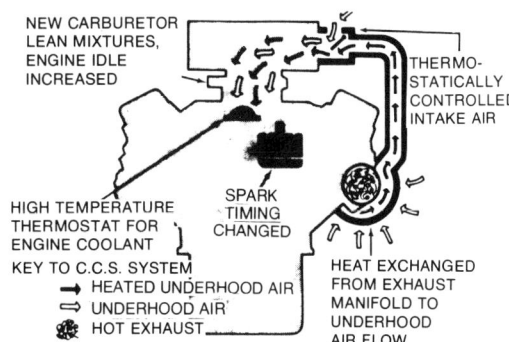

Schematic of the Controlled Combustion System (CCS)

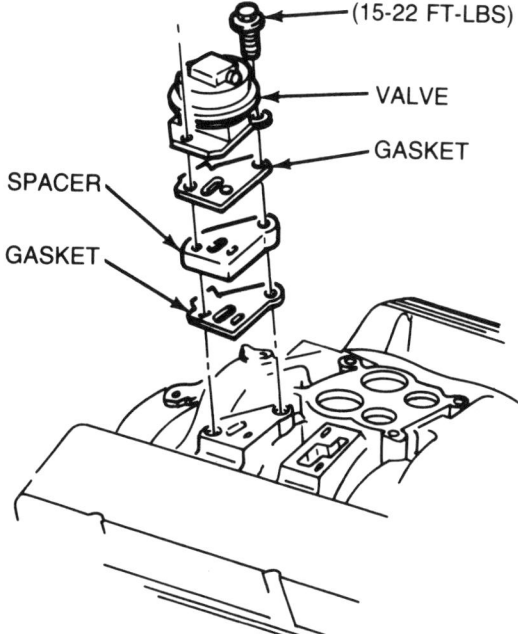

Typical EGR valve mounting location

TVS SWITCH REMOVAL AND INSTALLATION

1. Drain the radiator.
2. Disconnect the vacuum lines from the switch noting their locations. Remove the switch.
3. Apply sealer to the threaded portion of the new switch, and install it, torquing to 15 ft. lb.
4. Rotate the head of the switch to a position that will permit easy hookup of vacuum hoses. Then install vacuum hoses to the proper connectors.

Controlled Combustion System

The CCS system relies upon leaner air/fuel mixtures and altered ignition timing to improve combustion efficiency. A special air cleaner with a thermostatically controlled opening is used on most CCS equipped models to ensure that air entering the carburetor is kept at 100°F. This allows leaner carburetor settings and improves engine warm-up. A 15°F higher temperature thermostat is employed on CCS cars to further improve emission control.

SERVICE

Since the only extra component added with a CCS system is the thermostatically controlled air cleaner, there is no additional maintenance required; however, tune-up adjustments such as idle speed, ignition timing, and dwell become much more critical. Care must be taken to ensure that these settings are correct, both for trouble-free operation and a low emission level.

Computer Controlled Catalytic Converter System (C-4)

The C-4 System, installed on all 1980 cars sold in California, is an electronically controlled exhaust emissions system. The purpose of the system is to maintain the ideal air/fuel ratio at which the catalytic converter is most effective.

Major components of the system include an Electronic Control Module (ECM), an oxygen sensor, an electronically controlled carburetor, and a three-way oxidation reduction catalytic converter. The system also includes a maintenance reminder flag connected to the odometer which becomes visible in the instrument cluster at regular intervals, signaling the need for oxygen sensor replacement.

The oxygen sensor, installed in the exhaust manifold, generates a voltage which varies

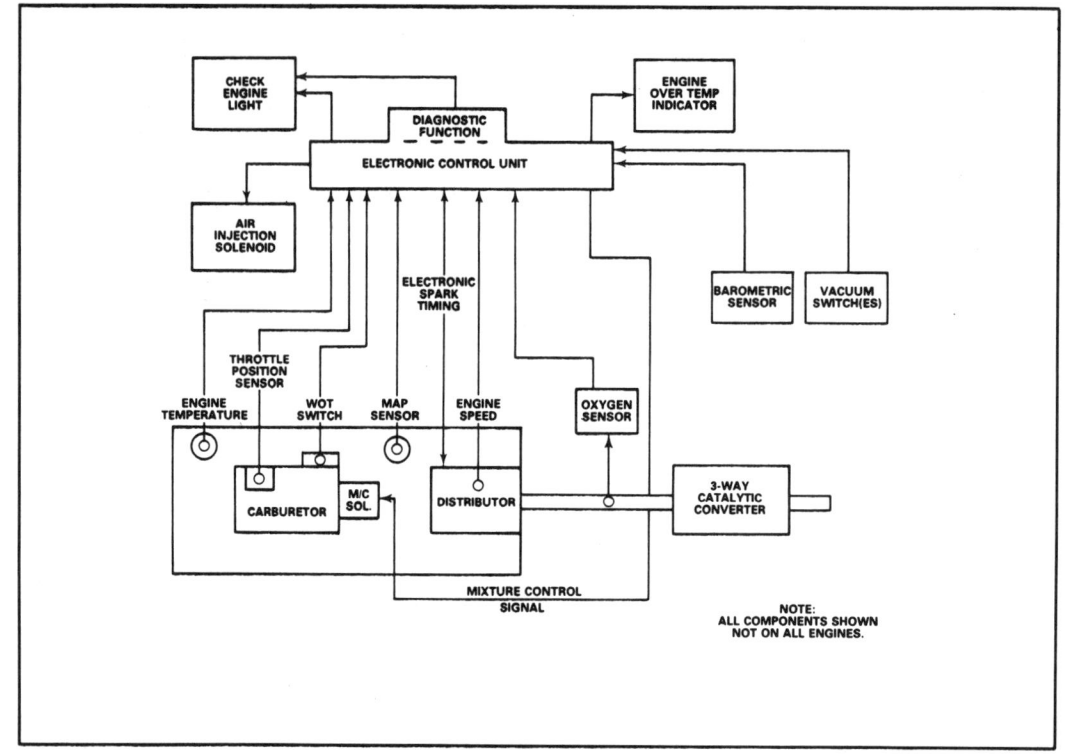

C-4 system schematic

with exhaust gas oxygen content. Lean mixtures (more oxygen) reduce voltage; rich mixtures (less oxygen) increase voltage. Voltage output is sent to the ECM.

An engine temperature sensor installed in the engine coolant outlet monitors engine coolant temperatures. Vacuum control switches and throttle position sensors also monitor engine conditions and supply signals to the ECM.

The Electronic Control Module receives input signals from all sensors. It processes these signals and generates a control signal sent to the carburetor. The control signal cycles between on (lean command) and off (rich command). The amount of on and off time is a function of the input voltage sent to the ECM by the oxygen sensor.

Rochester Dualjet E2ME and E4ME carburetors are used with the C-4 System. Basically, an electrically operated mixture control solenoid is installed in the carburetor float bowl. The solenoid controls the air/fuel mixture metered to the idle and main metering systems. Air metering to the idle system is controlled by an idle air bleed valve. It follows the movement of the mixture solenoid to control the amount of air bled into the idle system, enriching or leaning out the mixture as appropriate. Air/fuel mixture enrichment occurs when the fuel valve is open and the air bleed valve is closed. All cycling of this system, which occurs ten times per second, is controlled by the ECM. A throttle position switch informs the ECM of open or closed throttle operation. A number of different switches are used, varying with application. When the ECM receives a signal from the throttle switch, indicating a change of position, it immediately searches its memory for the last set of operating conditions that resulted in an ideal air/fuel ratio, and shifts to that set of conditions. The memory is continually updated during normal operation.

A "Check-Engine" light is included in the C-4 System installation. When a fault develops, the light comes on, and a trouble code is set into the ECM memory. However, if the fault is intermittent, the light will go out, but the trouble code will remain in the ECM memory as long as the engine is running. The trouble codes are used as a diagnostic aid, and are pre-programmed.

Unless the required tools are available, troubleshooting the C-4 System should be confined to mechanical checks of electrical connectors, vacuum hoses and the like. All

EMISSION CONTROLS AND FUEL SYSTEM

diagnosis and repair should be performed by a qualified mechanic.

Computer Command Control System

The Computer Command Control System, installed on all 1981 cars, is basically a modified version of the C-4 system. Its main advantage over its predecessor is that it can monitor and control a larger number of interrelated emission control systems.

This new system can monitor up to 15 various engine/vehicle operating conditions and then use this information to control as many as 9 engine related systems. The "System" is thereby making constant adjustments to maintain good vehicle performance under all normal driving conditions while at the same time allowing the catalytic converter to effectively control the emissions of NOx, HC and CO.

In addition, the "System" has a built in diagnostic system that recognizes and identifies possible operational problems and alerts the driver through a "Check Engine" light in the instrument panel. The light will remain ON until the problem is corrected. The "System" also has built in back-up systems that in most cases of an operational problem will allow for the continued operation of the vehicle in a near normal manner until the repairs can be made.

The CCC system has some components in common with the C-4 system, although they are not interchangeable. These components include the Electronic Control Module (ECM), which, as previously stated, controls many more functions than does its predecessor, an oxygen sensor system, an electronically controlled variable-mixture carburetor, a three-way catalytic converter, throttle position and coolant sensors, a Barometric Pressure Sensor (BARO), a Manifold Absolute Pressure Sensor (MAP) and a "Check Engine" light in the instrument panel.

Components unique to the CCC system include the Air Injection Reaction (AIR) management system, a charcoal canister purge solenoid, EGR valve controls, a vehicle speed sensor (in the instrument panel), a transmission converter clutch solenoid (only on models with automatic transmission), idle speed control and Electronic Spark Timing (EST).

The ECM, in addition to monitering sensors and sending out a control signal to the carburetor, also controls the following components or sub-systems: charcoal canister purge control, the AIR system, idle speed, automatic transmission converter lock-up, distributor ignition timing, the EGR valve, and the air conditioner converter clutch.

The EGR valve control solenoid is activated by the ECM in a fashion similar to that of the charcoal canister purge solenoid de-

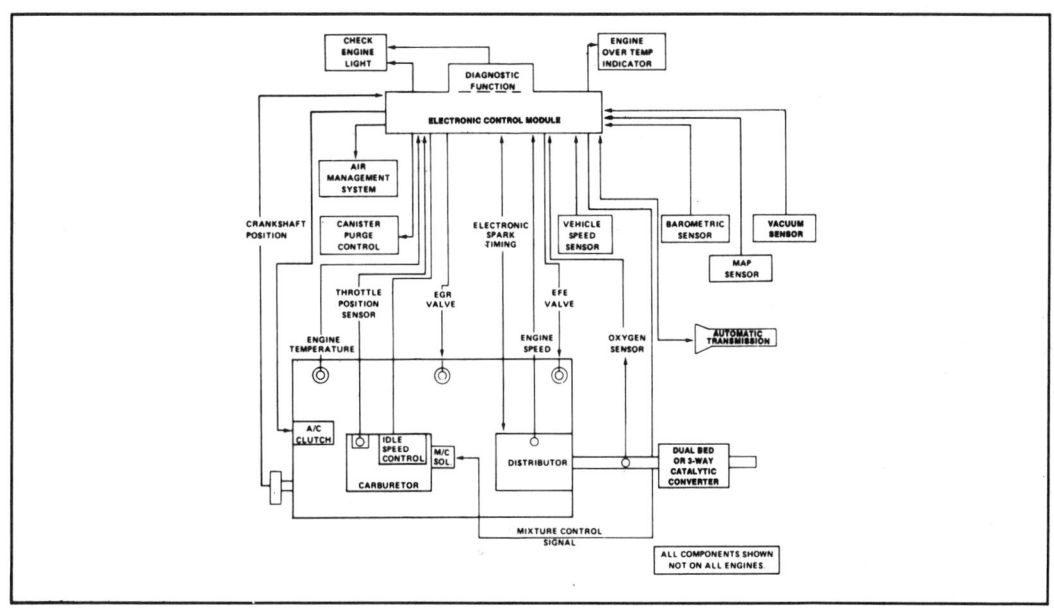

CCC system schematic

180 EMISSION CONTROLS AND FUEL SYSTEM

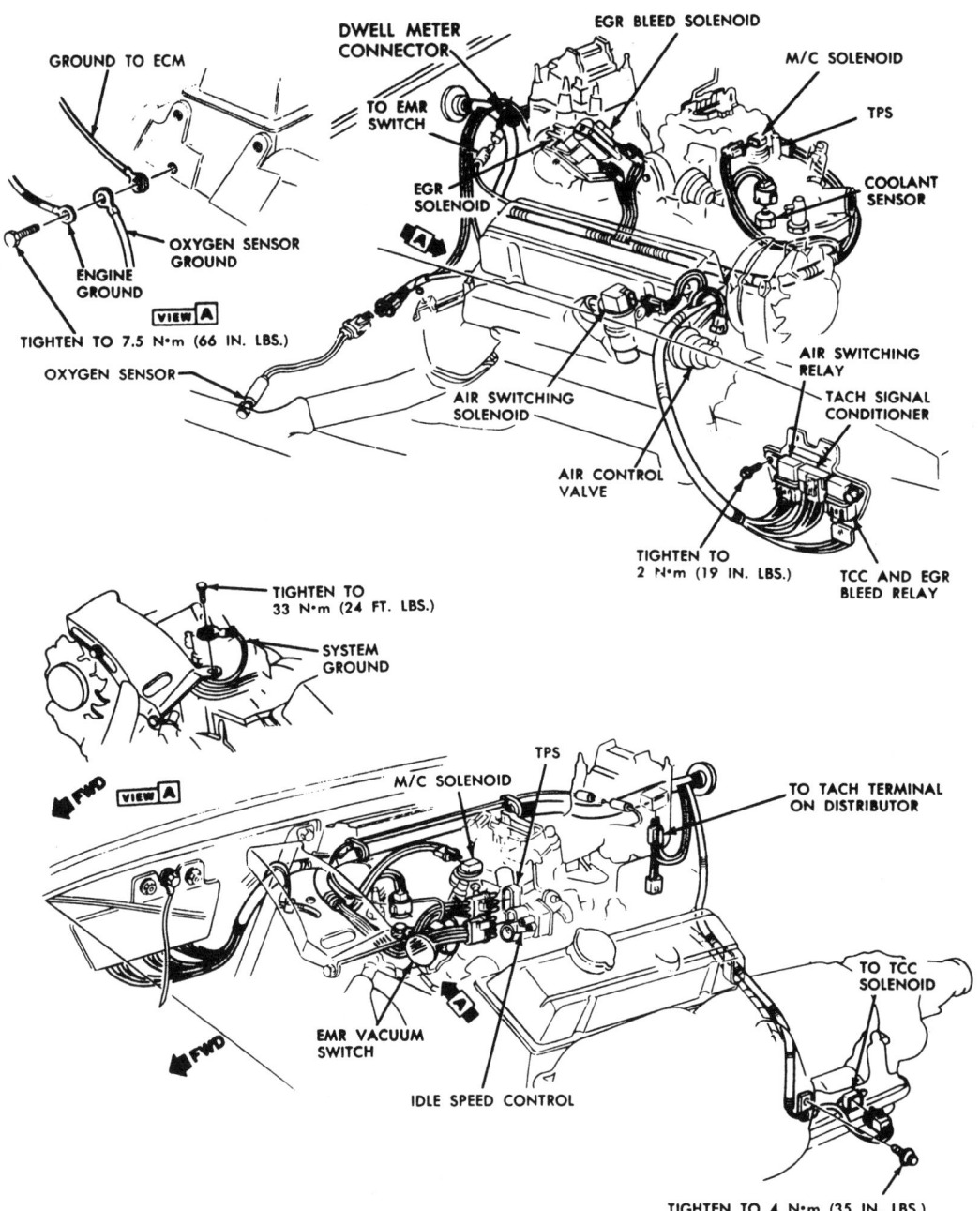

CCC component location—229 V6

scribed earlier in this chapter. When the engine is cold, the ECM energizes the solenoid, which blocks the vacuum signal to the EGR valve. When the engine is warm, the ECM de-energizes the solenoid and the vacuum signal is allowed to reach and then activate the EGR valve.

The Transmission Converter Clutch (TCC) lock is controlled by the ECM through an electrical solenoid in the automatic transmission. When the vehicle speed sensor in the dash signals the ECM that the car has attained the pre-determined speed, the ECM energizes the solenoid which then allows the torque converter to mechanically couple the engine to the transmission. When the brake pedal is pushed, or during deceleration or passing, etc., the ECM returns the transmission to fluid drive.

The idle speed control adjusts the idle

EMISSION CONTROLS AND FUEL SYSTEM

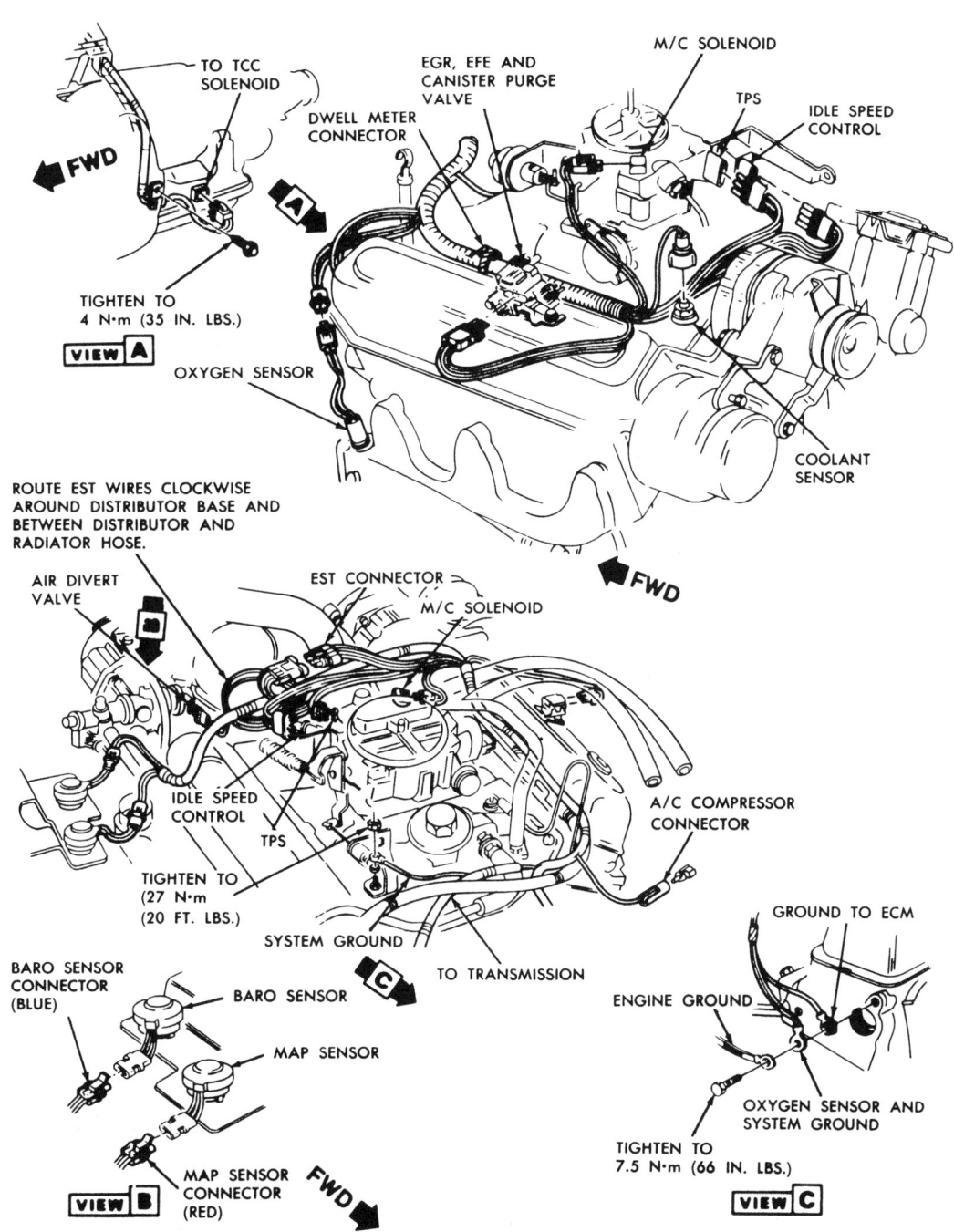

CCC component location—231 V6

speed to all particular engine load conditions and will lower the idle under no-load or low-load conditions in order to conserve fuel.

NOTE: *Not all engines use all systems. Control applications may differ.*

BASIC TROUBLESHOOTING

NOTE: *The following explains how to activate the Trouble Code signal light in the instrument cluster. This is not a full fledged C-4 or CCC system troubleshooting and isolation procedure.*

Before suspecting the C-4 or CCC system, or any of its components as being faulty, check the ignition system (distributor, timing, spark plugs and wires). Check the engine compression, the air cleaner and any of the emission control components that are not

182 EMISSION CONTROLS AND FUEL SYSTEM

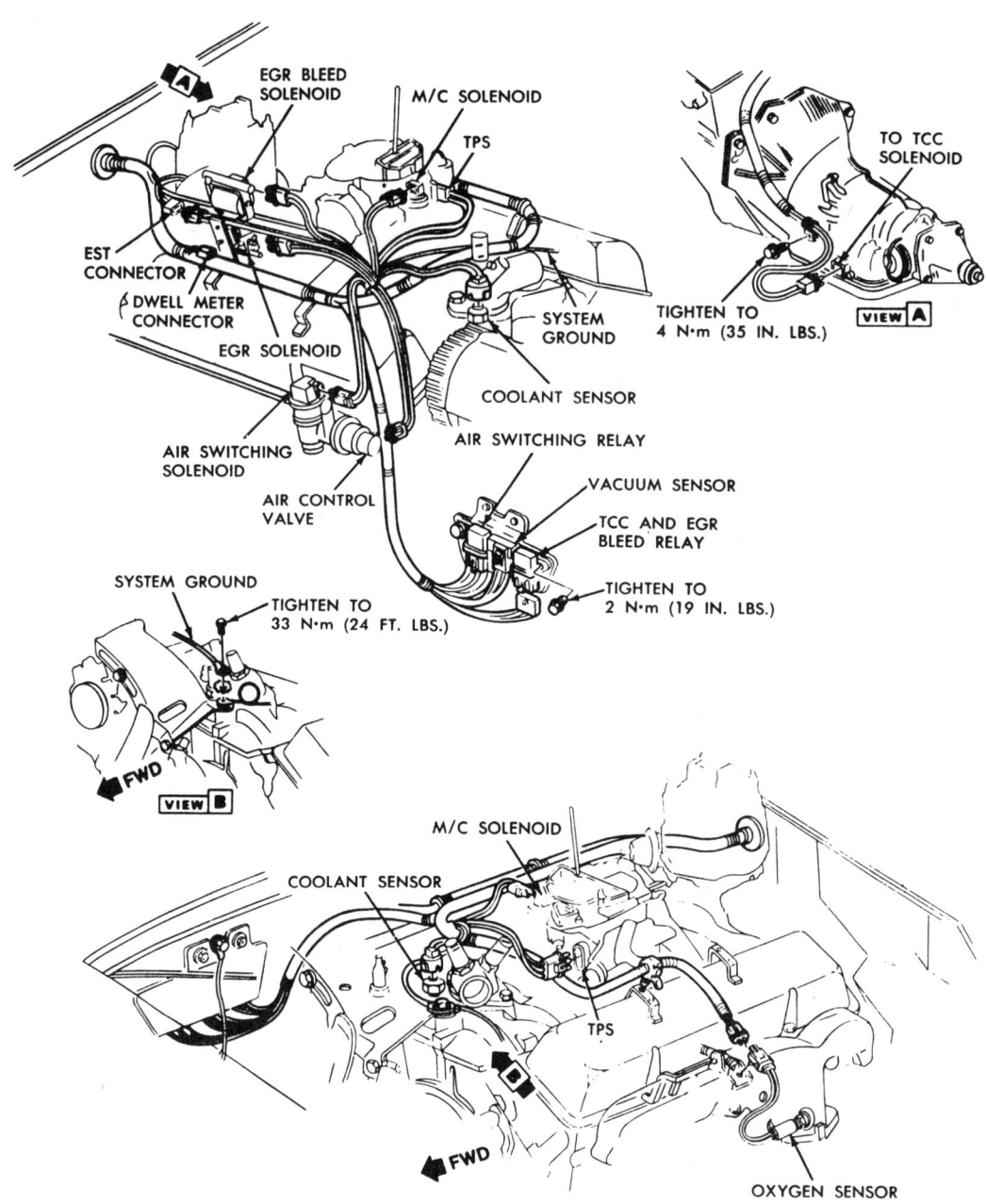

CCC component location—V8

controlled by the ECM. Also check the intake manifold, the vacuum hoses and hose connectors for any leaks. Check the carburetor mounting bolts for tightness.

The following symptoms could indicate a possible problem area with the C-4 or CCC systems:
1. Detonation
2. Stalling or rough idling when the engine is cold
3. Stalling or rough idling when the engine is hot
4. Missing
5. Hesitation
6. Surging
7. Poor gasoline mileage
8. Sluggish or spongy performance
9. Hard starting when engine is cold
10. Hard starting when the engine is hot
11. Objectionable exhaust odors
12. Engine cuts out
13. Improper idle speed (CCC only)

As a bulb and system check, the "Check Engine" light will come on when the ignition

EMISSION CONTROLS AND FUEL SYSTEM

switch is turned to the ON position but the engine is not started.

The "Check Engine" light will also produce the trouble code/codes by a series of flashes which translate as follows: When the diagnostic test lead (C-4) or terminal (CCC) under the instrument panel is grounded, with the ignition in the ON position and the engine not running, the "Check Engine" light will flash once, pause, and then flash twice in rapid succession. This is a Code 12, which indicates that the diagnostic system is working. After a long pause, the Code 12 will repeat itself two more times. This whole cycle will then repeat itself until the engine is started or the ignition switch is turned OFF.

When the engine is started, the "Check Engine" light will remain on for a few seconds and then turn off. If the "Check Engine" light remains on, the self-diagnostic system has detected a problem. If the test lead (C-4) or test terminal (CCC) is then grounded, the trouble code will flash (3) three times. If more than one problem is found to be in exsistance, each trouble code will flash (3) three times and then change to the next one. Trouble codes will flash in numerical order (lowest code number to highest). The trouble code series will repeat themselves for as long as the test leads or terminal remains grounded.

A trouble code indicates a problem with a given circuit. For example, trouble code 14 indicates a problem in the cooling sensor circuit. This includes the coolant sensor, its electrical harness and the Electronic Control Module (ECM).

Since the self-diagnostic system cannot diagnose every possible fault in the system, the absence of a trouble code does not necessarily mean that the system is trouble-free. To determine whether or not a problem with the system exists that does not activate a trouble code, a system performance check must be made. This job should be left to a qualified service technician.

In the case of an intermittant fault in the system, the "Check Engine" light will go out when the fault goes away, but the trouble code will remain in the memory of the ECM. Therefore, if a trouble code can be obtained even though the "Check Engine" light is not on, it must still be evaluated. It must be determined if the fault is intermittant or if the engine must be operating under certain conditions (acceleration, deceleration, etc.) before the "Check Engine" light will come on. In some cases, certain trouble codes will not be recorded in the ECM until the engine has been operated at part throttle for at least 5 to 18 minutes.

On the C-4 system, the ECM erases all trouble codes every time that the ignition is turned off. In the case of intermittant faults, a long term memory is desirable. This can be produced by connecting the orange connector/lead from terminal "S" of the ECM directly to the battery (or to a 'hot' fuse panel terminal). This terminal must always be disconnected immediately after diagnosis as it puts an undue strain on the battery.

On the CCC system, a trouble code will be stored until the terminal 'R' at the ECM has been disconnected from the battery for at least 10 seconds.

ACTIVATING THE TROUBLE CODE

On the C-4 system, activate the trouble code by grounding the trouble code test lead. Use the illustrations to help you locate the test lead under the instrument panel (usually a white and black wire with a green connector). Run a jumper wire from the lead to a suitable ground.

On the CCC system, locate the test ter-

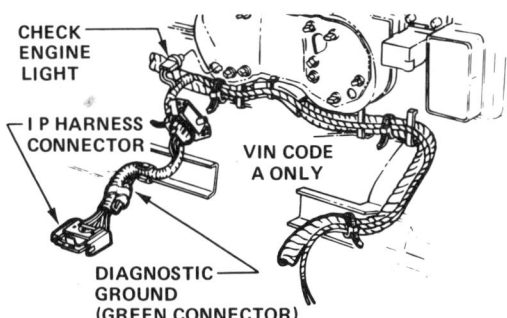

C-4 system diagnostic test lead location

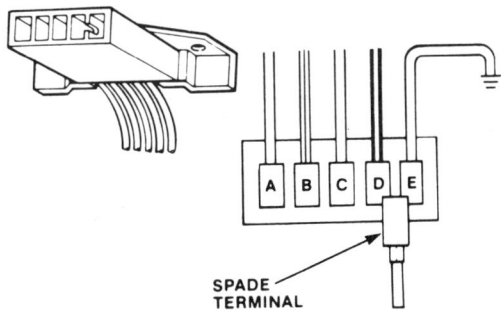

The CCC system diagnostic test terminal is located underneath the left side of the instrument panel

EMISSION CONTROLS AND FUEL SYSTEM

Trouble Code Identification Chart

NOTE: *Always ground the test lead/terminal AFTER the engine is running*

Trouble Code	Applicable System	Possible Problem Area
12	C-4, CCC	No reference pulses to the ECM. This is not stored in the memory and will only flash when the fault is present (not to be confused with the Code 12 discussed earlier).
13	C-4, CCC	Oxygen sensor circuit. The engine must run for at least 5 min. (18 min. on the C-4 equipped 231 V6) at part throttle before this code will show.
13 & 14 (at same time)	C-4	See code 43.
13 & 43 (at same time)	C-4	See code 43.
14	C-4, CCC	Shorted coolant sensor circuit. The engine must run 2–5 min. before this code will show.
15	C-4, CCC	Open coolant sensor circuit. The engine must run for at least 5 min. (18 min. on the C-4 equipped 231 V6) before this code will show.
21	C-4	Shorted wide open throttle switch and/or open closed-throttle switch circuit (when used).
	C-4, CCC	Throttle position sensor circuit. The engine must run for at least 10 sec. (25 sec.—CCC) below 800 rpm before this code will show.
21 & 22 (at same time)	C-4	Grounded wide open throttle switch circuit (231 V6).
22	C-4	Grounded closed throttle or wide open throttle switch circuit (231 V6).
23	C-4, CCC	Open or grounded carburetor mixture control (M/C) solenoid circuit.
24	CCC	Vehicle speed sensor circuit. The engine must for at least 5 min. at normal read speed before this code will show.
32	C-4, CCC	Barometric pressure sensor (BARO) circuit output is low.
32 & 55 (at same time)	C-4	Grounded +8V terminal or V(REF) terminal for BARO sensor, or a faulty ECM.
34	C-4	Manifold absolute pressure sensor (MAP) output is high. The engine must run for at least 10 sec. below 800 rpm before this code will show.
	CCC	Manifold absolute pressure sensor (MAP) circuit or vacuum sensor circuit. The engine must run for at least 5 min. below 800 rpm before this code will show.
35	CCC	Idle speed control circuit shorted. The engine must run for at least 2 sec. above ½ throttle before this code will show.

EMISSION CONTROLS AND FUEL SYSTEM

Trouble Code Identification Chart (cont.)

NOTE: *Always ground the test lead/terminal AFTER the engine is running*

Trouble Code	Applicable System	Possible Problem Area
42	CCC	Electronic spark timing (EST) bypass circuit grounded.
43	C-4	Throttle position sensor adjustment. The engine must run for at least 10 sec. before this code will show.
44	C-4, CCC	Lean oxygen sensor indication. The engine must run for at least 5 min. in closed loop (oxygen sensor adjusting carburetor mixture) at part throttle under load (drive car) before this code will show.
44 & 55 (at same time)	C-4, CCC	Faulty oxygen sensor circuit.
45	C-4, CCC	Rich oxygen sensor indication. The engine must run for at least 5 min. before this code will show (see 44 for conditions).
51	C-4, CCC	Faulty calibration unit (PROM) or improper PROM installation in the ECM. It will take at least 30 sec. before this code will show.
52 & 53	C-4	"Check Engine" light off: intermittant ECM problem. "Check Engine" light on: faulty ECM—replace.
52	C-4, CCC	Faulty ECM.
53	CCC	Faulty ECM.
54	C-4, CCC	Faulty mixture control solenoid circuit and/or faulty ECM.
55	C-4	Faulty throttle position sensor or ECM (all but 231 V6). Faulty oxygen sensor, open MAP sensor or faulty ECM (231 V6 only).
	CCC	Grounded +8V supply (terminal 19 on ECM connector), grounded 5V reference (terminal 21 on ECM connector), faulty oxygen sensor circuit or faulty ECM.

NOTE: *Not all codes will apply to every model.*

minal under the instrument panel (see illustration). Use a jumper wire and ground only the lead.

NOTE: *Ground the test lead/terminal according to the instructions given previously in the "Basic Troubleshooting" section.*

Mixture Control Solenoid (M/C)

The fuel flow through the carburetor idle main metering circuits is controlled by a mixture control (M/C) solenoid located in the carburetor. The M/C solenoid changes the air/fuel mixture to the engine by controlling the fuel flow through the carburetor. The ECM controls the solenoid by providing a ground. When the solenoid is energized, the fuel flow through the carburetor is reduced, providing a leaner mixture. When the ECM removes the ground, the solenoid is de-energized, increasing the fuel flow and providing a richer mixture. The M/C solenoid is energized and de-energized at a rate of 10 times per second.

Throttle Position Sensor (TPS)—1980–81

The throttle position sensor is mounted in the carburetor body and is used to supply

EMISSION CONTROLS AND FUEL SYSTEM

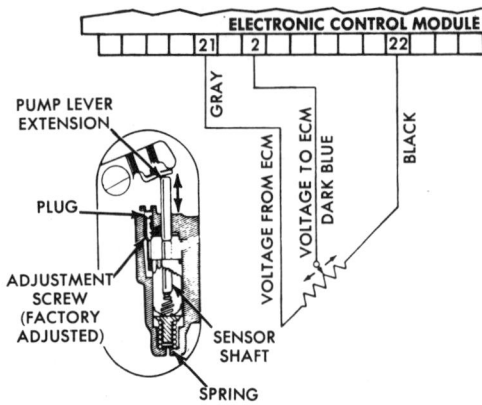

Throttle position sensor (TPS)

throttle position information to the ECM. The ECM memory stores an average of operating conditions with the ideal air/fuel ratios for each of those conditions. When the ECM receives a signal that indicates throttle position change, it immediately shifts to the last remembered set of operating conditions that resulted in an ideal air/fuel ratio control. The memory is continually being updated during normal operations.

Idle Speed Control (ISC)—1981 229 V6

The idle speed control does just what its name implies—it controls the idle. The ISC is used to maintain low engine speeds while at the same time preventing stalling due to engine load changes. The system consists of a motor assembly mounted on the carburetor which moves the throttle lever so as to open or close the throttle blades.

The whole operation is controlled by the ECM. The ECM monitors engine load to determine the proper idle speed. To prevent

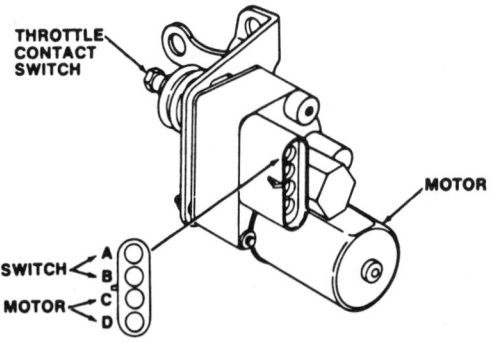

The Idle Speed Control (ISC) motor is attached to the carburetor

stalling, it monitors the air conditioning compressor switch, the transmission, the park/neutral switch and the ISC throttle switch. The ECM processes all this information and then uses it to control the ISC motor which in turn will vary the idle speed as necessary.

Electronic Spark Timing (EST)

All 1980 models with the 231 V6 engine and all 1981 models but those with the 229 V6 engine use EST. The EST distributor, as described in an earlier chapter, contains no vacuum or centrifugal advance mechanism and uses a seven terminal HEI module. It has four wires going to a four terminal connector in addition to the connectors normally found on HEI distributors. A reference pulse, indicating engine rpm is sent to the ECM. The ECM determines the proper spark advance for the engine operating conditions and then sends an 'EST' pulse back to the distributor.

Under most normal operating conditions, the ECM will control the spark advance. However, under certain operating conditions such as cranking or when setting base timing, the distributor is capable of operating without ECM control. This condition is called BYPASS and is determined by the BYPASS lead which runs from the ECM to the distributor. When the BYPASS lead is at the proper voltage (5), the ECM will control the spark. If the lead is grounded or open circuited, the HEI module itself will control the spark. Disconnecting the 4-terminal EST connector will also cause the engine to operate in the BYPASS mode.

Transmission Converter Clutch (TCC)

All 1981 models with an automatic transmission use TCC. The ECM controls the converter by means of a solenoid mounted in the transmission. When the vehicle speed reaches a certain level, the ECM energizes the solenoid and allows the torque converter to mechanically couple the transmission to the engine. When the operating conditions indicate that the transmission should operate as a normal fluid coupled transmission, the ECM will de-energize the solenoid. Depressing the brake will also return the transmission to normal automatic operation.

EMISSION CONTROLS AND FUEL SYSTEM

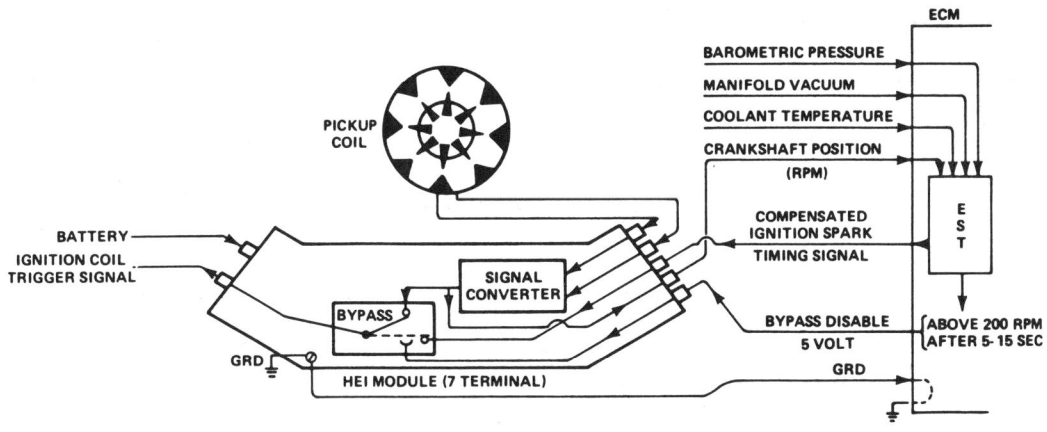

A schematic view of the EST circuitry

Catalytic Converter

The catalytic converter is a muffler-like container built into the exhaust system to aid in the reduction of exhaust emissions. The catalyst element consists of individual pellets or a honeycomb monolithic substrate coated with a noble metal such as platinum, palladium, rhodium or a combination. When the exhaust gases come into contact with the catalyst, a chemical reaction occurs which will reduce the pollutants into harmless substances like water and carbon dioxide.

There are essentially two types of catalytic converters: an oxidizing type and a three-way type. The oxidizing type is used on all 1975–80 models with the exception of those 1980 models built for Calif. It requires the addition of oxygen to spur the catalyst into reducing the engine's HC and CO emissions into H_2O and CO_2. Because of this need for oxygen, the AIR system is used with all these models.

The oxidizing catalytic converter, while effectively reducing HC and CO emissions, does little, if anything in the way of reducing NOx emissions. Thus, the three-way catalytic converter.

The three-way converter, unlike the oxidizing type, is capable of reducing HC, CO and NOx emissions; all at the same time. In theory, it seems impossible to reduce all three pollutants in one system since the reduction of HC and CO requires the addition of oxygen, while the reduction of NOx calls for the removal of oxygen. In actuality, the three-way system really can reduce all three pollutants, but only if the amount of oxygen in the exhaust system is precisely controlled. Due to this precise oxygen control requirement, the three-way converter system is used only in cars equipped with an oxygen sensor system (1980 Calif. cars and all 1981 models).

There are no service procedures required for the catalytic converter, although the converter body should be inspected occasionally for damage. Some models with the V-6 engine require a catalyst change at 30,000 mile intervals (consult your Owner's Manual).

PRECAUTIONS

1. Use only unleaded fuel.
2. Avoid prolonged idling; the engine should run on longer than 20 min. at curb idle and no longer than 10 min. at fast idle.
3. Do not disconnect any of the spark plug leads while the engine is running.
4. Make engine compression checks as quickly as possible.

CATALYST TESTING

At the present time threre is no known way to reliably test catalytic converter operation in the field. The only reliable test is a 12 hour and 40 min. "soak" test (CVS) which must be done in a laboratory.

An infrared HC/CO tester is not sensitive enough to measure the higher tailpipe emissions from a failing converter. Thus, a bad converter may allow enough emissions to escape so that the car is no longer in compliance with Federal or state standards, but will still not cause the needle on a tester to move off zero.

The chemical reactions which occur inside a catalytic converter generate a great deal of heat. Most converter problems can be traced to fuel or ignition system problems which cause unusually high emissions. As a result of

188 EMISSION CONTROLS AND FUEL SYSTEM

the increased intensity of the chemical reactions, the converter literally burns itself up.

A completely failed converter might cause a tester to show a slight reading. As a result, it is occasionally possible to detect one of these.

As long as you avoid severe overheating and the use of leaded fuels it is reasonably safe to assume that the converter is working properly. If you are in doubt, take the car to a diagnostic center that has a tester.

Oxygen Sensor

An oxygen sensor is used on all 1980 models built for Calif. and on all 1981 models. The sensor protrudes into the exhaust stream and moniters the oxygen content of the exhaust gases. The difference between the oxygen content of the exhaust gases and that of the outside air generates a voltage signal to the ECM. The ECM moniters this voltage and, depending upon the value of the signal received, issues a command to adjust for a rich or a lean condition.

No attempt should ever be made to measure the voltage output of the sensor. The current drain of any conventional voltmeter would be such that it would permanently damage the sensor. No jumpers, test leads or any other electrical connections should ever be made to the sensor. Use these tools ONLY on the ECM side of the wiring harness connector AFTER disconnecting it from the sensor.

REMOVAL AND INSTALLATION

The oxygen sensor must be replaced every 30,000 miles (48,000 km.). The sensor may be difficult to remove when the engine temperature is below 120°F (48°C). Excessive removal force may damage the threads in the exhaust manifold or pipe; follow the removal procedure carefully.

1. Locate the oxygen sensor. On the V8 engines, it is on the front of the left side exhaust manifold, just above the point where it connects to the exhaust pipe. On the V6 engines, it is on the inside of the exhaust pipe where it bends toward the back of the car.

NOTE: *On the V6 engine you may find it necessary to raise the front of the car and remove the oxygen sensor from underneath.*

2. Trace the wires leading from the oxygen sensor back to the first connector and then disconnect them (the connector on the V6 engine is attached to a bracket mounted

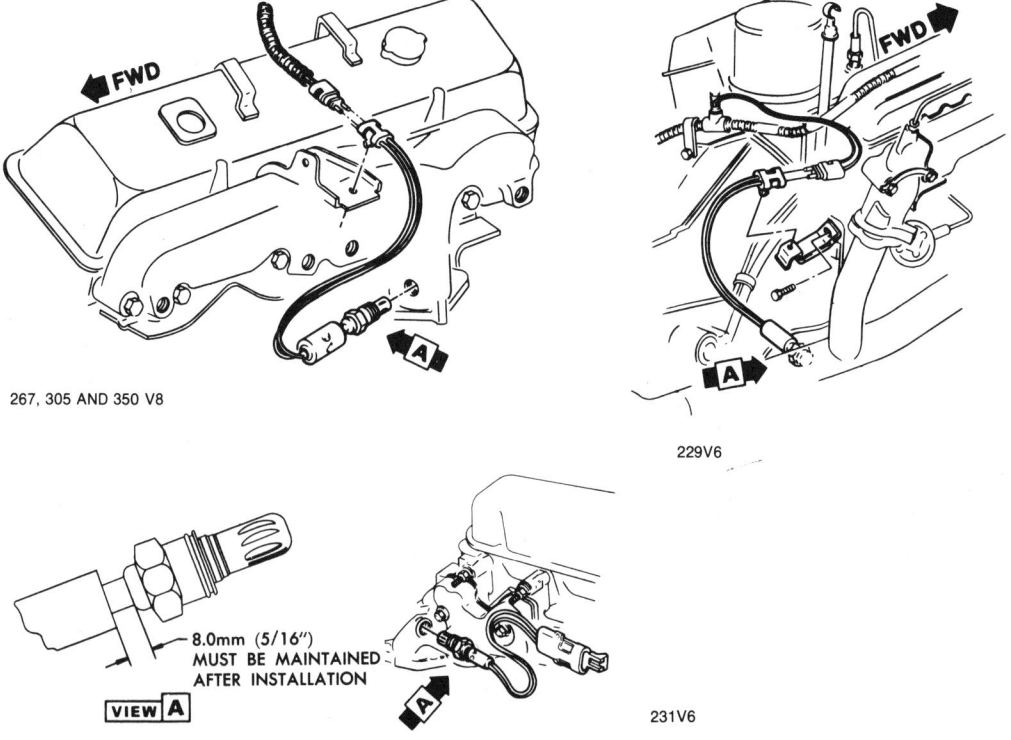

Oxygen sensor locations on all engines

on the right, rear of the engine block, while the connector on the V8 engine is attached to a bracket mounted on the top of the left side exhaust manifold).

3. Spray a commercial heat riser solvent onto the sensor threads and allow it to soak in for at least five minutes.

4. Carefully unscrew and remove the sensor.

5. To install, first coat the new sensor's threads with G.M. anti-seize compound no. 5613695 or the equivalent. This is *not* a conventional anti-seize paste. The use of a regular compound may electrically insulate the sensor, rendering it inoperative. You must coat the threads with an electrically conductive anti-seize compound.

6. Installation torque is 30 ft. lbs. (42 Nm.). Do not overtighten.

7. Reconnect the electrical connector. Be careful not to damage the electrical pigtail. Check the sensor boot for proper fit and installation. Install the air cleaner, if removed.

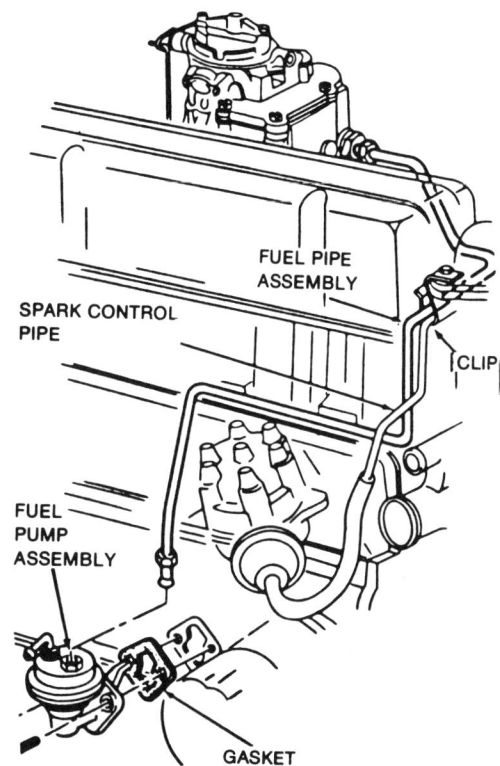
Fuel pump mounting—inline six cylinder

FUEL SYSTEM

Fuel Pump

The fuel pump is a single action AC diaphragm type. All fuel pumps used on inline sixes, V6 and V8 engines are of the diaphragm type and because of the design are serviced by replacement only. No adjustments or repairs are possible.

The pump is operated by an eccentric on the camshaft. On L6 engines, the eccentric acts directly on the pump rocker arm. On V6 and V8 engines, a pushrod between the camshaft eccentric and the fuel pump operates the pump rocker arm.

TESTING THE FUEL PUMP

Fuel pumps should always be tested on the vehicle. The larger line between the pump and tank is the suction side of the system and the smaller line, between the pump and carburetor is the pressure side. A leak in the pressure side would be apparent because of dripping fuel. A leak in the suction side is often only apparent because of a reduced volume of fuel delivered to the pressure side. However, fuel *may* leak out on the suction side when the engine is off.

1. Tighten any loose line connections and look for any kinks or restrictions. Inspect rubber hoses for cracks or leaks and replace

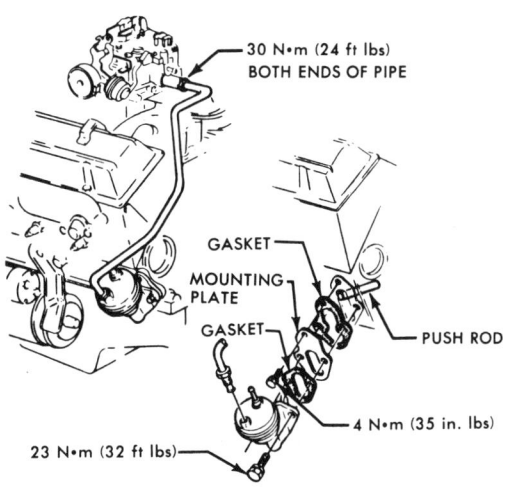
Fuel pump mounting—229 V6

if necessary. Inspect the fuel filter for clogging and clean or replace it as necessary.

2. Disconnect the fuel line at the carburetor. Disconnect the distributor-to-coil primary wire or, on HEI systems, the distributor connector. Place a container at the end of the fuel line and crank the engine a few revolutions. If little or no gasoline flows from the line, either the fuel pump is inoperative or

EMISSION CONTROLS AND FUEL SYSTEM

the line is plugged. Blow through the lines with compressed air and try the test again. Reconnect the line.

3. Attach a pressure gauge to the pressure side of the fuel line with a "Tee" fitting.

4. Run the engine and note the reading on the gauge. Stop the engine and compare the reading with the specifications listed in the "Tune-Up Specifications" chart. If the pump is operating properly, the pressure will be as specified and will be constant at idle speed. If pressure varies sporadically or is too high or low, the pump should be replaced.

5. Remove the pressure gauge.

REMOVAL AND INSTALLATION

NOTE: *When you connect the fuel pump outlet fitting, always use 2 wrenches to avoid damaging the pump.*

1. Disconnect the fuel intake and outlet lines at the pump and plug the pump intake line.

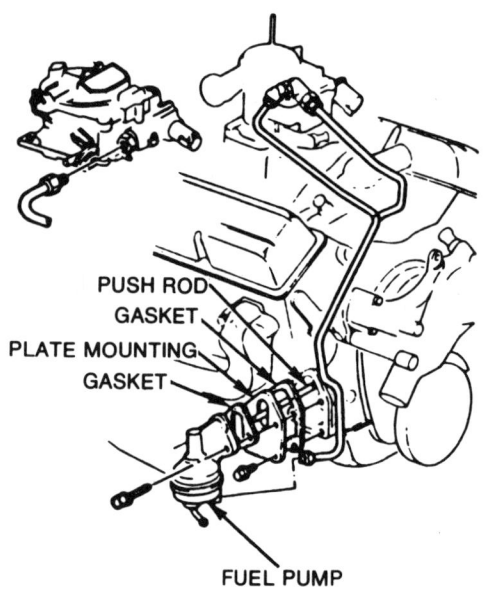

Fuel pump mounting—V8

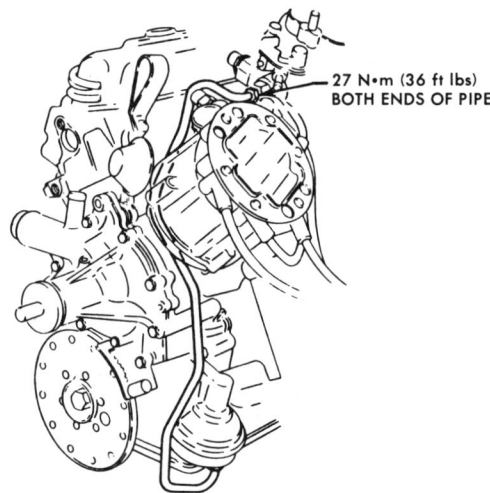

Fuel pump mounting—231 V6

2. On small-block V6 and V8 engines, remove the upper bolt from the right front mounting boss. Insert a longer bolt (⅜–16 ×2 in.) in this hole to hold the fuel pump pushrod.

3. Remove the two pump mounting bolts and lockwashers; remove the pump and its gasket.

4. If the rocker arm pushrod is to be removed from V6 or V8, remove the two adapter bolts and lockwashers and remove the adapter and its gasket.

5. Install the fuel pump with a new gasket reversing the removal procedure. Coat the mating surfaces with sealer.

6. Connect the fuel lines and check for leaks.

Carburetors

Since its introduction in 1967, the Camaro has used thirteen different carburetors:
- Carter YF 1 bbl—1967
- Rochester BV 1 bbl—1967
- Rochester MV 1 bbl—1968–76
- Rochester 2GV 2 bbl—1968–76
- Rochester 4MV 4 bbl—1968–74
- Holley 4150 4 bbl—1969–72
- Rochester 1ME 1 bbl—1977–79
- Rochester 2 GC 2 bbl—1975–79
- Rochester M4MC 4 bbl—1975–79
- Rochester M2ME 2 bbl—1980
- Rochester M4ME 4 bbl—1980
- Rochester E2ME 2 bbl—1980–81
- Rochester E4ME 4 bbl—1980–81

MODEL IDENTIFICATION

General Motors Rochester carburetors are identified by their model code. The first number indicates the number of barrels, while one of the last letters indicates the type of choke used. These are V for the manifold mounted choke coil, C for the choke coil mounted in the carburetor body, and E for electric choke, also mounted on the carburetor. Model codes ending in A indicate an altitude-compensating carburetor.

EMISSION CONTROLS AND FUEL SYSTEM

REMOVAL AND INSTALLATION
All Carburetors

1. Remove the air cleaner and its gasket.
2. Disconnect the fuel and vacuum lines from the carburetor.
3. Disconnect the choke coil rod, heated air line tube, or electrical connector.
4. Disconnect the throttle linkage.
5. On automatic transmission cars, disconnect the throttle valve linkage if so equipped.
6. If CEC equipped remove the CEC valve vacuum hose and electrical connector. Disconnect the EGR line, if so equipped.
7. Remove the idle stop solenoid, if so equipped.
8. Remove othe carburetor attaching nuts and/or bolts, gasket or insulator, and remove the carburetor.
9. Install the carburetor using the reverse of the removal procedure. Use a new gasket and fill the float bowl with gasoline to ease starting the engine.

OVERHAUL
All Types

Efficient carburetion depends greatly on careful cleaning and inspection during overhaul, since dirt, gum, water, or varnish in or on the carburetor parts are often responsible for poor performance.

Overhaul your carburetor in a clean, dust-free area. Carefully disassemble the carburetor, referring often to the exploded views and directions packaged with the rebuilding kit. Keep all similar and look-alike parts segregated during disassembly and cleaning to avoid accidental interchange during assembly. Make a note of all jet sizes.

When the carburetor is disassembled, wash all parts (except diaphragms, electric choke units, pump plunger, and any other plastic, leather, fiber, or rubber parts) in clean carburetor solvent. Do not leave parts in the solvent any longer than is necessary to sufficiently loosen the deposits. Excessive cleaning may remove the special finish from the float bowl and choke valve bodies, leaving these parts unfit for service. Rinse all parts in clean solvent and blow them dry with compressed air or allow them to air dry. Wipe clean all cork, plastic, leather, and fiber parts with a clean, lint-free cloth.

Blow out all passages and jets with compressed air and be sure that there are no restrictions or blockages. Never use wire or similar tools to clean jets, fuel passages, or air bleeds. Clean all jets and valves separately to avoid accidental interchange.

Check all parts for wear or damage. If wear or damage is found, replace the defective parts. Especially check the following:

1. Check the float needle and seat for wear. If wear is found, replace the complete assembly.
2. Check the float hinge pin for wear and the float(s) for dents or distortion. Replace the float if fuel has leaked into it.
3. Check the throttle and choke shaft bores for wear or an out-of-round condition. Damage or wear to the throttle arm, shaft, or shaft bore will often require replacement of the throttle body. These parts require a close tolerance of fit; wear may allow air leakage, which could affect starting and idling.

NOTE: *Throttle shafts and bushings are not included in overhaul kits. They can be purchased separately.*

4. Inspect the idle mixture adjusting needles for burrs or grooves. Any such condition requires replacement of the needle, since you will not be able to obtain a satisfactory idle.
5. Test the accelerator pump check valves. They should pass air one way but not the other. Test for proper seating by blowing and sucking on the valve. Replace the valve check ball and spring as necessary. If the valve is satisfactory, wash the valve parts again to remove breath moisture.
6. Check the bowl cover for warped surfaces with a straightedge.
7. Closely inspect the accelerator pump plunger wear and damage, replacing as necessary.
8. After the carburetor is assembled, check the choke valve for freedom of operation.

Carburetor overhaul kits are recommended for each overhaul. These kits contain all gaskets and new parts to replace those which deteriorate most rapidly. Failure to replace all parts supplied with the kit (especially gaskets) can result in poor performance later.

Some carburetor manufacturers supply overhaul kits of three basic types: minor repair; major repair; and gasket kits. Basically, they contain the following:

Minor Repair Kits:
- All gaskets
- Float needle valve

EMISSION CONTROLS AND FUEL SYSTEM

- All diagrams
- Spring for the pump diaphragm

Major Repair Kits:
- All jets and gaskets
- All diaphragms
- Float needle valve
- Pump ball valve
- Float
- Complete intermediate rod
- Intermediate pump lever
- Some cover hold-down screws and washers

Gasket Kits:
- All gaskets

After cleaning and checking all components, reassemble the carburetor, using new parts and referring to the exploded view. When reassembling, make sure that all screws and jets are tight in their seats, but do not overtighten as the tips will be distorted. Tighten all screws gradually, in rotation. Do not tighten needle valves into their seats; uneven jetting will result. Always use new gaskets. Be sure to adjust the float level when reassembling.

PRELIMINARY CHECKS (ALL CARBURETORS)

The following should be observed before attempting any adjustments.

1. Thoroughly warm the engine. If the engine is cold, be sure that it reaches operating temperature.
2. Check the torque of all carburetor mounting nuts and assembly screws. Also check the intake manifold-to-cylinder head bolts. If air is leaking at any of these points, any attempts at adjustment will inevitably lead to frustration.
3. Check the manifold heat control valve (if used) to be sure that it is free.
4. Check and adjust the choke as necessary.
5. Adjust the idle speed and mixture. If the mixture screws are capped, don't adjust them unless all other causes of rough idle have been eliminated. If any adjustments are performed that might possibly change the idle speed or mixture, adjust the idle and mixture again when you are finished.

Before you make any carburetor adjustments make sure that the engine is in tune. Many problems which are thought to be carburetor-related can be traced to an engine which is simply out-of-tune. Any trouble in these areas will have symptoms like those of carburetor problems.

Carter YF—1 BBI Carburetor

AUTOMATIC CHOKE ADJUSTMENT

1. Disconnect the choke rod from the choke lever.
2. Hold the choke valve closed and pull the rod up against the stop in the thermostat housing.
3. The top of the rod should be about one rod diameter above the top of the hole in the choke lever. If not, adjust the length of the rod by bending it at the bend.
4. Connect the choke rod at the lever.

HAND CHOKE ADJUSTMENT

1. Push in the hand choke knob until the knob is within 1/8 in. of the dash.
2. Loosen the cable clamp at the carburetor and adjust the cable until the choke is wide open.
3. Tighten the cable clamp and check the operation of the choke.

IDLE VENT ADJUSTMENT

1. With the choke open, back out the idle speed screw until it is free to close the throttle valve.
2. Insert a feeler gauge between the air horn and the vent valve. Adjust to get 0.065 in. clearance.

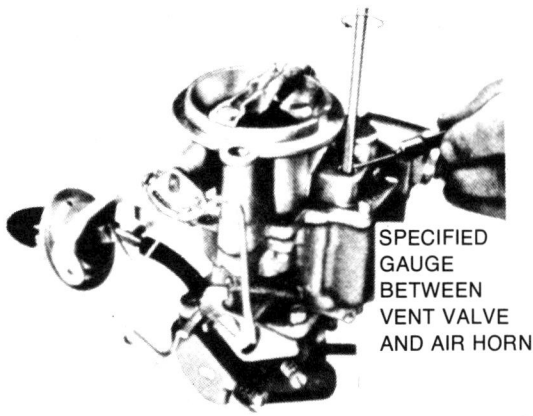

Adjusting idle vent (Carter YF) (© Chevrolet Motor Division)

FAST IDLE AND CHOKE VALVE ADJUSTMENT

1. Hold the choke valve closed.
2. Close the throttle and mark the position of the throttle lever tang on the fast idle cam.
3. The mark on the fast idle cam should align with the upper edge of the tang on the

EMISSION CONTROLS AND FUEL SYSTEM

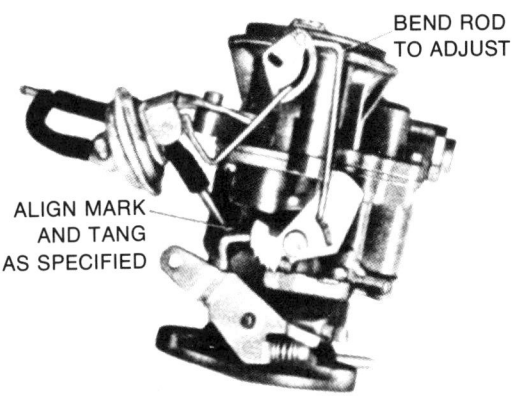

Choke rod adjustment (Carter YF) (© Chevrolet Motor Division)

throttle lever. If not, bend the choke rod as necessary.

CHOKE UNLOADER ADJUSTMENT

1. Open the throttle to the wide open position.
2. Using a rubber band, hold the choke valve closed.
3. Bend the unloader tang on the throttle lever to get the proper clearance (0.250 in.) between the lower edge of the choke valve and the air horn wall.

VACUUM BREAK ADJUSTMENT

1. Hold the vacuum break arm against its stop and hold the choke closed with a rubber band.
2. Bend the vacuum break link to establish a clearance of 2.220 in. (automatic transmission) or 0.240 in. (standard transmission) between the lower edge of the choke valve and the air horn wall.

FLOAT LEVEL ADJUSTMENT

1. Turn the bowl cover upside down and measure the float level by measuring the distance between the float (free end) and cover. This distance should be $7/32$ in.; if not, bend the lip of the float, not the float arm.
2. Hold the cover in the proper position (not upside down) and measure the float drop from the cover to the float bottom at the end opposite the hinge. This distance should be $1^3/_{16}$ in.
3. Make any necessary adjustments with the stop tab on the float arm.

ACCELERATOR PUMP ADJUSTMENT

1. Seat the throttle valve by backing off the idle speed screw.

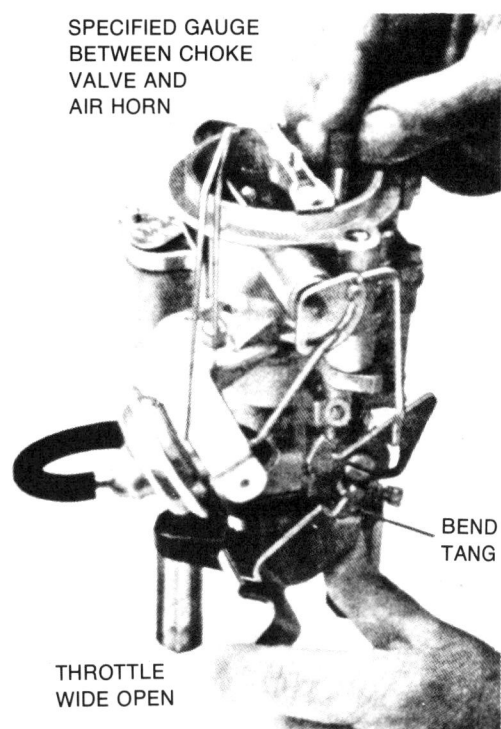

Choke unloader adjustment (Carter YF) (© Chevrolet Motor Division)

2. Hold the throttle valve closed.
3. Fully depress the diaphragm shaft and check the contact between the lower retainer and the lifter link.
4. This retainer (upper pump spring) should just contact the pump lifter link. Do not compress the spring.
5. Bend the pump connector link at its "U" bend to make corrections.

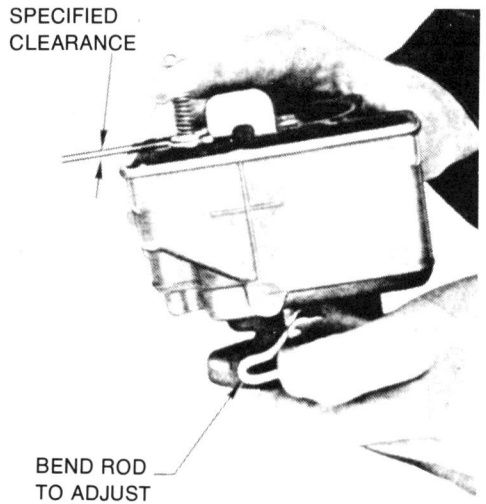

Accelerator pump adjustment (Carter YF) (© Chevrolet Motor Division)

EMISSION CONTROLS AND FUEL SYSTEM

Carter YF Specifications

Year	Model ①	Float Level (in.)	Idle Vent (in.)	Fast Idle Cam (in.)	Unloader (in.)	Choke
1967	4367S	7/32	0.065	0.015	0.250	Index
	4368S, 78S	7/32	0.065	0.015	0.250	Index
	4377S, 87S	7/32	0.065	0.015	0.250	Index

① Model number located on the tag or casting

METERING ROD ADJUSTMENT

1. Insert the metering rod through the metering jet and close the throttle valve. Press down on the upper pump spring until the pump bottoms.
2. The metering rod arm must rest on the pump lifter link; the rod eye should just slide over the arm pin.
3. To adjust, bend the metering rod arm.

Rochester BV—1 BBL Carburetor

AUTOMATIC CHOKE ADJUSTMENT

1. Disconnect the choke rod from the choke lever at the carburetor.
2. While holding the choke valve shut, pull the choke rod up against the stop in the thermostat housing.
3. Adjust the length of the choke rod so that the bottom edge of the choke rod is even with the top edge of the hole in the choke lever.
4. Check the linkage for freedom of operation.

IDLE VENT ADJUSTMENT

1. Position the carburetor lever on the low step of the fast idle cam.
2. The distance between the choke valve and the body casting should be 0.050 in.
3. If an adjustment is necessary, turn the valve with a screwdriver.

FAST IDLE AND CHOKE VALVE ADJUSTMENT

1. Position the end of the idle adjusting screw on the next to highest step of the fast idle cam.
2. A 0.050 in. feeler gauge should slide easily between the lower edge of the choke valve and the carburetor bore.
3. If necessary, bend the choke rod until the correct clearance is obtained.

Rochester BV Specifications

Year	Carburetor Identification ①	Float Level (in.)	Float Drop (in.)	Pump Rod (in.)	Idle Vent (in.)	Vacuum Break (in.)	Automatic Choke	Choke Rod (in.)	Choke Unloader (in.)	Fast Idle Speed
1967	7025000	19/32	1¾	—	0.050	0.140	—	0.090	0.350	—
	7022503	19/32	1¾	—	0.050	0.160	—	0.100	0.350	—
	7026028	19/32	1¾	—	0.050	0.140	—	0.090	0.350	—
	7026027	19/32	1¾	—	0.050	0.160	—	0.100	0.350	—
	7027110	¾	1¾	—	1	0.110	—	0.060	0.215	—
	7027101	¾	1¾	—	1	0.120	—	0.060	0.215	—

① The carburetor identification tag is located at the rear of the carburetor on one of the air horn screws

EMISSION CONTROLS AND FUEL SYSTEM

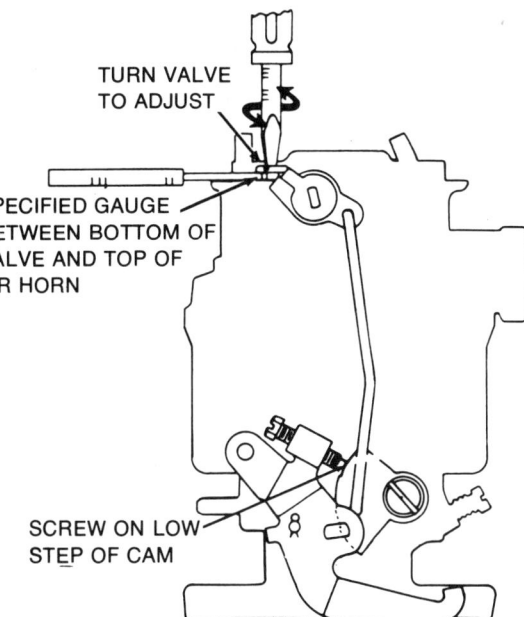

Idle vent adjustment (Rochester BV) (© Chevrolet Motor Division)

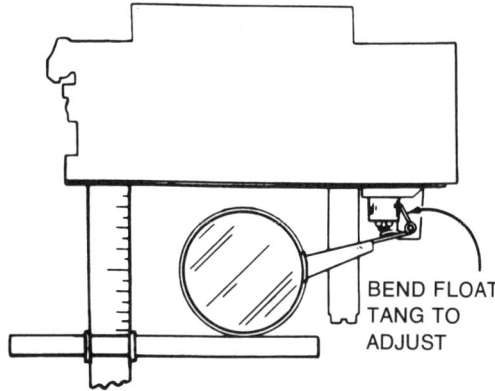

Adjusting float drop (Rochester BV) (© Chevrolet Motor Division)

UNLOADER ADJUSTMENT

1. Open the throttle to the wide open position.
2. A 0.230/0.270 in. gauge should slide freely between the lower edge of the choke valve and the bore of the carburetor.
3. If necessary, bend the throttle tang to obtain the proper clearance.

VACUUM BREAK ADJUSTMENT

1. Hold the diaphragm lever against the diaphragm body.
2. The clearance between the lower edge of the choke valve and the air horn wall should be 0.136–0.154 in. on Powerglide cars and 0.154–0.173 in. on manual cars.
3. Bend the diaphragm link, if necessary.

FLOAT LEVEL ADJUSTMENT

1. Remove the air cleaner.
2. Disconnect the fuel line, fast idle rod, cam-to-choke kick lever, vacuum hose at the diaphragm, and the choke rod at the choke lever.
3. Remove the bowl cover screws and carefully lift the cover off the carburetor.
4. Install a new gasket on the cover before making any adjustments.
5. Invert the cover assembly and measure the float level with a float gauge.
   NOTE: *Rebuilding kits include a float level gauge.*
6. Check float centering while holding the cover sideways. Use the same gauge as in Step five. The floats should not touch the gauge.
7. Hold the cover upright and measure the float drop. If the drop is more or less than 1¾ in., bend the stop tang until the drop is correct.
8. Install the cover and reconnect the lines and linkage in the reverse order of removal.

Rochester MV—1 BBL Carburetor

The model MV carburetor is a single bore, down-drift carburetor with an aluminum throttle body, automatic choke, internally balanced venting, and a hot idle compensating system for cars equipped with automatic transmissions. Newer models are also equipped with Combination Emission Control valves (C.E.C.) and an Exhaust Gas Recirculation (EGR) system. An electrically operated idle stop solenoid replaces the idle stop screw of older models.

The MV carburetor is used on six cylinder cars from 1968 and service procedures apply to all MV carburetors.

FAST IDLE ADJUSTMENT

NOTE: *The fast idle adjustment must be made with the transmission in Neutral.*

1. Position the fast idle lever on the high step of the fast idle cam.
2. Be sure that the choke is properly adjusted and in the wide open position with the engine warm.

EMISSION CONTROLS AND FUEL SYSTEM

3. Bend the fast idle lever until the specified speed is obtained.

CHOKE ROD (FAST IDLE CAM) ADJUSTMENT

NOTE: *Adjust the fast idle before making choke rod adjustments.*

1. Place the fast idle cam follower on the second step of the fast idle cam and hold it firmly against the rise to the high step.
2. Rotate the choke valve in the direction of a closed choke by applying force to the choke coil lever.
3. Bend the choke rod, at the point shown in the illustration, to give the specified opening between the lower edge (upper edge—1976), of the choke valve and the inside air horn wall.

NOTE: *Measurement must be made at the center of the choke valve.*

Choke Vacuum Break Adjustments

The adjustment of the vacuum break diaphragm unit insures correct choke valve opening after engine starting.

1. Remove the air cleaner on vehicles with THERM AC air cleaner; plug the sensor's vacuum take off port.
2. Using an external vacuum source, apply vacuum to the vacuum break diaphragm until the plunger is fully seated.
3. When the plunger is seated, push the choke valve toward the closed position.

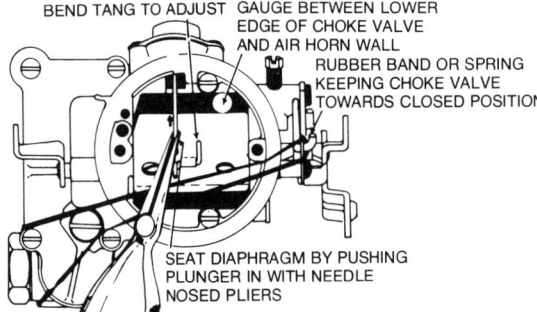

Vacuum break adjustment (MV) (© Chevrolet Motor Division)

CHOKE UNLOADER ADJUSTMENT

1. While holding the choke valve closed, apply pressure to the choke operating lever.
2. Turn the throttle lever to the wide open position.
3. Measure the distance between the lower edge of the choke plate and the air horn wall.
4. If an adjustment is necessary, bend the unloader tang on the throttle lever.

FLOAT LEVEL ADJUSTMENT

1. While holding the float retainer in place, push down on the outer end of the float arm.
2. Measure the distance from the top of the float bowl casting (no gasket) and the toe of the float.
3. Bend the float as necessary to obtain the specified measurement.

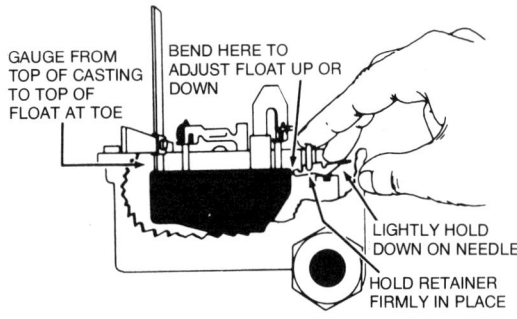

Float level adjustment (MV) (© Chevrolet Motor Division)

METERING ROD ADJUSTMENT

1. Back out the idle adjusting screw or idle stop solenoid to close the throttle valve.
2. Apply pressure to the power piston hanger and hold the piston against its stop.
3. While holding the power piston down, turn the metering rod holder over to the flat surface of the bowl casting until the metering rod lightly touches the inside edge of the bowl.
4. Measure the space between the bowl and the bottom of the metering rod holder. This dimension should be between 0.070 and 0.078 in.
5. Bend the metering rod holder if an adjustment is necessary.

CHOKE ROD ADJUSTMENT

1. Disconnect the choke rod from the upper choke lever and hold the choke valve closed.
2. Push the choke rod down to the bottom of its travel.
3. The top of the rod should be even with the bottom of the hole in the choke lever; bend the rod if necessary.

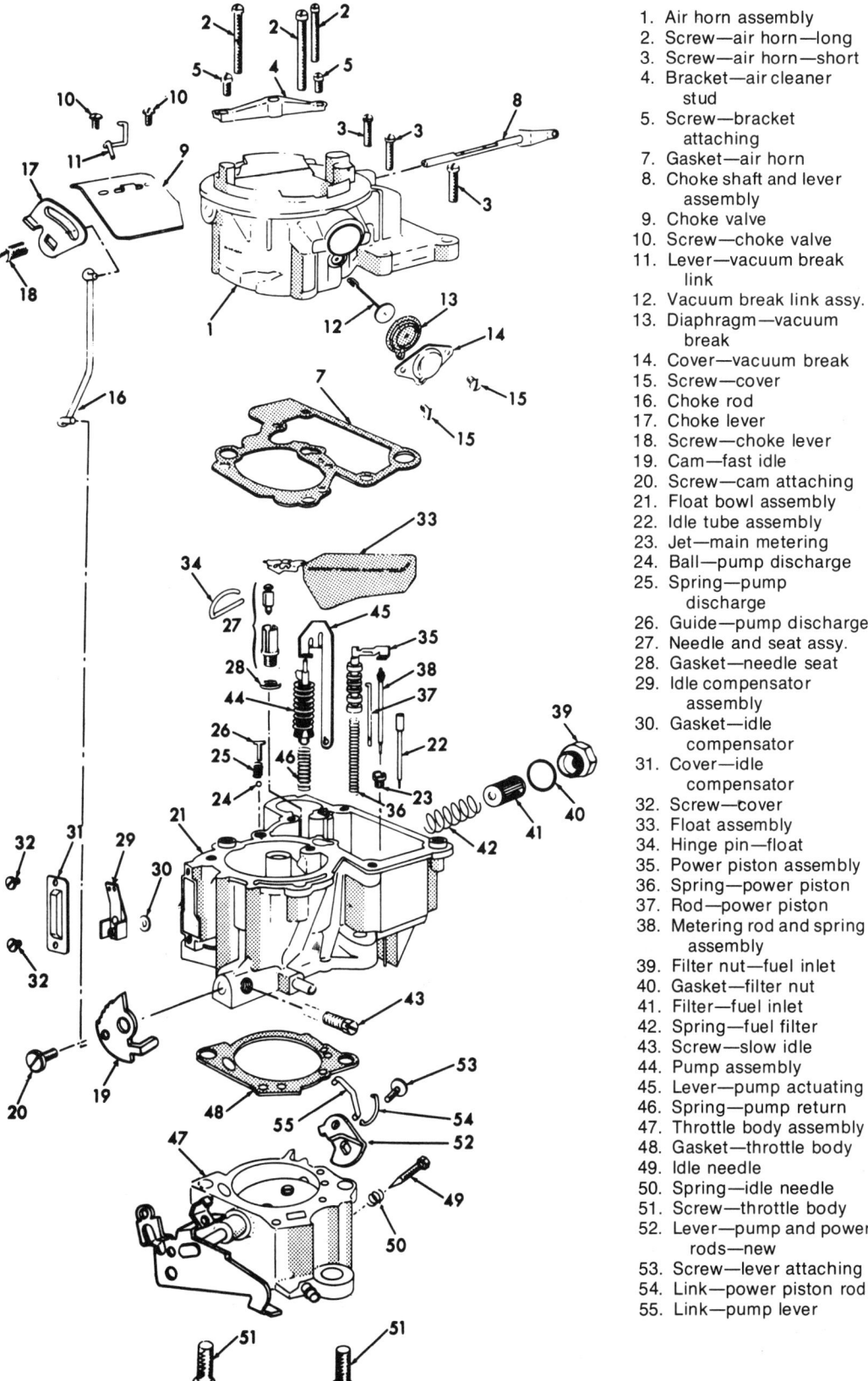

Exploded view of an MV carburetor © CHEVROLET MOTOR DIVISION

Rochester MV Specifications

Year	Carburetor Identification ①	Float Level (in.)	Metering Rod (in.)	Pump Rod	Idle Vent (in.)	Vacuum Break (in.)	Auxiliary Vacuum Break (in.)	Fast Idle Off Car (in.)	Choke Rod (in.)	Choke Unloader (in.)	Fast Idle Speed (rpm)
1968	7028014	9/32	0.120	—	0.050	0.245	—	1½	0.150	0.350	2400②
	7028015	9/32	0.130	—	0.050	0.275	—	1½	0.150	0.350	2400②
	7028017	9/32	0.130	—	0.050	0.275	—	1½	0.150	0.350	2400②
1969	7029014	¼	0.070	—	0.050	0.245	—	0.100	0.170	0.350	2400②
	7029015	¼	0.090	—	0.050	0.275	—	0.100	0.200	0.350	2400②
	7029017	¼	0.090	—	0.050	0.275	—	0.100	0.200	0.350	2400②
1970	7040014	¼	0.070	—	—	0.200	—	0.110	0.170	0.350	2400②
	7040017	¼	0.090	—	—	0.160	—	0.100	0.190	0.350	2400②
1971	7041014	¼	0.080	—	—	0.200	—	0.100	0.160	0.350	—
	7041017	¼	0.080	—	—	0.230	—	0.100	0.180	0.350	—
	7041023	1/16	—	—	—	0.200	—	0.110	0.120	0.350	—
1972	7042014	¼	0.080	—	—	0.190	—	—	0.125	0.500	2400②
	7042017	¼	0.078	—	—	0.225	—	—	0.150	0.500	2400②
1972	7042984	¼	0.078	—	—	0.190	—	—	0.125	0.500	2400②
	7042987	¼	0.076	—	—	0.225	—	—	0.150	0.500	2400②
1973	7043014	¼	0.080	—	—	0.300	—	—	0.245	0.500	1800②
	7043017	¼	0.080	—	—	0.350	—	—	0.275	0.500	1800②
1974	7044014	3/10	0.079	—	—	0.275	—	—	0.230	0.500	1800②③
	7044017	3/10	0.072	—	—	0.350	—	—	0.275	0.500	1800②③
	7044314	3/10	0.073	—	—	0.300	—	—	0.245	0.500	1800②③
1975	7045013	11/32	0.080	—	—	0.200	0.215	—	0.160	0.215	1800④
	7045012	11/32	0.080	—	—	0.350	0.312	—	0.275	0.275	1800④
	7045314	11/32	0.080	—	—	0.275	0.312	—	0.230	0.275	1800④
1976	17056012	11/32	0.084	—	—	0.140	0.265	—	0.100	0.260	⑤
	17056013	11/32	0.082	—	—	0.140	0.325	—	0.140	0.260	⑤
	17056014	—	—	—	—	—	—	—	—	—	—

① The carburetor identification tag is located at the rear of the carburetor on one of the air horn screws
② High step of cam
③ Without vacuum advance
④ 1700 rpm with automatic transmission in Neutral
⑤ 2100 rpm—49 states with transmission in Neutral; 2200 rpm—49 states with non-integral head; 1700 rpm—California

EMISSION CONTROLS AND FUEL SYSTEM

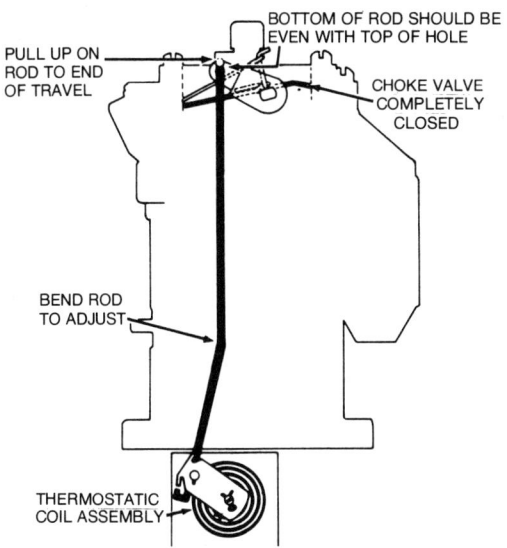

Choke rod adjustment (MV) (© Chevrolet Motor Division)

taining pin, gauge from the top of the casting to the top of the index point at the toe of the float.

3. If float level needs to be changed do it by bending the float arm just on the float side of the float needle.

FAST IDLE ADJUSTMENT

1. If the carburetor has a stepped fast idle cam, put the cam follower on the high step of the cam. If the cam has a smooth contour, open the throttle slightly and rotate the cam to its highest position, then release throttle.

2. Support the lever with a pair of pliers, and bend the tang in or out to achieve specified rpm. Perform the adjustment with engine hot and choke open.

CHOKE COIL LEVER ADJUSTMENT

NOTE: *This adjustment requires a plug gauge or other metal rod of .120" diameter.*

1. Place the fast idle cam follower on the highest step of the cam or rotate the cam to its highest possible position. Close the choke all the way and hold.

2. Insert the plug gauge through the small hole in the outer end of the choke lever. Bend the link at the lowest point of the curved portion until the gauge will enter the hole in the carburetor casting.

Rochester 1ME—1 BBL Carburetors

FLOAT LEVEL ADJUSTMENT

1. Push down on the end of the float arm and against the top of the float needle to hold the retaining pin firmly in place.

2. While holding the position of the re-

Rochester ME Specifications

Year	Carburetor Identification	Float Level (in.)	Metering Rod (in.)	Pump Rod	Idle Vent (in.)	Vacuum Break (in.)	Auxiliary Vacuum Break (in.)	Fast Idle Off Car (in.)	Choke ① Rod (in.)	Choke Unloader (in.)	Fast Idle Speed (rpm) ②
1977	17057013	3/8	.070	—	—	.125	—	—	1 CCW	.375	2000
	17057014	3/8	.070	—	—	.120	—	—	2 CCW	.325	2000
	17057310	3/8	.070	—	—	—	—	—	Index	—	1800
1978	17058013	3/8	.080	—	—	.200	—	—	Index	.200	2000
	17058014	5/16	.160	—	—	.200	—	—	Index	.200	2100
	17058314	3/8	.160	—	—	.243	—	—	Index	.245	2000
1979	17059013	—	—			Information not available					
	17059014	—	—			Information not available					
	17059314	—	—			Information not available					

① Choke adjustment—Index, CCW—counterclockwise in notches, or CW—clockwise in notches
② Transmission in Neutral

CHOKE ADJUSTMENT

1. Place the fast idle cam follower on the high step of the cam or rotate the cam until it is at the highest position.
2. Slightly loosen the three screws which retain the choke cover just enough to turn the cover—don't loosen them more than necessary, or the lever may slip out of the tang inside.
3. Turn the cover until the mark on the cover lines up with the appropriate mark on the choke housing—see specifications.

METERING ROD ADJUSTMENT

1. Hold the throttle wide open. Push downward on the metering rod until it can be slid out of the slot in the holder. Slide the rod out of the holder and remove it from the main metering jet.
2. Back out solenoid hex screw until the throttle can be closed all the way.
3. Remove float bowl gasket.
3. Holding power piston down and throttle closed, swing the metering rod holder over the flat surface of the bowl casting next to the throttle bore. Measure the distance from the flat surface to the outer end of the rod holder with the specified gauge (see specifications), or a metal rod of equivalent diameter.
5. Bend the horizontal portion of the rod holder where it joins the vertical portion until the gauge just passes between the holder and surface of the bowl casting with power piston bottomed.

Rochester 2GC, 2GV—2 BBL Carburetors

These procedures are for both the 1¼ and 1½ models; where there are differences these are noted. The 1½ model has larger throttle bores and an additional fuel feed circuit to make it suitable for use on the 350 V8s.

FAST IDLE ADJUSTMENT

On 2GC and 2GV models the fast idle is set automatically when the curb idle and mixture is set.

FAST IDLE CAM ADJUSTMENT

1. Turn the idle screw onto the second step of the fast idle cam, abutting against the top step.
2. Hold the choke valve toward the closed position and check the clearance between the

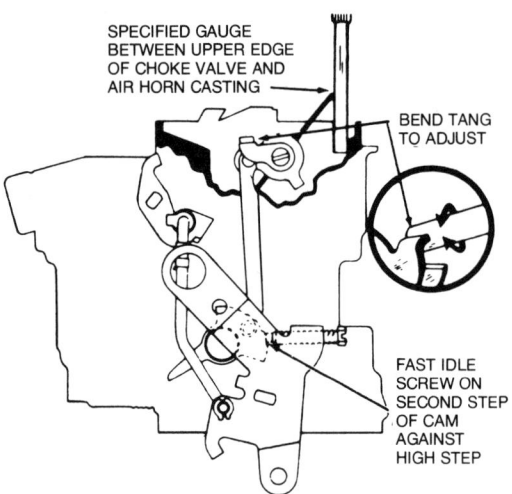

Fast idle cam adjustment (2GV) (© Chevrolet Motor Division)

upper edge of the choke valve and the air horn wall.
3. If this measurement varies from specifications, bend the tang on the choke lever.

CHOKE UNLOADER ADJUSTMENT

1. Hold the throttle valves wide open and use a rubber band to hold the choke valve toward the closed position.
2. Measure the distance between the upper edge of the choke valve and the air horn wall.
3. If this measurement is not within specifications, bend the unloader tang on the throttle lever to correct it.

ACCELERATOR PUMP ROD ADJUSTMENT

1. Back out the idle stop screw and close the throttle valves in their bores.
2. Measure the distance from the top of the air horn to the top of the pump rod.
3. Bend the pump rod at angle to correct this dimension.

FLOAT LEVEL ADJUSTMENT

Invert the air horn and, with the gasket in place and the needle seated, measure the level as follows:
On nitrophyl floats, measure from the air horn gasket to the lip on the toe of the float.
On brass floats, measure from the air horn gasket to the lower edge of the float seam.
Bend the float tang to adjust the level.

EMISSION CONTROLS AND FUEL SYSTEM

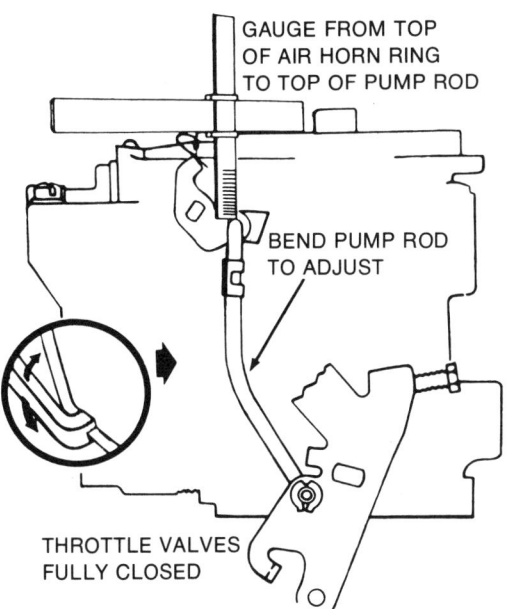

Accelerator pump rod adjustment (2GV)
(© Chevrolet Motor Division)

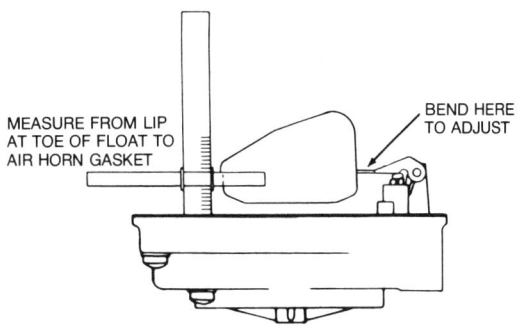

Float level adjustment—nitrophyl (2GV)
(© Chevrolet Motor Division)

On brass floats, measure from the air horn gasket to the bottom of the float.

Bend the float tang to adjust either type of float.

Rochester 4MC, 4MV, M4MC— 4 BBL Carburetors

The Rochester Quadrajet carburetor is a two stage, four-barrel downdrift carburetor. The designation MC or MV refers to the type of choke system the carburetor is designed for. The MV model is equipped with a manifold thermostatic choke coil. The MC model has

FLOAT DROP ADJUSTMENT

Holding the air horn right side up, measure float drop as follows:

On nitrophyl floats, measure from the air horn gasket to the lip at the toe of the float.

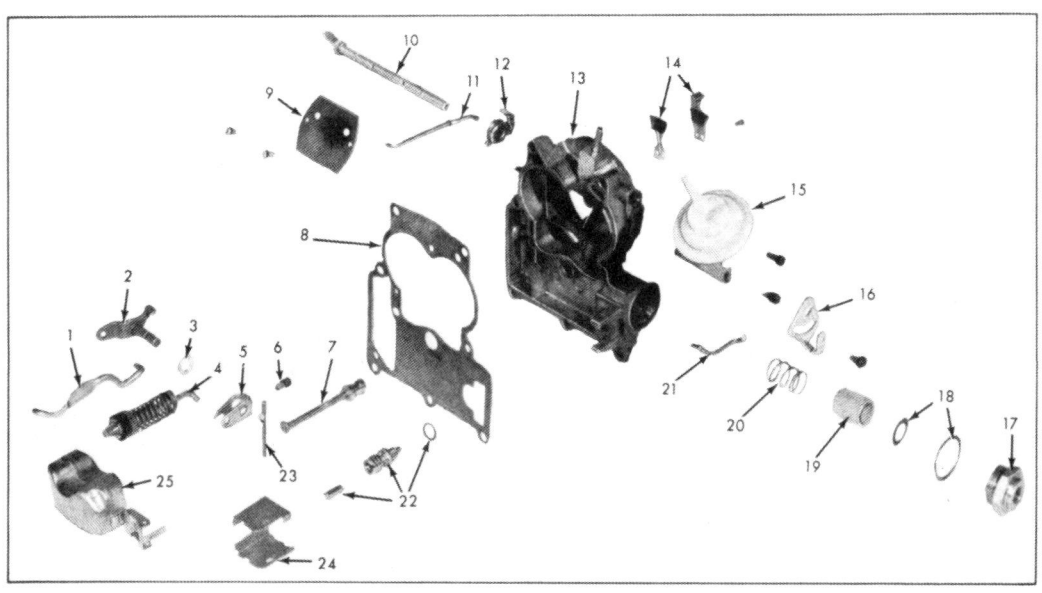

1. Pump rod
2. Pump outlet lever
3. Accelerator pump
4. Washer
5. Pump inner lever
6. Pump inner lever retainer
7. Power piston
8. Air horn-to-bowl gasket
9. Choke valve
10. Choke rod
11. Choke shaft
12. Choke kick lever
13. Air horn
14. Vent valve and shield
15. Vacuum diaphragm
16. Choke lever
17. Diaphragm link
18. Fuel inlet nut
19. Gaskets
20. Fuel filter
21. Filter spring
22. Float needle and seat
23. Float hinge pin
24. Splash shield
25. Float

Exploded view of 2GV (1¼) air horn (© Chevrolet Motor Division)

Rochester 2GC, 2GV Specifications

Year	Carburetor Identification ①	Float Level (in.)	Float Drop (in.)	Pump Rod (in.)	Idle Vent (in.)	Vacuum Break (in.)	Automatic ② Choke	Choke Rod (in.)	Choke Unloader (in.)	Fast Idle Speed
1967	7027101	3/4	1 3/4	1 1/8	1.000	0.120	—	0.060	0.215	—
	7027103	3/4	1 3/4	1 1/8	1.000	0.120	—	0.060	0.215	—
	7027110	3/4	1 3/4	1 1/8	1.000	0.110	—	0.060	0.215	—
	7027112	3/4	1 3/4	1 1/8	1.000	0.110	—	0.060	0.215	—
	7037103	3/4	1 3/4	1 1/8	1.000	0.130	—	0.060	0.215	—
	7037110	3/4	1 3/4	1 1/8	1.000	0.110	—	0.060	0.215	—
	7037112	3/4	1 3/4	1 1/8	1.000	0.110	—	0.060	0.215	—
1968	7028110	3/4	1 3/4	1 1/8	1.000	0.100	—	0.060	0.200	—
	7028101	3/4	1 3/4	1 1/8	1.000	0.100	—	0.060	0.200	—
1968	7028112	3/4	1 3/4	1 1/8	1.000	0.100	—	0.060	0.200	—
	7028103	3/4	1 3/4	1 1/8	1.000	0.100	—	0.060	0.200	—
1969	7029101	27/32	1 3/4	1 1/8	0.020	0.100	—	0.060	0.215	—
	7029103	27/32	1 3/4	1 1/8	0.020	0.100	—	0.060	0.215	—
	7029110	27/32	1 3/4	1 1/8	0.020	0.100	—	0.060	0.215	—
	7029112	27/32	1 3/4	1 1/8	0.020	0.100	—	0.060	0.215	—
	7029102	3/4	1 3/4	1 13/32	0.020	0.215	—	0.085	0.275	—
	7029104	3/4	1 3/4	1 13/32	0.020	0.215	—	0.085	0.275	—
	7029127	3/4	1 3/4	1 13/32	0.020	0.215	—	0.085	0.275	—
	7029129	3/4	1 3/4	1 13/32	0.020	0.215	—	0.085	0.275	—
	7029117	3/4	1 3/4	1 13/32	0.020	0.215	—	0.085	0.275	—
	7029118	3/4	1 3/4	1 13/32	0.020	0.215	—	0.085	0.275	—
	7029119	5/8	1 3/4	1 13/32	0.020	0.215	—	0.085	0.275	—
	7029120	5/8	1 3/4	1 13/32	0.020	0.215	—	0.085	0.275	—
1970	7040110	27/32	1 3/4	1 1/8	0.020	0.100	—	0.060	0.215	—
	7040112	27/32	1 3/4	1 1/8	0.020	0.100	—	0.060	0.215	—

Rochester 2GC, 2GV Specifications (cont.)

Year	Carburetor Identification ①	Float Level (in.)	Float Drop (in.)	Pump Rod (in.)	Idle Vent (in.)	Vacuum Break (in.)	Automatic ② Choke	Choke Rod (in.)	Choke Unloader (in.)	Fast Idle Speed
1970	7040101	27/32	1 3/4	1 1/8	0.020	0.125	—	0.060	0.160	—
	7040103	27/32	1 3/4	1 1/8	0.020	0.125	—	0.060	0.225	—
	7040114	23/32	1 3/8	1 17/32	0.020	0.200	—	0.085	0.325	—
	7040116	23/32	1 3/8	1 17/32	0.020	0.200	—	0.085	0.325	—
	7040113	23/32	1 3/8	1 17/32	0.020	0.215	—	0.085	0.275	—
	7040115	23/32	1 3/8	1 17/32	0.020	0.215	—	0.085	0.275	—
	7040118	23/32	1 3/8	1 17/32	0.020	0.215	—	0.085	0.325	—
	7040120	23/32	1 3/8	1 17/32	0.020	0.215	—	0.085	0.325	—
	7040117	23/32	1 3/8	1 17/32	0.020	0.215	—	0.085	0.325	—
	7040119	23/32	1 3/8	1 17/32	0.020	0.215	—	0.085	0.325	—
1971	7041024	1/16	—	—	—	0.140	—	0.080	0.350	—
	7041101	13/16	1 3/4	1 3/64	—	0.110	—	0.075	0.215	—
	7041110	13/16	1 3/4	1 3/64	—	0.080	—	0.040	0.215	—
	7041102	25/32	1 3/8	1 5/32	—	0.170	—	0.100	0.325	—
	7041114	25/32	1 3/8	1 5/32	—	0.170	—	0.100	0.325	—
	7041113	23/32	1 3/8	1 5/32	—	0.180	—	0.100	0.325	—
	7041127	23/32	1 3/8	1 5/32	—	0.180	—	0.100	0.325	—
	7041118	23/32	1 3/8	1 5/32	—	0.170	—	0.100	0.325	—
	7041181	5/8	1 3/4	1 3/8	—	0.120	—	0.080	0.180	—
	7041182	5/8	1 3/4	1 3/8	—	0.120	—	0.080	0.180	—
1972	7042111	23/32	1 9/32	1 1/2	—	0.180	—	0.100	0.325	—
	7042831	23/32	1 9/32	1 1/2	—	0.180	—	0.100	0.325	—
	7042112	23/32	1 9/32	1 1/2	—	0.170	—	0.100	0.325	—
	7042832	23/32	1 9/32	1 1/2	—	0.170	—	0.100	0.325	—
	7042100	25/32	1 31/32	1 5/16	—	0.080	—	0.040	0.215	—

Rochester 2GC, 2GV Specifications (cont.)

Year	Carburetor Identification ①	Float Level (in.)	Float Drop (in.)	Pump Rod (in.)	Idle Vent (in.)	Vacuum Break (in.)	Automatic ② Choke	Choke Rod (in.)	Choke Unloader (in.)	Fast Idle Speed
1972	7042820	25/32	1 31/32	1 5/16	—	0.080	—	0.040	0.215	—
	7042101	25/32	1 31/32	1 5/16	—	0.110	—	0.075	0.215	—
	7042821	25/32	1 31/32	1 5/16	—	0.110	—	0.075	0.215	—
1973	7043100	21/32	1 9/32	1 5/16	—	0.080	—	0.150	0.215	—
	7043101	21/32	1 9/32	1 5/16	—	0.080	—	0.150	0.215	—
	7043120	21/32	1 9/32	1 5/16	—	0.080	—	0.150	0.215	—
	7043105	21/32	1 9/32	1 5/16	—	0.080	—	0.150	0.215	—
1973	7043112	19/32	1 9/32	1 7/16	—	0.130	—	0.245	0.325	—
	7043111	19/32	1 9/32	1 7/16	—	0.140	—	0.200	0.250	—
1974	7043100	21/32	1 9/32	1 5/16	—	0.080	—	0.150	0.215	—
	7043101	21/32	1 9/32	1 5/16	—	0.080	—	0.150	0.215	—
	7043120	21/32	1 9/32	1 5/16	—	0.080	—	0.150	0.215	—
	7043105	21/32	1 9/32	1 5/16	—	0.080	—	0.150	0.215	—
	7043112	19/32	1 9/32	1 7/16	—	0.130	—	0.245	0.325	—
	7043111	19/32	1 9/32	1 7/16	—	0.140	—	0.200	0.250	—
1975	7045111	21/32	31/32	1 5/8	—	0.130	—	—	0.350	—
	7045112	21/32	31/32	1 5/8	—	0.130	—	—	0.350	—
1976	17056111	9/16	1 9/32	1 21/32	—	0.140	—	—	0.325	—
	17056112	9/16	1 9/32	1 21/32	—	0.140	—	—	0.325	—
	17056412	9/16	1 9/32	1 11/16	—	0.140	—	—	0.325	—
1977	17057111	19/32	1 9/32	1 21/32	—	0.130 ③	Index	—	0.325	—
	17057108	19/32	1 9/32	1 21/32	—	0.130 ③	Index	—	0.325	—
	17057412	21/32	1 9/32	1 21/32	—	0.140 ③	1/2 CCW	—	0.325	—
1978	17058102	15/32	1 9/32	1 17/32	0	0.130 ④	Index	—	0.325	—
	17058103	15/32	1 9/32	1 17/32	0	0.130 ④	Index	—	0.325	—

Rochester 2GC, 2GV Specifications (cont.)

Year	Carburetor Identification ①	Float Level (in.)	Float Drop (in.)	Pump Rod (in.)	Idle Vent (in.)	Vacuum Break (in.)	Automatic ② Choke	Choke Rod (in.)	Choke Unloader (in.)	Fast Idle Speed
1978	17058104	15/32	19/32	1 21/32	0	0.130 ③	Index	—	0.325	—
	17058105	15/32	19/32	1 21/32	0	0.130 ③	Index	—	0.325	—
	17058107	15/32	19/32	1 17/32	0	0.130 ③	Index	—	0.325	—
	17058109	15/32	19/32	1 17/32	0	0.130 ③	Index	—	0.325	—
	17058404	1/2	19/32	1 21/32	0	0.140 ③	1/2 CCW	—	0.325	—
	17058405	1/2	19/32	1 21/32	0	0.140 ③	1/2 CCW	—	0.325	—
1979	17059135	—	—	Information not available						
	17059134	—	—	Information not available						
	17059434	—	—	Information not available						

① The carburetor identification tag is located at the rear of the carburetor on one of the air horn screws
② Index or notches clockwise (CW) or counterclockwise (CCW)
③ .160 after 22,500 miles or first tune-up
④ .150 after 22,500 miles or first tune-up

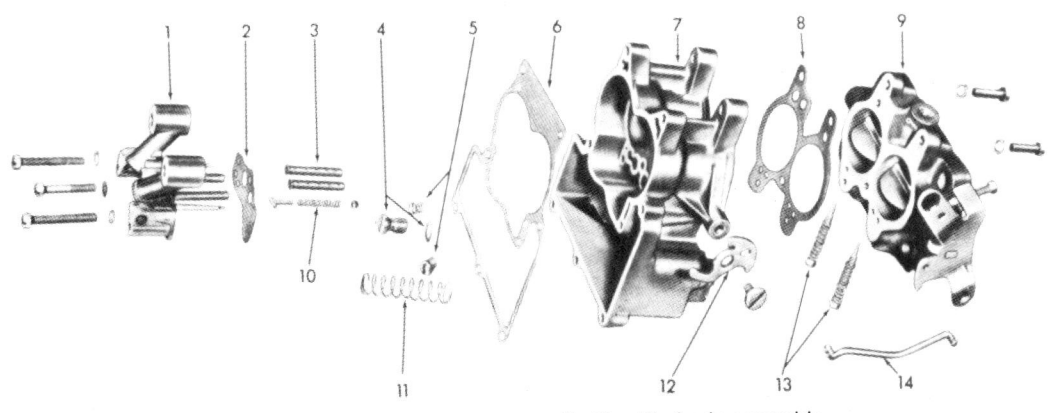

1. Cluster assembly
2. Gasket
3. Splash shield—main well
4. Power valve assembly
5. Main jets
6. Air horn gasket
7. Bowl assembly
8. Throttle body-to-bowl gasket
9. Throttle body assembly
10. Pump discharge check assembly
11. Accelerator pump spring
12. Fast idle cam
13. Idle mixture screws
14. Choke rod

Exploded view of 2GV (1¼) float bowl (© Chevrolet Motor Division)

a choke housing and coil mounted on the side of the float bowl.

The primary side of the carburetor is equipped with 1⅜ diameter bores and a triple venturi with plain tube nozzles. During off idle and part throttle operation, the fuel is

206 EMISSION CONTROLS AND FUEL SYSTEM

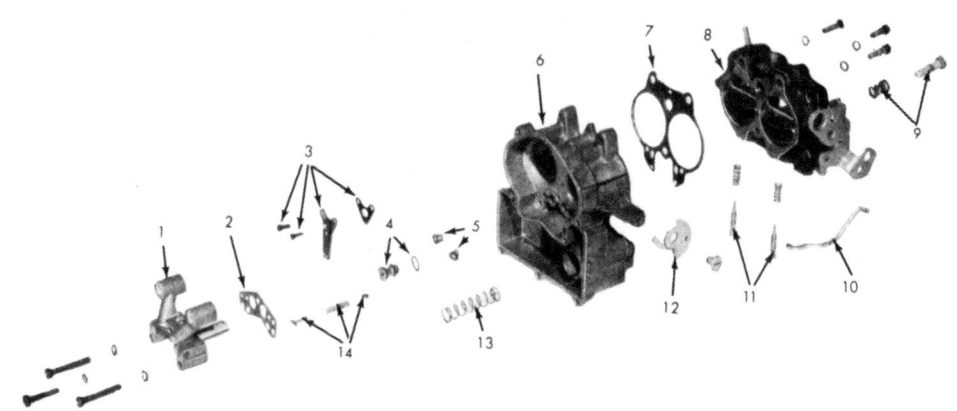

1. Cluster assembly
2. Cluster gasket
3. Hot idle compensator
4. Power valve assembly
5. Main jets
6. Bowl assembly
7. Throttle body-to-bowl gasket
8. Throttle body assembly
9. Idle speed screw
10. Choke rod
11. Idle mixture screws
12. Fast idle cam
13. Accelerator pump spring
14. Pump discharge check assembly

Exploded view of 2GV (1½) float bowl (© Chevrolet Motor Division)

metered through tapered metering rods operating in specially designed jets positioned by a manifold vacuum responsive piston.

The secondary side of the carburetor contains two 2¼ bores. An air valve is used on the secondary side for metering control and supplements the primary bores.

The secondary air valve operates tapered metering rods which regulate the fuel in constant proportion to the air being supplied.

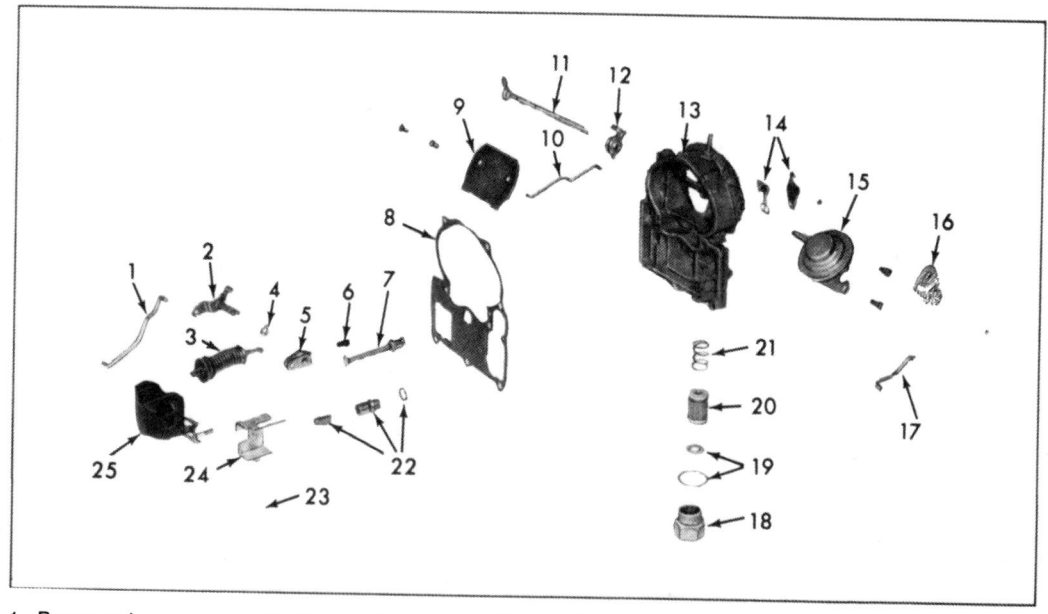

1. Pump rod
2. Pump outer lever
3. Washer
4. Accelerator pump
5. Pump inner lever
6. Pump inner lever retainer
7. Power piston
8. Air horn-to-bowl gasket
9. Choke valve
10. Choke shaft
11. Choke rod
12. Choke kick lever
13. Air horn
14. Vent valve and shield
15. Vacuum diaphragm
16. Choke lever
17. Fuel inlet nut
18. Gaskets
19. Fuel filter
20. Filter spring
21. Diaphragm link
22. Float needle and seat
23. Float hinge pin
24. Splash shields
25. Float

Exploded view of 2GV (1½) air horn (© Chevrolet Motor Division)

EMISSION CONTROLS AND FUEL SYSTEM

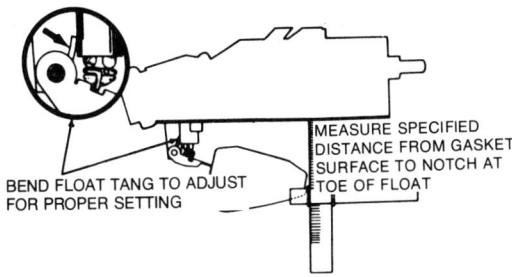

Float drop adjustment—nitrophyl (2GV) (© Chevrolet Motor Division)

ACCELERATOR PUMP

1. Close the primary throttle valves by backing out the slow idle screw and making sure that the fast idle cam follower is off the steps of the fast idle cam.
2. Bend the secondary throttle closing tang away from the primary throttle lever.
3. With the pump in the appropriate hole in the pump lever, measure from the top of the choke valve wall to the top of the pump stem.
4. To adjust, bend the pump lever while supporting it with a screwdriver.
5. After adjusting, readjust the secondary throttle tang and the slow idle screw.

IDLE VENT ADJUSTMENT

NOTE: *This adjustment is not required on 1977–79 carburetors.*

After adjusting the accelerator pump rod as specified above, open the primary throttle valve enough to just close the idle vent. Measure from the top of the choke valve wall to the top of the pump plunger stem. If adjustment is necessary, bend the wire tang on the pump lever.

FLOAT LEVEL

With the air horn assembly upside down, measure the distance from the air horn gasket surface (gasket removed) to the top of the float at the toe. Measure at a point 3/16" back from the top of the float on 1977–79 carburetors.

NOTE: *Make sure the retaining pin is firmly held in place and that the tang of the float is firmly against the needle and seat assembly.*

FAST IDLE

1. Position the fast idle lever on the high step of the fast idle cam. Disconnect and plug the vacuum hose at the EGR valve.
2. Be sure that the choke is wide open and the engine warm.
3. Turn the fast idle screw to gain the proper fast idle rpm.

CHOKE ROD ADJUSTMENT

Position the cam follower on the second step of the fast idle cam, touching the high step. Close the choke valve directly on models up to 1976. On 1977 models, remove the choke thermostatic cover, and then hold the choke closed by pushing upward on the choke coil lever. Gauge the clearance between the lower edge of the choke valve and the carburetor body on models to 1975, and between the upper edge of the choke valve and the carburetor body on 1976 and 1977 models. Bend the choke rod to obtain the specified clearance. On 1977 models, install the choke thermostatic cover and adjust it to specification when the adjustment is complete. This adjustment requires sophisticated special tools on 1978 and later models, and so is not included here.

AIR VALVE DASHPOT ADJUSTMENT

Seat the vacuum break diaphragm. On 1977–79 models, this requires plugging the bleed purge hole on the back of the diaphragm with tape, and the use of an external vacuum source. Hold the air valve tightly closed on all models. Gauge the clearance between the dashpot rod and the end of the slot in the air valve lever. Bend the rod to adjust. Remove the tape from the bleed purge hole.

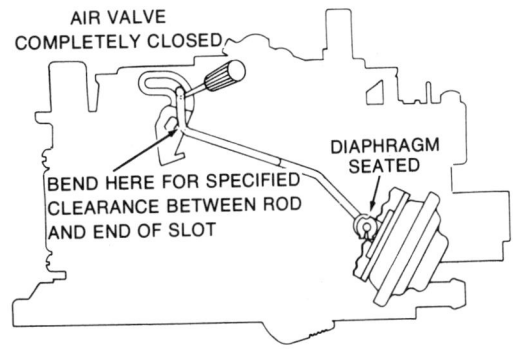

Air valve dashpot adjustment (4MV) (© Chevrolet Motor Division)

CHOKE COIL ROD

1967–76

1. Close the choke valve by rotating the choke coil lever counterclockwise.

EMISSION CONTROLS AND FUEL SYSTEM

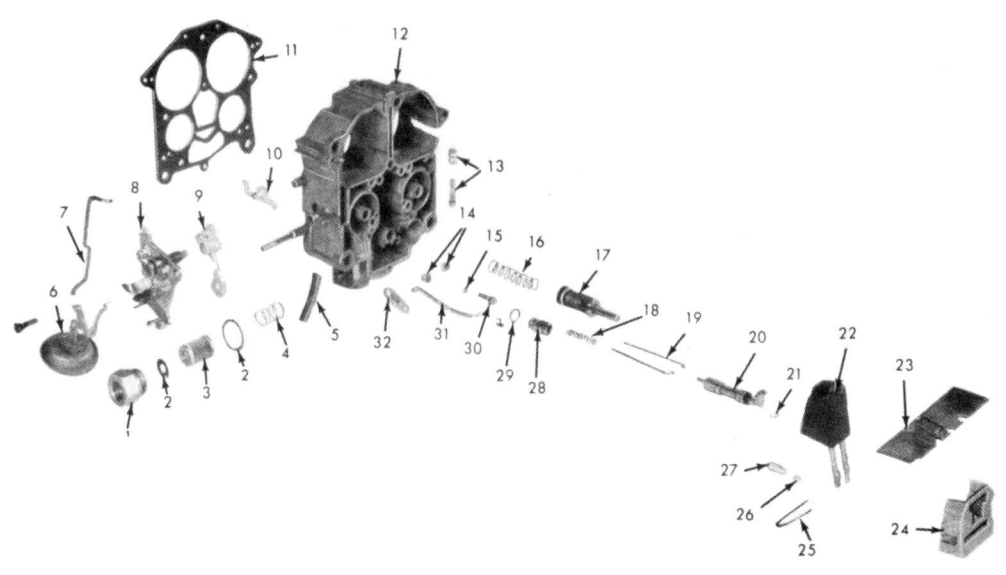

1. Fuel inlet nut
2. Gasket
3. Fuel filter
4. Fuel filter spring
5. Vacuum break hose
6. Vacuum diaphragm
7. Air valve dashpot
8. Choke control bracket
9. Fast idle cam
10. Secondary throttle lockout
11. Throttle body-to-bowl gasket
12. Float bowl assembly
13. Idle speed screw
14. Primary jets
15. Pump discharge ball
16. Pump return spring
17. Accelerator pump
18. Power piston spring
19. Primary metering rods
20. Power piston
21. Metering rod retainer
22. Float
23. Secondary air baffle
24. Float bowl insert
25. Float hinge pin
26. Float needle pull clip
27. Float needle
28. Float needle seat
29. Needle seat gasket
30. Discharge ball retainer
31. Choke rod
32. Choke lever

Exploded view of float bowl (4MV) (© Chevrolet Motor Division)

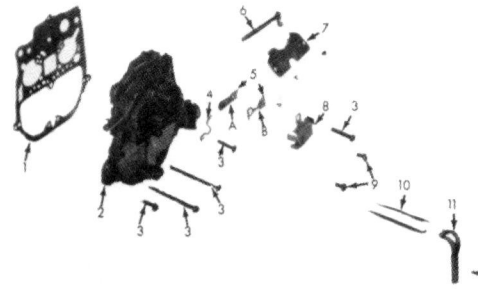

1. Air horn-to-bowl gasket
2. Air horn assembly
3. Air horn-to-bowl retaining screws
4. Idle vent valve lever
5. Idle vent valve
   a. Bimetal
   b. Spring
6. Choke shaft and lever
7. Choke valve
8. Idle vent shield
9. Countersunk air horn retaining screws
10. Secondary metering rods
11. Metering rod hanger

Exploded view of 4MV air horn (© Chevrolet Motor Division)

EMISSION CONTROLS AND FUEL SYSTEM

2. Disconnect the thermostatic coil rod from the upper lever.

3. Push down on the rod until it contacts the bracket of the coil.

4. The rod must fit in the notch of the upper lever.

5. If it does not, it must be bent on the curved portion just below the upper lever.

CHOKE COIL LEVER AND CHOKE THERMOSTATIC COIL

1977-79

1. Remove the three mounting screws and retainers, and pull the thermostatic coil cover assembly off the choke housing and set it aside.

2. Place the fast idle cam follower on the high step of the cam and then push up on the thermostatic coil tang in the choke housing until the choke is closed.

3. Insert a .120″ plug gauge or rod of that diameter into the hole in the housing located just below the lever. With the choke closed, the lever should just touch the gauge.

4. Adjust the choke rod by changing the angle of the bend it makes just below the choke itself, if necessary.

5. Then, install the coil cover back on the choke housing, making sure that the thermostatic coil engages the tang. Install the three retainers and screws, but do not tighten. With the fast idle cam follower still on the high step of the cam, rotate the cover assembly counterclockwise until the choke closes. Set all models 2 notches lean except 1977 models with manual transmission; set these three notches lean. Hold the position of the housing while tightening screws evenly.

VACUUM BREAK

1967-76

1. Fully seat the vacuum break diaphragm using an outside vacuum source.

2. Open the throttle valve enough to allow the fast idle cam follower to clear the fast idle cam.

3. The end of the vacuum break rod should be at the outer end of the slot in the vacuum break diaphragm plunger.

4. The specified clearance should register from the lower end of the choke valve to the inside air horn wall.

5. If the clearance is not correct, bend the vacuum break link.

1977

NOTE: *Adjustment procedures for 1978 and later models require the use of an expensive and sophisticated special tool, so procedures are not included here.*

1. Remove the choke thermostatic cover. Place fast idle cam follower on high step of cam.

2. Where there is a purge bleed hole on the back of the choke vacuum break, put tape over the hole. Then, seat the diaphragm using an outside vacuum source.

3. Push the inside choke coil lever counter-clockwise until the tang on the vacuum break lever touches the tang on the vacuum break plunger stem.

4. Place a gauge of the following diameter between the upper edge of the choke butterfly and the inside wall of the air horn:
- California Engines: .165″
- All Other Engines: .160″

5. If the dimension is incorrect, adjust the screw on the vacuum break plunger stem until all play is taken up and choke butterfly just touches the gauge when its held vertically.

6. Reconnect the vacuum line to vacuum break port of carburetor, remove tape from purge hole (if applied) and reinstall and adjust choke thermostat (see above).

CHOKE UNLOADER ADJUSTMENT

NOTE: *Performing this adjustment on 1978 and later models requires sophisticated special tools, so the procedure is not included here.*

On 1977 models, make sure the choke thermostatic spring is properly adjusted (see above). Close the choke valve and secure it with a rubber band hooked to the vacuum break lever. Open the primary throttles all the way. Then measure the distance between the air horn and edge of the choke butterfly. On models up to and including 1976, use the bottom side of the butterfly for this measurement; on 1977 models, use the top side. Bend the fast idle lever tang to achieve the proper opening of the choke.

SECONDARY LOCKOUT ADJUSTMENT

1967-76

Completely open the choke valve and rotate the vacuum break lever clockwise. Bend the lever if the measurement between the lever and the secondary throttle exceeds specifications. Close the choke and gauge the distance between the lever and the secondary throttle shaft pin. Bend the lever to adjust.

1977-79

1. See illustration below.

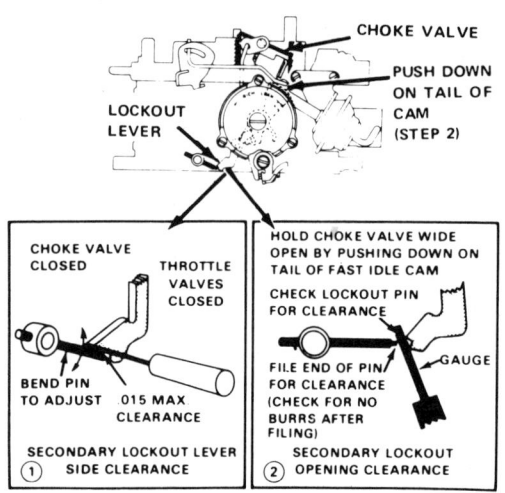

Secondary Lockout adjustment procedure (1977-79) (© Chevrolet Motor Division)

AIR VALVE SPRING ADJUSTMENT

NOTE: *Loosening and tightening the locking screw to adjust the air valve spring requires a hex wrench on 1977 and later model carburetors.*

Remove all spring tension by loosening the locking screw and backing out the adjusting screw. Close the air valve and turn the adjusting screw in until the torsion spring touches the pin on the shaft, and then turn it the additional number of turns specified. Secure the locking screw.

SECONDARY CLOSING ADJUSTMENT

This adjustment assures proper closing of the secondary throttle plates.

1. Set the idle as per instructions in the appropriate car section. Make sure that the fast idle cam follower is not resting on the fast idle cam.
2. There should be 0.020 in. clearance between the secondary throttle actuating rod and the front of the slot on the secondary throttle lever with the closing tang on the throttle lever resting against the actuating lever.
3. Bend the tang on the primary throttle actuating rod to adjust.

SECONDARY OPENING ADJUSTMENT

1. Open the primary throttle valves until the actuating link contacts the upper tang on the secondary lever.
2. With two point-linkage, the bottom of the link should be in the center of the secondary lever slot.
3. With three point linkage, there should be 0.070 in. clearance between the link and the middle tang.
4. Bend the upper tang on the secondary lever to adjust as necessary.

Rochester 4MV, 4MC, M4MC Specifications

Year	Carburetor Identification ①	Float Level (in.)	Air Valve Spring	Pump Rod (in.)	Idle Vent (in.)	Vacuum Break (in.)	Secondary Opening (in.)	Choke Rod (in.)	Choke Unloader (in.)	Fast Idle Speed (rpm)
1967	7027202	9/32	7/8 turn	13/32	3/8	0.160	0.015	0.100	0.260	—
	7027203	9/32	7/8 turn	13/32	3/8	0.200	0.015	0.100	0.300	—
	7027200	9/32	7/8 turn	13/32	3/8	0.160	0.015	0.100	0.300	—
	7027201	9/32	7/8 turn	13/32	3/8	0.240	0.015	0.100	0.300	—
	7027202	9/32	7/8 turn	13/32	3/8	0.160	0.015	0.100	0.260	—
	7027203	9/32	7/8 turn	13/32	3/8	0.200	0.015	0.100	0.300	—
1968	7028212	9/32	3/8 turn	9/32	3/8	0.160	0.010	0.100	0.260	—

Rochester 4MV, 4MC, M4MC Specifications (cont.)

Year	Carburetor Identification ①	Float Level (in.)	Air Valve Spring	Pump Rod (in.)	Idle Vent (in.)	Vacuum Break (in.)	Secondary Opening (in.)	Choke Rod (in.)	Choke Unloader (in.)	Fast Idle Speed (rpm)
1968	7028213	9/32	3/8 turn	9/32	3/8	0.245	0.010	0.100	0.300	—
	7028229	9/32	7/8 turn	9/32	3/8	0.245	0.010	0.100	0.300	—
	7028208	9/32	3/8 turn	9/32	3/8	0.160	0.010	0.100	0.260	—
	7028207	9/32	3/8 turn	9/32	3/8	0.245	0.010	0.100	0.300	—
	7028219	9/32	7/8 turn	9/32	3/8	0.245	0.010	0.100	0.300	—
	7028218	3/16	7/8 turn	9/32	3/8	0.160	0.010	0.100	0.300	—
	7028217	3/16	7/8 turn	9/32	3/8	0.245	0.010	0.100	0.300	—
	7028210	3/16	7/8 turn	9/32	3/8	0.160	0.010	0.100	0.300	—
	7028211	3/16	7/8 turn	9/32	3/8	0.245	0.010	0.100	0.300	—
	7028216	3/16	7/8 turn	9/32	3/8	0.160	0.010	0.100	0.300	—
	7028209	3/16	7/8 turn	9/32	3/8	0.245	0.010	0.100	0.300	—
1969	7029203	7/32	7/16 turn	5/16	3/8	0.245	0.015	0.100	0.450	—
	7029202	7/32	7/16 turn	5/16	3/8	0.180	0.015	0.100	0.450	—
	7029207	3/16	13/16 turn	5/16	3/8	0.245	0.015	0.100	0.450	—
	7029215	1/4	13/16 turn	5/16	3/8	0.245	0.015	0.100	0.450	—
	7029204	1/4	13/16 turn	5/16	3/8	0.180	0.015	0.100	0.450	—
1970	7040202	1/4	7/16 turn	5/16	—	0.245	—	0.100	0.450	—
	7040203	1/4	7/16 turn	5/16	—	0.275	—	0.100	0.450	—
	7040207	1/4	13/16 turn	5/16	—	0.275	—	0.100	0.450	—
	7040200	1/4	13/16 turn	5/16	—	0.245	—	0.100	0.450	—
	7040201	1/4	13/16 turn	5/16	—	0.275	—	0.100	0.450	—
	7040204	1/4	13/16 turn	5/16	—	0.245	—	0.100	0.450	—
	7040205	1/4	13/16 turn	5/16	—	0.275	—	0.100	0.450	—
1971	7041200	1/4	7/16 turn	—	—	0.260	—	0.100	—	—
	7041202	1/4	7/16 turn	—	—	0.260	—	0.100	—	—

Rochester 4MV, 4MC, M4MC Specifications (cont.)

Year	Carburetor Identification ①	Float Level (in.)	Air Valve Spring	Pump Rod (in.)	Idle Vent (in.)	Vacuum Break (in.)	Secondary Opening (in.)	Choke Rod (in.)	Choke Unloader (in.)	Fast Idle Speed (rpm)
1971	7041204	1/4	7/16 turn	—	—	0.260	—	0.100	—	—
	7041212	1/4	7/16 turn	—	—	0.260	—	0.100	—	—
	7041201	1/4	7/16 turn	—	—	0.275	—	0.100	—	—
	7041203	1/4	7/16 turn	—	—	0.275	—	0.100	—	—
	7041205	1/4	7/16 turn	—	—	0.275	—	0.100	—	—
	7041213	1/4	7/16 turn	—	—	0.275	—	0.100	—	—
1972	7042202	1/4	1/2 turn	3/8	—	0.215	—	0.100	0.450	—
	7042203	1/4	1/2 turn	3/8	—	0.215	—	0.100	0.450	—
	7042902	1/4	1/2 turn	3/8	—	0.215	—	0.100	0.450	—
	7042903	1/4	1/2 turn	3/8	—	0.215	—	0.100	0.450	—
1973	7043212	7/32	1 turn	13/32	—	0.250	—	0.430	0.450	—
	7043213	7/32	1 turn	13/32	—	0.250	—	0.430	0.450	—
1974	7044202	1/4	7/8 turn	13/32 ②	—	0.230	—	0.430	0.450	1600 ③– 1300 ④
	7044203	1/4	7/8 turn	13/32 ②	—	0.230	—	0.430	0.450	1600 ③– 1300 ④
	7044208	1/4	1 turn	13/32 ②	—	0.230	—	0.430	0.450	1600 ③– 1300 ④
	7044209	1/4	1 turn	13/32 ②	—	0.230	—	0.430	0.450	1600 ③– 1300 ④
	7044502	1/4	7/8 turn	13/32 ②	—	0.230	—	0.430	0.450	1600 ③– 1300 ④
	7044503	1/4	7/8 turn	13/32 ②	—	0.230	—	0.430	0.450	1600 ③– 1300 ④
1975	7045202	15/32	7/8 turn	0.275 ⑤	—	0.180 ⑥	—	0.300	0.325	—
	7045203	15/32	7/8 turn	0.275 ⑤	—	0.180 ⑥	—	0.300	0.325	—
	7045208	15/32	7/8 turn	0.275 ⑤	—	0.180 ⑥	—	0.300	0.325	—
	7045209	15/32	7/8 turn	0.275 ⑤	—	0.180 ⑥	—	0.300	0.325	—

EMISSION CONTROLS AND FUEL SYSTEM

Rochester 4MV, 4MC, M4MC Specifications (cont.)

Year	Carburetor Identification ①	Float Level (in.)	Air Valve Spring	Pump Rod (in.)	Idle Vent (in.)	Vacuum Break (in.)	Secondary Opening (in.)	Choke Rod (in.)	Choke Unloader (in.)	Fast Idle Speed (rpm)
1976	17056202	13/32	7/8 turn	9/32	—	0.185	—	0.325	0.325	—
	17056203	13/32	7/8 turn	9/32	—	0.170	—	0.325	0.325	—
	17056528	13/32	7/8 turn	9/32	—	0.185	—	0.325	0.325	—
1977	17057203	15/32	7/8	9/32 ⑤	—	0.160	—	0.325	0.280	1300
	17057202	15/32	—	9/32 ⑤	—	0.160	—	0.325	—	1600 ⑤
	17057502	15/32	7/8	9/32 ⑤	—	0.165	—	0.325	0.280	1600 ⑤
1978	17058203	15/32	7/8	9/32	—	0.179	—	0.314	0.277	⑦
	17058202	15/32	7/8	9/32	—	0.179	—	0.314	0.277	⑦
	17058502	15/32	7/8	9/32	—	0.187	—	0.314	0.277	⑦
1979	17059203	15/32	7/8	1/4	—	0.157	—	0.243	0.243	⑦
	17059207	15/32	7/8	1/4	—	0.157	—	0.243	0.243	⑦
	17059216	15/32	7/8	1/4	—	0.157	—	0.243	0.243	⑦
	17059217	15/32	7/8	1/4	—	0.157	—	0.243	0.243	⑦
	17059218	15/32	7/8	1/4	—	0.164	—	0.243	0.243	⑦
	17059222	15/32	7/8	1/4	—	0.164	—	0.243	0.243	⑦
	17059502	15/32	7/8	1/4	—	0.164	—	0.243	0.243	⑦
	17059504	15/32	7/8	1/4	—	0.164	—	0.243	0.243	⑦
	17059582	15/32	7/8	11/32	—	0.203	—	0.243	0.314	⑦
	17059584	15/32	7/8	11/32	—	0.203	—	0.243	0.314	⑦
	17059210	15/32	1	9/32	—	0.157	—	0.243	0.243	⑦
	17059211	15/32	1	9/32	—	0.157	—	0.243	0.243	⑦
	17029228	15/32	1	9/32	—	0.157	—	0.243	0.243	⑦

① The carburetor identification tag is located at the rear of the carburetor on mne of the air horn screws
② Without vacuum advance
③ With automatic transmission; vacuum advance connected and EGR disconnected and the throttle positioned on the high step of cam
④ With manual transmission; without vacuum advance and the throttle positioned on the high step of cam
⑤ Inner pump rod location
⑥ Front vacuum break given; rear—0.170 in.
⑦ See engine compartment sticker

214 EMISSION CONTROLS AND FUEL SYSTEM

Holley 4150—4 BBL Carburetor

The 4150 carburetor has been both an end and center inlet design.

CHOKE ADJUSTMENT

The model 4150 employs a remotely located choke. To adjust, disconnect the choke rod at the choke lever and secure the choke lever shut. Bend the rod so that when the rod is depressed to the contact stop, the top is even with the bottom of the hole in the choke lever.

FLOAT LEVEL ADJUSTMENT

Position the car on a flat, level surface and start the engine. Remove the sight plugs and check to see that the fuel level reaches the bottom threads of the sight plug port. A tolerance of $1/32$ in. is acceptable. To change the level, loosen the fuel inlet needle locking screw and adjust the nut. Turning it clockwise lowers the fuel level and counterclockwise raises it. Turn the nut $1/6$ of a turn for each $1/16$ in. desired change. Open the primary throttle slightly to assure a stabilized adjusting condition on the secondaries. There is no required float drop adjustment.

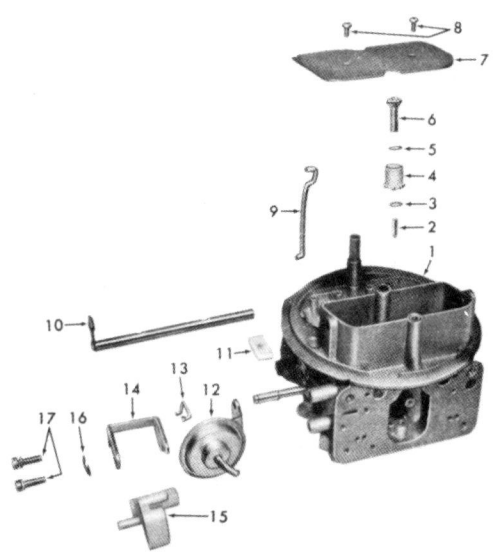

1. Main body assembly
2. Pump discharge needle
3. Pump discharge nozzle gasket
4. Pump discharge nozzle
5. Pump discharge nozzle screw gasket
6. Pump discharge nozzle screw
7. Choke valve
8. Choke valve screw
9. Choke rod
10. Choke shaft and lever
11. Choke rod seal
12. Vacuum break
13. Vacuum break link
14. Choke lever
15. Fast idle cam
16. Choke lever retainer
17. Vacuum break screw

Exploded view of main body assembly (Holley) (© Chevrolet Motor Division)

Float level adjustment (Holley) (© Chevrolet Motor Division)

FAST IDLE ADJUSTMENT

Open the throttle and place the choke plate fast idle lever against the top step of the fast idle cam. Bend the fast idle lever to obtain the specified throttle plate opening.

CHOKE UNLOADER ADJUSTMENT

Adjustment should be made with the engine not running. Fully open and secure the throttle plate. Force the choke valve toward a closed position, so that contact is made with the unloader tang. Bend the choke rod to gain the specified clearance between the main body and the lower edge of the choke valve.

ACCELERATOR PUMP ADJUSTMENT

With the engine off, block the throttle open and push the pump lever down. Clearance between the pump lever arm and the spring adjusting nut should be 0.015 in. minimum. Turn the screw or nut to adjust this clearance.

SECONDARY THROTTLE VALVE ADJUSTMENT

Close the throttle plates, and then turn the adjustment screw until it contacts the throttle lever. Advance the screw ½ turn more.

EMISSION CONTROLS AND FUEL SYSTEM

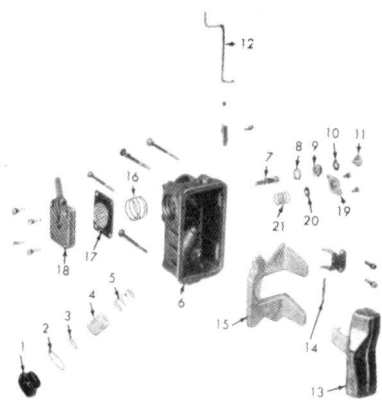

1. Fuel inlet nut
2. Inlet nut gasket
3. Fuel filter gasket
4. Fuel filter
5. Fuel filter spring
6. Fuel bowl
7. Inlet needle and seat assembly
8. Adjusting nut gasket
9. Fuel inlet adjusting nut
10. Inlet nut lock screw gasket
11. Inlet nut lock screw
12. Vent valve lever
13. Float
14. Float hinge pin
15. Fuel displacement block
16. Pump diaphragm spring
17. Pump diaphragm (primary only)
18. Pump cover
19. Vent valve cover
20. Vent valve
21. Vent valve spring

Exploded view of fuel bowl assembly (Holley) (© Chevrolet Motor Division)

AIR VENT VALVE ADJUSTMENT

Close the throttle valves and open the choke valve so that the throttle arm is free of the idle screw. Bend the air vent valve rod to obtain the specified clearance between the choke valve and seat. Advance the idle speed

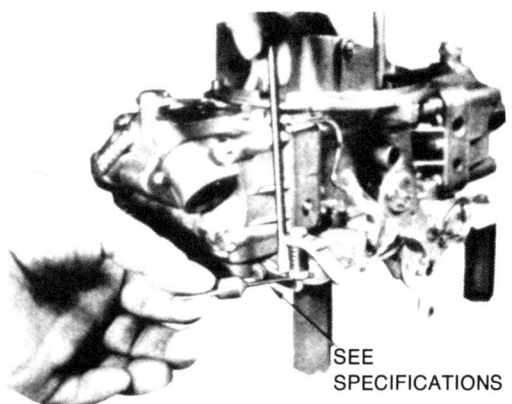

Accelerator pump adjustment (Holley) (© Chevrolet Motor Division)

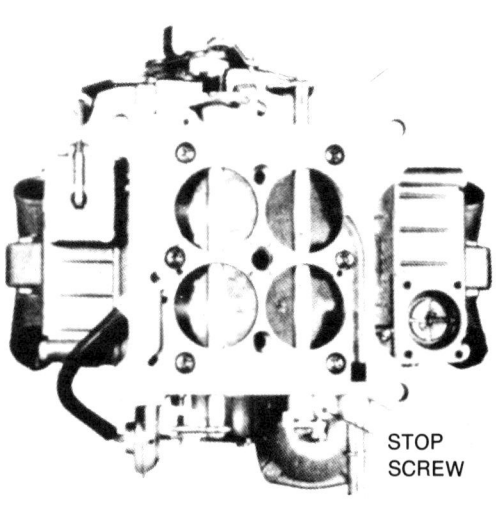

Secondary throttle valve adjustment (Holley) (© Chevrolet Motor Division)

Holley 4150 Specifications

Year	Carburetor Identification ①	Float Level (in.)	Float Drop (in.)	Pump Rod (in.)	Idle Vent (in.)	Vacuum Break (in.)	Automatic Choke	Choke Rod (in.)	Choke Unloader (in.)	Fast Idle Speed
1968–69	V8—302, 396 (4150)	B②	B②	0.015	—	0.350	—	—	0.350	—
1970	4150—350, 396	0.350	—	0.015	—	0.350	—	—	0.350	—
1971	4150—350	③	②	0.015	—	0.350	—	—	0.350	—
1972	4150—350 (Z28)	③	②	0.015	—	0.350	—	—	0.350	—

① Located on a tag attached to the carburetor or on the casting or choke plate
② Float adjustment: Fuel level should be plus or minus 1/32 in. with threads at bottom of sight holes. To adjust turn adjusting nut on top of bowl clockwise to lower, counterclockwise to raise.
③ Float centered in bowl
A—Primary 0.170, Secondary 0.300
B—Primary 0.350, Secondary 0.500

EMISSION CONTROLS AND FUEL SYSTEM

screw until it touches the throttle lever, and then advance it 1½ turns.

VACUUM BREAK ADJUSTMENT

Secure the choke valve closed and the vacuum break against the stop. Bend the vacuum break link to gain the specified clearance between the main body and the lower edge of the choke valve.

Rochester M2ME and E2ME—2 BBL Carburetors

FLOAT ADJUSTMENT

1. Remove the air horn from the throttle body.
2. Using your fingers, hold the retainer in place and then push the float down into light contact with the needle.
3. Measure the distance from the toe of the float (furthest from the hinge) to the top of the carburetor (gasket removed).
4. To adjust, remove the float and gently bend the arm to specifications. After adjustment, check the float alignment in the chamber. On engines equipped with the C-4 or the CCC system, where the float level varies more than 1/16 in. from specifications, adjust the float as follows.

Float too high:
1. Hold the retainer firmly in place and then push down the center of the float pontoon until the correct setting is obtained.

Float too low:
1. Lift out the meter rods and remove the solenoid connector screw.

2. Turn the lean mixture solenoid screw clockwise until the screw is bottomed lightly in the float bowl. *Count and record the number of turns before the screw is bottomed.*
3. Turn the screw counterclockwise and remove it. Lift the solenoid and the connector from the float bowl.
4. Remove the float and bend the arm up to adjust it. Put the float back in and check its alignment.
5. Installation is in the reverse order of removal. Make sure that the solenoid lean mixture screw is backed out of the float bowl EXACTLY the same number of turns as were recorded in Step 2.

PUMP ADJUSTMENT

NOTE: *All 1980–81 engines equipped with the C-4 or the CCC system have a non-adjustable pump lever. No adjustments are either necessary or possible.*

1. With the throttle closed and the fast idle screw off the steps of the fast idle cam, measure the distance from the air horn casting to the top of the pump stem.
2. To adjust the lever, support if firmly with a screwdriver and then bend it to obtain the proper specifications.
3. When the adjustment is correct, open and close the throttle a few times to check the linkage movement and alignment.

CHOKE COIL LEVER ADJUSTMENT

NOTE: *To complete this procedure you will need a Stat Cover Retainer kit; available at most auto parts suppliers.*

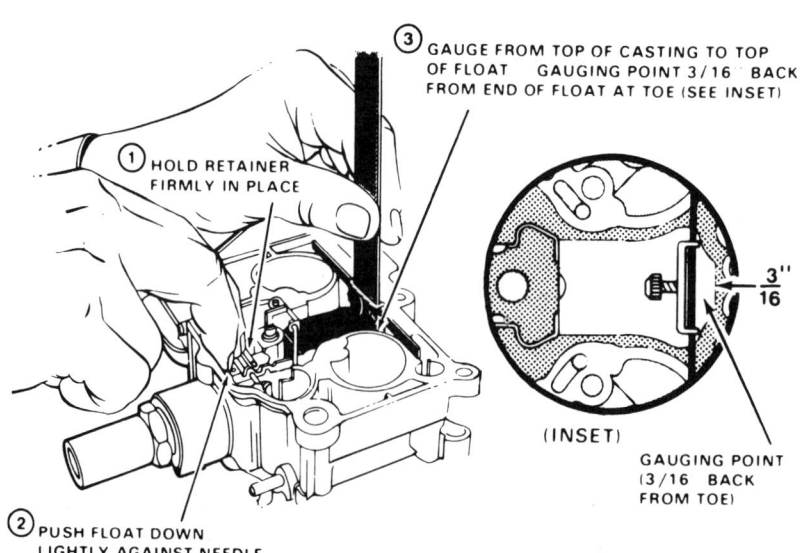

Adjusting the float—M2ME, E2ME

EMISSION CONTROLS AND FUEL SYSTEM

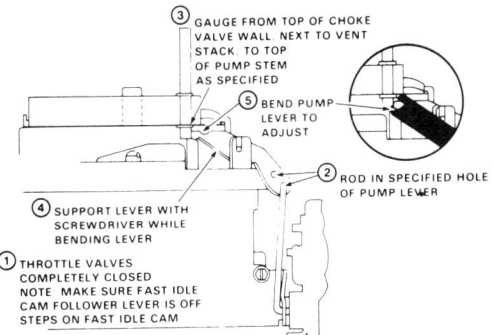

Pump adjustment—M2ME, E2ME (all but C-4 or CCC)

FAST IDLE ADJUSTMENT

1. Set the ignition timing and curb idle speed. Disconnect and plug any hoses as directed on the emission control sticker.
2. Place the fast idle screw on the highest step of the fast idle cam.
3. Start the engine and adjust the engine speed to specifications with the fast idle screw.

FAST IDLE CAM (CHOKE ROD) ADJUSTMENT

NOTE: *A special angle gauge should be used. If it is not available, an inch measurement can be used.*

1. Adjust the choke coil lever and the fast idle as previously detailed.
2. Rotate the degree scale until it is zeroed.
3. Close the choke valve completely and place the magnet on top of it.
4. Center the bubble.
5. Rotate the scale so that the specified degree is opposite the pointer.
6. Place the fast idle screw on the second step of the cam, against the rise of the high step.
7. Close the choke by pushing up on the choke coil lever or the vacuum break lever

1. Drill out and remove the rivets which retain the choke housing cover and then remove the thermostatic cover and coil assembly from the choke housing.
2. Place the fast idle cam follower on the high step of the fast idle cam.
3. Close the choke valve by pushing up on the thermostatic coil tang (counterclockwise).
4. Insert a drill or gauge of the specified size into the hole in the choke housing. The lower edge of the choke lever should be just touching the side of the gauge.
5. If the choke lever is not touching the side of the gauge, bend the choke rod until you see that it does.

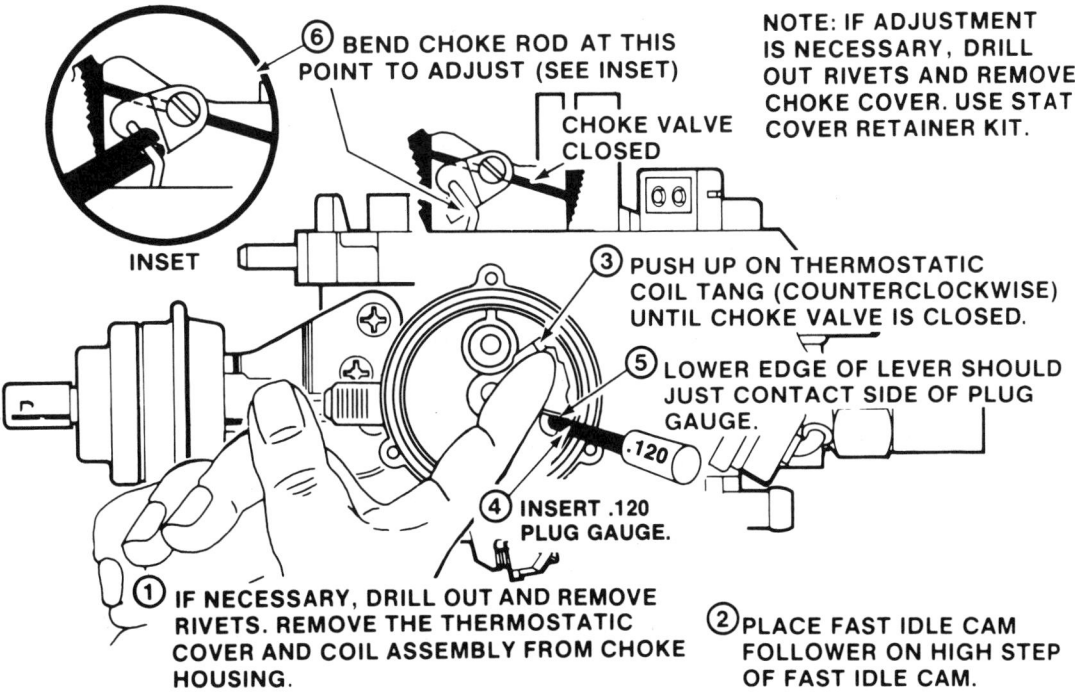

Adjusting the choke coil lever—M2ME, E2ME

218 EMISSION CONTROLS AND FUEL SYSTEM

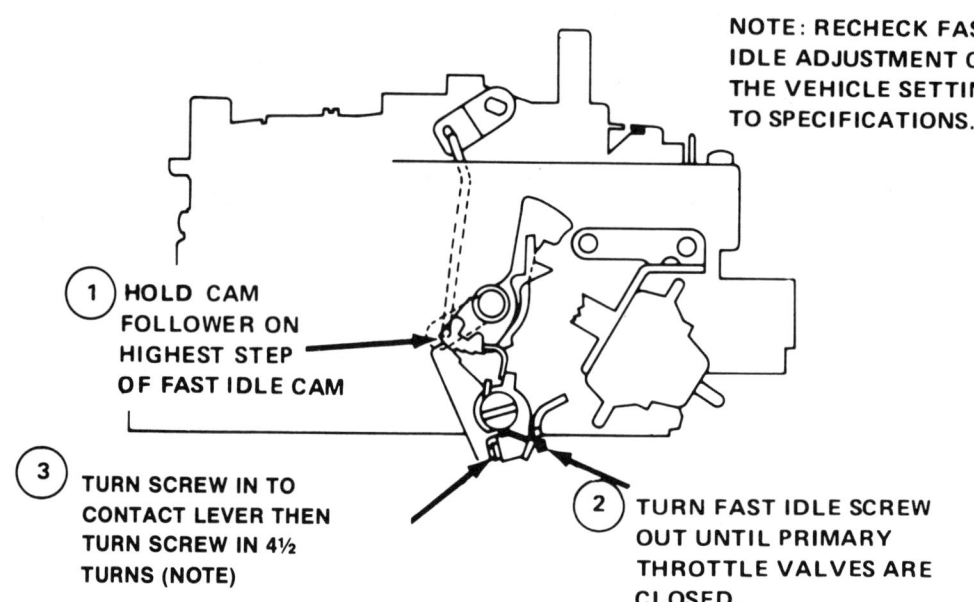

Adjusting the fast idle with the carburetor off the car—M2ME, E2ME

tang. You may hold it in position with a rubber band.

8. To adjust, bend the tang on the fast idle cam until the bubble is centered.

FRONT VACUUM BREAK ADJUSTMENT

1. Follow Steps 1–5 of the "Fast Idle Cam Adjustment" procedure.

2. Set the choke vacuum disphragm using an outside vacuum source.

3. Close the choke valve by pushing up on the choke coil lever or the vacuum break lever. You may hold it in position with a rubber band.

4. To adjust, turn the screw in or out until the bubble in the gauge is centered.

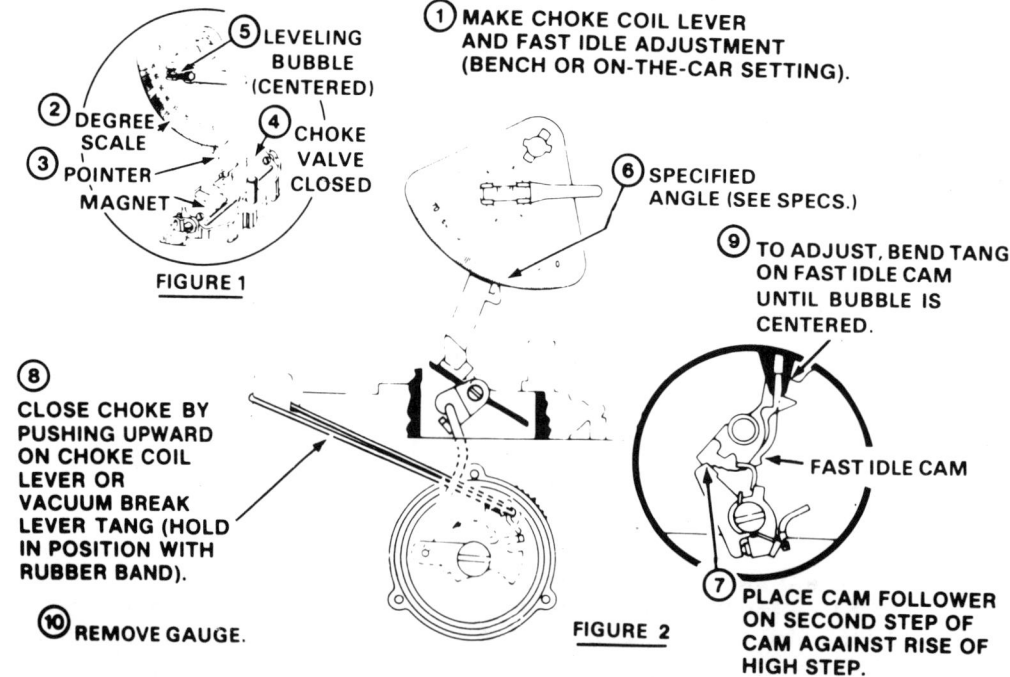

Fast idle cam (choke rod) adjustment—M2ME, E2ME

EMISSION CONTROLS AND FUEL SYSTEM

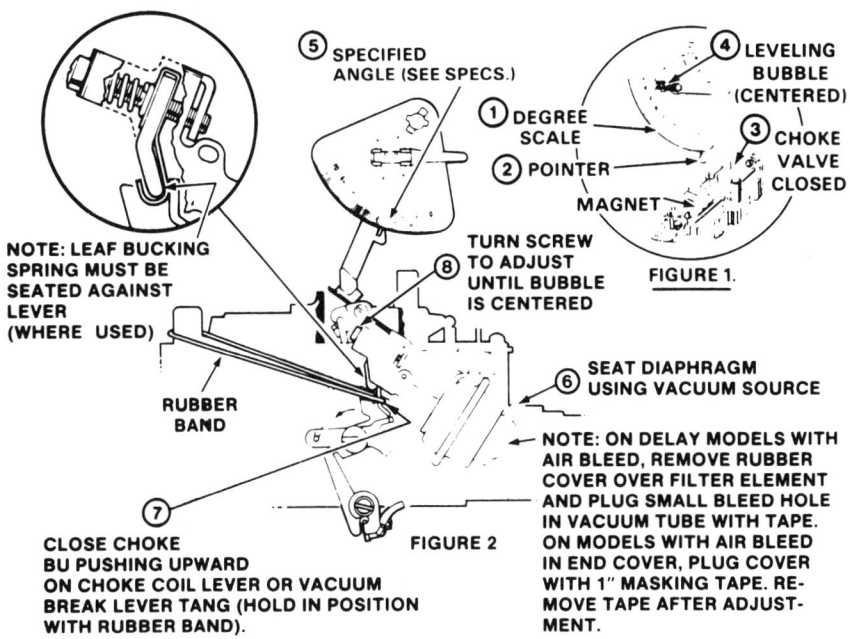

Front vacuum break adjustment—M2ME, E2ME

REAR VACUUM BREAK ADJUSTMENT

1. Follow Steps 1-3 of the "Front Vacuum Break Adjustment" procedure.
2. To adjust, use a ⅛ in. Allen wrench to turn the screw in the rear cover until the bubble is centered. After adjusting, apply silicone sealant RTV over the screw head to seal the setting.

UNLOADER ADJUSTMENT

1. Follow Steps 1-5 of the "Fast Idle Cam Adjustment" procedure.
2. If they have been previously removed, install the choke thermostatic cover and the coil assembly into the choke housing.
3. Close the choke valve by pushing up on the tang on the vacuum break lever (you may hold it with a rubber band).

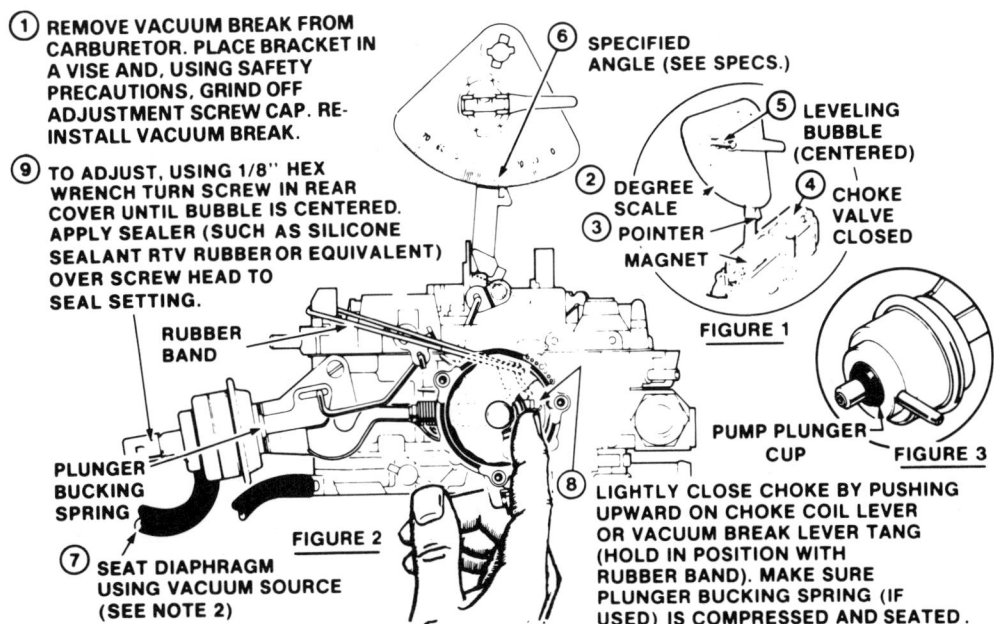

Rear vacuum break adjustment—M2ME, E2ME

EMISSION CONTROLS AND FUEL SYSTEM

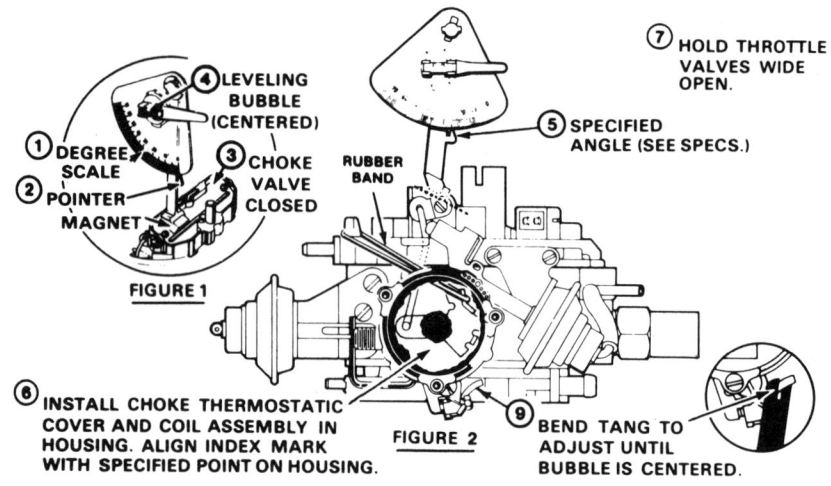

Unloader adjustment—M2ME, E2ME

Rochester M2ME, E2ME Specifications

Year	Carburetor Identification ①	Float Level (in.)	Choke Rod (deg./in.)	Choke Unloader (deg./in.)	Vacuum Break Lean or Front (deg./in.)	Vacuum Break Rich or Rear (deg./in.)	Pump Rod (in.)	Choke Coil Lever (in.)	Automatic Choke (notches)
1980	17080108	3/8	38/0.243	38/0.243	25/0.142	—	5/16 ②	0.120	Fixed
	17080110	3/8	38/0.243	38/0.243	25/0.142	—	5/16 ②	0.120	Fixed
	17080130	5/16	38/0.243	38/0.243	25/0.142	—	5/16 ②	0.120	Fixed
	17080131	5/16	38/0.243	38/0.243	25/0.142	—	5/16 ②	0.120	Fixed
	17080132	5/16	38/0.243	38/0.243	25/0.142	—	5/16 ②	0.120	Fixed
	17080133	5/16	38/0.243	38/0.243	25/0.142	—	5/16 ②	0.120	Fixed
	17080138	3/8	38/0.243	38/0.243	25/0.142	—	5/16 ②	0.120	Fixed
	17080140	3/8	38/0.243	38/0.243	25/0.142	—	5/16 ②	0.120	Fixed
	17080493	5/16	38/0.139	38/0.243	25/0.117	—/0.179	Fixed	0.120	Fixed
	17080495	5/16	38/0.139	38/0.243	25/0.117	—/0.179	Fixed	0.120	Fixed
	17080496	5/16	38/0.139	38/0.243	25/0.117	—/0.203	Fixed	0.120	Fixed
	17080498	5/16	38/0.139	38/0.243	25/0.117	—/0.203	Fixed	0.120	Fixed
1981	17080185	9/32	24.5/0.139	38/0.243	19/0.103	14/0.071	1/4 ②	0.120	Fixed
	17080187	9/32	24.5/0.139	38/0.243	19/0.103	14/0.071	1/4 ②	0.120	Fixed

Rochester M2ME, E2ME Specifications (cont.)

Year	Carburetor Identification ①	Float Level (in.)	Choke Rod (deg./in.)	Choke Unloader (deg./in.)	Vacuum Break Lean or Front (deg./in.)	Vacuum Break Rich or Rear (deg./in.)	Pump Rod (in.)	Choke Coil Lever (in.)	Automatic Choke (notches)
1981	17080191	9/32	24.5/0.139	38/0.243	18/0.096	18/0.096	¼ ②	0.120	Fixed
	17080491	5/16	24.5/0.139	38/0.243	21/0.117	35/0.220	Fixed	0.120	Fixed
	17080496	5/16	24.5/0.139	38/0.243	21/0.117	33/0.203	Fixed	0.120	Fixed
	17080498	5/16	24.5/0.139	38/0.243	21/0.117	33/0.203	Fixed	0.120	Fixed
	17081130	3/8	20/0.110	38/0.243	25/0.142	—	Fixed	0.120	Fixed
	17081131	3/8	20/0.110	38/0.243	25/0.142	—	Fixed	0.120	Fixed
	17081132	3/8	20/0.110	38/0.243	25/0.142	—	Fixed	0.120	Fixed
	17081133	3/8	20/0.110	38/0.243	25/0.142	—	Fixed	0.120	Fixed
	17081138	3/8	20/0.110	40/0.260	25/0.142	—	Fixed	0.120	Fixed
	17081140	3/8	20/0.110	40/0.260	25/0.142	—	Fixed	0.120	Fixed
	17081191	5/16	24.5/0.139	38/0.243	28/0.139	24/0.136	Fixed	0.120	Fixed
	17081192	5/16	24.5/0.139	38/0.243	28/0.139	24/0.136	Fixed	0.120	Fixed
	17081194	5/16	24.5/0.139	38/0.243	21/0.117	24/0.136	Fixed	0.120	Fixed
	17081196	5/16	24.5/0.139	38/0.243	28/0.139	24/0.136	Fixed	0.120	Fixed
	17081197	5/16	18/0.096	38/0.243	28/0.139	24/0.136	Fixed	0.120	Fixed
	17081198	3/8	24.5/0.139	38/0.243	28/0.139	24/0.136	Fixed	0.120	Fixed
	17081199	3/8	18/0.096	38/0.243	28/0.139	24/0.136	Fixed	0.120	Fixed

① The carburetor identification number is stamped on the float bowl, next to the fuel inlet nut.
② inner hole

4. Hold the primary throttle valves wide open.
5. To adjust, bend the tang on the fast idle lever until the bubble on the gauge is centered.

Rochester M4ME and E4ME—4 BBL Carburetors

NOTE: *Float, pump, choke coil lever, fast idle, fast idle cam (choke rod), front and rear vacuum break and unloader adjustments on these two carburetors are identical to those detailed in the preceding "M2ME and E2ME" section. Please refer to them. There are, however, a number of procedures that apply only to these 4 bbl carburetors.*

AIR VALVE ROD ADJUSTMENT

1. Using an outside vacuum source, seat the choke vacuum disphragm. Put a piece of tape over the purge bleed hole if so equipped.

222 EMISSION CONTROLS AND FUEL SYSTEM

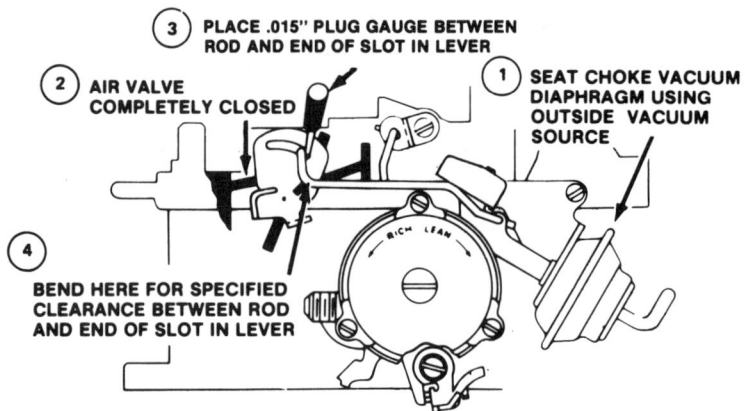

Adjusting the air valve rod—M4ME, E4ME

2. Close the air valve completely.
3. Insert the gauge between the rod and the end of the slot in the lever.
4. Bend the rod to adjust the clearance.

SECONDARY LOCKOUT ADJUSTMENT

1. Pull the choke wide open by pushing out on the choke lever.
2. Open the throttle until the end of the secondary actuating lever is opposite the toe of the lockout lever.
3. Measure the clearance between the lockout lever and the secondary lever.
4. Bend the lockout pin until the clearance is in accordance with the proper specifications.

SECONDARY CLOSING ADJUSTMENT

1. Make sure that the idle speed is set to the proper specifications.
2. The choke valve should be wide open with the cam follower off of the steps of the fast idle cam.
3. There should be 0.020 in. clearance between the secondary throttle actuating rod and the front of the slot on the secondary throttle lever with the closing tang on the throttle lever resting against the actuating lever.
4. To adjust, bend the secondary closing tang on the primary throttle actuating rod.

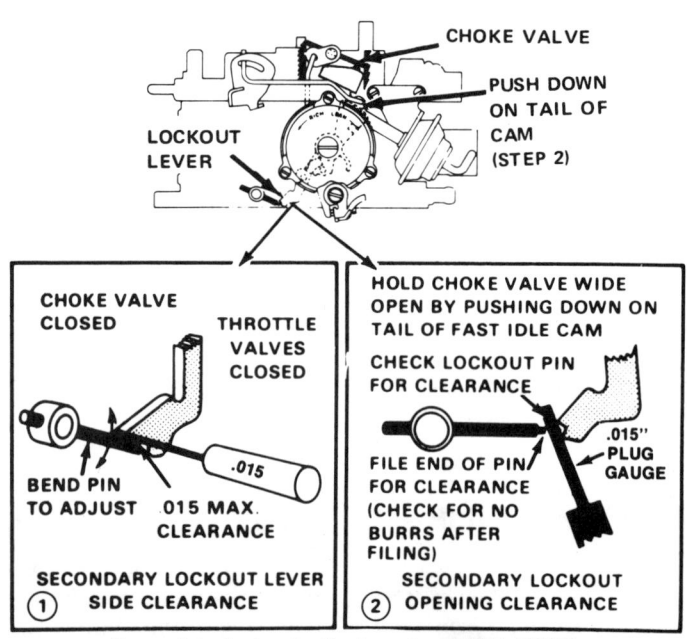

Secondary lockout adjustment—M4ME, E4ME

Rochester M4ME, E4ME Specifications

Year	Carburetor Identification ①	Float Level (in.)	Air Valve Spring (turn)	Pump Rod (in.)	Primary Vacuum Break (deg./in.)	Secondary Vacuum Break (in.)	Secondary Opening (in.)	Choke Rod (deg./in.)	Choke Unloader (deg./in.)	Fast Idle Speed ② (rpm)
1980	17080202	7/16	7/8	1/4 ③	27/0.157	—	⑤	20/0.110	38/0.243	⑥
	17080204	7/16	7/8	1/4 ③	27/0.157	—	⑤	20/0.110	38/0.243	⑥
	17080207	7/16	7/8	1/4 ③	27/0.157	—	⑤	20/0.110	38/0.243	⑥
	17080228	7/16	7/8	9/32 ③	30/0.179	—	⑤	20/0.110	38/0.243	⑥
	17080243	3/16	9/16	9/32 ③	16/0.016	0.083	⑤	14.5/0.074	30/0.179	⑥
	17080274	15/32	5/8	5/16 ④	20/0.110	0.164	⑤	16/0.083	33/0.203	⑥
	17080282	7/16	7/8	11/32 ④	25/0.142	—	⑤	20/0.110	38/0.243	⑥
	17080284	7/16	7/8	11/32 ④	25/0.142	—	⑤	20/0.110	38/0.243	⑥
	17080502	1/2	7/8	Fixed	–/0.136	0.179	⑤	20/0.110	38/0.243	⑥
	17080504	1/2	7/8	Fixed	–/0.136	0.179	⑤	20/0.110	38/0.243	⑥
	17080542	3/8	9/16	Fixed	–/0.103	0.066	⑤	14.5/0.074	38/0.243	⑥
	17080543	3/8	9/16	Fixed	–/0.103	0.129	⑤	14.5/0.074	38/0.243	⑥
1981	17081202	11/32	7/8	Fixed	26/0.149	—	⑤	20/0.110	38/0.243	⑦
	17081203	11/32	7/8	Fixed	26/0.149	—	⑤	20/0.110	38/0.243	⑦
	17081204	11/32	7/8	Fixed	26/0.149	—	⑤	20/0.110	38/0.243	⑦
	17081207	11/32	7/8	Fixed	26/0.149	—	⑤	20/0.110	38/0.243	⑦
	17081216	11/32	7/8	Fixed	26/0.149	—	⑤	20/0.110	38/0.243	⑦
	17081217	11/32	7/8	Fixed	26/0.149	—	⑤	20/0.110	38/0.243	⑦
	17081218	11/32	7/8	Fixed	26/0.149	—	⑤	20/0.110	38/0.243	⑦
	17081242	5/16	7/8	Fixed	17/0.090	0.077	⑤	24.5/0.139	38/0.243	⑦
	17081243	1/4	7/8	Fixed	19/0.103	0.090	⑤	24.5/0.139	38/0.243	⑦

① The carburetor identification number is stamped on the float bowl, near the secondary throttle lever.
② With manual transmission; w/o vacuum advance and the throttle positioned on the high step of the cam
③ Inner hole
④ Outer hole
⑤ No measurement necessary on two point linkage; see text
⑥ 4 turns after contacting lever for preliminary setting
⑦ 4½ turns after contacting lever for preliminary setting

224 EMISSION CONTROLS AND FUEL SYSTEM

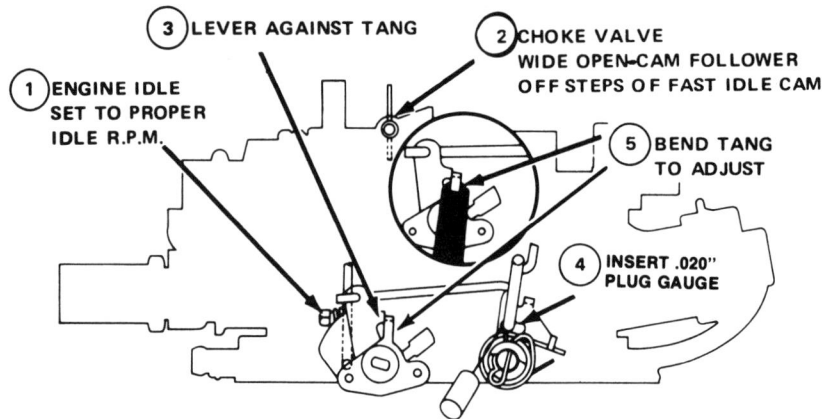

Secondary closing adjustment—M4ME, E4ME

SECONDARY OPENING ADJUSTMENT

1. Open the primary throttle valves until the actuating link contacts the upper tang on the secondary lever.
2. With the two point linkage, the bottom of the link should be in the center of the secondary lever slot.
3. With the three point linkage, there should be 0.070 in. clearance between the link and the middle tang.
4. To adjust, bend the upper tang on the secondary lever.

AIR VALVE SPRING ADJUSTMENT

To adjust the air valve spring windup, loosen the Allen head lockscrew and then turn the adjusting screw counterclockwise so as to remove all spring tension. With the air valve closed, turn the adjusting screw clockwise the specified number of turns after the tor-

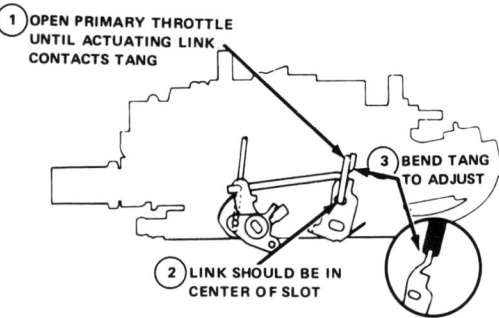

Secondary opening adjustment—M4ME, E4ME

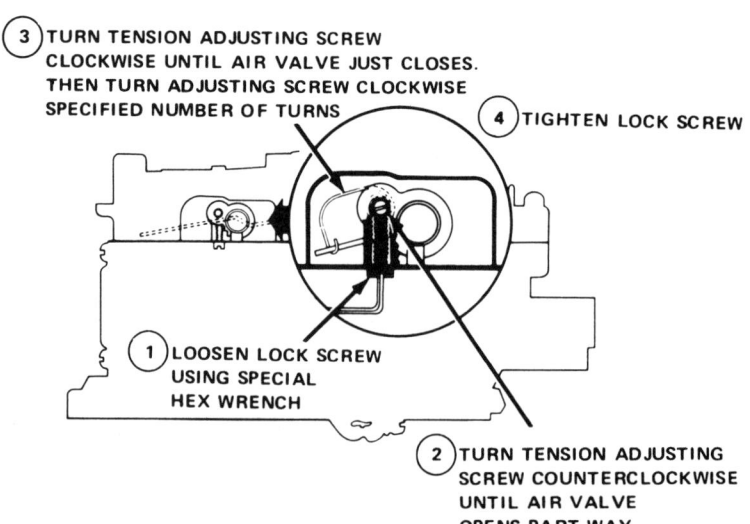

Adjusting the air valve spring—M4ME, E4ME

EMISSION CONTROLS AND FUEL SYSTEM

sion spring contacts the pin on the shaft. Hold the adjusting screw in this position and tighten the lockscrew.

Fuel Tank

REMOVAL AND INSTALLATION

1. Disconnect the battery ground cable.
2. Disconnect the meter wire at the rear wiring harness connector.
3. Push out the grommet and pull the wire through the hole in the trunk floor pan.
4. Raise the car and drain the tank. There are no drain plugs so siphoning is necessary. On 1970 and later cars, the filler neck is too long for siphoning so fuel will have to be siphoned or pumped out through the fuel feed line.
5. Disconnect the fuel line hose from the gauge unit pick-up line. Disconnect the vapor return hose on 1971 and later models.
6. Remove the gauge ground wire screw from the floor pan.
7. Remove the tank strap bolts and carefully lower the tank.
8. To install, reverse this removal procedure.

Chassis Electrical

HEATER

Heater Blower
REMOVAL AND INSTALLATION

1967-69

1. Disconnect the battery ground cable.
2. Disconnect the hoses and wiring from the fender skirt.
3. Remove the wheel opening trim.
4. Remove the rocker panel molding.
5. Loosen the rear lower fender-to-body bolt.
6. Remove the nine rearmost fender skirt attaching screws.
7. Pull the lower rear edge of the fender out. Pull the skirt down. Place a block of wood between the fender and the skirt.
8. Remove the blower-to-case attaching screws. Remove the blower assembly.
9. Remove the blower wheel retaining nut. Separate the blower and motor.
10. Reverse the procedure to install. The open end of the blower should be away from the motor.

1970-77

1. Disconnect the battery ground cable.
2. Disconnect the hoses and wiring from the fender skirt.
3. Remove all the fender skirt attaching bolts except those attaching the skirt to the radiator support.
4. Pull out, then down, on the skirt. Place a block between the skirt and fender.
5. Remove the blower-to-case attaching screws. Remove the blower assembly.
6. Remove the blower wheel retaining nut and separate the motor and wheel.
7. Reverse the procedure to install. The open end of the blower should be away from the motor. Use new sealer on the blower case flange.

1978-81

1. Disconnect the negative battery cable.
2. Tag and disconnect any electrical connections at the motor.
3. Remove the heater front module screws and nuts.
4. Lift off the front module and the motor.
5. Installation is in the reverse order of removal. Replace all sealer.

Heater Core
REMOVAL AND INSTALLATION

1967 Except Air-Conditioned Cars

1. Disconnect the battery ground cable and drain the radiator.
2. Remove the heater hoses from the core. The top hose connects to the water pump and

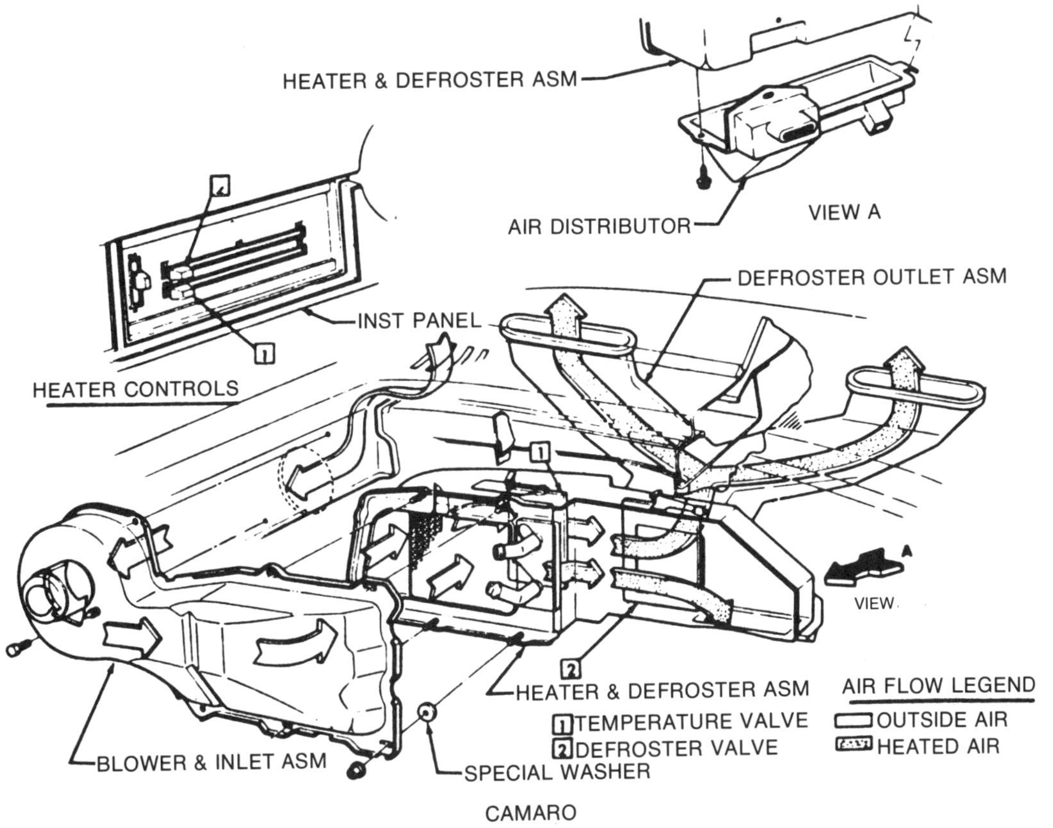

CHASSIS ELECTRICAL 227

Heater airflow diagram (© Chevrolet Motor Division)

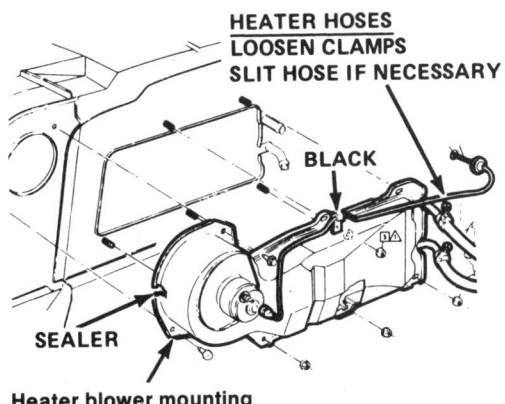

Heater blower mounting

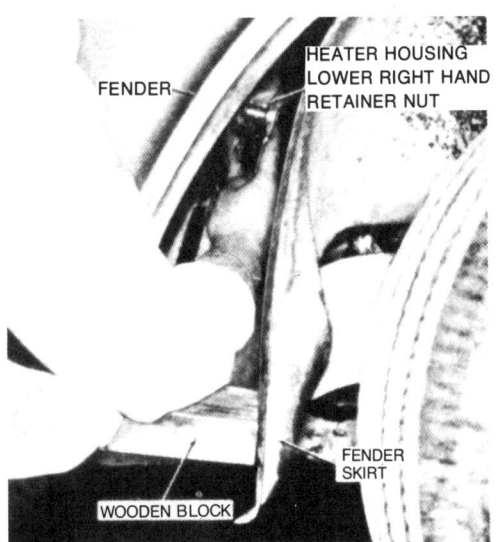

Providing access to blower motor bolts (© Chevrolet Motor Division)

the lower hose goes to the thermostat housing.
3. Remove the cables and all electrical connections from the heater and defroster assembly.
4. Remove the nuts from the core case studs located on the firewall.
5. From inside the car, remove the case-to-firewall mounting screws and also the heater and defroster assembly.
6. Remove the retaining springs and core.
7. Install the core and retaining springs, making sure the core-to-case sealer is in good shape.
8. Complete the installation by reversing the removal procedure.

228 CHASSIS ELECTRICAL

1968-77 Except Air-Conditioned Cars

1. Disconnect the battery ground cable.
2. Drain the radiator.
3. Disconnect the heater hoses. Plug the core inlet and outlet.
4. Remove the nuts from the air distributor duct studs on the firewall.
5. On post-1969 Camaros: remove the glove box and radio, then the defroster duct-to-distributor duct screw.
6. Pull the defroster duct out of the way, and then pull the distributor duct from the firewall mounting. Remove the resistor wires. Lay the duct on the floor.
7. Remove the core assembly from the distributor duct.
8. Reverse the procedure to install. Use new sealer on the duct flange, if necessary.

1978-81

1. Disconnect the negative battery cable. Drain the radiator. Disconnect heater hoses.
2. Remove the nuts that attach the heater case to the firewall from the firewall side. Then, remove the screws from inside the car.
3. Remove the glovebox and door. Remove the screws attaching the heater outlet duct to the heater case, and remove the duct.
4. Remove the defroster screw. Pull the heater case out. The core may now be pulled out of the case.
5. Reverse the removal procedure to install. Use new seals between the heater case and firewall.

1967-81 Air Conditioned Cars

Removal of the heater core from air-conditioned cars requires the opening (evacuation) of the refrigerant lines. These lines contain pressurized Freon gas, capable of inflicting serious injury upon contact. Do not, under any circumstance, disconnect or loosen any refrigerant hose. This should be attempted only by a qualified refrigeration repairman. To avoid the possibility of accidents, heater core removal on air-conditioned cars, and all other air-conditioning service procedures have been deleted from this book.

Radio

REMOVAL AND INSTALLATION

1. Disconnect the battery ground cable.
2. Remove the ash tray and the ash tray housing as necessary.
3. Remove the knobs, controls, washers,

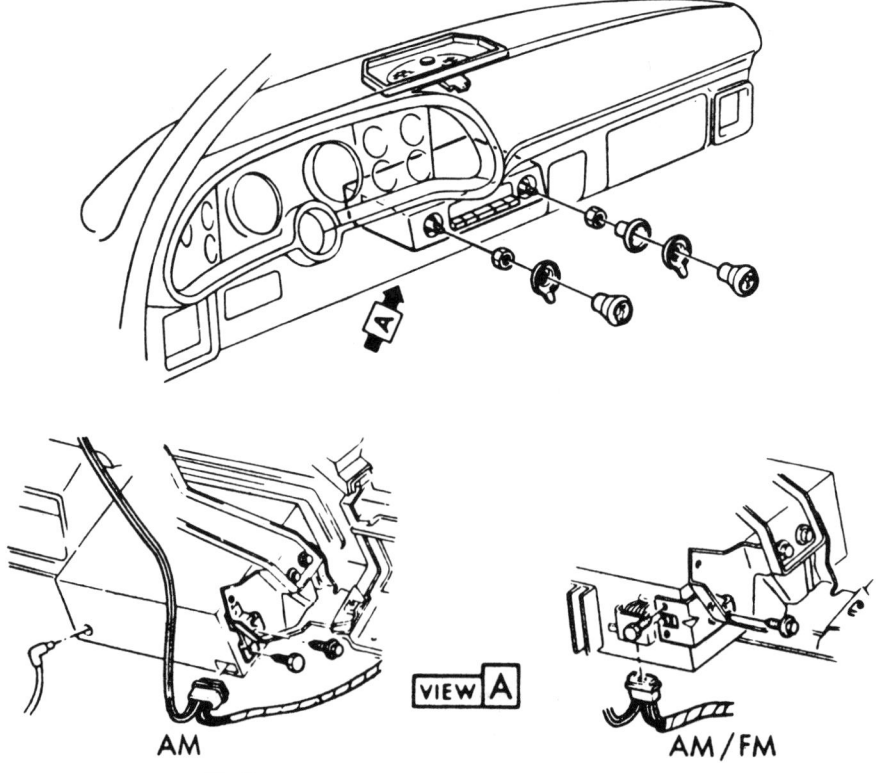

Radio mounting (© Chevrolet Motor Division)

trim plate, and nuts from the radio. Using a deep well socket, remove the control shaft nuts and washers.

4. Remove the hoses from the center air-conditioning duct as necessary.

5. On 1967–76 vehicles only, disconnect all wiring leads. Remove all screws and nuts from the radio mount(s), and then push the radio forward until the control shafts clear the instrument panel. On 1967–76 vehicles, turn the radio upside down (dial toward front of vehicle) and remove it. On 1976–79 vehicles, pull the radio out just far enough to disconnect wiring, and disconnect it. Then, tilt the radio so the dial faces the front of the car and remove it.

6. Installation is the reverse of removal. Be careful not to apply power to the radio until the speaker harness is connected.

WINDSHIELD WIPERS

Blade and Arm
REPLACEMENT

If the wiper assembly has a press type release tab at the center, simply depress the tab and remove the blade. If the blade has no release tab, use a screwdriver to depress the spring at the center. This will release the assembly. To install the assembly, position the blade over the pin at the tip of the arm and press until the spring retainer engages the groove in the pin.

To remove the element, either depress the release button or squeeze the spring type retainer clip at the outer end together, and slide the blade element out. Just slide the new element in until it latches.

Removal of the wiper arms requires the use of a special tool, G.M. J8966 or its equivalent. Versions of this tool are generally available in auto parts stores.

1. Insert the tool under the wiper arm and lever the arm off the shaft.

NOTE: *Raising the hood on most later models will facilitate easier wiper arm removal.*

2. Disconnect the washer hose from the arm (if so equipped). Remove the arm.

3. Installation is in the reverse order of removal. The proper park position for the arms is with the blades approximately 2 in. (50 mm) above the lower molding of the windshield. Be sure that the motor is in the park position before installing the arms.

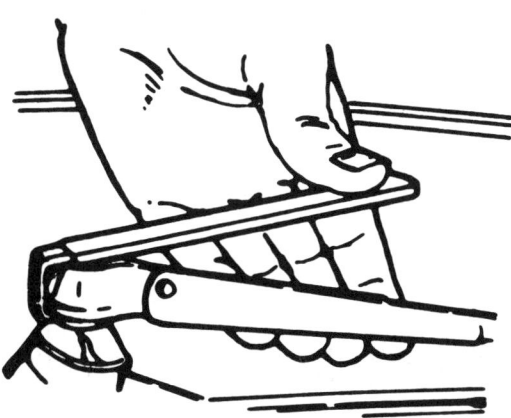

Remove the wiper arm with the special tool

Wiper Motor
REMOVAL AND INSTALLATION
1967

1. Make certain that the wiper motor is in the park position.

2. Disconnect the washer hoses and electrical connectors.

3. Remove the three motor bolts. Pull the wiper motor assembly from the cowl opening and loosen the nuts retaining the drive rod ball stud to the crank arm.

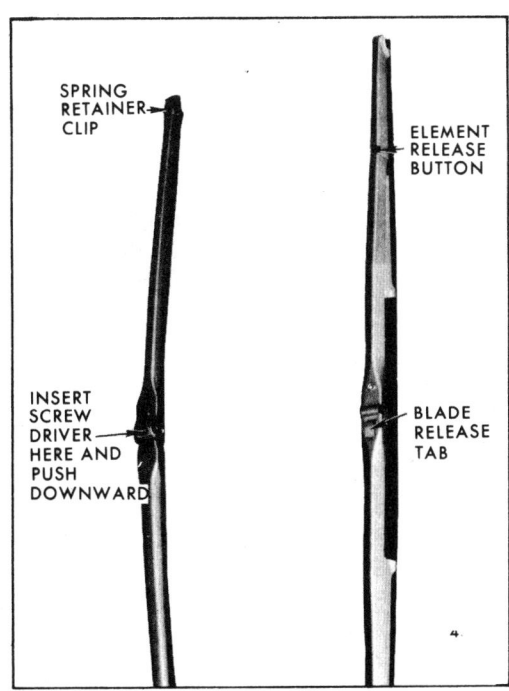

The two methods of releasing wiper blade assemblies

CHASSIS ELECTRICAL

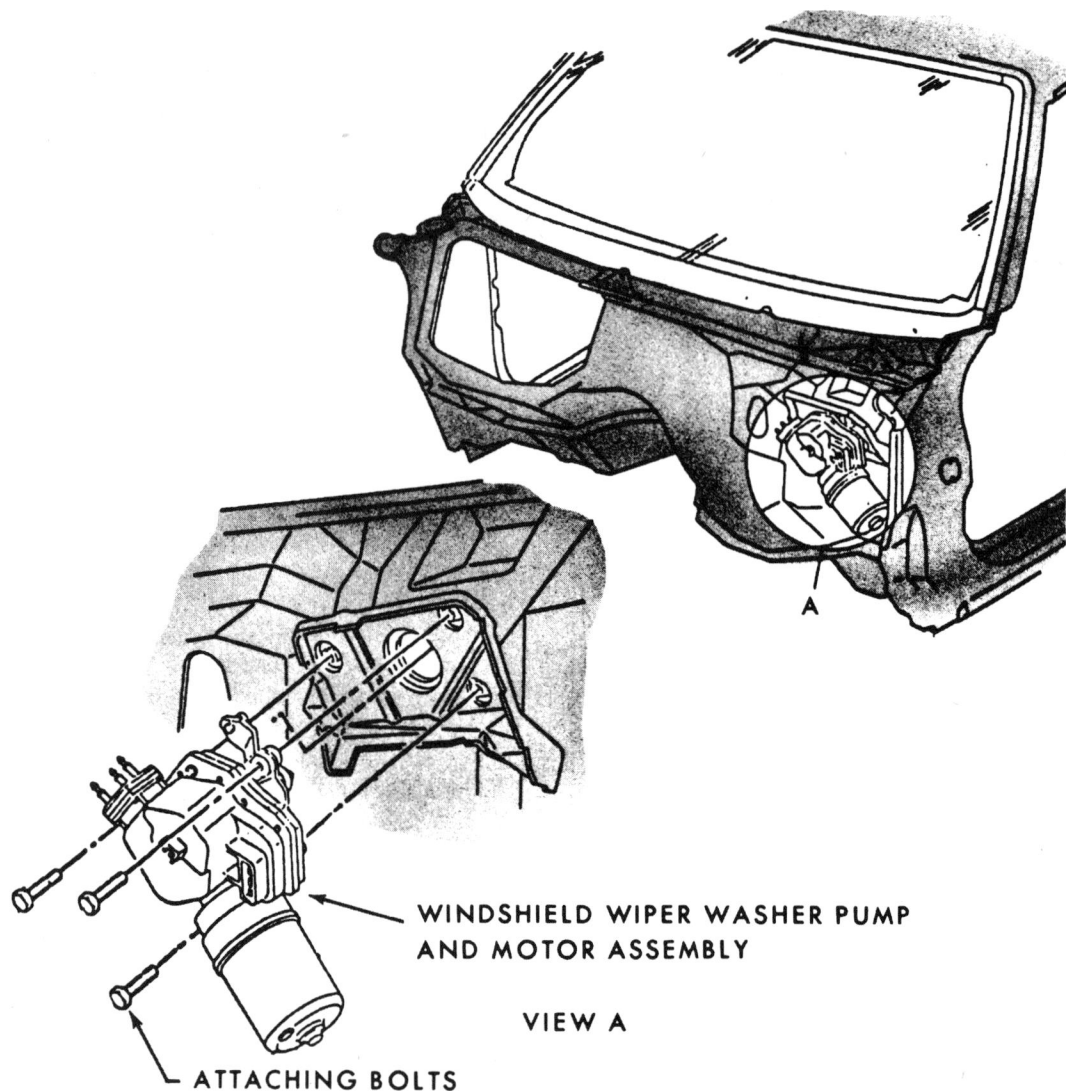

Windshield wiper motor mounting—round motor

4. Reverse the procedure to install, checking the sealing gaskets at the motor. Make sure the motor is in the park position before installation.

1968-70

1. Make sure that the wiper motor is in the park position.
2. Disconnect the washer hoses and electrical connectors.
3. Remove the plenum chamber grille or access cover. Remove the nut retaining the crank arm to the motor assembly.
4. Remove the retaining screws or nuts and remove the motor. Do not allow the motor to hang by the drive link.
5. Reverse the procedure to install, checking the sealing gaskets at the motor. Make sure the motor is in the park position before installation.

1971-81

NOTE: *Your car may be equipped with either a round motor or a rectangular motor.*

1. Remove the screen or grille that covers the cowl area.
2. Working under the hood, disconnect the motor wiring. Then, reach through the cowl opening and loosen, but do not remove, the nuts which attach the transmission drive link to the motor crank arm. Then, disconnect the drive link from the crank arm.
3. Remove the three motor attaching

CHASSIS ELECTRICAL 231

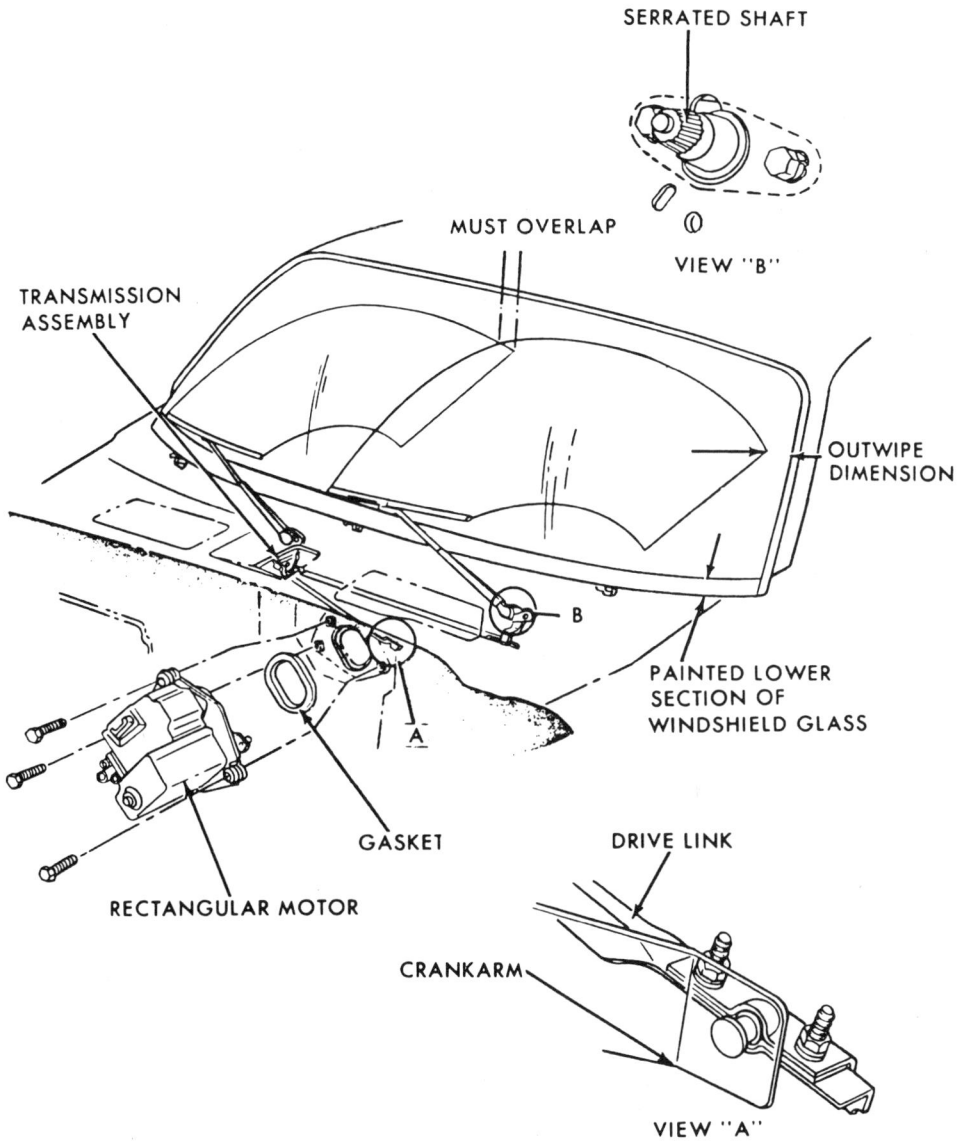

Windshield wiper motor mounting—rectangular motor

screws, and remove the motor, guiding the crank arm through the hole.

4. Installation is in the reverse order of removal. The motor must be in the park position before assembling the crank arm to the transmission drive link(s).

Linkage

REMOVAL AND INSTALLATION

1967-70

1. Make sure that the wiper motor is in the park position.
2. Disconnect the battery ground cable.
3. Remove the wiper arm and blade assemblies from the transmission. On the articulated left arm assemblies, remove the carburetor type clip retaining the pinned arm to the blade arm.
4. Remove the plenum chamber air intake grille or screen.
5. Loosen the nuts retaining the drive rod ball stud to the crank arm and detach the drive rod from the crank arm.
6. Remove the transmission retaining screws. Lower the transmission and drive rod assemblies into the plenum chamber.
7. Remove the transmission and linkage

232 CHASSIS ELECTRICAL

from the plenum chamber through the cowl opening.

8. Reverse the procedure to install, making sure the wiper blade assemblies are installed in the park position. On recessed wiper arms, this occurs at ⅜ in. from the top of the reveal molding.

1971–81

1. Remove the wiper arms and blades. Remove the cowl screen or grille.
2. Disconnect the wiring from the wiper motor. Loosen, but do not remove the nuts which attach the transmission drive link to the motor crank arm. Then, disconnect the drive link from the arm.
3. Remove the transmission-to-body attaching screws from both the right and left sides of the car.
4. Guide the transmissions and linkage out through the cowl opening.
5. Installation is the reverse of removal.

INSTRUMENT CLUSTER

REMOVAL AND INSTALLATION

1967–68

1. Disconnect the negative battery cable. Remove the clock shaft knob if so equipped.
2. Remove the support screws from the lower mast jacket.
3. Remove the support bolts from the upper mast jacket and allow the steering wheel to rest on the seat.
CAUTION: *Remove the upper and lower supports to prevent distortion of the mast jacket.*

4. Remove the attaching screws from the face of the instrument cluster and partially remove the assembly.
5. Disconnect the speedometer cable, the speed warning device (if so equipped), and the chassis wiring harness connector. Check the speedometer cable and lubricate it if necessary.
6. Remove the instrument cluster from the car.
7. To install, reverse the removal procedure.

1969

1. Disconnect the battery ground cable.
2. Remove the instrument panel pad.
3. Remove the air-conditioning connections.
4. Remove the radio brace attachments.
5. Lower the steering column.
6. Remove the attaching screw from the instrument cluster.
7. Disconnect the speedometer cable, the wiring for the speed warning device (if so equipped), and any other connections.
8. Remove the cluster assembly from the car.
9. To install, reverse the removal procedure, making sure all the connections are clean and tight. It may be a good idea to lubricate the speedometer cable at this time.

1967–69 Center Console

1. Disconnect the negative battery cable.
2. Remove the retaining screws and lift the cover from the assembly.

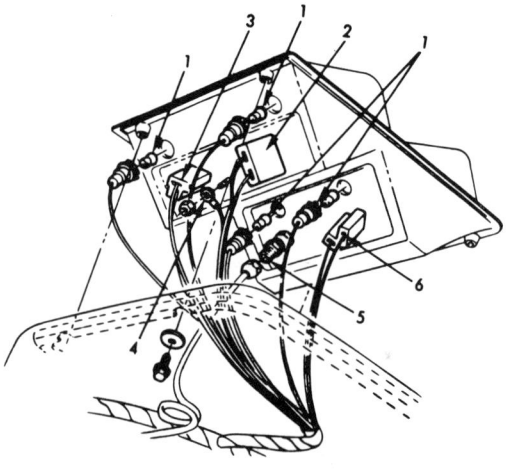

1. Cluster lamps
2. Ammeter conn.
3. Temp. gauge conn.
4. Ground wire
5. Oil gauge conn.
6. Fuel gauge conn.

Center console—1968–69

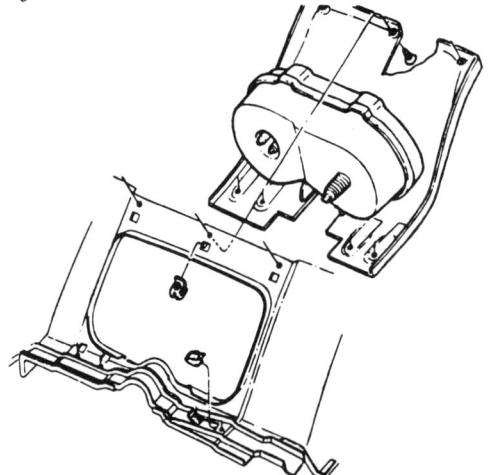

1967–68 instrument cluster mounting (© Chevrolet Motor Division)

CHASSIS ELECTRICAL 233

3. Remove the screws holding each gauge mounting plate to the instrument housing.

4. Carefully remove the gauge plate from the housing and disconnect all connections from the rear of the gauges.

5. To install, reverse the removal procedure, making sure that the oil line fitting to the oil gauge is tight and not leaking.

1970-81

1. Disconnect the battery ground cable.

2. Remove the six screws holding the trim cover beneath the steering column. Remember to remove the two screws above the ashtray.

3. Reach behind the cluster and press in the retainer button on the headlamp switch shaft while pulling on the switch knob.

4. Remove the retaining nut from the switch.

5. Remove the cigarette lighter element, disconnect the lighter wire, and unscrew the retainer from the housing.

6. Look up under the lower edge of the cluster and remove the screw from either side of the steering column.

7. Remove the four screws from the front of the carrier.

8. Remove the screw holding the wiper switch ground wire. It is located under the wiper switch.

9. Detach the connector plugs and remove the carrier.

10. Remove the eight lens screws and the four cluster screws.

11. Disconnect the transmission indicator (PRNDL) from the column.

12. Depress the speedometer cable housing tang on the rear of the cluster and tilt the cluster forward.

13. Remove the connectors from the printed circuit and clock, and free the wiring harness from the cluster.

14. Lift out the cluster.

15. To install, reverse the removal procedure, making sure that all connections are clean and tight, and that the printed circuits are placed with the metallic side to the bulb sockets. It would be a good idea to lubricate the speedometer cable at this time.

1970-81 Optional Instrument Cluster

To remove all bulbs, instruments (except speedometer), and printed circuits, it is not necessary (unless air-conditioned) to remove the cluster. The instruments are installed and removed from the rear of the cluster. On cars with air-conditioning, it will be necessary to remove the cluster to remove the ammeter, fuel, and temperature gauges.

NOTE: *When performing any operation behind the cluster, disconnect the battery ground cable first.*

Speedometer Cable Replacement

1. Reach behind the instrument cluster and push the speedometer cable casing toward the speedometer while depressing the retaining spring on the back of the instrument cluster case. Once the retaining spring has released, hold it in while pulling outward on the casing to disconnect the casing from the speedometer.

2. Remove the cable casing sealing plug from the dash panel. Then, pull the casing down from behind the dash and remove the cable.

3. If the cable is broken and cannot be entirely removed from the top, support the car securely, and then unscrew the cable casing connector at the transmission. Pull the bottom part of the cable out, and then screw the connector back onto the transmission.

4. Lubricate the new cable. Insert it into the casing until it bottoms. Push inward while rotating it until the square portion at the bottom engages with the coupling in the transmission, permitting the cable to move in another inch or so. Then, reconnect the cable casing to the speedometer and install the sealing plug into the dash panel.

Ignition Switch

NOTE: *All Camaros made in 1969 and later are equipped with ignition switches which are mounted in the steering column. Removal and installation procedures for these models can be found in Chapter 8.*

REMOVAL AND INSTALLATION
1967-68

1. Disconnect the battery ground cable. Put the ignition switch in the Accessory (ACC) position.

2. Insert a wire into the small hole in the face of the lock cylinder. Push in on the wire to depress the plunger. Continue turning the key until the cylinder can be removed from the switch.

3. Remove the switch bezel nut, and then pull the switch out from under the dash.

234 CHASSIS ELECTRICAL

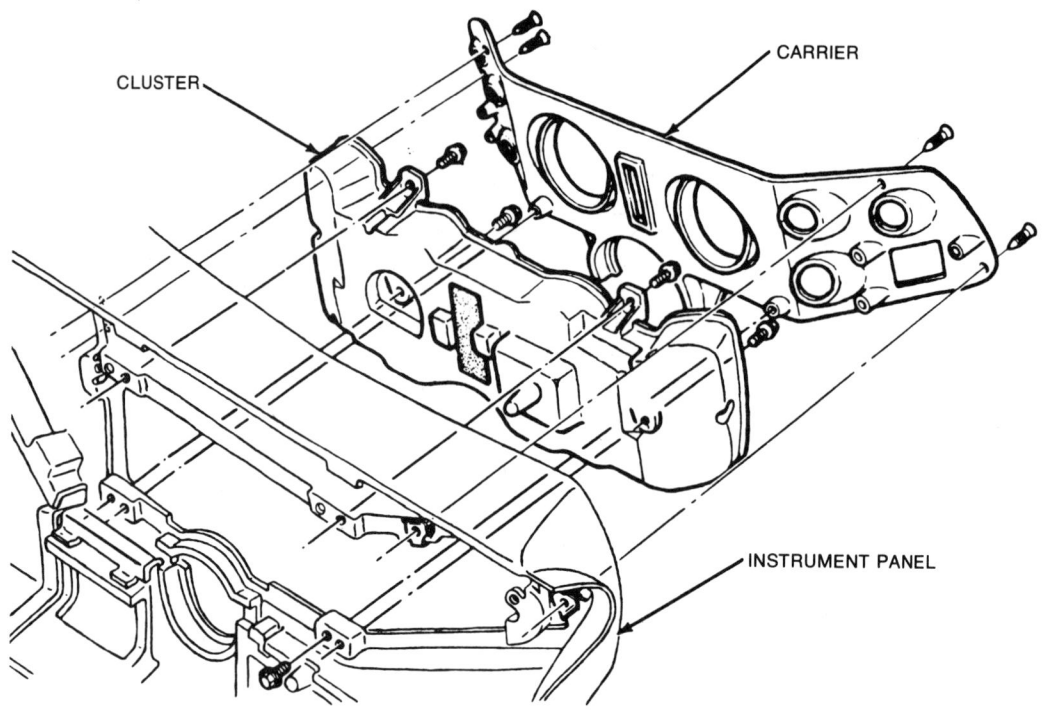

Instrument cluster mounting—1970–81

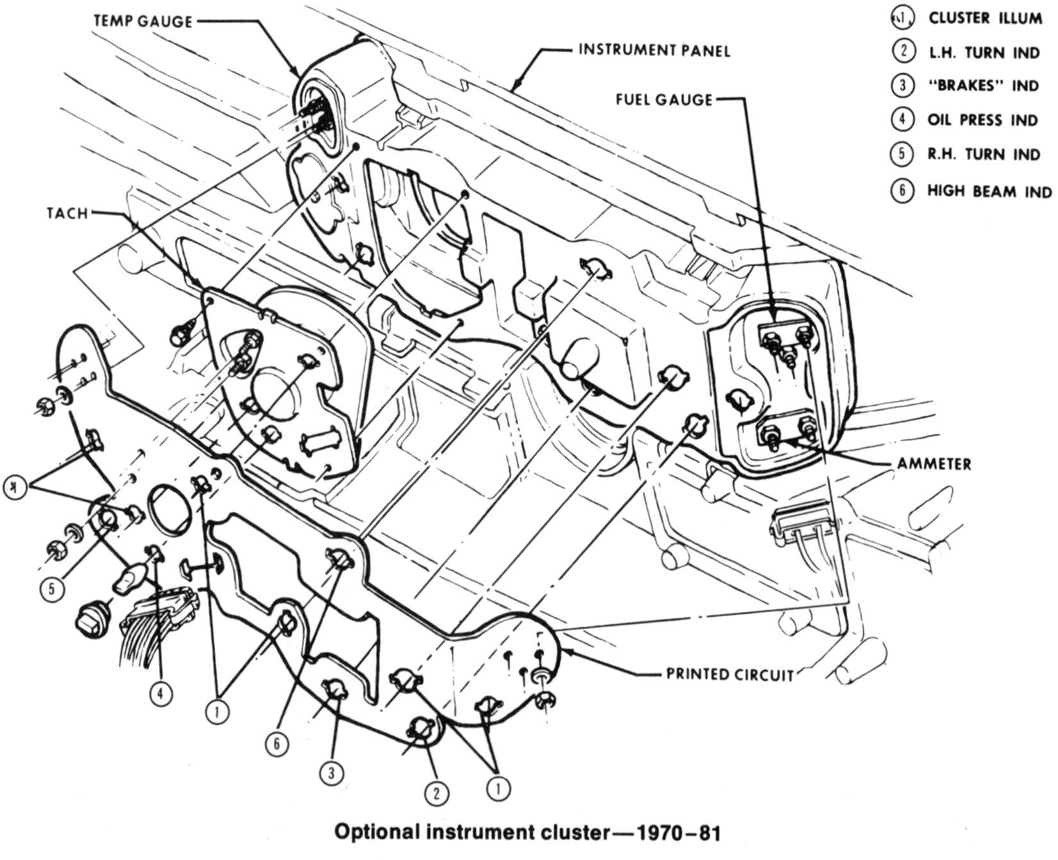

Optional instrument cluster—1970–81

4. Go in from the front of the switch with a screwdriver and unsnap the theft resistant locking tangs on the connector and then unplug the connector.

5. Installation is in the reverse order of removal.

SEAT BELT SYSTEM

Warning Buzzer and Light—1972-73

Beginning January 1, 1972, all cars are required to have a warning system which operates a buzzer and a warning light if either the driver's or the right-hand front passenger's seat belts are not fastened when the seats are occupied and the car is in forward motion.

On Chevrolet products, this system consists of seat belt retractor switches, pressure sensitive front seat switches, a parking brake switch (manual transmission), or a transmission switch (automatic transmission), a warning light, and a buzzer.

The seat belt warning system is wired through the 20 amp "Gauges" fuse.

The warning light is located in the instrument cluster; and the buzzer, which is shared with the ignition key warning system, is taped to the instrument cluster wiring harness.

The warning system is activated when the ignition switch is ON, the front seats are occupied, and the seat belts are left in their retractors. Only when the front seat belts are extended and properly fastened will the warning light and buzzer stop.

Seat Belt/Starter Interlock—1974-75

As required by law, all 1974 and some 1975 Chevrolet passenger cars cannot be started until the front seat occupants are seated and have fastened their seat belts. If the proper sequence is not followed, the engine cannot be started.

If, after the car is started, the seat belts are unfastened, a warning buzzer and light will be activated in a similar manner to that described above for 1972-73 models.

The shoulder harness and lap belt are permanently fastened together, so that they both must be worn. The shoulder harness uses an inertia-lock reel to allow freedom of movement under normal driving conditions.

NOTE: *This type of reel locks up when the car decelerates rapidly, as during a crash.*

The lap belts use the same rachet-type retractors that the 1972-73 models use.

The switches for the interlock system have been removed from the lap belt retractors and placed in the belt buckles. The seat sensors remain the same as those used in 1972-73.

For ease of service, the car may be started from outside, by reaching in and turning the key, but without depressing the seat sensors.

In case of system failure, an over-ride switch is located under the hood. This is a "one start" switch and it must be reset each time it is used.

DISABLING THE INTERLOCK SYSTEM

Since the requirement for the interlock system was dropped during the 1975 model year, those systems installed on cars built earlier may now be legally disabled. The seat belt warning light is still required.

1. Disconnect the negative battery cable.
2. Locate the interlock harness connector under the left side of the instrument panel on or near the fuse block. It has orange, yellow, and green leads.
3. Cut and tape the ends of the green wire on the body side of the connector.
4. Remove the buzzer from the fuse block or connector.

LIGHTING

Headlights

REMOVAL AND INSTALLATION

1. Unscrew the four retaining screws and remove the headlight bezel.
2. Remove the headlight bulb retaining screws. These are the screws which hold the retaining ring for the bulb to the front of the car. Do not touch the two headlight aiming screws, at the top and the side of the retaining ring (these screws will have different heads), or the headlight aim will have to be re-adjusted.
3. Pull the bulb and ring forward and then separate them. Unplug the electrical connector from the rear of the bulb.
4. Plug the new bulb into the electrical connector. Install the bulb into the retaining ring and then install the ring and the bulb. Install the headlight bezel.

236 CHASSIS ELECTRICAL

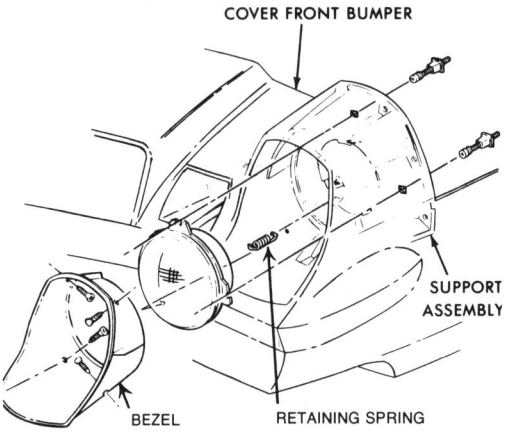

Exploded view of a typical headlight assembly (the bezel may differ on certain models)

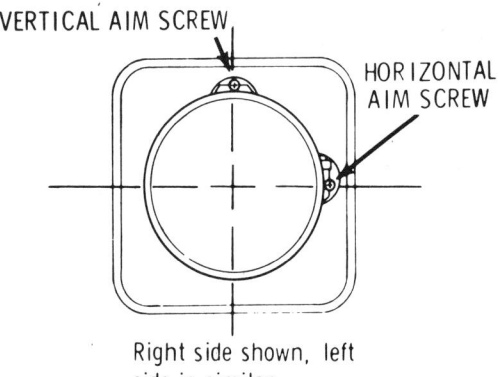

Headlight adjusting screws locations

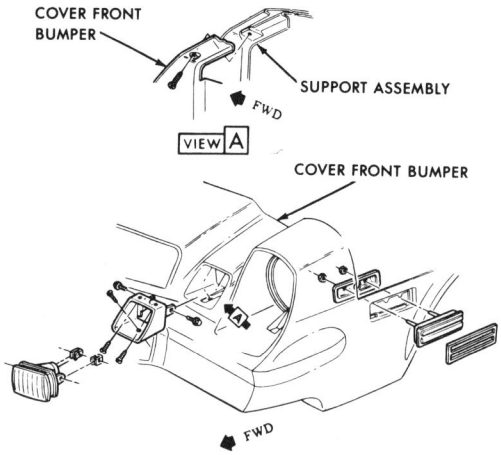

When replacing the headlight, it is always a good idea to check the other points of illumination

CIRCUIT PROTECTION

Fusible Links

A fusible link is a protective device used in an electrical circuit. When the current in-

Light Bulb Specifications

Unit	Candlepower or Wattage	Trade Number
Headlamp unit (1977–81)	—	6014
Headlamp unit—high-beam (1970–76)	60	6014 ('76—6012)
Headlamp unit—low-beam (1970–76)	60	6014
Headlamp unit—high-beam (1967–69)	55	6012
Headlamp unit—low-beam (1967–69)	45	6012
Parking lamp and turn signal (1977–81)	—	1157NA
Parking lamp and turn signal (1969–76)	3—32	1157NA
Parking lamp and turn signal (1967–68)	4—32	1157NA, 1034A ('67)
Tail, stop and turn signal (1969–81)	3—32	1157
Tail, stop and turn signal (1967–68)	4—32	1157
Back-up lamp	32	1156
Instrument illumination lamps	2	194
Temperature indicator	2	194
Oil pressure indicator	2	194
Generator indicator	2	194
High-beam indicator	2	194
Turn signal indicator	2	194
Check engine (1981)	2	194
Heater or A/C control panel (1979–81)	2	194
Heater or A/C control panel (1977–78)	1	171
Heater or A/C control panel (1971–76)	1	1445
Heater or A/C control panel (1967–70)	2	1895
Glove box lamps (1977–81)	—	1891/194
Glove box lamps (1967–76)	2	1895/194 ('72—1893)
Dome lamp (1977–81)	5	561
Dome and courtesy lamps (cartridge) (1967–76)	12	211
Dome and courtesy lamps (bayonet) (1967–76)	6	631
Seat separator courtesy lamp	6	212
Side marker (front and rear)	2	194
License plate lamp	4	67 ('75–'81—168)
Radio dial lamp—AM (1977–81)	2	194
Radio dial lamp—AM (1972–76)	3	1816
Radio dial lamp—AM (1970–71)	2	293

Light Bulb Specifications (cont.)

Unit	Candle-power or Wattage	Trade Number
Radio dial lamp—AM (1967–69)	2	1893
Radio dial lamp—AM/FM or stereo (1977–81)	—	216
Radio dial lamp—FM and tape (1967–76)	2	1893
Tape player lens illumination lamp (1977–81)	—	1893
Tape player lens illumination lamp (1967–76)	1	216
Stereo indicator lamp①	3	2182D
Automatic transmission indicator lamp	2	194
Brake alarm lamp	2	194
Luggage compartment lamp	15	1003
Underhood lamp	15	93
Indicator—wash fluid level	3	168
Seat belt warning lamp	2	194
Map lamp (mirror) (1970–76)	4	563 ('73—631)
Map lamp (mirror) (1969)	6	562
Clock lamp	3	168 ('72—1895)
Headlight motor warning lamp (1967)	2	257
Windshield wiper/washer switch (1977–81)	2	194

Unless otherwise noted, figures apply to all years.
① 1977–81—stereo radio uses Drake 66; stereo tape uses DS 410 (LED)

creases beyond a certain amperage, the fusible metal of the wire link will melt, thus breaking the electrical circuit and preventing further damage to any other components or wiring. Whenever a fusible link is melted because of a short circuit, correct the cause before installing a new one. Most Camaros have four fusible links.

REPLACING FUSIBLE LINKS

1. Disconnect both battery cables. If the link is connected to the junction block or starter solenoid, disconnect it.
2. Cut the wiring harness right behind the link connector(s) and remove.
3. Strip insulation off the harness wire back ½".
4. Position a clip around new link and wiring harness or new connector and crimp it securely. Then, solder the connection, using rosin core solder and sufficient heat to guarantee a good connection. Repeat for the remaining connection.
5. Tape all exposed wiring with electrical tape. Where necessary, connect the link to the junction block or starter solenoid. Reconnect battery.

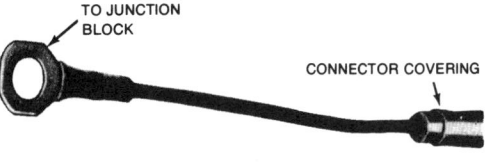

Fusible links before and after a short circuit

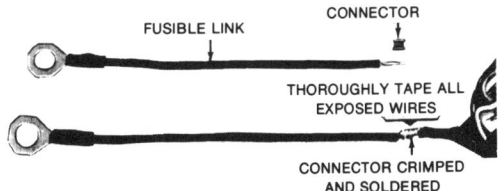

New fusible links are spliced to the wire

Circuit Breakers

A circuit breaker in the light switch protects the headlight circuit. A separate 30 amp breaker mounted on the firewall protects the power window, seat, and power top circuits. Circuit breakers open and close rapidly to protect the circuit if current is excessive.

Fuses and Flashers

The fusebox is located under the instrument panel on the left side. The turn signal flasher

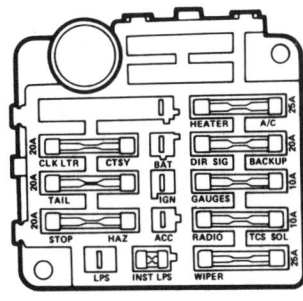

Fuse box—1971–79 (amperage figures may differ with individual models)

CHASSIS ELECTRICAL

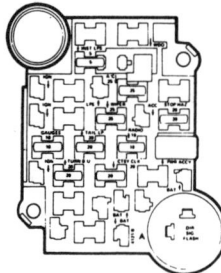

Fuse box—1980-81

Fuses

Year	Components	Amps
1967	Wiper	20
	Back-up lamp and gauges	10
	Heater, A/C	25
	Radio	10
	Instrument lamps	4
	Stop and tail lamps	20
	Clock, lighter, courtesy lamps, hazard warning	20
1968-70	Wiper/washer, 3 spd A/T downshift	25
	Back-up lamp, turn signal, cruise control master defogger, heater (exc. 1968)	20
	A/C, transmission control spark solenoid (1970)	25
	Radio, power window	10
	Tail, marker and fender lamps	20
	Instrument lamps	4
	Gauges and tell-tale lamps	10
	Stop and hazard	20
	Clock, lighter, courtesy lamps, dome and luggage lamps	20
1971-74	Radio, T.S.C. solenoid, rear defogger, glove box lamp	10
	Wiper	25
	Stop and hazard warning lamps	20
	Turn signals, back-up lights	20
	Heater, A/C	25
	Instrument lamps, anti-diesel relay, dome lamp	3
	Gauges, warning lamps	10
	Clock, lighter, courtesy lamps	20
	Tail, license, luggage, sidemarker, parking lamps	20
1975-79	Radio, idle stop solenoid	10
	Wiper	25
	Stop and hazard lamps	20
	Turn signals, back-up lights	20
	Heater, A/C	25
	Instrument lamps, radio dial light, heater dial light, wiper light	4
	Gauge warning lights, cruise control, rear defogger, fuel gauge, headlight buzzer, seat belt warning buzzer	10
	Glove box light, dome lamp, luggage lamp, clock, lighter, courtesy lights, key warning buzzer	20
	Tail, parking and side marker lights, underhood lamp, license lamp	20
1980-81	Radio, idle stop solenoid	10
	Electronic control module (1981)	10
	Wiper	25
	Stop and hazard lights	20
	Turn signal, back-up lights	20
	Heater, A/C	25
	Inst. lamps, radio dial lamp, heater dial light, W/S wiper lamp, audio alarm buzzer	5
	Gauges, warning lights, cruise control, fuel gauge, headlight buzzer, seat belt warning buzzer	10
	Glove box light, dome lamp, luggage light, clock, lighter, courtesy lights, key warning buzzer, closed loop	20
	Tail, parking and side marker lights, underhood lamp, license lamp	20
	Choke heater	20

is under the dash to the right of the steering column. The hazard flasher is under the dash, to the left of the steering column. On all 1980–81 models, both the turn signal flasher and the hazard flasher are located at the lower left hand and the upper right hand corners of the fuse block respectively. There is an inline fuse for the underhood/spotlamp circuit. The fusebox is marked to indicate fuse size and the circuit(s) protected on 1971 and later cars.

WIRING DIAGRAMS

Wiring diagrams have been left out of this book. As cars have become more complex, and available with longer and longer option lists, wiring diagrams have grown in size and complexity also. It has become virtually impossible to provide a readable reproduction in a reasonable number of pages. Information on ordering wiring diagrams from the vehicle manufacturer can be found in the owners manual.

Clutch and Transmission

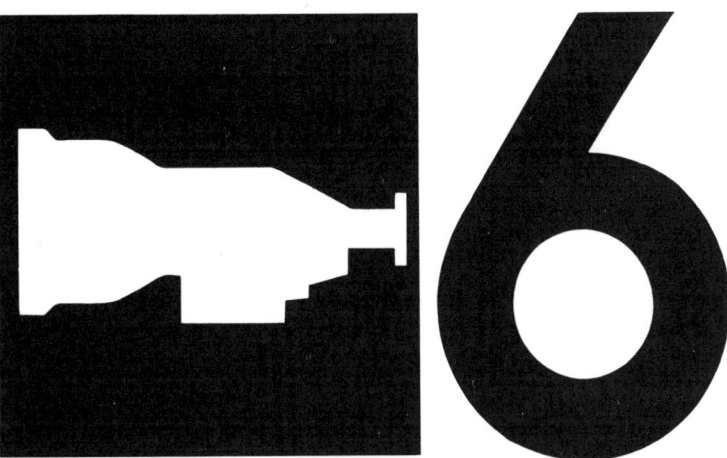

MANUAL TRANSMISSION

Understanding the Manual Transmission and Clutch

Because of the way the gasoline engine breathes, it can produce torque, or twisting force, only within a narrow speed range. Most modern engines must turn at about 2,500 rpm to produce their peak torque. By 4,500 rpm they are producing so little torque that continued increases in engine speed produce no power increases.

The transmission and clutch are employed to vary the relationship between engine speed and the speed of the wheels so that adequate engine power can be produced under all circumstances. The clutch allows engine torque to be applied to the transmission input shaft gradually, due to mechanical slippage. The car can, consequently, be started smoothly from a full stop.

The transmission changes the ratio between the rotating speeds of the engine and the wheels by the use of gears. Three-speed or four-speed transmissions are most common. The lower gears allow full engine power to be applied to the rear wheels during acceleration at low speeds.

The clutch driven plate is a thin disc, the center of which is splined to the transmission input shaft. Both sides of the disc are covered with a layer of material which is similar to brake lining and which is capable of allowing slippage without roughness or excessive noise.

The clutch cover is bolted to the engine flywheel and incorporates a diaphragm spring which provides the pressure to engage the clutch. The cover also houses the pressure plate. The driven disc is sandwiched between the pressure plate and the smooth surface of the flywheel when the clutch pedal is released, thus forcing it to turn at the same speed as the engine crankshaft.

The transmission contains a mainshaft which passes all the way through the transmission, from the clutch to the driveshaft. This shaft is separated at one point, so that front and rear portions can turn at different speeds.

Power is transmitted by a countershaft in the lower gears and reverse. The gears of the countershaft mesh with gears on the mainshaft, allowing power to be carried from one to the other. All the countershaft gears are integral with that shaft, while several of the mainshaft gears can either rotate independently of the shaft or be locked to it. Shifting from one gear to the next causes one of the gears to be freed from rotating with the shaft, and locks another to it. Gears are locked and

240 CLUTCH AND TRANSMISSION

unlocked by internal dog clutches which slide between the center of the gear and the shaft. The forward gears usually employ synchronizers: friction members which smoothly bring gear and shaft to the same speed before the toothed dog clutches are enged.

The clutch is operating properly if:
1. It will stall the engine when released with the vehicle held stationary.
2. The shift lever can be moved freely between first and reverse gears when the vehicle is stationary and the clutch disengaged.

A clutch pedal free-play adjustment is incorporated in the linkage. If there is about 1–2 in. of motion before the pedal begins to release the clutch, it is adjusted properly. Inadequate free-play wears all parts of the clutch releasing mechanisms and may cause slippage. Excessive free-play may cause inadequate release and hard shifting of gears.

Some clutches use a hydraulic system in place of mechanical linkage. If the clutch fails to release, fill the clutch master cylinder with fluid to the proper level and pump the clutch pedal to fill the system with fluid. Bleed the system in the same way as a brake system. If leaks are located, tighten loose connections or overhaul the master or slave cylinder as necessary.

Identification

See Chapter 2, which lists the basic types of manual transmissions and the various locations of their serial numbers. By finding the serial number on your transmission and comparing its location with the information there, you can readily determine the type of gearbox used.

Linkage Adjustment

COLUMN SHIFT

1967–68

1. Located on the left side of the transmission case are two levers. Manipulate these levers until the transmission is in neutral. Depress the clutch pedal, start the engine, and release the pedal slowly. If the car fails to move and engine is still running with the pedal fully released, the transmission is in neutral. If the car moves, the transmission is in gear and the levers should be repositioned until neutral is found. Loosen the swivel nuts on both shift rods.
2. Move the shift lever (on the column) to the neutral position. Raise the hood and lo-

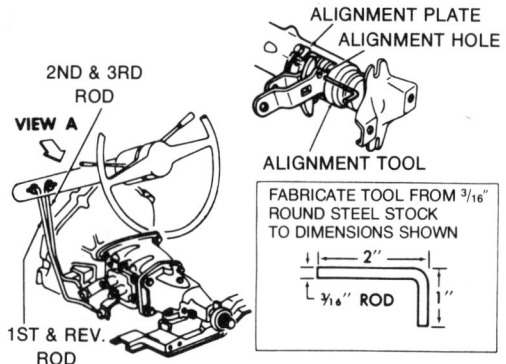

Shift linkage (column) adjustment for 1967–69 cars (© Chevrolet Motor Division)

cate the shifter tube levers on the steering column. Align the first and reverse lever with the second and third lever. Using a pin (use a large L-shaped Allen wrench), hold these levers in alignment (most cars have alignment holes in the levers and an alignment plate) until the linkage is connected.
3. Make the final adjustments to align the shift rods and levers at the transmission into the neutral position. Road-test the car and check the shifting operation. If the adjustment is correct, the alignment pin should pass freely through all alignment holes. If not, readjustment is necessary.

1969

1. Turn the ignition switch to the "off" position.
2. Loosen the swivel nuts on both shift rods.
3. Place the column-mounted shift lever in the reverse position. There are two levers located on the side of the transmission case. The lever to the front of the transmission controls second and third gears while the other lever controls first and reverse. Place this first and reverse lever into the reverse position. Push up on the first/reverse shift rod until the column lever is in the reverse detent position. Tighten the swivel nut.
4. Place the column lever and the transmission levers (located on the side of the case) in neutral (to determine neutral, see Step One for 1967–68 cars). The shift tube levers are located on the steering column mast jacket. Make sure the column lever is in neutral and hold it in this position by inserting a pin through the alignment holes in the shift tube levers (a 3/16 in Allen wrench is perfect).
5. Hold the second/third shift rod steady

CLUTCH AND TRANSMISSION

(to prevent a change in adjustment) and tighten the swivel locknut.

6. Remove the alignment pin from the shift tube levers and shift the column shift lever to the reverse position. Turn the ignition key to "lock" and check the ignition interlock control. If it binds, leave the control in "lock" and readjust the first/reverse rod at the swivel.

7. Move the column lever through the gear positions and return it to neutral. The alignment pin should pass freely through the alignment holes of the shift tube levers. If it doesn't, loosen the swivel nuts and readjust.

1970-72

1. Place the shift lever (on the column) in reverse and the ignition switch in "off."
2. Raise the car and support it with floor stands.
3. Loosen the locknuts on the shift rod swivels. Pull down slightly on the first/reverse control rod on the lower steering column to remove any slack. Tighten the locknut at the transmission lever.
4. Unlock the ignition switch and shift the column lever into neutral. Position the shift tube levers (located on the lower steering column) in neutral by aligning the lever alignment holes. Hold them in this position by inserting a 3/16 in. Allen wrench through the alignment holes.
5. Hold the second/third shift rod steady and tighten the rod locknut.
6. Remove the alignment tool from the shift tube levers and check the shifting operation.
7. Place the column lever in reverse and check the movement of the ignition key. In reverse and only reverse, the key must turn freely in and out of "lock."

FLOOR SHIFT

1967—Saginaw 3 Speed and Muncie 4 Speed

1. Place the transmission levers (located on the left side plate of the transmission) in neutral. The lever closest to the bellhousing operates second and third gears while the other lever controls first and reverse. Check for neutral in the manner described in Step one of "Linkage Adjustment—Column Shift."
2. Place the floor-mounted shift lever into neutral and insert the locating pin into the notch of the shift lever and bracket assembly.

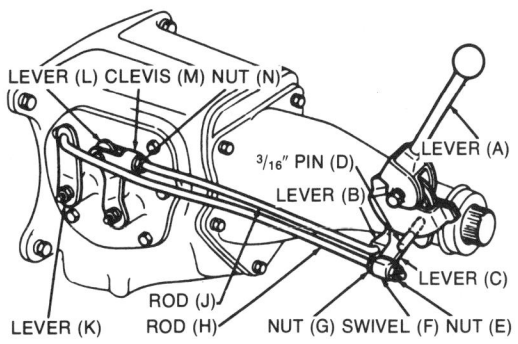

1967 three-speed (Saginaw) linkage adjustment
(© Chevrolet Motor Division)

On the four-speed, connect the reverse rod to the lever and secure with a retainer.

3. Loosely install the nut and clevis on the end of the shift rod and attach the other end of the rod to the lever located beneath the shift lever bracket. Secure the assembly with a retainer.
4. After attaching the rod to the lever, move the lever against the locating pin and adjust the clevis (U-shaped shackle) to the transmission lever until the clevis pin passes freely through the holes. Place a washer on the pin and secure it with a cotter pin. Prevent the clevis from turning by tightening the nut.
5. Install a nut, a swivel, and another nut on the other shift rod. Attach the other end of this rod to the other transmission lever and secure it with a retainer.
6. Located beneath the floor-mounted shift lever are two levers (three on a four-speed), each connected to a shift rod. The first lever and rod were connected in Step Three. Move the second lever against the locating pin and attach the swivel to this lever, then secure it with a retainer. Tighten both nuts against the swivel.
7. Remove the locating pin and check the shift operation. Adjust the clevis and swivel if readjustment is necessary.

1967—Warner T-16 3 Speed

1. Place the transmission levers in neutral. Verify the neutral setting in the manner described in Step One of "Linkage Adjustment—Column Shift."
2. Place the floor-mounted shift lever in neutral along with the two levers directly below it. Hold the levers in neutral by inserting a locating pin into the lever bracket assembly (3/16 in. Allen wrench).
3. Insert the longer rod into the transmis-

sion lever and secure it with a retainer. Attach the swivel end of the rod to the other lever and secure it with a retainer. Repeat this procedure for the shorter rod.

4. Remove the locating pin and check the shifter operation.

1968-69—3 Speed and 4 Speed

1. On 1969 models, turn the ignition key to the "off" position.

2. Loosen the swivel locknuts on the shift rods. On 1969 models, it will be necessary to loosen the locknut on the back drive rod.

3. Place the shift levers on the side of the transmission and the shift lever in the car in neutral. Lock the car shift lever in neutral by placing a pin in the notch of the lever and bracket assembly directly below the shift lever.

4. Move the shift rod nut against the swivel on each rod, then tighten the locknut against the other side of the swivel. Remove the locating pin and check the shifting operation.

5. On 1968 and 1969 models with a Muncie four-speed, readjust the reverse rod by shortening it three turns of the jam nut. On 1969 models, shift into reverse. Push up on the back drive control rod in order to place the column mechanism in the reverse position. Pull down slightly on the rod to remove any slack and tighten the jam nut. Place the ignition switch in "lock." The switch should not bind when moved in and out of "lock"; if it does, readjust the back control rod. Check the shifting operation and correct it if necessary.

1970-81—3 Speed and 4 Speed

1. Turn the ignition switch "off" ("lock" for 1970 cars), raise the car, and support it on jackstands.

2. Loosen the swivel locknuts on all shift rods and on the back drive control rod.

3. Place the transmission shift levers (on the side of the transmission) in neutral.

4. Place the floor shift lever in neutral and lock it in this position by installing a pin into the lever bracket assembly directly below the shift lever.

5. Move the shift rod nut up against the swivel on each shift rod and hold it in place by tightening the locknuts.

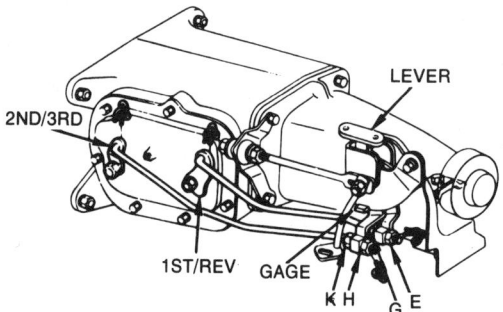

1968 three-speed linkage (© Chevrolet Motor Division)

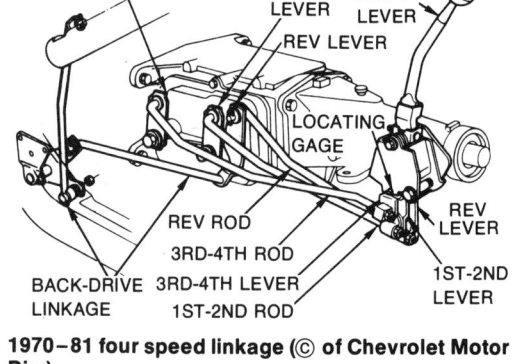

1970–81 four speed linkage (© of Chevrolet Motor Div.)

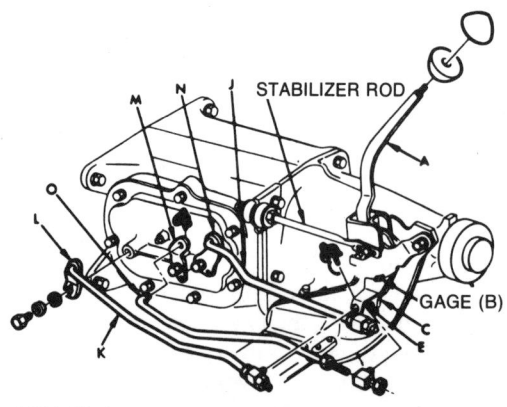

1967–68 four-speed linkage (© Chevrolet Motor Division)

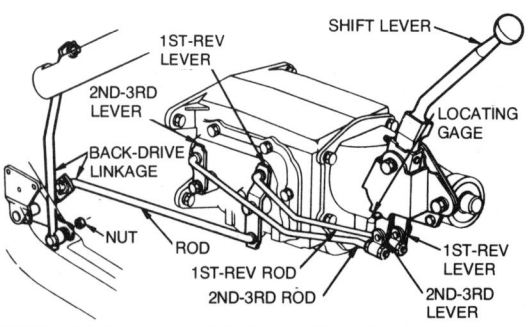

1969–81 three speed linkage (© of Chevrolet Motor Div.)

CLUTCH AND TRANSMISSION

6. Remove the locating pin from the control bracket assembly and shift the transmission into reverse. On 1971 and later models, place the ignition key in "lock." To remove any slack in the steering column mechanism, pull down on the back drive rod and tighten the nut. When in reverse, it must be possible to easily turn the ignition key in and out of the "lock" position. If any binding exists, leave the key in "lock" and readjust the back drive control rod.

7. Check the shifting operation and readjust if necessary.

CLUTCH SWITCH ADJUSTMENT AND REPLACEMENT

A clutch-operated neutral safety switch was used beginning in 1970. The ignition switch must be in the "start" position and the clutch must be fully depressed before the car will start. The switch mounts to the clutch pedal arm. Removal of this switch is obvious and simple. This switch cannot be adjusted.

REMOVAL AND INSTALLATION

3 Speed and 4 Speed—1967-69

REMOVAL

1. Raise the car and remove the driveshaft. On floor-shift models, remove the trim plate and shifter boot.
2. On 1968-69 models, it may be necessary to disconnect the exhaust pipe at the manifold.
3. Disconnect the speedometer cable and, on floor-shift models, disconnect the back-up light switch.
4. Remove the crossmember-to-frame bolts. On floor-shift models, remove the bolts holding the control lever support to the crossmember.
5. Remove the transmission mount bolts.
6. Using a suitable jack and a block of wood (to be placed between the jack and the engine), raise the engine slightly and remove or relocate the crossmember.
7. Remove the shift levers from the transmission side cover.
8. On floor-shift models, remove the stabilizer rod (if so equipped) situated between the shift lever assembly and the transmission.
9. Remove the transmission-to-bellhousing bolts. Remove the top bolts first and insert guide pins into the holes, then remove the bottom bolts.
10. Remove the transmission.

INSTALLATION

1. Lift the transmission into position and insert the mainshaft into the bellhousing.
2. Install the transmission-to-bellhousing bolts and lockwashers, and torque them to 50 ft. lbs.
3. Install the transmission shift levers to the side cover. On floor-shift models, install the stabilizer rod (if so equipped).
4. Raise the engine slightly, position the crossmember, and install the bolts.
5. Install the transmission mount bolts. On floor-shift models, install the bolts holding the shift lever support to the crossmember.

CAUTION: *Lubricate the tailshaft bushing before the driveshafts are installed.*

6. Install the driveshaft and, if removed, install the exhaust pipe to manifold.
7. Connect the speedometer cable and, on floor-shift cars, connect the backup light.
8. Fill the transmission with lubricant.

3 Speed and 4 Speed—1970-81

REMOVAL

1. On floor-shift models, remove the shift knob and console trim plate.
2. Raise the car and support it with floor stands.
3. Disconnect the speedometer cable and the TCS switch wiring.
4. Remove the driveshaft.
5. Remove the bolts securing the transmission mounts to the crossmember and also those bolts securing the crossmember to the frame. Remove the crossmember.
6. Remove the shift levers from the side of the transmission.
7. Disconnect the back drive rod from the bellcrank.
8. Remove the bolts from the shift control assembly and carefully lower the assembly until the shift lever clears the rubber shift boot. Remove the assembly from the car.
9. Remove the transmission-to-bellhousing bolts and lift the transmission from the car.

INSTALLATION

1. Lift the transmission and insert the mainshaft into the bellhousing.
2. Install and torque the transmission-to-clutch housing bolts and lockwashers.
3. Install the shift lever.
4. Install the shift levers to the transmission side cover.

CLUTCH AND TRANSMISSION

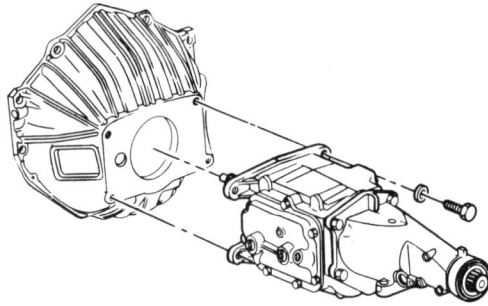

Typical transmission mounting

5. Connect the back drive rod to the bellcrank.

6. Raise the engine high enough to position the crossmember. Install and tighten the crossmember-to-frame bolts and transmission mounts to crossmember bolts.

7. Install the driveshaft.

8. Connect the speedometer cable and TCS wiring.

9. Fill the transmission with the specified lubricant. If applicable, install the console trim plate and shift knob. Adjust the linkage.

CLUTCH

Understanding the Clutch

The purpose of the clutch is to disconnect and connect engine power from the transmission. A car at rest requires a lot of engine torque to get all that weight moving. An internal-combustion engine does not develop a high starting torque (unlike steam engines), so it must be allowed to operate without any load until it builds up enough torque to move the car. Torque increases with engine rpm. The clutch allows the engine to build up torque by physically disconnecting the engine from the transmission, relieving the engine of any load or resistance. The transfer of engine power to the transmission (the load) must be smooth and gradual; if it weren't, drive line components would wear out or break quickly. This gradual power transfer is made possible by gradually releasing the clutch pedal. The clutch disc and pressure plate are the connecting link between the engine and transmission. When the clutch pedal is released, the disc and plate contact each other (clutch engagement), physically joining the engine and transmission. When the pedal is pushed in, the disc and plate separate (the clutch is disengaged), disconnecting the engine from the transmission.

The clutch assembly consists of the flywheel, the clutch disc, the clutch pressure plate, the throwout bearing and fork, the actuating linkage and the pedal. The flywheel and clutch pressure plate (driving members) are connected to the engine crankshaft and rotate with it. The clutch disc is located between the flywheel and pressure plate, and splined to the transmission shaft. A driving member is one that is attached to the engine and transfers engine power to a driven member (clutch disc) on the transmission shaft. A driving member (pressure plate) rotates (drives) a driven member (clutch disc) on contact and, in so doing, turns the transmission shaft. There is a circular diaphragm spring within the pressure plate cover (transmission side). In a relaxed state (when the clutch pedal is fully released), this spring is convex; that is, it is dished outward toward the transmission. Pushing in the clutch pedal actuates an attached linkage rod. Connected to the other end of this rod is the throwout bearing fork. The throwout bearing is attached to the fork. When the clutch pedal is depressed, the clutch linkage pushes the fork and bearing forward to contact the diaphragm spring of the pressure plate. The outer edges of the spring are secured to the pressure plate and are pivoted on rings so that when the center of the spring is compressed by the throwout bearing, the outer edges bow outward and, by so doing, pull the pressure plate in the same direction—away from the clutch disc. This action separates the disc from the plate, disengaging the clutch and allowing the transmission to be shifted into another gear. A coil type clutch return spring attached to the clutch pedal arm permits full release of the pedal. Releasing the pedal pulls the throwout bearing away from the diaphragm spring resulting in a reversal of spring position. As bearing pressure is gradually released from the spring center, the outer edges of the spring bow inward, pushing the pressure plate into closer contact with the clutch disc. As the disc and plate move closer together, friction between the two increases and slippage is reduced until, when full spring pressure is applied (by fully releasing the pedal), the speed of the disc and plate are the same. This stops all slipping, creating a direct connection between the plate and disc which results in the transfer of power from the engine to the transmission. The clutch disc is now rotating with the pressure plate at engine speed and,

CLUTCH AND TRANSMISSION

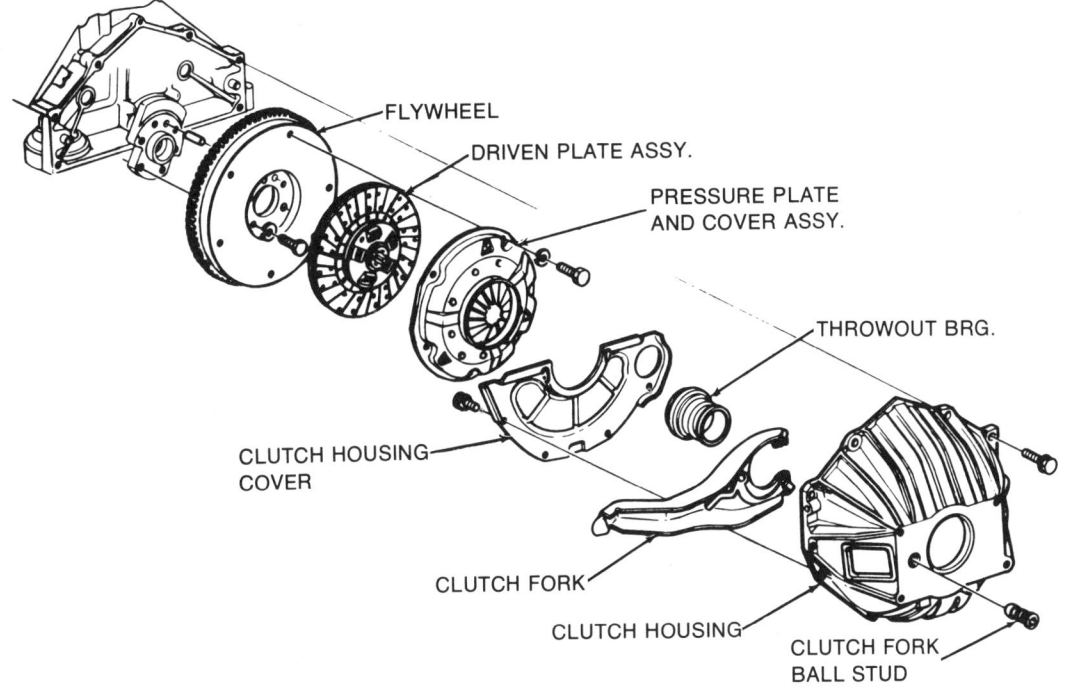

Clutch and flywheel assembly (exploded view) (© Chevrolet Motor Division)

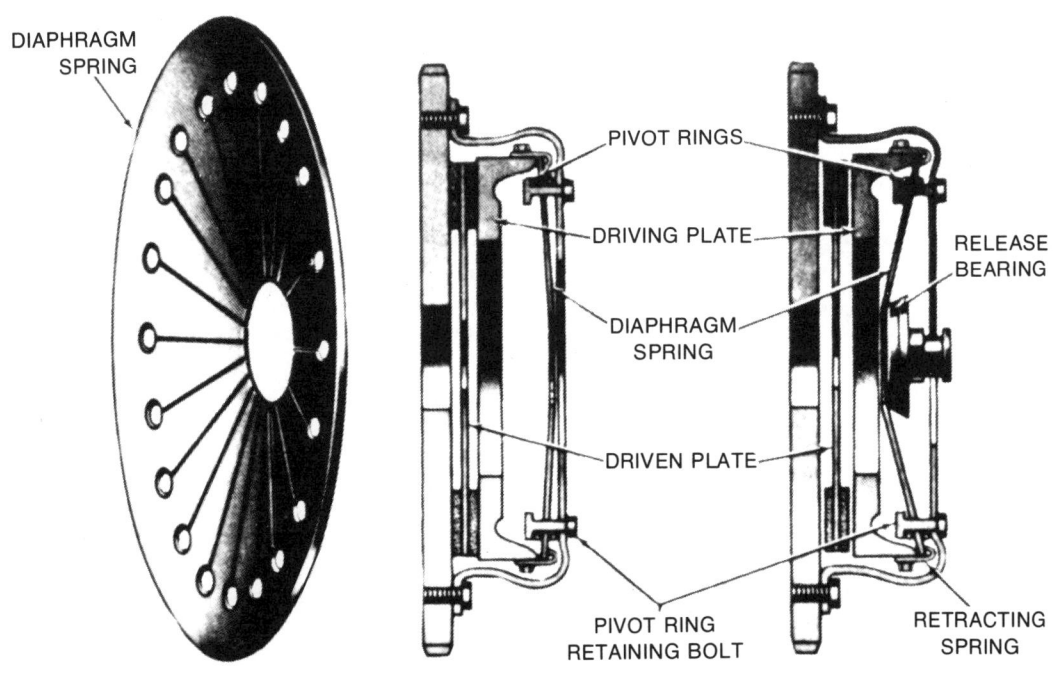

Operation of diaphragm spring clutch (© Chevrolet Motor Division)

246 CLUTCH AND TRANSMISSION

because it is splined to the transmission shaft, the shaft now turns at the same engine speed. Understanding clutch operation can be rather difficult at first; if you're still confused after reading this, consider the following analogy. The action of the diaphragm spring can be compared to that of an oil can bottom. The bottom of an oil can is shaped very much like the clutch diaphragm spring and pushing in on the can bottom and then releasing it produces a similar effect. As mentioned earlier, the clutch pedal return spring permits full release of the pedal and reduces linkage slack due to wear. As the linkage wears, clutch free-pedal travel will increase and free-travel will decrease as the clutch wears. Free-travel is actually throwout bearing lash.

The diaphragm spring type clutches used in Camaros are available in two different designs: flat diaphragm springs or bent springs. The bent fingers are bent back to create a centrifugal boost ensuring quick reengagement at higher engine speeds. This design enables pressure plate load to increase as the clutch disc wears and makes low pedal effort possible even with a heavy-duty clutch. The throwout bearing used with the bent finger design is 1¼ in. long and is shorter than the bearing used with the flat finger design. These bearings are not interchangeable. If the longer bearing is used with the bent finger clutch, free-pedal travel will not exist. This results in clutch slippage and rapid wear.

The transmission varies the gear ratio between the engine and rear wheels. It can be shifted to change engine speed as driving conditions and loads change. The transmission allows disengaging and reversing power from the engine to the wheels.

CLUTCH CROSS-SHAFT LUBRICATION

Once every 36,000 miles, or sooner if necessary, remove the plug, install a fitting and lubricate with a water-resistant EP (Extreme Pressure) chassis lubricant.

Linkage Inspection

A clutch may have all the symptoms of going bad when the real trouble lies in the linkage. To avoid the unnecessary replacement of a clutch, make the following linkage checks:

 a. Start the engine and depress the clutch pedal until it is about ½ in. from the floor mat and move the shift lever between first and reverse (first and second on a four-speed) several times. If this can be done smoothly without any grinding, the clutch is releasing fully. If the shifting is not smooth, the clutch is not releasing fully and adjustment is necessary.

 b. Check the condition of the clutch pedal bushings for signs of sticking or excessive wear.

 c. Check the throwout bearing fork for proper installation on the ball stud. The fork could possibly be pulled off the ball if not properly lubricated.

 d. Check the cross-shaft levers for distortion or damage.

 e. Check the car for loose or damaged motor mounts. Bad motor mounts can cause the engine to shift under acceleration and bind the clutch linkage at the cross-shaft. There must be some clearance between the cross-shaft and motor mount.

 f. Check the throwout bearing clearance between the clutch spring fingers and the front bearing retainer on the transmission. If there is no clearance, the fork may be improperly installed on the ball stud or the clutch disc may be worn out.

Linkage Adjustment

Only one adjustment is necessary to compensate for all normal clutch wear. Depress the clutch pedal and slowly release it. If adjusted correctly, the throwout bearing should begin to disengage the clutch diaphragm spring levers when the top of the pedal pad is 1–1⅛ in. from the floor mat. The car should begin to move forward. If clutch engagement begins at a point noticeably greater than 1⅛ in. from the floor mat or less than 1 in. from the floor mat, this free-play measurement must be adjusted as follows:

1967–69

1. Disconnect the pedal return spring at the fork.
2. Hold the clutch pedal against the rubber stop and loosen the locknut.
3. Turn the adjusting rod out and against clutch fork until the throwout bearing lightly contacts the pressure plate fingers.
4. Turn the rod into the swivel three times and tighten the locknut.
5. Install the clutch spring and check pedal free-play (1–1⅛ in.).

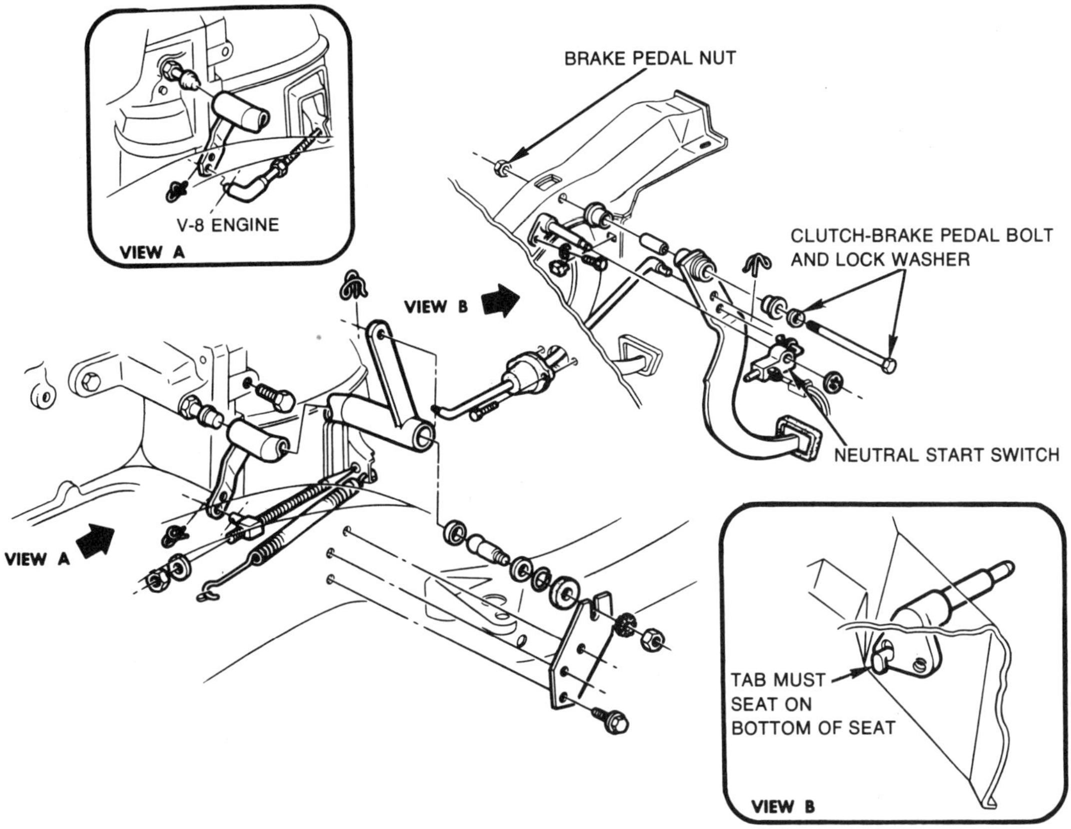

CLUTCH AND TRANSMISSION

Clutch pedal upper and lower linkage (© Chevrolet Motor Division)

1970-81

The clutch on these models can be adjusted as outlined above or by the alternate procedure below.

1. Disconnect the return spring at the clutch fork.
2. Hold the pedal against the rubber bumper on the dash brace.

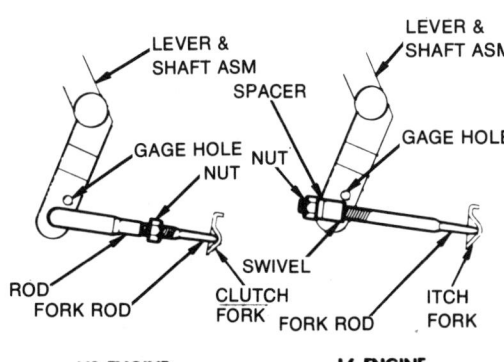

Adjusting the clutch pedal free-play. Gauge hole present only on 1970 and later cars (© Chevrolet Motor Division)

3. Push the clutch fork so the throwout bearing lightly contacts the pressure plate fingers.
4. Loosen the locknut and adjust the length of the rod so that the swivel or rod can slip freely into the gauge hole in the lever. Increase the length of the rod until all free-play is removed.
5. Remove the rod or swivel from the gauge hole and insert it in the lower hole on the lever. Install the retainer and tighten the locknut.
6. Install the return spring and check free-play measurement from the floor mat to top of the pedal pad. It should measure 1⅛–1⅜ in. 1967–74; ¾–1½ in. 1975–76; 1–1½ in. 1977; .85–1.45 in. 1978–81.

REMOVAL

1. Support engine and remove the transmission.
2. Disconnect the clutch fork push rod and spring.
3. Remove the flywheel housing.

248 CLUTCH AND TRANSMISSION

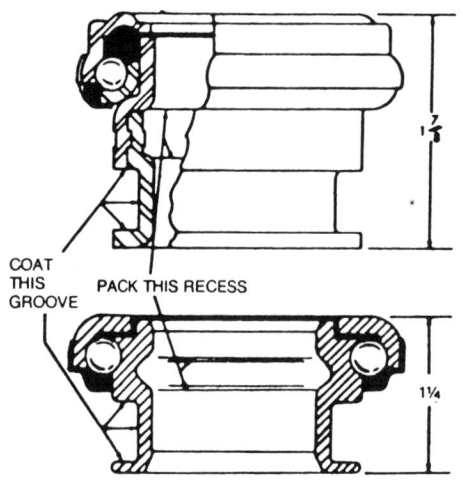

Clutch release bearing lubrication—flat finger type (top), bent finger type (bottom)

4. Slide the clutch fork from the ball stud and remove the fork from the dust boot. The ball stud is threaded into the clutch housing and may be replaced, if necessary.

5. Install an alignment tool to support the clutch assembly during removal. Mark the flywheel and clutch cover for reinstallation, if they do not already have "X" marks.

6. Loosen the clutch-to-flywheel attaching bolts evenly, one turn at a time, until spring pressure is released. Remove the bolts and clutch assembly.

INSTALLATION

1. Clean the pressure plate and flywheel face.

2. Support the clutch disc and pressure plate with an alignment tool. The driven disc is installed with the damper springs on the transmission side. On some 1967 6-cylinder engines, the clutch disc is installed in a reverse manner with the damper springs to the flywheel side.

3. Turn the clutch assembly until the mark on the cover lines up with the mark on the flywheel, then install the bolts. Tighten down evenly and gradually to avoid distortion.

4. Remove the alignment tool.

5. Lubricate the ball socket and fork fingers at the release bearing end with high melting-point grease. Lubricate the recess on the inside of the throwout bearing and throwout fork groove with a light coat of graphite grease.

6. Install the clutch fork and dust boot into the housing. Install the throwout bearing to the throwout fork. Install the flywheel housing. Install the transmission.

7. Connect the fork push rod and spring. Lubricate the spring and pushrod ends.

8. Adjust the shift linkage and clutch pedal free-play.

AUTOMATIC TRANSMISSION

Understanding Automatic Transmission

The automatic transmission allows engine torque and power to be transmitted to the rear wheels within a narrow range of engine operating speeds. The transmission will allow the engine to turn fast enough to produce plenty of power and torque at very low speeds, while keeping it at a sensible rpm at high vehicle speeds. The transmission performs this job entirely without driver assistance. The transmission uses a light fluid as the medium for the transmission of power. This fluid also works in the operation of various hydraulic control circuits and as a lubricant. Because the transmission fluid performs all of these three functions, trouble within the unit can easily travel from one part to another. For this reason, and because of the complexity and unusual operating principles of the transmission, a very sound understanding of the basic principles of operation will simplify troubleshooting.

THE TORQUE CONVERTER

The torque converter replaces the conventional clutch. It has three functions:

1. It allows the engine to idle with the vehicle at a standstill—even with the transmission in gear.

2. It allows the transmission to shift from range to range smoothly, without requiring that the driver close the throttle during the shift.

3. It multiples engine torque to an increasing extent as vehicle speed drops and throttle opening is increased. This has the effect of making the transmission more responsive and reduces the amount of shifting required.

The torque converter is a metal case which is shaped like a sphere that has been flattened on opposite sides. It is bolted to the rear end of the engine's crankshaft. Generally, the entire metal case rotates at engine speed and serves as the engine's flywheel.

CLUTCH AND TRANSMISSION

The case contains three sets of blades. One set is attached directly to the case. This set forms the torus or pump. Another set is directly connected to the output shaft, and forms the turbine. The third set is mounted on a hub which, in turn, is mounted on a stationary shaft through a one-way clutch. This third set is known as the stator.

A pump, which is driven by the converter hub at engine speed, keeps the torque converter full of transmission fluid at all times. Fluid flows continuously through the unit to provide cooling.

The torus is turning faster than the turbine. It picks up fluid at the center of the converter and, through centrifugal force, slings it outward. Since the other edge of the converter moves faster than the portions at the center, the fluid picks up speed.

The fluid then enters the outer edge of the turbine blades. It then travels back toward the center of the converter case along the turbine blades. In impinging upon the turbine blades, the fluid loses the energy picked up in the torus.

If the fluid were now to immediately be returned directly into the torus, both halves of the converter would have to turn at approximately the same speed at all times, and torque input and output would both be the same.

In flowing through the torus and turbine, the fluid picks up two types of flow, or flow in two separate directions. It flows through the turbine blades, and it spins with the engine. The stator, whose blades are stationary when the vehicle is being accelerated at low speeds, converts one type of flow into another. Instead of allowing the fluid to flow straight back into the torus, the stator's curved blades turn the fluid almost 90° toward the direction of rotation of the engine. Thus the fluid does not flow as fast toward the torus, but is already spinning when the torus picks it up. This has the effect of allowing the torus to turns much faster than the turbine. This difference in speed may be compared to the difference in speed between the smaller and larger gears in any gear train. The result is that engine power output is higher, and engine torque is multiplied.

As the speed of the turbine increases, the fluid spins faster and faster in the direction of engine rotation. As a result, the ability of the stator to redirect the fluid flow is reduced. Under cruising conditions, the stator is eventually forced to rotate on its one-way clutch in the direction of engine rotation. Under these conditions, the torque converter begins to behave almost like a solid shaft, with the torus and turbine speeds being almost equal.

THE PLANETARY GEARBOX

The ability of the torque converter to multiply engine torque is limited. Also, the unit tends to be more efficient when the turbine is rotating at relatively high speeds. Therefore, a planetary gearbox is used to carry the power output the turbine to the driveshaft to make the most efficient use of the converter.

Planetary gears function very similarly to conventional transmission gears. However, their construction is different in that three elements make up one gear system, and in that all three elements are different from one another. The three elements are: an outer gear that is shaped like a hoop, with teeth cut into the inner surface; a sun gear, mounted on a shaft and located at the very center of the outer gear; and a set of three planet gears, held by pins in a ring-like planet carrier and meshing with both the sun gear and the outer gear. Either the outer gear or the sun gear may be held stationary, providing more than one possible torque multiplication factor for each set of gears. Also, if all three gears are forced to rotate at the same speed, the gearset forms, in effect, a solid shaft.

Most modern automatics use the planetary gears to provide either a single reduction ratio of about 1.8:1, or two reduction gears; a low of about 2.5:1, and an intermediate of about 1.5:1. Bands and clutches are used to hold various portions of the gearsets to the transmission case or to the shaft on which they are mounted. Shifting is accomplished, then, by changing the portion of each planetary gearset which is held to the transmission case or to the shaft.

THE SERVOS AND ACCUMULATORS

The servos are hydraulic pistons and cylinders. They resemble the hydraulic actuators used on many familiar machines, such as bulldozers. Hydraulic fluid enters the cylinder, under pressure, and forces the piston to move to engage the band or clutches.

The accumulators are used to cushion the engagement of the servos. The transmission fluid must pass through the accumulator on the way to the servo. The accumulator housing contains a thin piston which is sprung away from the discharge passage of the accu-

250 CLUTCH AND TRANSMISSION

mulator. When fluid passes through the accumulator on the way to the servo, it must move the piston against spring pressure, and this action smooths out the action of the servo.

THE HYDRAULIC CONTROL SYSTEM

The hydraulic pressure used to operate the servos comes from the main transmission oil pump. This fluid is channeled to the various servos through the shift valves. There is generally a manual shift valve which is operated by the transmission selector lever and an automatic shift valve for each automatic upshift the transmission provides: i.e., two-speed automatics have a low-high shift valve, while three-speeds will have a 1–2 valve, and a 2–3 valve.

There are two pressures which effect the operation of these valves. One is the governor pressure which is affected by vehicle speed. The other is the modulator pressure which is affected by intake manifold vacuum or throttle position. Governor pressure rises with an increase in vehicle speed, and modulator pressure rises as the throttle is opened wider. By responding to these two pressures, the shift valves cause the upshift points to be delayed with increased throttle opening to make the best use of the engine's power output.

Most transmissions also make use of an auxiliary circuit for downshifting. This circuit may be actuated by the throttle linkage or the vacuum line which actuates the modulator, or by a cable or solenoid. It applies pressure to a special downshift surface on the shift valve or valves.

The transmission modulator also governs the line pressure, used to actuate the servos. In this way, the clutches and bands will be actuated with a force matching the torque output of the engine.

There are two basic automatic transmissions. The first is the two-speed Powerglide which was available until mid-1973. The second type is the three-speed Turbo Hydra-Matic, which is available in four load capacities, Turbo Hydra-Matic 200, 250, 350, and 400.

Identification

The four types of pan gaskets used on the automatic transmissions used in the Camaro are pictured below for ready identification.

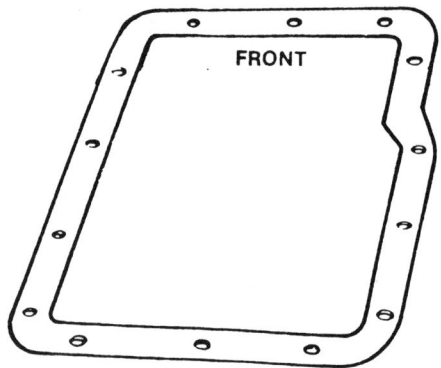

GM Powerglide

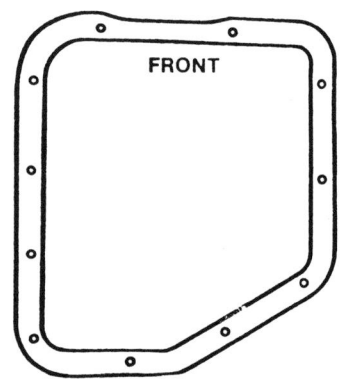

GM Turbo Hydra-Matic 200

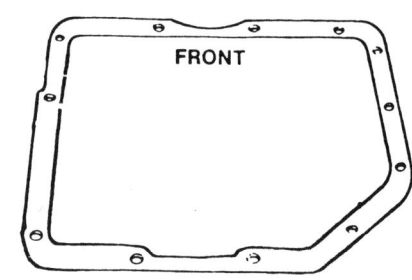

GM Turbo Hydra-Matic 250, 350, 375B

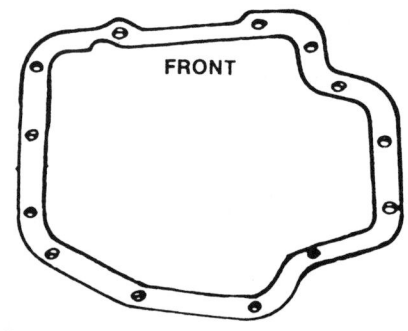

GM Turbo Hydra-Matic 400

CLUTCH AND TRANSMISSION

Pan Removal and Installation, Fluid and Filter Change

The fluid should be changed with the transmission warm. A 20 minute drive at highway speeds should accomplish this.

1. Raise and support the vehicle, preferably in a level attitude.
2. With Turbo Hydra-Matic 250 or 350, support the transmission and remove the support crossmember.
3. Place a large pan under the transmission pan. Remove all the front and side pan bolts. Loosen the rear bolts about four turns.
4. Pry the pan loose and let it drain.
5. Remove the pan and gasket. Clean the pan thoroughly with solvent and air dry it. Be very careful not to get any lint from rags in the pan.
6. Remove the strainer to valve body screws, the strainer, and the gasket. Most 350 transmissions will have a throw-away filter instead of a strainer. On the 400 transmission, remove the filter retaining bolt, filter, and intake pipe O-ring.
7. If there is a strainer, clean it in solvent and air dry.
8. Install the new filter or cleaned strainer with a new gasket. Tighten the screws to 12 ft. lbs. On the 400, install a new intake pipe O-ring and a new filter, tightening the retaining bolt to 10 ft. lbs.
9. Install the pan with a new gasket. Tighten the bolts evenly to 12 ft. lbs. (8 for Powerglide and Torque Drive).
10. Lower the car and add the proper amount of DEXRON® or DEXRON® II automatic transmission fluid through the dipstick tube.
11. Start the engine in Park and let it idle. Do not race the engine. Shift into each shift lever position, shift back into Park, and check the fluid level on the dipstick. The level should be ¼ in. below ADD. Be very careful not to overfill. Recheck the level after the car has been driven long enough to thoroughly warm up the transmission. Add fluid as necessary. The level should then be at FULL.

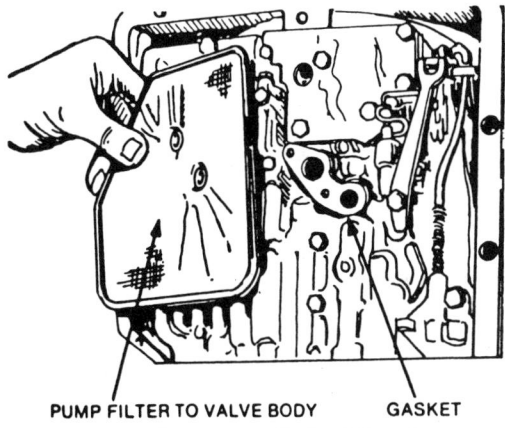

Removing the filter on the Turbo 350

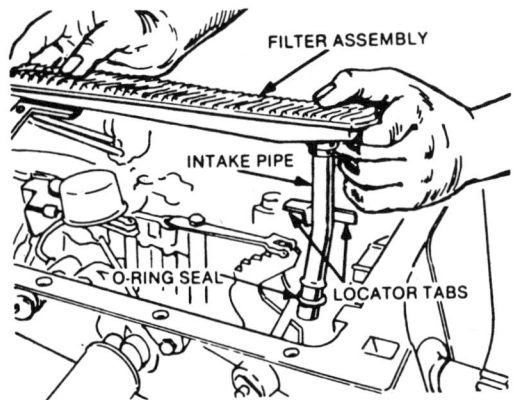

Removing the filter, intake pipe and O-ring on the 400

Shift Linkage Adjustment
POWERGLIDE COLUMN SHIFT

1. The shift tube and lever assembly must be free in the mast jacket.
2. Lift the selector lever toward the steering wheel and allow the selector lever to be positioned in Drive by the transmission detent.
3. Release the selector lever. The lever should be prevented from engaging low, unless the lever is lifted.
4. Lift the selector lever toward the steering wheel and allow the lever to be positioned in Neutral by the transmission detent.
5. Release the selector lever. The selector lever should now be kept from engaging Reverse unless the lever is lifted. If the linkage is adjusted correctly, the selector lever should be prevented from moving beyond both the neutral detent and the Drive detent unless the lever is lifted to pass over the mechanical stop in the steering column.

If adjustment is necessary, perform the following steps:

6. Adjust the linkage by loosening the adjustment clamp at the cross-shaft. Place the transmission lever in Drive by rotating the lever counterclockwise to the Low detent, and then clockwise one detent to Drive.

252 CLUTCH AND TRANSMISSION

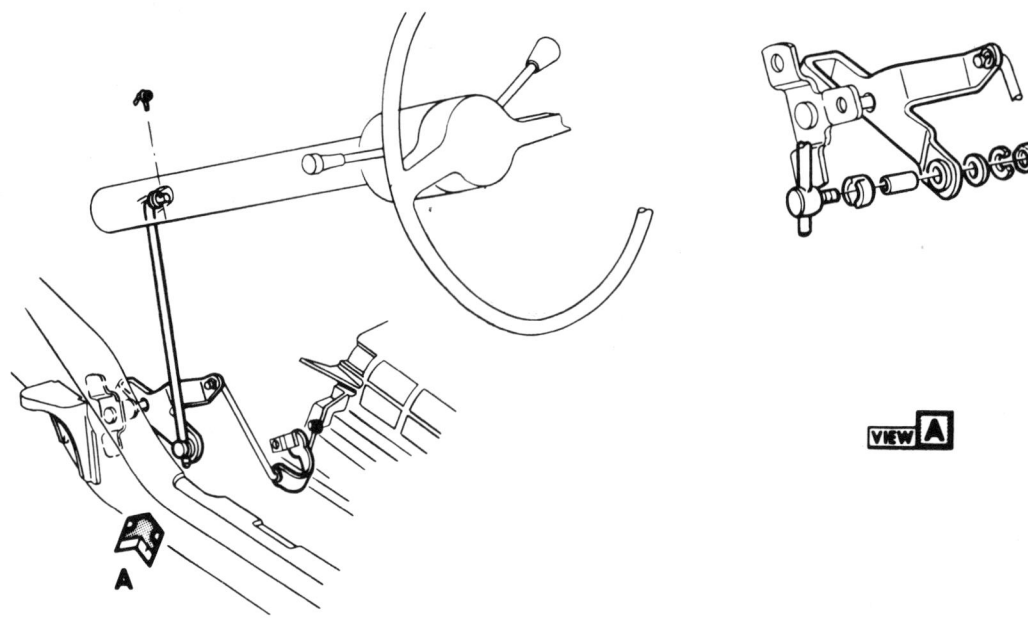

Column shift linkage adjustment—1967-69 Powerglide

7. Place the selector lever in Drive and remove any free-play by holding the cross-shaft up and pulling the shift rod downward.
8. Tighten the clamp and check the adjustment.

On 1969-73 cars, carry out the following additional steps:

9. Place the shift lever in Park and the ignition switch in lock. Loosen the backdrive rod clamp nut. Remove any lash in the column and tighten the clamp nut.
10. When the selector lever is in Park, the ignition key should move freely into lock. Lock position should be obtainable only when the transmission is in Park.

POWERGLIDE FLOOR SHIFT—1967

1. Loosen the adjustment nuts at the swivel. Place the transmission lever in the Drive position by moving it counterclockwise to the Low detent, and then clockwise one detent position to Drive.
2. Place the floorshift lever in Drive. Hold the floorshift unit lower operating lever forward against the shift lever detent.
3. Place a 0.094 in. spacer between the rear nut and the swivel. Tighten the rear nut against the spacer.
4. Remove the spacer and tighten the front nut against the swivel, locking the swivel between the nuts.

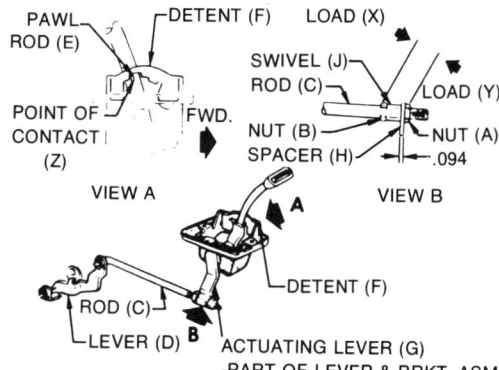

Floor shift linkage adjustment—1967 Powerglide

POWERGLIDE FLOOR SHIFT—1968-73

1968 and later cars use a cable-type shift linkage.

1. Place the shift lever in Drive.
2. Disconnect the cable from the transmission lever. Place the transmission lever in Drive by rotating the lever counterclockwise to the Low detent, and then clockwise one detent to Drive.
3. Measure the distance from the rearward face of the attaching bracket to the center of the cable attaching pin. If this distance is not 5.5 in., loosen and move the cable end stud nut to obtain the correct measurement.

NOTE: *1969 and later models require an additional backdrive adjustment.*

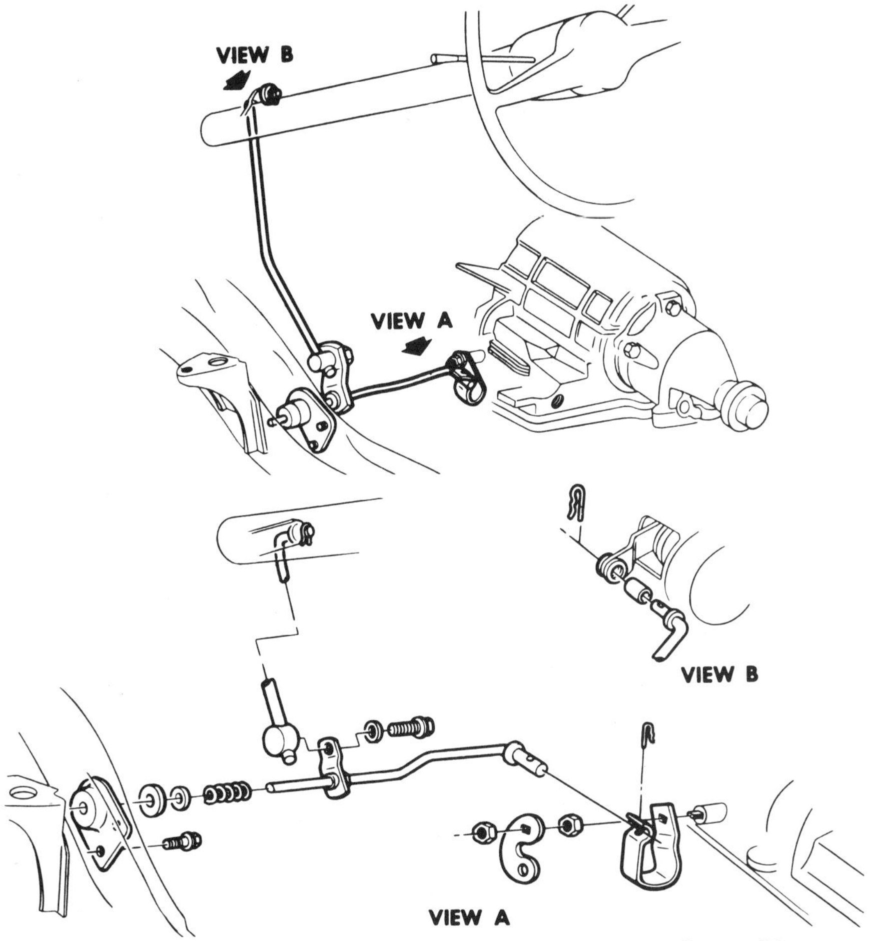

CLUTCH AND TRANSMISSION

Column shift linkage adjustment—1970 and later Powerglide

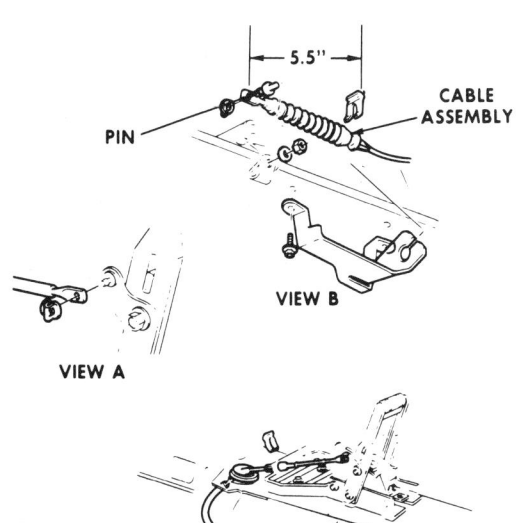

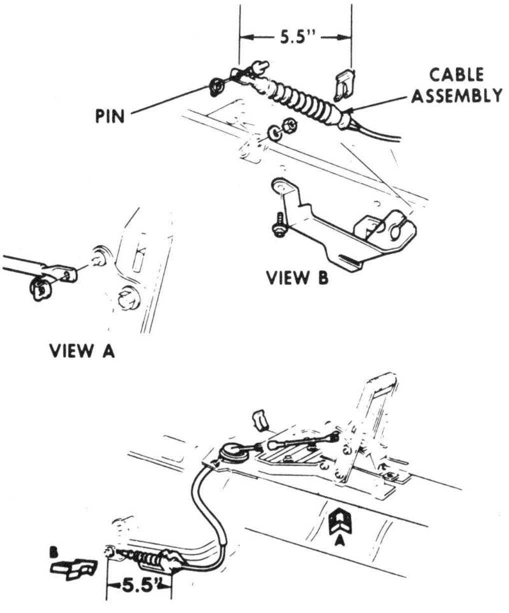

Floor shift linkage adjustment—1968-72 Powerglide

4. Place the shift lever in Park and the ignition switch in the Lock position.
5. Loosen and adjust the backdrive rod.
6. With the selector lever in Park, the ignition key should move freely into the Lock position. Lock position should not be obtainable in any transmission position other than Park.

TURBO HYDRA-MATIC COLUMN AND FLOOR SHIFT LINKAGE ADJUSTMENT THROUGH 1974

Linkages used on Turbo Hydra-Matic transmissions are similar to those used on Powerglides. Adjustments are the same, except that the transmission lever is adjusted to Drive by moving the lever clockwise to the Low detent, and then counterclockwise two detent positions to Drive.

CLUTCH AND TRANSMISSION

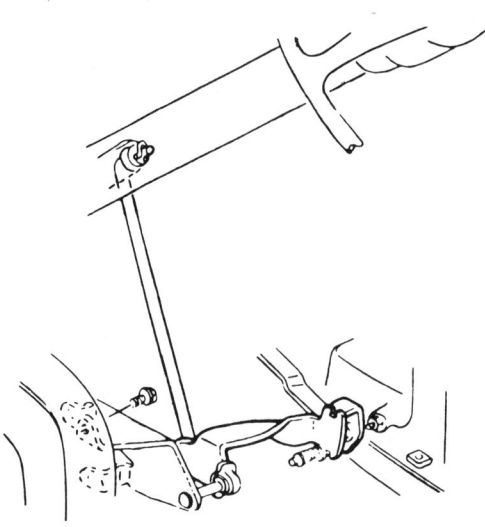

Column shift linkage components—Turbo Hydra-matic

COLUMN SHIFT (EXCEPT TURBO HYDRA-MATIC 200)

1. Loosen the swivel at the lower end of the rod that comes from the column.

2. On 1973 and later models, set the transmission lever in the Neutral detent by turning the lever counterclockwise to the L1 detent, then clockwise three positions. On models through 1972, set the lever in the Drive detent by turning the lever counterclockwise to the L1 detent, then clockwise two positions.

3. Put the column lever in Neutral for 1973 and later models, and in Drive for models through 1972. The important thing here is not where the indicator points but that the lever be in the correct position.

4. Tighten the swivel. Readjust the neutral start switch as necessary.

5. Check that the key cannot be removed and that the wheel is not locked with the key in RUN. Check that the key can be removed in LOCK with the lever in Park, and that the steering wheel is locked.

TURBO HYDRA-MATIC 200

1. Remove the screw and washer from the swivel assembly on the rod which activates the transmission shift lever.

2. Put the transmission shift lever in neutral by turning it counterclockwise to L1 detent and then clockwise three detent positions. Put the transmission selector lever in neutral as determined by the mechanical stop in the steering column assembly—do not use the indicator pointer.

3. Turn the swivel until it lines up directly with the hole in the shift lever, and install screw and washer. You should not have to force the transmission lever to move in either direction to install the screw.

4. Adjust the transmission indicator pointer and neutral start switch.

5. Check that the key cannot be removed from the "run" position if the transmission selector is in "Reverse" and that the key can be removed with the selector in "Park." Make sure the lever will not move from "Park" position with key out of ignition.

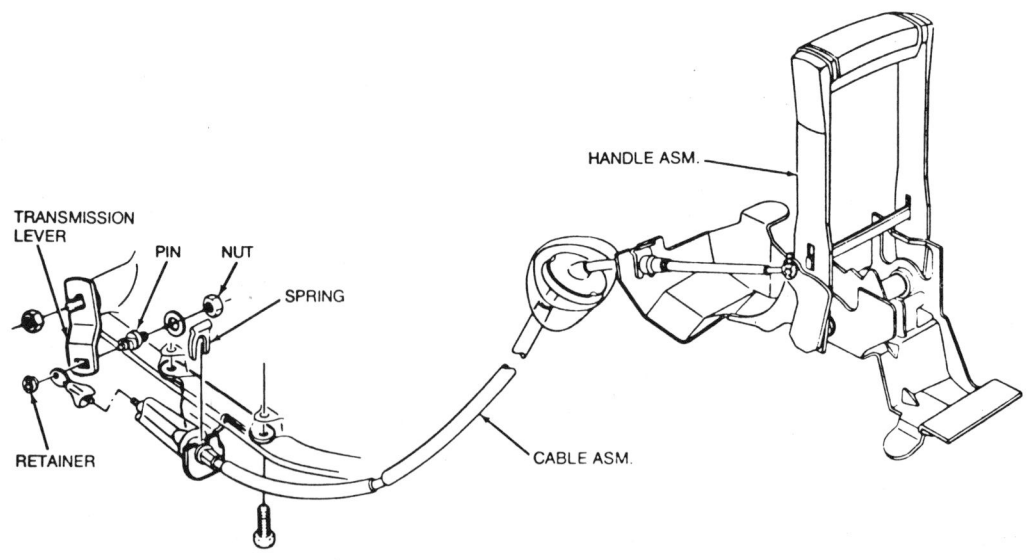

Floor shift linkage components—Turbo Hydra-matic

CLUTCH AND TRANSMISSION 255

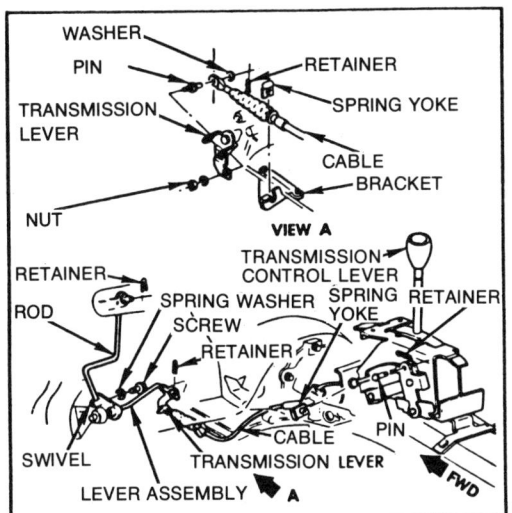

Floor shift linkage adjustment—1973 and later Turbo Hydra-matic

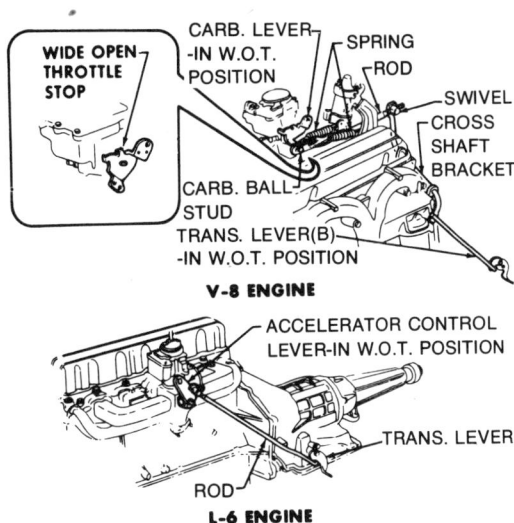

Throttle valve linkage adjustment (© Chevrolet Motor Division)

1975 AND LATER CARS WITH CABLE LINKAGE

1. Loosen the swivel at the lower end of the rod that comes from the steering column.
2. Loosen the pin at the transmission end of the cable.
3. Set the floorshift lever in the Drive detent.
4. Set the transmission lever in the Drive detent by moving it counterclockwise to the L1 detent, then clockwise three detent positions.
5. Tighten the nut on the pin at the transmission end of the cable.
6. Put the floorshift lever in Park and the ignition switch in LOCK.
7. Pull down lightly on the rod from the column and tighten its clamp nut.

Throttle Valve Linkage Adjustment

POWERGLIDE 1967–73 6 CYLINDER

1. Depress the accelerator pedal.
2. The bellcrank on 6 cylinder engines must be at the wide open throttle position.
3. The dash lever at the firewall must be $1/64$–$1/16$ in. off its lever stop.
4. The transmission lever must be against the transmission internal stop.
5. Adjust the linkage to simultaneously obtain the conditions in Steps 1–4.

POWERGLIDE 1967–73 V8

1. Remove the air cleaner.
2. Disconnect the accelerator linkage at the carburetor.

3. Disconnect both return springs.
4. Pull the throttle valve upper rod forward until the transmission is through the detent.
5. Open the carburetor to the wide open throttle position. Adjust the swivel on the end of the upper throttle valve rod so that the carburetor reaches wide open throttle position at the same time that the ball stud contacts the end of the slot in the upper throttle valve rod. A tolerance of $1/32$ in. is allowable.

Detent Cable Adjustment

TURBO HYDRA-MATIC 250, 350

These transmissions utilize a downshift cable between the carburetor and the transmission.

1. Pry up on each side of the detent cable snap-lock with a small pry bar to release the

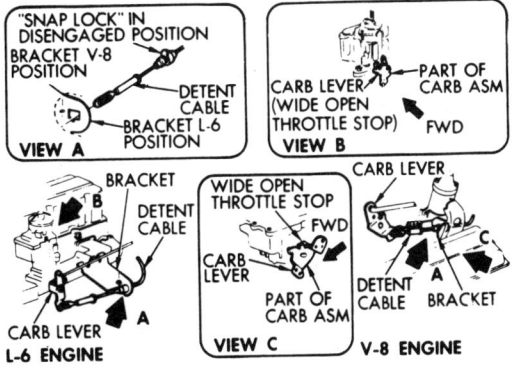

Detent cable adjustment—Turbo Hydra-matic 350 (250 similar)

CLUTCH AND TRANSMISSION

lock. On cars equipped with a retaining screw, loosen the detent cable screw.

2. Squeeze the locking tabs and disconnect the snap-lock assembly from the throttle bracket.

3. Place the carburetor lever in the wide open throttle position. Make sure that the lever is against the wide open stop. On cars with Quadrajet carburetors, disengage the secondary lock-out before placing the lever in the wide open position.

NOTE: *The detent cable must be pulled through the detent position.*

4. With the carburetor lever in the wide open position, push the snap-lock on the cable or else tighten the retaining screw.

NOTE: *Do not lubricate the detent cable.*

1973 AND LATER

The detent cable on these models adjusts itself the first time the accelerator pedal is pushed to the floor.

Detent Switch Adjustment

Turbo Hydra-Matic 400 transmissions are equipped with an electrical detent, or downshift switch operated by the throttle linkage.

1968

1. Place the carburetor lever in the wide open position.
2. Position the automatic choke so that it is off.
3. Fully depress the switch plunger.
4. Adjust the switch mounting to obtain a distance of 0.05 in. between the switch plunger and the throttle lever paddle.

1969 AND LATER

1. Pull the detent switch driver rearward until the hole in the switch body aligns with the hole in the driver. Insert a 0.092 in. diameter pin through the aligned holes to hold the driver in position.

2. Loosen the mounting bolt.

3. Press the switch plunger as far forward as possible. This will preset the switch for adjustment, which will occur on the first application of wide open throttle.

4. Tighten the mounting bolt and remove the pin.

Neutral Safety Switch Replacement

The neutral safety switch prevents the engine from being started in any transmission position except Neutral or Park. The switch is located on the upper side of the steering column under the instrument panel on column shift cars, and inside the shift console on floor shift models.

1. Remove the console for access on floor shift models.
2. Disconnect the electrical connectors.
3. Remove the neutral switch.
4. Place 1967–70 column shift lever models in Drive, and 1971 and later models in neutral. Locate the lever tang against the transmission selector plate on column shift models. Place 1967 through early 1972 floor shift models in Drive, and mid-1972 and later models in Park.
5. Align the slot in the contact support with the hole in the switch. Insert a 3/32 place. The switch is now aligned in Drive position.

NOTE: *1973 and later neutral safety switches have a shear-pin installed to aid in proper switch alignment so that insertion of a pin is unnecessary. Moving the shift lever from Neutral shears the pin.*

6. Place the contact support drive slot over the drive tang. Install the switch mounting screws.
7. Remove the aligning pin. Connect the electrical wiring, and replace the console.
8. Set the parking brake and hold your foot on the service brake pedal. Check to see that the engine will start only in Park or Neutral.

Band Adjustments

There are no band adjustments possible or required for the Turbo Hydra-Matic 350 or 400.

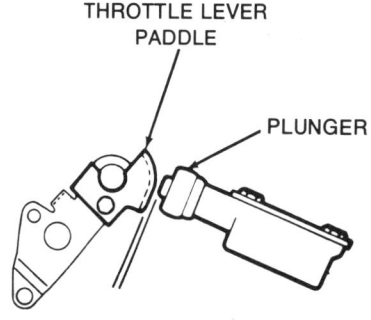

Detent switch Adjustment—1968–72 Turbo Hydra-Matic 400 (© Chevrolet Motor Division)

CLUTCH AND TRANSMISSION

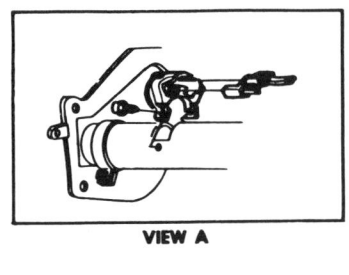
VIEW A

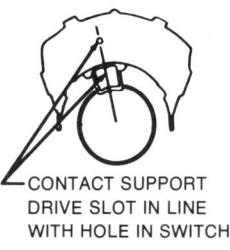
CONTACT SUPPORT DRIVE SLOT IN LINE WITH HOLE IN SWITCH

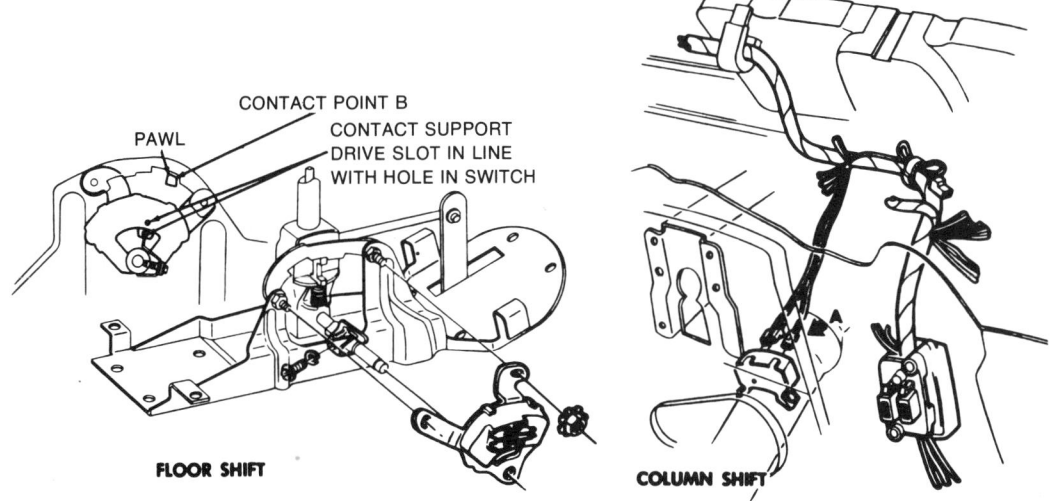

Typical neutral safety switch installation (© Chevrolet Motor Division)

LOW BAND—POWERGLIDE AND TORQUE DRIVE

The low band must be adjusted at the first required fluid change or whenever there is slippage.

1. Position the shift lever in Neutral.
2. Remove the protective cap from the adjusting screw on the left side of the transmission.
3. Loosen the locknut ¼ turn and hold it with a wrench during the entire adjusting procedure.
4. Tighten the adjusting nut to 70 in. lbs, using a 7/32 allen wrench.
5. Back off the adjusting nut *exactly* three turns for a band used less than 6,000 miles. Back off *exactly* four turns for a band used 6,000 miles or more.
6. Torque the locknut to 15 ft lbs and replace the cap.

INTERMEDIATE BAND—TURBO HYDRA-MATIC 250

The intermediate band must be adjusted with every required fluid change or whenever there is slippage.

1. Position the shift lever in Neutral.
2. Loosen the locknut on the right side of the transmission and tighten the adjusting screw to 30 in. lbs.
3. Back the screw out three turns and then tighten the locknut to 15 ft. lbs.

Drive Train

DRIVELINE

Driveshaft and U-Joints

The driveshaft (propeller shaft) is a long steel tube that transmits engine power from the transmission to the rear axle assembly. It is connected to, and revolves with, the transmission output shaft (remember, the transmission shaft is connected to and revolves with the engine crankshaft) whenever the transmission is put into gear. With the transmission in neutral, the driveshaft does not move. Located at each end of the driveshaft is a flexible joint that rotates with the shaft. These flexible joints, known as U-joints (universal joints) perform an important function. The rear axle assembly moves with the car. It moves up and down with every bump or dip in the road. The driveshaft by itself is a rigid tube incapable of bending. When combined with the flexing capabilities of the U-joints, however, it can do so. A slip joint is coupled to the front of the driveshaft by a universal joint. This U-joint allows the yoke (slip joint) to move up and down with the car. The yoke is a cylinder containing splines that slides over and meshes with the splines on the transmission output shaft. When the rear axle moves up and down, the yoke slides back and forth a small amount on the transmission shaft. Therefore, it combines with the U-joints in allowing the driveshaft to move with the movements of the car. The rear universal joint is secured to a companion flange which is attached to, and revolves with, the rear axle drive pinion.

A U-joint consists of a cross piece (trunnion) and, on each of the four ends, a dust seal and a series of needle bearings that fit into a bearing cup. Each U-joint connects one yoke with another and the bearings allow the joints to revolve within each yoke. A Camaro U-joint is secured to the yoke in one of two ways. Dana and Cleveland shafts use a conventional snap-ring to hold each bearing

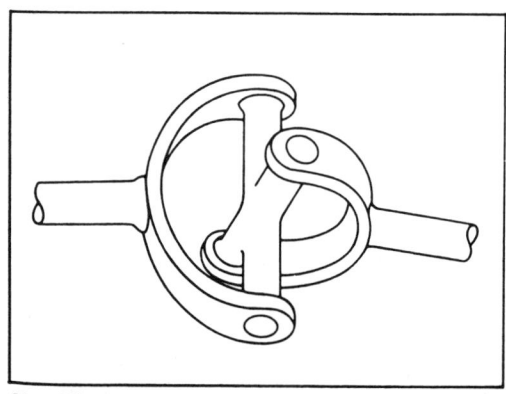

Simplified example of a universal joint (© Chevrolet Motor Division)

DRIVE TRAIN

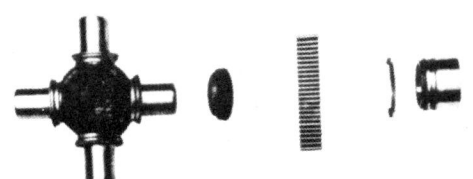

Driveshaft trunnion (Saginaw) (© Chevrolet Motor Division)

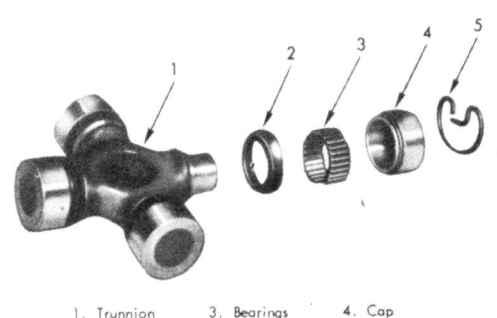

1. Trunnion 3. Bearings 4. Cap
2. Seal   5. Snap Ring

Driveshaft trunnion (Dana) (© Chevrolet Motor Division)

cup in the yoke. The snap-ring fits into a groove located in each yoke end just on top of each bearing cup. The Saginaw design shaft secures its U-joints in another way. Nylon material is injected through a small hole in the yoke and flows along a circular groove between the U-joint and the yoke, creating a synthetic snap-ring. Disassembly of the Saginaw U-joint requires the joint to be pressed from the yoke. This results in damage to the bearing cups and destruction of the nylon rings. Replacement kits include new bearing cups and conventional snap-rings to replace the original nylon rings. These replacement rings must go inboard of the yoke in contrast to outboard mounting of the Dana and Cleveland designs. Previous service to the Saginaw U-joints can be recognized by the presence of snap-rings inboard of the yoke.

Bad U-joints, requiring replacement, will produce a clunking sound when the car is put into gear. This is due to worn needle bearings or a scored trunnion end possibly caused by improper lubrication during assembly. Camaro U-joints require no periodic maintenance and therefore have no lubrication fittings. A clunking sound can also be produced by two other components. The Camaro three-speed automatic transmission has a real seal that prevents the transmission from lubricating the front slip joint. All other transmissions allow a slight lubrication of this slip joint because they contain a different type of rear seal. If a driveline clunk should develop in a Camaro with a three-speed automatic, clean the slip joint and pack it with one tablespoon of chassis lube. A similar clunk can be the result of improper rear end gear lash but, due to its complexity, should be checked only after checking the more probable causes.

Some driveshafts (generally heavy-duty applications) use a damper as part of the slip joint. This vibration damper can not be serviced separately from the slip joint. If either component goes bad, the two must be replaced as a unit.

Driveshaft

REMOVAL

1. Raise the vehicle and safely support it on jackstands. Paint a reference line from the rear end of the driveshaft to the companion flange so that they can be reassembled in the same position.
2. Disconnect the rear universal joint by removing the U-bolts, retaining straps, or the flange bolts.
3. To prevent loss of the needle bearings, tape the bearing caps to the trunnion.

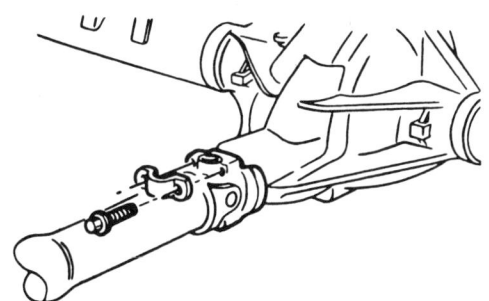

Strap-type retainer on driveshaft (© Chevrolet Motor Division)

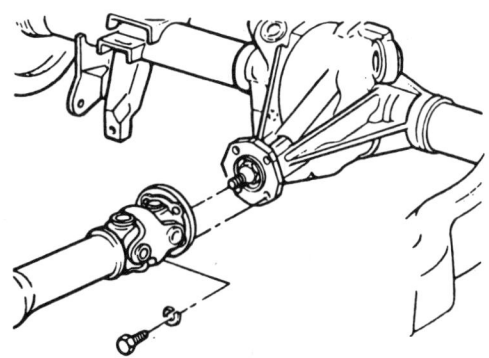

Driveshaft flange attachment (© Chevrolet Motor Division)

4. Remove the driveshaft from the transmission by sliding it rearward.

NOTE: *Do not be alarmed by oil leakage at the transmission output shaft. This oil is there to lubricate the splines of the front yoke.*

INSTALLATION

1. Check the yoke seal in the transmission case extension and replace it if necessary. See the transmission section for replacement procedures.
2. Position the driveshaft and insert the front yoke into the transmission so that the splines mesh with the splines of the transmission shaft.
3. Using reference marks made during removal, align the driveshaft with the companion flange and secure it with U-bolts or, retaining straps.

U-Joint Overhaul

1. Remove the driveshaft as explained above and remove the snap-rings from the ends of the bearing cup.
2. After removing the snap-rings, place the driveshaft on the floor and place a large diameter socket under one of the bearing cups. Tap on the bearing opposite this one with a hammer and a drift. This will push the trunnion through the yoke enough to force the bearing cup out of the yoke and into the socket. Repeat this procedure for the other bearing cups. If a hammer fails to loosen the cups, a press may be necessary.

NOTE: *A Saginaw driveshaft secures its U-joints in a different manner than the conventional snap-rings of the Dana and Cleveland designs.*

Nylon is injected through a small hole in the yoke and flows along a circular groove between the U-joint and the yoke, thus creating

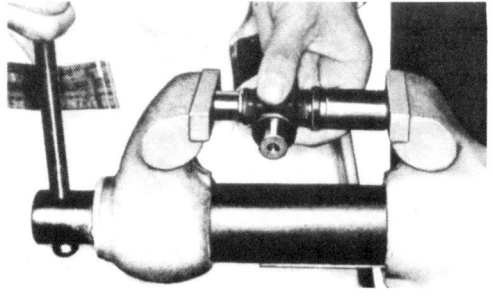

Installing U-joint trunnion seal (© Chevrolet Motor Division)

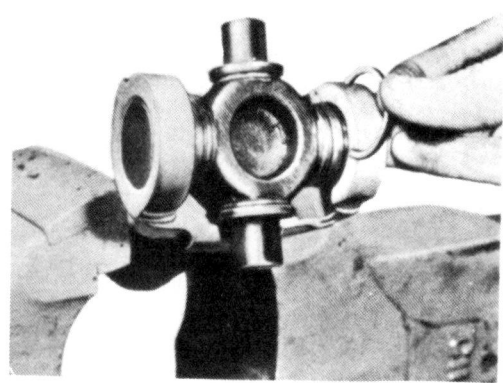

Installing trunnion snap ring (© Chevrolet Motor Division)

a synthetic snap-ring. Disassembly of this Saginaw U-joint requires the joint to be pressed from the yoke. If a press is not available, it may be carefully hammered out using the same procedure (step two) as the Dana design, although it may require more force to break the nylon ring. Either method, press or hammer, will damage the bearing cups and destroy the nylon rings. Replacement kits include new bearing cups and conventional metal snap-rings to replace the original nylon rings.

3. Thoroughly clean the entire U-joint assembly with solvent. Inspect for excessive wear in the yoke bores and on the four ends of the trunnion. The needle bearings should not be scored, broken, or loose in their cups. Bearing cups may suffer slight distortion during removal and should be replaced.
4. Pack the bearings with chassis lube (lithium base) and completely fill each trunnion end with the same lubricant.
5. Place new dust seals on the trunnions with the cavity of the seal toward the end of the trunnion. Care must be taken to avoid distortion of the seal. A suitable size socket and a vise can be used to press on the seal.
6. Insert one bearing cup about a quarter of the way into the yoke and place the trunnion into the yoke and bearing cup. Install another bearing cup, press in both cups, and install the snap-rings. Snap-rings on the Dana and Cleveland shafts must go on the outside of the yoke while the Saginaw shaft requires that the rings go on the inside of the yoke. The gap in the Saginaw rings must face toward the yoke. Once installed, the trunnion must move freely in the yoke.

NOTE: *The Saginaw shaft uses two different sizes of bearing cup at the differential end. The larger cups (the ones with the groove) fit into the driveshaft yoke.*

DRIVE TRAIN

REAR AXLE

Identification

The rear axle number is located in the right or left axle tube adjacent to the carrier. See the Rear Axle Codes chart at the end of the chapter for information on determining axle ratio from letter codes.

Axle Shaft

Axle shafts are the last link in the chain of components working to transmit engine power to the rear wheels. The splined end of each shaft meshes with the internal splines of each differential side gear. As the side gears turn, so do the axle shafts, and, since they are also connected, so do the wheels. Each shaft passes through the side gear and is locked into place by a "C" lock. As the name implies, the "C" lock is a flat, C-shaped piece of metal that fits into a groove at the end of the shaft. A round pinion shaft is wedged in between the end of the shafts. This pinion shaft prevents the shafts from sliding inward and makes the "C" locks functional by pushing them tightly against each side gear. Removing this pinion shaft allows the shafts to slide inward making the "C" locks accessible for removal. Once the "C" locks are removed, the axle shafts can be pulled from the car. The wheel end of each shaft is flanged and pressed into it are five wheel lug bolts serving to hold on the wheel. Each axle shaft is supported by an axle bearing (wheel bearing) and oil seal located within the axle shaft housing just to the outside of the brake backing plate.

REMOVAL AND INSTALLATION

1. Raise the vehicle and remove the wheels and brake drums.
2. Thoroughly clean the area around the differential carrier cover.
3. Place a drain pan under the carrier and then remove the cover.
4. Remove the differential pinion shaft lockscrew and the differential pinion shaft.
5. Push the flanged end of the axle shaft toward the center of the vehicle and remove the "C" lock from the end of the shaft.
6. Remove the axle shaft from the housing, being careful not to damage the oil seal.
7. Remove the oil seal by inserting the button end of the axle shaft behind the steel case of the oil seal. Pry the seal loose from the bore.
8. Seat the legs of the bearing puller behind the bearing. Seat a washer against the bearing and hold it in place with a nut. Use a slide hammer to pull the bearing.
9. Pack the cavity between the seal lips with wheel bearing lubricant and lubricate a new wheel bearing with same.
10. Use a suitable driver and install the bearing until it bottoms against the tube. Install the oil seal.
11. Slide the axle shaft into place. Be sure that the splines on the shaft do not damage the oil seal. Make sure that the splines engage the differential side gear.
12. Install the axle shaft, C-lock on the inner end of the axle shaft and push the shaft outward so that the C-lock seats in the differential side gear counterbore.
13. Position the differential pinion shaft

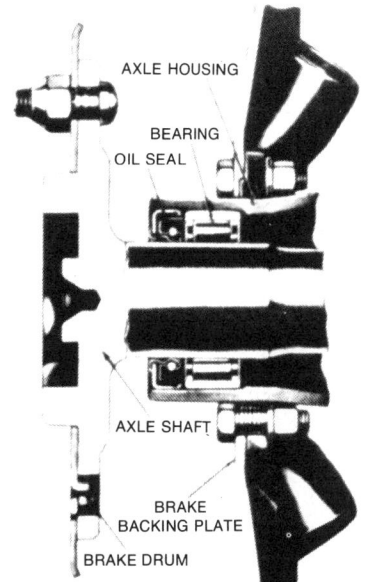

Axle housing components (© Chevrolet Motor Division)

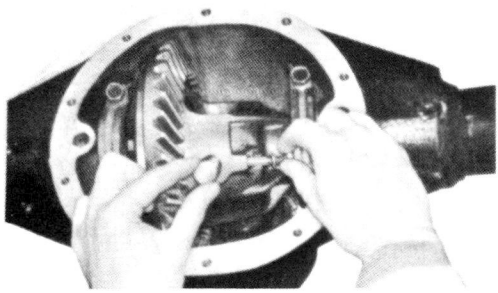

Removing differential pinion shaft (© Chevrolet Motor Division)

DRIVE TRAIN

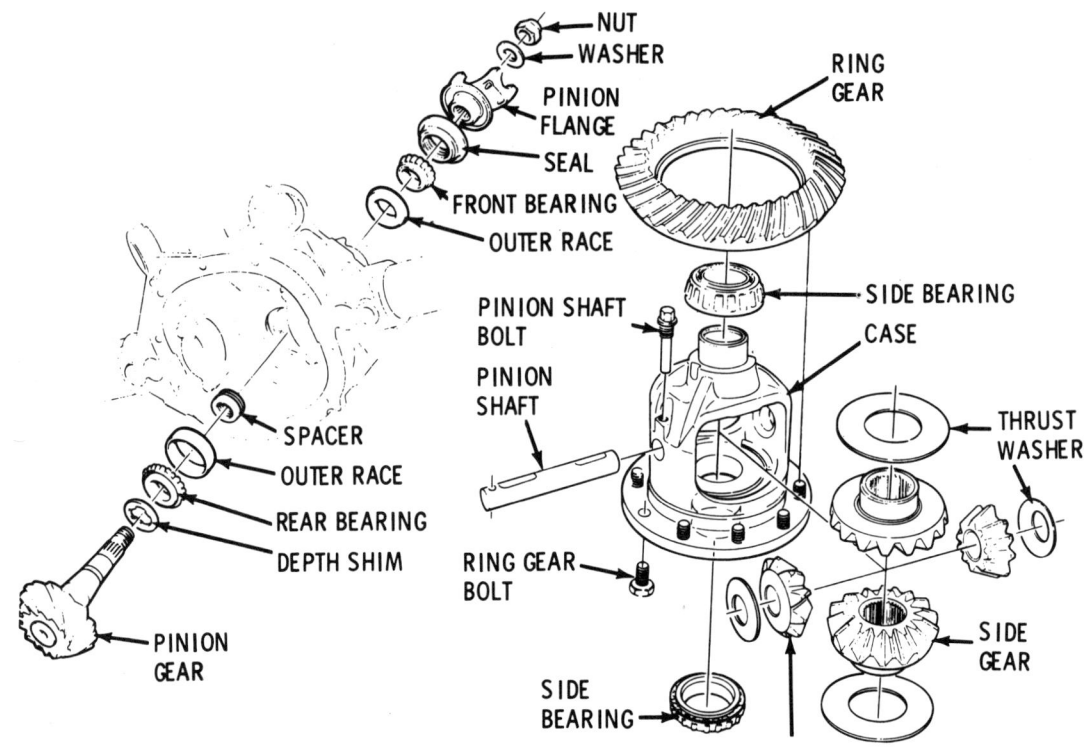

Exploded view of the rear axle

through the case and pinions, aligning the hole in the case with the hold for the lockscrew.

14. Use a new gasket and install the carrier cover. Be sure that the gasket surfaces are clean before installing the gasket and cover.

15. Fill the axle with lubricant to the bottom of the filler hole.

16. Install the brake drum and wheels and lower the car. Check for leaks and road test the car.

Rear Axle Codes

1967

(3.08 ratio)	PA
(3.36 ratio)	PB
4 Speed "350" (3.31 ratio)	PC
Positraction (3.07 ratio)	PD
Positraction (3.08 ratio)	PE
Positraction (3.31 ratio)	PF
Positraction (3.36 ratio)	PG
Positraction (3.55 ratio) (small ring gear)	PH
Positraction (3.55 ratio) (large ring gear)	PI
Positraction (3.73 ratio)	PJ
4 Speed Trans (3.55 ratio)	PK
4 Speed Close-Ratio (3.55 ratio)	PL
(3.73 ratio)	PM
w/Metallic Brakes (3.07 ratio)	PN

Rear Axle Codes (cont.)

1967

Positraction w/Metallic Brakes (3.07 ratio)	PO
w/Metallic Brakes (3.31 ratio)	PP
w/Metallic Brakes (3.55 ratio) (large ring gear)	PQ
Positraction w/Metallic Brakes (3.31 ratio)	PR
Positraction w/Metallic Brakes (3.55 ratio) (large ring gear)	PS
w/Metallic Brakes (3.73 ratio)	PT
Positraction w/Metallic Brakes (3.73 ratio)	PU
(3.07 ratio)	PV

1968

(2.56 ratio) (small ring gear)	BA
Positraction (2.56 ratio) (small ring gear)	BB
(3.36 ratio)	BC
Positraction (3.36 ratio)	BD
(2.73 ratio)	BI
(3.07 ratio)	BL
(3.55 ratio)	BN
(3.31 ratio)	BM
Positraction (2.73 ratio) (large ring gear)	BQ
(3.73 ratio)	BO
(2.73 ratio)	BP
Positraction (3.07 ratio)	BR
Positraction (3.31 ratio)	BS
Positraction (3.35 ratio)	BT
Positraction (3.37 ratio)	BU
Positraction (4.10 ratio)	BV
Positraction (4.56 ratio)	BW
Positraction (4.88 ratio)	BX
Positraction (2.73 ratio) (large ring gear)	BY

Rear Axle Codes (cont.)

1967

(2.73 ratio)	BZ
(3.08 ratio)	PA
(3.31 ratio)	PB
Positraction (3.08 ratio)	PE
Positraction (3.07 ratio)	PG
Positraction (3.55 ratio) (small ring gear)	PH
(3.55 ratio)	PK
(2.56 ratio) (large ring gear)	PN
w/Metallic Brakes Positraction (2.56 ratio) (large ring gear)	PO
(3.07 ratio)	PP
Positraction (3.31 ratio)	PR
(2.56 ratio) (large ring gear)	PY
Positraction (2.73 ratio) (small ring gear)	PX
Positraction (2.56 ratio) (large ring gear)	PZ
Camaro (3.55 ratio)	QE
(3.55 ratio) (large ring gear)	Q2
Positraction (3.55 ratio) (large ring gear)	Q3
(3.55 ratio) (small ring gear)	Q9
(3.55 ratio)	QE
w/Disc Brakes—Front and Rear (4.88 ratio)	QN
w/Disc Brakes—Front and Rear (2.56 ratio)	QS
w/Disc Brakes—Front and Rear (2.73 ratio)	QT
w/Disc Brakes—Front and Rear (3.07 ratio)	QU
w/Disc Brakes—Front and Rear (3.31 ratio)	QV
w/Disc Brakes—Front and Rear (3.55 ratio)	QW
w/Disc Brakes—Front and Rear (3.73 ratio)	QX
w/Disc Brakes—Front and Rear (4.10 ratio)	QY
w/Disc Brakes—Front and Rear (4.56 ratio)	QZ

1969

(2.56 ratio)	BA
Positraction (2.56 ratio)	BB
(3.36 ratio)	BC
Positraction (3.36 ratio)	BD
(2.73 ratio)	BI
(3.07 ratio)	BL
(3.31 ratio)	BM
(3.55 ratio)	BN
(3.73 ratio)	BO
(2.73 ratio)	BP
Positraction (2.73 ratio)	BQ
Positraction (3.07 ratio)	BR
Positraction (3.31 ratio)	BS
Positraction (3.55 ratio)	BT
Positraction (3.73 ratio)	BU
Positraction (4.10 ratio)	BV
Positraction (4.56 ratio)	BW
Positraction (4.88 ratio)	BX
(3.08 ratio)	PA
(2.56 ratio)	PB
Positraction (2.56 ratio)	PC
Positraction (3.08 ratio)	PE
Positraction (2.73 ratio)	PX
(2.56 ratio)	PY
Positraction (2.56 ratio)	PZ
Positraction (2.56 ratio)	QS
Positraction (2.73 ratio)	QT
Positraction (3.07 ratio)	QU
Positraction (3.31 ratio)	QV
Positraction (3.55 ratio)	QW

1969

Positraction (3.73 ratio)	QX
Positraction (4.10 ratio)	QY
Positraction (4.56 ratio)	QZ
Positraction (4.88 ratio)	QN

1970

(2.73 ratio)	COC
Positraction (2.73 ratio)	COD
(3.08 ratio)	COE
Positraction (3.08 ratio)	COF
(3.07 ratio)	COS
Positraction (3.07 ratio)	COT
(3.31 ratio)	COU
Positraction (3.31 ratio)	COV
Positraction (3.55 ratio)	COX
Positraction (3.73 ratio)	COZ
(4.10 ratio)	COO
(2.73 ratio)	CRX
Positraction (2.73 ratio)	CRY
Positraction (3.08 ratio)	CRI

1971

(3.08)	GX
Positraction (3.08)	GY
(2.73)	GZ
Positraction (2.73)	CA
(4.10)	CB
(3.73)	CG
(3.42)	CK
Positraction (3.42)	CJ

1972

(3.08)	GX
Positraction (3.08)	GY
(2.73)	GZ
Positraction (2.73)	CA
(4.10)	CB
(3.73)	CG
(3.42)	CK
Positraction (3.42)	CJ

1973–74

(3.42)	CL
Positraction (3.42)	CM
(3.08)	GX
Positraction (3.08)	GY
(2.73)	GZ
Positraction (2.73)	CA
(4.10)	CB
(3.73)	CG

1975–77

(2.56)	PH or PT
(2.73)	PA, PU, 2PA, 2PU
(3.08)	PC, PW, 2PC, 2PW
(3.42)	PZ or PY

NOTE: *On 1978 and later axles, the axle numerical ratio is indicated in place of a code.*

Suspension and Steering

FRONT SUSPENSION

The front suspension is designed to allow each wheel to compensate for changes in the road surface level without appreciably affecting the opposite wheel. Each wheel is independently connected to the frame by a steering knuckle, ball joint assemblies, and upper and lower control arms. The control arms are specifically designed and positioned to allow the steering knuckles to move in a prescribed three dimensional arc. The front wheels are held in proper relationship to each other by two tie rods which are connected to steering arms on the knuckles and to an intermediate rod.

Coil chassis springs are mounted between the spring housings on the frame or front end sheet metal and the lower control arms. Ride control is provided by double, direct acting, shock absorbers mounted inside the coil springs and attached to the lower control arms by bolts and nuts. The upper portion of each shock absorber extends through the upper control arm frame bracket and is secured with two grommets, two grommet retainers, and a nut.

Side roll of the front suspension is controlled by a spring steel stabilizer shaft. It is mounted in rubber bushings which are held to the frame side rails by brackets. The ends of the stabilizer are connected to the lower control arms by link bolts isolated by rubber grommets.

The upper control arm is attached to a cross shaft through isolating rubber bushings. The cross shaft, in turn, is bolted to frame brackets.

A ball joint assembly is riveted to the outer end of the upper arm. It is pre-loaded by a rubber spring to insure proper seating of the ball in the socket. The upper ball joint is attached to the steering knuckle by a torque prevailing nut.

The inner ends of the lower control arm have pressed-in bushings. Bolts, passing through the bushings, attach the arm to the frame. The lower ball joint assembly is a press fit in the arm and attaches to the steering knuckle with a torque prevailing nut.

Rubber grease seals are provided at ball socket assemblies to keep dirt and moisture from entering the joint and damaging bearing surfaces.

Shock Absorbers
TESTING

Visually inspect the shock absorber. If there is evidence of leakage and the shock absorber is covered with oil, the shock is defective and should be replaced.

SUSPENSION AND STEERING

If there is no sign of excessive leakage (a small amount of weeping is normal) bounce the car at one corner by pressing down on the fender or bumper and releasing. When you have the car bouncing as much as you can, release the fender or bumper. The car should stop bouncing after the first rebound. If the bouncing continues past the center point of the bounce more than once, the shock absorbers are worn and should be replaced.

REMOVAL AND INSTALLATION

1. Raise the car, and with an open end wrench hold the upper stem of the shock absorber from turning. Remove the upper stem retaining nut, retainer and grommet.
2. Remove the two bolts retaining the lower shock absorber pivot to the lower control arm and then pull the shock out through the bottom of the control arm.
3. With the lower retainer and the rubber grommet in place over the upper stem, install the shock (fully extended) back through the lower control arm.
4. Install the upper grommet, retainer and nut onto the upper stem.
5. Hold the upper stem from turning with an open end wrench and then tighten the retaining nut.
6. Reinstall the retainers on the lower end of the shock.

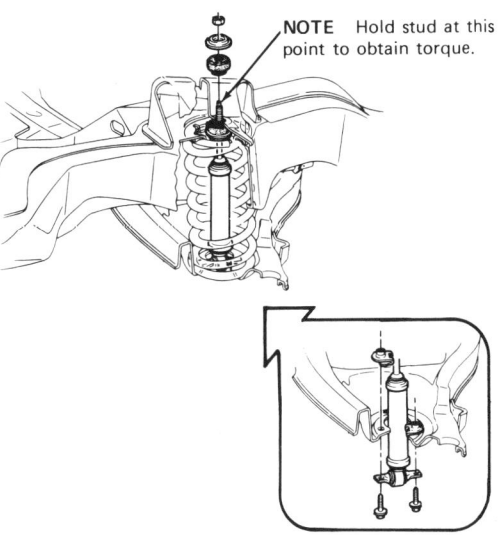

Shock absorber mounting locations

Coil Springs

CAUTION: *The coil springs are under a considerable amount of tension. Be extremely careful when removing or installing them; they can exert enough force to cause serious injury.*

REMOVAL AND INSTALLATION

1. Remove the shock absorber. Disconnect the stabilizer bar.
2. Support the car at the frame so the control arms hang free.

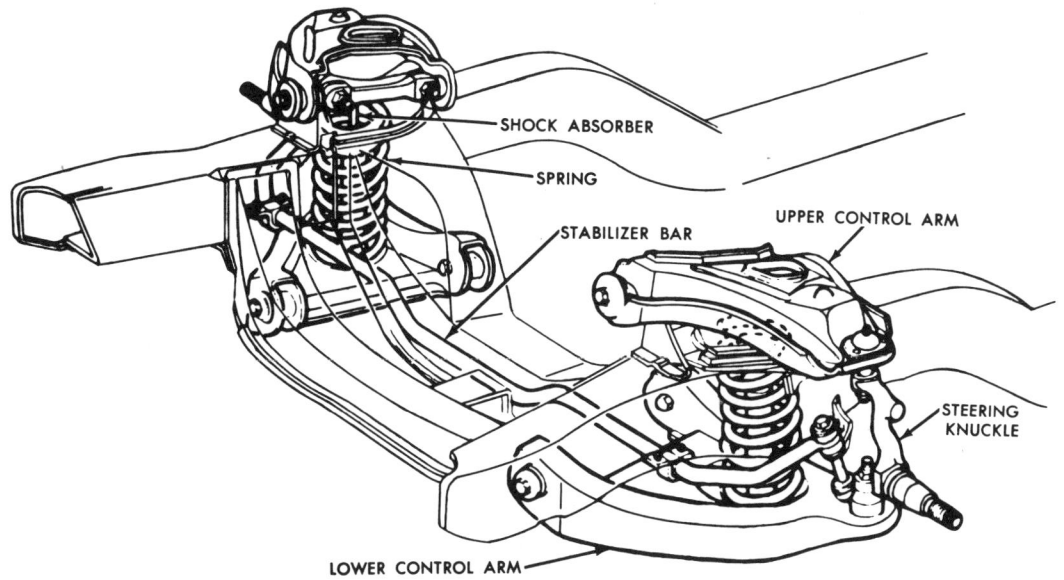

Front suspension (© Chevrolet Motor Division)

266 SUSPENSION AND STEERING

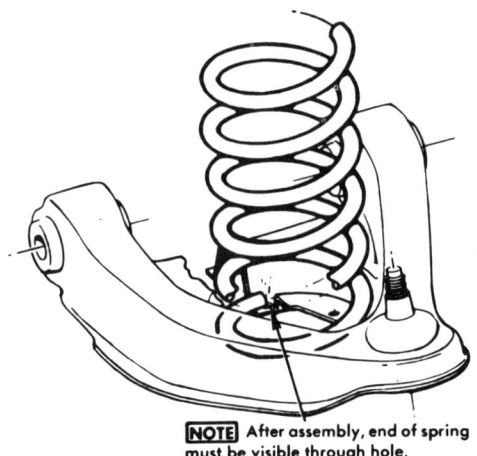

NOTE: After assembly, end of spring must be visible through hole.

Positioning coil spring (© Chevrolet Motor Division)

3. Support the inner end of the control arm with a floor jack. (Dealers have a device that cradles the inner bushings).
4. Raise the jack enough to take the tension off the lower control arm pivot bolts.
5. Chain the spring to the lower control arm.
6. Remove first the rear, then the front pivot bolt.
7. Cautiously lower the jack until all spring tension is released.
8. Note the way in which the spring is installed in relation to the drain holes on the control arm and remove it.
9. On installation, position the spring to the control arm and raise it into place.
10. Install the pivot bolts and torque the nuts to 100 ft. lbs. for all 1974 and later models. Torque all models through 1973 to 85 ft. lbs.
11. Replace the shock absorber and stabilizer bar.

Ball Joints

INSPECTION

NOTE: *Before performing this inspection, make sure that the wheel bearings are adjusted correctly and that the control arm bushings are in good condition.*

1. Raise the car by placing the jack under the lower control arm at the spring seat.
2. Raise the car until there is a 1–2 in. clearance under the wheel.
3. Insert a bar under the wheel and pry upward. If the wheel raises more than ⅛ in., the ball joints are worn. Determine whether the upper or lower ball joint is worn by visual inspection while prying on the wheel.

NOTE: *Due to the distribution of forces in the suspension, the lower ball joint is usually the defective joint. Because of this, 1974 and later Camaros are equipped with wear indicators on the lower ball joint. As long as the indicator extends below the ball stud seat, replacement is unnecessary.*

UPPER BALL JOINT REPLACEMENT

1967–70

1. Support the car by placing a jack under the outer end of the lower control arm.
2. Remove the wheel and tire assembly.
3. Remove the cotter pin and nut from the stud.
4. Remove the stud from the steering knuckle.
5. Cut off the ball joint rivets with a chisel.
6. It may be necessary to enlarge the stud attaching holes in the control arm to accept the larger ⁵⁄₁₆ in. bolts. Inspect and clean the tapered hole in the steering knuckle. If the hole is damaged or deformed, the knuckle *must* be replaced.
7. Install the new joint and connect the stud to the steering knuckle. When installing the stud nut, never back off on the nut to align the cotter pin holes; always tighten the nut to the next hole.
8. Replacement ball joints may not include the lube fitting. If not, install a self-threading fitting into the tapped hole.

1971–81

1. Raise the vehicle and support securely. Support the lower control arm securely. Remove the tire and wheel.
2. Remove the upper ball stud cotter pin and loosen ball stud nut *just one turn.*
3. Procure a special tool designed to press out '71 and later Chevrolet ball joints. Locate the tool between upper and lower ball joints and press the joints out of the steering knuckle. Remove the tool.
4. Remove the ball joint stud nut, and separate the joint from the steering knuckle. Lift the upper arm up and place a block of wood between the frame and the arm to support it.
5. With the control arm in the raised position, drill a hole ¼ in. deep into each rivet. Use a ⅛ in. drill bit.
6. Use a ½ in. drill bit and drill off the heads of each rivet.

SUSPENSION AND STEERING

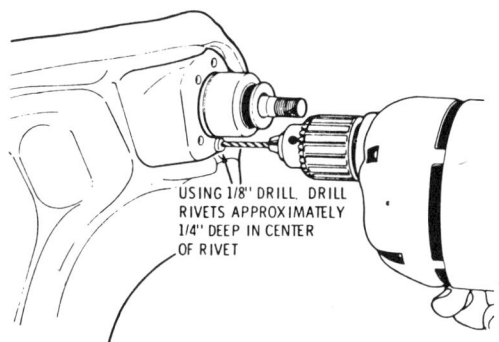

Drill the upper ball joint rivets—1971–81

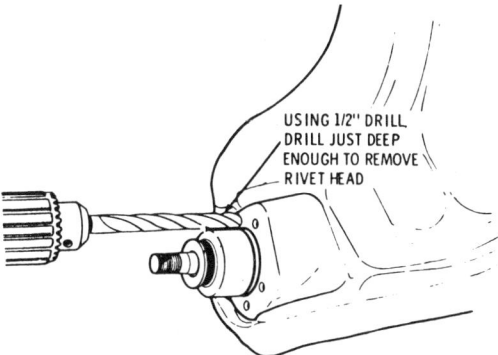

Drill the upper ball joint rivet heads—1971–81

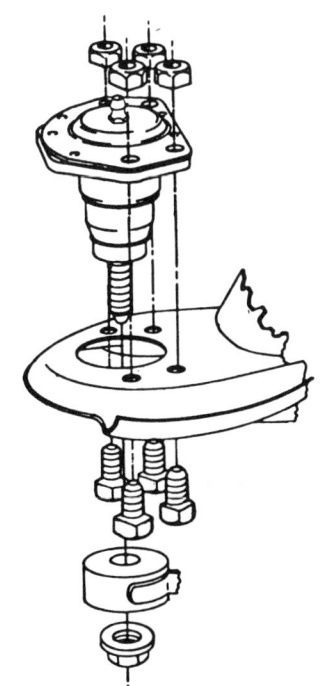

When installing the new upper ball joints, make sure that the nuts are on top (1971–81)

7. Punch out the rivets using a small punch and then remove the ball joint.

8. Install the new ball joint using fasteners that meet Chevrolet specifications. Bolts should come in from the bottom with the nuts going on top. Torque to 10 ft. lbs.

9. Turn the ball stud cotter pin hole to the fore and aft position. Remove the block of wood from between the upper control arm and frame.

10. Clean and inspect the steering knuckle hole. Replace the steering knuckle if any out of roundness is noted.

11. Insert the ballstud into the steering knuckle, and install and torque the stud nut to 60 ft. lbs. Install a new cotter pin. *If nut must be turned to align cotter pin holes, tighten it further. Do not back off!*

12. Install a lube fitting, and fill the joint with fresh grease.

13. Remove lower control arm support and lower the car.

LOWER BALL JOINT REPLACEMENT
1967–70

1. Raise the car and support securely. Support the lower control arm with a floor jack.

2. Remove the wheel. If the vehicle has disc brakes, remove the caliper assembly.

3. Remove the lower ball stud. Then, using a tool designed for such work, press the ball stud out of the steering knuckle. Wire the steering knuckle out of the way so you'll have more room.

Removing the lower ball joint with a special tool (© Chevrolet Motor Division)

268 SUSPENSION AND STEERING

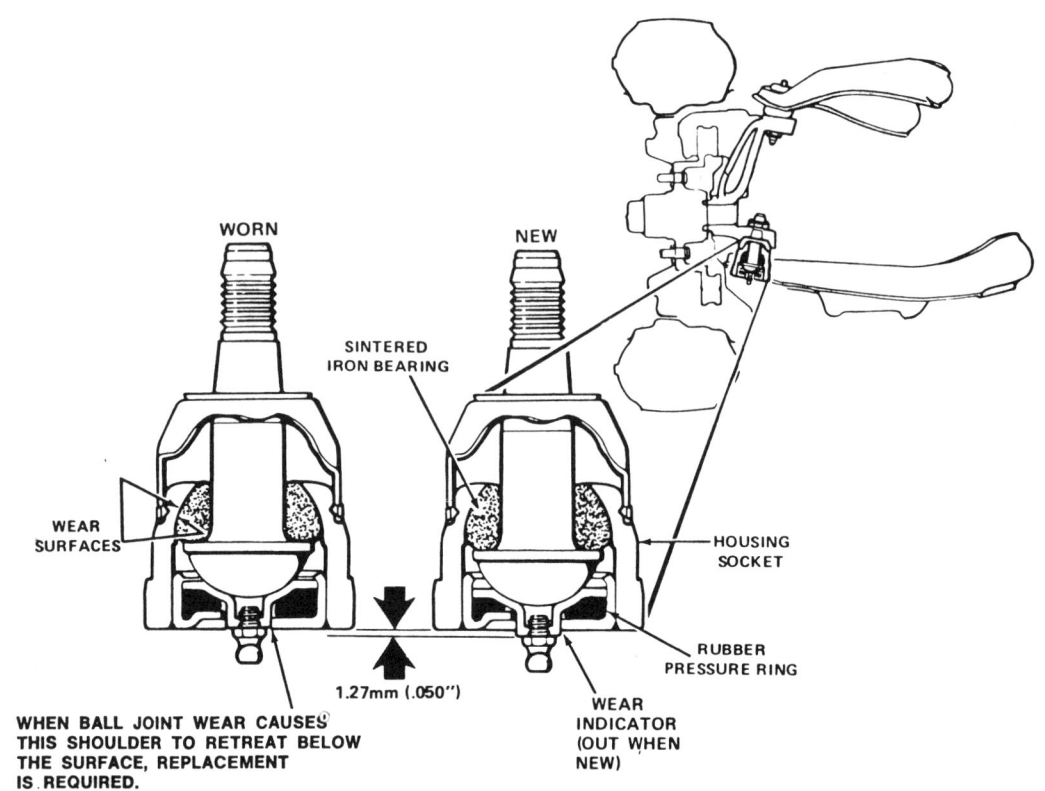

Lower ball joint wear indicator—1974 and later

4. Press the joint out of the control arm with a tool designed for that purpose.

5. Start the replacement joint into the control arm with the air vent in the rubber boot facing inboard.

6. Set the joint in the control arm, pressing it in with a tool designed for that purpose.

7. Install the stud into the steering knuckle, and install attaching nut and new cotter pin.

8. Reinstall caliper assembly (as necessary) and wheel, remove the jack supporting the control arm, and lower the car.

1971–81

NOTE: *On Camaros equipped with the wear indicating ball joint, Chevrolet recommends replacement of both upper and lower ball joints if only the lower ball joint is bad.*

1. Raise the vehicle and support it securely. Support the lower control arm with a jack.

2. Remove the lower ball stud cotter pin, and loosen the ball stud nut just one turn.

3. Install a special tool designed for such work between the two ball studs, and press the stud downward in the steering knuckle. Then, remove the stud nut.

4. Pull the tire outward and at the same time upward, with your hands on the bottom (of the tire), to free the steering knuckle from the ball stud. Then, remove the wheel.

5. Lift up on the upper control arm and place a block of wood between it and the frame. Be careful not to put any tension on the brake hose in doing this.

6. Press the ball joint out of the lower control arm with a tool made for that purpose. You may have to disconnect the tie rod at the steering knuckle to do this.

7. To install, position the new ball joint, with the vent in the rubber boot facing inward, onto the lower control arm. Press the joint fully into the control arm with a tool designed for this.

8. Turn the ball stud cotter pin hole so it is fore and aft.

9. Remove the block of wood holding the upper control arm out of the way, and inspect the tapered hole in the steering knuckle. Remove any dirt from the hole. If the hole is out of round or there is other noticeable damage, replace the entire steering knuckle.

SUSPENSION AND STEERING

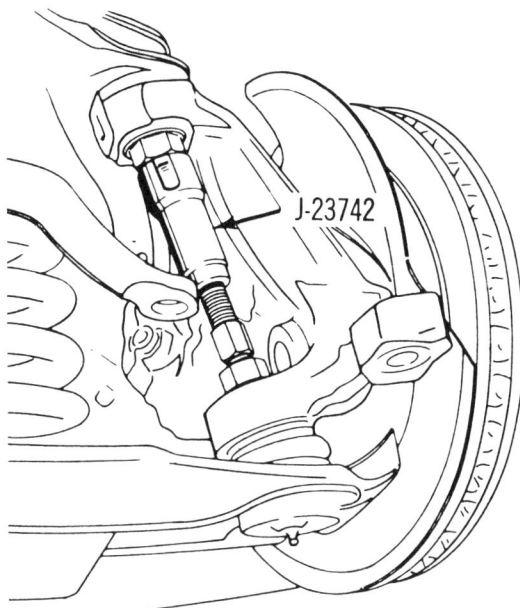

Disconnecting the lower ball joint—1980 shown, others similar

10. Insert the ballstud into the steering knuckle, install the stud nut, and torque it to 83 ft. lbs. Install a new cotter pin, aligning cotter pin holes in nut and stud *only* through further tightening. *Do not loosen the nut from the torque position.*

11. Install a lube fitting and lube the joint. Reconnect tie rod (as necessary), install wheel, remove the jack supporting the lower control arm and lower the car.

Upper Control Arm
REMOVAL AND INSTALLATION

1. Raise the vehicle on a hoist.
2. Support the outer end of the lower control arm with a jack.
3. Remove the wheel.
4. Separate the upper ball joint from the steering knuckle as described above under "Upper Ball Joint Replacement."
5. Remove the control arm shaft-to-frame nuts.
   NOTE: *Tape the shims together and identify them so that they can be installed in the positions from which they were removed.*
6. Remove the bolts which attach the control arm shaft to the frame and remove the control arm. Note the positions of the bolts.
7. Install in the reverse order of removal. Make sure that the shaft-to-frame bolts are installed in the same position they were in before removal and that the shims are in their original positions. Use free running nuts (not locknuts) to pull serrated bolts through the frame. Then install locknuts. Tighten the thinner shim pack first. After the car has been lowered to the ground, bounce the front end to center the bushings and then tighten the bushing collar bolts to 45 ft. lbs. Tighten the shaft-to-frame bolts to 80 ft. lbs. on Camaros through 1973; 1974 and later Camaros require 90 ft. lbs. The control arm shaft nuts are tightened to 65 ft. lbs. through 1974; on 1975 and later models tighten to 75 ft. lbs.

Lower Control Arm
REMOVAL AND INSTALLATION

1. Remove the spring as described earlier.
2. Remove the ball stud from the steering knuckle as described earlier.
3. Remove the control arm pivot bolts and the control arm.
4. To install, reverse the above procedure. If any bolts are to be replaced, do so with bolts of equal strength and quality.

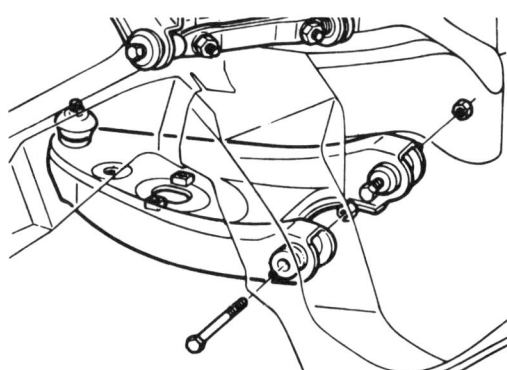

Lower control arm attachment bolts (© Chevrolet Motor Division)

Front End Alignment
CASTER, CAMBER, AND TOE-IN

Caster is the angle at which the front steering axis tilts either forward or backward from a vertical position. Positive caster is a backward tilt while a forward tilt is negative caster. Caster angle on the Camaro suspension cannot be seen with the eye, it requires the use of instruments. Caster angle can, however, be visualized. If you look down from the top of the upper control arm to the ground, you notice that the upper and lower ball joints do not line up (unless a 0 degree

270 SUSPENSION AND STEERING

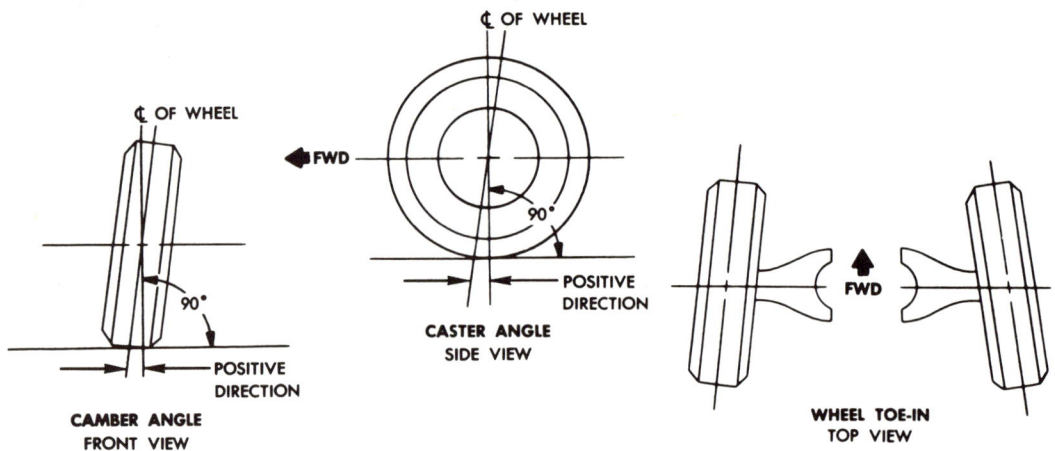

Camber, caster, and toe-in (© CHEVROLET MOTOR DIVISION)

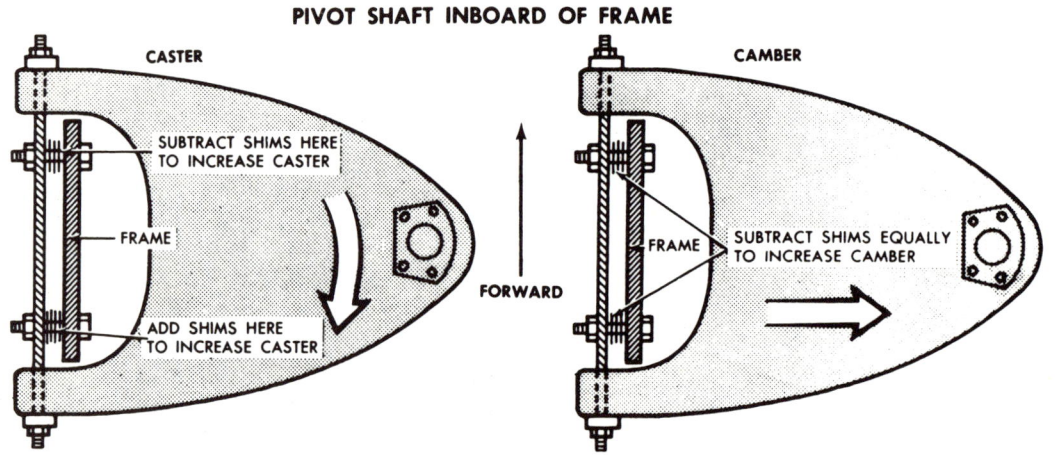

Caster and camber adjustment (© Chevrolet Motor Division)

caster angle existed). With any angle (other than 0 degrees), one ball joint would be slightly ahead or slightly to the rear of the other. If you had a positive angle, the lower ball joint would be slightly ahead (more to the front of the car) of the upper ball joint.

The front wheels will tilt outward or inward at the top depending on whether the camber is positive or negative. Camber angle then is the amount (in degrees) that a wheel tilts from a perfectly vertical position. When the wheels tilt outward at the top, it has positive camber; camber is negative when the wheel tilts inward at the top.

Toe-in, measured in fractions of an inch, is the turning in of the front of the front wheels. The front wheels must roll parellel to each other; if they don't uneven tire wear will result.

When performing a front wheel alignment, the mechanic checks all three of these measurements and makes any necessary adjustments. Since one adjustment affects each of the others, they must be adjusted in a specific order: caster, camber, and then toe-in. Proper wheel alignment is necessary for ease and stability of steering and controlling tire wear.

Adjustment of caster and camber is carried out by adding or subtracting shims between the upper control arm shaft and the frame bracket. Camber is adjusted by adding or subtracting shims from both the front and rear of the shaft. Adding shims decreases positive camber. Caster is adjusted by adding or subtracting shims from one end of the shaft. Moving one shim to the front bolt from the rear bolt will decrease positive caster. To adjust, loosen the shaft-to-frame nuts and add or subtract shims as necessary. Torque the nuts to 55 ft. lbs. when the adjustment is final. At least two bolt threads should be pro-

Wheel Alignment Specifications

Year	Model	Caster Range (deg)	Caster Pref Setting (deg)	Camber Range (deg)	Camber Pref Setting (deg)	Toe-in (in.)	Steering Axis Inclin (deg)	Wheel Pivot Ratio Inner Wheel	Wheel Pivot Ratio Outer Wheel
1967	All	0 to 1P	½P	¼N to ¾P	¼P	⅛ to ¼	8¾	20	18¾
1968–69	All	0 to 1P	½P	¼N to ¾P	½P	⅛ to ¼	8¾	20	NA
1970–71	All	0 to 2P	1P	¼N to 1¾P	¾P	⅛ to ¼	10 to 11	20	NA
1972	Camaro	½N to ½P	0	½P to 1½P	1P	⅛ to ¼	9 to 10	NA	NA
	Camaro (Z28)	1½N to ½N	1N	¼P to 1¼P	¾P	⅛ to ¼	9¼ to 10¼	NA	NA
1973	Camaro	1N to 1P	0	¼P to 1¾P	1P	1/16 to 5/16	10½	NA	NA
	Camaro (Z28)	2N to 0	1N	1½N to 0	¾N	1/16 to 5/16	10½	NA	NA
1974	Camaro	½N to ½P	0	½ to 1½P	1P	⅛ to ¼	9½	NA	NA
	Camaro (Z28)	1½N to ½N	1N	¼ to 1¼P	¾P	⅛ to ¼	9¾	NA	NA
1975	Camaro	½N to ½P	0	½N to 1½P	1P	0 to ⅛	10½	NA	NA
1976	Camaro	½P to 1½P	1P	¼ to 1¾P	1P	1/16 to 3/16	10½	NA	NA
1977	Camaro	½N to 3P	1P	½N to 2½P	1P	0–⅛	10½	NA	NA
1978	Camaro	1N to 3P	1P	½N to 2½P	1P	1/16–3/16	10½	NA	NA
1979–81	Camaro	0 to 2P	1P	1/5N to 1⅘P	1P	1/16–¼	10.35①	NA	NA

N Negative   P Positive   NA Not available
① At 1 degree camber

truding from the shim pack. The difference between the front and rear shim pack should never exceed ⅖ in.

Toe-in is adjusted after the caster and camber adjustments are carried out. Adjust the toe-in by loosening the clamps on the tie-rod sleeves, and turning the sleeves an equal amount in the opposite direction, to maintain wheel spoke alignment while adjusting.

REAR SUSPENSION

In 1967, Camaro used a pair of single leaf springs and two shock absorbers each mounted to the spring seat. The 1967 models had problems with rear axle hop during periods of hard acceleration. To prevent this hop, Chevrolet relocated the shock absorbers on later Camaros. On all 1968 and later Camaros, the right shock is mounted in front of the axle while the left shock is mounted behind the axle.

The rear axle assembly is attached to multi-leaf springs by "U" bolts. The spring front eyes are attached to the frame at the front hangers, through rubber bushings. The rear ends of the springs are attached to the frame by the use of shackles which allow the spring to "change its length" while the vehicle is in motion. Control arms are not used with leaf springs.

SUSPENSION AND STEERING

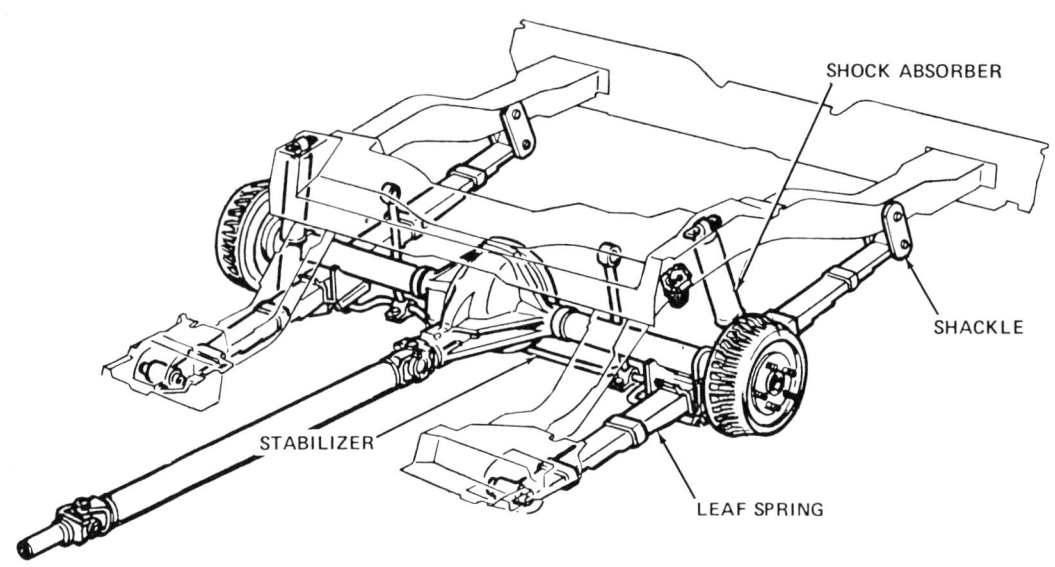

Rear suspension

Leaf Springs

REMOVAL

1. Raise the rear of the car enough for the axle assembly to hang freely. Place jackstands under both frame side rails near the front of the spring.
2. Remove the spring tension by raising the axle assembly.
3. Remove the lower bolt from the shock absorber.
4. Loosen the bolt holding the spring eye to its bracket.
5. Remove the spring retainer bracket. On later models this may require lowering the axle further.
6. Remove the parking brake cable from the retainer bracket mounted on the spring-mounted plate.
7. Remove the retaining nuts from the lower spring plate to the axle bracket.
8. Remove both upper and lower rubber spring pads and the spring plate.
9. Place a jack under the spring and remove the lower bolt from the rear shackle. Remove the spring from the car. Remove the shackle upper bolt and shackle bushings from the frame.

INSTALLATION

NOTE: *When replacing bolts or other suspension components, use only Chevrolet replacement parts or parts of equal strength and quality.*

1. Position the front mounting bracket to the front eye of the spring.
2. Install the bolt so that the bolt head is toward the center of the car.
3. Place the shackle upper bushings in the frame and position the shackles up to the bushings and loosely install the bolt and nut.
4. Install the bushing in the rear eye of the spring, lift the spring up the shackles and loosely install the shackle bolt and nut.

IMPORTANT: *The parking brake cable must be on the underside of the spring.*

5. Raise the front of the spring and position the bracket to the underbody, making sure that the tab on the bracket is inserted into the slot on the body.
6. Loosely install the spring-to-underbody bracket.
7. Place the spring upper cushion between the spring and axle bracket aligning the cushion ribs with the bracket ribs.
8. Place the lower spring cushion on the spring locating dowel.
9. Place the lower mounting plate over the dowel on the spring lower pad and loosely install the nuts.
10. Position the shock absorber to the spring plate and loosely install the bolt and nut to the eye of the spring, making sure the head of the bolt is toward the front of the car.
11. Position and secure the parking brake cable in the cable bracket.
12. Lower the car and tighten the bolts.

SUSPENSION AND STEERING 273

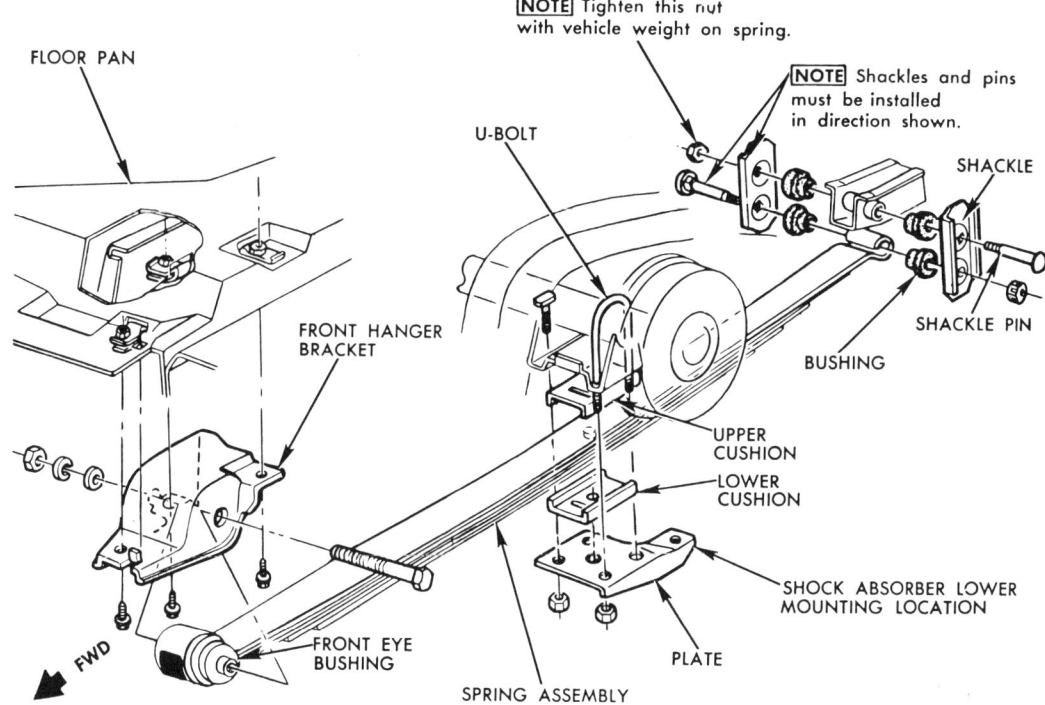

Exploded view of the leaf spring

Shock Absorbers

TESTING

If the ride of your car has become increasingly bouncy or fluid leakage can be observed on the shock absorber, it's time to replace them. Push up and down on the rear bumper several times and then let go. If the car continues to move up and down the shocks aren't doing their job.

REMOVAL AND INSTALLATION

1967-69

1. Raise the rear of the car and support the rear axle assembly.
2. Remove the lower mounting bolt.
3. Remove the upper bracket mounting screws and also the shock and bracket.
4. Remove the nut, retainer, grommet, gasket, and bracket from the shock rod.
5. Inspect the grommets and gasket, and replace them if they are worn or rotted.

To install, reverse the removal procedures.

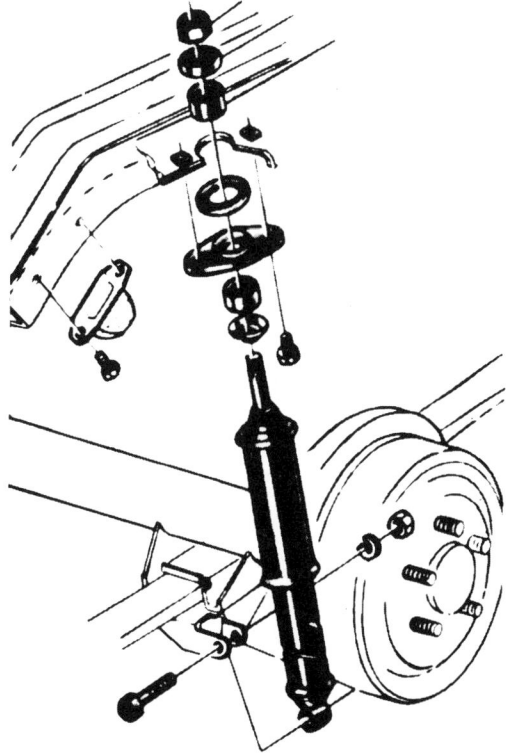

1967-69 shock absorber mounting (© Chevrolet Motor Division)

SUSPENSION AND STEERING

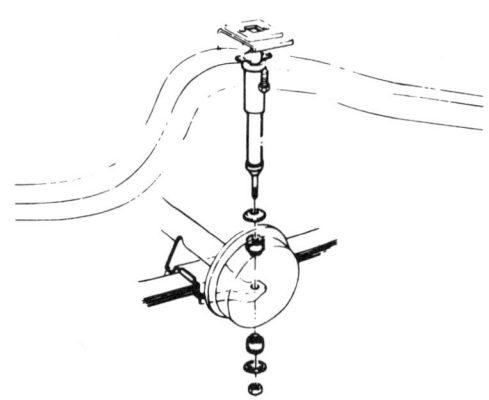

1970 and later shock absorber mounting (© Chevrolet Motor Division)

1970-81

1. Raise the car and support the rear axle.
2. Remove the lower nut, retainer, and grommet.
3. Remove the upper bolts and lift out the shock.

To install, reverse the removal procedure.

STEERING

Camaros have recirculating ball type steering. Forces are transmitted from a worm to a sector gear through ball bearings. Relay type steering linkage is used with a pitman arm connected to one end of the relay rod. The other end of the relay rod is connected to an idle arm which is attached to the frame. The relay rod is connected to the steering arms by two adjustable tie rods. All Camaros are equipped with a collapsible steering column designed to collapse on impact, thereby reducing possible chest injuries during accidents. When making any repairs to the steering column or steering wheel, excessive pressure or force capable of collapsing the column must be avoided. Beginning 1969, the ignition lock, ignition switch, and an antitheft system were built into each column. The key cannot be removed unless the transmission is in "Park" (automatic) or Reverse (manual) with the switch in the "Lock" position. Placing the lock in the "Lock" position activates a rod within the column which locks the steering wheel and shift lever. On floorshift models, a back drive linkage between the floorshift and the column produces the same effect.

Steering Wheel

CAUTION: *Steering columns are collapsible. When replacing the wheel, do not hammer or exert any force against the column.*

STANDARD WHEEL REPLACEMENT

1967-69

1. Disconnect the battery ground cable.
2. Disconnect the column wiring harness from the chassis wiring harness.
3. Remove the horn button cap or ornament and retainer.
4. Remove the receiving cup, spring, bushing, and pivot ring.
5. Remove the steering wheel nut and washer.
6. Install a puller and turn the puller bolt clockwise to remove the wheel.
7. Make sure that the turn signal lever is in the Neutral position before installing the wheel; otherwise, damage may be done to the control.
8. With the turn signal and horn assemblies in place, position the wheel on the shaft and install the washer and nut.
9. Install the spring (dish side up), pivot ring, bushing, and receiving cup.
10. Install the retainer and horn button cap or ornament.
11. Connect the wiring.

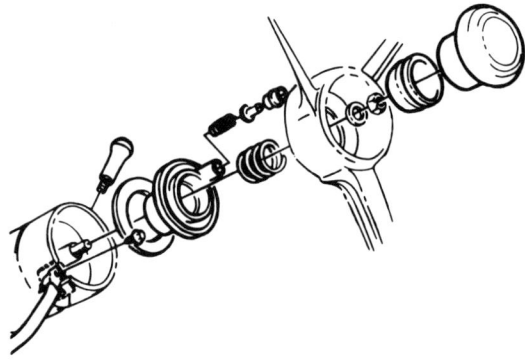

1967-69 standard steering wheel and related parts (© Chevrolet Motor Division)

1970

1. Disconnect the battery ground cable.
2. Remove the wheel shroud.
3. Remove the three spacer screws and also the spacer, plate, and spring.
4. Remove the shaft nut.
5. Install a wheel puller and turn the puller bolt clockwise to remove the wheel.
6. Position the eyelet and insulator in the horn contact tower.
7. Position the wheel on the shaft and

SUSPENSION AND STEERING 275

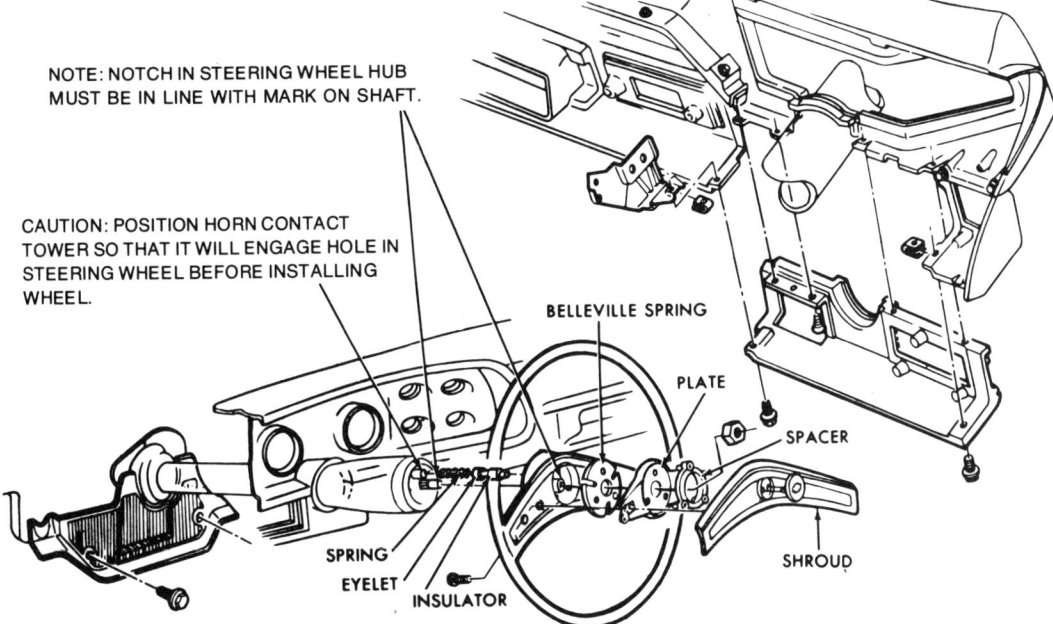

1970 steering wheel and steering column (© **Chevrolet Motor Division**)

align the notch in the wheel hub with the mark on the shaft.

IMPORTANT: *The horn contact tower must engage the hole in the steering wheel.*

8. Install and tighten the wheel nut.
9. Install the belleville spring with the concave side down, followed by the plate and spacer. Install the spacer screws.
10. Install the wheel shroud and secure it with two screws.
11. Connect the battery cable.

1971–81

1. Disconnect the battery ground cable.
2. Remove the wheel shroud (curved outside cover) and horn contact lead assembly.

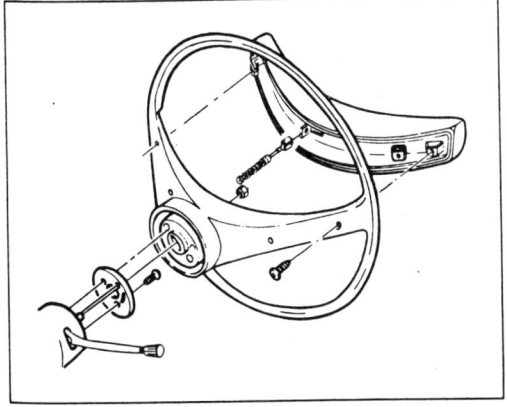

1971 and later standard steering wheel components (© **Chevrolet Motor Division**)

3. Remove the steering wheel nut.
4. Install the wheel puller, turn the puller bolt clockwise, and remove the wheel.
5. Set the turn signal lever in a neutral position and tighten the wheel onto the shaft. Overtightening the nut may cause the wheel to rub.
6. Place the shroud onto the wheel while guiding the horn lead into the turn signal tower.
7. Install the shroud screws and connect the battery.

DELUXE WHEEL REPLACEMENT

1968–69

1. Disconnect the battery ground cable.
2. On 1968 models, disconnect the steering column wiring from the chassis wiring harness.
3. Remove the screws from the underside of the wheel.
4. Lift off the steering wheel shroud and disconnect the horn wires.
5. Remove the nut and washer securing the wheel to the shaft.
6. Install a wheel puller, turn the puller bolt clockwise, and remove the wheel.
7. Position the turn signal cam and horn contact, install the wheel to the shaft, and secure them with a washer and nut.
8. Position the horn wires and, on 1968 models, attach the horn buttons.

276 SUSPENSION AND STEERING

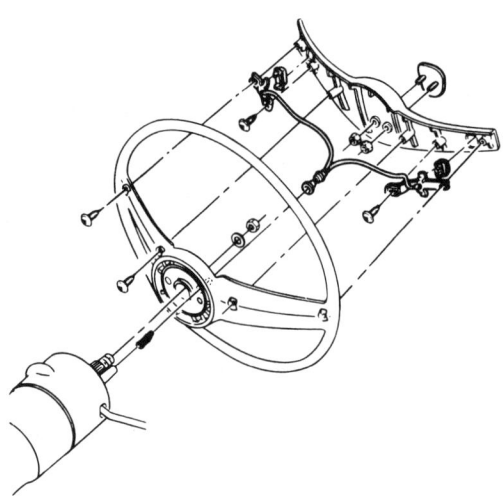

1969 deluxe steering wheel and horn components (© Chevrolet Motor Division)

9. Install the shroud.
10. Install the screws on the underside of the wheel and, on 1968 models, connect the column wiring.
11. Connect the battery cable.

CUSHIONED RIM WHEEL

1971–81

1. Disconnect the battery ground cable.
2. Remove the horn button cap. Remove snap ring.
3. Remove the steering wheel nut.
4. Remove the upper horn insulator, receiver, and belleville spring.
5. Install the wheel puller, turn the puller bolt clockwise, and remove the wheel.
6. Place the turn signal lever in a Neutral position, position the wheel to the shaft, and tighten the nut.

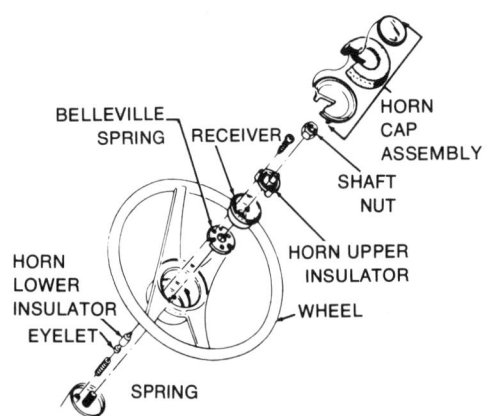

1971 and later cushioned rim wheel (© Chevrolet Motor Division)

7. Position the horn lower insulator, eyelet, and spring in the horn contact tower. Install the belleville spring, receiver, and horn upper insulator.
8. Install the horn button cap and connect the battery cable.

Turn Signal Switch

REMOVAL AND INSTALLATION

1967–68

1. Disconnect the battery ground cable.
2. Disconnect the signal switch wiring from the wiring harness under the instrument panel.
3. Remove the steering wheel.
4. If applicable, remove the shift lever.
5. Remove the four-way flasher lever arm.
6. If equipped with an automatic transmission, remove the dial indicator housing and lamp assembly from the column.
7. Remove the mast jacket lower trim cover.
8. Remove the C-ring and washers from the upper steering shaft.
9. Loosen the signal switch screws, move the switch counterclockwise, and remove it from the mast jacket.
10. Remove the upper support bracket assembly.

CAUTION: *Support the column; do not allow it to be suspended by the lower reinforcement only.*

11. Remove the wiring harness protector and clip, and then reinstall the support bracket and finger-tighten the bolts.
12. Remove the shift lever bowl from the mast jacket and disconnect it from the wiring harness.
13. Remove the three lockplate screws, being careful not to lose the three springs.
14. Disassemble the switch and upper bearing housing from the switch cover.
15. Insert the upper bearing housing assembly and switch assembly into the switch cover.
16. Align the switch and bearing housing with the mounting holes in the cover and install the three mounting screws.
17. Slide the springs onto the screws and install the lockplate over the springs. Tighten the screws three turns into the lockplate.
18. Position the switch wire through the shift lever bowl and place the upper end assembly on top of the bowl.
19. Place the shift lever bowl and signal

switch assembly on top of the jacket, inserting the lockplate tangs into the slots.

20. Push down on the cover assembly and turn clockwise to lock the assembly into position.
21. Tighten the signal mounting screws.
22. Remove the mast jacket support bracket, then install the wiring, wiring cover and clip, and install and tighten the support bracket.
23. Install a C-ring onto the shaft.
24. Install the dial indicator and lamp assembly on the column if so equipped.
25. Install the mast jacket lower trim cover if so equipped.
26. Install the four-way flasher knob and the turn signal lever.
27. Install the shift lever.
28. Install the steering wheel.
29. Connect the wiring and battery cable.

1969-81

1. Remove the steering wheel.
2. Remove the trim cover from the column.
3. Remove the steering column cover from the shaft by removing the three screws or by prying it out with a screwdriver (1976 and later models).
4. Using a compressing tool, compress the lockplate. With the plate compressed, pry out the snap-ring from its shaft groove and throw it away.
5. Slide the cancelling cam, spring, and washer off the shaft.
6. Remove the turn signal lever.
7. Push the four-way flasher knob in and unscrew it.
8. Remove the three switch mounting screws.
9. Pull the switch connector out of the bracket and wrap it with tape to prevent it from snagging.
10. If applicable, place tilt columns in the low and remove the harness cover.
11. Remove the switch.
12. To install, reverse the removal procedure, being sure to use only the specified nuts and bolts. Using screws that are slightly too long could prevent the column from collapsing during a collision.
13. When installing the cancelling cam, spring, and washer, make sure that the switch is in neutral and that the flasher knob is out.
14. Use a compressing tool to compress the lockplate and install a new snap-ring.

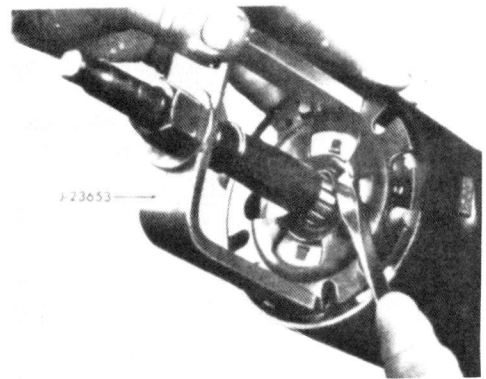

Using a special tool to remove the lockplate retaining ring on 1969 and later cars (© Chevrolet Motor Division)

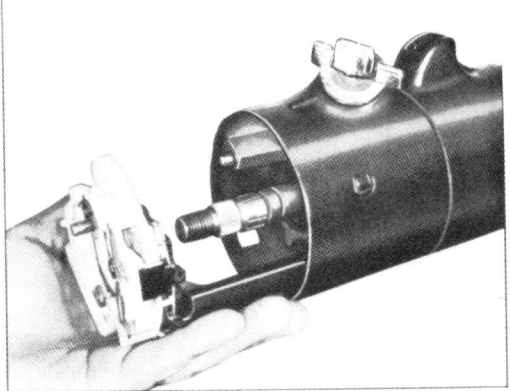

Removing the turn signal switch assembly (© Chevrolet Motor Division)

Lock Cylinder

REMOVAL AND INSTALLATION

1969-81

1. Remove the steering wheel and the directional signal switch. It is not necessary to pull the wiring harness out of the column. See the applicable procedures above.
2. Place the lock cylinder in "Lock" (up to 1970), or "Run" (1971-81).
3. Insert a small screwdriver into the turn signal housing slot. Keeping the screwdriver to the right side of the slot, break the housing flash loose and depress the spring latch at the lower end of the lock cylinder. Remove the lock cylinder.

NOTE: *Considerable force may be necessary to break this casting flash, but be careful not to damage any other parts. When ordering a new lock cylinder, specify a cylinder assembly. This will save assem-*

278 SUSPENSION AND STEERING

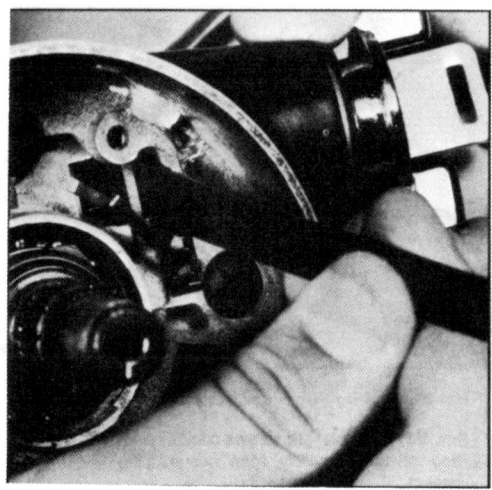

Depressing the lock cylinder retainer (1969 and later cars) (© Chevrolet Motor Division)

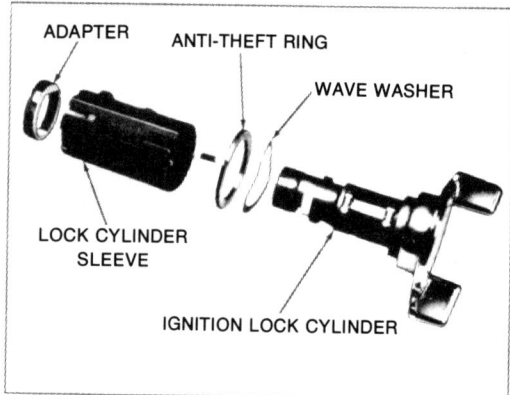

Exploded view of ignition lock assembly (© Chevrolet Motor Division)

bling the cylinder washer, sleeve, and adaptor.

4. To install, hold the lock cylinder sleeve and rotate the knob clockwise against the stop. Insert the cylinder into the housing, aligning the key and keyway. On 1969–76 cars hold a 0.070 in. drill between the lock bezel and the housing. On 1977–81 cars, push the cylinder into abutment of cylinder and sector. Rotate the cylinder counterclockwise, maintaining a light pressure until the drive section of the cylinder mates with the sector. Push in until the snap-ring pops into the grooves. Remove the drill. Check the operation of the cylinder. Install the direction signal switch and steering wheel.

DISASSEMBLE

1. Place lock in "run".
2. Remove lock plate, turn signal switch and buzzer switch (see service manual.)
3. Remove screw & lock cylinder. **CAUTION:** If screw is dropped on removal, it could fall into the column, requiring complete disassembly to retrieve the screw.

Power Steering Pump

REMOVAL AND INSTALLATION

1. Remove the hoses at the pump and tape the openings shut to prevent contamination. Position the disconnected lines in a raised position to prevent leakage.
2. Remove the pump belt.
3. Loosen the retaining bolts and any braces, and remove the pump.
4. Install the pump on the engine with the retaining bolt handtight.
5. Connect and tighten the hose fittings.
6. Refill the pump with fluid and bleed by turning the pulley counterclockwise (viewed from the front). Stop the bleeding when air bubbles no longer appear.
7. Install the pump belt on the pulley and adjust the tension.

ASSEMBLE

1. Rotate as shown, align cylinder key with keyway in housing.
2. Push lock all the way in.
3. Install screw. Tighten to 4.5 N·m for regular columns—2.5 N·m for adjustable columns.

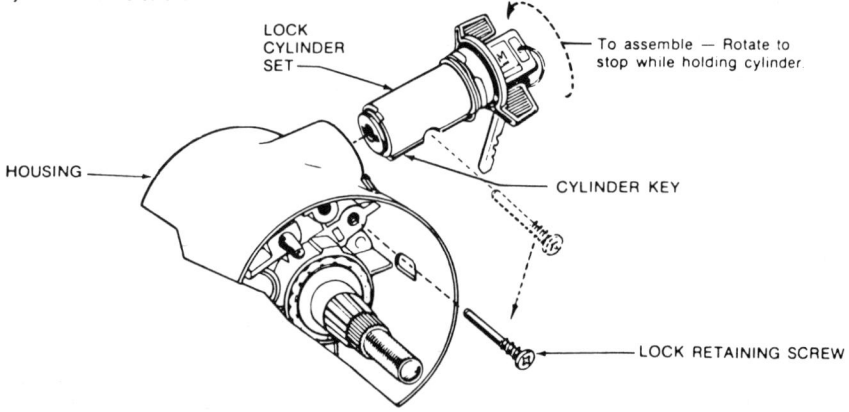

Lock cylinder removal—1979 shown, others similiar

SUSPENSION AND STEERING

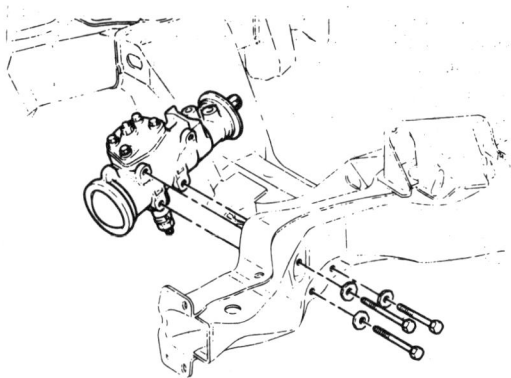

Typical steering gear mounting

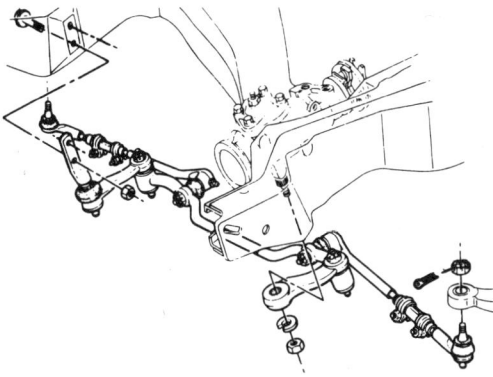

Late model steering linkage

BLEEDING

1. Fill the fluid reservoir.
2. Let the fluid stand undisturbed for two minutes, then crank the engine for about two seconds. Refill reservoir if necessary.
3. Repeat Steps 1 and 2 above until the fluid level remains constant after cranking the engine.
4. Raise the front of the car until the wheels are off the ground, then start the engine. Increase the engine speed to about 1,500 rpm.
5. Turn the wheels to the left and right, checking the fluid level and refilling if necessary.

Tie Rod Ends

REMOVAL AND INSTALLATION

1. Raise the vehicle and support securely.
2. Remove the cotter pins from the ball studs and remove the castellated nuts.
3. Remove the outer ball stud by tapping on the steering arm at the tie rod end with a heavy hammer on the other side of the steering arm as a backing. If necessary, pull downward on the tie rod to disconnect it from the steering arm.
4. Remove the inner ball stud from the relay rod using a similar procedure.
5. Remove the tie rod end or ends to be replaced by loosening the clamp bolt and unscrewing them.
6. Lubricate tie rod threads with chassis grease and install new tie rod end(s). Make sure both ends are an equal distance from the tie rod and tighten clamp bolts.
7. Make sure ball studs, tapered surfaces, and all threaded surfaces are clean and smooth, and free of grease. Install seals on ball studs. Install ball stud in steering arm and relay rod.
8. Rotate both inner and outer tie rod housings rearward to the limit of ball joint travel before tightening clamps. Make sure clamp slots and sleeve slots are aligned before tightening clamps. Make sure tightened bolts will be in horizontal position to 45 degrees upward (in the forward direction) when the tie rod is in its normal position. Make sure the tie rod end stays in position relative to the rod during the tightening operation. Tighten the clamps, and then return the assembly to the center of its travel.
9. Install ball stud nuts and torque to 35 ft. lbs. Then tighten (*do not loosen*) further as required to align cotter pin holes in studs and nuts. Install new cotter pins.
10. Lubricate new tie rod ends and lower the vehicle.

Brakes

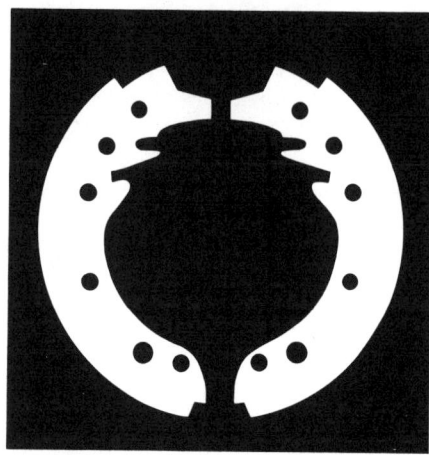

BRAKE SYSTEM

All Camaros are equipped with two separate and independent brake systems, a front brake system and a rear brake system. This independence originates at the master cylinder. The master cylinder, mounted on the firewall, consists of two separate fluid reservoirs. They are independent of one another; fluid cannot pass from one to the other although they are contained within the same housing. The front reservoir supplies fluid to the front brakes only while the rear reservoir and outlet connects to the rear brakes. If a leak developed in either system, front or rear, the fluid level in the good system would provide enough pressure to stop the car. Situated below the reservoirs is a cylinder housing a primary and a secondary piston and springs. Fluid from the reservoirs drains down into this cylinder and the pistons—mechanically activated by the brake pedal—exert pressure on the fluid transmitting it through the brake lines to the wheel cylinders at each wheel. The fluid pressure then enters each wheel cylinder or caliper (disc brakes) and forces the pistons outward. These pistons are linked to the brake shoes or, as with disc brakes, contact the brake pads. When the pistons move, so do the shoes or pads. The pads contact a round flat disc and the shoes move outward to contact a round metal drum surrounding them. The disc or drum is attached to the revolving wheel and the friction of the lining or pads against it slows the revolving wheel to a stop. With use, brake linings and pads gradually wear down and, if not replaced in time, their metal support plates (shoes) are exposed to contact and damage the drum or disc. The pad or lining surface attached to the metal shoe wears away and, eventually, braking ability decreases to a point requiring shoe and lining or pad replacement.

Self-adjusting drum brakes were standard equipment on all 1967–69 Camaros. Front disc brakes were optional during these three years but became standard equipment on 1970 and later models. The drum brakes are the Duo-Servo, single-anchor (the brake shoes pivot on one anchor pin) type having bonded brake linings; that is, the linings are bonded rather than riveted to the metal shoes. The wheel cylinders each contain two pistons. Dirt and moisture are kept out of the cylinder by a rubber boot positioned over each end. The wheel cylinders are nonadjustable.

Beginning 1967, all cars were equipped with a brake pipe distribution and switch assembly mounted below the master cylinder. This assembly is approximately rectangular;

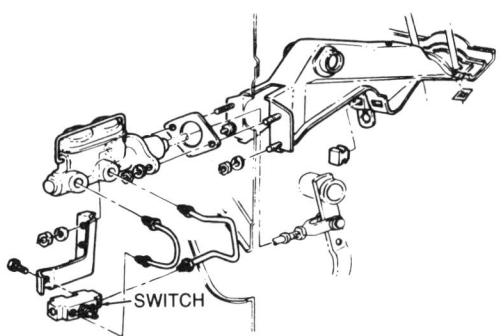

Brake pipe distribution and switch assembly (1967–69) (© Chevrolet Motor Division)

attached to the top are two brake lines (one for the front system and one for the rear) coming from the master cylinder. Fluid comes from the master cylinder, passes through this assembly, and exits to the wheels through two outlet lines mounted at each end of the assembly. An electrical switch is situated at top center on the assembly. At the top of the switch is a wire going to the parking brake light on the instrument panel and at the bottom of the switch (within the assembly) is a retractable pin which, when contacted, activates the light on the dash. Directly below the switch pin and running the length of the assembly is a passageway or cylinder housing a piston. Connected to each end of this cylinder is the fluid outlet line going to the wheels. Fluid exits the master cylinder through its two outlet lines and then passes through the distribution assembly and out the outlet lines to the wheels. As long as no leaks exist within the system, fluid passes through the inlet ports and flows into the passageway containing the piston. This fluid exerts an equal pressure at each end of the piston thereby keeping the piston centered in one location. The piston is flat along its top except for a depression or dip in the center. When no leaks exist, this dip is directly beneath the electrical switch activator pin. If a leak develops within one of the systems (front or rear), fluid pressure at one end of the piston drops and the piston is forced to one end of its cylinder. The piston moves off center and the elevated area of the piston now contacts the switch pin and activates the light on the dash warning the driver that a leak has occurred. Brake pedal free-play will increase but the remaining system (front or rear) will stop the car. When the leaking system is repaired and the lines are bled of any air, then the piston will return to its central position and the switch will be reset to the off position causing the light to go out. This light will continue to go on but only when the parking brake is applied.

From 1967 to 1970, all Camaros equipped with air conditioning, an 8⅞ in. rear axle ring gear (1969), or disc brakes (except four-wheel disc brakes), have a pressure regulator valve (called a metering valve on later disc brake cars) mounted on the left frame side rail (drum brake cars) or beneath the master cylinder (disc brake cars). On drum brake cars, this valve operates off the rear brake line but on disc brake cars, it is connected to the front brake line. This valve controls the hydraulic pressure to the rear brakes (drum brake cars) or to the front brakes (disc brake cars) so that front and rear brakes apply at the same time. It guards against early lock-up of the front or rear wheels during brake application. On disc brake cars, a pin on the end of this valve (underneath rubber boot) must be held down (this allows the valve to remain open) during bleeding operations. To depress the pin, press in on the rubber boot.

Beginning in 1970, front disc brakes were standard equipment on the Camaro. Valving included the brake pipe distribution and switch assembly and the metering valve described above. 1971 and later cars are equipped with a combination valve mounted below the master cylinder. This valve is the combination of the brake failure warning switch, metering valve, and the proportioning valve, all in one assembly. This valve is

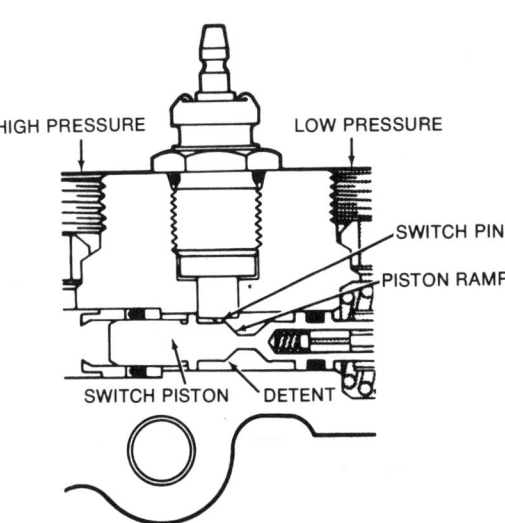

Brake pipe distribution and switch assembly as it appears during a pressure leak in the rear brake system (© Chevrolet Motor Division)

282 BRAKES

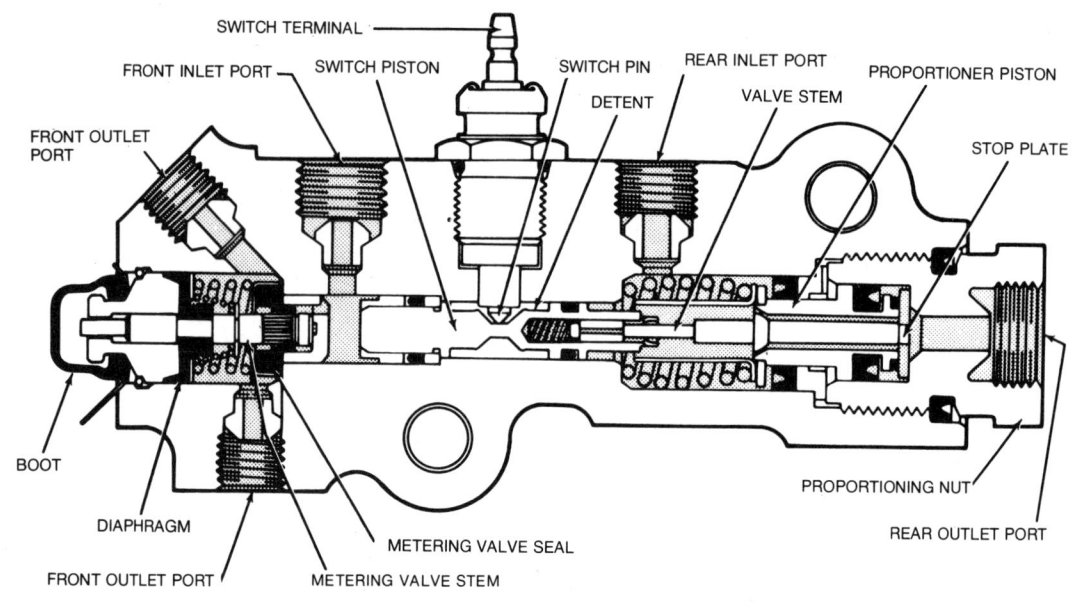

Typical combination valve (© Chevrolet Motor Division)

nonadjustable and non-serviceable; it must be replaced when defective. The proportioning valve (new in 1971) prevents early rear wheel lockup during quick, "panic" stops. Brake line fluid pressure is permitted to increase up to a certain point. When this point is reached, the valve begins to limit the amount of pressure going to the rear brakes. This prevents the rear brakes from locking up before the front disc brakes. If a leak occurs in the front system, a bypass within this valve sends full pressure to the rear brakes. This is especially effective during a quick, "panic" stop in a light car. A sudden stop in a light car causes the front end to dip, resulting in weight transfer to the front, making the rear end even lighter and more susceptible to sliding. The proportioning valve does not work during normal stops. When bleeding the brakes, the combination valve must be held in the open position by pressing in on the pin at the end of the valve.

As mentioned earlier, front disc brakes were available only as an option from 1967 to 1969, with a very limited production of four-wheel disc brakes in 1969. The 1967 and 1968 brakes of the four-piston, fixed-caliper type; in 1969 a change was made to a new single-piston, sliding-caliper type, while retaining the four-piston type for the four-wheel disc models. In 1970, the sliding-caliper type became standard front wheel equipment and remains unchanged to date. The fixed-caliper type consists of the caliper, a rotating disc, a splash shield, and a mounting bracket. The caliper contains four pistons and two brake shoes (pads) with riveted linings. Behind each piston is a spring; assembled with each piston is a rubber seal and dust boot so that fluid can be kept in while keeping dirt and moisture out. A retaining pin, secured by a cotter pin, passes through each caliper half and both shoes to hold everything together. One caliper half with brake shoe is mounted to the inside of the disc while the other half is mounted to the outside of the disc. As the brakes are applied, fluid pressure behind each piston forces the pistons outward aginst each pad (shoe); each pad then contacts a side of the rotating disc and the friction created stops the car. The sliding-caliper type consists of a one-piece housing, bored on the inboard side for a single piston. A rubber seal within this bore retains fluid and prevents it from seeping between the piston and the cylinder. Stepping on the brake pedal causes fluid pressure to force the piston and shoe outward to contact the inboard surface of the disc. This causes the caliper to slide inward on four bushings and two bolts, thereby forcing the outboard pad (shoe and lining) against the outer surface of the disc.

The Duo-Servo drum brakes are used on all cars with front disc brakes. Rear brake design has remained unchanged since 1967. Power brakes have been available as an option on all Camaros. This type of brake reduces pedal effort through the use of engine vacuum.

HYDRAULIC SYSTEM

Master Cylinder

REMOVAL AND INSTALLATION

1. Disconnect and plug the hydraulic line(s) at the master cylinder.
2. Remove the two retaining nuts and lockwashers that hold the cylinder to the firewall.

NOTE: *On non-power brakes, disconnect the push rod at the brake pedal.*

3. Remove the master cylinder, gasket, and rubber boot.
4. Position the master cylinder on the firewall, making sure the push rod goes through the rubber boot into the piston.

NOTE: *On non-power brakes, reconnect the push rod clevis to the brake pedal. If so equipped, thread jam nut down to push rod shoulder, thread clevis down to jam nut, and torque nut (against clevis) to 14 ft. lbs.*

5. Install the nuts and lockwashers.
6. Install the hydraulic line(s), then check brake pedal free-play.
7. Bleed the brakes as described later in this chapter.

NOTE: *Cars having disc brakes do not have a check valve in the front outlet port*

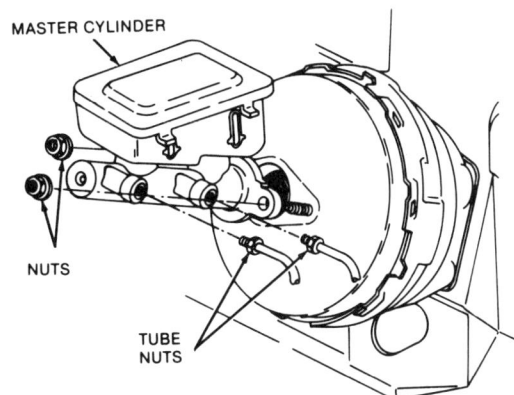

Typical master cylinder mounting for cars equipped with power brakes

of the master cylinder. If one is installed, front discs will immediately wear out due to residual hydraulic pressure holding the pads against the rotor.

OVERHAUL

1. Remove the master cylinder from the car.
2. Remove the mounting gasket and boot, and the main cover. Empty the cylinder of all fluid.
3. Place the cylinder in a vise and remove the pushrod retainer and the secondary piston stop bolt that are found inside the front reservoir.
4. Remove the retaining ring and primary piston assembly.
5. Direct compressed air into the piston stop screw hole to force the secondary piston,

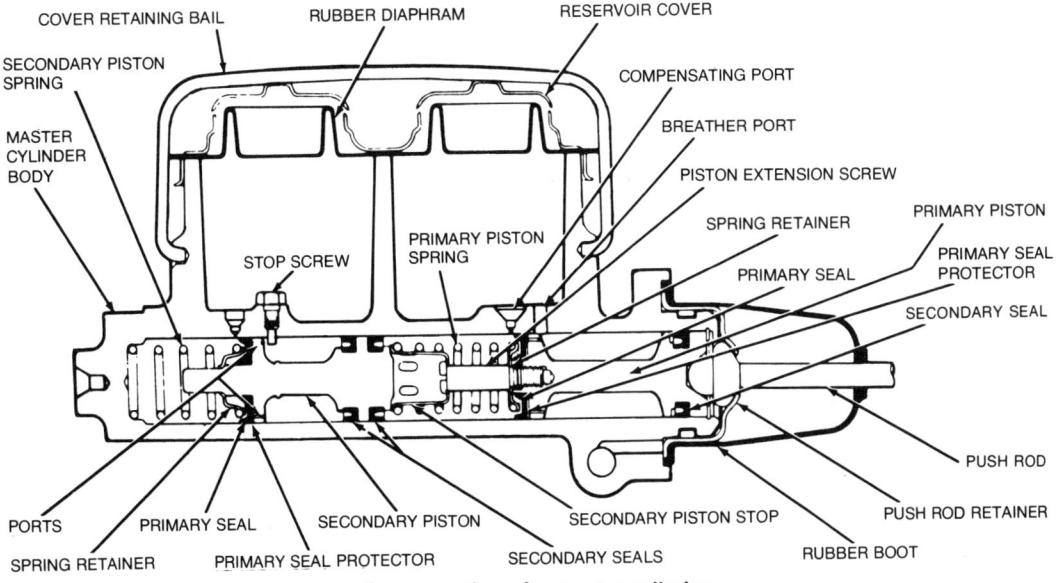

Cross section of a master cylinder

284 BRAKES

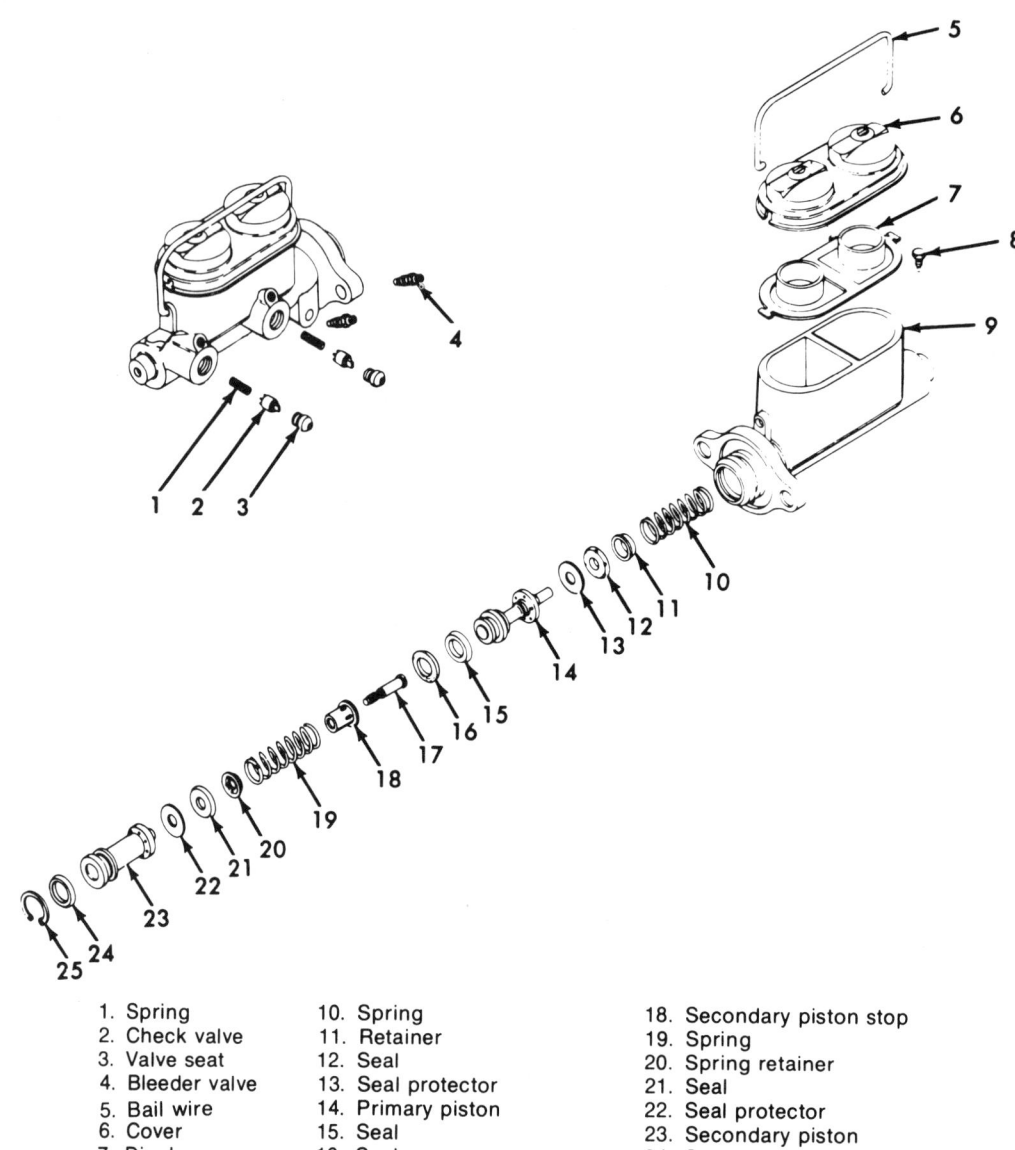

1. Spring
2. Check valve
3. Valve seat
4. Bleeder valve
5. Bail wire
6. Cover
7. Diaphragm
8. Stopscrew
9. Body
10. Spring
11. Retainer
12. Seal
13. Seal protector
14. Primary piston
15. Seal
16. Seal
17. Piston extension screw
18. Secondary piston stop
19. Spring
20. Spring retainer
21. Seal
22. Seal protector
23. Secondary piston
24. Seal
25. Retaining ring

Exploded view of a master cylinder. Some 1980 models and all 1981 models no longer use the bails to retain the reservoir cap.

spring, and retainer from the cylinder bore. If compressed air isn't available, use a hooked wire to pull out the secondary piston.

6. Check the brass tube fitting inserts and, if damaged, remove them; if not, leave them in place.

7. If insert replacement is necessary, thread a No. 6-32 x 5/8 in. self-tapping screw into the insert. Hook the end of the screw with a claw hammer and pull out the insert.

8. An alternative (but more troublesome) way to remove the inserts is to drill out the outlet holes with a 13/64 in. drill and then thread them with a 1/4 in.-20 tap. Position a thick washer over the hole to serve as a spacer and then thread a 1/4 in.-20 x 3/4 in. hex-head bolt into the insert and tighten the bolt until the insert is free.

9. Use only *denatured alcohol* or brake fluid and compressed air to clean the parts. Slight rust may be removed with crocus cloth.

CAUTION: *Do not polish the aluminum bore of type "A" cylinders with any type of* abrasive. Never use any mineral-based solvents (gasoline, kerosene, etc.) for cleaning. It will quickly deteriorate rubber parts.

10. Replace the brass tube inserts by positioning them in their holes and threading a brake line tube nut into the outlet hole. Turn down the nut until the insert is seated.

11. Check the piston assemblies for correct identification and, when satisfied, position the replacement secondary seals in the twin grooves of the secondary piston.

12. The outside seal is correctly placed when its lips face the flat end of the piston.

13. Slip the primary seal and its protector over the end of the secondary piston opposite the secondary seals. The flat side of this seal should face the piston's compensating hole flange.

14. Replace the primary piston assembly with the assembled piece in the overhaul kit.

15. Coat the cylinder bore and the secondary piston's inner and outer seals with brake fluid. Assemble the secondary piston spring to its retainer and place them over the end of the primary seal.

16. Insert the combined spring and piston assembly into the cylinder and, using a pencil, seat the spring against the end of the bore.

17. Coat the primary piston seals with brake fluid and push it (push rod receptacle end out) into the cylinder.

18. Hold the piston in and snap the retaining ring into place.

19. Continue to hold the piston down to make sure that all components are seated and insert the secondary piston stop screw in its hole in the bottom of the front reservoir. Torque the screw to 25–40 in. lbs.

20. Install the reservoir diaphragm and cover.

21. It will save time to bleed the cylinder before installing it in the car. Do so in the following manner:
    a. Install plugs in the outlet ports.
    b. Place the unit in a vise with the front end tilted slightly downward. *DO NOT OVERTIGHTEN* the vise.
    c. Fill both reservoirs with clean fluid.
    d. Using a smooth, round rod (try the eraser end of a pencil), push in on the primary piston.
    e. Release the pressure on the rod and watch for air bubbles in the fluid. Keep repeating this until the bubles disappear.
    f. Loosen the vise and position the cylinder so the front end if tilted slightly upward. Repeat steps "d" and "e."
    g. Place the diaphragm cover on the reservoir.

NOTE: *Master cylinder overhaul on cars with power brakes is the same as above.*

Combination Valve
REMOVAL AND INSTALLATION

1. Disconnect the battery negative cable.
2. Disconnect the electrical lead from the switch.
3. Place rags under the unit to absorb any spilled brake fluid.
4. Clean any dirt from the hydraulic lines and the switch/valve assembly. Disconnect the hydraulic lines from the assembly. If necessary, loosen the line connections at the master cylinder. Tape the open line ends to prevent the entrance of dirt.
5. Remove the mounting screws and remove the switch/valve assembly.
6. Make sure that the new unit is clean and free of dust and lint. If in doubt, wash the new unit in clean brake fluid.
7. Place the new unit in position and install it to its mounting bracket with screws.
8. Remove the tape from the hydraulic lines and connect them to the unit. If necessary, tighten the line connections at the master cylinder.
9. Connect the electrical lead.
10. Connect the battery negative cable.
11. Bleed the brake systems.

Brake Bleeding

The hydraulic brake system must be bled any time one of the lines is disconnected or any

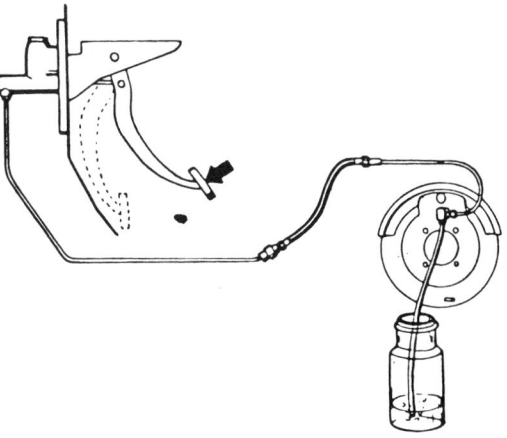

Bleeding the brake system

time air enters the system. If the brake pedal feels spongy upon application, and goes almost to the floor but regains height when pumped, air has entered the system. It must be bled out. Check for leaks that would have allowed the entry of air and repair them before bleeding the system. The correct bleeding sequence is: right wheel cylinder, left rear, right front, and left front. If the master cylinder is equipped with bleeder valves, bleed them first then go to the wheel cylinder nearest the master cylinder (left front) followed by the right front, left rear, and right rear.

MANUAL BLEEDING

This method of bleeding requires two people, one to depress the brake pedal and the other to open the bleeder screws.

1. Clean the top of the master cylinder, remove the cover and fill the reservoirs with clean fluid. To prevent squirting fluid, replace the cover.

IMPORTANT: *On cars with front disc brakes, it will be necessary to hold in the metering valve pin during the bleeding procedure. The metering valve is located beneath the master cylinder and the pin is situated under the rubber boot on the end of the valve housing. This may be taped in or held by an assistant.*

CAUTION: *Never reuse brake fluid which has been bled from the system.*

2. Fill the master cylinder with brake fluid.
3. Install a box-end wrench on the bleeder screw on the right rear wheel.
4. Attach a length of small diameter, clear vinyl tubing to the bleeder screw. Submerge the other end of the rubber tubing in a glass jar partially filled with clean brake fluid. Make sure the rubber tube fits on the bleeder screw snugly or you may be squirted with brake fluid when the bleeder screw is opened.
5. Have your friend slowly depress the brake pedal. As this is done, open the bleeder screw half a turn and allow the fluid to run through the tube. Close the bleeder screw, then return the brake pedal to its fully released position.
6. Repeat this procedure until no bubbles appear in the jar. Refill the master cylinder.
7. Repeat this procedure on the left rear, right front, and left front wheels, in that order. Periodically refill the master cylinder so it does not run dry.
8. If the brake warning light is on, depress the brake pedal firmly. If there is no air in the system, the light will go out.

FRONT DISC BRAKES

Disc Brake Pads

INSPECTION

Brake pads should be inspected once a year or at 7,500 miles, whichever occurs first. Check both ends of the outboard shoe, looking in at each end of the caliper; then check the lining thickness on the inboard shoe, looking down through the inspection hole. Lining should be more than .020″ thick above the rivet (so that the lining is thicker than the metal backing). Keep in mind that any applicable state inspection standards that are more stringent take precedence. All four pads must be replaced if one shows excessive wear.

NOTE: *All 1979 and later models have a wear indicator that makes a noise when the linings wear to a degree where replacement is necessary. The spring clip is an integral part of the inboard shoe and lining. When the brake pad reaches a certain degree of wear, the clip will contact the rotor and produce a warning noise.*

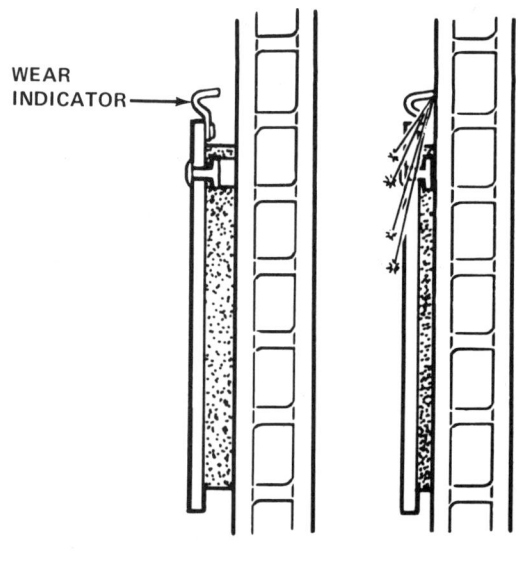

Front disc brake pad wear indicator—1979 and later

BRAKES

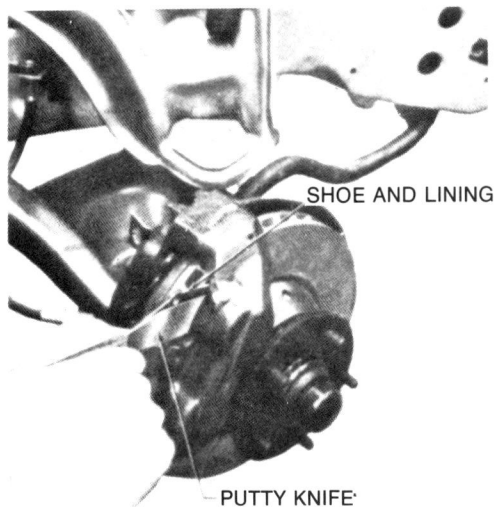

Replacing brake pads—1967–68 and 1969 four-wheel disc cars (© Chevrolet Motor Division)

REMOVAL AND INSTALLATION

1967–68

1. Siphon off about two-thirds of the brake fluid from a full master cylinder.
   CAUTION: *The insertion of the thicker replacement pads will push the caliper pistons back into their bores and will cause a full master cylinder to overflow causing paint damage. In addition to siphoning fluid, it would be wise to keep the cylinder cover on during pad replacement.*
2. Raise the car and support it with jackstands. Remove the wheels.
   NOTE: *Replacing the pads on just one wheel will result in uneven braking. Always replace the pads on both wheels.*
3. Extract and discard the pad retaining pin cotter key.
4. Remove the retaining pin and, while removing one pad, insert its replacement before the piston has time to move outward. If you were too slow and the pistons were too fast, it will be necessary to use a wide-bladed putty knife to hold in the pistons while inserting the new pads. If this gives you difficulty open the bleeder screw on that caliper and release some of the fluid, but do not allow the fluid to drain from the master cylinder. This may reduce the pressure and make it easier to push in on the pistons. After removing the outboard pad, inspect it and compare it with the inboard pad. They may be slightly different; if so, make sure that the replacement pads are installed correctly.

5. After installing the new pads, install the retaining pin and insert a new cotter pin.
6. Refill the master cylinder and bleed the system if necessary.

1969–81

1. Siphon off about two-thirds of the brake fluid from a full master cylinder.
   CAUTION: *The insertion of the thicker replacement pads will push the piston back into its bore and will cause a full master cylinder to overflow causing paint damage. In addition to siphoning off fluid it would be wise to keep the cylinder cover on during pad replacement.*
2. Raise the car and support it with jackstands. Remove the wheels.
   NOTE: *Replacing the pads on just one wheel will result in uneven braking. Always replace the pads on both wheels.*
3. Install a C-clamp on the caliper so that the solid side of the clamp rests against the back of the caliper and so the screw end rests against the metal part (shoe) of the outboard pad.

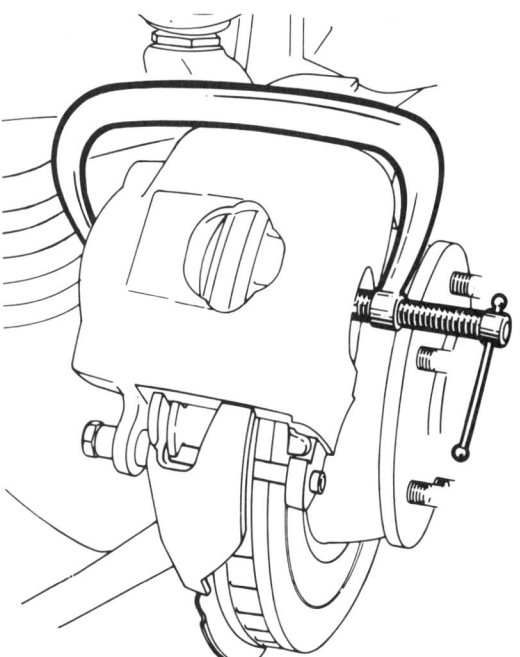

Use a C-clamp to seat the caliper piston

4. Tighten the clamp until the caliper moves enough to bottom the piston in its bore. Remove the clamp.
5. Remove the two allen-head caliper mounting bolts enough to allow the caliper to be pulled off the disc.

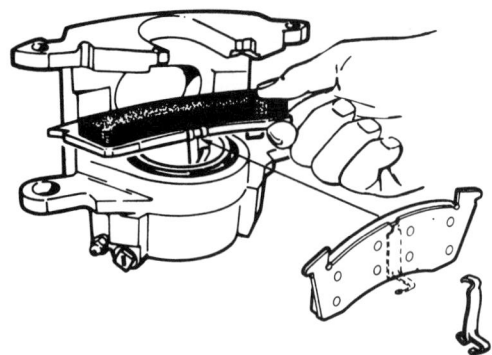

Installing the shoe support spring—1970-81

6. Remove the inboard pad and loosen the outboard pad. Place the caliper where it won't strain the brake hose. It would be best to wire it out of the way.

7. Remove the pad support spring clip from the piston.

8. Remove the two bolt ear sleeves and the four rubber bushings from the ears.

9. Brake pads should be replaced when they are worn to within 1/32 in. of the rivet heads.

10. Check the inside of the caliper for leakage and the condition of the piston dust boot.

11. Lubricate the two new sleeves and four bushings with a silicone spray.

12. Install the bushings in each caliper ear. Install the two sleeves in the two inboard ears.

13. Install the pad support spring clip and the old pad into the center of the piston. You will then push this pad down to get the piston flat against the caliper. This part of the job is a pain and requires an assistant. While the assistant holds the caliper and loosens the bleeder valve to relieve pressure, you get a pry bar and try to force the old pad in to make the piston flush with the caliper surface. When it is flush, close the bleeder valve so that no air gets into the system.

NOTE: *On models with wear sensors, make sure the wear sensor is toward the rear of the caliper.*

14. Place the outboard pad in the caliper with its top ears over the caliper ears and the bottom tab engaged in the caliper cutout.

15. After both pads are installed, lift the caliper and place the bottom edge of the outboard pad on the outer edge of the disc to make sure that there is no clearance between the tab on the bottom of the shoes and the caliper abutment.

16. Place the caliper over the disc, lining

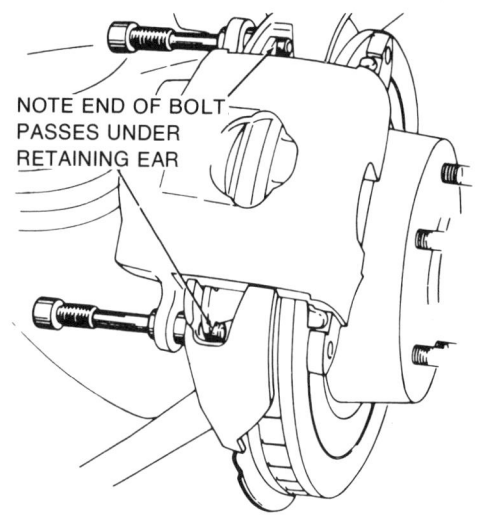

Caliper bolts must go under the pad retaining ears (© Chevrolet Motor Division).

up the hole in the caliper ears with the hole in the mounting bracket. Make sure that the brake hose is not kinked.

17. Start the caliper-to-mounting bracket bolts through the sleeves in the inboard caliper ears and through the mounting bracket making sure that the ends of the bolts pass under the retaining ears of the inboard shoe.

18. Push the mounting bolts through to engage the holes in the outboard shoes and the outboard caliper ears and then threading them into the mounting bracket.

19. Torque the mounting bolts to 35 ft. lbs. Pump the brake pedal to seat the linings against the rotors.

20. With a pair of channel lock pliers placed on the notch on the caliper housing, bend the caliper upper ears until no clearance exists between the shoe and the caliper housing.

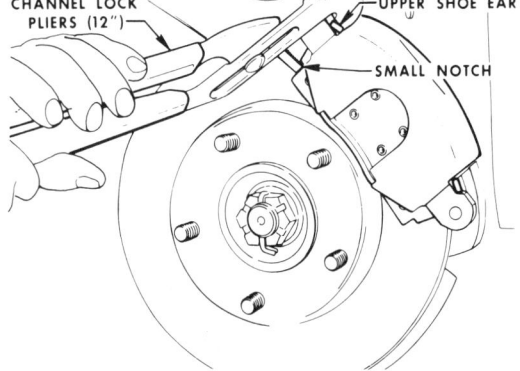

Use pliers to fit the brake pad to the caliper housing

BRAKES

21. Install the wheels, lower the car, and refill the master cylinder with fluid. Pump the brake pedal to make sure that it is firm. If it is not, bleed the brakes.

CALIPER REPLACEMENT AND OVERHAUL

1967-68

1. Raise the car and support it on jackstands.
2. Remove the tire and wheel assembly from the side on which the caliper is being removed.
3. Disconnect the brake hose at the support bracket. Tape the end of the line to prevent contamination.
4. Remove the cotter pin from the brake pad retaining pin and remove the pin.
5. Remove the brake pads and identify them as inboard or outboard if they are being reused.
6. Remove the U-shaped retainer from the hose fitting and pull the hose from the bracket.
7. Remove the two caliper retaining bolts and also the caliper from its mounting bracket.
8. Separate the caliper halves. Remove the two O-rings from the fluid transfer holes in the caliper.
9. Push the piston all the way down into the caliper. Using the piston as a fulcrum, place a screwdriver under the steel ring in the boot and pry the boot from the caliper half.
10. Remove the pistons and springs, being careful not to damage the seal.
11. Remove the boot and seal from the piston.
12. Clean all metal components with clean brake fluid or denatured alcohol.

CAUTION: *Do not use gasoline, kerosene, or any other mineral-based solvent for cleaning. These solvents form an oily film on the parts which leads to fluid contamination and the deterioration of rubber parts.*

13. Blow out all fluid passages with an air hose.
14. Discard and replace all rubber parts.
15. Inspect all bores for scoring and pitting and replace if necessary. Minor flaws can be removed with very fine crocus cloth but do so with a circular motion.
16. Using a feeler gauge, check the clearance of the piston in its bore. If the bore is not damaged and the clearance exceeds the

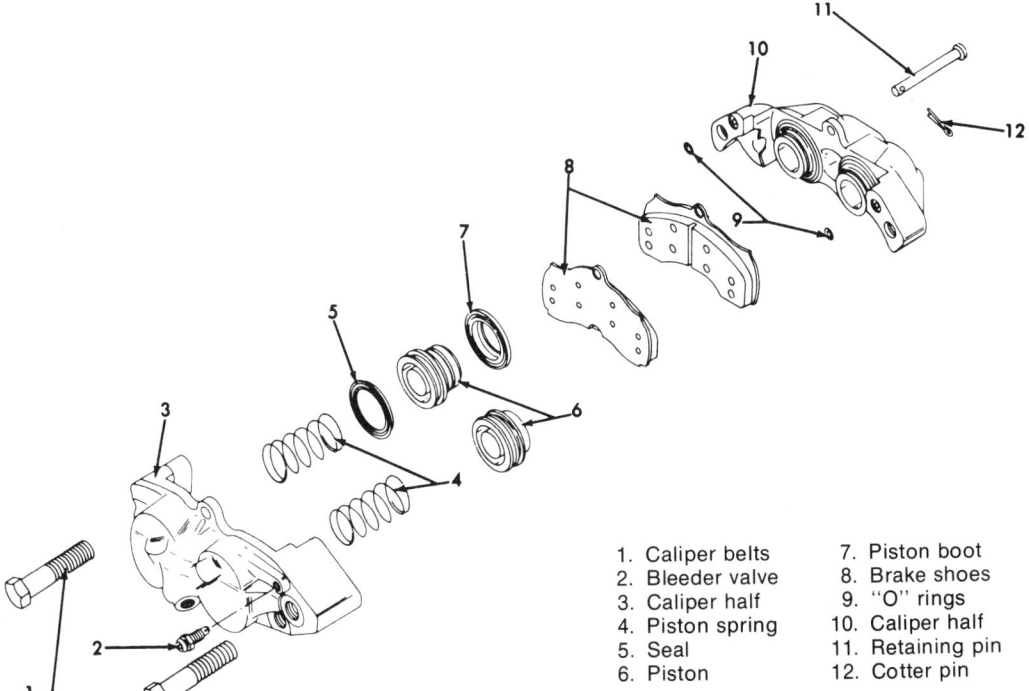

1. Caliper belts
2. Bleeder valve
3. Caliper half
4. Piston spring
5. Seal
6. Piston
7. Piston boot
8. Brake shoes
9. "O" rings
10. Caliper half
11. Retaining pin
12. Cotter pin

Exploded view of the caliper assembly (1967-68 models and 1969 models with four-wheel disc brakes)
(© CHEVROLET Motor Division)

maximum limit below, then the piston must be replaced.

Bore Diameter	Clearance
2 1/16 in.	0.0045–0.010 in.
1 7/8 in.	0.0045–0.010 in.
1 3/8 in.	0.0035–0.009 in.

17. Insert the seal in the piston groove nearest the flat end of the piston. The seal lip must face the large end of the piston. The lips must be in the groove and may not extend beyond.
18. Place the spring in the piston bore.
19. Coat the seal with clean brake fluid.
20. Install the piston assembly into the bore, being careful not to damage the seal lip on the edge of the bore.
21. Install the boot into the piston groove closest to the concave end of the piston.
22. The fold in the boot must face the seal end of the piston.
23. Push the pistons to the bottom of the bore and check for smooth piston movement. The end of the piston must be flush with the end of the bore. If it is not, check the installation of the seal.
24. Seat the piston boot so that its metal ring is even in the counterbore. The ring is even in the counterbore. The ring must be flush or below the machined face of the caliper. If the ring is seated unevenly dirt and moisture could get into the bore.
25. Insert the O-rings around the fluid transfer holes at both ends of the caliper halves.
26. Lubricate the bolts with brake fluid, connect the caliper halves, and torque the bolts to 130 ft. lbs.
27. While holding in the brake pistons with a putty knife, mount the caliper over the disc. Be careful not to damage the piston boots on the edge of the disc.
28. Install the two mounting bolts and torque them to 130 ft. lbs.
29. Install the brake pads. If the same pads are being reused, return them to their original places (outboard or inboard) as marked during removal. New pads will usually have an arrow on the back indicating the direction of disc rotation. See "Brake Pad Replacement" for details.
30. Install the brake hose into the caliper, passing the female end through the support bracket.
31. Make sure that the tube line is clean and connect the brake line nut to the caliper.

32. Install the hose fitting into the support bracket and install the U-shaped retainer. Turn the steering wheel from side to side to make sure that the hose doesn't interfere with the tire. If it does, turn the hose end one or two points in the bracket until the interference is eliminated.
33. After performing the above check, install the steel tube connector and tighten it.
34. Bleed the brakes as instructed earlier in this chapter.
35. Install the wheels and lower the car.

1969–81

1. Perform the removal steps for pad replacement.
2. Disconnect the brake hose and plug the line.
3. Remove the U-shaped retainer from the fitting.
4. Pull the hose from the frame bracket and remove the caliper with the hose attached.
5. Clean the outside of the caliper with denatured alcohol.
6. Remove the brake hose and discard the copper gasket.
7. Remove the brake fluid from the caliper.
8. Place clean rags inside the caliper opening to catch the piston when it is released.
9. Apply compressed air to the caliper fluid inlet hole and force the piston out of its bore. Do not blow the piston out; use just enough pressure to ease it out.
10. Use a screwdriver to pry the boot out of the caliper. Avoid scratching the bore.
11. Remove the piston seal from its groove in the caliper bore. *Do not use a metal tool of any type for this operation.*
NOTE: *Replace (do not reuse) the boot, piston seal, rubber bushings, and sleeves.*
12. Blow out all passages in the caliper and bleeder valve. Clean the piston and piston bore with fresh brake fluid.
13. Examine the piston for scoring, scratches, or corrosion. If any of these conditions exist, the piston must be replaced because it is plated and cannot be refinished.
14. Examine the bore for the same defects. Light rough spots may be removed by rotating crocus cloth, using finger pressure, in the bore. Do not polish with an in-and-out motion or use any other abrasive.
15. Lubricate the piston bore and the new

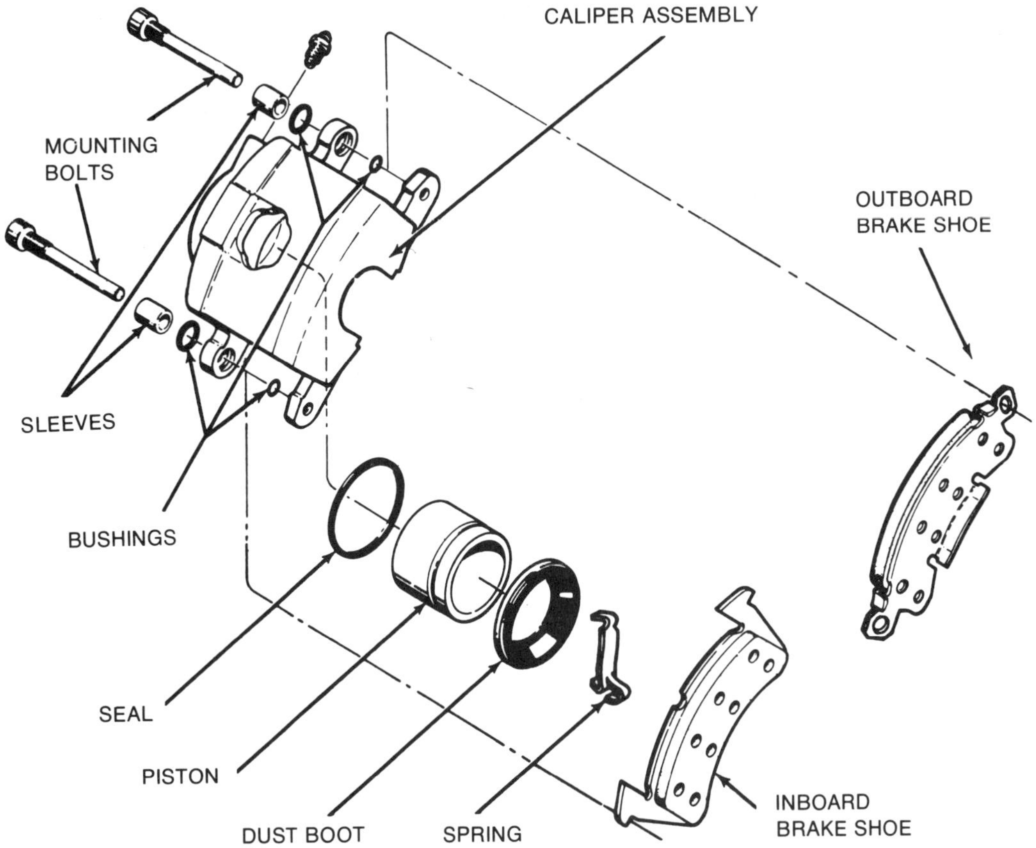

Exploded view of the single piston caliper

rubber parts with fresh brake fluid. Position the seal in the piston bore groove.

16. Lubricate the piston with brake fluid and assemble the boot into the piston groove so that the fold faces the open end of the piston.

17. Insert the piston into the bore, taking care not to unseat the seal.

18. Force the piston to the bottom of the bore. (This will require a force of 50–100 lbs). Seat the boot lip around the caliper counterbore. Proper seating of the boot is very important for sealing out contaminants.

19. Install the brake hose into the caliper with a new copper gasket.

20. Lubricate the new sleeves and rubber bushings. Install the bushings in the caliper ears. Install the sleeves so that the end toward the disc pad is flush with the machined surface.

NOTE: *Lubrication of the sleeves and bushings is essential to insure the proper operation of the sliding caliper design.*

21. Install the shoe support spring in the piston.

22. Install the disc pads in the caliper and remount the caliper on the hub (see "Disc Pad Replacement").

23. Reconnect the brake hose to the steel brake line. Install the retainer clip. Bleed the brakes (see "Brake Bleeding").

24. Replace the wheels, check the brake fluid level, check the brake pedal travel, and road-test the vehicle.

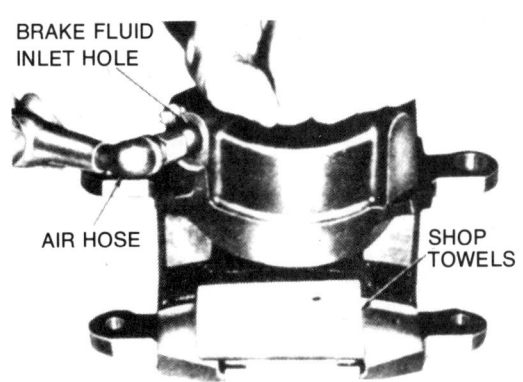

Removing piston from caliper (© Chevrolet Motor Division)

292 BRAKES

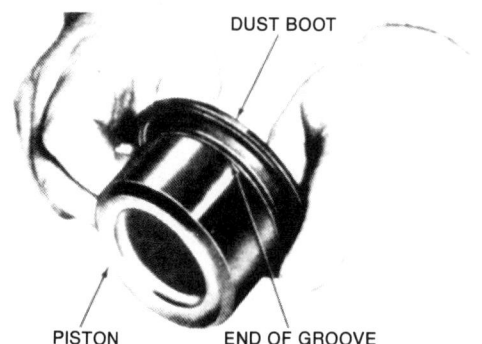

Placing the boot on the piston (© Chevrolet Motor Division)

Brake Disc

DISC INSPECTION

1. Tighten the spindle nut to remove all wheel bearing play.
2. Install a dial indicator on the caliper so that its feeler will contact the disc about 1 in. below its outer edge.
3. Turn the disc and observe the runout reading. If the reading exceeds 0.002 in. (.004 in. total reading), the disc should be replaced.
4. Measure the thickness of the rotor at 5 points around the circumference. Tolerance is .0005 in.

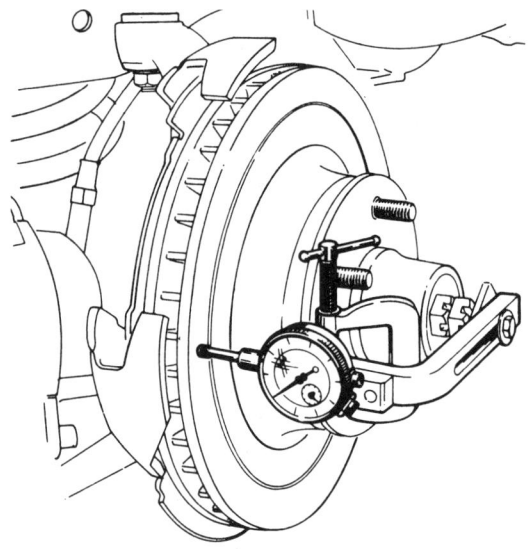

Use a dial indicator to determine brake disc runout

5. Minimum thickness dimensions are cast into the caliper for reference.

DISC REPLACEMENT

1. Raise the car, support it with jackstands, and remove the wheel and tire assembly.

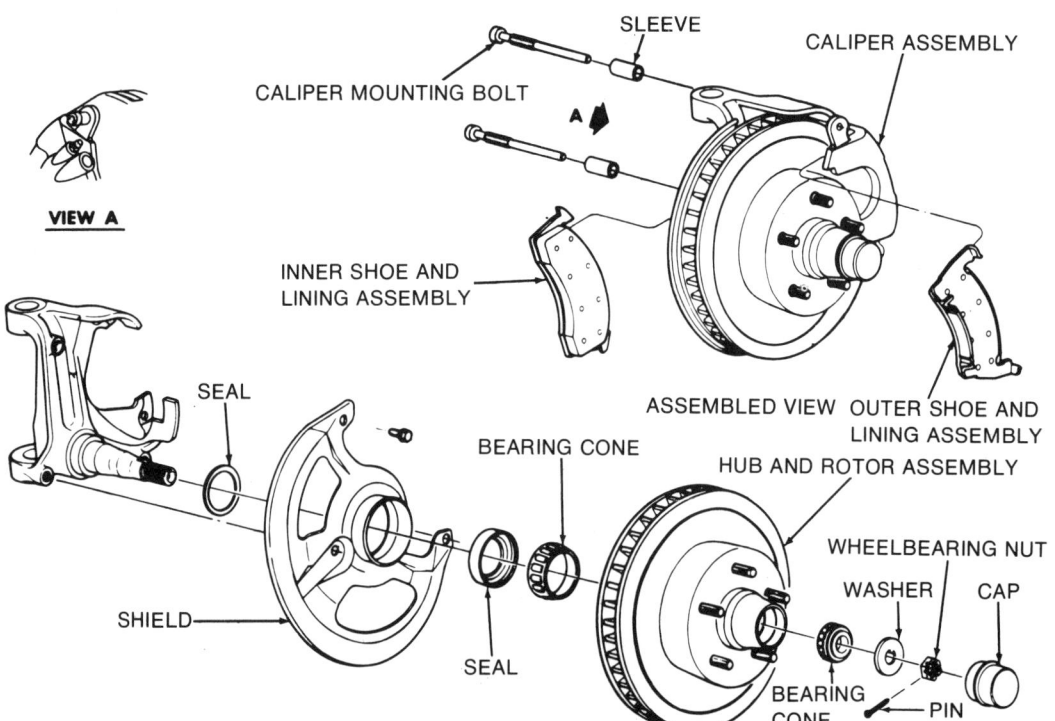

Exploded view of the disc brake assembly

2. Remove the brake caliper as previously outlined.
3. Drill out the five rivets holding the disc to the hub.
4. Remove the disc.
5. Remove the rivet stubs from the hub.
6. Install the disc on the hub, aligning the lug bolts with the holes in the disc.
7. Install the brake caliper and shoes as previously outlined.
8. Bleed the brakes, install the wheel, and lower the car. Adjust front wheel bearings as described at the end of this chapter.

Wheel Bearings

Properly adjusted bearings have a slightly loose feeling. Wheel bearings must never be preloaded. Preloading will damage bearings and eventually spindles. If the bearings are too loose, they should be cleaned, inspected, and then adjusted.

Hold the tire at the top and bottom and move the wheel in and out of the spindle. If the movement is greater than 0.008 in. (0.005 in. 1974 and later), the bearings are too loose.

ADJUSTMENT

1. Raise and support the car by the lower control arm.
2. Remove the hub cap, then remove the dust cap from the hub.
3. Remove the cotter pin and spindle nut.
4. Spin the wheel forward by hand. Tighten the nut until snug to fully seat the bearings.
5. Back off the nut ¼–½ turn until it is just loose, then tighten it finger-tight.
6. Loosen the nut until either hole in the spindle lines up with a slot in the nut and then insert the cotter pin. This may appear to be too loose, but it is the correct adjustment. The spindle nut should not be even fingertight.
7. Proper adjustment creates 0.001–0.008 in. (0.001–0.005 in. 1974 and later) of endplay.

REMOVAL AND INSTALLATION
1967–69

1. Remove the wheel and tire assembly, and the brake drum or brake caliper.
2. On those cars with disc brakes, remove the hub and disc as an assembly. Remove the caliper mounting bolts and insert a block between the brake pads as the caliper is removed. Remove the caliper and wire it out of the way.
3. Pry out the grease cap, cotter pin, spindle nut, and washer, then remove the hub. Do not drop the wheel bearings.
4. Remove the outer roller bearing assembly from the hub. The inner bearing assembly will remain in the hub and may be removed after prying out the inner seal. Discard the seal.
5. Clean all parts in solvent (air dry) and check for excessive wear or damage.
6. Using a hammer and drift, remove the bearing cups from the hub. When installing new cups, make sure they are not cocked and that they are fully seated against the hub shoulder.
7. Using a high melting point bearing lubricant, pack both inner and outer bearings.
8. Place the inner bearing in the hub and install a new inner seal, making sure the seal flange faces the bearing cup.
9. Carefully install the wheel hub over the spindle.
10. Using your hands, firmly press the outer bearing into the hub. Install the spindle washer and nut, and adjust as instructed above.

1970–81

1. Remove the hub and disc assembly as described in Steps 1–3 above.
2. Remove the outer roller bearing assembly from the hub. The inner bearing assembly can be removed after prying out the inner seal. Discard the seal.
3. Wash all parts in solvent and check for excessive wear or damage.
4. To replace the outer or inner race, knock out the old race with a hammer and brass drift. New races must be installed squarely and evenly to avoid damage.
5. Pack the bearings with a high meltingpoint bearing lubricant.
6. Lightly grease the spindle and the inside of the hub.
7. Place the inner bearing in hub race and install a new grease seal.
8. Carefully install the hub and disc assembly.
9. Install the outer wheel bearing.
10. Install the washer and nut and adjust the bearings according to the procedure outlined above.
11. Install the caliper and torque the mounting bolts to 35 ft. lbs.

12. Install the dust cap and the wheel and tire assembly, then lower the car to the ground.

PACKING

Clean the wheel bearings thoroughly with solvent and check their condition before installation.

CAUTION: *Do not blow the bearing dry with compressed air as this would allow the bearing to turn without lubrication.*

Apply a sizable daub of lubricant to the palm of one hand. Using your other hand, work the bearing into the lubricant so that the grease is pushed through the rollers and out the other side. Keep rotating the bearing while continuing to push the lubricant through it.

FRONT AND REAR DRUM BRAKES

BRAKE DRUM REPLACEMENT

1. Raise and support the car.
2. Remove the wheel or wheels.
3. Pull the brake drum off. It may be necessary to gently tap the rear edges of the drum to start it off the studs.
4. If extreme resistance to removal is encountered, it will be necessary to retract the adjusting screw. Knock out the access hole in the brake drum and turn the adjuster to retract the linings away from the drum.
5. Install a replacement hole cover before reinstalling drum.
6. Install the drums in the same position on the hub as removed. Adjust front wheel bearings as described at the end of this chapter.

DRUM INSPECTION

1. Check the drums for any cracks, scores, grooves, or an out-of-round condition. Replace if cracked. Slight scores can be removed with fine emery cloth while extensive scoring requires turning the drum on a lathe.
2. Never have a drum turned more than 0.060 in.

BRAKE SHOE ADJUSTMENT

Rotate the star wheel adjuster until a slight drag is felt between the shoes and drum, then back off 1¼ turns on the adjusting wheel. Put the car in reverse and, while backing up, firmly apply the brakes. This will allow the self-adjusters to complete the adjustment.

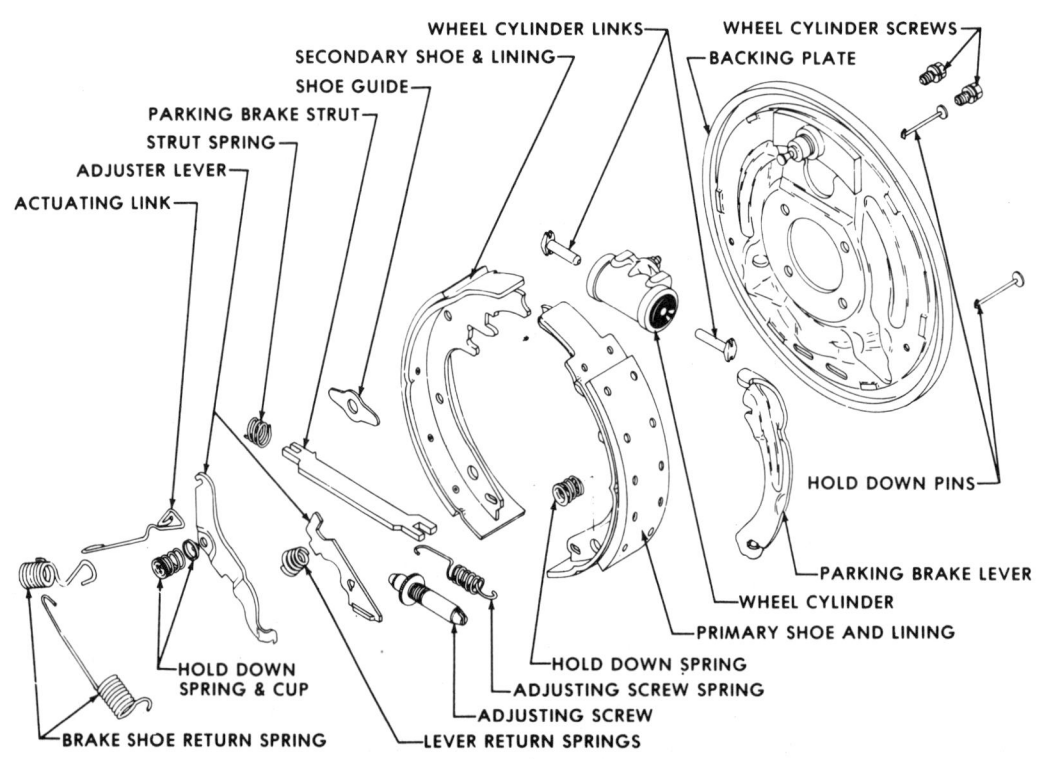

Exploded view of the drum brake

BRAKES

BRAKE SHOE REPLACEMENT

1. Raise the car and support it on jackstands.
2. Slacken the parking brake cable.
3. Remove the rear wheel and brake drum. The front wheel and drum may be removed as a unit by removing the spindle nut and cotter pin.
4. Free the brake shoe return springs, actuator pull-back spring, hold-down pins and springs, and actuator assembly.

NOTE: *Special tools available from auto supply stores will ease removal of the spring and anchor pin, but the job may still be done with common hand tools.*

5. On the rear wheels, disconnect the adjusting mechanism and spring, and remove the primary shoe. The primary shoe has a shorter lining than the secondary and is mounted at the front of the wheel.
6. Disconnect the parking brake lever from the secondary shoe and remove the shoe. Front wheel shoes may be removed together.
7. Clean and inspect all brake parts.
8. Check the wheel cylinders for seal condition and leaking.
9. Repack wheel bearings and replace the seals.
10. Inspect the replacement shoes for nicks or burrs, lubricate the backing plate contact points, brake cable and levers, and adjusting screws and then assemble.
11. Make sure that the right and left-hand adjusting screws are not mixed. You can prevent this by working on one side at a time. This will also provide you with a reference for reassembly. The star wheel should be nearest to the secondary shoe when correctly installed.
12. To install, reverse the removal procedure. When completed, make an initial adjustment as previously described.

NOTE: *Maintenance procedures for the metallic lining option are the same as those for standard linings. Do not substitute these linings in standard drums, unless they have been honed to a 20 micro-inch finish and equipped with special heat-resistant springs.*

Wheel Cylinders

OVERHAUL

As is the case with master cylinders, overhaul kits for wheel cylinders are readily available. When rebuilding and installing wheel cylin-

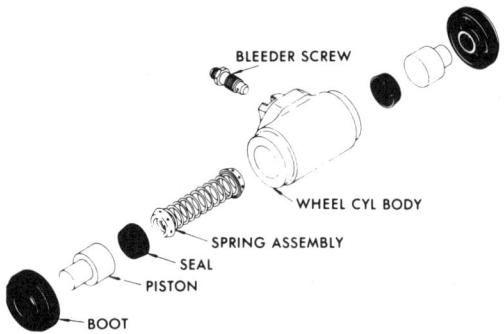

Exploded view of a typical wheel cylinder (© Chevrolet Motor Division)

ders, avoid getting any contaminants into the system. Always install clean, new high-quality brake fluid. If dirty or improper fluid has been used, it will be necessary to drain the entire system, flush the system with proper brake fluid, replace all rubber components, refill, and bleed the system.

1. Remove the rubber boots from the cylinder ends with pliers. Discard the boots.
2. Remove and discard the pistons and cups.
3. Wash the cylinder and metal parts in denatured alcohol or clean brake fluid.

CAUTION: *Never use a mineral-based solvent such as gasoline, kerosene, or paint thinner for cleaning purposes. These solvents will swell rubber components and quickly deteriorate them.*

4. Allow the parts to air dry or use compressed air. Do not use rags for cleaning since lint will remain in the cylinder bore.
5. Inspect the piston and replace it if it shows scratches.
6. Lubricate the cylinder bore and counterbore with clean brake fluid.
7. Install the rubber cups (flat side out) and then the pistons (flat side in).
8. Insert new boots into the counterbores by hand. Do not lubricate the boots.
9. Install the wheel cylinder to the backing plate and connect all push rods and springs. Connect the brake line, install the brake drum, and bleed the brakes.

REMOVAL AND INSTALLATION

1. Remove the brake drum as described above.
2. Clean all dirt away from around the brake line connection, and disconnect the brake line.
3. Remove the wheel cylinder from the backing plate.

296 BRAKES

4. Install the wheel cylinder onto the backing plate.
5. Connect the brake pipe. Torque the connection to 100 in. lbs.
6. Install brake shoes, drum, and wheel, and flush and bleed brakes.

Wheel Bearings

Refer to the "Front Disc Brakes—Wheel Bearings" section for removal and installation, adjustment and packing procedures.

PARKING BRAKE

All Camaros are equipped with a foot-operated ratchet type parking brake. A cable assembly connects this pedal to an intermediate cable by means of an equalizer. Adjustment is made at the equalizer. The intermediate cable connects with two rear cables and each of these cables enters a rear wheel.

Cable

ADJUSTMENT

1. Raise the rear of the car and support it with jackstands.
2. Push down on the parking brake pedal so that it is two notches (clicks) from the fully released position.
3. Loosen the forward equalizer check nut and adjust the rear nut as necessary to obtain a light drag when the rear wheel is turned forward.
4. Tighten both check nuts.
5. Fully release the parking brake lever and check to see that there is no drag present when the rear wheel is turned forward.
6. Lower the car.
7. If the parking brake has to be forcibly released, clean and lubricate the cables and equalizer, and also the parking brake assembly, then check the cables for straightness and kinks.

REMOVAL AND INSTALLATION
1967–70

There are three parking brake cables: the front cable runs between the pedal assembly and the looped center cable; the center cable is a large loop, each end connected to the short rear cables and the center (forward) attached to the front cable with the equalizer; the rear cables are attached to brake shoe actuating levers.

FRONT CABLE

With the parking brake in the released position, remove the equalizer nut from the equalizer. Remove the cable retainer from the inside of the frame rail and disconnect

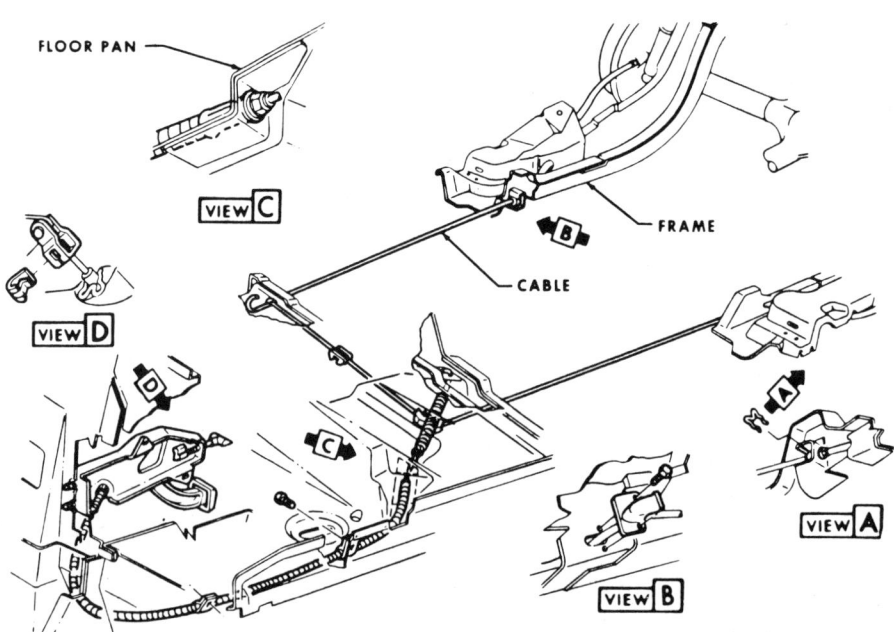

Parking brake cable assembly—1971–76

Brake Specifications
(All measurements are given in in.)

Year	Master Cylinder		Wheel Cylinder			Brake Disc or Drum Diameter		
			Front			Front		
	Disc	Drum	Disc	Drum	Rear	Disc	Drum	Rear
'67	1.000	1.0 ①	1.875	1.125	0.875	11.0	9.5	9.5
'68	1.125	1.0	2.063	1.125	0.875	11.0	9.5	9.5
'69	1.125	1.0	2.938	1.125	0.875	11.0	9.5	9.5
'70–'72	1.125 ②	—	2.938	—	0.875	11.0	—	9.5
'73	1.000 ③	—	2.938	—	0.875	11.0	—	9.5
'74	1.000 ③	—	2.938	—	0.875	11.0	—	9.5
'75	1.000 ③	—	2.938	—	0.875	11.0	—	9.5
'76	1.000 ③	—	2.938	—	0.938	11.0	—	9.5
'77	0.9375 ③	—	2.938	—	0.9375	11.0	—	9.5
'78	0.9375 ③	—	2.938	—	0.9375	11.0	—	9.5
'79–'81	1.000 ③	—	2.9375	—	0.9375	11.0	—	9.5

① 0.875 with metallic linings
② 1.000 with power disc brakes
③ 1.125 with power assist brakes
— Not applicable

the other end of the cable from the brake lever assembly. Remove the cable.

CENTER CABLE

With the parking brake in the released position, remove the equalizer assembly. Remove the center cable from the guides and then disconnect it from the rear cable.

REAR CABLE

Disconnect the forward end from the center cable, remove the frame retainers, and remove the rear end of the cable from the brake actuating levers. In order to do this the brake drum and shoes must be removed. After replacing the cables, the brakes must be adjusted as described in the previous section.

1971–76

FRONT CABLE

Remove the cable return spring and the equalizer assembly. Remove the cable retaining nut from the frame end. Remove the cable end from the pedal lever and remove the cable retaining bracket. Remove the left kick pad and scuff plate. Pull up the floor mat to expose the retaining clips, remove them, and withdraw the front cable through the hole.

REAR CABLE

Remove the front cable return spring and equalizer assembly. Unhook the cable from the guide and separate the cables so that either can be removed. Remove the clip from the cable near the front leaf spring bushing. Remove the cable bracket from the body rail near the front leaf spring bushing. Pull the cable through the opening where the cable bracket was located. Remove the brake drum and remove the end of the cable from the parking brake lever by compressing the spring and lifting the knobbed end from the lever. Compress the locking fingers with a

298 BRAKES

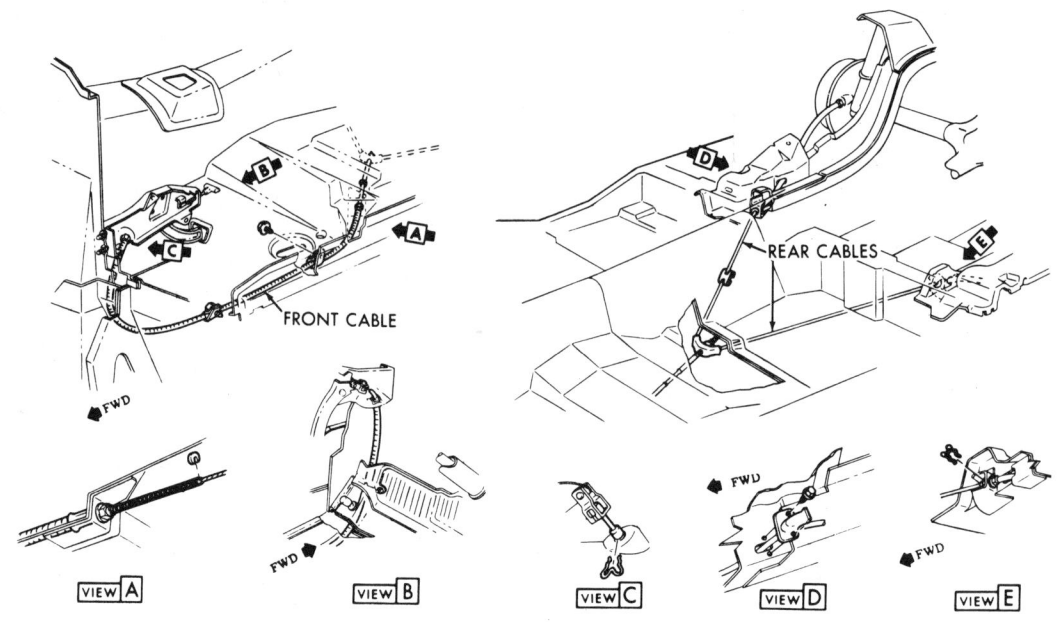

Parking brake cable assembly—1977–81

box wrench and pull the cable through the hole in the brake plate.

1977–79

FRONT

Remove the adjusting nut from the equalizer. Remove the retainer clip from the rear portion of the front cable at the frame and from the lever arm. Disconnect the front brake cable from the parking brake lever. Remove the cable. On some models, it may be easier to install the new cable if a heavy cord is tied to either end of the cable to guide it through the openings. Reverse the removal procedure to install the new cable, and then adjust the parking brake.

REAR

Remove the cable clip retainers. Loosen the adjusting nut. Disengage the rear cable at the connector. Bend the retaining fingers and disengage the cable at the brake shoe operating lever. Remove the assembly from the vehicle. Install the new cable by reversing the removal procedure, and then adjust the parking brake.

Body

You can repair most minor auto body damage yourself. Minor damage usually falls into one of several categories: (1) small scratches and dings in the paint that can be repaired without the use of body filler, (2) deep scratches and dents that require body filler, but do not require pulling, or hammering metal back into shape and (3) rust-out repairs. The repair sequences illustrated in this chapter are typical of these types of repairs. If you want to get involved in more complicated repairs including pulling or hammering sheet metal back into shape, you will probably need more detailed instructions. Chilton's *Minor Auto Body Repair, 2nd Edition* is a comprehensive guide to repairing auto body damage yourself.

TOOLS AND SUPPLIES

The list of tools and equipment you may need to fix minor body damage ranges from very basic hand tools to a wide assortment of specialized body tools. Most minor scratches, dings and rust holes can be fixed using an electric drill, wire wheel or grinder attachment, half-round plastic file, sanding block, various grades of sandpaper (#36, which is coarse through #600, which is fine) in both wet and dry types, auto body plastic, primer, touch-up paint, spreaders, newspaper and masking tape.

Most manufacturers of auto body repair products began supplying materials to professionals. Their knowledge of the best, most-used products has been translated into body repair kits for the do-it-yourselfer. Kits are available from a number of manufacturers and contain the necessary materials in the required amounts for the repair identified on the package.

Kits are available for a wide variety of uses, including:
- Rusted out metal
- All purpose kit for dents and holes
- Dents and deep scratches
- Fiberglass repair kit
- Epoxy kit for restyling.

Kits offer the advantage of buying what you need for the job. There is little waste and little chance of materials going bad from not being used. The same manufacturers also merchandise all of the individual products used—spreaders, dent pullers, fiberglass cloth, polyester resin, cream hardener, body filler, body files, sandpaper, sanding discs and holders, primer, spray paint, etc.

CAUTION: *Most of the products you will be using contain harmful chemicals, so be extremely careful. Always read the complete label before opening the containers. When*

300 BODY

you put them away for future use, be sure they are out of children's reach!

Most auto body repair kits contain all the materials you need to do the job right in the kit. So, if you have a small rust spot or dent you want to fix, check the contents of the kit before you run out and buy any additional tools.

ALIGNING BODY PANELS

Doors

There are several methods of adjusting doors. Your vehicle will probably use one of those illustrated.

Whenever a door is removed and is to be reinstalled, you should matchmark the position of the hinges on the door pillars. The holes of the hinges and/or the hinge attaching points are usually oversize to permit alignment of doors. The striker plate is also moveable, through oversize holes, permitting up-and-down, in-and-out and fore-and-aft movement. Fore-and-aft movement is made by adding or subtracting shims from behind the striker and pillar post. The striker should be adjusted so that the door closes fully and remains closed, yet enters the lock freely.

DOOR HINGES

Don't try to cover up poor door adjustment with a striker plate adjustment. The gap on each side of the door should be equal and uniform and there should be no metal-to-metal contact as the door is opened or closed.

1. Determine which hinge bolts must be loosened to move the door in the desired direction.
2. Loosen the hinge bolt(s) just enough to allow the door to be moved with a padded pry bar.
3. Move the door a small amount and check the fit, after tightening the bolts. Be sure that there is no bind or interference with adjacent panels.
4. Repeat this until the door is properly positioned, and tighten all the bolts securely.

Hood, Trunk or Tailgate

As with doors, the outline of hinges should be scribed before removal. The hood and trunk can be aligned by loosening the hinge bolts in their slotted mounting holes and moving the hood or trunk lid as necessary.

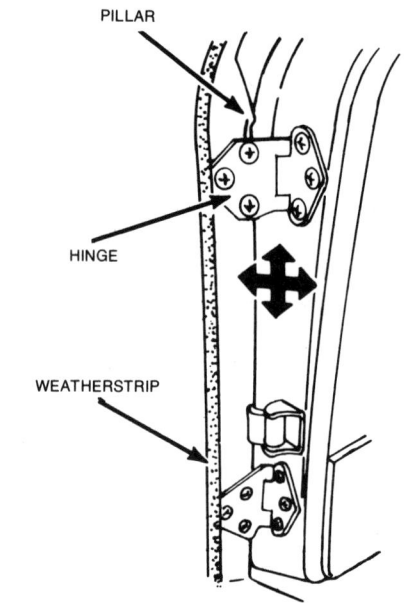
Door hinge adjustment

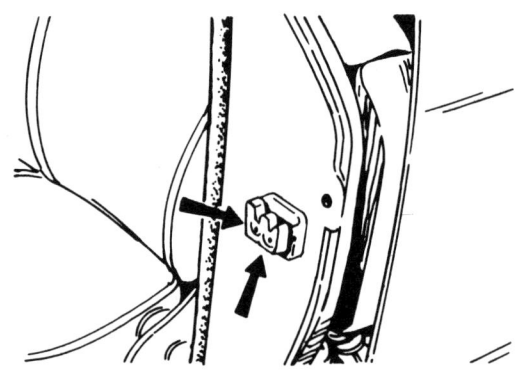
Move the door striker as indicated by arrows

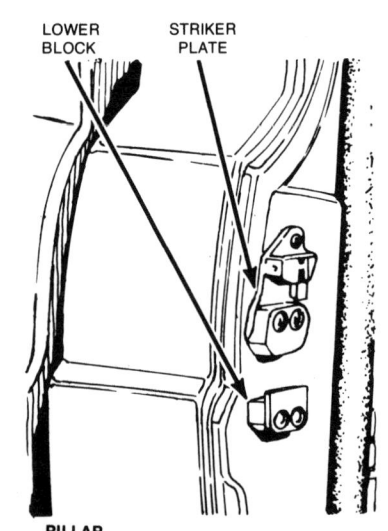
Striker plate and lower block

BODY 301

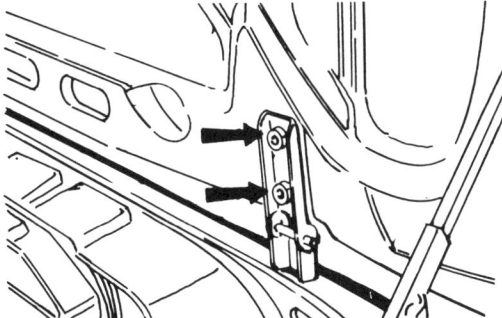

Loosen the hinge boots to permit fore-and-aft and horizontal adjustment

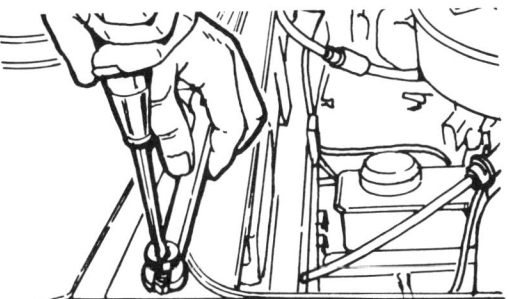

The hood is adjusted vertically by stop-screws at the front and/or rear

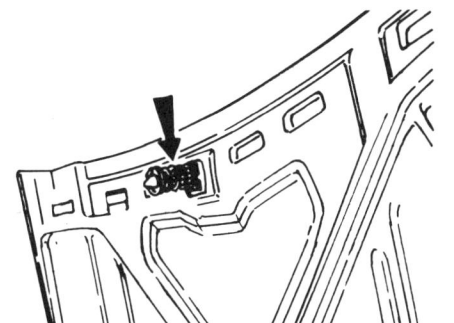

The hood pin can be adjusted for proper lock engagement

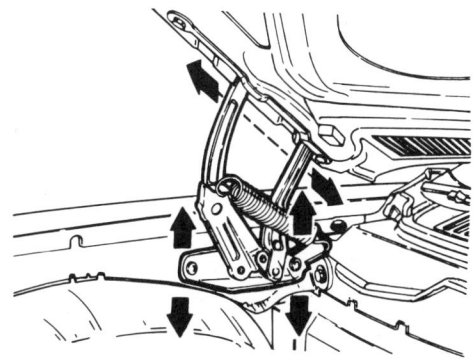

The height of the hood at the rear is adjusted by loosening the bolts that attach the hinge to the body and moving the hood up or down

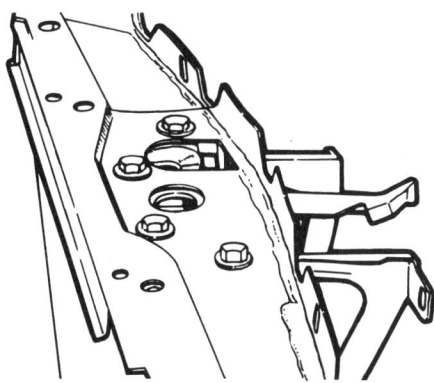

The base of the hood lock can also be repositioned slightly to give more positive lock engagement

The hood and trunk have adjustable catch locations to regulate lock engagement. Bumpers at the front and/or rear of the hood provide a vertical adjustment and the hood lockpin can be adjusted for proper engagement.

The tailgate on the station wagon can be adjusted by loosening the hinge bolts in their slotted mounting holes and moving the tailgate on its hinges. The latchplate and latch striker at the bottom of the tailgate opening can be adjusted to stop rattle. An adjustable bumper is located on each side.

RUST, UNDERCOATING, AND RUSTPROOFING

Rust

Rust is an electrochemical process. It works on ferrous metals (iron and steel) from the inside out due to exposure of unprotected surfaces to air and moisture. The possibility of rust exists practically nationwide—anywhere humidity, industrial pollution or chemical salts are present, rust can form. In coastal areas, the problem is high humidity and salt air; in snowy areas, the problem is chemical salt (de-icer) used to keep the roads clear, and in industrial areas, sulphur dioxide is present in the air from industrial pollution and is changed to sulphuric acid when it rains. The rusting process is accelerated by high temperatures, especially in snowy areas, when vehicles are driven over slushy roads and then left overnight in a heated garage.

Automotive styling also can be a contributor to rust formation. Spot welding of panels creates small pockets that trap moisture and form an environment for rust formation. Fortunately, auto manufacturers have been working hard to increase the corrosion protection of their products. Galvanized sheet metal enjoys much wider use, along with the increased use of plastic and various rust retardant coatings. Manufacturers are also designing out areas in the body where rust-forming moisture can collect.

To prevent rust, you must stop it before it gets started. On new vehicles, there are two ways to accomplish this.

First, the car or truck should be treated with a commercial rustproofing compound. There are many different brands of franchised rustproofers, but most processes involve spraying a waxy "self-healing" compound under the chassis, inside rocker panels, inside doors and fender liners and similar places where rust is likely to form. Prices for a quality rustproofing job range from $100–$250, depending on the area, the brand name and the size of the vehicle.

Ideally, the vehicle should be rustproofed as soon as possible following the purchase. The surfaces of the car or truck have begun to oxidize and deteriorate during shipping. In addition, the car may have sat on a dealer's lot or on a lot at the factory, and once the rust has progressed past the stage of light, powdery surface oxidation rustproofing is not likely to be worthwhile. Professional rustproofers feel that once rust has formed, rustproofing will simply seal in moisture already present. Most franchised rustproofing operations offer a 3–5 year warranty against rust-through, but will not support that warranty if the rustproofing is not applied within three months of the date of manufacture.

Undercoating should not be mistaken for rustproofing. Undercoating is a black, tar-like substance that is applied to the underside of a vehicle. Its basic function is to deaden noises that are transmitted from under the car. It simply cannot get into the crevices and seams where moisture tends to collect. In fact, it may clog up drainage holes and ventilation passages. Some undercoatings also tend to crack or peel with age and only create more moisture and corrosion attracting pockets.

The second thing you should do immediately after purchasing the car is apply a paint sealant. A sealant is a petroleum based product marketed under a wide variety of brand names. It has the same protective properties as a good wax, but bonds to the paint with a chemically inert layer that seals it from the air. If air can't get at the surface, oxidation cannot start.

The paint sealant kit consists of a base coat and a conditioning coat that should be applied every 6–8 months, depending on the manufacturer. The base coat must be applied before waxing, or the wax must first be removed.

Third, keep a garden hose handy for your car in winter. Use it a few times on nice days during the winter for underneath areas, and it will pay big dividends when spring arrives. Spraying under the fenders and other areas which even car washes don't reach will help remove road salt, dirt and other build-ups which help breed rust. Adjust the nozzle to a high-force spray. An old brush will help break up residue, permitting it to be washed away more easily.

It's a somewhat messy job, but worth it in the long run because rust often starts in those hidden areas.

At the same time, wash grime off the door sills and, more importantly, the under portions of the doors, plus the tailgate if you have a station wagon or truck. Applying a coat of wax to those areas at least once before and once during winter will help fend off rust.

When applying the wax to the under parts of the doors, you will note small drain holes. These holes often are plugged with undercoating or dirt. Make sure they are cleaned out to prevent water build-up inside the doors. A small punch or penknife will do the job.

Water from the high-pressure sprays in car washes sometimes can get into the housings for parking and taillights, so take a close look. If they contain water merely loosen the retaining screws and the water should run out.

Repairing Scratches and Small Dents

Step 1. This dent (arrow) is typical of a deep scratch or minor dent. If deep enough, the dent or scratch can be pulled out or hammered out from behind. In this case no straightening is necessary

Step 2. Using an 80-grit grinding disc on an electric drill grind the paint from the surrounding area down to bare metal. This will provide a rough surface for the body filler to grab

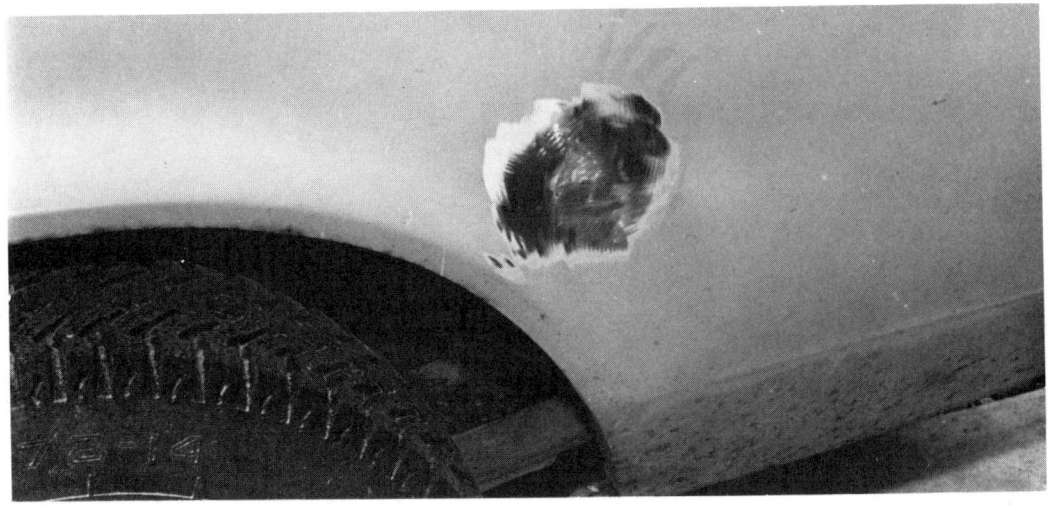

Step 3. The area should look like this when you're finished grinding

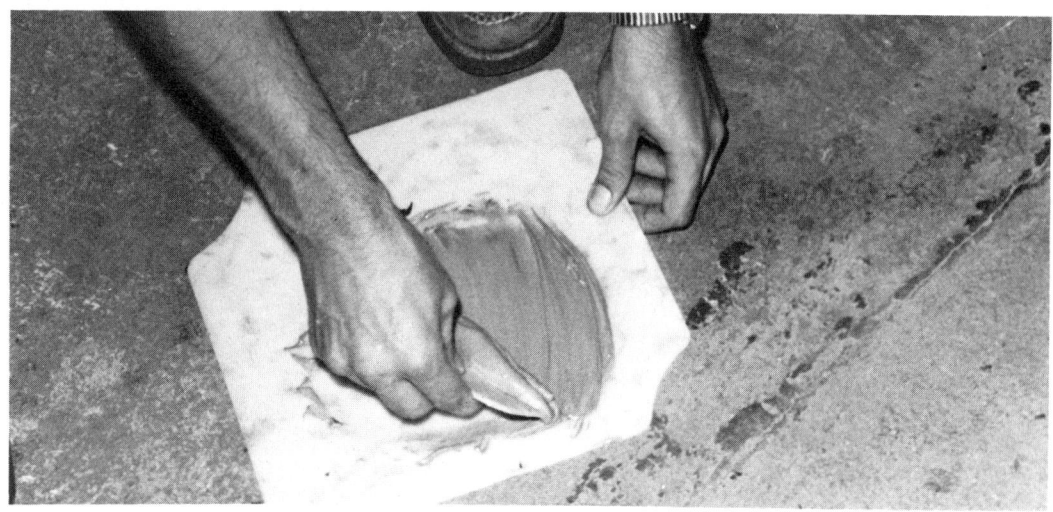

Step 4. Mix the body filler and cream hardener according to the directions

Step 5. Spread the body filler evenly over the entire area. Be sure to cover the area completely

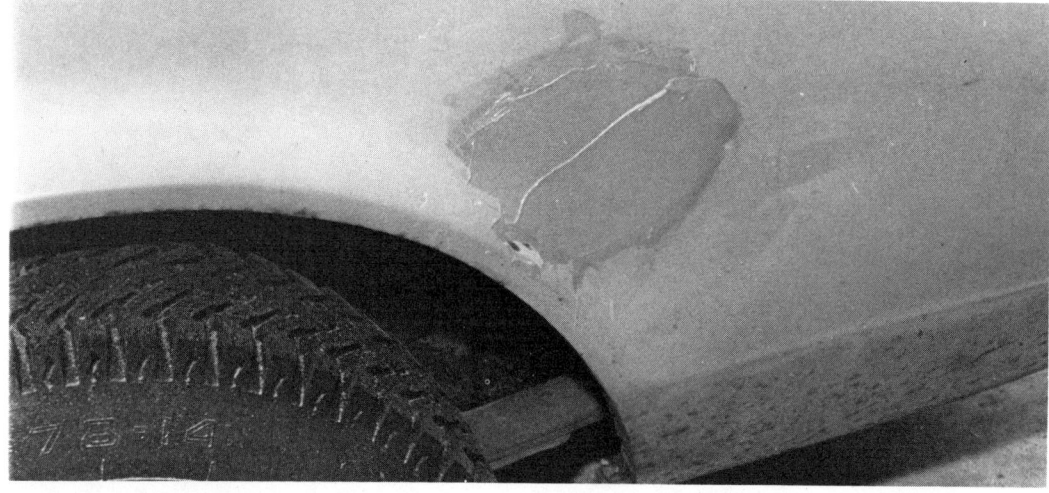

Step 6. Let the body filler dry until the surface can just be scratched with your fingernail

Step 7. Knock the high spots from the body filler with a body file

Step 8. Check frequently with the palm of your hand for high and low spots. If you wind up with low spots, you may have to apply another layer of filler

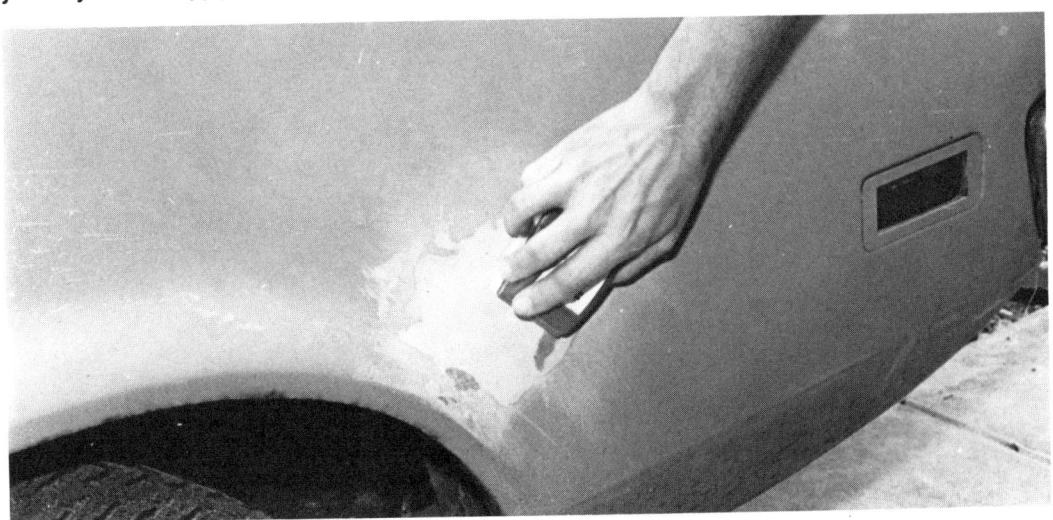

Step 9. Block sand the entire area with 320 grit paper

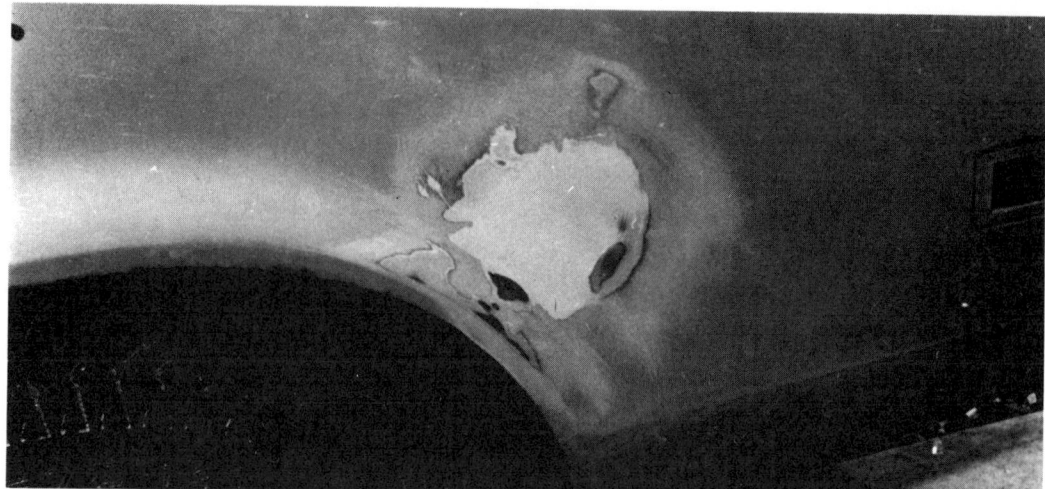

Step 10. When you're finished, the repair should look like this. Note the sand marks extending 2—3 inches out from the repaired area

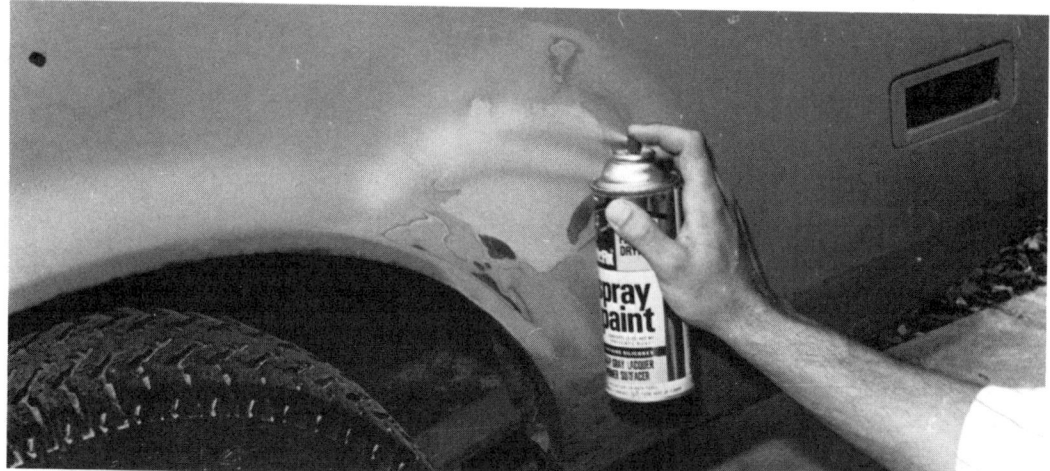

Step 11. Prime the entire area with automotive primer

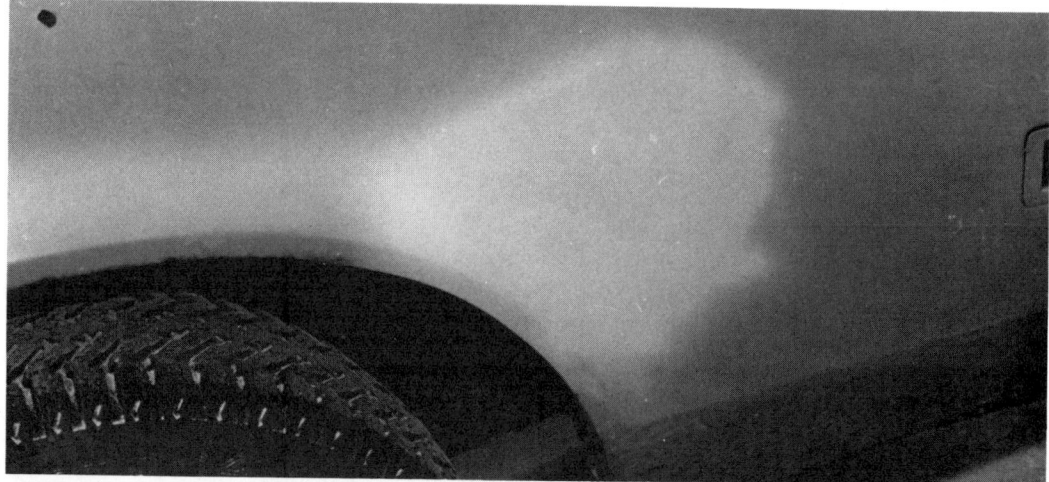

Step 12. The finished repair ready for the final paint coat. Note that the primer has covered the sanding marks (see Step 10). A repair of this size should be able to be spotpainted with good results

BODY

REPAIRING RUST HOLES

One thing you have to remember about rust: even if you grind away all the rusted metal in a panel, and repair the area with any of the kits available, *eventually* the rust will return. There are two reasons for this. One, rust is a chemical reaction that causes pressure under the repair from the inside out. That's how the blisters form. Two, the back side of the panel (and the repair) is wide open to moisture, and unpainted body filler acts like a sponge. That's why the best solution to rust problems is to remove the rusted panel and install a new one or have the rusted area cut out and a new piece of sheet metal welded in its place. The trouble with welding is the expense; sometimes it will cost more than the car or truck is worth.

One of the better solutions to do-it-yourself rust repair is the process using a fiberglass cloth repair kit (shown here). This will give a strong repair that resists cracking and moisture and is relatively easy to use. It can be used on large or small holes and also can be applied over contoured surfaces.

Step 1. Rust areas such as this are common and are easily fixed

Step 2. Grind away all traces of rust with a 24-grit grinding disc. Be sure to grind back 3—4 inches from the edge of the hole down to bare metal and be sure all traces of rust are removed

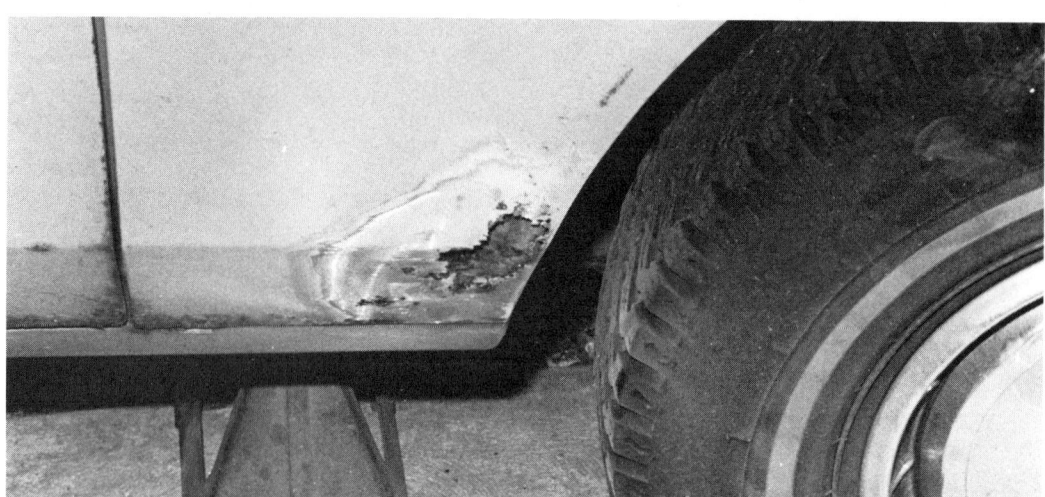

Step 3. Be sure all rust is removed from the edges of the metal. The edges must be ground back to un-rusted metal

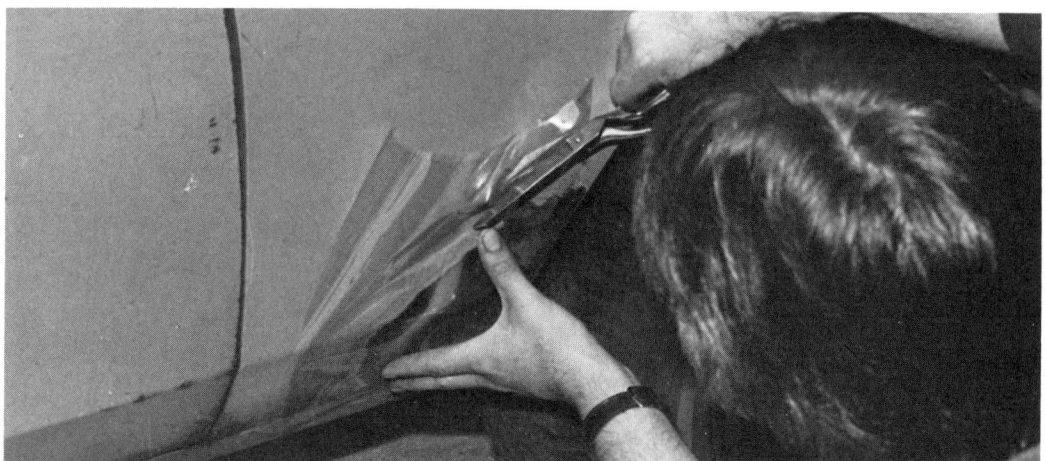

Step 4. If you are going to use release film, cut a piece about 2" larger than the area you have sanded. Place the film over the repair and mark the sanded area on the film. Avoid any unnecessary wrinkling of the film

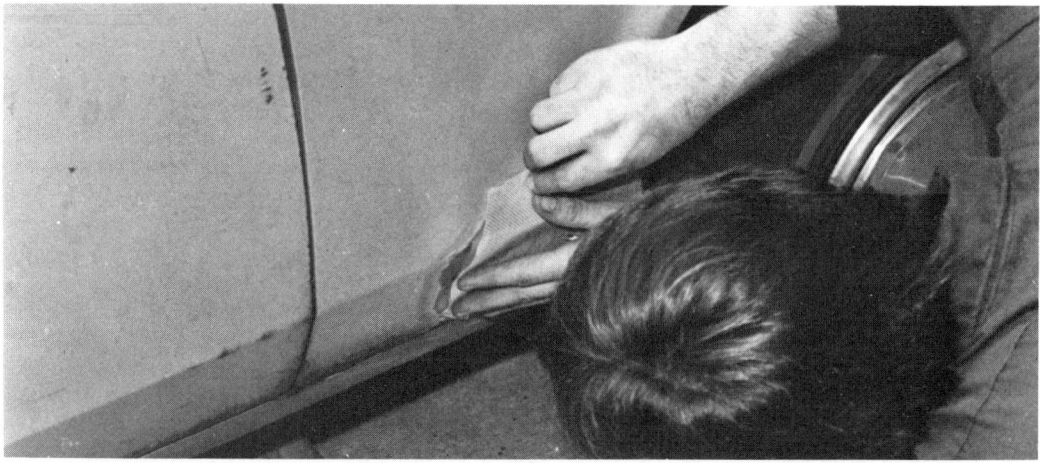

Step 5. Cut 2 pieces of fiberglass matte. One piece should be about 1" smaller than the sanded area and the second piece should be 1" smaller than the first. Use sharp scissors to avoid loose ends

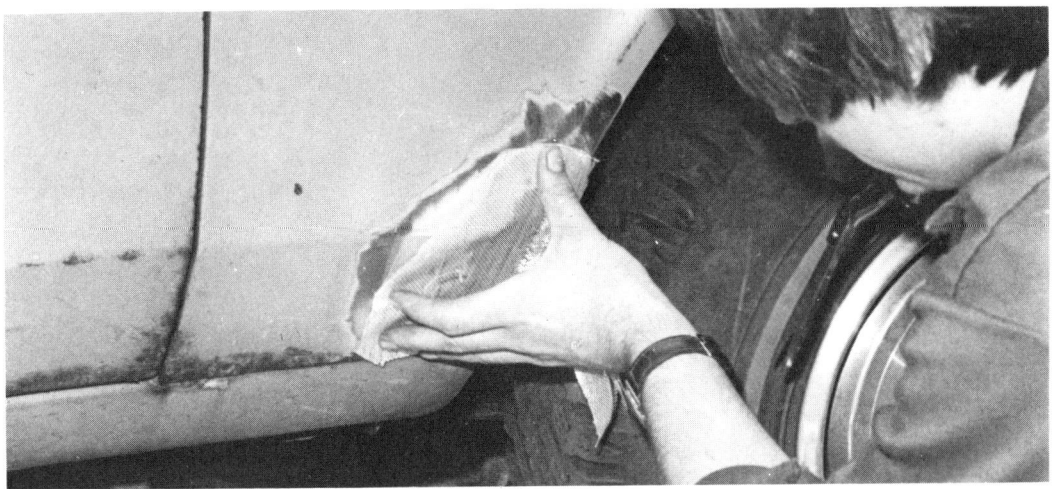

Step 6. Check the dimensions of the release film and cloth by holding them up to the repair area

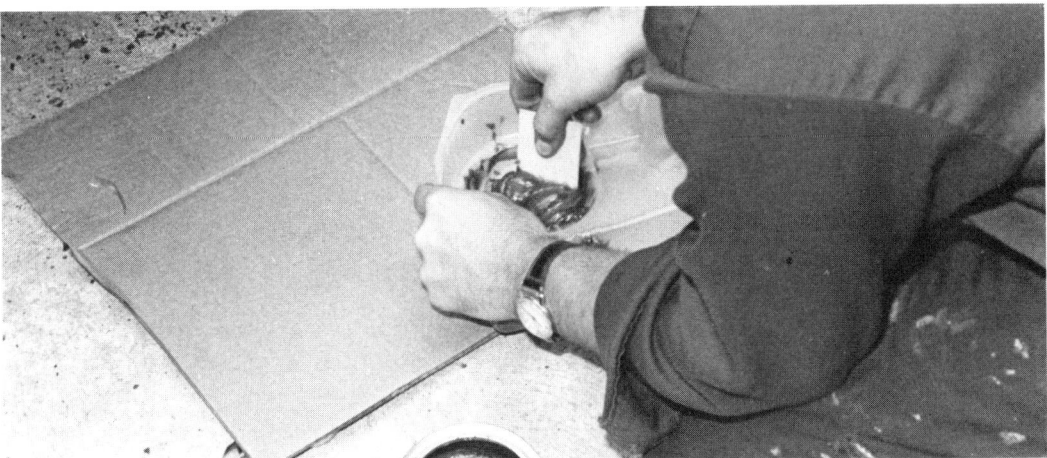

Step 7. Mix enough repair jelly and cream hardener in the mixing tray to saturate the fiberglass material or fill the repair area. Follow the directions on the container

Step 8. Lay the release sheet on a flat surface and spread an even layer of filler, large enough to cover the repair. Lay the smaller piece of fiberglass cloth in the center of the sheet and spread another layer of repair jelly over the fiberglass cloth. Repeat the operation for the larger piece of cloth. If the fiberglass cloth is not used, spread the repair jelly on the release film, concentrated in the middle of the repair

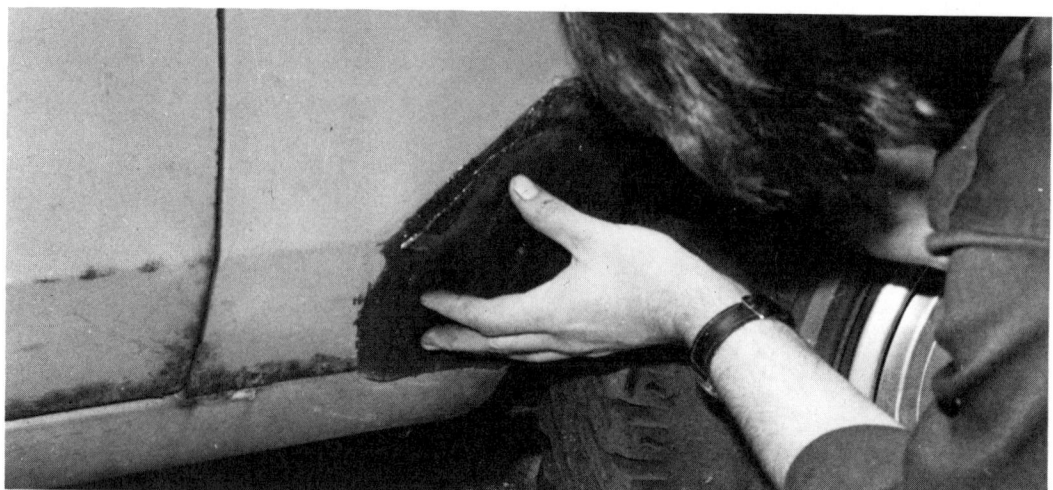
Step 9. Place the repair material over the repair area, with the release film facing outward

Step 10. Use a spreader and work from the center outward to smooth the material, following the body contours. Be sure to remove all air bubbles

Step 11. Wait until the repair has dried tack-free and peel off the release sheet. The ideal working temperature is 65—90° F. Cooler or warmer temperatures or high humidity may require additional curing time

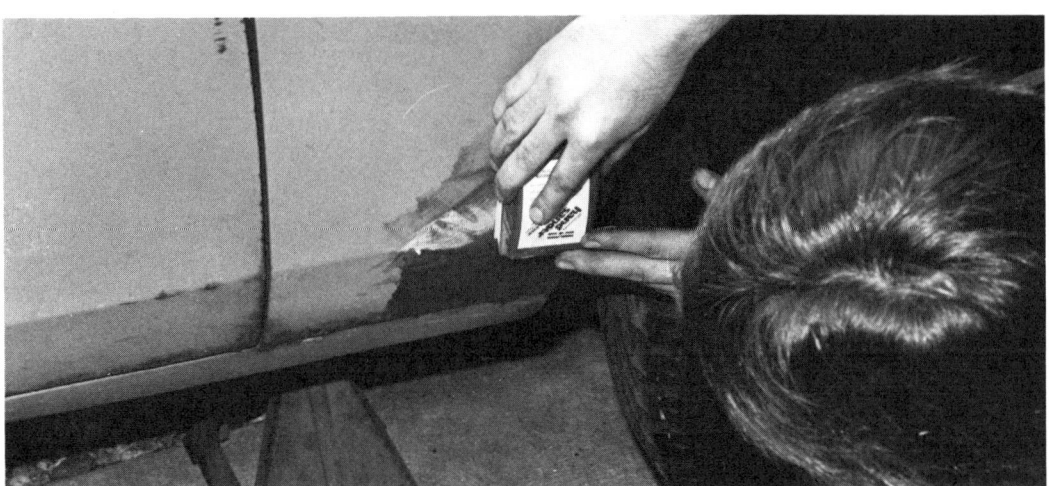

Step 12. Sand and feather-edge the entire area. The initial sanding can be done with a sanding disc on an electric drill if care is used. Finish the sanding with a block sander

Step 13. When the area is sanded smooth, mix some topcoat and hardener and apply it directly with a spreader. This will give a smooth finish and prevent the glass matte from showing through the paint

Step 14. Block sand the topcoat with finishing sandpaper

Step 15. To finish this repair, grind out the surface rust along the top edge of the rocker panel

Step 16. Mix some more repair jelly and cream hardener and apply it directly over the surface

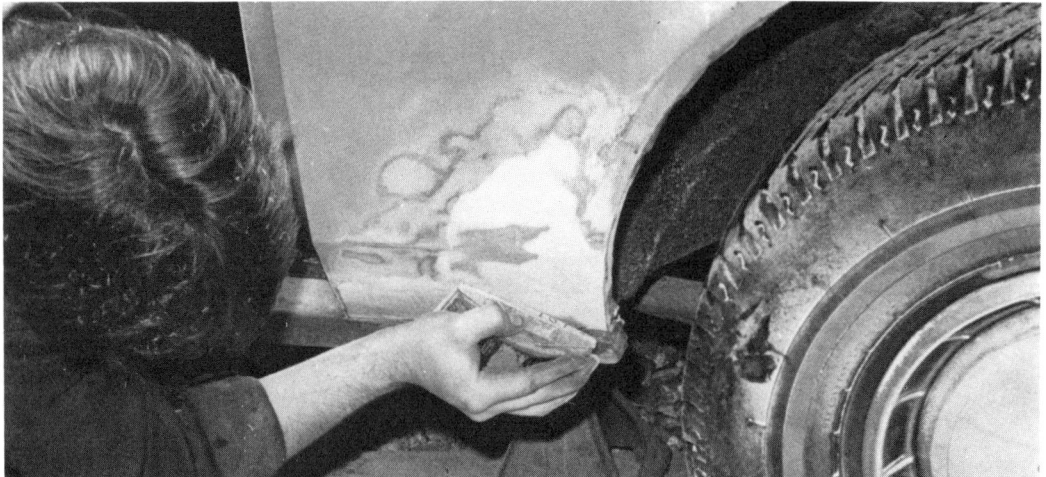

Step 17. When it dries tack-free, block sand the surface smooth

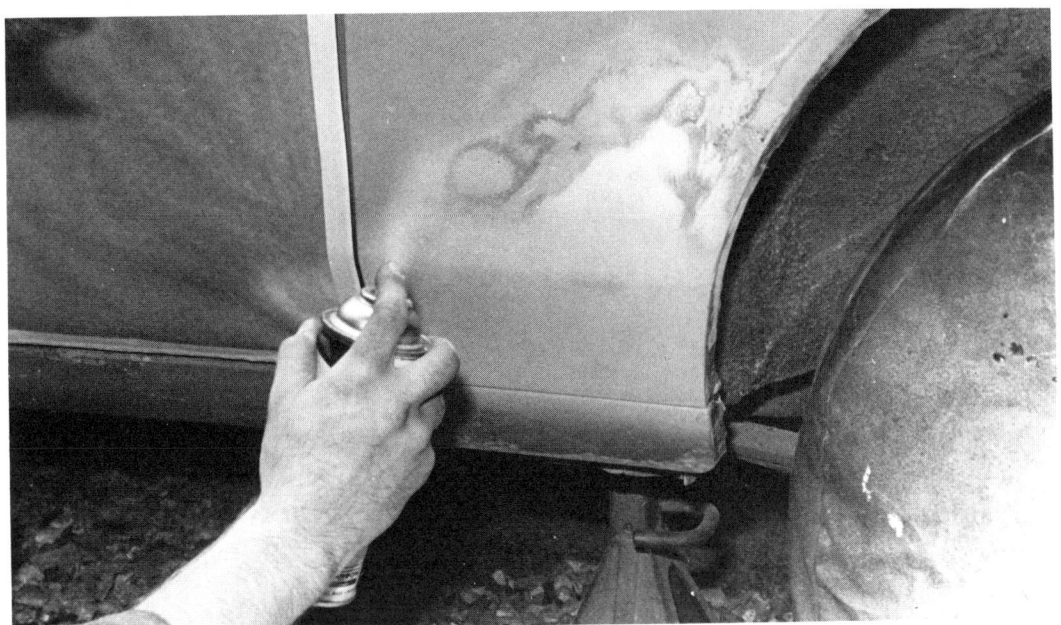

Step 18. If necessary, mask off adjacent panels and spray the entire repair with primer. You are now ready for a color coat

AUTO BODY CARE

There are hundreds—maybe thousands—of products on the market, all designed to protect or aid your car's finish in some manner. There are as many different products as there are ways to use them, but they all have one thing in common—the surface must be clean.

Washing

The primary ingredient for washing your car is water, preferably "soft" water. In many areas of the country, the local water supply is "hard" containing many minerals. The little rings or film that is left on your car's surface after it has dried is the result of "hard" water.

Since you usually can't change the local water supply, the next best thing is to dry the surface before it has a chance to dry itself.

Into the water you usually add soap. Don't use detergents or common, coarse soaps. Your car's paint never truly dries out, but is always evaporating residual oils into the air. Harsh detergents will remove these oils, causing the paint to dry faster than normal. Instead use warm water and a non-detergent soap made especially for waxed surfaces or a liquid soap made for waxed surfaces or a liquid soap made for washing dishes by hand.

Other products that can be used on painted surfaces include baking soda or plain soda water for stubborn dirt.

Wash the car completely, starting at the top, and rinse it completely clean. Abrasive grit should be loaded off under water pressure; scrubbing grit off will scratch the finish. The best washing tool is a sponge, cleaning mitt or soft towel. Whichever you choose, replace it often as each tends to absorb grease and dirt.

Other ways to get a better wash include:
- Don't wash your car in the sun or when the finish is hot.
- Use water pressure to remove caked-on dirt.
- Remove tree-sap and bird effluence immediately. Such substances will eat through wax, polish and paint.

One of the best implements to dry your car is a turkish towel or an old, soft bath towel. Anything with a deep nap will hold any dirt in suspension and not grind it into the paint.

Harder cloths will only grind the grit into the paint making more scratches. Always start drying at the top, followed by the hood and trunk and sides. You'll find there's always more dirt near the rocker panels and wheelwells which will wind up on the rest of the car if you dry these areas first.

Cleaners, Waxes and Polishes

Before going any farther you should know the function of various products.

Cleaners—remove the top layer of dead pigment or paint.

Rubbing or polishing compounds—used to remove stubborn dirt, get rid of minor scratches, smooth away imperfections and partially restore badly weathered paint.

Polishes—contain no abrasives or waxes; they shine the paint by adding oils to the paint.

Waxes—are a protective coating for the polish.

CLEANERS AND COMPOUNDS

Before you apply any wax, you'll have to remove oxidation, road film and other types of pollutants that washing alone will not remove.

The paint on your car never dries completely. There are always residual oils evaporating from the paint into the air. When enough oils are present in the paint, it has a healthy shine (gloss). When too many oils evaporate the paint takes on a whitish cast known as oxidation. The idea of polishing and waxing is to keep enough oil present in the painted surface to prevent oxidation; but when it occurs, the only recourse is to remove the top layer of "dead" paint, exposing the healthy paint underneath.

Products to remove oxidation and road film are sold under a variety of generic names—polishes, cleaner, rubbing compound, cleaner/polish, polish/cleaner, self-polishing wax, pre-wax cleaner, finish restorer and many more. Regardless of name there are two types of cleaners—abrasive cleaners (sometimes called polishing or rubbing compounds) that remove oxidation by grinding away the top layer of "dead" paint, or chemical cleaners that dissolve the "dead" pigment, allowing it to be wiped away.

Abrasive cleaners, by their nature, leave thousands of minute scratches in the finish, which must be polished out later. These should only be used in extreme cases, but are usually the only thing to use on badly oxidized paint finishes. Chemical cleaners are much milder but are not strong enough for severe cases of oxidation or weathered paint.

The most popular cleaners are liquid or paste abrasive polishing and rubbing compounds. Polishing compounds have a finer abrasive grit for medium duty work. Rubbing compounds are a coarser abrasive and for heavy duty work. Unless you are familiar with how to use compounds, be very careful. Excessive rubbing with any type of compound or cleaner can grind right through the paint to primer or bare metal. Follow the directions on the container—depending on type, the cleaner may or may not be OK for your paint. For example, some cleaners are not formulated for acrylic lacquer finishes.

When a small area needs compounding or heavy polishing, it's best to do the job by hand. Some people prefer a powered buffer for large areas. Avoid cutting through the paint along styling edges on the body. Small, hand operations where the compound is applied and rubbed using cloth folded into a thick ball allow you to work in straight lines along such edges.

To avoid cutting through on the edges when using a power buffer, try masking tape. Just cover the edge with tape while using power. Then finish the job by hand with the tape removed. Even then work carefully. The paint tends to be a lot thinner along the sharp ridges stamped into the panels.

Whether compounding by machine or by hand, only work on a small area and apply the compound sparingly. If the materials are spread too thin, or allowed to sit too long, they dry out. Once dry they lose the ability to deliver a smooth, clean finish. Also, dried out polish tends to cause the buffer to stick in one spot. This in turn can burn or cut through the finish.

WAXES AND POLISHES

Your car's finish can be protected in a number of ways. A cleaner/wax or polish/cleaner followed by wax or variations of each all provide good results. The two-step approach (polish followed by wax) is probably slightly better but consumes more time and effort. Properly fed with oils, your paint should never need cleaning, but despite the best polishing job, it won't last unless it's protected with wax. Without wax, polish must be renewed at least once a month to prevent oxidation. Years ago (some still swear by it today), the best wax was made from the Brazilian palm, the Carnuba, favored for its vegetable base and high melting point. However, modern synthetic waxes are harder, which means they protect against moisture better, and chemically inert silicone is used for a long lasting protection. The only problem with silicone wax is that it penetrates all layers of paint. To repaint or touch up a panel or car protected by silicone wax, you have to completely strip the finish to avoid "fish-eyes."

Under normal conditions, silicone waxes will last 4–6 months, but you have to be careful of wax build-up from too much waxing. Too thick a coat of wax is just as bad as no wax at all; it stops the paint from breathing.

Combination cleaners/waxes have become popular lately because they remove the old layer of wax plus light oxidation, while putting on a fresh coat of wax at the same time. Some cleaners/waxes contain abrasive cleaners which require caution, although many cleaner/waxes use a chemical cleaner.

Applying Wax or Polish

You may view polishing and waxing your car as a pleasant way to spend an afternoon, or as a boring chore, but it has to be done to keep the paint on your car. Caring for the paint doesn't require special tools, but you should follow a few rules.

1. Use a good quality wax.
2. Before applying any wax or polish, be sure the surface is completely clean. Just because the car looks clean, doesn't mean it's ready for polish or wax.
3. If the finish on your car is weathered, dull, or oxidized, it will probably have to be compounded to remove the old or oxidized paint. If the paint is simply dulled from lack of care, one of the non-abrasive cleaners known as polishing compounds will do the trick. If the paint is severely scratched or really dull, you'll probably have to use a rubbing compound to prepare the finish for waxing. If you're not sure which one to use, use the polishing compound, since you can easily ruin the finish by using too strong a compound.
4. Don't apply wax, polish or compound in direct sunlight, even if the directions on the can say you can. Most waxes will not cure properly in bright sunlight and you'll probably end up with a blotchy looking finish.
5. Don't rub the wax off too soon. The result will be a wet, dull looking finish. Let the wax dry thoroughly before buffing it off.
6. A constant debate among car enthusiasts is how wax should be applied. Some maintain pastes or liquids should be applied in a circular motion, but body shop experts have long thought that this approach results in barely detectable circular abrasions, especially on cars that are waxed frequently. They advise rubbing in straight lines, especially if any kind of cleaner is involved.
7. If an applicator is not supplied with the wax, use a piece of soft cheesecloth or very soft lint-free material. The same applies to buffing the surface.

SPECIAL SURFACES

One-step combination cleaner and wax formulas shouldn't be used on many of the special surfaces which abound on cars. The one-step materials contain abrasives to achieve a clean surface under the wax top coat. The abrasives are so mild that you could clean a car every week for a couple of years without fear of rubbing through the paint. But this same level of abrasiveness might, through repeated use, damage decals used for special trim effects. This includes wide stripes, wood-grain trim and other appliques.

Painted plastics must be cleaned with care. If a cleaner is too aggressive it will cut through the paint and expose the primer. If bright trim such as polished aluminum or chrome is painted, cleaning must be performed with even greater care. If rubbing compound is being used, it will cut faster than polish.

Abrasive cleaners will dull an acrylic finish. The best way to clean these newer finishes is with a non-abrasive liquid polish. Only dirt and oxidation, not paint, will be removed.

Taking a few minutes to read the instructions on the can of polish or wax will help prevent making serious mistakes. Not all preparations will work on all surfaces. And some are intended for power application while others will only work when applied by hand.

Don't get the idea that just pouring on some polish and then hitting it with a buffer will suffice. Power equipment speeds the operation. But it also adds a measure of risk. It's very easy to damage the finish if you use the wrong methods or materials.

Caring for Chrome

Read the label on the container. Many products are formulated specifically for chrome, but others contain abrasives that will scratch the chrome finish. If it isn't recommended for chrome, don't use it.

Never use steel wool or kitchen soap pads to clean chrome. Be careful not to get chrome cleaner on paint or interior vinyl surfaces. If you do, get it off immediately.

Troubleshooting

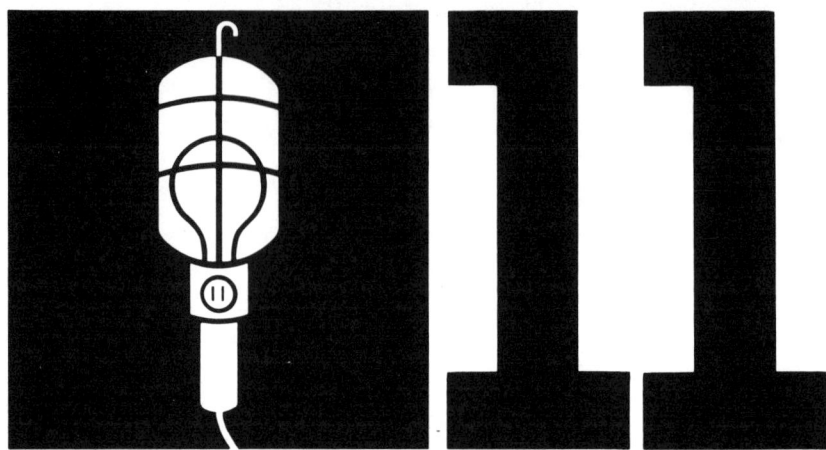

This section is designed to aid in the quick, accurate diagnosis of automotive problems. While automotive repairs can be made by many people, accurate troubleshooting is a rare skill for the amateur and professional alike.

In its simplest state, troubleshooting is an exercise in logic. It is essential to realize that an automobile is really composed of a series of systems. Some of these systems are interrelated; others are not. Automobiles operate within a framework of logical rules and physical laws, and the key to troubleshooting is a good understanding of all the automotive systems.

This section breaks the car or truck down into its component systems, allowing the problem to be isolated. The charts and diagnostic road maps list the most common problems and the most probable causes of trouble. Obviously it would be impossible to list every possible problem that could happen along with every possible cause, but it will locate MOST problems and eliminate a lot of unnecessary guesswork. The systematic format will locate problems within a given system, but, because many automotive systems are interrelated, the solution to your particular problem may be found in a number of systems on the car or truck.

USING THE TROUBLESHOOTING CHARTS

This book contains all of the specific information that the average do-it-yourself mechanic needs to repair and maintain his or her car or truck. The troubleshooting charts are designed to be used in conjunction with the specific procedures and information in the text. For instance, troubleshooting a point-type ignition system is fairly standard for all models, but you may be directed to the text to find procedures for troubleshooting an individual type of electronic ignition. You will also have to refer to the specification charts throughout the book for specifications applicable to your car or truck.

TOOLS AND EQUIPMENT

The tools illustrated in Chapter 1 (plus two more diagnostic pieces) will be adequate to troubleshoot most problems. The two other tools needed are a voltmeter and an ohmmeter. These can be purchased separately or in combination, known as a VOM meter.

In the event that other tools are required, they will be noted in the procedures.

TROUBLESHOOTING 317

Troubleshooting Engine Problems

See Chapters 2, 3, 4 for more information and service procedures.

Index to Systems

System	To Test	Group
Battery	Engine need not be running	1
Starting system	Engine need not be running	2
Primary electrical system	Engine need not be running	3
Secondary electrical system	Engine need not be running	4
Fuel system	Engine need not be running	5
Engine compression	Engine need not be running	6
Engine vacuum	Engine must be running	7
Secondary electrical system	Engine must be running	8
Valve train	Engine must be running	9
Exhaust system	Engine must be running	10
Cooling system	Engine must be running	11
Engine lubrication	Engine must be running	12

Index to Problems

Problem: Symptom	Begin at Specific Diagnosis, Number
Engine Won't Start:	
Starter doesn't turn	1.1, 2.1
Starter turns, engine doesn't	2.1
Starter turns engine very slowly	1.1, 2.4
Starter turns engine normally	3.1, 4.1
Starter turns engine very quickly	6.1
Engine fires intermittently	4.1
Engine fires consistently	5.1, 6.1
Engine Runs Poorly:	
Hard starting	3.1, 4.1, 5.1, 8.1
Rough idle	4.1, 5.1, 8.1
Stalling	3.1, 4.1, 5.1, 8.1
Engine dies at high speeds	4.1, 5.1
Hesitation (on acceleration from standing stop)	5.1, 8.1
Poor pickup	4.1, 5.1, 8.1
Lack of power	3.1, 4.1, 5.1, 8.1
Backfire through the carburetor	4.1, 8.1, 9.1
Backfire through the exhaust	4.1, 8.1, 9.1
Blue exhaust gases	6.1, 7.1
Black exhaust gases	5.1
Running on (after the ignition is shut off)	3.1, 8.1
Susceptible to moisture	4.1
Engine misfires under load	4.1, 7.1, 8.4, 9.1
Engine misfires at speed	4.1, 8.4
Engine misfires at idle	3.1, 4.1, 5.1, 7.1, 8.4

Sample Section

Test and Procedure	Results and Indications	Proceed to
4.1—Check for spark: Hold each spark plug wire approximately ¼" from ground with gloves or a heavy, dry rag. Crank the engine and observe the spark.	If no spark is evident:	4.2
	If spark is good in some cases:	4.3
	If spark is good in all cases:	4.6

TROUBLESHOOTING

Specific Diagnosis

This section is arranged so that following each test, instructions are given to proceed to another, until a problem is diagnosed.

Section 1—Battery

Test and Procedure	Results and Indications	Proceed to
1.1—Inspect the battery visually for case condition (corrosion, cracks) and water level. *Inspect the battery case*	If case is cracked, replace battery:	1.4
	If the case is intact, remove corrosion with a solution of baking soda and water (**CAUTION:** *do not get the solution into the battery*), and fill with water:	1.2
1.2—Check the battery cable connections: Insert a screwdriver between the battery post and the cable clamp. Turn the headlights on high beam, and observe them as the screwdriver is gently twisted to ensure good metal to metal contact. *TESTING BATTERY CABLE CONNECTIONS USING A SCREWDRIVER*	If the lights brighten, remove and clean the clamp and post; coat the post with petroleum jelly, install and tighten the clamp:	1.4
	If no improvement is noted:	1.3
1.3—Test the state of charge of the battery using an individual cell tester or hydrometer.	If indicated, charge the battery. **NOTE:** *If no obvious reason exists for the low state of charge (i.e., battery age, prolonged storage)*, proceed to:	1.4

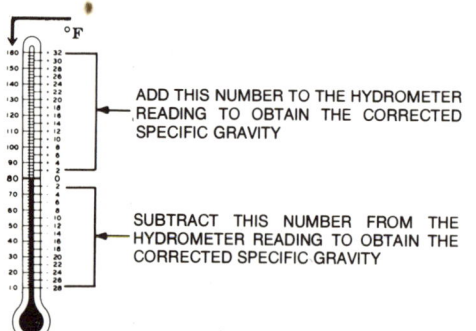

Specific Gravity (@ 80° F.)

Minimum	Battery Charge
1.260	100% Charged
1.230	75% Charged
1.200	50% Charged
1.170	25% Charged
1.140	Very Little Power Left
1.110	Completely Discharged

The effects of temperature on battery specific gravity (left) and amount of battery charge in relation to specific gravity (right)

Test and Procedure	Results and Indications	Proceed to
1.4—Visually inspect battery cables for cracking, bad connection to ground, or bad connection to starter.	If necessary, tighten connections or replace the cables:	2.1

TROUBLESHOOTING

Section 2—Starting System
See Chapter 3 for service procedures

Test and Procedure	Results and Indications	Proceed to
Note: Tests in Group 2 are performed with coil high tension lead disconnected to prevent accidental starting.		
2.1—Test the starter motor and solenoid: Connect a jumper from the battery post of the solenoid (or relay) to the starter post of the solenoid (or relay).	If starter turns the engine normally:	2.2
	If the starter buzzes, or turns the engine very slowly:	2.4
	If no response, replace the solenoid (or relay).	3.1
	If the starter turns, but the engine doesn't, ensure that the flywheel ring gear is intact. If the gear is undamaged, replace the starter drive.	3.1
2.2—Determine whether ignition override switches are functioning properly (clutch start switch, neutral safety switch), by connecting a jumper across the switch(es), and turning the ignition switch to "start".	If starter operates, adjust or replace switch:	3.1
	If the starter doesn't operate:	2.3
2.3—Check the ignition switch "start" position: Connect a 12V test lamp or voltmeter between the starter post of the solenoid (or relay) and ground. Turn the ignition switch to the "start" position, and jiggle the key.	If the lamp doesn't light or the meter needle doesn't move when the switch is turned, check the ignition switch for loose connections, cracked insulation, or broken wires. Repair or replace as necessary:	3.1
	If the lamp flickers or needle moves when the key is jiggled, replace the ignition switch.	3.3

Checking the ignition switch "start" position

STARTER RELAY (IF EQUIPPED)

2.4—Remove and bench test the starter, according to specifications in the engine electrical section.	If the starter does not meet specifications, repair or replace as needed:	3.1
	If the starter is operating properly:	2.5
2.5—Determine whether the engine can turn freely: Remove the spark plugs, and check for water in the cylinders. Check for water on the dipstick, or oil in the radiator. Attempt to turn the engine using an 18" flex drive and socket on the crankshaft pulley nut or bolt.	If the engine will turn freely only with the spark plugs out, and hydrostatic lock (water in the cylinders) is ruled out, check valve timing:	9.2
	If engine will not turn freely, and it is known that the clutch and transmission are free, the engine must be disassembled for further evaluation:	Chapter 3

320 TROUBLESHOOTING

Section 3—Primary Electrical System

Test and Procedure	Results and Indications	Proceed to
3.1—Check the ignition switch "on" position: Connect a jumper wire between the distributor side of the coil and ground, and a 12V test lamp between the switch side of the coil and ground. Remove the high tension lead from the coil. Turn the ignition switch on and jiggle the key.	If the lamp lights:	3.2
	If the lamp flickers when the key is jiggled, replace the ignition switch:	3.3
	If the lamp doesn't light, check for loose or open connections. If none are found, remove the ignition switch and check for continuity. If the switch is faulty, replace it:	3.3

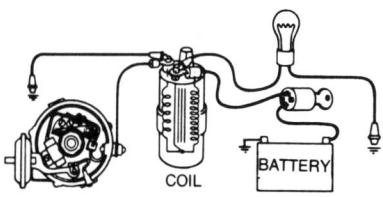

Checking the ignition switch "on" position

3.2—Check the ballast resistor or resistance wire for an open circuit, using an ohmmeter. See Chapter 3 for specific tests.	Replace the resistor or resistance wire if the resistance is zero. **NOTE:** *Some ignition systems have no ballast resistor.*	3.3

 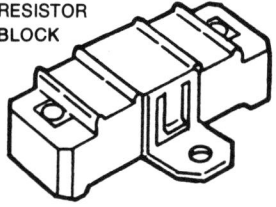

Two types of resistors

3.3—On point-type ignition systems, visually inspect the breaker points for burning, pitting or excessive wear. Gray coloring of the point contact surfaces is normal. Rotate the crankshaft until the contact heel rests on a high point of the distributor cam and adjust the point gap to specifications. On electronic ignition models, remove the distributor cap and visually inspect the armature. Ensure that the armature pin is in place, and that the armature is on tight and rotates when the engine is cranked. Make sure there are no cracks, chips or rounded edges on the armature.	If the breaker points are intact, clean the contact surfaces with fine emery cloth, and adjust the point gap to specifications. If the points are worn, replace them. On electronic systems, replace any parts which appear defective. If condition persists:	3.4

TROUBLESHOOTING   321

Test and Procedure	Results and Indications	Proceed to
3.4—On point-type ignition systems, connect a dwell-meter between the distributor primary lead and ground. Crank the engine and observe the point dwell angle. On electronic ignition systems, conduct a stator (magnetic pickup assembly) test. See Chapter 3.	On point-type systems, adjust the dwell angle if necessary. **NOTE:** *Increasing the point gap decreases the dwell angle and vice-versa.*	3.6
	If the dwell meter shows little or no reading;	3.5
	On electronic ignition systems, if the stator is bad, replace the stator. If the stator is good, proceed to the other tests in Chapter 3.	

Dwell is a function of point gap

3.5—On the point-type ignition systems, check the condenser for short: connect an ohmeter across the condenser body and the pigtail lead.	If any reading other than infinite is noted, replace the condenser	3.6

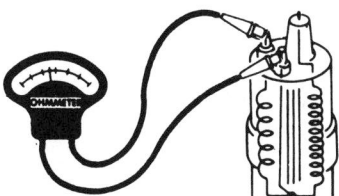

Checking the condenser for short

3.6—Test the coil primary resistance: On point-type ignition systems, connect an ohmmeter across the coil primary terminals, and read the resistance on the low scale. Note whether an external ballast resistor or resistance wire is used. On electronic ignition systems, test the coil primary resistance as in Chapter 3.	Point-type ignition coils utilizing ballast resistors or resistance wires should have approximately 1.0 ohms resistance. Coils with internal resistors should have approximately 4.0 ohms resistance. If values far from the above are noted, replace the coil.	4.1

Check the coil primary resistance

TROUBLESHOOTING

Section 4—Secondary Electrical System
See Chapters 2–3 for service procedures

Test and Procedure	Results and Indications	Proceed to
4.1—Check for spark: Hold each spark plug wire approximately ¼" from ground with gloves or a heavy, dry rag. Crank the engine, and observe the spark.	If no spark is evident:	4.2
	If spark is good in some cylinders:	4.3
	If spark is good in all cylinders:	4.6

Check for spark at the plugs

4.2—Check for spark at the coil high tension lead: Remove the coil high tension lead from the distributor and position it approximately ¼" from ground. Crank the engine and observe spark. **CAUTION: This test should not be performed on engines equipped with electronic ignition.**	If the spark is good and consistent:	4.3
	If the spark is good but intermittent, test the primary electrical system starting at 3.3:	3.3
	If the spark is weak or non-existent, replace the coil high tension lead, clean and tighten all connections and retest. If no improvement is noted:	4.4
4.3—Visually inspect the distributor cap and rotor for burned or corroded contacts, cracks, carbon tracks, or moisture. Also check the fit of the rotor on the distributor shaft (where applicable).	If moisture is present, dry thoroughly, and retest per 4.1:	4.1
	If burned or excessively corroded contacts, cracks, or carbon tracks are noted, replace the defective part(s) and retest per 4.1:	4.1
	If the rotor and cap appear intact, or are only slightly corroded, clean the contacts thoroughly (including the cap towers and spark plug wire ends) and retest per 4.1:	
	If the spark is good in all cases:	4.6
	If the spark is poor in all cases:	4.5

Inspect the distributor cap and rotor

TROUBLESHOOTING 323

Test and Procedure	Results and Indications	Proceed to
4.4—Check the coil secondary resistance: On point-type systems connect an ohmmeter across the distributor side of the coil and the coil tower. Read the resistance on the high scale of the ohmmeter. On electronic ignition systems, see Chapter 3 for specific tests.	The resistance of a satisfactory coil should be between 4,000 and 10,000 ohms. If resistance is considerably higher (i.e., 40,000 ohms) replace the coil and retest per 4.1. **NOTE:** *This does not apply to high performance coils.*	

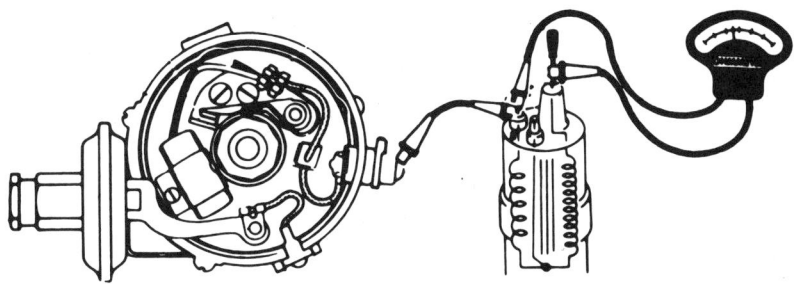

Testing the coil secondary resistance

4.5—Visually inspect the spark plug wires for cracking or brittleness. Ensure that no two wires are positioned so as to cause induction firing (adjacent and parallel). Remove each wire, one by one, and check resistance with an ohmmeter.	Replace any cracked or brittle wires. If any of the wires are defective, replace the entire set. Replace any wires with excessive resistance (over 8000Ω per foot for suppression wire), and separate any wires that might cause induction firing.	4.6

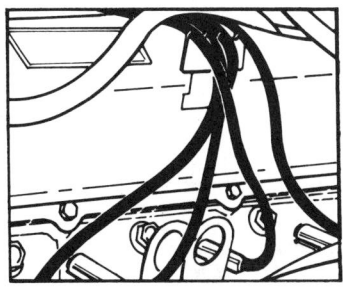 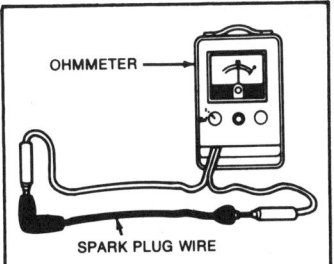 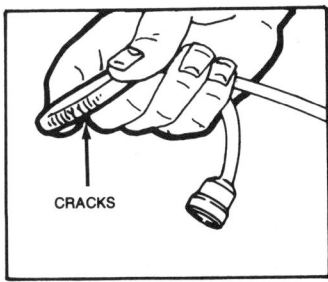

Misfiring can be the result of spark plug leads to adjacent, consecutively firing cylinders running parallel and too close together

On point-type ignition systems, check the spark plug wires as shown. On electronic ignitions, do not remove the wire from the distributor cap terminal; instead, test through the cap

Spark plug wires can be checked visually by bending them in a loop over your finger. This will reveal any cracks, burned or broken insulation. Any wire with cracked insulation should be replaced

4.6—Remove the spark plugs, noting the cylinders from which they were removed, and evaluate according to the color photos in the middle of this book.	See following.	See following.

324 TROUBLESHOOTING

Test and Procedure	Results and Indications	Proceed to
4.7—Examine the location of all the plugs.	The following diagrams illustrate some of the conditions that the location of plugs will reveal.	4.8

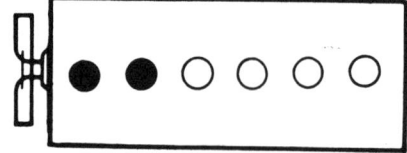

Two adjacent plugs are fouled in a 6-cylinder engine, 4-cylinder engine or either bank of a V-8. This is probably due to a blown head gasket between the two cylinders

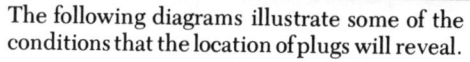

The two center plugs in a 6-cylinder engine are fouled. Raw fuel may be "boiled" out of the carburetor into the intake manifold after the engine is shut-off. Stop-start driving can also foul the center plugs, due to overly rich mixture. Proper float level, a new float needle and seat or use of an insulating spacer may help this problem

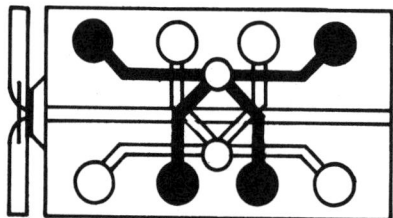

An unbalanced carburetor is indicated. Following the fuel flow on this particular design shows that the cylinders fed by the right-hand barrel are fouled from overly rich mixture, while the cylinders fed by the left-hand barrel are normal

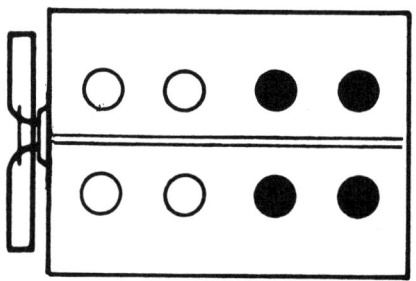

If the four rear plugs are overheated, a cooling system problem is suggested. A thorough cleaning of the cooling system may restore coolant circulation and cure the problem

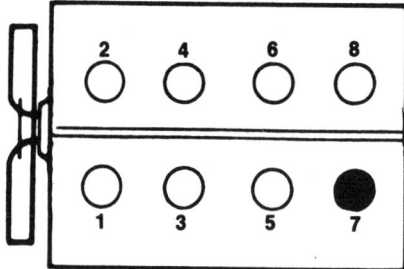

Finding one plug overheated may indicate an intake manifold leak near the affected cylinder. If the overheated plug is the second of two adjacent, consecutively firing plugs, it could be the result of ignition cross-firing. Separating the leads to these two plugs will eliminate cross-fire

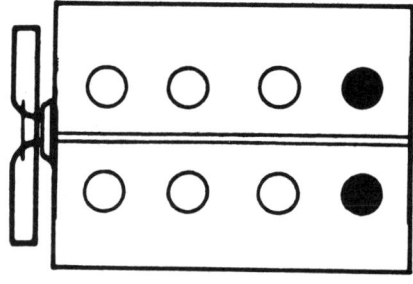

Occasionally, the two rear plugs in large, lightly used V-8's will become oil fouled. High oil consumption and smoky exhaust may also be noticed. It is probably due to plugged oil drain holes in the rear of the cylinder head, causing oil to be sucked in around the valve stems. This usually occurs in the rear cylinders first, because the engine slants that way

TROUBLESHOOTING

Test and Procedure	Results and Indications	Proceed to
4.8—Determine the static ignition timing. Using the crankshaft pulley timing marks as a guide, locate top dead center on the compression stroke of the number one cylinder.	The rotor should be pointing toward the No. 1 tower in the distributor cap, and, on electronic ignitions, the armature spoke for that cylinder should be lined up with the stator.	4.8
4.9—Check coil polarity: Connect a voltmeter negative lead to the coil high tension lead, and the positive lead to ground (**NOTE:** *Reverse the hook-up for positive ground systems*). Crank the engine momentarily.	If the voltmeter reads up-scale, the polarity is correct:	5.1
	If the voltmeter reads down-scale, reverse the coil polarity (switch the primary leads):	5.1
	Checking coil polarity	

Section 5—Fuel System
See Chapter 4 for service procedures

Test and Procedure	Results and Indications	Proceed to
5.1—Determine that the air filter is functioning efficiently: Hold paper elements up to a strong light, and attempt to see light through the filter.	Clean permanent air filters in solvent (or manufacturer's recommendation), and allow to dry. Replace paper elements through which light cannot be seen:	5.2
5.2—Determine whether a flooding condition exists: Flooding is identified by a strong gasoline odor, and excessive gasoline present in the throttle bore(s) of the carburetor.	If flooding is not evident:	5.3
	If flooding is evident, permit the gasoline to dry for a few moments and restart.	
	If flooding doesn't recur:	5.7
	If flooding is persistent:	5.5
	If the engine floods repeatedly, check the choke butterfly flap	
5.3—Check that fuel is reaching the carburetor: Detach the fuel line at the carburetor inlet. Hold the end of the line in a cup (not styrofoam), and crank the engine.	If fuel flows smoothly:	5.7
	If fuel doesn't flow (**NOTE:** *Make sure that there is fuel in the tank*), or flows erratically:	5.4
	Check the fuel pump by disconnecting the output line (fuel pump-to-carburetor) at the carburetor and operating the starter briefly	

TROUBLESHOOTING

Test and Procedure	Results and Indications	Proceed to
5.4—Test the fuel pump: Disconnect all fuel lines from the fuel pump. Hold a finger over the input fitting, crank the engine (with electric pump, turn the ignition or pump on); and feel for suction.	If suction is evident, blow out the fuel line to the tank with low pressure compressed air until bubbling is heard from the fuel filler neck. Also blow out the carburetor fuel line (both ends disconnected):	5.7
	If no suction is evident, replace or repair the fuel pump: NOTE: *Repeated oil fouling of the spark plugs, or a no-start condition, could be the result of a ruptured vacuum booster pump diaphragm, through which oil or gasoline is being drawn into the intake manifold (where applicable).*	5.7
5.5—Occasionally, small specks of dirt will clog the small jets and orifices in the carburetor. With the engine cold, hold a flat piece of wood or similar material over the carburetor, where possible, and crank the engine.	If the engine starts, but runs roughly the engine is probably not run enough. If the engine won't start:	5.9
5.6—Check the needle and seat: Tap the carburetor in the area of the needle and seat.	If flooding stops, a gasoline additive (e.g., Gumout) will often cure the problem:	5.7
	If flooding continues, check the fuel pump for excessive pressure at the carburetor (according to specifications). If the pressure is normal, the needle and seat must be removed and checked, and/or the float level adjusted:	5.7
5.7—Test the accelerator pump by looking into the throttle bores while operating the throttle. **Check for gas at the carburetor by looking down the carburetor throat while someone moves the accelerator**	If the accelerator pump appears to be operating normally:	5.8
	If the accelerator pump is not operating, the pump must be reconditioned. Where possible, service the pump with the carburetor(s) installed on the engine. If necessary, remove the carburetor. Prior to removal:	5.8
5.8—Determine whether the carburetor main fuel system is functioning: Spray a commercial starting fluid into the carburetor while attempting to start the engine.	If the engine starts, runs for a few seconds, and dies:	5.9
	If the engine doesn't start:	6.1

TROUBLESHOOTING

Test and Procedure	Results and Indications	Proceed to
5.9—Uncommon fuel system malfunctions: See below:	If the problem is solved:	6.1
	If the problem remains, remove and recondition the carburetor.	

Condition	Indication	Test	Prevailing Weather Conditions	Remedy
Vapor lock	Engine will not restart shortly after running.	Cool the components of the fuel system until the engine starts. Vapor lock can be cured faster by draping a wet cloth over a mechanical fuel pump.	Hot to very hot	Ensure that the exhaust manifold heat control valve is operating. Check with the vehicle manufacturer for the recommended solution to vapor lock on the model in question.
Carburetor icing	Engine will not idle, stalls at low speeds.	Visually inspect the throttle plate area of the throttle bores for frost.	High humidity, 32–40° F.	Ensure that the exhaust manifold heat control valve is operating, and that the intake manifold heat riser is not blocked.
Water in the fuel	Engine sputters and stalls; may not start.	Pump a small amount of fuel into a glass jar. Allow to stand, and inspect for droplets or a layer of water.	High humidity, extreme temperature changes.	For droplets, use one or two cans of commercial gas line anti-freeze. For a layer of water, the tank must be drained, and the fuel lines blown out with compressed air.

Section 6—Engine Compression
See Chapter 3 for service procedures

Test and Procedure	Results and Indications	Proceed to
6.1—Test engine compression: Remove all spark plugs. Block the throttle wide open. Insert a compression gauge into a spark plug port, crank the engine to obtain the maximum reading, and record.	If compression is within limits on all cylinders:	7.1
	If gauge reading is extremely low on all cylinders:	6.2
	If gauge reading is low on one or two cylinders: (If gauge readings are identical and low on two or more adjacent cylinders, the head gasket must be replaced.)	6.2

Checking compression

6.2—Test engine compression (wet): Squirt approximately 30 cc. of engine oil into each cylinder, and retest per 6.1.	If the readings improve, worn or cracked rings or broken pistons are indicated:	See Chapter 3
	If the readings do not improve, burned or excessively carboned valves or a jumped timing chain are indicated: NOTE: *A jumped timing chain is often indicated by difficult cranking.*	7.1

328 TROUBLESHOOTING

Section 7—Engine Vacuum
See Chapter 3 for service procedures

Test and Procedure	Results and Indications	Proceed to
7.1—Attach a vacuum gauge to the intake manifold beyond the throttle plate. Start the engine, and observe the action of the needle over the range of engine speeds.	See below.	See below

INDICATION: normal engine in good condition

Proceed to: 8.1

Normal engine
Gauge reading: steady, from 17–22 in./Hg.

INDICATION: sticking valves or ignition miss

Proceed to: 9.1, 8.3

Sticking valves
Gauge reading: intermittent fluctuation at idle

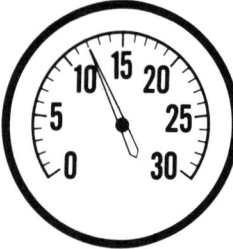

INDICATION: late ignition or valve timing, low compression, stuck throttle valve, leaking carburetor or manifold gasket

Proceed to: 6.1

Incorrect valve timing
Gauge reading: low (10–15 in./Hg) but steady

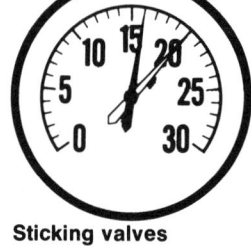

INDICATION: improper carburetor adjustment or minor intake leak.

Proceed to: 7.2

Carburetor requires adjustment
Gauge reading: drifting needle

INDICATION: ignition miss, blown cylinder head gasket, leaking valve or weak valve spring

Proceed to: 8.3, 6.1

Blown head gasket
Gauge reading: needle fluctuates as engine speed increases

INDICATION: burnt valve or faulty valve clearance. Needle will fall when defective valve operates

Proceed to: 9.1

Burnt or leaking valves
Gauge reading: steady needle, but drops regularly

INDICATION: choked muffler, excessive back pressure in system

Proceed to: 10.1

Clogged exhaust system
Gauge reading: gradual drop in reading at idle

INDICATION: worn valve guides

Proceed to: 9.1

Worn valve guides
Gauge reading: needle vibrates excessively at idle, but steadies as engine speed increases

White pointer = steady gauge hand   Black pointer = fluctuating gauge hand

TROUBLESHOOTING 329

Test and Procedure	Results and Indications	Proceed to
7.2—Attach a vacuum gauge per 7.1, and test for an intake manifold leak. Squirt a small amount of oil around the intake manifold gaskets, carburetor gaskets, plugs and fittings. Observe the action of the vacuum gauge.	If the reading improves, replace the indicated gasket, or seal the indicated fitting or plug: If the reading remains low:	8.1 7.3
7.3—Test all vacuum hoses and accessories for leaks as described in 7.2. Also check the carburetor body (dashpots, automatic choke mechanism, throttle shafts) for leaks in the same manner.	If the reading improves, service or replace the offending part(s): If the reading remains low:	8.1 6.1

Section 8—Secondary Electrical System
See Chapter 2 for service procedures

Test and Procedure	Results and Indications	Proceed to
8.1—Remove the distributor cap and check to make sure that the rotor turns when the engine is cranked. Visually inspect the distributor components.	Clean, tighten or replace any components which appear defective.	8.2
8.2—Connect a timing light (per manufacturer's recommendation) and check the dynamic ignition timing. Disconnect and plug the vacuum hose(s) to the distributor if specified, start the engine, and observe the timing marks at the specified engine speed.	If the timing is not correct, adjust to specifications by rotating the distributor in the engine: (Advance timing by rotating distributor opposite normal direction of rotor rotation, retard timing by rotating distributor in same direction as rotor rotation.)	8.3
8.3—Check the operation of the distributor advance mechanism(s): To test the mechanical advance, disconnect the vacuum lines from the distributor advance unit and observe the timing marks with a timing light as the engine speed is increased from idle. If the mark moves smoothly, without hesitation, it may be assumed that the mechanical advance is functioning properly. To test vacuum advance and/or retard systems, alternately crimp and release the vacuum line, and observe the timing mark for movement. If movement is noted, the system is operating.	If the systems are functioning: If the systems are not functioning, remove the distributor, and test on a distributor tester:	8.4 8.4
8.4—Locate an ignition miss: With the engine running, remove each spark plug wire, one at a time, until one is found that doesn't cause the engine to roughen and slow down.	When the missing cylinder is identified:	4.1

Section 9—Valve Train
See Chapter 3 for service procedures

Test and Procedure	Results and Indications	Proceed to
9.1—Evaluate the valve train: Remove the valve cover, and ensure that the valves are adjusted to specifications. A mechanic's stethoscope may be used to aid in the diagnosis of the valve train. By pushing the probe on or near push rods or rockers, valve noise often can be isolated. A timing light also may be used to diagnose valve problems. Connect the light according to manufacturer's recommendations, and start the engine. Vary the firing moment of the light by increasing the engine speed (and therefore the ignition advance), and moving the trigger from cylinder to cylinder. Observe the movement of each valve.	Sticking valves or erratic valve train motion can be observed with the timing light. The cylinder head must be disassembled for repairs.	See Chapter 3
9.2—Check the valve timing: Locate top dead center of the No. 1 piston, and install a degree wheel or tape on the crankshaft pulley or damper with zero corresponding to an index mark on the engine. Rotate the crankshaft in its direction of rotation, and observe the opening of the No. 1 cylinder intake valve. The opening should correspond with the correct mark on the degree wheel according to specifications.	If the timing is not correct, the timing cover must be removed for further investigation.	See Chapter 3

Section 10—Exhaust System

Test and Procedure	Results and Indications	Proceed to
10.1—Determine whether the exhaust manifold heat control valve is operating: Operate the valve by hand to determine whether it is free to move. If the valve is free, run the engine to operating temperature and observe the action of the valve, to ensure that it is opening.	If the valve sticks, spray it with a suitable solvent, open and close the valve to free it, and retest. If the valve functions properly: If the valve does not free, or does not operate, replace the valve:	10.2 10.2
10.2—Ensure that there are no exhaust restrictions: Visually inspect the exhaust system for kinks, dents, or crushing. Also note that gases are flowing freely from the tailpipe at all engine speeds, indicating no restriction in the muffler or resonator.	Replace any damaged portion of the system:	11.1

TROUBLESHOOTING

Section 11—Cooling System
See Chapter 3 for service procedures

Test and Procedure	Results and Indications	Proceed to
11.1—Visually inspect the fan belt for glazing, cracks, and fraying, and replace if necessary. Tighten the belt so that the longest span has approximately ½" play at its midpoint under thumb pressure (see Chapter 1).	Replace or tighten the fan belt as necessary:	11.2

Checking belt tension

11.2—Check the fluid level of the cooling system.	If full or slightly low, fill as necessary:	11.5
	If extremely low:	11.3
11.3—Visually inspect the external portions of the cooling system (radiator, radiator hoses, thermostat elbow, water pump seals, heater hoses, etc.) for leaks. If none are found, pressurize the cooling system to 14–15 psi.	If cooling system holds the pressure:	11.5
	If cooling system loses pressure rapidly, reinspect external parts of the system for leaks under pressure. If none are found, check dipstick for coolant in crankcase. If no coolant is present, but pressure loss continues:	11.4
	If coolant is evident in crankcase, remove cylinder head(s), and check gasket(s). If gaskets are intact, block and cylinder head(s) should be checked for cracks or holes. If the gasket(s) is blown, replace, and purge the crankcase of coolant: NOTE: *Occasionally, due to atmospheric and driving conditions, condensation of water can occur in the crankcase. This causes the oil to appear milky white. To remedy, run the engine until hot, and change the oil and oil filter.*	12.6
11.4—Check for combustion leaks into the cooling system: Pressurize the cooling system as above. Start the engine, and observe the pressure gauge. If the needle fluctuates, remove each spark plug wire, one at a time, noting which cylinder(s) reduce or eliminate the fluctuation.	Cylinders which reduce or eliminate the fluctuation, when the spark plug wire is removed, are leaking into the cooling system. Replace the head gasket on the affected cylinder bank(s).	

Pressurizing the cooling system

TROUBLESHOOTING

Test and Procedure	Results and Indications	Proceed to
11.5—Check the radiator pressure cap: Attach a radiator pressure tester to the radiator cap (wet the seal prior to installation). Quickly pump up the pressure, noting the point at which the cap releases.	If the cap releases within ±1 psi of the specified rating, it is operating properly:	**11.6**
	If the cap releases at more than ±1 psi of the specified rating, it should be replaced:	**11.6**

Checking radiator pressure cap

Test and Procedure	Results and Indications	Proceed to
11.6—Test the thermostat: Start the engine cold, remove the radiator cap, and insert a thermometer into the radiator. Allow the engine to idle. After a short while, there will be a sudden, rapid increase in coolant temperature. The temperature at which this sharp rise stops is the thermostat opening temperature.	If the thermostat opens at or about the specified temperature:	**11.7**
	If the temperature doesn't increase: (If the temperature increases slowly and gradually, replace the thermostat.)	**11.7**
11.7—Check the water pump: Remove the thermostat elbow and the thermostat, disconnect the coil high tension lead (to prevent starting), and crank the engine momentarily.	If coolant flows, replace the thermostat and retest per 11.6:	**11.6**
	If coolant doesn't flow, reverse flush the cooling system to alleviate any blockage that might exist. If system is not blocked, and coolant will not flow, replace the water pump.	

Section 12—Lubrication
See Chapter 3 for service procedures

Test and Procedure	Results and Indications	Proceed to
12.1—Check the oil pressure gauge or warning light: If the gauge shows low pressure, or the light is on for no obvious reason, remove the oil pressure sender. Install an accurate oil pressure gauge and run the engine momentarily.	If oil pressure builds normally, run engine for a few moments to determine that it is functioning normally, and replace the sender.	—
	If the pressure remains low:	**12.2**
	If the pressure surges:	**12.3**
	If the oil pressure is zero:	**12.3**
12.2—Visually inspect the oil: If the oil is watery or very thin, milky, or foamy, replace the oil and oil filter.	If the oil is normal:	**12.3**
	If after replacing oil the pressure remains low:	**12.3**
	If after replacing oil the pressure becomes normal:	—

TROUBLESHOOTING 333

Test and Procedure	Results and Indications	Proceed to
12.3 — Inspect the oil pressure relief valve and spring, to ensure that it is not sticking or stuck. Remove and thoroughly clean the valve, spring, and the valve body.	If the oil pressure improves: If no improvement is noted:	— **12.4**
12.4 — Check to ensure that the oil pump is not cavitating (sucking air instead of oil): See that the crankcase is neither over nor underfull, and that the pickup in the sump is in the proper position and free from sludge.	Fill or drain the crankcase to the proper capacity, and clean the pickup screen in solvent if necessary. If no improvement is noted:	**12.5**
12.5 — Inspect the oil pump drive and the oil pump:	If the pump drive or the oil pump appear to be defective, service as necessary and retest per 12.1:	**12.1**
	If the pump drive and pump appear to be operating normally, the engine should be disassembled to determine where blockage exists:	**See Chapter 3**
12.6 — Purge the engine of ethylene glycol coolant: Completely drain the crankcase and the oil filter. Obtain a commercial butyl cellosolve base solvent, designated for this purpose, and follow the instructions precisely. Following this, install a new oil filter and refill the crankcase with the proper weight oil. The next oil and filter change should follow shortly thereafter (1000 miles).		

TROUBLESHOOTING EMISSION CONTROL SYSTEMS

See Chapter 4 for procedures applicable to individual emission control systems used on specific combinations of engine/transmission/model.

TROUBLESHOOTING THE CARBURETOR
See Chapter 4 for service procedures

Carburetor problems cannot be effectively isolated unless all other engine systems (particularly ignition and emission) are functioning properly and the engine is properly tuned.

TROUBLESHOOTING

Condition	Possible Cause
Engine cranks, but does not start	1. Improper starting procedure 2. No fuel in tank 3. Clogged fuel line or filter 4. Defective fuel pump 5. Choke valve not closing properly 6. Engine flooded 7. Choke valve not unloading 8. Throttle linkage not making full travel 9. Stuck needle or float 10. Leaking float needle or seat 11. Improper float adjustment
Engine stalls	1. Improperly adjusted idle speed or mixture **Engine hot** 2. Improperly adjusted dashpot 3. Defective or improperly adjusted solenoid 4. Incorrect fuel level in fuel bowl 5. Fuel pump pressure too high 6. Leaking float needle seat 7. Secondary throttle valve stuck open 8. Air or fuel leaks 9. Idle air bleeds plugged or missing 10. Idle passages plugged **Engine Cold** 11. Incorrectly adjusted choke 12. Improperly adjusted fast idle speed 13. Air leaks 14. Plugged idle or idle air passages 15. Stuck choke valve or binding linkage 16. Stuck secondary throttle valves 17. Engine flooding—high fuel level 18. Leaking or misaligned float
Engine hesitates on acceleration	1. Clogged fuel filter 2. Leaking fuel pump diaphragm 3. Low fuel pump pressure 4. Secondary throttle valves stuck, bent or misadjusted 5. Sticking or binding air valve 6. Defective accelerator pump 7. Vacuum leaks 8. Clogged air filter 9. Incorrect choke adjustment (engine cold)
Engine feels sluggish or flat on acceleration	1. Improperly adjusted idle speed or mixture 2. Clogged fuel filter 3. Defective accelerator pump 4. Dirty, plugged or incorrect main metering jets 5. Bent or sticking main metering rods 6. Sticking throttle valves 7. Stuck heat riser 8. Binding or stuck air valve 9. Dirty, plugged or incorrect secondary jets 10. Bent or sticking secondary metering rods. 11. Throttle body or manifold heat passages plugged 12. Improperly adjusted choke or choke vacuum break.
Carburetor floods	1. Defective fuel pump. Pressure too high. 2. Stuck choke valve 3. Dirty, worn or damaged float or needle valve/seat 4. Incorrect float/fuel level 5. Leaking float bowl

TROUBLESHOOTING

Condition	Possible Cause
Engine idles roughly and stalls	1. Incorrect idle speed 2. Clogged fuel filter 3. Dirt in fuel system or carburetor 4. Loose carburetor screws or attaching bolts 5. Broken carburetor gaskets 6. Air leaks 7. Dirty carburetor 8. Worn idle mixture needles 9. Throttle valves stuck open 10. Incorrectly adjusted float or fuel level 11. Clogged air filter
Engine runs unevenly or surges	1. Defective fuel pump 2. Dirty or clogged fuel filter 3. Plugged, loose or incorrect main metering jets or rods 4. Air leaks 5. Bent or sticking main metering rods 6. Stuck power piston 7. Incorrect float adjustment 8. Incorrect idle speed or mixture 9. Dirty or plugged idle system passages 10. Hard, brittle or broken gaskets 11. Loose attaching or mounting screws 12. Stuck or misaligned secondary throttle valves
Poor fuel economy	1. Poor driving habits 2. Stuck choke valve 3. Binding choke linkage 4. Stuck heat riser 5. Incorrect idle mixture 6. Defective accelerator pump 7. Air leaks 8. Plugged, loose or incorrect main metering jets 9. Improperly adjusted float or fuel level 10. Bent, misaligned or fuel-clogged float 11. Leaking float needle seat 12. Fuel leak 13. Accelerator pump discharge ball not seating properly 14. Incorrect main jets
Engine lacks high speed performance or power	1. Incorrect throttle linkage adjustment 2. Stuck or binding power piston 3. Defective accelerator pump 4. Air leaks 5. Incorrect float setting or fuel level 6. Dirty, plugged, worn or incorrect main metering jets or rods 7. Binding or sticking air valve 8. Brittle or cracked gaskets 9. Bent, incorrect or improperly adjusted secondary metering rods 10. Clogged fuel filter 11. Clogged air filter 12. Defective fuel pump

TROUBLESHOOTING FUEL INJECTION PROBLEMS

Each fuel injection system has its own unique components and test procedures, for which it is impossible to generalize. Refer to Chapter 4 of this Repair & Tune-Up Guide for specific test and repair procedures, if the vehicle is equipped with fuel injection.

TROUBLESHOOTING ELECTRICAL PROBLEMS

See Chapter 5 for service procedures

For any electrical system to operate, it must make a complete circuit. This simply means that the power flow from the battery must make a complete circle. When an electrical component is operating, power flows from the battery to the component, passes through the component causing it to perform its function (lighting a light bulb), and then returns to the battery through the ground of the circuit. This ground is usually (but not always) the metal part of the car or truck on which the electrical component is mounted.

Perhaps the easiest way to visualize this is to think of connecting a light bulb with two wires attached to it to the battery. If one of the two wires attached to the light bulb were attached to the negative post of the battery and the other were attached to the positive post of the battery, you would have a complete circuit. Current from the battery would flow to the light bulb, causing it to light, and return to the negative post of the battery.

The normal automotive circuit differs from this simple example in two ways. First, instead of having a return wire from the bulb to the battery, the light bulb returns the current to the battery through the chassis of the vehicle. Since the negative battery cable is attached to the chassis and the chassis is made of electrically conductive metal, the chassis of the vehicle can serve as a ground wire to complete the circuit. Secondly, most automotive circuits contain switches to turn components on and off as required.

Every complete circuit from a power source must include a component which is using the power from the power source. If you were to disconnect the light bulb from the wires and touch the two wires together (don't do this) the power supply wire to the component would be grounded before the normal ground connection for the circuit.

Because grounding a wire from a power source makes a complete circuit—less the required component to use the power—this phenomenon is called a short circuit. Common causes are: broken insulation (exposing the metal wire to a metal part of the car or truck), or a shorted switch.

Some electrical components which require a large amount of current to operate also have a relay in their circuit. Since these circuits carry a large amount of current, the thickness of the wire in the circuit (gauge size) is also greater. If this large wire were connected from the component to the control switch on the instrument panel, and then back to the component, a voltage drop would occur in the circuit. To prevent this potential drop in voltage, an electromagnetic switch (relay) is used. The large wires in the circuit are connected from the battery to one side of the relay, and from the opposite side of the relay to the component. The relay is normally open, preventing current from passing through the circuit. An additional, smaller, wire is connected from the relay to the control switch for the circuit. When the control switch is turned on, it grounds the smaller wire from the relay and completes the circuit. This closes the relay and allows current to flow from the battery to the component. The horn, headlight, and starter circuits are three which use relays.

It is possible for larger surges of current to pass through the electrical system of your car or truck. If this surge of current were to reach an electrical component, it could burn it out. To prevent this, fuses, circuit breakers or fusible links are connected into the current supply wires of most of the major electrical systems. When an electrical current of excessive power passes through the component's fuse, the fuse blows out and breaks the circuit, saving the component from destruction.

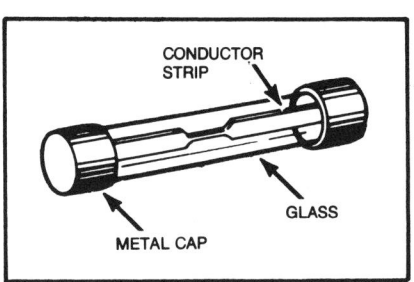

Typical automotive fuse

A circuit breaker is basically a self-repairing fuse. The circuit breaker opens the circuit the same way a fuse does. However, when either the short is removed from the circuit or the surge subsides, the circuit breaker resets itself and does not have to be replaced as a fuse does.

A fuse link is a wire that acts as a fuse. It is normally connected between the starter relay and the main wiring harness. This connection is usually under the hood. The fuse link (if installed) protects all the

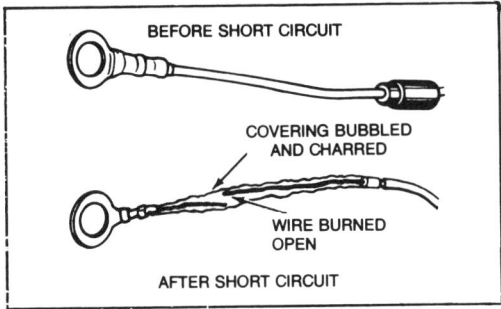

Most fusible links show a charred, melted insulation when they burn out

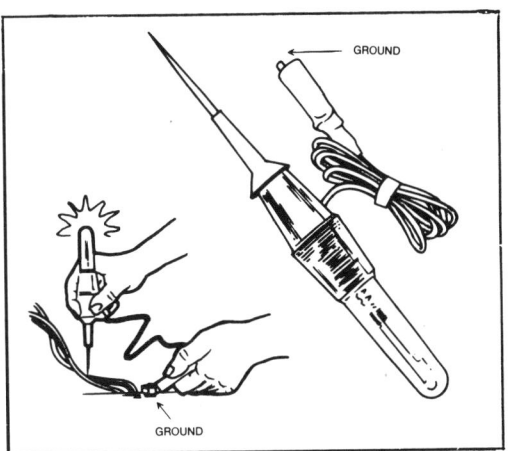

The test light will show the presence of current when touched to a hot wire and grounded at the other end

chassis electrical components, and is the probable cause of trouble when none of the electrical components function, unless the battery is disconnected or dead.

Electrical problems generally fall into one of three areas:

1. The component that is not functioning is not receiving current.
2. The component itself is not functioning.
3. The component is not properly grounded.

The electrical system can be checked with a test light and a jumper wire. A test light is a device that looks like a pointed screwdriver with a wire attached to it and has a light bulb in its handle. A jumper wire is a piece of insulated wire with an alligator clip attached to each end.

If a component is not working, you must follow a systematic plan to determine which of the three causes is the villain.

1. Turn on the switch that controls the inoperable component.
2. Disconnect the power supply wire from the component.
3. Attach the ground wire on the test light to a good metal ground.
4. Touch the probe end of the test light to the end of the power supply wire that was disconnected from the component. If the component is receiving current, the test light will go on.

NOTE: *Some components work only when the ignition switch is turned on.*

If the test light does not go on, then the problem is in the circuit between the battery and the component. This includes all the switches, fuses, and relays in the system. Follow the wire that runs back to the battery. The problem is an open circuit between the battery and the component. If the fuse is blown and, when replaced, immediately blows again, there is a short circuit in the system which must be located and repaired. If there is a switch in the system, bypass it with a jumper wire. This is done by connecting one end of the jumper wire to the power supply wire into the switch and the other end of the jumper wire to the wire coming out of the switch. If the test light lights with the jumper wire installed, the switch or whatever was bypassed is defective.

NOTE: *Never substitute the jumper wire for the component, since it is required to use the power from the power source.*

5. If the bulb in the test light goes on, then the current is getting to the component that is not working. This eliminates the first of the three possible causes. Connect the power supply wire and connect a jumper wire from the component to a good metal ground. Do this with the switch which controls the component turned on, and also the ignition switch turned on if it is required for the component to work. If the component works with the jumper wire installed, then it has a bad ground. This is usually caused by the metal area on which the component mounts to the chassis being coated with some type of foreign matter.

6. If neither test located the source of the trouble, then the component itself is defective. Remember that for any electrical system to work, all connections must be clean and tight.

TROUBLESHOOTING

Troubleshooting Basic Turn Signal and Flasher Problems
See Chapter 5 for service procedures

Most problems in the turn signals or flasher system can be reduced to defective flashers or bulbs, which are easily replaced. Occasionally, the turn signal switch will prove defective.

F = Front   R = Rear   ● = Lights off   ○ = Lights on

Condition		Possible Cause
Turn signals light, but do not flash	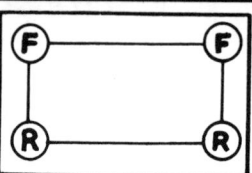	Defective flasher
No turn signals light on either side	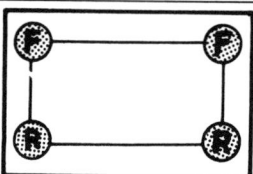	Blown fuse. Replace if defective. Defective flasher. Check by substitution. Open circuit, short circuit or poor ground.
Both turn signals on one side don't work	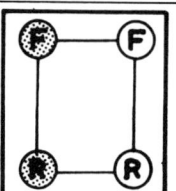	Bad bulbs. Bad ground in both (or either) housings.
One turn signal light on one side doesn't work	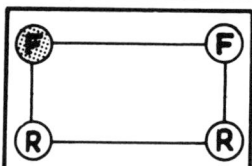	Defective bulb. Corrosion in socket. Clean contacts. Poor ground at socket.
Turn signal flashes too fast or too slowly	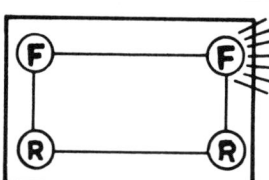	Check any bulb on the side flashing too fast. A heavy-duty bulb is probably installed in place of a regular bulb. Check the bulb flashing too slowly. A standard bulb was probably installed in place of a heavy-duty bulb. Loose connections or corrosion at the bulb socket.
Indicator lights don't work in either direction		Check if the turn signals are working. Check the dash indicator lights. Check the flasher by substitution.
One indicator light doesn't light	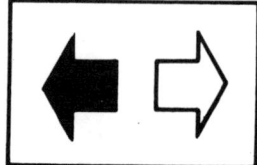	On systems with one dash indicator: See if the lights work on the same side. Often the filaments have been reversed in systems combining stoplights with taillights and turn signals. Check the flasher by substitution. On systems with two indicators: Check the bulbs on the same side. Check the indicator light bulb. Check the flasher by substitution.

Troubleshooting Lighting Problems
See Chapter 5 for service procedures

Condition	Possible Cause
One or more lights don't work, but others do	1. Defective bulb(s) 2. Blown fuse(s) 3. Dirty fuse clips or light sockets 4. Poor ground circuit
Lights burn out quickly	1. Incorrect voltage regulator setting or defective regulator 2. Poor battery/alternator connections
Lights go dim	1. Low/discharged battery 2. Alternator not charging 3. Corroded sockets or connections 4. Low voltage output
Lights flicker	1. Loose connection 2. Poor ground. (Run ground wire from light housing to frame) 3. Circuit breaker operating (short circuit)
Lights "flare"—Some flare is normal on acceleration—If excessive, see "Lights Burn Out Quickly"	High voltage setting
Lights glare—approaching drivers are blinded	1. Lights adjusted too high 2. Rear springs or shocks sagging 3. Rear tires soft

Troubleshooting Dash Gauge Problems

Most problems can be traced to a defective sending unit or faulty wiring. Occasionally, the gauge itself is at fault. See Chapter 5 for service procedures.

Condition	Possible Cause

COOLANT TEMPERATURE GAUGE

Gauge reads erratically or not at all	1. Loose or dirty connections 2. Defective sending unit. 3. Defective gauge. To test a bi-metal gauge, remove the wire from the sending unit. Ground the wire for an instant. If the gauge registers, replace the sending unit. To test a magnetic gauge, disconnect the wire at the sending unit. With ignition ON gauge should register COLD. Ground the wire; gauge should register HOT.

AMMETER GAUGE—TURN HEADLIGHTS ON (DO NOT START ENGINE). NOTE REACTION

Ammeter shows charge Ammeter shows discharge Ammeter does not move	1. Connections reversed on gauge 2. Ammeter is OK 3. Loose connections or faulty wiring 4. Defective gauge

TROUBLESHOOTING

Condition	Possible Cause
OIL PRESSURE GAUGE	
Gauge does not register or is inaccurate	1. On mechanical gauge, Bourdon tube may be bent or kinked. 2. Low oil pressure. Remove sending unit. Idle the engine briefly. If no oil flows from sending unit hole, problem is in engine. 3. Defective gauge. Remove the wire from the sending unit and ground it for an instant with the ignition ON. A good gauge will go to the top of the scale. 4. Defective wiring. Check the wiring to the gauge. If it's OK and the gauge doesn't register when grounded, replace the gauge. 5. Defective sending unit.
ALL GAUGES	
All gauges do not operate All gauges read low or erratically All gauges pegged	1. Blown fuse 2. Defective instrument regulator 3. Defective or dirty instrument voltage regulator 4. Loss of ground between instrument voltage regulator and frame 5. Defective instrument regulator
WARNING LIGHTS	
Light(s) do not come on when ignition is ON, but engine is not started Light comes on with engine running	1. Defective bulb 2. Defective wire 3. Defective sending unit. Disconnect the wire from the sending unit and ground it. Replace the sending unit if the light comes on with the ignition ON. 4. Problem in individual system 5. Defective sending unit

Troubleshooting Clutch Problems

It is false economy to replace individual clutch components. The pressure plate, clutch plate and throwout bearing should be replaced as a set, and the flywheel face inspected, whenever the clutch is overhauled. See Chapter 6 for service procedures.

Condition	Possible Cause
Clutch chatter	1. Grease on driven plate (disc) facing 2. Binding clutch linkage or cable 3. Loose, damaged facings on driven plate (disc) 4. Engine mounts loose 5. Incorrect height adjustment of pressure plate release levers 6. Clutch housing or housing to transmission adapter misalignment 7. Loose driven plate hub
Clutch grabbing	1. Oil, grease on driven plate (disc) facing 2. Broken pressure plate 3. Warped or binding driven plate. Driven plate binding on clutch shaft
Clutch slips	1. Lack of lubrication in clutch linkage or cable (linkage or cable binds, causes incomplete engagement) 2. Incorrect pedal, or linkage adjustment 3. Broken pressure plate springs 4. Weak pressure plate springs 5. Grease on driven plate facings (disc)

Troubleshooting Clutch Problems (cont.)

Condition	Possible Cause
Incomplete clutch release	1. Incorrect pedal or linkage adjustment or linkage or cable binding 2. Incorrect height adjustment on pressure plate release levers 3. Loose, broken facings on driven plate (disc) 4. Bent, dished, warped driven plate caused by overheating
Grinding, whirring grating noise when pedal is depressed	1. Worn or defective throwout bearing 2. Starter drive teeth contacting flywheel ring gear teeth. Look for milled or polished teeth on ring gear.
Squeal, howl, trumpeting noise when pedal is being released (occurs during first inch to inch and one-half of pedal travel)	Pilot bushing worn or lack of lubricant. If bushing appears OK, polish bushing with emery cloth, soak lube wick in oil, lube bushing with oil, apply film of chassis grease to clutch shaft pilot hub, reassemble. NOTE: Bushing wear may be due to misalignment of clutch housing or housing to transmission adapter
Vibration or clutch pedal pulsation with clutch disengaged (pedal fully depressed)	1. Worn or defective engine transmission mounts 2. Flywheel run out. (Flywheel run out at face not to exceed 0.005") 3. Damaged or defective clutch components

Troubleshooting Manual Transmission Problems
See Chapter 6 for service procedures

Condition	Possible Cause
Transmission jumps out of gear	1. Misalignment of transmission case or clutch housing. 2. Worn pilot bearing in crankshaft. 3. Bent transmission shaft. 4. Worn high speed sliding gear. 5. Worn teeth or end-play in clutch shaft. 6. Insufficient spring tension on shifter rail plunger. 7. Bent or loose shifter fork. 8. Gears not engaging completely. 9. Loose or worn bearings on clutch shaft or mainshaft. 10. Worn gear teeth. 11. Worn or damaged detent balls.
Transmission sticks in gear	1. Clutch not releasing fully. 2. Burred or battered teeth on clutch shaft, or sliding sleeve. 3. Burred or battered transmission mainshaft. 4. Frozen synchronizing clutch. 5. Stuck shifter rail plunger. 6. Gearshift lever twisting and binding shifter rail. 7. Battered teeth on high speed sliding gear or on sleeve. 8. Improper lubrication, or lack of lubrication. 9. Corroded transmission parts. 10. Defective mainshaft pilot bearing. 11. Locked gear bearings will give same effect as stuck in gear.
Transmission gears will not synchronize	1. Binding pilot bearing on mainshaft, will synchronize in high gear only. 2. Clutch not releasing fully. 3. Detent spring weak or broken. 4. Weak or broken springs under balls in sliding gear sleeve. 5. Binding bearing on clutch shaft, or binding countershaft. 6. Binding pilot bearing in crankshaft. 7. Badly worn gear teeth. 8. Improper lubrication. 9. Constant mesh gear not turning freely on transmission mainshaft. Will synchronize in that gear only.

Condition	Possible Cause
Gears spinning when shifting into gear from neutral	1. Clutch not releasing fully. 2. In some cases an extremely light lubricant in transmission will cause gears to continue to spin for a short time after clutch is released. 3. Binding pilot bearing in crankshaft.
Transmission noisy in all gears	1. Insufficient lubricant, or improper lubricant. 2. Worn countergear bearings. 3. Worn or damaged main drive gear or countergear. 4. Damaged main drive gear or mainshaft bearings. 5. Worn or damaged countergear anti-lash plate.
Transmission noisy in neutral only	1. Damaged main drive gear bearing. 2. Damaged or loose mainshaft pilot bearing. 3. Worn or damaged countergear anti-lash plate. 4. Worn countergear bearings.
Transmission noisy in one gear only	1. Damaged or worn constant mesh gears. 2. Worn or damaged countergear bearings. 3. Damaged or worn synchronizer.
Transmission noisy in reverse only	1. Worn or damaged reverse idler gear or idler bushing. 2. Worn or damaged mainshaft reverse gear. 3. Worn or damaged reverse countergear. 4. Damaged shift mechanism.

TROUBLESHOOTING AUTOMATIC TRANSMISSION PROBLEMS

Keeping alert to changes in the operating characteristics of the transmission (changing shift points, noises, etc.) can prevent small problems from becoming large ones. If the problem cannot be traced to loose bolts, fluid level, misadjusted linkage, clogged filters or similar problems, you should probably seek professional service.

Transmission Fluid Indications

The appearance and odor of the transmission fluid can give valuable clues to the overall condition of the transmission. Always note the appearance of the fluid when you check the fluid level or change the fluid. Rub a small amount of fluid between your fingers to feel for grit and smell the fluid on the dipstick.

If the fluid appears:	It indicates:
Clear and red colored	Normal operation
Discolored (extremely dark red or brownish) or smells burned	Band or clutch pack failure, usually caused by an overheated transmission. Hauling very heavy loads with insufficient power or failure to change the fluid often result in overheating. Do not confuse this appearance with newer fluids that have a darker red color and a strong odor (though not a burned odor).
Foamy or aerated (light in color and full of bubbles)	1. The level is too high (gear train is churning oil) 2. An internal air leak (air is mixing with the fluid). Have the transmission checked professionally.
Solid residue in the fluid	Defective bands, clutch pack or bearings. Bits of band material or metal abrasives are clinging to the dipstick. Have the transmission checked professionally.
Varnish coating on the dipstick	The transmission fluid is overheating

TROUBLESHOOTING DRIVE AXLE PROBLEMS

First, determine when the noise is most noticeable.

Drive Noise: Produced under vehicle acceleration.

Coast Noise: Produced while coasting with a closed throttle.

Float Noise: Occurs while maintaining constant speed (just enough to keep speed constant) on a level road.

External Noise Elimination

It is advisable to make a thorough road test to determine whether the noise originates in the rear axle or whether it originates from the tires, engine, transmission, wheel bearings or road surface. Noise originating from other places cannot be corrected by servicing the rear axle.

ROAD NOISE

Brick or rough surfaced concrete roads produce noises that seem to come from the rear axle. Road noise is usually identical in Drive or Coast and driving on a different type of road will tell whether the road is the problem.

TIRE NOISE

Tire noise can be mistaken as rear axle noise, even though the tires on the front are at fault. Snow tread and mud tread tires or tires worn unevenly will frequently cause vibrations which seem to originate elsewhere; *temporarily, and for test purposes only,* inflate the tires to 40–50 lbs. This will significantly alter the noise produced by the tires, but will not alter noise from the rear axle. Noises from the rear axle will normally cease at speeds below 30 mph on coast, while tire noise will continue at lower tone as speed is decreased. The rear axle noise will usually change from drive conditions to coast conditions, while tire noise will not. Do not forget to lower the tire pressure to normal after the test is complete.

ENGINE/TRANSMISSION NOISE

Determine at what speed the noise is most pronounced, then stop in a quiet place. With the transmission in Neutral, run the engine through speeds corresponding to road speeds where the noise was noticed. Noises produced with the vehicle standing still are coming from the engine or transmission.

FRONT WHEEL BEARINGS

Front wheel bearing noises, sometimes confused with rear axle noises, will not change when comparing drive and coast conditions. While holding the speed steady, lightly apply the footbrake. This will often cause wheel bearing noise to lessen, as some of the weight is taken off the bearing. Front wheel bearings are easily checked by jacking up the wheels and spinning the wheels. Shaking the wheels will also determine if the wheel bearings are excessively loose.

REAR AXLE NOISES

Eliminating other possible sources can narrow the cause to the rear axle, which normally produces noise from worn gears or bearings. Gear noises tend to peak in a narrow speed range, while bearing noises will usually vary in pitch with engine speeds.

Noise Diagnosis

The Noise Is:	Most Probably Produced By:
1. Identical under Drive or Coast	Road surface, tires or front wheel bearings
2. Different depending on road surface	Road surface or tires
3. Lower as speed is lowered	Tires
4. Similar when standing or moving	Engine or transmission
5. A vibration	Unbalanced tires, rear wheel bearing, unbalanced driveshaft or worn U-joint
6. A knock or click about every two tire revolutions	Rear wheel bearing
7. Most pronounced on turns	Damaged differential gears
8. A steady low-pitched whirring or scraping, starting at low speeds	Damaged or worn pinion bearing
9. A chattering vibration on turns	Wrong differential lubricant or worn clutch plates (limited slip rear axle)
10. Noticed only in Drive, Coast or Float conditions	Worn ring gear and/or pinion gear

TROUBLESHOOTING

Troubleshooting Steering & Suspension Problems

Condition	Possible Cause
Hard steering (wheel is hard to turn)	1. Improper tire pressure 2. Loose or glazed pump drive belt 3. Low or incorrect fluid 4. Loose, bent or poorly lubricated front end parts 5. Improper front end alignment (excessive caster) 6. Bind in steering column or linkage 7. Kinked hydraulic hose 8. Air in hydraulic system 9. Low pump output or leaks in system 10. Obstruction in lines 11. Pump valves sticking or out of adjustment 12. Incorrect wheel alignment
Loose steering (too much play in steering wheel)	1. Loose wheel bearings 2. Faulty shocks 3. Worn linkage or suspension components 4. Loose steering gear mounting or linkage points 5. Steering mechanism worn or improperly adjusted 6. Valve spool improperly adjusted 7. Worn ball joints, tie-rod ends, etc.
Veers or wanders (pulls to one side with hands off steering wheel)	1. Improper tire pressure 2. Improper front end alignment 3. Dragging or improperly adjusted brakes 4. Bent frame 5. Improper rear end alignment 6. Faulty shocks or springs 7. Loose or bent front end components 8. Play in Pitman arm 9. Steering gear mountings loose 10. Loose wheel bearings 11. Binding Pitman arm 12. Spool valve sticking or improperly adjusted 13. Worn ball joints
Wheel oscillation or vibration transmitted through steering wheel	1. Low or uneven tire pressure 2. Loose wheel bearings 3. Improper front end alignment 4. Bent spindle 5. Worn, bent or broken front end components 6. Tires out of round or out of balance 7. Excessive lateral runout in disc brake rotor 8. Loose or bent shock absorber or strut
Noises (see also "Troubleshooting Drive Axle Problems")	1. Loose belts 2. Low fluid, air in system 3. Foreign matter in system 4. Improper lubrication 5. Interference or chafing in linkage 6. Steering gear mountings loose 7. Incorrect adjustment or wear in gear box 8. Faulty valves or wear in pump 9. Kinked hydraulic lines 10. Worn wheel bearings
Poor return of steering	1. Over-inflated tires 2. Improperly aligned front end (excessive caster) 3. Binding in steering column 4. No lubrication in front end 5. Steering gear adjusted too tight
Uneven tire wear (see "How To Read Tire Wear")	1. Incorrect tire pressure 2. Improperly aligned front end 3. Tires out-of-balance 4. Bent or worn suspension parts

HOW TO READ TIRE WEAR

The way your tires wear is a good indicator of other parts of the suspension. Abnormal wear patterns are often caused by the need for simple tire maintenance, or for front end alignment.

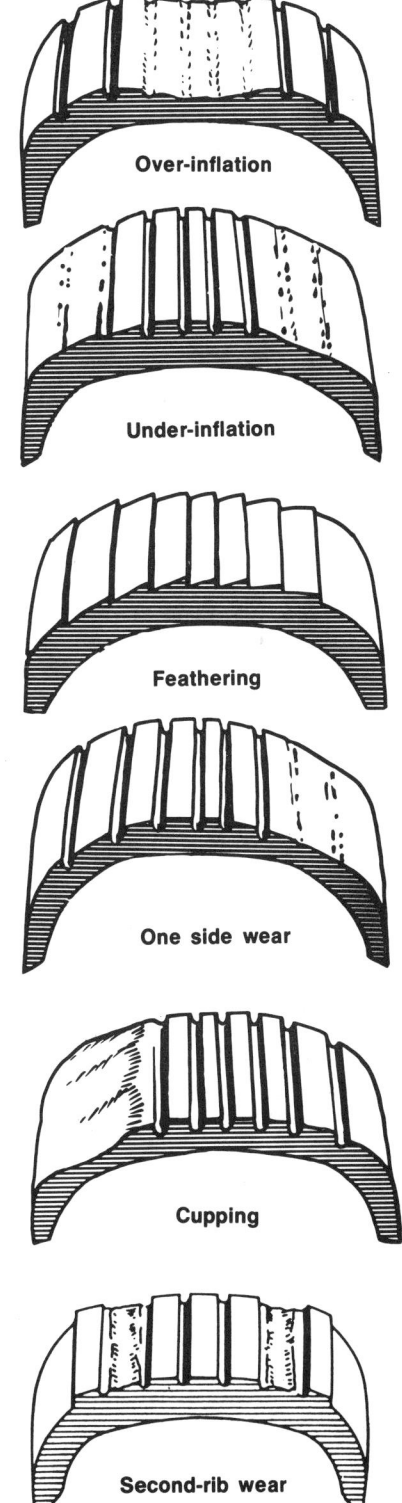

Excessive wear at the center of the tread indicates that the air pressure in the tire is consistently too high. The tire is riding on the center of the tread and wearing it prematurely. Occasionally, this wear pattern can result from outrageously wide tires on narrow rims. The cure for this is to replace either the tires or the wheels.

This type of wear usually results from consistent under-inflation. When a tire is under-inflated, there is too much contact with the road by the outer treads, which wear prematurely. When this type of wear occurs, and the tire pressure is known to be consistently correct, a bent or worn steering component or the need for wheel alignment could be indicated.

Feathering is a condition when the edge of each tread rib develops a slightly rounded edge on one side and a sharp edge on the other. By running your hand over the tire, you can usually feel the sharper edges before you'll be able to see them. The most common causes of feathering are incorrect toe-in setting or deteriorated bushings in the front suspension.

When an inner or outer rib wears faster than the rest of the tire, the need for wheel alignment is indicated. There is excessive camber in the front suspension, causing the wheel to lean too much putting excessive load on one side of the tire. Misalignment could also be due to sagging springs, worn ball joints, or worn control arm bushings. Be sure the vehicle is loaded the way it's normally driven when you have the wheels aligned.

Cups or scalloped dips appearing around the edge of the tread almost always indicate worn (sometimes bent) suspension parts. Adjustment of wheel alignment alone will seldom cure the problem. Any worn component that connects the wheel to the suspension can cause this type of wear. Occasionally, wheels that are out of balance will wear like this, but wheel imbalance usually shows up as bald spots between the outside edges and center of the tread.

Second-rib wear is usually found only in radial tires, and appears where the steel belts end in relation to the tread. It can be kept to a minimum by paying careful attention to tire pressure and frequently rotating the tires. This is often considered normal wear but excessive amounts indicate that the tires are too wide for the wheels.

Troubleshooting Disc Brake Problems

Condition	Possible Cause
Noise—groan—brake noise emanating when slowly releasing brakes (creep-groan)	Not detrimental to function of disc brakes—no corrective action required. (This noise may be eliminated by slightly increasing or decreasing brake pedal efforts.)
Rattle—brake noise or rattle emanating at low speeds on rough roads, (front wheels only).	1. Shoe anti-rattle spring missing or not properly positioned. 2. Excessive clearance between shoe and caliper. 3. Soft or broken caliper seals. 4. Deformed or misaligned disc. 5. Loose caliper.
Scraping	1. Mounting bolts too long. 2. Loose wheel bearings. 3. Bent, loose, or misaligned splash shield.
Front brakes heat up during driving and fail to release	1. Operator riding brake pedal. 2. Stop light switch improperly adjusted. 3. Sticking pedal linkage. 4. Frozen or seized piston. 5. Residual pressure valve in master cylinder. 6. Power brake malfunction. 7. Proportioning valve malfunction.
Leaky brake caliper	1. Damaged or worn caliper piston seal. 2. Scores or corrosion on surface of cylinder bore.
Grabbing or uneven brake action—Brakes pull to one side	1. Causes listed under "Brakes Pull". 2. Power brake malfunction. 3. Low fluid level in master cylinder. 4. Air in hydraulic system. 5. Brake fluid, oil or grease on linings. 6. Unmatched linings. 7. Distorted brake pads. 8. Frozen or seized pistons. 9. Incorrect tire pressure. 10. Front end out of alignment. 11. Broken rear spring. 12. Brake caliper pistons sticking. 13. Restricted hose or line. 14. Caliper not in proper alignment to braking disc. 15. Stuck or malfunctioning metering valve. 16. Soft or broken caliper seals. 17. Loose caliper.
Brake pedal can be depressed without braking effect	1. Air in hydraulic system or improper bleeding procedure. 2. Leak past primary cup in master cylinder. 3. Leak in system. 4. Rear brakes out of adjustment. 5. Bleeder screw open.
Excessive pedal travel	1. Air, leak, or insufficient fluid in system or caliper. 2. Warped or excessively tapered shoe and lining assembly. 3. Excessive disc runout. 4. Rear brake adjustment required. 5. Loose wheel bearing adjustment. 6. Damaged caliper piston seal. 7. Improper brake fluid (boil). 8. Power brake malfunction. 9. Weak or soft hoses.

Troubleshooting Disc Brake Problems (cont.)

Condition	Possible Cause
Brake roughness or chatter (pedal pumping)	1. Excessive thickness variation of braking disc. 2. Excessive lateral runout of braking disc. 3. Rear brake drums out-of-round. 4. Excessive front bearing clearance.
Excessive pedal effort	1. Brake fluid, oil or grease on linings. 2. Incorrect lining. 3. Frozen or seized pistons. 4. Power brake malfunction. 5. Kinked or collapsed hose or line. 6. Stuck metering valve. 7. Scored caliper or master cylinder bore. 8. Seized caliper pistons.
Brake pedal fades (pedal travel increases with foot on brake)	1. Rough master cylinder or caliper bore. 2. Loose or broken hydraulic lines/connections. 3. Air in hydraulic system. 4. Fluid level low. 5. Weak or soft hoses. 6. Inferior quality brake shoes or fluid. 7. Worn master cylinder piston cups or seals.

Troubleshooting Drum Brakes

Condition	Possible Cause
Pedal goes to floor	1. Fluid low in reservoir. 2. Air in hydraulic system. 3. Improperly adjusted brake. 4. Leaking wheel cylinders. 5. Loose or broken brake lines. 6. Leaking or worn master cylinder. 7. Excessively worn brake lining.
Spongy brake pedal	1. Air in hydraulic system. 2. Improper brake fluid (low boiling point). 3. Excessively worn or cracked brake drums. 4. Broken pedal pivot bushing.
Brakes pulling	1. Contaminated lining. 2. Front end out of alignment. 3. Incorrect brake adjustment. 4. Unmatched brake lining. 5. Brake drums out of round. 6. Brake shoes distorted. 7. Restricted brake hose or line. 8. Broken rear spring. 9. Worn brake linings. 10. Uneven lining wear. 11. Glazed brake lining. 12. Excessive brake lining dust. 13. Heat spotted brake drums. 14. Weak brake return springs. 15. Faulty automatic adjusters. 16. Low or incorrect tire pressure.

TROUBLESHOOTING

Condition	Possible Cause
Squealing brakes	1. Glazed brake lining. 2. Saturated brake lining. 3. Weak or broken brake shoe retaining spring. 4. Broken or weak brake shoe return spring. 5. Incorrect brake lining. 6. Distorted brake shoes. 7. Bent support plate. 8. Dust in brakes or scored brake drums. 9. Linings worn below limit. 10. Uneven brake lining wear. 11. Heat spotted brake drums.
Chirping brakes	1. Out of round drum or eccentric axle flange pilot.
Dragging brakes	1. Incorrect wheel or parking brake adjustment. 2. Parking brakes engaged or improperly adjusted. 3. Weak or broken brake shoe return spring. 4. Brake pedal binding. 5. Master cylinder cup sticking. 6. Obstructed master cylinder relief port. 7. Saturated brake lining. 8. Bent or out of round brake drum. 9. Contaminated or improper brake fluid. 10. Sticking wheel cylinder pistons. 11. Driver riding brake pedal. 12. Defective proportioning valve. 13. Insufficient brake shoe lubricant.
Hard pedal	1. Brake booster inoperative. 2. Incorrect brake lining. 3. Restricted brake line or hose. 4. Frozen brake pedal linkage. 5. Stuck wheel cylinder. 6. Binding pedal linkage. 7. Faulty proportioning valve.
Wheel locks	1. Contaminated brake lining. 2. Loose or torn brake lining. 3. Wheel cylinder cups sticking. 4. Incorrect wheel bearing adjustment. 5. Faulty proportioning valve.
Brakes fade (high speed)	1. Incorrect lining. 2. Overheated brake drums. 3. Incorrect brake fluid (low boiling temperature). 4. Saturated brake lining. 5. Leak in hydraulic system. 6. Faulty automatic adjusters.
Pedal pulsates	1. Bent or out of round brake drum.
Brake chatter and shoe knock	1. Out of round brake drum. 2. Loose support plate. 3. Bent support plate. 4. Distorted brake shoes. 5. Machine grooves in contact face of brake drum (Shoe Knock). 6. Contaminated brake lining. 7. Missing or loose components. 8. Incorrect lining material. 9. Out-of-round brake drums. 10. Heat spotted or scored brake drums. 11. Out-of-balance wheels.

TROUBLESHOOTING

Troubleshooting Drum Brakes (cont.)

Condition	Possible Cause
Brakes do not self adjust	1. Adjuster screw frozen in thread. 2. Adjuster screw corroded at thrust washer. 3. Adjuster lever does not engage star wheel. 4. Adjuster installed on wrong wheel.
Brake light glows	1. Leak in the hydraulic system. 2. Air in the system. 3. Improperly adjusted master cylinder pushrod. 4. Uneven lining wear. 5. Failure to center combination valve or proportioning valve.

Appendix

General Conversion Table

Multiply by	To convert	To	
2.54	Inches	Centimeters	.3937
30.48	Feet	Centimeters	.0328
.914	Yards	Meters	1.094
1.609	Miles	Kilometers	.621
6.45	Square inches	Square cm.	.155
.836	Square yards	Square meters	1.196
16.39	Cubic inches	Cubic cm.	.061
28.3	Cubic feet	Liters	.0353
.4536	Pounds	Kilograms	2.2045
3.785	Gallons	Liters	.264
.068	Lbs./sq. in. (psi)	Atmospheres	14.7
.138	Foot pounds	Kg. m.	7.23
1.014	H.P. (DIN)	H.P. (SAE)	.9861
—	To obtain	From	Multiply by

Note: 1 cm. equals 10 mm.; 1 mm. equals .0394".

Conversion—Common Fractions to Decimals and Millimeters

Common Fractions	Decimal Fractions	Millimeters (approx.)	Common Fractions	Decimal Fractions	Millimeters (approx.)	Common Fractions	Decimal Fractions	Millimeters (approx.)
1/128	.008	0.20	11/32	.344	8.73	43/64	.672	17.07
1/64	.016	0.40	23/64	.359	9.13	11/16	.688	17.46
1/32	.031	0.79	3/8	.375	9.53	45/64	.703	17.86
3/64	.047	1.19	25/64	.391	9.92	23/32	.719	18.26
1/16	.063	1.59	13/32	.406	10.32	47/64	.734	18.65
5/64	.078	1.98	27/64	.422	10.72	3/4	.750	19.05
3/32	.094	2.38	7/16	.438	11.11	49/64	.766	19.45
7/64	.109	2.78	29/64	.453	11.51	25/32	.781	19.84
1/8	.125	3.18	15/32	.469	11.91	51/64	.797	20.24
9/64	.141	3.57	31/64	.484	12.30	13/16	.813	20.64
5/32	.156	3.97	1/2	.500	12.70	53/64	.828	21.03
11/64	.172	4.37	33/64	.516	13.10	27/32	.844	21.43
3/16	.188	4.76	17/32	.531	13.49	55/64	.859	21.83
13/64	.203	5.16	35/64	.547	13.89	7/8	.875	22.23
7/32	.219	5.56	9/16	.563	14.29	57/64	.891	22.62
15/64	.234	5.95	37/64	.578	14.68	29/32	.906	23.02
1/4	.250	6.35	19/32	.594	15.08	59/64	.922	23.42
17/64	.266	6.75	39/64	.609	15.48	15/16	.938	23.81
9/32	.281	7.14	5/8	.625	15.88	61/64	.953	24.21
19/64	.297	7.54	41/64	.641	16.27	31/32	.969	24.61
5/16	.313	7.94	21/32	.656	16.67	63/64	.984	25.00
21/64	.328	8.33						

APPENDIX

Conversion—Millimeters to Decimal Inches

mm	inches	mm	inches	mm	inches	mm	inches	mm	inches
1	.039 370	31	1.220 470	61	2.401 570	91	3.582 670	210	8.267 700
2	.078 740	32	1.259 840	62	2.440 940	92	3.622 040	220	8.661 400
3	.118 110	33	1.299 210	63	2.480 310	93	3.661 410	230	9.055 100
4	.157 480	34	1.338 580	64	2.519 680	94	3.700 780	240	9.448 800
5	.196 850	35	1.377 949	65	2.559 050	95	3.740 150	250	9.842 500
6	.236 220	36	1.417 319	66	2.598 420	96	3.779 520	260	10.236 200
7	.275 590	37	1.456 689	67	2.637 790	97	3.818 890	270	10.629 900
8	.314 960	38	1.496 050	68	2.677 160	98	3.858 260	280	11.032 600
9	.354 330	39	1.535 430	69	2.716 530	99	3.897 630	290	11.417 300
10	.393 700	40	1.574 800	70	2.755 900	100	3.937 000	300	11.811 000
11	.433 070	41	1.614 170	71	2.795 270	105	4.133 848	310	12.204 700
12	.472 440	42	1.653 540	72	2.834 640	110	4.330 700	320	12.598 400
13	.511 810	43	1.692 910	73	2.874 010	115	4.527 550	330	12.992 100
14	.551 180	44	1.732 280	74	2.913 380	120	4.724 400	340	13.385 800
15	.590 550	45	1.771 650	75	2.952 750	125	4.921 250	350	13.779 500
16	.629 920	46	1.811 020	76	2.992 120	130	5.118 100	360	14.173 200
17	.669 290	47	1.850 390	77	3.031 490	135	5.314 950	370	14.566 900
18	.708 660	48	1.889 760	78	3.070 860	140	5.511 800	380	14.960 600
19	.748 030	49	1.929 130	79	3.110 230	145	5.708 650	390	15.354 300
20	.787 400	50	1.968 500	80	3.149 600	150	5.905 500	400	15.748 000
21	.826 770	51	2.007 870	81	3.188 970	155	6.102 350	500	19.685 000
22	.866 140	52	2.047 240	82	3.228 340	160	6.299 200	600	23.622 000
23	.905 510	53	2.086 610	83	3.267 710	165	6.496 050	700	27.559 000
24	.944 880	54	2.125 980	84	3.307 080	170	6.692 900	800	31.496 000
25	.984 250	55	2.165 350	85	3.346 450	175	6.889 750	900	35.433 000
26	1.023 620	56	2.204 720	86	3.385 820	180	7.086 600	1000	39.370 000
27	1.062 990	57	2.244 090	87	3.425 190	185	7.283 450	2000	78.740 000
28	1.102 360	58	2.283 460	88	3.464 560	190	7.480 300	3000	118.110 000
29	1.141 730	59	2.322 830	89	3.503 903	195	7.677 150	4000	157.480 000
30	1.181 100	60	2.362 200	90	3.543 300	200	7.874 000	5000	196.850 000

To change decimal millimeters to decimal inches, position the decimal point where desired on either side of the millimeter measurement shown and reset the inches decimal by the same number of digits in the same direction. For example, to convert 0.001 mm to decimal inches, reset the decimal behind the 1 mm (shown on the chart) to 0.001; change the decimal inch equivalent (0.039″ shown) to 0.000039″.

Tap Drill Sizes

National Fine or S.A.E.

Screw & Tap Size	Threads Per Inch	Use Drill Number
No. 5	44	37
No. 6	40	33
No. 8	36	29
No. 10	32	21
No. 12	28	15
1/4	28	3
5/16	24	1
3/8	24	Q
7/16	20	W
1/2	20	29/64
9/16	18	33/64
5/8	18	37/64
3/4	16	11/16
7/8	14	13/16
1 1/8	12	1 3/64
1 1/4	12	1 11/64
1 1/2	12	1 27/64

Tap Drill Sizes

National Coarse or U.S.S.

Screw & Tap Size	Threads Per Inch	Use Drill Number
No. 5	40	39
No. 6	32	36
No. 8	32	29
No. 10	24	25
No. 12	24	17
1/4	20	8
5/16	18	F
3/8	16	5/16
7/16	14	U
1/2	13	27/64
9/16	12	31/64
5/8	11	17/32
3/4	10	21/32
7/8	9	49/64
1	8	7/8
1 1/8	7	63/64
1 1/4	7	1 7/64
1 1/2	6	1 11/32

Decimal Equivalent Size of the Number Drills

Drill No.	Decimal Equivalent	Drill No.	Decimal Equivalent	Drill No.	Decimal Equivalent
80	.0135	53	.0595	26	.1470
79	.0145	52	.0635	25	.1495
78	.0160	51	.0670	24	.1520
77	.0180	50	.0700	23	.1540
76	.0200	49	.0730	22	.1570
75	.0210	48	.0760	21	.1590
74	.0225	47	.0785	20	.1610
73	.0240	46	.0810	19	.1660
72	.0250	45	.0820	18	.1695
71	.0260	44	.0860	17	.1730
70	.0280	43	.0890	16	.1770
69	.0292	42	.0935	15	.1800
68	.0310	41	.0960	14	.1820
67	.0320	40	.0980	13	.1850
66	.0330	39	.0995	12	.1890
65	.0350	38	.1015	11	.1910
64	.0360	37	.1040	10	.1935
63	.0370	36	.1065	9	.1960
62	.0380	35	.1100	8	.1990
61	.0390	34	.1110	7	.2010
60	.0400	33	.1130	6	.2040
59	.0410	32	.1160	5	.2055
58	.0420	31	.1200	4	.2090
57	.0430	30	.1285	3	.2130
56	.0465	29	.1360	2	.2210
55	.0520	28	.1405	1	.2280
54	.0550	27	.1440		

Decimal Equivalent Size of the Letter Drills

Letter Drill	Decimal Equivalent	Letter Drill	Decimal Equivalent	Letter Drill	Decimal Equivalent
A	.234	J	.277	S	.348
B	.238	K	.281	T	.358
C	.242	L	.290	U	.368
D	.246	M	.295	V	.377
E	.250	N	.302	W	.386
F	.257	O	.316	X	.397
G	.261	P	.323	Y	.404
H	.266	Q	.332	Z	.413
I	.272	R	.339		

APPENDIX

Anti-Freeze Chart

Temperatures Shown in Degrees Fahrenheit +32 is Freezing

Quarts of ETHYLENE GLYCOL Needed for Protection to Temperatures Shown Below

Cooling System Capacity Quarts	1	2	3	4	5	6	7	8	9	10	11	12	13	14
10	+24°	+16°	+4°	−12°	−34°	−62°								
11	+25	+18	+8	−6	−23	−47								
12	+26	+19	+10	0	−15	−34	−57°							
13	+27	+21	+13	+3	−9	−25	−45							
14			+15	+6	−5	−18	−34							
15			+16	+8	0	−12	−26							
16			+17	+10	+2	−8	−19	−34	−52°					
17			+18	+12	+5	−4	−14	−27	−42					
18			+19	+14	+7	0	−10	−21	−34	−50°				
19			+20	+15	+9	+2	−7	−16	−28	−42				
20				+16	+10	+4	−3	−12	−22	−34	−48°			
21				+17	+12	+6	0	−9	−17	−28	−41			
22				+18	+13	+8	+2	−6	−14	−23	−34	−47°		
23				+19	+14	+9	+4	−3	−10	−19	−29	−40		
24				+19	+15	+10	+5	0	−8	−15	−23	−34	−46°	
25				+20	+16	+12	+7	+1	−5	−12	−20	−29	−40	−50°
26					+17	+13	+8	+3	−3	−9	−16	−25	−34	−44
27					+18	+14	+9	+5	−1	−7	−13	−21	−29	−39
28					+18	+15	+10	+6	+1	−5	−11	−18	−25	−34
29					+19	+16	+12	+7	+2	−3	−8	−15	−22	−29
30					+20	+17	+13	+8	+4	−1	−6	−12	−18	−25

For capacities over 30 quarts divide true capacity by 3. Find quarts Anti-Freeze for the ⅓ and multiply by 3 for quarts to add.

For capacities under 10 quarts multiply true capacity by 3. Find quarts Anti-Freeze for the tripled volume and divide by 3 for quarts to add.

To Increase the Freezing Protection of Anti-Freeze Solutions Already Installed

Number of Quarts of ETHYLENE GLYCOL Anti-Freeze Required to Increase Protection

Cooling System Capacity Quarts	From +20° F. to					From +10° F. to					From 0° F. to			
	0°	−10°	−20°	−30°	−40°	0°	−10°	−20°	−30°	−40°	−10°	−20°	−30°	−40°
10	1¾	2¼	3	3½	3¾	¾	1½	2¼	2¾	3¼	¾	1½	2	2½
12	2	2¾	3½	4	4½	1	1¾	2½	3¼	3¾	1	1¾	2½	3¼
14	2¼	3¼	4	4¾	5½	1¼	2	3	3¾	4½	1	2	3	3½
16	2½	3½	4½	5¼	6	1¼	2½	3½	4¼	5¼	1¼	2¼	3¼	4
18	3	4	5	6	7	1½	2¾	4	5	5¾	1½	2½	3¾	4¾
20	3¼	4½	5¾	6¾	7½	1¾	3	4¼	5½	6½	1½	2¾	4¼	5¼
22	3½	5	6¼	7¼	8¼	1¾	3¼	4¾	6	7¼	1¾	3¼	4½	5½
24	4	5½	7	8	9	2	3½	5	6½	7½	1¾	3½	5	6
26	4¼	6	7½	8¾	10	2	4	5½	7	8¼	2	3¾	5½	6¾
28	4½	6¼	8	9½	10½	2¼	4¼	6	7½	9	2	4	5¾	7¼
30	5	6¾	8½	10	11½	2½	4½	6½	8	9½	2¼	4¼	6¼	7¾

Test radiator solution with proper hydrometer. Determine from the table the number of quarts of solution to be drawn off from a full cooling system and replace with undiluted anti-freeze, to give the desired increased protection. For example, to increase protection of a 22-quart cooling system containing Ethylene Glycol (permanent type) anti-freeze, from +20° F. to −20° F. will require the replacement of 6¼ quarts of solution with undiluted anti-freeze.

Index

A
Air cleaner, 15, 167
Air conditioning
    Sight glass inspection, 24
Alternator, 89
Automatic transmission
    Adjustment, 251, 256
    Filter change, 251
    Pan removal, 251
Axle
    Lubricant level, 29
Axle shaft
    Bearings and seals, 261

B
Ball joints, 266
Battery
    Jump starting, 43
    Maintenance, 17
Belt tension adjustment, 19
Body, 299
Body work, 299
Brakes
    Adjustment, 294, 296
    Bleeding, 285
    Caliper, 289
    Fluid level, 28
    Front brakes, 286
    Master cylinder, 283
    Parking brake, 296
    Rear brakes, 294
Bulbs, 236

C
Camber, 269
Camshaft and bearings, 132
Capacities, 33
Carburetor
    Adjustment, 71, 192
    Overhaul, 191
    Replacement, 191
Caster, 269
Catalytic converter, 187
Chassis lubrication, 40
Circuit breaker, 237
Clutch
    Adjustment, 246
    Replacement, 247
Coil (ignition), 67
Condenser, 57
Connecting rod and bearings, 133
Control arm
    Upper, 269
    Lower, 269
Cooling system, 23, 40
Crankcase ventilation (PCV), 16, 164
Cylinder head
    Removal and installation, 117
    Torque sequence, 119-20

D
Dents and scratches, 299
Differential
    Fluid change, 39
Distributor
    Removal and installation, 86
    Breaker points, 57
Door panels, 299
Drive axle, 261
Driveshaft, 258
Dwell angle, 61
Dwell meter, 61

E
Electrical
    Chassis, 226
    Engine, 83
Electronic ignition, 62, 85
Emission controls
    Air injection reactor system, 168
    Air management system, 170
    Anti-dieseling solenoid, 172
    Catalytic converter, 187
    Computer command control system, 179
    Computer controlled catalytic converter system, 177
    Controlled combustion system, 177
    Early fuel evaporation system, 174
    Electronic spark timing, 186
    Evaporative emission controls, 166
    Exhaust emission controls, 167
    Exhaust gas recirculation, 175
    Idle speed control, 186
    Mixture control solenoid, 185
    Oxygen sensor, 188
    Positive crankcase ventilation, 164
    Thermostatic air cleaner, 167
    Throttle position sensor, 185
    Transmission controlled spark, 173
    Transmission converter clutch, 186
Engine
    Camshaft, 132
    Cylinder head torque sequence, 119-20
    Design, 99
    Exhaust manifold, 127
    Front cover, 128
    Identification, 7
    Intake manifold, 125
    Oil recommendations, 36
    Pistons and rings, 133
    Rebuilding, 142
    Removal and installation, 106
    Rocker arm (or shaft), 123
    Specifications, 100
    Timing chain (or gears), 130
    Tune-up, 46

INDEX

Evaporative canister, 17, 166
Exhaust manifold, 127

F

Fan belt adjustment, 19
Firing order, 89
Fluid level checks
    Battery, 29
    Coolant, 28
    Engine oil, 26
    Master cylinder, 28
    Power steering pump, 29
    Rear axle, 29
    Transmission, 27
Fluid recommendations, 36
Front suspension
    Ball joints, 266
    Lower control arm, 269
    Upper control arm, 269
    Wheel alignment, 269
Front wheel bearing, 293
Fuel filter, 32
Fuel pump, 189
Fuel system, 189
Fuel tank, 225
Fuses and flashers, 237
Fusible links, 236

G

Gearshift linkage adjustment
    Automatic, 251, 256
    Manual, 240
Generator (see Alternator)

H

Hand brake, 296
Headlights, 235
Heater, 226
Heat riser, 19
History, 4
Hoses, 23

I

Identification
    Vehicle, 6
    Engine, 7
    Model, 4
    Transmission, 13
Idle speed and mixture, 71
Ignition switch, 233
Instrument cluster, 232
Intake manifold, 125

J

Jacking points, 44
Jump starting, 43

L

Light bulb specifications, 236
Lock cylinder, 277
Lower control arm, 269
Lubrication
    Chassis, 40
    Differential, 39
    Engine, 37
    Transmission, 39

M

Manifolds
    Intake, 125
    Exhaust, 127
Manual transmission, 239
Master cylinder, 283
Model identification, 4

N

Neutral safety switch, 256

O

Oil and fuel recommendations, 36
Oil change, 37
Oil filter (engine), 37
Oil pan, 136
Oil pump, 139
Oil level (engine), 26
Operation in foreign countries, 37

P

Parking brake, 296
Pistons and rings
    Installation, 133
    Positioning, 133
PCV valve, 16, 164
Points, 57
Power steering, 278
Power steering pump, 278

R

Radiator, 140
Radio, 228
Rear axle, 261
Rear suspension, 271
Regulator, 91
Rear main oil seal, 137
Rings, 133
Rocker arm (or shaft), 123
Routine maintenance, 15
Rust spots, 299

S

Scratches and dents, 299
Seat belts, 235
Serial number location, 6

Shock absorbers
  Front, 264
  Rear, 273
Spark plugs, 46
Spark plug wires, 57
Specifications
  Alternator and regulator, 93
  Battery and starter, 98
  Brakes, 297
  Camshaft, 115
  Capacities, 33
  Carburetor, 194, 198, 199, 202, 210, 215, 220, 223
  Crankshaft and connecting rod, 107
  Fuses, 238
  General engine, 100
  Light bulb, 236
  Piston and ring, 112-114
  Recommended lubricants, 38
  Torque, 117
  Tune-up, 47
  Valve, 103
  Wheel alignment, 271
Speedometer cable, 233
Springs
  Front, 265
  Rear, 272
Starter, 95
Steering
  Gear, 278
  Linkage, 279
  Wheel, 274

T

Thermostat, 141
Tie-rod, 279
Timing (ignition), 68
Timing chain or gear, 130
Timing cover, 128
Timing gear cover oil seal, 130
Tires, 31
Tools, 2
Towing, 44
Transmission
  Automatic, 248
  Manual, 239
  Fluid change, 39
Troubleshooting, 316
Tune-up
  Procedures, 46
  Specifications, 47
Turn signal switch, 276

U

U-joints, 258

V

Valves
  Adjustment, 70, 124
  Service, 123
  Specifications, 103
Vehicle identification, 6

W

Water pump, 140
Wheel alignment, 269
Wheel bearings, 42, 293, 296
Wheel cylinders, 295
Windshield wipers
  Arm, 229
  Blade, 25, 229
  Linkage, 231
  Motor, 229
Wiring diagrams, 238